W9-CSU-884

POLICE NATIONALE
ORLY

7 - SEP. 1999

A 299 FRANCE

DEPARTMENT OF IMMIGRATION
PERMITTED TO ENTER
AUSTRALIA.

24 APR 1986

on

For stay of

SYDNEY AIRPORT 54

IMMIGRATION DIVISION BANGKOK THAILAND
A
72
DEPARTED
- 6 FEB 1988
SIGNED

IMMIGRATION & ETHNIC AFFAIRS
...........Person
30 OCT 1989
DEPARTED
AUSTRALIA
SYDNEY 32

T R A V E L E R ' S
MEDITERRANEAN
FRANCE
C O M P A N I O N

中华人民共和国
东省公安厅

上陸許可
ADMITTED
15. FEB. 1986
4
Status:4-1-
Duration:
NARITA(N)
90 days

ADMITTED
OCT. 1988
Status: 4-1-16
Duration   180 days
Port: HANEDA
Signature

Nº 011278 Immigration Inspector

日本国

THE UNITED STATES
OF AMERICA
NONIMMIGRANT VISA

PASSED
Air Port

U.S. IMMIGRATION
170 HHW 1710

JUL 20 1998

HONG KONG
(1038)
- 7 JUN 1987
IMMIGRATION
OFFICER

The 2000–2001 Traveler's Companions
ARGENTINA • AUSTRALIA • BALI • CALIFORNIA • CANADA • CHILI • CHINA •
COSTA RICA • CUBA • EASTERN CANADA • ECUADOR • FLORIDA • HAWAII •
HONG KONG • INDIA • INDONESIA • JAPAN • KENYA • MALAYSIA & SINGAPORE •
MEDITERRANEAN FRANCE • MEXICO • NEPAL • NEW ENGLAND •
NEW ZEALAND • PERU • PHILIPPINES • PORTUGAL • RUSSIA • SOUTH AFRICA •
SOUTHERN ENGLAND • SPAIN • THAILAND • TURKEY • VENEZUELA •
VIETNAM, LAOS AND CAMBODIA • WESTERN CANADA

Traveler's MEDITERRANEAN FRANCE Companion
First published 1998
Second edition 2000
The Globe Pequot Press
246 Goose Lane, PO Box 480
Guilford, CT 06437 USA
www.globe.pequot.com

ISBN: 0-7627-0607-4

© 2000 The Globe Pequot Press, Guilford CT, USA

Created, edited and produced by
Allan Amsel Publishing, 53, rue Beaudouin
27700 Les Andelys, France.
E-mail: Allan.Amsel@wanadoo.fr
Editor in Chief: Allan Amsel
Editor: Anne Trager
Original design concept: Hon Bing-wah
Picture editor and designer: David Henry

AUTHOR'S ACKNOWLEDGMENTS
A small army of people helped me with this book, far more than I can possibly mention, but I
remember and thank them all. My special thanks go to Debra Zimmerman, Monique Hamot and
her family, Omblyne Salvy de Richemont, Lucie Peyraud, Tom and Mireille Johnston, Jean-Luc and
Sara Pujol, Emily Emerson and Arnaud Le Moing, Paule Artillan, Katia Zeitlan, Sylvie Grosgogeat,
Tink Denis-Hardenbol, Youlaine Mouaikel, Lysianne Boissy d'Anglas, Myriam Journet Fillaquier,
my colleague Nik Wheeler, and above all my marvelous wife Joanne, whose tireless help and
encouragement from beginning to end were essential to the completion of this book.

Printed by Samhwa Printing Co. Ltd., Seoul, South Korea

TRAVELER'S
MEDITERRANEAN
FRANCE
COMPANION

by David Burke

photographs by Nik Wheeler

The
Globe
Pequot
Press

GUILFORD

Contents

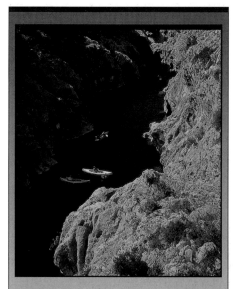

TOP SPOTS

Cruise the *Corniches* of the Riviera

YOU DON'T HAVE TO BE A MONTE-CARLO RALLY DRIVER TO TACKLE THE CORNICHES OF THE RIVIERA, but a cool hand at the wheel doesn't hurt. The Grande Corniche, the highest of the three parallel roads cut into the slopes of the Maritime Alps between Nice and Menton, presents you with breathtaking drops to the Mediterranean at every turn. On this road built by Napoléon in 1806, you can cruise at an altitude of 550 m (1,800 ft) and peer down dizzily at the Principality of Monaco, which looks like a miniature town in a model train set.

The Moyenne Corniche, the middle road built in the late 1920s, offers the best views of the elegant port towns of Villefranche-sur-Mer and Beaulieu and the Cap Ferrat peninsula, the section closest to Nice. It also provides the only access to the colorful medieval "perched village" of Èze clinging to a sheer, rocky peak overlooking the sea. The Corniche Inférieure,

the lower road, snakes in and out of coves along the coast where you can stop and take a dip in the Mediterranean. It was built by the Princes of Monaco in the seventeenth century when Roquebrune and Menton were under their rule.

The hard part of the drive is not navigating the *corniches* themselves, which are gently graded, but the steep connector roads between them, which zigzag up from the coast or plunge down from high. If you like roller coasters, you'll love this part of the ride.

For other kinds of thrills, be sure to make time for Monaco, 19 km (12 miles) east of Nice on the coast road. Its Exotic Garden has 6,000 varieties of cacti and succulents, and the aquarium at the Musée Océanographique (Oceanographic Museum) is one of the finest in the world. I recommend staying overnight if you can, to experience the Grand Casino of Monte-Carlo at its most glamorous. You may want to try your luck in its splendid *belle époque* gaming rooms, but if gambling is not for you, relax and watch the high-rollers in action.

The next day visit medieval Roquebrune and the flower-filled Italianate port of Menton before swinging up onto the Grande Corniche for the 32-km (20-mile) drive back to Nice. At La Turbie, at an altitude of 480 m (1,575 ft), pause at the towering monument the Trophée des Alpes built in 6 BC to commemorate Emperor Augustus' defeat of the last resisting Ligurian tribes. Another spectacular panorama awaits you — a vast sweep of Riviera coast and Corsica, 162 km (100 miles) across the sea.

For non-drivers, several tour operators in Nice offer daily coach excursions. Not as thrilling as driving it yourself, but close enough.

OPPOSITE: Evening on the red rock coast of the Esterel west of Cannes. ABOVE: The Route des Crêtes near Cassis, one of several hair-raising drives you can make along Mediterranean cliffs.

Attack a Fortified City

IF YOU'RE NOT A MEDIEVAL HISTORY BUFF ALREADY, THE MAJESTIC WALLED CITY OF CARCASSONNE IS ALMOST GUARANTEED TO MAKE YOU ONE. Visions of knights in armor, court jesters, damsels in distress, troubadours, jousts, and rumbling siege machines leap to mind as you approach this giant fortress in the heart of Languedoc. During the Hundred Years War, Edward the Black Prince brought his army here in hopes of conquering it. Legend has it that he took one look up the hill with the mighty walls looming above him and decided to lay siege somewhere else. Two sets of massive crenellated walls encircle the city, measuring three kilometers (almost two miles) in circumference on the outside, with 52 round towers. Between the two sets of walls is an open space, the *lices* (lists), where any attackers who made it over the outer wall would be killed by defenders raining projectiles down on them from the inner walls. It was this feature more than anything that made the fortress impregnable and earned it the nickname of "The Maid of Languedoc."

As you enter the city through the Porte Narbonnaise, the fortified main gate, lining the winding stone streets you will see meticulously restored medieval houses that have been converted into restaurants, hotels, and tourist shops. Regrettably, a lot of shops carry tasteless souvenir junk. But don't let that put you off, because the more you prowl about the Cité, as old Carcassonne is known, the more evocative it becomes.

Inside the city, be sure not to bypass the Château Comtal, the twelfth-century castle of the Trencavel family. They ruled Carcassonne, Béziers, and a large part of Languedoc until their downfall during the Albigensian Crusade (young Viscount Raymond-Roger Trencavel was murdered in this castle in 1209). Frequent guided walking tours start here daily and lead you through the castle and onto ramparts. Most impressive of this *tour de force* of medieval engineering are the views from the top of the high walls and towers.

You can take little tourist trains for a 20-minute circuit of the walls, well worth doing if you have the time. But if a choice has to be made, I prefer the defenders' point of view you get from the walking tour, with its marvelous panoramas of the Cité and the vine-covered hills around Carcassonne.

A main stop on the tourist trail, this historical wonder attracts more than 200,000 visitors a year, mostly in the summer. But if you choose

to brave the summer crowds, you will see it at its most magical, when it is illuminated at night. On July 14, Bastille Day, there is a tremendous fireworks display, and in August the town explodes with music, dance, crafts shows, and jousting tournaments during *Les Médiévales*, a costume pageant which recreates the atmosphere of a medieval fair.

Bouillabaisse by the Sea

IN MEDITERRANEAN FRANCE, WHERE DINING IS AKIN TO A RELIGIOUS EXPERIENCE, HAVING BOUILLABAISSE IS A VERITABLE EPIPHANY. This exuberant Provençal fish soup is made all along the coast, and many places claim to make the best. Maybe it's just the power of suggestion, but I always feel that foods and wines taste best in the place they originally came from — and when it comes to *bouillabaisse*, that place is Marseille.

Every morning on the Quai des Belges of Marseille's Vieux Port (Old Port), fishermen's wives sell their husbands' catch of the previous night. Fronting this lively scene is the Miramar Restaurant, an excellent seafood house run by the genial Minguella brothers, Pierre and Jean-Michel. Here you can sit on

At Carcassonne OPPOSITE, the largest fortified city in Europe, little tourist trains make it easy to circle the mighty walls. ABOVE: Outdoor restaurants at the Cours Saleya market in Nice.

the outdoor dining terrace and enjoy the view of the harbor and the basilica of Notre-Dame-de-la-Garde topped by a giant golden statue of the Virgin, "*La Bonne Mère*," who watches over all things *Marseillais*, including, clearly, the making of *bouillabaisse*.

The ritual begins with Pierre bringing a tray to your table with six fresh fish for you inspect. They will be *rascasse* (rockfish), *saint-pierre* (John Dory), *vive* (weever fish), *lotte* (monkfish), *congre* (conger eel), and *rouget* (red mullet), with a substitution or two possible, depending on the catch of the day. They go back to the kitchen and are boiled by brother Jean-Michel, the chef, in a previously prepared soup made from some of the same kinds of fish already mentioned plus other sea creatures, including *favouilles*, little green crabs that add a peppery flavor. While you wait expectantly for your meal, Pierre makes sure you have the right wine — a dry white from Cassis is the favorite in Marseille.

Your first course will be the creamy reddish tan fish soup, which you season to your taste with great dollops of *rouille*, a mayonnaise made with garlic, saffron, and pepper. You then rub as much fresh garlic as you can stand on some large croutons, add them to the tantalizing soup and dig in. Two or three filling bowls later, the six boiled fish arrive at the table. You know you can't possibly

eat this mountain of food, but you make a Herculean effort. And when you finally reach the point where you can't possibly eat another bite, you are amazed to see all that remains is a pile of cleanly picked bones.

Take a Roman Holiday

IF YOU HAD TRAVELED THROUGH MEDITERRANEAN FRANCE IN THE FIRST CENTURY AD — PROVINCIA ROMANA, AS IT WAS THEN CALLED — you would have seen roman arenas rocking to the cheers of thousands of spectators, parades under triumphal arches, crowded Roman baths, temples, aqueducts, and the villas of wealthy Roman landlords. Today as you travel through Provence you will not only be awed by the powerful architectural legacy left by Rome, but discover that many of these ancient marvels are kept constantly in use. Nîmes, the bullfighting capital of France, puts on more *corridas* than any city other than Madrid or Seville in its 20,000-seat Roman arena, along with rodeos, musical performances, and — as in the days of the Romans — circuses. In Nîmes's elegant Roman meeting house, the Maison Carrée, you can see the latest in modern art displayed on its 2,000-year-old walls, and at the Pont du Gard north of the city you can take a stroll on top of the

To complete your circuit of Roman cities in Provence, proceed 27 km (17 miles) to the southwest to Orange to see its Arc de Triomphe, the third largest Roman triumphal arch still standing, and especially the magnificent 10,000-seat Théâtre Antique, one of the best preserved Roman theaters anywhere; it puts on a distinguished series of operas in the summer.

Visit a Vineyard

FROM THE CÔTES DE PROVENCE WINE REGION NORTH OF SAINT-TROPEZ DOWN TO THE PYRÉNÉES, where Côtes du Roussillon, Banyuls and Collioure vineyards run into the foothills, Mediterranean France is a sea of vines, with only the occasional island of market gardens, orchards, and livestock areas. More than half France's wine comes from its Mediterranean regions, so the opportunities for visiting vineyards are practically unlimited.

The most prestigious wines of southern France come from Châteauneuf-du-Pape north of Avignon, where the fourteenth-century popes planted their vines on its pebble-covered slopes overlooking the Rhône. The most beautiful vineyard to visit and among the most highly respected is Château la Nerthe (04 90 83 70 11 E-MAIL lanerthe@wanadoo.fr. This elegant neoclassical mansion in a tree-shaded park is open to visitors weekdays from 8 AM to noon and 2 PM to 6 PM. As you walk through its atmospheric cellars, past hundreds of oak casks

ABOVE: The 2,000-year-old Roman arena in Arles is used regularly for bullfights, concerts, and special events. BELOW: Grapes thrive in most parts of Mediterranean France, making it far and away the nation's largest wine-producing area.

magnificent many-arched aqueduct that once carried Nîmes's water supply down from the mountains.

Nîmes calls itself "The Rome of France," but Arles, 30 km (19 miles) to the east, lays strong claims to the title as well. For a short time in the early fifth century, Arles even became the capital of the Roman Empire. It also has a 20,000-seat Roman arena that is used for bullfights and other events. Its Roman theater puts on plays in the summer, and you can walk through the moody necropolis of Les Alyscamps, the most important Roman and early Christian burial ground in France. At Glanum near Saint-Rémy, 24 km (15 miles) north of Arles, you can explore the archaeological site where digs have unearthed the traces of three ancient civilizations — Celto-Ligurian, Greek and Roman, one on top of the other. Take a two-minute walk down the road to the Mausoleum, a perfectly preserved monument to Emperor Augustus' grandsons, and admire the vivid bas-reliefs of hunting and battle scenes.

Like Saint-Rémy, Vaison-la-Romaine, 69 km (43 miles) to the north, has an active archaeological site to explore, along with a 6,000-seat amphitheater, which presents a summer-long program of music, dance and theatrical events.

and tens of thousands of aging bottles, you will learn about the 13 kinds of grape that are blended to make the robust red wines of the area. But you will not learn how it's done, because each vineyard has its own secret recipe.

This is only one of the many estates you can visit in Châteauneuf-du-Pape. The Tourist Office (04 90 83 71 08 at Place du Portail in the center of town provides a map and a list of estates and their visiting hours. In general, the *caves* are open weekdays, and on Saturdays by appointment only.

The winemakers are generally delighted to welcome you and let you sample their wares, in the hope that you will buy something, of course. But they are also most generous about sharing their deep knowledge with anyone who shows an interest. It's not always easy to meet people when you're on the road, but in Mediterranean France, visiting vineyards is a delightful solution to that problem.

Festive Follies

IN THE SUMMER, FRANCE'S CENTER OF CULTURAL GRAVITY SHIFTS TO THE SOUTH, AND IT IS NO EXAGGERATION TO SAY THAT ALL MEDITERRANEAN FRANCE BECOMES A FESTIVAL. From the month-long international theater festival at Avignon to the opera festivals of Orange and Aix-en-Provence, jazz in Nice and Antibes, classical programs in Prades, Saint-Rémy and Menton, and dance, film, photography, and folk arts festivals, the region is literally bursting with cultural delights. But no city in the South plays *la carte de la culture*, the culture card, with more vigor than Languedoc's bold, modern capital of Montpellier. While other cities content themselves with one major festival a summer, Montpellier puts on three.

Printemps des Comédiens (Springtime for Actors), a three-week festival starting early to mid-June, began in 1986 and built a name for itself as a showcase of Mediterranean theater. But in 1994, it widened its scope, and since then has presented creative productions from all over Europe, and more recently from Africa and Asia as well. The Licedei clown troupe from Saint Petersburg, Shakespeare's *Henry VI* directed by Stuart Seide, the Berlin Cabaret featuring transvestite Georgette Dee, Daniel Bedos's extravaganza *Al Anadalus* with a cast of 30 Spanish and Moroccan performers, marionettes, horses, falcons and snake charmers, and the African Royal de Luxe company's *Petits Contes Nègres* have been some of the offerings.

Festival International Montpellier Danse is one of the major dance festivals of Europe. Established in 1980, it attracts top companies such as the Béjart Ballet of Lausanne and an eclectic mix of artists from all over the world: Antonio Gadès, the Ballet of the Royal Khmer Academy, Twyla Tharp, the Moscow Dance Academy, José Montalvo, Joëlle Bouvier and Régis Obadia, the Alwin Nicolaïs-Murray Louis Dance Company. It is held for two weeks in late June and early July.

The largest of Montpellier's festivals is the Festival de Radio France, running from mid-July to early August. Since 1985 it has been featuring a bold mix of modern, classical and contemporary works performed by leading

French and international symphony and chamber orchestras, opera companies, and jazz and popular artists. Richard Strauss's first opera *Guntram*, Britten's *Rape of Lucretia*, the Helikon Theatre of Moscow's production of Offenbach's *Tales of Hoffman*, and works by American minimalist John Adams have been performed in recent years. Jazz and pop artists have included Michel Portal, the duo of Julia Migenes and Dee Dee Bridgewater, Leon Redbone, and the *klezmer* swing group Orient Express Moving Schnorers.

Further enhancing the high caliber of talent and the bright, often provocative content of its festivals, Montpellier stages its performances in a variety of unusual locales, such as the cathedral, the courtyard of the Fabre Museum, and the Château d'O. This is one of a number of extravagant mansions known as *folies* (follies) that were built in the countryside around Montpellier in the eighteenth century. Its large tree-lined, statue-filled park provides an elegant setting for an evening of music under the stars.

Events are often sold out, so be sure to reserve long in advance. For information contact the Montpellier Tourist Office (04 67 60 60 60 WEB SITE www.ville.montpellier.fr, Printemps des Comédiens (04 67 63 66 67 WEB SITE www.cge-ol.fr/printemps, Festival de Radio France (04 67 02 02 01 WEB SITE www.radiofrance.fr, or Montpellier Danse (04 67 60 83 60 WEB SITE www.montpellierdanse.com.

Pardon the Popes

EARLY IN THE FOURTEENTH CENTURY, IN ONE OF THE MORE BIZARRE TWISTS OF THE MIDDLE AGES, THE CHURCH SUDDENLY DESERTED ROME, THE CAPITAL OF WESTERN CHRISTIANITY, AND MOVED TO A SLEEPY TOWN ON THE EAST BANK OF THE RHÔNE. Avignon, a backwater of little previous distinction, woke up and found itself one of the richest and most important places in the world — and soon one of the most corrupt. Petrarch, who worked as a secretary for a cardinal, called Avignon "a sink of vice." About its masters he said, "Prostitutes swarm on the papal beds." But artists and architects also swarmed to Avignon, attracted by the hefty fees the popes were willing to pay to transform this town into a city worthy of the princes of the Church.

One look at Avignon today is all that's needed to convince you that they succeeded beyond their wildest dreams. One the most dramatic sights you will encounter in the South will be that of the hulking Palais des Papes (Papal Palace) that dominates Avignon.

OPPOSITE BOTTOM: The women of Arles, here in traditional costume, are famed for their beauty. OPPOSITE TOP: A wine festival in Cimiez, in the hills above Nice. ABOVE LEFT: Frescos by Matteo Giavonetti at the Papal Palace in Avignon. RIGHT: Clement VII, Pope of Avignon from 1378 to 1394, in the Musée du Petit Palais in Avignon.

It is one of the best preserved structures of the medieval period, with towers up to 50 m (160 ft) high. In addition, there are four kilometers (two and a half miles) of crenellated walls surrounding the city.

Inside the Papal Palace, only a few of the fourteenth-century frescos that decorated the walls remain, but the vastness of the Banquet Hall and other public rooms is something you will never forget. A few hundred yards across the wide square from the Papal Palace, the Petit Palais is a fourteenth-century cardinal's mansion which now houses a museum of medieval and early Renaissance painting and sculpture from Italy and from the fifteenth-century School of Avignon that emerged as a result of papal patronage. The collection includes an altarpiece by Enguerrand Quarton, the school's most brilliant painter. His masterpiece, the magnificent *Coronation of the Virgin*, can be seen across the river at the Musée Municipal in Villeneuve-lès-Avignon.

And so, notorious sinners though most of the seven popes of Avignon were, perhaps they deserve pardon in gratitude for the wealth of artistic and architectural treasures they left behind, and for making the City of the Popes one of the most intriguing places in France — an absolute "must" on any traveler's Southern itinerary.

Spend a Day at the Beach

THE ONE THING EVERYONE KNOWS ABOUT MEDITERRANEAN FRANCE IS THAT IT HAS SOME OF THE MOST BEAUTIFUL BEACHES IN THE WORLD — AND SOME OF THE MOST BEAUTIFUL PEOPLE IN THE WORLD ON THEM. Where to find them? Where else but Saint-Tropez? The ultimate draw of fashionable sun-lovers — and many of them in summer. These beaches are undoubtedly part of the French Riviera experience, whether to your taste or not. In Saint-Tropez, head for the Plage de Pampelonne, a five-kilometer (three-mile) stretch of sand west of town. Of the 30 beach clubs to choose from, try lunch at Club 55, near the memorial to the 1944 Allied landings, an ethereal eatery

attracting a chic clientele to its tables amid a grove of feathery tamarisk trees. It started as a canteen to feed Brigitte Bardot and the crew of *Et Dieu créa la femme (And God Created Woman)* in 1955, when "Saint-Trop" was turning from a "nice little modest town" into a scandalous coastal attraction famous for introducing the bikini and the first topless sunbathing in public.

Fewer people and more quietude are not so easy to find in Mediterranean France during the summer, even with 520 km (325 miles) of coastline. To be alone on a beach takes quite an effort. If you are agile, one place to try is along the Esterel Corniche. In Le Trayas, 16 km (10 miles) west of Cannes, you can scramble down the cliffs from the coast road to one of the tiny beach coves nestled among the red rocks of the colorful Esterel range. If that cove is already occupied, try the next one. There are many of them.

For long stretches of isolated beach, head for the western end of the Camargue, the Rhône River's broad delta. From the big marina of Port-Camargue, take the beach road seven kilometers (four miles) east to Le Phare de l'Espiguette, park your car by the lighthouse, and walk east between the dunes and the sea until you find a nook that is private enough for your taste. If you forget to bring your bathing suit, don't worry. The dress code is thoroughly relaxed out here in the dunes.

Land in an Eagle's Nest

IN LITERALLY HUNDREDS OF DIFFERENT PLACES THROUGHOUT THE REGION, AS YOU ROLL ALONG IN A CAR OR A TRAIN, YOUR EYE WILL CATCH THE OUTLINE OF SOMETHING AT THE TOP OF A STEEP HILL THAT YOU'D SWEAR WAS THE NEST OF A GIGANTIC BIRD. But as you move closer you make out a cluster of houses clinging precariously to the rim, and you see there's a village up there. These *nids d'aigle* or "eagle's nest" villages are among the most striking features of Mediterranean France. You will find them in all the hilly parts of the region from the Maritime Alps down to the Pyrénées. There are some 400 "perched villages," as they are also known, in the Côte d'Azur and Provence alone.

One of the most dramatic — and one of the most convenient to get to — is Peillon, daintily balanced atop a 376-m (1,234-ft) spur of rock 19 km (12 miles) northeast of Nice. Like the others, it was built in the Middle Ages, when large bands of bloodthirsty marauders roamed the countryside, and Saracen pirates could appear at any moment. A bird's-eye view was as much a matter of survival as a sturdy set of ramparts. Here, as in most medieval hilltop

OPPOSITE TOP: The pebbly beach of Nice, along the Promenade des Anglais. LEFT: "Lizarding" in the sun at Saint-Tropez. ABOVE: The town of Roussillon in the fashionable Lubéron.

towns, the outer walls of the houses ring the village at the top of a sheer cliff and double as defensive ramparts. They look harsh and forbidding, but once inside the main gate, you will find yourself in a pretty cobblestone square with a fountain, and you will discover this is a delightful village to explore, little changed architecturally since the Middle Ages. The few streets of the town are narrow and very steep, and it's easier to walk up the many flights of steps that lead you through passages under flower-decked stone houses. Visit the Chapelle des Pénitents Blancs (Chapel of the White Penitents) and see the frescos of the fifteenth-century School of Nice painter Giovanni Canavesio that depict the Passion of Christ.

If you lunch on the flowery terrace of the Auberge de La Madone, you can enjoy the view of Peillon's deep mountain valley while dining on outstanding Mediterranean cuisine. The inn also has 20 charming and comfortable

rooms, all with views, at rates ranging from moderate to expensive. They are much in demand. So if you think you might want to alight in this eagle's nest for a night, be sure to book ahead (04 93 79 91 17 FAX 04 93 79 99 36.

Other eagle's nest villages nearby are Peille, Sainte-Agnès, Gorbio, and Roquebrune, any one of them eminently worth visiting.

Cross Trails with Camargue Cowboys

THE CAMARGUE IS A MAGICAL PLACE THAT KEEPS COMING BACK IN THE DAYDREAMS OF ANYONE WHO'S BEEN THERE — a peaceable kingdom filled with flocks of pink flamingos wading in sun-splashed lagoons, sturdy black bulls tended by Gypsy-like cowboys, and acres of grasslands dotted with little white horses. You'll be swept off your feet by this wildlife paradise, where more than 400 species of birds make their home in the nature preserve of this 518-sq-km (200-sq-mile) delta of the Rhône River. While you sometimes catch a glimpse of these fine-feathered creatures from your car, the ideal way to observe them is from the top of a horse. On the numerous trails that ring the 13,000-hectare (32,000-acre) wildlife preserve, you can quietly steal close for a view of the nesting areas, and with a little luck have the thrill of finding a nest full of chicks. The horses are docile and know where to go, making any kind of skill unnecessary. So a horseback excursion into the Camargue is an adventure nobody should be afraid of. But if you know how to ride, you can do what my equestrian wife likes to do — take a spirited horse out onto the open ranges of the cattle ranches, or *manades*, that breed bulls for the non-lethal Provençal style of bullfighting.

More than 50 stables in the Camargue rent horses. For information, contact the Saintes-Maries-de-la-Mer Office of Tourism (04 90 97 82 55 E-MAIL saintes-maries@enprovence.com WEB SITE www.saintes-maries-de-la-mer.com. I recommend Domaine Paul Ricard (04 90 97 10 60, a 600-hectare (1,500-acre) horse stud in Méjanes on the northern edge of the Étang de Vaccarès, the large lagoon that is the center of the preserve. Their horses rent for 230 francs for a half-day, 350 francs for a full day.

OPPOSITE TOP: Saint-Jean-de-Buèges, a tiny "perched village" near Saint-Guilhem-le-Désert in Languedoc. LEFT: A non-lethal Provençal style of bullfighting is practiced in all the towns in and around the Camargue. RIGHT: Blessing of horses at the Camargue cowboys' festival held on May 26 in Les Saintes-Maries-de-la-Mer.

YOUR CHOICE

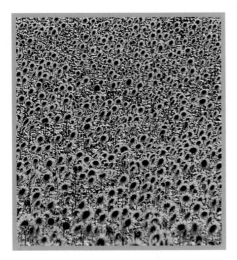

The Great Outdoors

From the high mountain valleys of the Alpes-Maritimes above Nice to the Pyrénées frontier with Spain, Mediterranean France has been blessed with some of the most dramatic scenery in the world, and the most intimate way to experience it is to walk it. You won't find an easier place to plan a walking trip than in France, because the Comité National des Sentiers de Grande Randonnée (National Committee for Long-Distance Hiking), or CNS, has figured it all out for you. The CNS publishes a series of booklets called *Topo-Guides des Grandes Randonnées*, excellently organized guides to the **long-distance hiking** trails in France with detailed topographical maps and symbols for shelters, water-points, and emergency telephones, as well as cultural information on the area. The *Topo-Guides* are in French, but the symbols are explained in English and are easy to follow. You can buy them at bookshops and sporting goods stores throughout France or from the CNS (01 44 89 93 93 WEB SITE www.ffrp.asso.fr, 14 rue Riquet, 75019 Paris. The average price is about 80 francs. To order them from outside France, contact the Maison de France of the French Government Tourist Office in your country (see TOURIST INFORMATION, page 363 in TRAVELERS' TIPS). The book *Walks in Provence*, published by Robinson McCarta, 122 King's Cross Road, London, describes several *grandes randonnées* (*GR's* for short) in the region.

Each *GR* has a number. One of the most popular, *GR-9*, runs from the Alps to the Mediterranean. It heads south from Grenoble in the French Alps and enters Provence north of Mont Ventoux, crosses the Parc Naturel Régional du Lubéron (Lubéron Regional Nature Park) and Cézanne's beloved Montagne Sainte-Victoire, descends through the Massif de la Sainte-Baume, where Mary Magdelen is said to have prayed, and the chestnut-covered hills of the Massif des Maures north of Saint-Tropez, and it ends on the shores of the Mediterranean near the marina village of Port Grimaud.

Another popular walk, the *GR-10*, starts at Banyuls-sur-Mer on Roussillon's dramatic Côte Vermeille (Vermilion Coast), climbs into vine-covered hills with a huge vista of the Mediterranean, and runs westward through the Pyrénées, deep into the Catalan homeland of the Cerdagne — the sunniest region in France, and all the way through the mountains to the Atlantic.

The **Cévennes** is a superb chain of mountains for hiking, particularly around Mont Lozère and Mont Aigoual, crisscrossed

OPPOSITE: The Grand Canyon of the Verdon River in the Alpes-de-Haute-Provence, the largest canyon in Europe. ABOVE: A field of sunflowers in Arles, as Van Gogh might have seen them.

by the *GR-6*, *GR-7*, *GR-60*, *GR-67*, and *GR-68*. This area was made famous by Robert Louis Stevenson in *Travels with a Donkey in the Cévennes*, his 1879 narrative of a 12-day, 220-km (140-mile) hike from Le Monastier to Saint-Jean-du-Gard with a lovable little beast named Modestine. Part of the *GR-70* is called *Le Chemin de Stevenson*.

The *GR-51*, the "Balcony of the Côte d'Azur," follows the coastal highlands from Castellar by the Italian Border north of Menton to Bormes-les-Mimosas on the Côte des Maures.

If you want to find out where the *GR's* are in any area you're interested in, look at the Kümmerly+Frey/Blay Foldex 1:250000 map, and you will see faint dotted lines labeled with the *GR* number that indicate the route (see GETTING AROUND, page 366 in TRAVELERS' TIPS).

In addition to the *grandes randonnées*, local tourist offices provide maps for *petites randonnées*, **short local hikes**, some quite spectacular, such as the *Sentier Nietzsche* in Èze, the footpath between the shore and the "perched village," 425 m (1,550 ft) up a steep hill above the Mediterranean. Other marvelous short hikes can be had in the red hills of the Esterel west of Cannes, the Saint-Tropez Peninsula, the Grand Canyon du Verdon, the mountains of La Sainte-Baume northeast of Marseille, the Calanques of Marseille, Montagne Sainte-Victoire near Aix, Mont Ventoux and the Dentelles de Montmirail in Northern Provence, the Camargue, the Cévennes, the Montagne de la Clape near Narbonne, the Cathar fortresses in the southern Corbières, Collioure and the Côte Vermeille, and a number of places in the Pyrénées.

For dedicated outdoors types who like to rough it in vast tracts of wilderness with nobody else for many miles around, Mediterranean France is not likely to be high on their list. To them, its coast would be unthinkably crowded and its national parks too easily accessible to tenderfoots strolling through the woods. On the other hand, if you don't mind seeing a few other people around from time to time while you roam through magnificent scenery, Mediterranean France certainly fills the bill.

Parc National du Mercantour (Mercantour National Park) in the Alpes-Maritimes north of Nice has 70,000 hectares (nearly 173,000 acres) of protected wildlife area where marmots, partridges, chamois, ibex, wild sheep, and other species can be seen. The Vallée des Merveilles (Valley of Marvels) is an enchanting valley in the heart of the Mercantour Park famed for its crystal-clear lakes and the 100,000 designs carved into its rocks by

Bronze Age shepherds. Travelers may hike in the park, but no cars, dogs, firearms, fires or camping are allowed (but there is plenty of camping in surrounding areas). For information about the park, contact Parc National du Mercantour (04 93 16 78 88, 23 rue d'Italie, 06000 Nice. The Mercantour's Internet site is currently under construction, but you can find information about it on the Internet site of the National Parks of France WEB SITE www.parcsnationaux-fr.com.

For information about the rugged 960-sq-km (600-sq-mile) **Cévennes National Park** in Languedoc, with its two big mountains, Mont Aigoual and Mont Lozère, and its magnificent Gorges of the Tarn, contact the Parc National des Cévennes (04 66 49 53 00 WEB SITE www.bsi.fr/pnc.

Another fine area for rambles is the **Parc Naturel Régional du Lubéron** (Lubéron Regional Nature Park) in eastern Provence, a 120,000-hectare (over 269,000-acre) expanse that includes the heavily wooded Lubéron range, the hilltop ruins of Fort de Buoux dating back to Ligurian times, the abandoned ochre mines of the Colorado de Rustrel, vineyards, farmlands, and orchards and 50 rural communities. For information, contact the Parc Naturel Régional du Lubéron (04 90 04 42 00 E-MAIL pnr.Lubéron@wanadoo.fr, 1 place Jean-Jaurès, 84000 Apt.

Sporting Spree

Mediterranean France is one of the most sports-oriented places in the world. Naturally, water sports leap first to mind, and for sailing, windsurfing, paragliding, waterskiing, snorkeling and scuba diving, this is paradise on earth. All are extremely popular and can be found at almost any resort town along the coast.

Sailboats can be rented with or without crews at most ports in the summer, and sailing schools are plentiful. The Fédération Française de Voile (FFV), the national sailing federation, lists 67 approved schools in Mediterranean France. Some of the main ports for sailing are Antibes, Cannes, Saint-Raphaël, Sainte-Maxime, Saint-Tropez, Le Lavandou, Porquerolles, Toulon, Sanary-sur-Mer, Cassis, Marseille, Port-Camargue (the largest pleasure boat port in Europe, with 4,500 berths), La Grande-Motte, Sète, Cap d'Agde, and Saint-Cyprien. For information about sailing, contact a local tourist office or the Fédération Française de Voile (01 44 05 81 00 WEB SITE www.ffv.fr, at 55 avenue Kléber, 75016 Paris.

The best places for **windsurfing** are Six-Fours-les-Plages west of Toulon, Fos-sur-Mer west of Marseille, and the lagoons along the coast of Languedoc and Roussillon.

Experienced **scuba divers** can find plenty of places along the coast to rent gear and beginners to take lessons. The Mecca of *la plongée* (scuba diving) is the Parc National de Port-Cros in the Îles d'Hyères. The entire island is a nature preserve, and it is surrounded by 1,800 hectares (4,320 acres) of protected underwater trails where divers can see a variety of flora and fauna. For information, contact the Parc National de Port-Cros (04 94 12 82 30 FAX 04 94 12 82 31 E-MAIL pnpc@wanadoo.fr WEB SITE www.parcsnationaux-fr.com, at Castel Sainte-Claire, rue Sainte-Claire, 83400 Hyères. They will provide a list of 17 dive clubs in and convenient to Port-Cros. Other especially active areas for scuba diving are Monaco, Cannes, Cassis, Marseille, Cap d'Agde, and on Roussillon's Côte Vermeille (Vermilion Coast), Collioure, Port-Vendres, and Banyuls. The central source for information about scuba diving is FFESSM (Fédération Française d'Études et de Sports Sous-marins (04 91 33 99 31 FAX 04 91 54 77 43, at 24 quai de Rive-Neuve, 13007 Marseille.

The one active water sport you will not be able to practice, however, is surfing. The waves in the Mediterranean are too mild.

The best way to view the wildlife of the Camargue, where more than 50 stables rent horses.

springtime, and for calm-water rafting, there are breathtaking floats through the most spectacular sections of the Gorges of the Tarn, from La Malène through Les Détroits (the Straits) and the Cirque des Baumes (the Amphitheater of the Caves) to Les Baumes-Hautes.

Since **tennis** was invented in France, it's no surprise to find it played everywhere. The main centers are Monte-Carlo, Cannes, and Cap d'Agde. The elegant Monte-Carlo Country Club has 23 courts and hosts a number of important tournaments, such as the Monte-Carlo Open in April. Cannes has a vast number of courts, clay and artificial, indoor and outdoor. The biggest tennis village in Europe is the Club International de Tennis in Cap d'Agde, with 43 courts and tennis instruction at all levels. They will arrange your accommodations. For summer, make your reservations in the early spring. For information, contact Club International de Tennis (04 67 01 03 60 FAX 04 67 26 77 18, 34300 Cap d'Agde. Despite the large number of courts in the region, you may have a difficult time finding one free in the high season unless you book it in advance.

Deep-sea fishing is available at many ports. At Sète, the biggest French fishing port in the Mediterranean, you can find charter or regularly scheduled boats to take you out day or night. No permit is necessary as long as your catch is for local consumption.

Freshwater fishing is popular at the large man-made Lac de Sainte-Croix in the Var, in the Alpes-de-Haute-Provence, and in mountain streams from the Alpes-Maritimes to the Cévennes and the Pyrénées.

The Verdon River running through the Grand Canyon du Verdon is the most dramatic place for **whitewater rafting**, **canoeing** or **kayaking**. Here you can barrel along on the swift-moving green water of the Verdon through a 21-km-long (13-mile) string of gorges the river has cut into the white limestone plateau of Haute-Provence, with depths ranging from 250 m to 700 m (800 ft to 2,500 ft). Thrillseekers can also pursue these sports in the gorges of the Hérault River near Saint-Guilhem-le-Désert west of Montpellier and in the Défilé de Pierre-Lys, a narrow, high-cliffed gorge in the foothills of the Pyrénées south of Quillan, where the Aude River offers exciting whitewater rafting and kayaking.

For experienced canoeists, the Tarn River in the Lozère between Florac and Sainte-Enimie offers a vigorous descent in the

Though France still lags behind English-speaking countries in numbers of **golf** courses, the sport has caught on in the past twenty years, and Mediterranean France is one of the best areas in France for it, with forty-four 18-hole courses, mainly in the Alpes-Maritimes, the Var, and along or near the Languedoc coast. Many were built during the 1980s and feature challenging layouts by Pete Dye, Ronald Fream, Robert Trent Jones, and other leading golf course architects. Golfers who like to tee off 12 months a year will find that the mild Mediterranean climate makes this dream a reality — except when the *mistral* and *tramontane* winds blow too fiercely in Provence and Languedoc, which can make it impossible to play. But the courses in the eastern Côte d'Azur are well protected from winds. Cannes has the greatest concentration of them, with nine 18-hole links within a half-hour's drive, including the stately, parasol pine-shaded Golf de Cannes-Mandelieu, the Côte d'Azur's oldest, founded by Grand Duke Michael of Russia in 1891.

The free 80-page booklet *Destination Golf Côte d'Azur*, produced jointly by the Comité Régional du Tourisme (CRT) Riviera-Côte d'Azur and the Comité Départemental du Tourisme du Var, profiles the 26 courses in the Alpes-Maritimes and the Var, and the CRT Riviera-Côte d'Azur's 43-page booklet *Golf Côte d'Azur Guide des Séjours* (in French,

ABOVE: On the *corniches* of the Riviera above Monaco. OPPOSITE: Canoeing is popular in the gorges of the Hérault River in Languedoc.

English and German) details dozens of golf package tours in the Alpes-Maritimes. The Comité Régional du Tourisme Provence-Alpes-Côte d'Azur's booklet *Guide des Golfs* includes the courses in Provence (Bouches-du-Rhône and Vaucluse) and Alpes-de-Haute-Provence as well as the Côte d'Azur. For golfers venturing west of the Rhône, the Comité Régional du Tourisme Languedoc-Roussillon publishes its 22-page annual booklet simply called *Golf* detailing the 26 courses in the region, 12 of them 18-hole *parcours*. To get these booklets or further information, see TOURIST INFORMATION, page 363 in TRAVELERS' TIPS, for the addresses and contact numbers of the Comité Régional du Tourisme Languedoc-Roussillon and the Comité Régional du Tourisme Riviera-Côte d'Azur.

For a free list of all the golf courses in France, contact the Fédération Française de Golf (01 41 49 77 00 FAX 01 41 49 77 01 WEB SITE www.FFG.org, at 68 rue Anatole-France, 92308 Levallois-Perret Cedex.

Some of the most important courses in Mediterranean France are:

Golf de Monte-Carlo (04 93 41 09 11 in Monaco, started in 1911 and spectacularly situated on a 900-m-high (2,950-ft) plateau overlooking the sea; package tours can be arranged through its owner, the SBM (04 92 16 20 00.

Golf de Cannes-Mandelieu (04 93 49 55 39 in Mandelieu (27 holes), owned by the Lucien Barrière Group; package tours can be arranged through their Majestic Hotel (04 92 98 77 00, in Cannes.

Golf de Cannes-Mougins (04 93 75 79 13 in Mougins.

Golf Club Opio Valbonne (04 93 12 00 08 in Valbonne.

Grasse Country Club (04 93 60 55 44 in Grasse.

Golf de Valescure (04 94 82 40 46 in Saint-Raphaël.

Golf de Sainte-Maxime (04 94 55 02 02 in Sainte-Maxime.

Golf de Barbaroux (04 94 69 63 63 in Brignoles, famed for its challenging layout by Pete Dye.

Golf Country Club de la Salette (04 91 27 12 16, another spectacularly lofty course, in the hills overlooking Marseille.

Golf Club de Nîmes-Campagne (04 66 70 17 37 in Nîmes.

Golf de la Grande-Motte (04 67 56 05 00 in La Grande-Motte (36 holes), a challenging layout designed by Robert Trent Jones in 1987 on the edge of the Camargue, where pink flamingos can be seen taking a dip in the water holes.

Golf de Montpellier-Massane (04 67 87 87 87 in Baillargues.

Golf du Cap d'Agde (04 67 26 54 40 in Cap d'Agde.

Golf de Saint-Cyprien (04 68 37 63 93 in Saint-Cyprien (27 holes).

Local tourist offices will help you make arrangements to play. Green fees range from 150 to 350 francs depending on day of the week and time of the year, with weekends and summer being the most expensive.

The best way to explore the Camargue is on horseback (see CROSS TRAILS WITH CAMARGUE COWBOYS, page 22 in TOP SPOTS), and there are more than 50 stables renting well-trained horses that knows the nature trails. **Horseback riding** is available in many other parts of Mediterranean France too. Other places where it is particularly popular are the Grand Canyon du Verdon, the "Lavender Alps" of Haute-Provence (so-called because of its vast expanses of lavender fields, blossoming fully in July), the Lubéron, the Cévennes and the Cathar Country of southern Languedoc, where you can explore the hilltop fortress that were the last refuges of the religious sect crushed in the thirteenth century by the Albigensian Crusade. Government tourist offices from the local to the regional level provide literature on *randonnées équestres* (equestrian rambles) and addresses of stables (known as *centres équestres* or *centres hippiques*) that rent horses and outfit excursions.

In the land of the Tour de France, you can be sure the **bicycle** is a well-serviced means of getting around. French Railways (SNCF) has bikes for rent at the baggage counters of most railroad stations. The bikes can be dropped off at another station later. Rental is about 50 francs a day and a deposit or credit card number is required. There are also plenty of private bicycle rental outlets, details of which can be obtained from the local tourist office. Cycling along the crowded coast roads during the summer is not recommended. Backcountry roads have much lighter traffic, and the drivers treat bikers with more consideration. The terrain tends to be very steep, though, as you get inland, and strong winds can come up suddenly. So don't do it unless you are in good shape. A helmet is highly recommended.

Again, the Alpes-de-Haute-Provence is popular for cycling. So are the lovely olive, truffle, and wine-growing area of La Drôme Provençale around Nyons, the Dentelles de Montmirail, the Lubéron, the Alpilles, the Camargue, the foothills of the Cévennes above Montpellier, the Corbières, and the Conflent,

the Cerdagne and the Vallespir in the Pyrénées. For information about cycling and suggested routes, contact Fédération Française de Cyclotourisme (01 44 16 88 88 FAX 01 44 16 88 99, 8 rue Jean-Marie Jego, 75013 Paris. They have a free introductory booklet with the names of local groups that organize bike tours, but it is only in French. For information in English, contact Cycliste Touring Club (CTC) ((44-483) 41 42 72 17 FAX (44-483) 41 42 69 94, at Cottaralle House, 69 Meadrow, Godalmeng, Surrey GU7 3HS, Great Britain.

Rock climbing is popular in the Calanques of Marseille, the Dentelles de Montmirail, and the Grand Canyon du Verdon.

Hang-gliding is popular in the Alpes-de-Haute-Provence and at Pic Saint-Loup near Saint-Martin-de-Londres north of Montpellier.

In the winter, there is good **skiing** in the Alpes-Maritimes at resorts such as Isola 2000, Valberg, and Gréolières-les-Neiges. They are close enough to Nice that in the spring you can easily ski and swim in the Mediterranean on the same day. For information, contact the Comité du Tourisme Riviera Côte d'Azur (04 93 37 78 78 WEB SITE www.crt-riviera.fr, at 55 promenade des Anglais, 06000 Nice. There are also numerous ski areas (*stations de ski*) in the eastern Pyrénées, including Font-Romeu, Eyne 2600, and Bolquère-Pyrénées in the Cerdagne, and Les Angles, Formiguères and Puyvalador in the Capcir. For information, contact the Comité Départemental du Tourisme des Pyrénées–Roussillon (04 68 34 29 94

WEB SITE www.pyrenees-orientales.com, at 7 quai de Lattre-de-Tassigny, BP 540, 66005 Perpignan.

For **spectator sports**, football (soccer, as Americans call it) is the most popular, and most cities have professional teams. In Marseille, going to Olympique de Marseille (OM) games at the Stade Vélodrome is virtually a religious event. In this big multi-ethnic city, the OM is one cause every *Marseillais* and *Marseillaise* can support, regardless of race, creed, or religion. Rugby is very popular in Languedoc, especially in Béziers, Narbonne, and Carcassonne.

The quintessential participatory sport of the region is *pétanque*, the bowling game practiced under the plane trees in town squares in all parts of our region, from Menton on the frontier of Italy to the Côte Vermeille in Roussillon north of Spain. The sport is outwardly quite simple, but requires a great deal of finesse. A little cork ball called a *cochonnet* is tossed onto the playing surface, and the object is to get one of your team's metal balls the closest to it. The game is a social ritual usually indulged in only by men of the region, but women are not excluded if they want to play. *Pétanque* can be a spectator sport also. A big tournament sponsored by the newspaper *La Marseillaise* is held in the Parc Borély in Marseille at the end of July.

Tennis instruction on one of the 43 courts of Club International de Tennis de Cap d'Agde.

The Open Road

For an area of its modest size — 525 km (325 miles) along the coast, extending inland 162 km (100 miles) or fewer in most parts — Mediterranean France offers an astounding diversity of terrain and culturally distinctive places to explore, and the best way to make their acquaintance is by car. The most important thing to remember in the summer is that you have to get off the coast to find anything resembling open roads, and the farther, the better, for unencumbered driving conditions. So put the big *autoroutes* (super highways) behind you, break out your Kümmerly+Frey/Blay Foldex map 1:250000 for the Provence–Côte d'Azur (Sheet 14) and the Languedoc-Roussillon (Sheet 10), and plunge into the heartlands.

The following itineraries will give you a taste of some of the drives you can take in Mediterranean France.

CÔTE D'AZUR

For a drive sure to please culture-vultures and lovers of mountain scenery alike, head up from Nice or Menton to the **Roya Valley** in the northeastern corner of the Alpes-Maritimes, along the Italian frontier. For the culturally curious, there is one dramatic hill village after another filled with medieval and Italianate baroque houses and churches. Most of the churches have frescoes painted from the thirteenth to the seventeenth century. The valleys of the Roya and its tributary the Bévéra are also famed for the splendid church organs that were built by Tuscan and Lombard craftsmen in the eighteenth and nineteenth centuries. Their sound quality is superb, and they are still in use today. For the nature lover, there is a delightful reward at the end of the road: the enchanting Vallée des Merveilles (Valley of the Marvels).

To reach this area from Nice, leave the city via boulevards Jean-Jaurès and Risso and drive 41 km (26 miles) to **Sospel** on D2204, or from Menton take D2566, a distance of 18 km (11 miles). Sospel is the crossroads of the area, with an eleventh-century bridge, a lovely ensemble of baroque churches and houses, and one of the famous organs in its cathedral. Next move on to lively **Breil-sur-Roya** overlooking a lake in the Roya River, with olive trees by the thousands dotting the surrounding hills. Nine kilometers (five and a half miles) to the north on N204 is **Saorge**, which clings to its amphitheater of steep hills "like a swallow's nest stuck to the side of a house," as one nineteenth-century traveler described it, and is

little changed today. **La Brigue** is yet another charming village in a lovely mountain setting with frescoes and one of those great antique organs in its church. On the outskirts of La Brigue is the chapel of **Notre-Dame-des-Fontaines**, known as the "Sistine Chapel of the Southern Alps" for its 25-panel fresco of the Life of Christ and the Last Judgment. This strikingly realistic series of late fifteenth-century murals is certainly the aesthetic highlight of the trip. The last town, 82 km (50 miles) from Nice, is **Tende**, the metropolis of the Upper Roya Valley, with 2,000 inhabitants living in tall, multistory slate-roofed houses running up its steep hills, a painted church, and another fine organ. But nature-lovers take heart: Tende is also the main jumping-off point for the **Vallée des Merveilles** (Valley of Marvels), a happy vale in the heart of the Parc National du Mercantour with a nine-kilometers-long (five-mile) chain of crystal-clear lakes. It lies at the foot of Mont Bégo, an important site of pilgrimage for the ancient Ligurian tribes of the Alpes-Maritimes. The valley is famed for its mysterious inscriptions etched into rocks by Bronze Age shepherds. Though there are an estimated 100,000 of them, they are very difficult to find. You would be wise to hire a guide in Tende or join a guided group heading out to the valley. The best time to visit the Vallée des Merveilles is from June to September. At other times the weather can be problematic.

In the hills directly to the west of Nice is a cluster of small towns and villages made famous by Picasso, Matisse, Renoir, Bonnard, Chagall, and others who lived and worked here. The drive starts two kilometers (one and a quarter miles) west of the Nice airport on the coast road. Take a right onto Route D36 just before reaching the Hippodrome (the racetrack), and head up to **Cagnes-sur-Mer**. It has a beautifully preserved medieval walled town, Haut-de-Cagnes. Pierre Auguste Renoir spent the last years of his life on his farm east of town; you can visit his home, which is lovingly maintained as the **Renoir Museum**. Continue north on D36 through fields of flowers and orange groves seven kilometers (four miles) to **Saint-Paul-de-Vence**, famed for the many artists and film stars who've stayed here, Bonnard, Picasso, Yves Montand and Simone Signoret among them. The town's star attractions are its sixteenth-century ramparts and art museum, the Fondation Maeght, which houses one of the great personal collections of twentieth-century painting and sculpture. Vence, a larger medieval walled town four kilometers (two and a half miles) north of Saint-Paul-de-Vence, is where Matisse

lived and worked, and it is famed for his Chapelle de la Rosaire. On the edge of a cliff five kilometers (three miles) west of Vence is the village of **Tourrettes-sur-Loup**, once a near-ghost town, brought back to life by weavers, jewelry designers, metal sculptors and potters, many of whose workshops are open to the public. A highly scenic side trip you can take from here is the 35-km (22-mile) swing along the dramatic **gorges of the Loup River**, with the ancient Saracen stronghold of Gourdon perched 500 m (1,640 ft) above the river. Resume your circuit of the art villages of the Côte d'Azur by driving down to **Biot**, a hill town a few kilometers in from the coast between Nice and Antibes. There you will find the Musée Fernand Léger, filled with his bold paintings, ceramics and tapestries, and the Verrerie de Biot, an outstanding glassblowing workshop, where artful glassware is created before your eyes and can be bought in the gift shop. In **Vallauris**, 12 km (7.5 miles) south of Biot, you can view the huge War and Peace frescoes Picasso painted in an abandoned

chapel in 1952, now the Musée National de la Guerre et de la Paix. Vallauris is also the largest ceramics manufacturing center in southern France, and there are pottery museums and workshops to be visited, with works to suit all tastes, including copies authorized by Picasso of works he created in Vallauris. The entire circuit including the side trip through the gorges of the Loup River and back to Nice is about 105 km (65 miles).

From nearby **Cannes** or **Grasse** you can get on the moody **Route Napoléon**, N85, and head north to the **Grand Canyon du Verdon**. This is the route the fallen Emperor took after escaping exile in Elba in 1815, and is a strange, barren piece of terrain. Once a rough shepherds' trail, today it is a well-paved secondary highway marked by plaques decorated with the Emperor's eagle. At **Castellane**, 80 km (50 miles) north of Cannes, head west to the

Tourrettes-sur-Loup is one of the finest crafts villages in the hills west of Nice, noted particularly for its weavers, metal workers, and jewelry makers.

Grand Canyon, the largest gorge in Europe, 21 km (13 miles) in length, with widths up to 1,500 m (5,000 ft) and depths to 700 m (2,500 ft). The two roads along either side of the canyon are equally dramatic, with perspectives that take your breath away. But if you only have time to drive one of them, I recommend the D23, the Corniche Sublime, on the southern rim where the best hotels and restaurants can be found. Hiking, rafting, and horseback riding are very popular in the canyon (see SPORTING SPREE, page 27). While in the area, you can also visit one of the premier crafts villages of southern France, **Moustiers-Sainte-Marie** at the western end of the gorge, famed for its creative ceramics studios.

For a break from the pace of life on the beaches and in the cafés and discos of Saint-Tropez, take a drive straight north to the **Massif des Maures**, a range of low mountains densely forested with chestnut, pine, and oak trees. Vineyards cover the foothills, and practically every village has its own wine cooperative, where you can sample tasty Côtes de Provence rosés. **La Garde-Freinet**, 20 km (12.5 miles) to the north of Saint-Tropez on D558, was once a stronghold of Saracen pirates and has retained its medieval atmosphere. If you hike past 1,000-year-old chestnut trees to the hilltop ruins of the Saracen fortress, you can see what a perfect place it was to watch for merchant ships along the coast. To the west of La Garde-Freinet follow the signs through a winding forest road to **Collobrières**, the chestnut capital, and stop at the Confiserie Azuréenne for *marrons glacés*, mouth-watering candied chestnuts. Nearby you'll find the impressive Chartreuse (Charterhouse) de la Verne. It was founded in the twelfth century, and some vestiges remain, but most buildings date from the seventeenth and eighteenth

centuries. They are under restoration by the Bethlehem monastic community. The views of the mountains are magnificent.

PROVENCE

One of my favorite drives is in the **Lubéron**, a 50-km-long (30-mile) valley covered with vineyards and fruit orchards and with a parallel ridge of wooded hills; it lies straight north of Aix-en-Provence and directly east of Avignon. It offers everything one could hope for in a drive, a delightful mixture of the beauty of nature and beauty that mankind has contributed to the region. Start your circuit in the picture-perfect hilltop town of **Gordes**, 35 km (22 miles) east of Avignon via N100, the central road of the Lubéron. In the largely Renaissance Gordes Château you can see a magnificent period fireplace, and in the countryside around town, hundreds of strange igloo-shaped huts made of flat stones and known as *bories*. A few kilometers outside of Gordes, the exquisite and perfectly preserved twelfth-century Cistercian Abbey of Sénanque sits deep in a lavender-filled valley. Concerts are held here in the summer. Drive east from Gordes 10 km (six miles) to the village of **Roussillon** and discover a town of a different color. The whole town sits on a plateau of ochre — which used to be mined in the area, and the buildings are several dozen different shades of oranges and reds. Twenty kilometers (12.5 miles) farther east is the **Colorado de Rustrel**, a huge abandoned open-pit ochre mine covering 15 sq km (10 sq miles), where the action of the weather has sculpted a wonderland of strange, multi-hued shapes. To the south is the Lubéron's central town of **Apt**, where the Saturday market is one of the liveliest and best provisioned in Provence. South of Apt, explore the long, low mountain range of the Lubéron that runs the length of the valley, with a densely forested Parc Naturel Régional du Lubéron (Lubéron Regional Nature Park) on its eastern end. To the west you will find vineyards and lavender farms and the hilltop towns of **Bonnieux**, **Lacoste** and **Oppède-le-Vieux**, which make for pleasant strolling. In the English-speaking world, this has been known as "Peter Mayle country" since 1989, when *A Year in Provence*, his lighthearted satire of this massively gentrified area, became a bestseller.

ABOVE: Dolmens, four-millenium-old megaliths believed to have been used as tombs, are numerous in the Cévennes. This one is in Lodève. OPPOSITE: The white limestone hills TOP of the Dentelles de Montmirail look like lace (*dentelle* in French) from a distance. Gordes BOTTOM, one of the meticulously restored hilltop towns of the chic Lubéron.

In **Northern Provence**, where it is the only mountain on the horizon, **Mont Ventoux** is known as "the Giant of Provence." At 1,912 m (6,265 ft), it has the most stupendous view in all of Provence and is the focus of fascinating drives. To get to Mont Ventoux, take D938 southeast from lively **Vaison-la-Romaine** to **Malaucène**, then D974 along the north slope of Ventoux. The drive to the top takes you from typically Mediterranean vegetation at the bottom through pine forests to bare pebbles above the tree line as you approach the observation point at the **Col des Tempêtes**, 21 km (13 miles) from Vaison. The view from the top is enormous — the Cévennes, Montagne Sainte-Victoire, Marseille, and the Mediterranean. On a very clear day right after a *mistral* wind you can see all the way down to Mount Canigou in the Pyrénées. From Mont Ventoux you can either follow D974 around the mountain or branch off to the east on D164 and drive 20 km (12.5 miles) to the lavender-growing capital of **Sault**, sensational in July when the fields are all in bloom. From Sault, the 40-km (25-mile) drive through the Gorge of the Nesque River to **Carpentras** is extremely dramatic.

Another exciting drive you can take from Vaison-la-Romaine is along the **Dentelles de Montmirail**, a chain of limestone hills 16 km (10 miles) long that runs north–south from just below Vaison-la-Romaine to Beaumes-de-Venise. The hills are topped by a jagged filigree of white rock that looks something like lace, *dentelle* in French, from a distance. Few of the peaks are

higher than 400 m (1,300 ft), but they look taller because of their cragginess. They are a favorite place of rock climbers. Flat and gently rolling vineyards lie to the west, lovely with the Dentelles as a backdrop. This is the heart of some of the finest wine country in the South. The vigorous reds of Gigondas and Vacqueyras and the delicious sweet apéritif wine Muscat de Beaumes-de-Venise have gained international renown. **Séguret**, 10 km (six miles) south of Vaison-la-Romaine, is a charming town of 714 inhabitants that clings to the western face of the Dentelles. It looks like Bethlehem in a Christmas crib, and in December, that is just what it becomes, when the townspeople dress in Biblical costumes and put on one of the liveliest Christmas pageants in Provence.

LANGUEDOC

In Languedoc, the roads are less traveled than in Provence and the Côte d'Azur, but the same principle holds here: the farther from the coast, the more open the roads. Using **Montpellier** as a base, short drives to the north or west of the city take you into the foothills of the Cévennes, where there are vineyards practically everywhere, fragrances of wild herbs and flowers, and long stretches of road lined by poplars. **Saint-Martin-de-Londres**, 27 km (19 miles) north of Montpellier on D986, has a lovely medieval town square and an eleventh-century church built by the monks of Saint-Guilhem, and there are interesting drives to nearby **Pic Saint-Loup**, a sharp-peaked

mountain that is a favorite of hang-gliders, and the **Grotte des Demoiselles**, a cave with vast galleries and huge sculpture-like stalagmites and stalactites, 19 km (12 miles) to the north. A few kilometers farther north at Ganges, take D25 west along the gorges of the Vis to **Saint-Maurice-Navacelles** and D130 north to the **Cirque de Navacelles**, a gigantic crater with an island in the middle that was created by a former course of the Vis River. Straight south of the Cirque de Navacelles via D25 and D9, a drive of about 45 km (28 miles), is **Saint-Guilhem-le-Désert**, a picturesque medieval village at the entrance the dramatic gorges of the Hérault River, built around its Romanesque abbey. A festival of religious music is held in the village throughout the summer. You can rent kayaks to ride down the rushing Hérault River, and there are exceptionally fine makers of Coteaux de Languedoc wines and *vins de pays* in this area.

These drives into the foothills of the Cévennes can be done as a day trip from Montpellier, but to get up into the real mountain scenery of the **Parc National des Cévennes** and see the stunning Gorges of the Tarn, you should figure on spending at least one night in the area. From Montpellier, take D986 north through Saint-Martin-de-Londres and Ganges, and continue on the same road as it winds up into the Cévennes National Park in the direction of **Mont Aigoual**, which offers a huge panorama of Mediterranean views from the observation platform at its peak (1,567 m or 5,145 ft).

Continuing on D986, **Meyrueis** is a pleasant valley town with good hotels and restaurants. It is 112 km (70 miles) from Montpellier. Switch now to D996 for the short drive to the Tarn River at Le Rozier. Here starts the 57-km (36-mile) drive along the famous **Gorges of the Tarn**. The most dramatic parts come early in the drive — the **Cirque des Baumes**, a bend in the river with sheer, mighty cliffs; **Point Sublime**, an observation point 400 m (1,300 ft) above the river and offering a breathtaking view; and **Les Détroits**, a narrow eight-kilometer (five-mile) straits between vertical cliffs and which you can descend in a boat from **La Malène**. While somewhat less spectacular, the rest of the gorges are quite lovely, with a few farms on little expanses of flat land on the far side of the river, and the charming medieval town of **Sainte-Enimie** in the middle, about halfway to Florac at the eastern end of the gorge.

To return to "civilization," take the **Corniche des Cévennes** (D9), which is only slightly less dramatic than the Gorges of the Tarn, to **Saint-Jean-du-Gard**, where Robert Louis Stevenson ended his famous trip with a donkey, and to **Anduze**, taking a ride on the *Train à Vapeur des Cévennes*, the old steam train that runs between them. If you then return to Montpellier, the whole circuit will have measured 320 km (200 miles).

OPPOSITE: The Monastery of Saint-Guilhem-le-Désert was founded by a former companion in arms of Charlemagne. ABOVE: The gorges of the Hérault River.

The **Corbières** is a sun-blasted range of rugged limestone hills in southern Languedoc famed for its potent red wines, savage beauty and cliff-top fortresses that are almost unbelievably dramatic. These "citadels of vertigo," as they have been dubbed, became the last refuges of the Cathars during the Albigensian Crusade in the thirteenth century. A fascinating driving tour of starts at Carcassonne (see ATTACK A FORTIFIED CITY, page 15 in TOP SPOTS) and takes in the five principal Cathar fortresses of this region, known by the Albigensian Crusaders as "The Five Sons of Carcassonne." **Puilaurens**, the closest, is 68 km (42 miles) south of Carcassonne via D118 and D117. This fortress, atop a 697-m-high (2,300-ft) sheer-cliffed peak, is in excellent condition, with its *donjon* (keep), four towers and crenellated walls intact, and there are superb views of Mont Canigou.

The largest and most dramatic of the "Five Sons" is **Peyrepertuse**. Its outer walls measure two and a half kilometers (one and a half miles) around, and it is topped by massive Château Saint-Georges, built by French kings in the late thirteenth century, after the fall of the Cathars. It has a breathtaking panorama of Corbières, the nearby Château of Quéribus, and the Mediterranean. Peyrepertuse towers over the little village of Duilhac, 42 km (26 miles) east of Puilaurens via D117, D7, and D14. The smaller but quite impressive fortress of **Quéribus**, eight kilometers (five miles) east of Peyrepertuse was the last island of Cathar resistance. It fell to the French in 1255.

Aguilar, the fourth of the five Cathar fortresses, is in Tuchan, 16 km (10 miles) east of Quéribus. The fifth fortress is **Termes**, in the heart of the Corbières. It is the least well preserved of the Cathar strongholds, but its site overlooking the gorges of the Terminet is very dramatic. Termes is 13 km (eight miles) west of Villerouge-Termenès via D613 and D40. From Aguilar, it is about 40 km (25 miles), with dramatic roads through the hills of the Corbières all the way.

ROUSSILLON

Roussillon, the relatively un-touristic southernmost part of Mediterranean France, offers the best chance to get off the beaten track and to explore a splendidly scenic part of France that has managed to hold onto its unique Catalan cultural identity. You will see road signs in Catalan as well as French, see Catalan flags everywhere, and hear the Catalan language being spoken. There are several fine driving itineraries, but to choose one that takes you into the Pyrénées as an example, start from Roussillon's capital of **Perpignan** and head southwest on D612 toward lofty Mont Canigou, snow-covered most of the year, to the Aspres, lightly populated foothills of the Pyrénées where the main points of interest are **Castelnou** and the **Prieuré de Serrabone** (Priory of Serrabone). Castelnou is a handsomely restored medieval walled village, its golden stone houses clustered around an eleventh-century fortress on the hill.

The village is known for its pottery, ironwork and other handicrafts, and for traditional Catalan food. To get to Castelnou, take D612 from Perpignan 14 km (nine miles) to Thuir and continue six kilometers (just under four miles) farther southwest on D48.

The Prieuré de Serrabone is the oldest Augustinian priory in Europe, started in 1082. It is very austere on the outside, but inside contains a dazzling ensemble of rose marble columns representing fantastic beasts' from the *Book of the Apocalypse*, itself a masterpiece of Romanesque art. The priory also has a botanical garden with more than 1,000 types of Mediterranean plants. It is open daily except public holidays from 10 AM to 5:45 PM. To get there from Castelnou, drive west on the very scenic D48, heading toward **Canigou**, and two smaller roads jog around to D618, the road Serrabone is on.

From Serrabone, take D618 to N116 and follow it west along the Têt River Valley to the Conflent, so named because of the several streams flowing into the river from nearby hills and mountains. Here we are in a peaceful valley of peach orchards and market gardens at the foot of majestic Mont Canigou, 2,784 m (9,140 ft) high, the symbol of the Catalan people. The main town is **Prades**, noted for the Pablo Casals Music Festival held from late July to mid-August, and for its tenth-century Abbey of Saint-Michel-de-Cuxa. Six kilometer (nearly four miles) south of Prades on N116 in a narrow valley where the Têt and Cady rivers flow together is the remarkable town of **Villefranche-de-Conflent**, entirely enclosed within the walls of a seventeenth-century fortress designed by Louis XIV's great military architect Sébastien Vauban. Yet despite its stern look from the outside, this little town of fewer than 300 year-round residents is one of the friendliest places you will ever find, thanks in large part to the bright, young team that runs its tourist and cultural programs, along with the crafts studios and cafés that are in full swing in the summer. Villefranche-de-Conflent is also where you connect with the *Petit Train Jaune* (*Little Yellow Train*) to the high mountain plateau of the Cerdagne, the homeland of the Catalan people deep in the Pyrénées. Eight kilometers (five miles) south of Villefranche-de-Conflent via D116 is the most dramatically situated of all Roussillon's Romanesque abbeys, **Saint-Martin-du-Canigou**, perched on a rocky spur on the very slope of Mont Canigou. Hikers can reach it by a steep, rugged trail, about half an hour's climb each way. It is not accessible by car, but Garage Villaceque (04 68 05 51 14, in Vernet-les-Bains provides jeep rides to the abbey for 170 francs per person.

Backpacking

The Côte d'Azur is one of the most famously expensive places in the world, particularly during the peak summer season, and for that reason, some cost-conscious travelers may think they should avoid Mediterranean France altogether. If so, they are mistaken. There are plenty of ways to keep costs down, even on the Côte d'Azur, and as you move onto the *arrière pays*, the backcountry, prices go down. They also drop noticeably as you travel from the east to the west along the Mediterranean crescent.

In general, food and lodging cost about a third less in Languedoc and Roussillon than they would in restaurants and hotels of comparable quality on the Côte d'Azur. As an additional benefit, the little hotels, youth hostels or camping grounds you choose to stay in to save money may be more relaxed and informal than expensive hotels, making it easier for you to meet hospitable French people and fellow travelers.

Camping is tremendously popular in Mediterranean France. Practically every town in this book has at least one camping ground. Most operate their own *camping municipal*,

OPPOSITE: Parasol pines on the Île de Porquerolles. ABOVE: The Languedoc coast's 160 km (100 miles) of fine sand beaches have plenty of camping grounds.

which can range from a modest site with basic sanitary facilities to deluxe spreads with swimming pools, tennis courts, restaurants, bars, supermarkets, laundromats, and plenty of shade trees. In addition to the municipal campsites, there are at least 1,000 privately owned camping grounds in the region. Like hotels, the Ministry of Tourism rates campsites by stars, from one to four, depending on location, facilities, and attractiveness of the site. The ones near the shore are generally the most expensive, and they tend to be *complet* (full) in the summer, so you should reserve as long as possible in advance. Four-star campsites run about the same price as a cheap hotel. On the Côte d'Azur, the most expensive area, a first-class site for a car and a caravan will cost about 150 francs, for a car and a two-person tent about 100 to 125 francs, and for a tent alone about 70 francs. Some especially popular areas for camping are Cagnes-sur-Mer and Villeneuve-Loubet-Plage west of Nice, Saint-Aygulf west of Fréjus, the Camargue and the whole coast of Languedoc and Roussillon, with vast numbers of camping grounds along the beaches in and around Cap d'Agde and along the coast near Béziers, Narbonne, and Perpignan (where Argelès-sur-Mer has 56 camping grounds with several thousand of emplacements). In the backcountry, the Alpes-de-Haute-Provence and the area of the Grand Canyon du Verdon have important concentrations of campsites, and they are also sprinkled liberally throughout the foothills of the Cévennes and the Pyrénées. Campers who want to rough it in the open countryside are strongly urged to get permission from the landowners so as to avoid possible bad feelings or worse. Information on camping grounds can be obtained from government tourist offices on all levels. For the addresses of regional and departmental tourist offices (which cover an area roughly equivalent to an English or American county), see TOURIST INFORMATION, page 363 in TRAVELERS' TIPS. The central source is the Fédération Française de Camping et Caravaning (01 42 72 84 08 E-MAIL ffcc@wanadoo.fr, 78 rue de Rivoli, 75004 Paris. Their annual *Guide Officiel Camping/Caravaning* lists all campsites in France with their government ratings, facilities, and prices. It is sold in most bookshops in France and at Maisons de France elsewhere (78 francs). You can also order it by mail and pay for it with Visa or Master Card. Michelin also publishes *Camping Caravaning France*, a selective guide to 3,500 camping sites nationwide (68 francs). For free information about camping and caravanning, contact the tourist offices of any

town or *département* you are thinking of stopping in. They all have up-to-date brochures about the camping grounds in their areas with full details about their facilities.

Inexpensive accommodations can be found at *auberges de jeunesse* (**youth hostels**), which offer single-sex dormitories for people of any age. Depending on the quality rating of the *auberge*, beds go for 40 to 50 francs in a night in modest one, 72 francs in the most luxurious *auberges*, breakfast included. Many have kitchen facilities or serve inexpensive meals, and they rent sheets and sleeping bags for nominal rates. Many accept reservations sent by fax from another hostel or through their central computer reservations system, but there are some that don't. To be sure to get a room in those ones, you have to go there between 8 AM and 10 AM, particularly in the busy summer season. Other possible drawbacks to watch for are curfews that some impose in the evening and locations far from town. For full information, contact the national youth hostel association in your home country; the Fédération Unie des Auberges de Jeunesse (FUAJ) (01 44 89 87 27 FAX 01 44 89 87 10 WEB SITE www.fuaj.org, at 27 rue Pajol, 75018 Paris, which has 19 youth hostels in Mediterranean France; or the Ligue Française des Auberges de la Jeunesse (LFAJ) (01 44 16 78 78 FAX 01 44 16 78 80 WEB SITE www.auberges-de-jeunesse.com, at 67 rue Vergniaud, 75013 Paris, which has seven. You must become a member of one of the youth hostel organizations, which you can do in your home country or at any youth hostel. The fee is 70 francs if you are under 26 or 100 francs if you are 26 or over. For people who are traveling alone, a youth hostel is the least expensive place to stay. But if there are a few of you, sharing an inexpensive hotel room can be as cheap or cheaper.

Though **bed and breakfasts** are not nearly as common in France as in the British Isles, the Fédération Nationale des Gîtes de France has a version called *Chambres & Tables d'Hôtes*. A *chambre d'hôte* offers a bedroom and breakfast in a private home, and a *table d'hôte* offers a home-cooked meal. They are mainly in rural villages and on working farms and vineyards. This is a very pleasant and comfortable way to enter into the life of a family and a community. *Chambre d'hôte* prices are generally in the 200 to 300 franc range for two people, with a big breakfast included. The annual *Chambres & Tables d'Hôtes* lists 21,000 bed and breakfasts throughout France and 2,750 of them that serve meals. The text is in French, but there are instructions in English and other European languages. It costs 140 francs and

can be purchased by mail, phone, fax, e-mail, or interactive web site (very good, in several languages) from the Maison des Gîtes de France (01 49 70 75 75 FAX 01 42 81 28 53 E-MAIL info@gites-de-france.fr WEB SITE www.gites-de-france.fr, at 59 rue Saint Lazare, 75009 Paris.

If you are a family or group, you may want to rent a *gîte*, a fully furnished and equipped country cottage or house in a village, which the Maison des Gîtes de France can also help you locate, and you can save money by doing your own cooking. *Gîtes* can be rented for a weekend, a week, or several weeks at a time. *Gîte* owners are generally local people who try to make you feel right at home in their community. Prices vary greatly depending on the size of the *gîte*, its location, and the season. There is an extra charge for linens. It goes without saying that the *gîtes* nearest the Mediterranean tend to be the most expensive.

Renting a *gîte* takes planning and must be done early. To do so, buy one of the Maison des Gîtes de France's guides. After you have selected a *gîte*, contact the owner directly. There is a guide for each of France's 95 *départements*, including the 12 covered in this book (see TOURIST INFORMATION, page 363 in TRAVELERS' TIPS, for an overview of the localities in each *département*). Each guide costs 40 to 80 francs (depending on the number of *gîtes)*, plus postage, and can be ordered by mail, phone, e-mail, or over the web. The text is in French, but there are introductory instructions in English and other major languages and color photos of each *gîte*.

Tourist offices also have their own lists of rental properties in the area.

For **reasonably priced hotels**, you would be wise to lay out 100 francs for the annual guide of the Logis de France group, a federation of family-run hotel-restaurants. There are hundreds of them in Mediterranean France. They range in price from inexpensive to moderate, usually between 200 and 350 francs for a double room depending on their location, classification and facilities. You can buy the guide in most book or newspaper shops in France or you can order it from the Fédération Nationale des Logis de France (01 45 84 70 00 FAX 01 45 83 59 66 WEB SITE www.logis-de-france.fr, at 83 avenue d'Italie, 75013 Paris. Their central reservation number is (01 45 84 83 84.

For more information about hotels, see ACCOMMODATION, page 368 in TRAVELERS' TIPS.

Getting around Mediterranean France by **public transportation** is not very expensive, and substantial discounts are available. People under 26 and over 60 are eligible for discounts of up to 50% on main line trains, and a program called *"Prix Découvertes"* gives a 60% discount to anyone who makes a train reservation 30 to 60 days in advance (*Prix Découvertes J30*), and a 40% discount for

Paella in Languedoc's main fishing port of Sète.

reservations made eight to 30 days in advance (*Prix Découvertes J8*). Train service along the coast is excellent. You could easily hop from town to town and rent bikes at the train station to get around locally (see SPORTING SPREE, page 27). Getting inland on public transportation is another story. There are buses, and while not too expensive, their service is very irregular. Most local people here drive their own cars. If you're tempted to **hitchhike** on the big highways, don't. Instead you should choose secondary and smaller roads, if at all.

Living It Up

EXCEPTIONAL HOTELS

Cannes, Nice, Cap d'Antibes, Cap-Ferrat, Monte-Carlo — their very names set your head spinning with visions of the high life — Cary Grant and Grace Kelly wheeling along the Riviera, Onassis-sized yachts draped with Beautiful People, a *croupier* pushing a tottering stack of chips across the table, hopefully in your direction. The Côte d'Azur is where luxury tourism was invented in the extravagant Belle Époque of the late nineteenth century, and for those who demand palatial hotels, gourmet restaurants, and elegant boutiques — and have the deep pockets to afford them — this area remains one of the most satisfying places on earth. But even if you don't happen to be a millionaire, you may want to have a splurge. While there are plenty of places to do it elsewhere in Mediterranean France, on the Côte d'Azur, there is truly an embarrassment of choices.

Take hotels: we could easily name two dozen between Monaco and Saint-Tropez whose splendid location, architecture, gorgeous decor, and lavish and impeccable service put them not only in the luxury category, but breathtakingly so. Among them are the Hôtel de Paris and its sister-hotel the Hermitage in Monaco, the Château de La Chèvre d'Or in Èze, the Voile d'Or and the Grand Hôtel du Cap-Ferrat in Cap-Ferrat, the Réserve de Beaulieu and the Métropole in Beaulieu-sur-Mer, the Negresco in Nice, the Hôtel du Cap in Cap d'Antibes, the Carlton and the Martinez in Cannes, the Byblos, the Résidence de la Pinède, and the Bastide de Saint-Tropez in Saint-Tropez, to name just a dozen. Here we are talking about hotels that run 1,500 francs a night and up.

Away from the Côte d'Azur, there are few such supremely deluxe hotels. In Avignon, the Hôtel d'Europe and the Mirande fill the bill, as does Aix's elegant Villa Gallici, and Marseille has its marvelous Petit Nice. In Languedoc and

Roussillon, there are few hotels in the deluxe category (four stars in the official government ratings), and only one of them, the Hôtel de la Cité in Carcassonne, could hold its own with the best of the ones on the Côte d'Azur. However, sophisticated inns of grand rustic elegance abound in the countryside in Provence as well as the Côte d'Azur. The famous Oustaù de Baumanière in Les Baux is the prototype of the luxury rural inn, and its fellow members in the prestigious Relais & Châteaux group are well represented in Mediterranean France. A heavy concentration of upscale country inns is found in the Alpilles, a popular resort area in the hills northeast of Arles, where the Oustaù de Baumanière is located. Other rural hostelries of great comfort and rustic elegance are the Château de Trigance, an eleventh-century castle near the Grand Canyon du Verdon, the Bastide de Moustiers in the same area, and the Mas du Langoustier, a rambling pink ochre hotel on its own private cove in a remote corner of the island of Porquerolles in the Îles d'Hyères, one of the most serenely restful spots you are ever likely to find.

EXCEPTIONAL RESTAURANTS

Gourmets will have no trouble finding culinary pleasure in Mediterranean France, and as with hotels and *le luxe* in general, the Côte d'Azur leads the way. Mediterranean France's current temple of *gourmandise* is Alain Ducasse's Louis XV Restaurant at the Hôtel de Paris in Monte-Carlo. But Maître

Ducasse is far from the only extraordinarily fine chef in the region. Just to mention some of the others who have gained international fame, there are Roger Vergé in Mougins, Dominique Le Stanc and Alain Llorca in Nice, Jacques Maximin in Vence, Jacques Chibois in Grasse, Christian Willer and Francis Chauveau in Cannes, Laurent Tarridec in Saint-Tropez, Jean-Paul and Gérald Passédat in Nice, Jean-André Charial in Les Baux, Christian Étienne in Avignon, Pierre and Jany Gleize in Château-Arnoux, Jean-Pierre Cazals in Port-Camargue, Jacques and Laurent Pourcel in Montpellier, and Franck Putelat in Carcassonne. This is a far from exhaustive list. A dozen or more first-rate chefs could easily be added. The point is that, if you can afford it, cuisine of the highest quality is within your reach in practically all parts of Mediterranean France, but especially to the east of the Rhône. For information on Mediterranean cuisine, see GALLOPING GOURMETS, page 56.

NIGHTLIFE

Nightlife is generally linked to the casino, and often the casino *is* the nightlife. Menton is an example, where the Club 06 at the Casino de Menton puts on the only floor show in town.

The big, famous casinos are in Monte-Carlo, which has three operating in the winter and four in the summer; Nice with one; Juan-les-Pins with one; and Cannes with two, including the Casino Croisette, the most active of all, with up to 10,000 visitors a day in the height of the summer season. Casinos can be found practically everywhere along the coast. They may not all have roulette, baccarat and *chemin de fer*, but wherever you go, you'll never be far from the clink and whir of *machines à sous*, as slot machines are called, or electronic draw poker, which is the rage now. Little Port-Barcarès in Roussillon, in its desperation to have a casino, ran an old cruise ship up onto its beach and converted it into one. Casinos are not confined to the racy cities along the coast. Even dignified cities inland have them, such as Digne-les-Bains and Aix-en-Provence.

For nightclubs, discos and musical bars on the Côte d'Azur, the leading towns are Monaco, Nice, Cannes, and Saint-Tropez; Antibes's beach and entertainment quarter of Juan-les-Pins deserves special mention for its five discos and innumerable music bars and cafés that are jumping until three or four o'clock in the morning.

Marseille also has a dynamic nightlife, with a number of musical bars and discos on the east side of the Vieux Port and lively cafés on the Cours Julien.

In the big university towns of Aix-en-Provence and Montpellier, each with about 50,000 students, there are good discos and music clubs geared to the young scholars' tastes.

Belle époque flair on the Côte d'Azur at the Casino of Monte-Carlo OPPOSITE, at La Rotonde at Nice's Hôtel Negresco ABOVE LEFT and at Monaco's Hôtel Hermitage RIGHT, with a winter garden designed by Gustave Eiffel.

Family Fun

In some places, taking a trip with children in tow can be an ordeal, but in Mediterranean France there is no end of activities to keep the little nippers amused. The numerous beaches along the 525 km (325 miles) of coastline are the most obvious kid-pleasers, and the facilities for water sports and most other sports are staggering (see SPORTING SPREE, page 27). But there is a lot more than sports and sand castles to provide excitement for children, and luckily most of it is fun for parents as well.

FUN ON THE WATER

In a number of places, there are short ferryboat rides to islands, such as the Îles de Lérins off Cannes, the Îles d'Hyères and the Château d'If, the island fortress where Alexandre Dumas's fictional Count of Monte-Cristo was kept prisoner. It is a short trip from the Vieux Port (Old Port) of Marseille. For kids, the boat ride is a thrill, the idea of being on an island is exciting, and you can make a complete experience of it with a picnic and a swim. From Marseille or Cassis, you can also take a boat ride to the Calanques de Marseille, a string of dramatic fjords cut into white limestone cliffs along the coast. In the Camargue, you can take barge tours of wildlife areas every day in the summer from Les Saintes-Maries-de-la-Mer and Aigues-Mortes, and in Languedoc there are barge cruises on the restful, tree-shaded Canal du Midi and connecting bodies of water.

ABOVE: A folklore festival in Fontvieille near Arles. RIGHT: A Catalan barbecue in Céret, a town in the cherry tree-covered Vallespir foothills of the Pyrénées.

They can be taken from Sète, Agde, Béziers, and Narbonne. You could also rent a house boat and pilot it yourself.

SCENIC TRAIN RIDES

Short train trips can be taken from Nice to the Alpes-de-Haute-Provence on the colorful *Train des Pignes* (*Pine Cone Train*), from Anduze to Saint-Jean-du-Gard on the *Train à Vapeur des Cévennes*, from Narbonne to Bize-Minervois on the *Autorail Touristique du Minervois* with stops at a Gallo-Roman pottery museum and an olive-oil cooperative on the way, and in the Pyrénées the *Petit Train Jaune* takes you from Villefranche-de-Conflent through the magnificent mountain scenery of the Cerdagne. It has open cars in the summer.

FUN IN THE WILD

A must for any family is the **Camargue**, the wide delta of the Rhône River. Its wetlands are home to huge flocks of pink flamingos and 400 other species of birds and its ranges are trod by little white horses, as well as black bulls that are bred for non-lethal Provençal-style bullfighting, herded by cowboys (see CROSS TRAILS WITH CAMARGUE COWBOYS, page 22 in TOP SPOTS). You can rent horses to explore the nature trails or rent bicycles to ride along the sea dike that runs for 20 km (12.5 miles) between the large central pond of the wildlife reserve, the Étang de Vaccarès, and the Mediterranean. There are also 60 km (40 miles) of fine sand beaches in the Camargue.

Another place where you are sure to see plenty of wildlife is the **African Reserve of Sigean** south of Narbonne. It has 3,500 African animals of 157 species including lions, elephants, hippos and giraffes, living on a simulated African plain on the Languedoc coast.

UNDERWATER LIFE

To see ocean-living creatures, be sure to visit the aquarium of the Musée Océanographique (Oceanographic Museum) in Monaco, one of the world's finest. It has 90 tanks with 450 different species of fish, a truly hypnotic experience. The Arago Laboratory in Banyuls-sur-Mer on the Côte Vermeille (Vermilion Coast) in Roussillon also has a first-rate aquarium. It has 39 tanks containing 250 species of creatures from the waters off the Languedoc coast. Marineland in La Brague on the coast road just east of Antibes puts on the biggest aquatic animal show in Europe, and next door is a large fairground with water slides, miniature golf, and other kid-pleasing pastimes.

CANYONS AND CAVES

For natural wonders, a drive along the Grand Canyon du Verdon in the Alpes-de-Haute-Provence offers spectacular views of the largest canyon in Europe. For the more adventurous members of the family, there are **kayaking** and **whitewater rafting** trips down the river, and for the younger or less adventurous ones, the large Lake of Sainte-Croix at the western end of the canyon offers swimming and boating. Horses can be rented for rides in and around the canyon. For information about the Grand Canyon du Verdon, check with the local tourist office at Castellane, Moustiers-Sainte-Marie, or Digne-les-Bains, or with the Comité Départemental du Tourisme des Alpes-de-Haute-Provence (see TOURIST INFORMATION, page 363 in TRAVELERS' TIPS), which provides information on all sports in the area.

Another very beautiful canyon to explore by kayak or raft is the Gorges of the Tarn River in the Lozère *département* in the Cévennes. For information contact the Comité Départemental du Tourisme de la Lozère (see TOURIST INFORMATION, page 363 in TRAVELERS' TIPS).

Caves are fascinating places for children to explore, and there are two large, mysterious ones in the foothills of the Cévennes above Montpellier — the **Grotte des Demoiselles** near the medieval town of Saint-Martin-de-Londres, which has huge galleries 50 m (165 ft) high, and the **Grotte de Clamouse** near the medieval monastery of Saint-Guilhem-le-Désert. There are even bigger ones up in the Cévennes — **L'Aven Armand** and the **Grotte de Dargilan** near Meyrueis. L'Aven Armand has a subterranean gallery that the Notre-Dame Cathedral would easily fit into. At Fontaine-de-Vaucluse east of Avignon, you will find the **Monde Souterrain de Norbert Casteret** (Underground World of Norbert Casteret), a series of caves with underground rivers and waterfalls, and chambers filled with stalagmites and stalactites collected by the famed speleologist. The Fontaine-de-Vaucluse is a mysterious spring at the foot of a steep cliff from which water gushes downhill to form the Sorgue River. Despite numerous scientific explorations, including three by Commander Jacques Cousteau, nobody has been able to determine the source of this water.

CASTLES AND FORTRESSES

A most original trained-animal show, **Aigles de Beaucaire** (Eagles of Beaucaire) is a full-costume medieval pageant featuring free-flying eagles, falcons, and vultures. It is held four times a day in the summer at the Château de Beaucaire, the imposing shell of an eleventh-century castle on the west bank of the Rhône.

People of all ages love medieval castles, and one of the most dramatic and best-preserved examples, Good King René's **Château de Tarascon**, sits directly across the river from Beaucaire on the east bank of the Rhône. Its interior gives you a good sense of what it was like to live in a castle.

Even more dramatic fortresses are to be found in Languedoc. They include **Carcassonne**, the largest medieval fortress city in Europe with two rings of high crenellated walls (see ATTACK A FORTIFIED CITY, page 15 in TOP SPOTS), and **Peyrepertuse**, a huge ruined Cathar fortress atop a steep hill in the rugged Corbières (see THE OPEN ROAD, page 32). No child will ever forget these places. In Roussillon, the **Fortress of Salses** near Perpignan is a massive, sinister-looking fort with walls 15 m (almost 50 ft) thick; it was built by the Spanish in the late sixteenth century and is well-preserved and fascinating to explore. **Villefranche-de-Conflent** is a completely walled town in a Pyrénées valley, its ramparts designed in the seventeenth century by Louis XIV's famed military engineer Sébastien Vauban. There is a 1,000-step tunneled staircase to hilltop Fort Liberia that the kids will enjoy climbing. Two other impressive walled cities are **Aigues-Mortes**, a perfectly preserved thirteenth-century port on the western edge of the Camargue that was built for the Crusades, and **Avignon**, whose ring of crenellated ramparts was built by the popes of Avignon in the fourteenth century, along with their gigantic Papal Palace.

GLIMPSE PREHISTORY

Two places where children can have fascinating glimpses into prehistory are at the **Terra Amata Museum** near the old port in Nice, where the actual shelters of Paleolithic men who hunted here 400,000 years ago have been incorporated into the museum, and true-to-life tableaus show the way they lived; and the **Centre Européen de la Préhistoire** in Tautavel near Perpignan. This is a modern museum of prehistory that contains the oldest human skull found in Europe, that of a nomadic hunter know as Tautavel Man. It is 450,000 years old.

The Festival of Saint-Louis at the walled city of Aigues-Mortes in honor of the town's founder, King Louis IX.

GETTING AROUND WITH CHILDREN

Traveling with children doesn't have to cost you a fortune. In France hotel rooms are generally rented by the room, not the number of people staying in it, though there will be a small extra charge for additional cots. For information on camping, youth hostels and other budget accommodations, see BACKPACKING, page 39.

A wonderful side-benefit of traveling as a family is that, as everywhere, French people warm up to strangers with children.

Cultural Kicks

Though the first images of Mediterranean France that leap to mind are of sunny beaches, palm-lined avenues and the high life, you could have a thoroughly rewarding trip through the region without setting foot on a beach or in a deluxe restaurant, four-star hotel, or casino. After Paris and the Île de France, no other part of France — and few places of comparable size anywhere — is as rich in cultural attractions as this.

THE ARCHITECTURAL LEGACY

The Mediterranean region was the first part of France to be exposed to Western Civilization, thanks to the Greeks who established a colony in Marseille in the seventh century BC and spread out to Arles, Toulon, Nice, and Agde in succeeding centuries. The Greek towns were eventually taken over by the Romans, whose architectural legacy is very rich in the Cimiez section of Nice, in Fréjus and particularly in the Rhône Valley, where Nîmes, Arles, Orange, Saint-Rémy-de-Provence and Vaison-la-Romaine have extensive **Roman remains**, including large arenas and theaters that are still in

regular use (see TAKE A ROMAN HOLIDAY, page 16 in TOP SPOTS). There are archaeological museums with important collections from the Roman period in all these places and in Marseille, Agde and Narbonne, the original capital of the Roman province.

From the Middle Ages, there is an even more extensive artistic and architectural legacy, with **Romanesque churches** and abbeys in every part of the region, from Côte d'Azur to the Pyrénées. Some of the most important Romanesque churches are the cathedrals and basilicas of Saint-Victor in Marseille, Saint-Sauveur in Aix, Saint-Trophime in Arles, Notre-Dame-de-Nazareth in Vaison-la-Romaine, Saint-Nazaire in Carcassonne, and Sainte-Eulalie et Sainte-Julie in Elne. Among the most aesthetically distinguished abbeys are Le Thoronet in the Var, Sénanque and Silvacane in Provence, Saint-Gilles near Camargue, Saint-Guilhem-le-Désert west of Montpellier, Fontfroide near Narbonne, Lagrasse in the Corbières and Serrabone, Saint-Michel-de-Cuxa and Saint-Martin-du-Canigou in the Pyrénées in Roussillon. Carcassonne, Aigues-Mortes, and Avignon are the quintessential **medieval cities** of Mediterranean France, the latter possessing an important museum of medieval paintings as well as its architectural treasures. There are also medieval hilltop villages, so-called **"perched villages,"** by the hundreds, with fascinating buildings, sculptures, and paintings from the period. In fact, other than the new beach resorts created since the 1960s, there are few towns of any size that *don't* have Romanesque remains of some kind.

The **Gothic style** came late to the South, but left the largest ecclesiastical structures in the region — the basilica in Saint-Maximin-la-Sainte-Baume and the cathedrals of Saint-Just in Narbonne and Saint-Jean in Perpignan.

Other architectural styles that are well-represented in the region are the **neoclassic** and **baroque** in Menton; the **hill towns** of the Roya Valley, Nice, Grasse, Marseille, Aix, Avignon, Uzès, Montpellier, and Pézenas; the *belle époque* "wedding cake" style in Monaco, Nice, and Cannes; and **contemporary styles** (i.e., post World War II) in Marseille, Nîmes, and Montpellier. For more information on all these periods, see LIFE AND ART, page 83 in THE REGION AND ITS PEOPLE.

MUSEUMS

The art museums of the region are also remarkably rich, particularly in twentieth-century art, since many of the greatest painters of the century settled here and saw fit to lavish their works on the area, including

such giants of modern painting as Picasso, Matisse, and Chagall. Nice has the most art museums, and they are of extraordinarily high quality. The **Matisse Museum**, the **Chagall Museum**, **MAMAC** (Museum of Modern and Contemporary Art), and the **Museum of Naive Art** are especially worth visiting. In Saint-Paul-de-Vence, the **Fondation Maeght** has a dazzling collection of modern painting (Matisse, Chagall, Bonnard, Kandinsky) and sculpture (Calder, Giacometti, Miro), and Matisse's famous **Chapel of the Rosary** is just up the road in Vence. The **Renoir Museum** is in nearby Cagnes-sur-Mer, the **Léger Museum** is in Biot, and Picasso's huge *War and Peace fresco* is in Vallauris. A short distance away is the **Picasso Museum** in Antibes's Château Grimaldi, which has many important works not only by Picasso, but by Léger, de Staël, Klein, Alechinsky, and numerous other modern painters and sculptors. Saint-Tropez's **Annonciade Museum** has a superb collection of Pointillist, Nabi and Fauve paintings, and the **Granet Museum** in Aix has eight small paintings by native son Paul Cézanne. Marseille's **Cantini Museum** and Arles's **Réattu Museum** have prestigious collections of modern art, and in Montpellier, the **Fabre Museum** has several paintings by native son Frédéric Bazille, one of the founders of Impressionism, and by Veronese, Poussin, David, Delacroix, Courbet, and others. Perpignan's **Hyacinthe Rigaud Museum**, named for the Perpignan native who was the

leading portrait artist of Louis XIV's court, has a fascinating and highly eclectic collection ranging from medieval Catalan altarpieces to work by contemporary Catalan painter Antoni Tàpies, along with three sketches by another Catalan artist who worked in this very building, Pablo Picasso.

This prolific genius is abundantly represented in one of the most remarkable small art museums you will ever see, the **Museum of Modern Art** of Céret. The little town of Céret in the eastern foothills of the Pyrénées is known as the "Mecca of Cubism" because of the critical work Picasso and Braque did in that style in Céret, and its museum contains works from the Cubist Period to the present, including paintings by Chagall, Dufy and Miro, drawings by Matisse and sculptures by Maillol, a native of Roussillon, and 53 items by Picasso, including a delightful series of ceramic bowls decorated with bullfighting scenes. For more information on art see LIFE AND ART, page 83 in THE REGION AND ITS PEOPLE.

THE PERFORMING ARTS
Classical music, opera, dance, and theater are alive and well in Nice, Monaco, Marseille, and Montpellier off-season and practically everywhere in the summer. For information

OPPOSITE: The Jardin de la Fontaine in Nîmes. ABOVE: *Les Baigneuses* at the Renoir Museum in Cagnes-sur-Mer, the last home of Pierre-Auguste Renoir.

about performing arts festivals, see MAJOR FESTIVALS AND EVENTS, page 375 in TRAVELERS' TIPS, and for the exact schedule of events, check with the appropriate regional, *départemental*, or local tourist authority (see TOURIST INFORMATION, page 363 in TRAVELERS' TIPS).

Shop till You Drop

TOWN AND COUNTRY MARKETS

The most fun to be had shopping in Mediterranean France is in the open-air markets. These can be food markets, antique and bric-a-brac markets, or Provençal markets, in which food, handicrafts, household products and clothing are sold. All towns have at least one market a week, and no matter how sleepy it may be the rest of the week, the town wakes up on market day.

Nice has a big, colorful, tremendously lively food and flower markets six mornings a week on the Cours Saleya amid the pastel baroque buildings of Old Nice, and on Mondays the antique and bric-a-brac dealers take over the space. **Antibes** is another city with an extremely lively market, this being a Provençal one held every morning except Monday in its large market pavilion and nearby streets by the walls of the medieval town. **Cannes** has one of my favorite food markets, the Marché Forville, a jolly pink stucco pavilion exuding the happy flavors and aromas of Provence — fresh herbs, olives, cheeses, honey, fruits and vegetables,

flowers — likewise open every morning except Monday. Other towns and cities with especially lively markets are **Saint-Tropez**, **Aix-en-Provence** — which has three — and **Apt**, **Arles**, **Saint-Rémy-de-Provence**, **Vaison-la-Romaine**, **Nyons**, **Uzès** (the loveliest of all Provençal markets, in my opinion), **Narbonne**, and **Céret**.

HANDICRAFTS

For handicrafts, the main towns in the hills west of Nice are **Vence** and **Saint-Paul-de-Vence**, where you can find a wide range of crafts — pottery, jewelry, weaving, metal sculpture — **Tourrettes-sur-Loup**, known particularly for its weavers, **Biot** for blown glass, and **Vallauris** for pottery. Another creative center for pottery and for earthenware is **Moustiers-Sainte-Marie** in the Alpes-de-Haute-Provence.

Marseille and **Aix** are noted for their *santons*, "little saints" in Provençal — these are small sculpted figures of Provençal peasants, used in Christmas cribs. They are seen everywhere in markets and souvenir shops.

Another distinctive product of the region is the bright-colored block-printed fabric in paisley, floral, or geometrical patterns seen in all Provençal markets, either as yard goods or made into tablecloths and napkin sets, dresses, skirts, pocket books, and other products. The leading maker of these traditional Provençal fabrics and products is Souleiado. The company is based in Tarascon and has retail shops in Nice, Cannes, Saint-Tropez, Toulon,

Marseille, Aix, Arles, Les Baux, Saint-Rémy, Avignon, Orange, Nîmes, Montpellier, and other towns in the region.

ANTIQUES

For antiques, **Isle-sur-la-Sorgue** east of Avignon is the leading purveyor. You will also find good antique shopping in **Marseille**, **Aix**, **Avignon**, **Nice**, **Antibes**, **Saint-Tropez**, **Toulon**, **Montpellier**, and **Perpignan**.

PERFUME AND LUXURY GOODS

The perfume capital of France is **Grasse**, where you can buy scents directly from Molinard, Galimard, Fragonard, and other manufacturers. For luxury goods of all kinds, your best hunting grounds will be **Monte-Carlo**, **Cannes**, and **Saint-Tropez**.

Short Breaks

Mediterranean France is an ideal place to take a long weekend or short vacation. No matter what you crave — cultural kicks, sporting sprees (golf, tennis, scuba diving, a boat trip), the great outdoors (a short walking, bicycling, or horseback trip through exciting countryside), living it up in playgrounds of the rich, or simply relaxing in exquisitely restful surroundings — this area is likely to have what it takes to give you a memorable and uplifting escape from the routine.

There are a dozen towns and cities that are easy to get to by plane or train where you could spend a richly rewarding short break; culturally, gastronomically and otherwise. For the high life, you need only go to **Cannes** and **Monte-Carlo**. For high life, art and architectural treasures, and a real city to explore, there is the Côte d'Azur's capital of **Nice**. The peaceful old port of **Menton** has particular charm to those who love gardens. A very satisfying break could be spent in the art-rich hill towns of **Vence**, **Saint-Paul-de-Vence**, or **Cagnes-sur-Mer**, all of which have superb cuisine and lodging, with visits to the nearby crafts towns of Tourrettes-sur-Loup, Biot, and Vallauris. The old port of **Antibes**, its luxurious cape and its beach and nightlife Mecca of Juan-les-Pins make a lively combination of historical, nostalgic, and nocturnal fun. For a mixture of gastronomy, historical treasures and the spectacular scenery of the Calanques of Marseille, a weekend in **Marseille** and **Cassis** would be hard to beat. Other excellent destinations for short breaks are **Aix-en-Provence**, **Avignon** and its neighbors of Villeneuve-lès-Avignon and Châteauneuf-du-Pape, **Arles** and the

neighboring Camargue, **Nîmes**, the nearby Pont du Gard and **Uzès**, **Narbonne**, **Perpignan**, **Carcassonne**, and **Montpellier**. Any one of these places offers a memorable experience in itself and has surrounding areas that are well worth exploring.

If you'd like a more rural escape, I suggest the Lubéron, easily reached from Avignon, where **Gordes** has the most to offer in the way of food and accommodations, or **Vaison-la-Romaine** in Northern Provence, with excursions to the olive capitol of Nyons, Mont Ventoux and the wine-rich Dentelles de Montmirail. This area is most easily reached from Montélimar or Orange.

Two spots where you can totally unwind from the pressures of life are the **Mas du Langoustier**, a cheerful hotel with exceptionally fine Provençal cuisine in a remote little cove on the delightful island of Porquerolles, and the medieval **Château de Trigance**, a storybook castle perched atop the village of the same name in a wide, quiet valley near the dramatic Grand Canyon du Verdon, beautifully converted into a Relais & Châteaux hotel and restaurant.

For art lovers, the excellent collections in the museums in Nice, Cagnes-sur-Mer, Saint-Paul-de-Vence, Vence, and Antibes make them obvious options for aesthetically intense breaks. A weekend in **"Cézanne Country"** is another idea. Here you will base yourself in Paul Cézanne's native city of Aix-en-Provence and see the important places of his childhood, the last studio he worked in, perfectly preserved, his beloved Montagne Sainte-

OPPOSITE: There's no shortage of art on the Côte d'Azur, here on the port at Saint-Tropez LEFT and in the pottery capital of Vallauris RIGHT. Boating on the Canal du Midi ABOVE.

Festive Flings

The Mediterranean has always been a festive part of the world, going back at least to the days of the ancient Greeks, with their Dionysian revels, and the French corner of the Mediterranean is certainly no exception. Celebrations here fall into four different categories — traditional, arts, modern special events, and bullfighting *ferias*.

TRADITIONAL FESTIVALS

Festivals of tradition are fêtes of long standing, usually associated with a religious holiday, a local saint's day, a celebration of a local hero or heroic event, a harvest or wine festival. The most important religious festivals take place in winter and spring, following the Christian calendar, from Christmas to Easter.

The **Christmas season** is celebrated with special fervor in Provence, where Christianity first came to France. In December, Marseille has a market for *santons*, the sculpted "little saints" used in *crèches*, or Christmas cribs, which are a specialty of the region. The town of Séguret in the Vaucluse transforms itself into a living *crèche*, with the whole town in costume. On Christmas eve, the traditional Shepherd's Mass takes place at Allauch near Marseille. Midnight masses are held at the grotto at La Sainte-Baume, where Mary Magdalene is said to have prayed, and many other places throughout the region. The **Fête du Citron**, the lemon festival, is held in Menton in early February, when citrus fruits by the thousands are used to decorate parade floats. **Carnaval** in Nice soon follows with a two-week blast of parades, music, theater and dancing in the streets, culminating in a massive fireworks display. On Good Friday, there are processions by several religious brotherhoods in Roussillon. The **Procession of the Penitents of the Sanch** in Perpignan ("*sanch*" being Catalan for *sang*, or blood), is the most dramatic because of the red hoods they wear.

The beginning of May brings the **Fête des Gardians** at Arles, a big rodeo with cowboys from the Camargue, held at the Roman Arena. Nearby Saint-Rémy puts on the **Fête de la Transhumance**, a shepherds' festival in which thousands of sheep are driven through the center of the old town.

Victoire and the red earth landscape around it, and eight small paintings by Cézanne in the Granet Museum. The Aix Tourist Office has the itinerary carefully mapped out for you. The Arles Tourist Office has done the same for "**Van Gogh Country**," which includes the places he frequented and painted in Arles, in the Camargue and the Crau, and in nearby Saint-Rémy — where Van Gogh had himself committed in a mental hospital for a year, and orchards of gnarled olive trees and rows of cypresses, instantly recognizable from paintings. Unfortunately, however, there is only one painting by Van Gogh in the Mediterranean France region, at the Musée Angladon-Dubrujeaud in Avignon.

A less-known, but exciting area for lovers of Modern Art is the delightful medieval port of Collioure south of Perpignan, known as "**The Cradle of Fauvism**" because of the work Matisse and Derain did there in 1905 and 1906, and the nearby Pyrénées hill town of Céret, dubbed "**The Mecca of Cubism**" because of the work Picasso and Braque did there a few years later. Céret's Museum of Modern Art has a first-rate collection of art from Cubism to the present. Both towns are easily reached from Perpignan by either car or public transport.

For an extended break of four or five days, you could take in the impressive concentration of **Roman vestiges** in an around Nîmes, Arles, Saint-Rémy, Vaison-la-Romaine and Orange (see TAKE A ROMAN HOLIDAY, page 16 in TOP SPOTS).

You could also tailor your short break around a special event or holiday, such as the **Gypsy Pilgrimage** to the Camargue in late May or one of the big **bullfighting festivals** in Nîmes, Arles or Béziers, or for that matter, any of the festivals or special events listed in FESTIVE FLINGS, below. There's no end of marvelous short trips to be made in this region.

ABOVE: King Louis IX on his feast day of August 25 at Aigues-Mortes. RIGHT: The Eagles of Beaucaire, a medieval-style birds of prey show at the Château de Beaucaire on the Rhône.

Saint-Tropez has its two **Bravades** in mid-May and in mid-June, the first to honor their patron saint, Torpes, the second to celebrate a heroic defense of the town against the Spanish in the seventeenth century, with parades in fanciful sailors' uniforms and firing of noisy muskets.

The most exciting religious event of the year is the **Gypsy Pilgrimage** to Les Saintes-Maries-de-la-Mer in the Camargue on May 24 and 25, when Gypsies come from all over Europe to carry a statue of their patron saint, the Black Saint Sara, down to the sea. There is lots of Gypsy music and dancing. The **Fête de Saint-Pierre** honoring Saint Peter, the patron saint of fisherman, is celebrated in many ports in early July, nowhere more vigorously than in Sète, where water jousts are among the featured events.

On July 14, Cannes celebrates **Bastille Day** with a tremendous fireworks display on the Croisette. The same day, the mighty walled city of Carcassonne explodes with light, sound and fireworks, and in the first two weeks in August follows it up with **Les Médiévales**, a program of medieval pageants, jousting, crafts shows, and musical events. Late in August, Aigues-Mortes, another walled city, celebrates the **Fête de Saint-Louis** with a medieval pageant and nearby Sète with another round of water jousting.

Arles's **Fête des Prémices du Riz**, the rice harvest festival, is held the second week of September.

In the fall, every town and village that makes wine has its **Fête du Vin** with music, dancing in the village square and, of course, lots of wine tasting. The wine capital of Béziers puts on its **Fête du Vin Nouveau** the third Sunday in October on the grand tree-shaded Allées Paul-Riquet that reminds everyone of Las Ramblas in Barcelona.

ARTS FESTIVALS

Arts festivals are held year round, but the big season is clearly the summer, when music, theater, dance, folk and visual arts programs abound in the region. If you look at arts sections of *Libération*, *Le Monde* or one of the other national newspapers, you will find 20 festivals or big musical events to choose from here on an average summer day. Montpellier is the most active city, with one major theater, music, and dance festival after another. It starts with **Printemps des Comédiens**, a French and European theater festival, early to mid-June. A huge dance festival, the **Festival International Montpellier Danse**, follows for two weeks in late June and early July, presenting leading companies all over the world. For the rest of the summer, every suitable setting for music from the cathedral to the city's ultramodern music halls is taken over by the eclectic programs of classical and avant-garde music, opera, chamber music, and jazz of the **Festival de Radio France**. Many of the concerts are broadcast live by Radio France (see FESTIVE FOLLIES, page 18 in TOP SPOTS).

Meanwhile, starting in early July, at the month-long **Festival d'Avignon**, the City of the Popes cuts loose with performances by hundreds of theater companies, dance troupes and orchestras from all over the world, and street entertainers on the café-lined Place de l'Horloge. An hour away, Aix-en-Provence presents it prestigious **Festival International d'Art Lyrique et de Musique** for opera and classical music. On the Côte d'Azur, the **Nice Jazz Festival** takes over the Roman Arena in Cimiez for two weeks in early July, and the **Festival International de Jazz (Jazz à Juan)** at Juan-les-Pins follows it right away, with the greatest names in jazz, blues and R&B at both places. **L'Été Vaison** features dance, music, and theater in the Roman theater of Vaison-la-Romaine, and at the 10,000-seat Roman Théâtre Antique in Orange, the **Chorégies d'Orange** is one of the world's top opera events. **Organa**, an international organ festival, takes place at Saint-Rémy from July through September, and La Roque d'Anthéron's **Festival International de Piano** is held at the Abbeye de Silvacane the first three weeks of August.

MODERN SPECIAL EVENTS

Many of the modern festive events are associated with sports. Monte-Carlo figures heavily in this category with its **car rally** in January, **circus festival** in February, **tennis open** in April, and **Grand Prix de Monaco** Formula-1 car racing in May. The other leading place for special events is Cannes. The **Cannes Film Festival** in May gets most of the attention, but that's just the tip of the iceberg. Festivals and major trade shows are going on practically all the time.

The **Nioulargue** is a tremendous international sailing event at Saint-Tropez at the end of September. Huge old yachts, former America's Cup champions and challengers, and racers of other classes participate. There are races between boats of different ages and classes.

BULLFIGHTING

Bullfighting needs a category all of its own. It is the rage in southern Provence and Languedoc, where Nîmes, Arles, and Béziers are the great centers of *la tauromachie*. Only Madrid and Seville have more *corridas* than Nîmes, where the **Feria de Pentecôte**, held in the Roman arena in late May, is France's biggest bullfighting event. There is music and street dancing and partying around the clock, with impromptu *bodegas* set up all over town. Nîmes revels in *la tauromachie* all over again the third week of September at the **Feria des Vendanges**, the harvest festival. Arles has its big **Corrida de Pâques** at Easter

Every town and village has at least one big festival a year. OPPOSITE: The *sardana*, the traditional Catalan dance, at a *sardana* festival in Collioure. ABOVE: A rustic local festival in tiny Saint-Etienne-des-Grès in the Alpilles.

and, like Nîmes, plenty of normal bullfights throughout the summer. Most of the bullfighting is Spanish style, with all the colorful pageantry, where they kill the bull at the end. But a Provençal style of bullfighting is also practiced in this part of France. Here young men dare death by trying to pluck a rosette, *la cocarde*, from between the bull's horns. But at the end of the match, the bull stays alive and is allowed to go back home to the Camargue.

There are bullfights in both styles in Saint-Rémy, the Camargue, and many other places. Béziers has its **Feria**, Spanish style, on August 14 and 15, with the running of the bulls through the streets, parades, the *corrida*, and partying all night.

For a more complete listing of the various festivals and special events, see MAJOR FESTIVALS AND EVENTS, page 375 in TRAVELERS' TIPS.

Galloping Gourmets

In the sixteenth century, Alonso Vasquez, a Mediterranean man, traveled to Flanders and was dismayed by what people ate and didn't eat there. It was "the land where there grows neither thyme, nor lavender, figs, olives, melons, or almonds; where parsley, onions and lettuce have neither juice nor taste; where dishes are prepared, strange to relate, with butter from cows instead of olive oil."

Vasquez's manner of expression may have a quaint ring, but the idea behind it is strictly contemporary. *Gault-Millau Magazine* called our present moment in culinary history "*L'Heure du Midi*" (The Hour of the South) and said, "Long eclipsed by the 'values' of the North where butter, cream and meat in abundance reigned, fish, tomatoes and olive oil have little by little regained their place… in the sun."

Meanwhile, the *Wine Spectator* named Alain Ducasse the best chef in the world. He is the chef of Monte-Carlo's Louis XV Restaurant and the most highly regarded practitioner of Mediterranean cuisine.

The food is delicious, but what brought it into vogue, particularly in America, were the health benefits associated with "the Mediterranean Diet." When it was scientifically demonstrated that the mixture of bread, olive oil, and tannic wine acts as a magic potion against cardiovascular disease, the stampede to olive oil and French red wine was on.

Alain Ducasse, a serene man, completely unfazed by the kingly position into which his cooking has thrust him, rejects the notion that this is a fad. "Mediterranean cuisine is not a phenomenon of fashion," he says. "It has always seduced everyone, as it seduced me, because it is real, essential, universal, and because it was born — and it is not just by chance — in the cradle of Western civilization."

The essentials of Mediterranean cuisine are simple, and that is part of its charm. They are olive oil, wine, garlic, tomatoes, herbs from Provence — thyme, rosemary, sage, savory, marjoram, oregano, basil, and parsley, fresh Mediterranean fish, fresh Provençal vegetables and, from time to time, meat. The key to success is judicious application of the oil, herbs, garlic, and wine to subtly flavor the fish and vegetables without obliterating their own natural savor.

VEGETABLES

In the cuisine of the leading chefs of the region, Ducasse, Roger Vergé, Jacques Maximin and others, the vegetable is the star of the show. *Petits farcis* are stuffed tomatoes, peppers, onions, eggplants, zucchinis, and even zucchini blossoms, *fleurs de courgette*. Various fillings are used, depending on the season and the imagination of the chef. *Beignets de fleurs de courgette* are deep-fried zucchini-blossom fritters. *Ratatouille* ("ra-ta-tweee," not "ra-ta-too-ey" as it is sometimes mispronounced) is a cooked dish of sliced eggplant, zucchini, tomatoes, peppers, and onions seasoned with garlic and herbs. It is usually served cold in the summer. *Soupe au pistou* is a popular vegetable soup with basil, garlic, and olive oil. *Mesclun*, also spelled *mesclum*, is a mixture of several tender salad greens, grown mainly in the back country of Nice. The Cours Saleya market in Nice is the best place to find it. *Salade Niçoise*, the famous salad of tuna, anchovies, black olives and lettuce, is sold everywhere. *Truffles* come mainly from the Tricastin in Northern Provence, where Valréas is its big market town. Since the lower Rhône Valley and the Durance Valleys are the leading vegetable-producing areas of France, you are sure to find and abundance of fresh Provençal legumes.

SEAFOOD

Due to overfishing in the Mediterranean, local fish has become quite expensive, and much of the seafood you find in the markets and restaurants is actually trucked in from the Atlantic. But Mediterranean people are willing to pay the higher price, because their seafood has more flavor, they claim. The important Mediterranean fish to look out for

are *rouget* (red mullet), *saint-pierre* (John Dory), *loup de mer* (sea bass), *requin* (shark, a local variety, very tender), *turbot*, *rascasse* (scorpion fish of the rockfish family, essential for *bouillabaisse*), *chapon de mer* (a rockfish-like cousin of the *rascasse*).

The biggest French fishing port on the Mediterranean is Sète on the Languedoc coast. Most shellfish come from this coast too. The *moules* and *huîtres* (mussels and oysters) from Bouzigues are especially well-known. You will also find local *crevettes* (shrimp), *langoustines* (large crayfish), *tourteaux* (crabs), and at outlandish prices, the occasional *langouste*, a clawless spiny lobster. *Encornet* or *seiche* (squid, cuttlefish) and *poulpe* (octopus) are widely available. Restaurants often have *"Petite Friture"* on the menu as an *entrée* (the French term for first course). This is a heaping platter of little deep-fried whitebait, enough for a light lunch with bread and a green salad.

Bouillabaisse is the classic Mediterranean fish soup. It originated in the Marseille area, but is available all along the coast, generally at very hefty prices. The dish was created to give fishermen's families a way to eat the fish of little value in the catch that otherwise would have been thrown away. But now that there is no such thing as a cheap Mediterranean fish, you will not find the real thing for less than about 200 francs per serving. But it is an enormous feast and an unforgettable experience, especially when served right at the port or with a view of the coast.

Bourride is a soup of white fish, onions, tomatoes, garlic, herbs and olive oil, seasoned with *aïoli* (garlic mayonnaise); it is generally much cheaper than *bouillabaisse*, but delicious too, and served all along the coast. It is a specialty of Sète.

Soupe des Pêcheurs (fishermen's soup) is a general term for fish stews also found on the menu.

The fish dish called *aïoli* is a heaping platter of boiled salted codfish, snails, and vegetables that arrives steaming at the table and is served with the garlic mayonnaise after which the feast is named.

Brandade de morue, a mousse of salt cod with garlic and cream or olive oil, is another reasonably priced dish that is widely available. It is a specialty of Nîmes.

The different areas all have their own local specialties, and none more than Nice, where the great fish dish you will see on the menu is *stockfisch*, also called *stocaficada* or *estoficado*. This can be either a flattened dried codfish or a purée of codfish with olive oil, tomatoes, black olives, peppers, potatoes, onions, garlic, and herbs.

The beautiful Catalan port of Collioure is famous for its anchovies (*anchois*), which are grilled right on the beach.

Recommendations about where to find local specialties will be found in the destination chapters.

Before moving on to the meat, let me put in a word for a personal favorite: grilled sea bass with fennel (*loup de mer grillé au fenouil*), a naturally delicious fish, so simple to prepare that only a very careless chef could go wrong.

MEAT

Roast lamb (*agneau*) is a great favorite, lamb from Sisteron in the Alpes-de-Haute-Provence being the most highly prized. Chicken (*poulet*) is usually served roasted or cooked in a tomato sauce (*à la Provençale*). *Pintade* (guinea hen) is

The flavors of the South, Provençal herbs LEFT and shellfish RIGHT in Saint-Tropez.

another favorite bird. *Daube*, a stew of braised chunks of meat, usually beef, with various vegetables, is common in most of the region. Some local specialties are *saucisson d'Arles*, a salami-like dried pork and beef sausage; *gardiane*, a stew made from the meat of bulls in the Camargue and upper Languedoc (sometimes from bulls killed in the bull ring); and in Marseille and the lower Rhône, *pieds et paquets*, sheep's feet and little packets of sheep's entrails cooked in tomatoes, olive oil and wine, much more savory than it sounds.

During hunting season, especially as you get into the mountains, many restaurants feature *gibier* (game) — *sanglier* (wild boar), *marcassin* (young boar), *chevreuil* (venison), *lièvre* (hare), *faisan* (pheasant), *perdrix* (partridge), *caille* (quail).

Cassoulet is not typically Mediterranean cuisine, but since our boundaries extend as far west as Carcassonne and Castelnaudary, two of the main cities for this dish, we include it. It is a casserole of baked white beans and a combination of meats, such as duck, goose, mutton, pork, and sausage, and is very hearty and filling.

In Roussillon the traditional Catalan dish is *cargolade*, a mixed grill of snails, lamb, and sausage cooked over vine clippings, a complicated meal to prepare, rarely made today.

SAUCES, DRESSINGS, AND DIPS

Aïoli is garlic mayonnaise. *Anchoïade* is an anchovy, garlic, and olive oil sauce. *Pistou* is a basil, garlic, and olive oil sauce. *Rouille* is a mayonnaise of olive oil, garlic and hot peppers, served with bread, usually with *bouillabaisse* and fish soups. *Tapenade* is a paste of black olives, olive oil, garlic, anchovies, capers and lemon juice, served either with bread as an appetizer or used in cooking.

CHEESES

The cheeses of Mediterranean France come mainly from the ring of mountains surrounding the region and can be purchased fresh from their makers in the wonderful outdoor markets at Apt, Aix, Carpentras, Uzès, and other places. **Annot** and **Banon** in the Alpes-de-Haute-Provence are noted for their sheep and goat cheeses. *Picodon* is a small, hard, flat, disc of goat cheese aged in brandy from northern Provence.

Pélardon is a little disc of goat cheese from the Cévennes, often sold in a blend of olive oil and *eau-de-vie*. **Tomme Arlésienne**, also called **Tomme de Camargue**, is made from a blend of cow and goat milk flavored with savory; it is popular in upper Languedoc and Arles.

PASTAS AND BREADS

Pasta is popular everywhere, especially in Old Nice, where delicious *gnocchi*, pizza, and their own local onion pizza called *pissaladière* can be found at every turn, as can *pan bagnat* (*salade Niçoise* on a roll) and *socca* (crêpes made from chickpea flour). *Fougasse*, a flat, latticed, pizza crust-like bread flavored with olives, onions, anchovies, herbs or spices, is available in most *boulangeries* in Provence. It is great for picnics.

DESSERTS, SWEETS, AND PASTRIES

Provence being France's largest fruit-growing area, a large candied-fruit production has developed. The leading places for *fruits confits* (candied fruit) are Apt in the Lubéron, Saint-Rémy, and the Nice area. Nice also makes a tart called a *tourte aux blettes* filled with raisins, Swiss chard, and pine nuts. Saint-Tropez has its famous *Tarte Tropézienne*, a tart filled with confectioners cream. *Calissons d'Aix* are little flat biscuits of almond, honey, and melon paste made in Aix. *Navettes de Saint-Victor* are tubular orange-flavored biscuits made by a famous eighteenth-century bakery in Marseille. The great chocolate candy-maker is **Puyricard** near Aix, whose products are sold throughout the region. There are many kinds of **honey** available, and lavender honey in particular is fantastic.

WINE

As with Mediterranean cooking, these have been exciting years for the area's wines. Since the 1960s, there has been a revolution in wine-making in the South. With only a few prestigious exceptions before that revolution — Châteauneuf-du-Pape, Bandol, Fitou — the area was known mainly for the vast quantities of "plonk," cheap red wine, it produced. The other main product of Southern vineyards was rosés, a whole category of wine once sneered at by connoisseurs. That situation has changed over the past 25 years, as the South has responded to the affluent French public's increasing demand for quality wines and a corresponding drop in the market for plonk. The wines of the South have improved drastically, as wine makers have followed a strategy of high quality and low yields. Both red wines and that formerly despised category of rosés have gained a good deal of respect.

Mediterranean France has been making wine since the sixth century BC, when the Greeks taught the local Ligurians that there was something else that could be done with grapes besides eat them. It is the oldest wine-making area in France and by far the largest.

By the time of the Pax Romana, when the Empire's bread and circuses needed prodigious quantities of wine, the whole sweep of Provincia Gallia Narbonensis was planted in vines, except for the eastern flank, where the land was not suitable. Today, other than the Alpes-Maritimes — where there are only two very small wine-growing areas, the high mountains, and a few sections where there are only orchards, rice fields or cattle ranches, vineyards can be found just about everywhere. In most places, the soil is so poor and the climate so hot and dry that the hardy grapevine is the only plant that can survive.

Since individual wine-growing areas will be discussed as we come upon them, we will only give a brief geographical overview here.

There are three major wine-growing regions in Mediterranean France. In Northern Provence, the Rhône Valley is known mainly for its **Côtes du Rhône** wines, most of them reds, of which **Châteauneuf-du-Pape** is the best known *Appellation d'Origine Contrôlée (AOC)*, and in fact was the first *AOC* ever created. (The *AOC* is a strict set of government standards that guarantees a wine's place of origin, the varieties of grapes used, and production methods and quantities allowable; it tends to promote quality, but is not in itself a guarantee of quality.) Newer *AOC*s in Northern Provence are **Coteaux du Tricastin** and **Côtes du Ventoux**, similar to Côtes du Rhône, but lighter. West of the Rhône, the villages of **Tavel** and **Lirac** are famed for their rosés.

The second major region is the Côte d'Azur's Var département, where the *AOC* is **Côtes de Provence**, and the area of Provence around Aix, where **Coteaux d'Aix-en-Provence** wines are grown. Both make mostly rosés and between them produce more than half of

France's *AOC* rosé wine. In 1995, a former sub-area of Coteaux d'Aix-en-Provence in the hills of the Alpilles gained the right to an *appellation* of its own — *AOC* **Baux-de-Provence**. It produces mostly red wines. Within this large overall region, there are also three small, but very prestigious *AOC*s — **Bandol**, famed for its vigorous reds, **Cassis** known for its dry whites, and **Palette**, a tiny *AOC* area with only two vineyards in Meyreuil south of Aix, making highly prized reds, whites and rosés.

The third major region is Languedoc-Roussillon, the largest and currently the most dynamic wine-producing region in France. It makes mostly reds. Moving from north to south, its main *AOC* table wines are **Costières de Nîmes** in the area around Nîmes, followed by **Coteaux du Languedoc**, covering a large area along the coast and up into the foothills of the Cévennes, with twelve different locally labeled areas (La Clape, Faugères, Picpoul de Pinet, etc.). Continuing southward, we come to the **Minervois**, the overlapping **Corbières** and **Fitou** areas, and **Côtes du Roussillon**.

Most areas in Languedoc and Roussillon have graduated to *AOC* status since the 1960s, some in very recent years.

Languedoc and Roussillon wine makers have also put great effort into improving their *vins de pays*, pleasant little country wines without all the regulations of the *AOC*s. **Vin de Pays d'Oc** from the Hérault department of Languedoc has built a large following in France in the past few years. You should not hesitate to try it.

In Roussillon, the predominant *AOC* table wine is **Côtes du Roussillon**, but there are two

Sausages LEFT from Arles and olives RIGHT at the Saturday morning market in Uzès.

small, highly prestigious *AOCs* you should know about — **Collioure** from vineyards on the steep hillsides of the Côte Vermeille, which produce some of the most subtly flavorful reds of southern France, and **Blanquette** et **Crémant de Limoux**, sparkling white wines from the charming town of Limoux in the hills west of the Corbières. Sparkling wines were made here before the process of putting bubbles in wine made its way up to Champagne.

Languedoc and Roussillon also produce a number of *vins doux naturels*, or sweet apéritif wines, most notably those of **Rivesaltes** and **Banyuls**.

For the tourist, the existence of thousands of vineyards presents a unique opportunity to enrich his or her travels. Wine makers are more than happy to have people visit their *caves*. You will have the chance to experience what wine writer Hugh Johnson calls "the unique complex of sensual, aesthetic and intellectual rewards that only wine of all products can offer: it is a perfect expression of modern civilization at its best. There is simply nothing that so perfectly encapsulates pleasure, social well-being, and aesthetic exploration at the same time."

Special Interests

There are many special interests that can be pursued in the region, either by stopping in one place to participate in an educational program or by pursuing your particular passion as you travel along.

CULINARY LESSONS

Given the enormous interest that Mediterranean cuisine has generated in recent years, many travelers may welcome a chance to learn how to prepare it. A fine place to learn the secrets of Provençal cooking is internationally renowned chef Roger Vergé's **École du Moulin** in the pretty village of Mougins overlooking Cannes. Classes are held in a specially designed teaching kitchen upstairs at the Restaurant L'Amandier in the center of Mougins. The sessions are about two-and-a-half hours long and cost 300 francs per session or 1,350 francs for a series of five. Classes are held Tuesday through Saturday. For information or bookings, contact the school at (04 93 75 35 70 or FAX 04 93 90 18 55 E-MAIL mougins@relaischateaux.fr WEB SITE www.relaischateaux.fr/mougins, or write to them at Restaurant l'Amandier, 06250 Mougins.

In La Cadière-d'Azur, in the heart of Bandol wine country between Marseille and Toulon, chef René Bérard (a fellow member of Roger Vergé in the distinguished order of Maître Cuisiniers de France) offers a four-day course at **Hostellerie Bérard**, all day Monday through Thursday, year round, except in July and August. This is a hands-on course that includes trips to regional food markets, to the hills to pick Provençal herbs, to vineyards to taste wine, and to a local olive oil mill. The January programs include special truffle options. The students reside at the lovely Hostellerie Bérard. The cost of the four-day course and accommodations is 6,500 francs for one person in a single room, 5,460 francs per person for two people sharing a room. The price includes the course, five nights in the hotel (Sunday night through Friday morning), dinner Sunday night and breakfast and lunch daily. For more information, contact the Hostellerie Bérard (04 94 90 11 43 FAX 04 94 90 01 94 E-MAIL berard@hotel-berard.com WEB SITE www.hotel-berard.com. The mailing address is: F-83740 La Cadière-d'Azur.

VISITING VINEYARDS

As noted, vineyards abound in the region, and stopping in to visit them is one of the most enjoyable things you can do. The most dynamic wine-making area at the moment is Languedoc, and if you would like to have an organized tour there, a group of eight leading vineyards has banded together as the **Club des Grands Vins de Châteaux de Languedoc**, and they make all the land arrangements (hotels, meals and ground transportation, everything first-class) for visitors to tour their *châteaux*. They include the Abbaye de Valmagne, a breathtaking medieval abbey in the vicinity of Mèze on the Basin de Thau, where prestigious Coteaux du Languedoc wines are made, and the distinguished Château de Lastours in the Corbières south of Narbonne. A three-day tour costs 3,480 francs, a four-day tour 4,415 francs. For information, contact Jean Viennet at the Château de Raissac (04 67 28 15 61 FAX 04 67 28 19 75, 34500 Béziers.

HOUSEBOATING

Houseboats can be rented in the canals to the west of the Rhône. From Beaucaire, you can cruise along the northern edge of the Camargue on the Canal du Rhône à Sète past the medieval walled city of Aigues-Mortes and the ancient island cathedral of Maguelone to the bustling fishing port of Sète. From there you can continue south through the Bassin de Thau and enter the Canal du Midi, which wends its peaceful, tree-lined way by Béziers, the Oppidum d'Ensérune, and Carcassonne.

There are several places where you can rent houseboats; principally **Beaucaire, Saint-Gilles**, **Port-de-Colombiers** near Béziers, **Argens-Minervois**, and **Castelnaudary**. Addresses and phone numbers of rental companies can be found in the chapter on Languedoc. For more information, contact the Comité Régional du Tourisme du Languedoc-Roussillon (see TOURIST INFORMATION, page 363 in TRAVELERS' TIPS). To make boat rental arrangements in the United States before coming to France, get in touch with Le Boat ((201) 236-2333 TOLL-FREE (800) 992-0291 FAX (201) 236-1214 E-MAIL leboatinc@worldnet.att.net WEB SITE www.leboat.com, 10 South Franklin Street (Suite 204B), Ramsey, New Jersey 07446, which represents the Crown Blue Line in America. In Great Britain, the Crown Blue Line is represented by Andrew Brock Travel Ltd. ((1572) 821 330 FAX (1572) 821 072

E-MAIL ABROCK3650@aol.com, 54 High Street East, Uppingham, Rutland LE15 9PZ. Ask for their helpful booklet *French Country Cruises*.

NUDIST COLONIES

Nudism, or *naturisme* as *naturistes* prefer to call it, is very popular in Mediterranean France, both at the shore and in the mountains. **Héliopolis** on the Île du Levant in the Îles d'Hyères is the granddaddy of French nudist colonies. It started in the 1930s and is still going strong. But by far the largest is **Port Ambonne** at Cap d'Agde, where 25,000 to 30,000 nudists are in residence in midsummer,

and there are hotels, camping grounds, restaurants, banks, and supermarkets for nudists. For information, contact the Fédération Française de Naturisme (01 47 64 32 82 FAX 01 47 64 32 63 WEB SITE www.ffn-naturisme.com, 65 rue Tocqueville, 75017 Paris. They will send you a free brochure on all the nudist resorts and camps in France with text in the five major European languages. To get it sent to you overseas, you must mail them three international mail coupons, which are available in post offices in your country.

HEALTH SPAS

You will notice that many towns in the region have the suffix *-les-bains* added to their names, as in **Digne-les-Bains**, **Amélie-les-Bains**, **Molitg-les-Bains**, and so forth, many of them in the Pyrénées. These and many others without *les bains* in their names are natural springs where treatment facilities have been

ABOVE: The bells of the fortified church of Les Saintes-Maries-de-la-Mer. TOP RIGHT: A plumed escort at the African Reserve of Sigean near Narbonne. LOWER RIGHT and OVERLEAF: Cruising on the Canal du Midi.

established to take advantage of the minerals in the spas' waters to cure various medical conditions — respiratory, arthritic, urinary, and so forth. Some of the mineral springs have been in use since the time of the Romans. For information, contact the Fédération Thermale et Climatique Française (01 43 25 11 85 FAX 01 46 34 07 45, 16 rue Estrapade, 75005 Paris.

Another kind of water treatment available in several places along the coast is *thalassothérapie*, which uses salt water, massage, mud baths with algae solutions, and exercises for its curative and stress-relieving ends. These include treatments for a wide range of conditions, from rheumatism to smoking to the stresses of the modern world to simply getting in shape. There are modern centers at the Marina Baie des Anges in **Villeneuve-Loubet** near Nice, **Antibes**, **Fréjus**, **Saint-Raphaël**, **Port-Camargue**, and **La Grande-Motte**. For information, contact Maison de La Thalassothérapie (01 45 72 38 38 FAX 01 45 72 40 60, 5 rue Denis Poisson, 75017 Paris. The most gorgeous thalassotherapy center is **Les Thermes Marins de Monte-Carlo** at the Hôtel de Paris in Monaco. For information, contact them at ((377) 92 16 40 40 FAX (377) 92 16 49 49 E-MAIL thermes@sbm.mn, or by mail at 2 avenue de Monte-Carlo, BP 215, Monte-Carlo, 98004 Monaco Cedex.

LANGUAGE COURSES

If you'd like to study French, the **Institut de Français** (04 93 01 88 44 FAX 04 93 76 92 17 E-MAIL instfran@aol.com WEB SITE www .institutedefrancais.com, 06230 Villefranche-sur-Mer, offers intensive courses for adults in two-to four-week cycles. In Aix-en-Provence, you can take four-week intensive French courses in June, July, and September at the **Institut d'Études Françaises pour Étudiants Étrangers** (04 42 21 70 90 FAX 04 42 23 02 64 E-MAIL ina.de-bruin@iufee.u-3mrs.fr WEB SITE www.u-3mrs.fr, Université Aix-Marseille III, 23 rue Gaston-de-Soporta, 13625 Aix-en-Provence.

GARDEN VISITS

For those with a special interest in horticulture, the most important gardens are the Jardin Botanique Exotique and the Jardin des Colombières in Menton, the Jardin Exotique in Monaco and the one in Èze, the gardens of the Ephrussi de Rothschild in Cap-Ferrat, the Jardin Thuret in Cap d'Antibes, Princess Pauline's Garden and the Noailles Gardens in Grasse, and the Jardins Olbius-Riquier in Hyères.

THE RELIGIOUS HERITAGE

Christianity first established itself in France in the Mediterranean area, and important remains of Gallo-Roman and very early medieval churches and monasteries are to be found in the Îles de Lérins, Fréjus, Marseille and Arles in Provence, and in Elne and Serrabone in Roussillon. The Romanesque results of the full flowering of the medieval monastic movement can be found as you travel throughout the region (see LIFE AND ART, page 83 in THE REGION AND ITS PEOPLE).

Mediterranean France also played a crucial role in Jewish history in France, particularly during the Middle Ages, when the Kingdom of France expelled the Jews and they took refuge in the papal lands of the Comtat Venaissin in what is now the Vaucluse. The oldest synagogue in France is in Carpentras, and there are other vestiges of the medieval Jewish presence in Cavaillon, Avignon, and other places in the Comtat. For a fascinating free brochure on the subject entitled *The Road of Jewish Heritage in the South of France*, contact the Comité Départemental du Tourisme de Vaucluse (see TOURIST INFORMATION, page 363 in TRAVELERS' TIPS).

Taking a Tour

For people who prefer to let the travel professionals lay out their itineraries and handle all the logistics, a number of companies offer package deals in southern France. Because of their bargaining power with airlines and hotels, the arrangements they make are often less expensive than they would be if you made the same bookings on your own.

ALLEZ FRANCE

This friendly British outfit offers a wide range of trips — golf vacations, wine tours, mobile-home vacations, short breaks in Nice, Antibes, Juan-les-Pins, the Grand Canyon du Verdon — and a large selection of rental apartments, cottages and villas, with color photos of them in their brochure. Allez France ((44 1903) 742 345 FAX (44 1903) 745 044 WEB SITE www .greatescapes.co.uk is at 27 West Street, Storrington, West Sussex RH20 4DZ.

THE FRENCH EXPERIENCE

This French-owned New York company offers prearranged self-drive tours in the main regions of tourist interest in France, including Provence and the Côte d'Azur. Each tour lasts one-week and can be extend by adding another week-long tour, such as "A Week in Provence" and "Along the French Riviera."

They also book houseboats and *gîtes*. The French Experience ((212) 896-1115 FAX (212) 986-3808 E-MAIL info@frenchexperience.com WEB SITE www.frenchexperience.com is at 370 Lexington Avenue, New York, New York 10017.

AMERICAN EXPRESS

Another organization that can arrange just about anything for you is American Express. For information on their services, call them in your local area or from anywhere in the United States at ((900) 990-0400 (there is a phone charge of 50 cents a minute). Their offices and correspondents in Mediterranean France can book local sightseeing trips, coach excursions, boat trips, and rental and chauffeur-driven cars on an *à la carte* basis. For information about travel arrangements, get in touch with them at their main office in the region at (04 93 16 53 51 FAX 04 93 16 53 42, 11 promenade des Anglais, 06000 Nice.

GOLF TOURS

InterGolf offers golf tours to the French Riviera from the United States. For information, contact them at (/FAX (770) 518-1272 TOLL-FREE (800) 468-0051 WEB SITE www.golf.com/travel/intergolf, PO Box 500608, Atlanta, Georgia 31150-0608.

ORGANIZED BIKING AND WALKING TOURS

For outstanding biking and walking trips in Provence, contact Butterfield & Robinson

((416) 864-1354 TOLL-FREE (800) 678-1147 FAX (416) 864-0541 WEB SITE www.butterfield.com, 70 Bond Street, Toronto, Ontario M5B 1X3 Canada. The group leaders are bright and knowledgeable, the food and accommodations top-of-the-line, and their brochure is a work of art. It goes without saying that these trips are far from cheap. The company also rents country homes in Provence and the Côte d'Azur.

CULTURAL AND EDUCATIONAL PROGRAMS

For information on the full range of cultural and educational programs available in Mediterranean France — crafts workshops, art and music classes, studies of the French language and culture, and so forth — contact the Cultural Service of the French Embassy or Consulate nearest you.

There are always plenty of archaeology projects under way in Provence and Languedoc in need of summer volunteers. To find out what these projects are, write to the Direction des Antiquités Préhistoriques et Historiques, 21 boulevard du Roi-René, 13617 Aix-en-Provence, or 5bis rue de la Salle l'Évêque, 34000 Montpellier.

A vineyard in the Hérault, France's most productive winemaking *département*.

Welcome to Mediterranean France

IF YOU COME TO THE SOUTH OF FRANCE in the long, hot days of summer, you will hear a shrill rasping chant in the background wherever you go: the ceaseless song of the cicada. "*Le soleil me fait chanter*" chirps the noisy insect — "The sun makes me sing." Provençal children smile. They know what many Northerners have been thrilled to discover later in life — Van Gogh, Matisse, and Chagall among them: In Mediterranean France, the sun makes everything sing.

This is clearly the sun's country. It's hot and dry in the summer and, like the rest of the Mediterranean basin, warm the year round. In all four of its regions, the Côte d'Azur, Provence, Languedoc, and Roussillon, you will find 3,000 hours of sunshine a year, and temperatures that rarely drop below 11°C (52°F) even in the winter, a stark contrast to Paris and the rest of Northern France known for its cold and overcast days. Geography and climate have conspired to make this 10% of France's surface a paradise for nature lovers, sports enthusiasts, and sun worshipers who come south to "lizard themselves," as the French say, on the beaches.

Mediterranean France is shaped like a giant Greek amphitheater, ideally oriented south and east, facing the sun and sea. Nine chains of mountains wall in this crescent-shaped arena, flanked on either side by the two greatest ranges in Europe, the Alps and the Pyrénées. The seven other ranges, including the Alpes-de-Haute-Provence and the Cévennes, with heights up to 1,700 m (5,580 ft), are only 200 km (125 miles) or less from the shore in most places. The nearly unbroken rampart 700 km (440 miles) long locks in the Mediterranean warmth and provides a barrier against the cold drafts of the north.

But the Mediterranean Sea, the region's other boundary, has always provided a gateway to the outside world through the dozens of ports scattered along 520 km (325 miles) of coastline between Italy and Spain. Since this region fronts on the sea that was the Cradle of Western Civilization, it has a cultural heritage as brilliant as its weather.

The seeds were planted by Greek seafarers who arrived in the seventh century BC with the vine, the olive tree, and Ionian ideas. They established towns along the coast and a style of eating, drinking, and making merry that characterizes Mediterranean France to this day. To them we must add the other peoples who brought their influences to the area — Romans, early Christians, Catalans, Italians, Cathars from the Balkans, Protestants from Switzerland and Germany and the Gauls, Celts and Franks from what is now Northern France.

The other main route of travel between the Mediterranean coast of France and the outside world has always been the Rhône River and its valley, the only corridor between North and South. The Greeks used it for trade, the Romans to conquer Northern Europe, and the Northern French to invade the South.

The valley also acts as a massive ventilating system, for it is down the Rhône that the *Mistral*, the "Master Wind," hurls itself from the North. This wind can be fierce and sometimes dangerous. But it is also responsible for the famed sparklingly clear days and nights that Van Gogh captured so brilliantly in his sunflower paintings and his *Starry Night*.

While I can't hope to fully convey all the human dimensions of an area that has been shaped by 2,600 years of evolution and cross-cultural

pollination, I have tried to point out the major influences that have created the distinctive cultures of the Côte d'Azur, Provence, Languedoc, and Roussillon. I think of Mediterranean France as a gigantic tapestry with its threads of history woven into the fabric of today. Where else can you watch a modern dance program in the courtyard of the fourteenth-century Palace of the Popes, wine and dine in a beautifully restored Romanesque abbey, or attend a bullfight in a 2,000-year-old Roman arena? To me, this area's greatest appeal has always been the relaxed, natural Mediterranean blend of the very old and the very new. My travels in this part of the world have given me some of the most pleasurable moments in my life, and I hope, as historian Fernand Braudel puts it, that "a little of this joy and a great deal of Mediterranean sunlight will shine from the pages of this book."

OPPOSITE: Entrevaux in the Alpes-de-Haute-Provence, fortified by Louis XIV to defend France's Var River frontier with the Duchy of Savoy.
ABOVE: Collioure, a magnet for painters since the days of Matisse.

The Region and its People

AS THE CROSSROADS BETWEEN ITALY AND SPAIN, the Mediterranean basin and Northern Europe, this region had no choice but to have a tumultuous life. Since the days of the Greeks and Romans, the main currents of Western European history have swept back and forth through here — Charlemagne, the Albigensian Crusade, the popes of Avignon, Napoléon, the World War II Allied landings, the European Union today. This is by no means a simple story. But if it seems at times too crowded with actors and events, it may help you to keep in mind that only a few important powers have dominated the region over its 3,000 years of history. They were the Greeks, the Romans, three houses of medieval lords, and, from the thirteenth century onward, the Kingdom, Empire and Republic of France. To these we should add the pervasive influence of the Roman Catholic Church, a major factor in art and architecture, politics, and all aspects of social behavior from the latter years of the Roman Empire to the present.

THE FIRST MILLION YEARS

The first human beings to set foot in Europe crossed the Straits of Gibraltar from Africa a million years ago. Not surprisingly, they wasted no time getting up to the Côte d'Azur. Stone tools and bone fragments from 950,000 years ago found in a cave at Roquebrune-Cap-Martin are the oldest evidence of human presence in Europe. 500,000 years later, Tautavel Man hunted in the valleys north of Roussillon, where his skull, the oldest discovered in Europe, was found in a cave north of Perpignan, along with bones of the elephants, woolly rhinoceroses, and deer that were his prey. Similar refuse from Stone Age hunters' feasts was found in a cave at Terra Amata at the foot of Mount Boron in Nice. Though other hunters undoubtedly roamed the hills and valleys of Mediterranean France over much of the period, no evidence of their presence during the next few hundred thousand years has surfaced. But in 1985 the next important trace of prehistoric man's activities in the area came to light — cave drawings skillfully depicting penguins, seals, and land animals that were discovered in a grotto near Marseille. These paintings, 18,000 to 27,000 years old, predate those at Lascaux in Périgord by up to 13,000 years. The paintings were discovered by scuba diver Henri Cosquer in a cave that was submerged when the level of the Mediterranean rose after the last Ice Age.

In 1994 another astounding discovery was made at Combe d'Arc in the Ardèche northwest of Avignon: four large caves containing over four hundred clear, extremely skillful paintings of mammoths, rhinos, lions, oxen, a red hyena, and the only panther and owls recorded in prehistoric cave paintings. These have been carbon-dated at 32,000 years old — the oldest European artwork ever found. This area was the northernmost part of Europe inhabited by humans in those chilly times.

Around 6,000 BC, sheep were domesticated in southwest Provence, and hunting gave way to pastoral life. The oldest pottery yet discovered in Western Europe also appeared in Provence at this time. But the strangest reminders of early Man's presence are to be found in Vallée des Merveilles in the Alpes-Maritimes, where Bronze Age shepherds scratched more than 100,000 complex abstract designs into the rocks.

By 1,000 BC, Ligurian tribes from northern Italy were farming and raising animals throughout Provence, and living in fortified hilltop settlements known as *oppida*. West of the Rhône, native Iberians followed the same pattern, always settling well in from the coast, partly for practical reasons — staying away from malarial swamps and pirates — but also from a deep-seated peasant distrust of the sea. "*Lauso la mare e tente'n terro*," goes an old Provençal saying — "Praise the sea and stay on land." The Ligurians' oppidum of Entremont near Aix and the Iberians' oppidum of Ensérune between Béziers and Narbonne, now well-excavated archaeological sites, grew into large towns. In the seventh century BC, Celts from northern Germany migrated south, married Ligurians and joined them in their bucolic lifestyle. But the next group to arrive came by the sea. They were an adventurous lot with a Dionysian outlook who introduced the characteristic Mediterranean spirit that permeates the region to this day.

THE GREEKS

Around 600 BC, Greek seafarers from Phocaea in Asia Minor came upon a magnificent harbor framed by white limestone hills so reminiscent of the Ionian coast that it must have made their hearts leap. Legend has it that the Phocaeans — not to be confused with the Phoenicians who were a Semitic people from Lebanon — landed in the middle of a ceremony in which Gyptis, the daughter of the area's Ligurian chief, was in the process of choosing a husband. But when she saw

the handsome Greek leader Protis, she looked no farther. Not only did her father give his consent to the marriage, but he threw in the harbor as her dowry. The Greeks named the harbor Massalia, which later became known as Marseille. It is the oldest city in France. The only other French cities close to it in age are the colonies Massalia founded in the next two centuries: Nikaia (Nice), Monoikos (Monaco), Antipolis (Antibes), Athenopolis (Saint-Tropez), Telunion (Toulon), and Agathe (Agde). The Greeks set up trading posts, *comptoirs*, in the lower Rhône at Arles, Avignon and Orange to barter with local Celto-Ligurians. But more importantly, the Greeks introduced two farm products from back home that would become essential elements in the diet, the economy, and the character of the region. "From the first millennium before Christ," writes historian Fernand Braudel, "the civilization of the

vine and the olive tree spread westwards from the eastern part of the sea. This basic unity was established far back in time, nature and man working to the same end."

During the Punic Wars in the third century BC, the Massalian Greeks united with the up-and-coming Romans against Carthage, Massalia's principal trade rival, but the Celto-Ligurians did not. They allowed Hannibal to pass freely through their lands as he marched his army and elephants from Spain to Italy in 214 BC. When Carthage went down to defeat in 201 BC, Rome annexed its former colonies in Spain. But since some of the Celto-Ligurian tribes continued to be troublesome, securing a reliable overland route between Italy and Spain turned out to a thorny problem for the Romans. While their Greek allies were better positioned to crack down on the troublemakers from their settlements along the coast, they had little interest in military matters and preferred to let the Romans come in and handle the tribes, a bit of negligence for which they would pay dearly one day.

THE ROMANS

In 124 BC, at Massalia's instigation, a Roman army attacked the Celto-Ligurian oppidum on the plateau of Entremont, home to a tough bunch of warriors who used to chop off the heads of their enemies and hang them on their front doors. But they were no match for the disciplined Roman legions, who plowed Entremont under. The following year, Consul Caius Sextius Calvinus built the first full-scale Roman settlement in Gaul on the plain below Entremont at the site of a thermal spring. Originally called "Aquae Sextiae" (the waters of Sextius), over the years its name shrank to Aix.

Within the next few years, the Romans moved permanently into Vaison-la-Romaine, Narbonne and Carcassonne, and in 102 BC, the Roman general Marius wiped out a vast horde of Teutonic invaders in a battle near Aix where an estimated 100,000 men, women and children were killed and another 100,000 taken prisoner. The victory gave its name to the ridge from which Marius observed the battle, Montagne Sainte-Victoire, and the name Marius has been a Provençal favorite ever since.

In 49 BC, the cat finally swallowed the canary. Marseille made the mistake of supporting Julius Caesar's rival general Pompey in their civil war, and in revenge, Caesar stripped Marseille of its colonies and transferred Rome's trade to the ports that had sided with him. Narbonne, Fréjus, and

Portrait of Hadrian in the Roman quarter of Puymin in Vaison-la-Romaine LEFT and Roman friezes at the Glanum archeological site in Saint-Rémy-de-Provence RIGHT, mementos of five centuries of Roman rule.

Nice profited handsomely, but the greatest beneficiary was Arles, which supplanted its mother city of Marseille as the dominant port linking the Rhône and the Mediterranean. Narbonne, Rome's main port on the western sweep of the Mediterranean, became the capital of the newly created Provincia Romana Narbonensis, and when Augustus (Caesar) wiped out the last Celto-Ligurian tribe that had failed to capitulate in 14 BC, Provincia Romana Narbonensis was seamlessly integrated into the economy and culture of the Italian peninsula.

Under the Pax Romana, the Golden Age of security and prosperity (golden, that is, for the lucky half who didn't happen to be slaves), the frontiers of the Roman Empire stretched from Scotland to Armenia, and the Romans could truly call the Mediterranean *Mare Nostrum*, "our sea." Though much of what they built in Provincia Romana has disappeared, enough remains to give a picture of their style of living during the first two centuries AD. The large arenas of Arles and Nîmes, the theaters of Cimiez in Nice, Vaison-la-Romaine and Orange, and the Pont du Gard aqueduct which fed the baths of Nîmes testify to the paramount role of sensual enjoyment and entertainment in their daily lives, and since they only worked half-days, they had plenty of time to indulge these tastes. Towns such as Vaison-la-Romaine and Glanum near Saint-Rémy grew wealthy from agriculture, while cities at main crossroads prospered from trade, most notably Aix, situated at the intersection of the Aurelian and Decumanus Ways, and Nîmes at the northern end of the Domitian Way to Spain. Nîmes was colonized by ex-legionnaires, as were Narbonne and Orange. The former soldiers were given land grants as a reward for past services and as a way to keep them from getting involved in revolts.

Whatever modest inroads Christianity might have made in the first three centuries AD, it was not until the conversion of Emperor Constantine in the early fourth century that the religion really caught on. Provençal legend has it that Constantine was on his way from Arles to Rome to try to put down a revolt when he had a vision at La Croix-Valmer near Saint-Tropez: a cross in the sky and a sign that said, *"in hoc signo vinces"* ("in this sign you will conquer"). He went on to victory, then converted, and many a Provençal followed suit. In 314, he presided over the first council of bishops held in France at his palace at Arles, one of his favorite cities. In the early fifth century the first Christian monastery, Saint-Victor, was built in Marseille. But even as early as Constantine's time, dry rot had set into the top-heavy, inefficient, slave-based economy, and barbarians were nibbling at the outer edges of the Empire. Constantine shifted the capital from Rome to Constantinople, and in AD 395 the Empire split permanently into East and West. The Visigoths, Ostrogoths, and Huns put Rome to sack several times in the following century, and in AD 476, the date marking the fall of the empire, the last Western Roman emperor, one Romulus Augustulus, was chased out of Rome by the Goths, bringing five centuries of political unity in Provincia Romana to an end.

THE MIDDLE AGES

The Middle Ages is the 1,000-year period from the fall of the Roman Empire to the end of feudalism and the rise of the absolute monarchy in the late fifteenth century. In some parts of Europe, this was a time of almost unmitigated chaos. Mediterranean France would experience its greatest period but also its most tragic defeat at this time.

Unfortunately, the history of this period unfolds in untidy ways, with trails that crisscross and go in many directions. But they all come together eventually with the emergence of the Kingdom of France, Europe's first nation-state, as the dominant power in the South.

After Rome's collapse, one barbarian tribe after another crossed the Alps and rampaged through Provence. Without Roman protection, the region found itself shattered into hundreds of city states and smaller localities, all trying to defend themselves from the hordes. By the sixth century, Caius Sextius Calvinus's once-thriving town of Aix was reduced to a pile of rubble.

The attacks from the east eventually ran their course, only to be replaced by a new cycle of invasions starting in the eighth century, when the Saracens, Spain's Moslem conquerors, crossed the Pyrénées. Their seemingly invincible armies swept a wide path of devastation across Languedoc and Provence and advanced northward until they were finally stopped by Charles Martel and the Franks at the Battle of Poitiers in AD 732. As Martel and his army pursued the Saracens south, the people of the *Midi* became acquainted with their fellow Christians from the North. It was not a happy experience. Martel sacked the cities of the South so brutally that the people of Arles begged the Saracens to come back and save them.

Charles Martel's son, Pepin the Short, made himself king in AD 751 and maintained Frankish domination of the South. His son Charlemagne expanded the kingdom into an empire covering most of Western Europe, which he ruled with an iron hand from his capital, Aix-la-Chapelle (Aachen in today's Northern Germany). Charlemagne's influence was such that he had himself crowned Emperor by the pope personally in Rome in AD 800, in order to symbolize the union of Church and Empire.

After Charlemagne's death, the empire was divided into three kingdoms — one in France, one in Germany, and a short-lived middle kingdom between them that was soon carved up and absorbed by the French and German kingdoms. Lords owning land to the west of the Rhône became vassals of the king of France and those to the east of it vassals of the king of Germany, who later took the title of Holy Roman Emperor. But as the feudal system developed, a number of the vassals grew richer and more powerful than the kings themselves and ruled their lands with de facto independence. Such was the case with the two powerful ruling houses that emerged in the South — the Counts of Toulouse and the Counts of Barcelona.

The Counts of Toulouse, who had been granted their fief by Charlemagne himself, extended their sway over all of Languedoc from the Garonne to the Rhône, and, by the eleventh century, a large part of northern Provence as well. The Counts of Barcelona started from scratch. After making their fortune from iron mining and advanced metalworking techniques in their Catalan homeland in the Pyrénées, they established themselves as the Counts of Barcelona and Roussillon, and by the early twelfth century had themselves crowned Kings of Aragon. They oversaw a sea-trading empire with ports in Barcelona, Majorca, Collioure, Perpignan, and Montpellier which rivaled those of Venice and Genoa. When Count Raimond Bérenger I married Douce de Gévaudan, the daughter of the Count of Provence, in 1112 and added the ports of Provence to his holdings, the western Mediterranean became known as "a Catalan lake."

THE AGE OF THE TROUBADOURS

The rule of the Counts of Toulouse and Barcelona ushered in a period of political stability, the economy came to life, and with the support of rich lords and the burgeoning monastic movement, the region launched into a glorious artistic period, with churches and monasteries going up everywhere. Architects studied the Roman models around them, and proceeding from the medieval axiom, "Architecture is applied geometry," created the sublime southern Romanesque style which is seen in Saint-Michel-de-Cuxa in Roussillon, Fontfroide in the Corbières, the Cistercian Abbeys of Silvacane, Sénanque and Le Thoronet in Provence, and the Church of Saint-Trophime in Arles. There are also hundreds of lesser-known gems from the period found from the Pyrénées to the remote valleys of the Alpes-Maritimes. From the eleventh to the thirteenth centuries, "The Age of the Troubadours" developed at the open-minded courts of the South. Toulouse, Barcelona, Aix-en-Provence, Carcassonne, and Les Baux welcomed poets and applauded the ingenious lyrics they sang to the high-born ladies there. The Southern "Courts of Love" reached a level of cultural refinement never before approached in Western Europe, and the troubadour singing in the mellow accents of the *Midi* replaced the warrior as the popular hero of the day. While the official language of the clergy and upper classes remained Latin, three vernaculars, all closely related, developed in southern France. They were Provençal, Catalan, and the Langue d'Oc, so-called because the word for "yes," was "*oc*," from the Latin "*hoc*" (as opposed to the Langue d'Oïl spoken in Paris, in which "yes" was "*oïl*," from the Latin "*ille*"). So widely accepted were these vernaculars as the languages of poetry that Dante, who traveled in Provence, considered writing his *Divine Comedy* in Provençal.

These new cultural centers in the South created cultural links not only among themselves, but also with Italy and Spain and with Jewish thinkers and Arabs, who were far more advanced in science and medicine than the Europeans. This rich exchange intensified when the Crusades began in 1095 and traffic between east and west increased dramatically. Montpellier, home of the great medical school of the Middle Ages, got its head start through its Arab contacts.

The "what ifs" of history are always stimulating to speculate about — and the great one of this region's history is "What if the Catalan-Occitan-Provençal culture had continued to knit together and ended up by forming a nation?" Imagine a country stretching from Catalonia to the Maritime Alps, with Barcelona, Montpellier, Toulouse, Marseille, and Nice as its centers of production, commerce, and culture. But that was not to be. Ironically, it was the very quality we admire most about this Southern culture — its openness to new ideas and different people — that would become its undoing. Because this openness also extended to new ideas about religion, and that was a realm the Church of Rome considered its exclusive jurisdiction.

At the end of the twelfth century, the Church, which had become so rich and self-involved that it had lost touch with the people, suddenly woke up to the fact that it had a full-blown "heresy" on its hands in Languedoc.

THE ALBIGENSIAN CRUSADE

The heretics were called Cathars, from *cathari*, meaning "pure" in Greek, and were also known in France as Albigensians, because Albi in northern Languedoc was one of the religion's main centers. A dualistic religion that grew out of the Manichaean belief in two divine forces, one good and the other evil, the Cathar movement developed in the Balkans in the eleventh century and spread rapidly through Languedoc in the twelfth century, due in large part to the interest of ladies of noble families, since in the Cathar religion, women were seen as equals to men in the eyes of God. The religion advocated Bible study in the vernacular, direct personal communication with God, and austerity — ecclesiastical wealth and power being especially evil — all of which were extremely threatening ideas to Rome. The Church tried but failed in its efforts to persuade the lords of Languedoc to root out the "heretics" (often the lords' own wives and relatives), and when the papal legate dealing with the heresy was murdered at the door of the Abbey of Saint-Gilles in 1208 by a follower of the Count of Toulouse, Pope Innocent III seized on the incident to enlist the Northern nobility in a crusade. He offered them the same incentives offered in the crusades against the Moslems in the Holy Land — the right to any lands taken from the heretics or their defenders and entry into Heaven for any who died in the process. In the cold light of history, the Albigensian Crusade has gone down as a cynical land grab by the northern aristocracy and a political power play by the Church.

In 1209 an army of 50,000 Northerners (some estimates go much higher) invaded Languedoc. It was led by "God's Madman," Simon de Montfort, perhaps the most hate-inspiring man in all of French history, though Arnaud-Amaury, the Crusade's Papal Legate, may have been even worse. Arnaud-Amaury is reported to have said when asked how to distinguish the heretics from the faithful during the siege of Béziers, "Kill them all. God will recognize His own."

Béziers fell in 1209, Carcassonne next, and year after year, de Montfort and his men murdered and burned their way through Languedoc. King Pedro II of Aragon finally broke away from a crusade of his own against the Moslems in Spain to come to the aid of his relation by marriage, Count Raymond VI of Toulouse. But in 1213 King Pedro was killed at the Battle of Muret, and the Southerners went down to catastrophic defeat. While all hope of victory ended that day for the Cathars, many took to the dramatic hilltop fortresses in the Corbières known as the "Five Sons of Carcassonne," which did not fall until mid-century. To track down individual heretics, put them on trial and send them to the stake if convicted, the Church created an new agency that would later to go to greater fame in Spain — the Inquisition.

After the defeat of the Cathars, Aragon signed the Treaty of Corbeil in 1258, giving up its claims to all lands north of Roussillon, and the Kingdom of France took title to the Count of Toulouse's lands. Further extending France's presence in the South, in 1241, King Louis IX (later canonized as

Saint Louis), purchased a piece of land on the western shore of the Camargue from a local monastery and built the port of Aigues-Mortes for his Crusades to the Holy Land. This was the Kingdom of France's first foothold on the Mediterranean coast, and a signal, if another one was needed, that the North had come South to stay.

THE FLOWERING OF PROVENCE

Five years later, in 1246, King Louis's crafty younger brother, Charles of Anjou, made himself Count of Provence by marrying Count Raimond Bérenger V's daughter Beatrice, a sister of Louis's wife Marguerite. (To give an idea of how much prestige the Count of Provence enjoyed, his two other daughters married King Henry III of England and the Holy Roman Emperor.) Two decades later, through arms and papal intrigue, Charles of Anjou made himself

King of Naples, and for the better part of the next two centuries, the Angevin dynasty would be far more occupied with holding onto its hotly contested kingship of Naples than in governing the lands in Provence.

In 1274, ever solicitous of good relations with the pope, Charles entered into an agreement with his nephew King Philip III (the Bold) of France to transfer to the Papacy most of the rural lands in Northern Provence formerly owned by the Count of Toulouse, as a delayed reward for the Church's role in the Albigensian Crusade. In 1309, Philip IV (the Fair) persuaded French-born Pope Clement V to leave Rome, then in the throes of anarchy, and move to the Comtat Venaissin, the Church's property in Provence where the French could offer him protection with their strongholds across the Rhône. So, in the greatest shock of the Middle Ages, the Papacy moved from the Eternal City to this hitherto unnoticed corner of the

world. Later popes moved into Avignon and built its huge Papal Palace, and in 1348, the year of the plague that killed half the population of southern France, Pope Clement VI "purchased" the city of Avignon from the beautiful, flamboyant Queen Jeanne of Naples, the Countess of Provence. In fact, this was her bargain with the Papacy to buy her way out of the charge of murdering her husband, Andrew of Hungary. The Church never paid for its purchase, but Queen Jeanne went back to Naples relieved of her immediate problem.

This sort of cynical merchandising of divine pardon infuriated poet Francesco Petrarch, who worked for a cardinal in Avignon. He called the city "a sink of vice" and said, "Everything there breathes a lie — the air, the earth, the houses, and especially the bedrooms." Venal souls though they

The Papal Palace in Avignon, the seat of the Catholic Church when the Popes abandoned Rome in the fourteenth century.

The Region and its People

were, one can't help being grateful to the Popes of Avignon for their palace, the ramparts around the city, and the fine body of fourteenth-century paintings they commissioned.

Seven popes reigned during the "Babylonian Captivity" from 1309 to 1377, followed by two anti-popes, the last one leaving Avignon in 1409. The Church would continue to own Avignon and the Comtat Venaissin, however, for another three centuries — until the French Revolution took them over in a peaceful transition in 1791.

In 1382, Queen Jeanne of Naples ended her scandal-ridden life true to fashion by being murdered by one of her cousins. A struggle for power broke out in the House of Anjou, and Duke

Amadeus VII of Savoy took advantage of it for his own ends. In 1388, he persuaded Jean Grimaldi, the Angevin governor of Provence's County of Nice, to bring Nice under the protection of the House of Savoy, thus giving the landlocked duchy in the Italian Alps the port on the Mediterranean it coveted. Nice's five centuries of Savoyard rule before joining France in 1860 would give it the distinctively Italian flavor it has to this day.

The last Angevin Count of Provence was the colorful "Good King" René, who presided over the most artistic court in Europe in Aix-en-Provence from 1434 to 1480. His title of "king" came from his claim to the throne of Naples, which had been lost by the House of Anjou before his time. As for "good," taxpayers in Provence found that a questionable title, too. They grumbled about the tax money he squandered on schemes to recover the lost throne and his lavish spending on the arts. René was a poet, a painter, a composer, a scientist, adept in all the classical languages and several modern ones — a throwback to the great days of the troubadours and a precursor of the Renaissance man. A body of myth later credited him with painting the famous *Burning Bush* triptych (Nicholas Froment actually painted it), in which the sleek, well-fed king appears in one of the side panels. He did however, introduce the silkworm and the muscat grape to Provence, and they created prosperity for years to come. We can still savor his grapes in the delicious apéritif wine, Muscat de Beaumes-de-Venise.

René also built the mighty Tarascon castle on the Rhône facing the French King's castle across the river at Beaucaire. As Count of Provence, René was still a vassal of the Holy Roman Emperor, and the Rhône was, as it had been since the breakup of Charlemagne's realm, the frontier between the Kingdom of France and the Holy Roman Empire, one of the last remaining vestiges of the feudal period.

Good King René died in 1480, and the glory days of Provençal culture with him. His nephew and heir Charles of Maine died without heirs the following year, and willed Provence to the Kingdom of France. Reinvigorated by their triumph over the English in the Hundred Years War, which had ended thirty years earlier, the French kings were in the process of unifying the country under strong centralized royal authority. The feudal system was over.

THE FRENCH IN THE SOUTH

Under French rule, Provence was governed by a viceroy but had its own local assembly, the Parliament of Aix, which had powers of taxation. Provençals had traditionally bemoaned two local scourges, the blustery *mistral* and the flood-prone Durance. Now they added a third — the tax-prone Parliament of Aix. In 1539, the death of Provençal and Languedoc culture was put into law by the Edict of Villers-Cotterêts. It established French, the *Langue d'Oïl*, as the only language to be used in official communications — a blatant act of Northern cultural imperialism which automatically reduced Southerners to second-class citizenship.

At the same time, Protestantism took root in the South, always France's most fertile ground for "heresy." It spread rapidly in Provence and Languedoc, and as in the time of the Albigensian Crusade, repression was not long in coming. The Wars of Religion were a series of intermittent wars between Catholics and Protestants in many parts of France in the late sixteenth century. They started in 1542 with the massacre of the Vaudois sect in the Lubéron, 2,000 executed and 800 sold as galley slaves in this crackdown by the crown and the Parliament of Aix. As in the time of the Cathars, the violence in Languedoc was especially grave. Appalling acts of brutality were committed by both sides, but the Protestants, who were greatly outnumbered, got the worst of it, and thousands died in their strongholds of Nîmes, Aigues-Mortes, and Montpellier. Tens of thousands went into exile or took to the Cévennes Mountains for refuge. The violence finally ended in 1598 when King Henry IV, a Protestant who had tactically converted to Catholicism, issued the Edict of Nantes, which guaranteed toleration of Protestantism and allowed Protestants to keep several fortified places as safeguards.

In the seventeenth century, Cardinal Richelieu reactivated the persecutions. As secretary of state and then chief minister to Louis XIII from 1616 to 1642, he worked obsessively to impose the power of the crown over all areas of French life, and since the Huguenots were seen as per se disloyal to the Catholic king, they had to be brought to heel. In 1622, Louis XIII invaded Montpellier, the leading center of Protestantism in the South, and once more it became the scene of terrible bloodshed. Territorial expansion was another of Richelieu's priorities, and in the South, he focused on Roussillon. In a war with Spain in the 1640s, Louis XIII led a long siege against Perpignan in which the defenders earned the nickname of "rat eaters." Hearing that Perpignan had finally fallen, the Cardinal died a happy man in 1642.

In 1659, France and Spain settled on the Pyrénées as their border. Catalonia was split in two, Roussillon going to France, the rest remaining under Spanish rule. The Catalans had supported France in the war, hoping to be rewarded with all of Catalonia as a buffer state between France and Spain. But their hopes were betrayed for France's geopolitical aims.

"The Great Century," as the seventeenth century is known, was a time for grand projects, the Palace of Versailles being the grandest, but from an engineering point of view, the great project of the South was more than its equal. In 1666, Louis XIV and his chief minister Colbert gave Baron Pierre-Paul Riquet of Béziers authorization to go ahead on the construction of the Canal du Midi, a barge canal linking the Atlantic and the Mediterranean by way of Toulouse and the Garonne. It had been a dream since the time of the Romans, but the mountains had defied all previous plans. After fifteen years of construction with up to 10,000 workers at a time, the largest and most ingenious engineering feat of the century was completed in 1681, bringing new prosperity to Languedoc, since it could now ship its wine and grain to any place in the world.

But only a few years later Louis XIV visited destruction on the land. In 1685, he revoked the Edict of Nantes, and once again Montpellier and Nîmes were under attack. Many took refuge in the Cévennes, and countless Protestants left France for good — a loss to the country of many of its most industrious people.

In his long reign from 1643 to 1715, Louis XIV led France into one foreign war after another, most with little to show at the end. But his last war brought France a valuable property in the South, the Principality of Orange, which had been owned by the Dutch royal family since the early sixteenth century. It was ceded to France by the Treaty of Utrecht in 1713.

The Sun King also put his brilliant military architect Sébastien Vauban to work on a vast fortress-building program. Vauban's forts and ramparts dot Mediterranean France from Antibes and Entrevaux on France's eastern frontier with Savoy to the far south along France's recently acquired Pyrénées border with Spain at Villefranche-de-Conflent, Mont-Louis, and other key spots in the mountains. Along with Roman ruins, Romanesque abbeys and walled hilltop villages,

Vauban's constructions rank as the most dominant architectural features of Mediterranean France.

The military projects of Louis XIV cost a fortune, however, and the ruinous state in which he left France at his death in 1715 would be one of the main causes of the downfall of the Kingdom in 1789.

Despite religious and other wars and several plagues, including one that killed more than half Marseille's population in 1720, Provence and Languedoc prospered under French rule in the seventeenth and eighteenth centuries. Marseille became France's main commercial port, while Montpellier, after losing its shipping business to Marseille, went on to new prosperity in textile manufacturing. Toulon prospered as France's main naval base and Antibes as France's easternmost port. But the greatest beneficiary of *La Paix Française* was the Provençal capital of Aix, whose dozens of elegant seventeenth-and eighteenth-century residences speak volumes about the sweetness of life before the Revolution.

OPPOSITE: Louis XIV in an unlikely pose at the Promenade du Peyrou in Montpellier. ABOVE: *Belle époque* splendor at the Casino of Monte-Carlo.

REVOLUTION AND EMPIRE

The French Revolution brought on considerable bloodshed and destruction of the Church's and nobles' property in Aix, where an estimated 8,000 clergy and aristocrats lost their lives. But while there were isolated incidents of violence elsewhere, compared to many other parts of France, the level of destructiveness was relatively mild. In the cities, the "reds" of the urban proletariat welcomed the Revolution, but the rural majority showed little enthusiasm for it, remaining "whites" — royalists — in their hearts. Administratively, the Revolution brought far-reaching changes. In 1790, the large historical provinces of France — Brittany, Aquitaine, Provence, and the rest — were abolished and divided into a number of smaller, county-sized administrative units called *départements* with directors, *préfets*, appointed by the central government in Paris. The aim was to keep political power out of the hands of the landowning aristocrats who had formerly controlled the regions. By weakening regional authority, the Revolutionary government gave itself more of a stranglehold over the country than the kings ever had. Provence was divided into four parts, once-proud Aix was stripped of its capital status and proletarian Marseille became the capital of the newly created *département* (county) of Bouches-du-Rhône. In 1791 the Revolution further extended its grip on southern France by taking control of the papal properties of Avignon and the Comtat Venaissin. With Orange and the Lubéron added to it, this became the *département*, or county, of the Vaucluse.

In 1792 a troupe of 500 volunteer militiamen, "reds" from Marseille, marched to Paris to join the Revolution. Waving tricolored flags, they sang a new tune called "The Song of the Army of the Rhine," whose melodramatic and bloodthirsty words caught the spirit of the times. By the time they reached Paris people were calling the song *La Marseillaise*.

With the execution of the king, an armed rebellion against the Revolution broke out in the South, and French royalists joined with the British to seize the military port of Toulon. A 23-year-old artillery officer named Napoléon Bonaparte distinguished himself in 1793 by his brilliant tactics in the retaking of Toulon and was promoted to brigadier general. This was one of the Corsican's few happy associations on the mainland of Mediterranean France. Other than General Masséna, his *"enfant chéri de la victoire"* ("beloved child of victory"), who was from Nice, Napoléon had little use for Southerners. As fighting men, they lacked the level of zest he required, and as royalists, they were not to be trusted by a man who wanted to be Emperor. The people of the South had little

use for Napoléon either. In 1815, after escaping his exile in Elba and landing at Golfe-Juan between Cannes and Antibes, he had to sneak through the mountains of Provence on a shepherd's trail for fear of being betrayed to the royal authorities.

THE NINETEENTH CENTURY

In the 1830s, France, which had lost most of its original colonies to the English during the late eighteenth century, made itself a colonial power again, first in Algeria, then expanding further into Africa and the Far East. As "The Gateway to Africa and the Orient," Marseille thrived as never

before, especially after the opening of the Suez Canal in 1869.

France's last major territorial expansion in Europe came in 1860, when Napoléon III made a deal with the House of Savoy to provide French military forces to help Savoy dislodge Austria from northern Italy in exchange for Savoy giving France its rights to the County of Nice. In a referendum held the same year, Nice voted to join France, much to the chagrin of Nice-born Italian patriot Giuseppe Garibaldi, and Menton and Roquebrune, former possessions of Monaco, followed suit. This was one of Napoléon III's few foreign policy successes. Had it failed, Nice would probably be the western-most city in Italy today.

By the time Nice and Menton joined France, they were already popular wintering places for the English upper classes, as was Cannes. After the original casino in Monte-Carlo was built in the 1860s, royalty and the rich flocked to the gaming tables, and the Riviera launched into the extravaganza of luxurious living typical of this period known as La Belle Époque. The age of mass tourism was born on the Côte d'Azur.

The late nineteenth century also saw the emergence of a serious literary movement in Provence, where Poet Frédéric Mistral and his followers were struggling to revive the grand tradition of Southern poetry. Centered in Arles, the Félibrige was a literary group that started creating works in the Occitan languages, Langue d'Oc and Provençal, dialects of the great days of the troubadours. Mistral won the Nobel Prize for Literature 1904 and left a legacy of renewed pride in

and throughout the region dates from this troubled period.

THE WAR YEARS

In World War I, the South shared the tragedy of the rest of France, losing 25% of its young men in the conflict, but was spared the devastation suffered by the Northeastern area. As France's largest port and a major industrial city, Marseille continued to prosper, but on the Côte d'Azur the war put an end to the lavish Belle Époque period. The biggest spenders, Czar Nicholas and the Russian aristocracy, were lost to the Russian Revolution, and other royal visitors stayed away

the Occitan culture that had been systematically suppressed since the Edict of Villers-Cotterêts.

In the 1870s phylloxera, a virulent infestation of plant lice from vines imported from America, devastated most of the vineyards throughout France. Provence and Languedoc suffered tremendous losses. In 1874 there were two and a half million hectares (six million acres) of vineyards under cultivation in Languedoc-Roussillon, but by 1900 only one and a half million hectares (four million acres) remained. Resistant root stock from America brought a slow recovery, but for the growers the disruption of the market was devastating. By the time the vines recovered in the early part of the century all the power was in the hands of middlemen, *négociants*, who squeezed the growers so unmercifully that a general revolt broke out in Languedoc in 1907. The widespread development of wine cooperatives in Languedoc

for the duration. In the 1920s, celebrity artists and writers such as Matisse, Scott Fitzgerald, and Cocteau set the tone. The new vogue of sunbathing became the rage, along with the old habit of spending money, until the Great Depression put a damper on those wild and carefree days.

During the first three years of World War II, Mediterranean France suffered no physical damage, but after the Germans occupied the South in November, 1942, extensive destruction followed. It started with the French Navy scuttling its own fleet in the harbor of Toulon to keep it from falling into German hands, and the region's ports and industrial cities were bombed extensively by the Allies. The Germans dynamited Marseille's Panier quarter, a casbah-like immigrant neighborhood that harbored *Résistance*

Aigues-Mortes, the Kingdom of France's first port on the Mediterranean.

fighters, and just before the Allied landings in Provence, blew up the port of Saint-Tropez. In Arles, the two houses Van Gogh had lived in were leveled by allied bombs. On August 15, 1944, the Allies made Normandy-style landings on the beaches of Saint-Tropez and the coast of the Maures and, with strong support from the *Résistance* in Marseille, Toulon and Nice, quickly drove the Germans and Italians out.

TODAY'S MEDITERRANEAN FRANCE

The post-War period has seen a radical transformation of Mediterranean France, touching every aspect of the way people live. The population of the region, now six and a half million, has doubled in the towns and cities along the coast. A huge building boom that started in the 1960s on the Côte d'Azur and spread along the coast has resulted in tens of thousands of new structures going up, and unfortunately, aesthetics has been the last thing most of their builders have had in mind. The area east of the Rhône, including the large cities of Nice, Marseille and Toulon, has become one of the most densely populated areas in France. But within it there are enormous discrepancies between the built-up coastal areas and the inland rural areas. After the War, *désertification* — the abandonment of villages — set in as the population migrated to the cities. Once-thriving villages became ghost towns and have only been saved from extinction by crafts people who settled there from the 1960s onward (in Tourrettes-sur-Loup near Vence, for example) or by purchasers of second homes (*à la* Peter Mayle in the chic Lubéron).

To the west of the Rhône, a De Gaulle and Pompidou government program to develop the coast resulted in two dozen modern middle-class beach resort towns springing up, but there is still much more open space between them than on the Côte d'Azur. The inland areas of Languedoc-Roussillon are also more open because of the volume of agriculture in the region. The population density there is far below the national average.

Mediterranean France has also seen tremendous economic growth and change since the 1960s, with 70% of today's work force now employed in service occupations. With 250 million overnight stays registered each year in the Provence-Alpes-Côte d'Azur region and 100 million in Languedoc-Roussillon, tourism supplies the most jobs and income, and Cannes, Montpellier, Monaco and Nice have developed major convention centers and other facilities to attract business tourism to compensate for the seasonal nature of vacation tourism. The many high-technology operations that have installed themselves in the region, drawn by the prestigious universities in

Montpellier, Aix-Marseille and Nice, have also become a major factor in the region's economy. Sophia-Antipolis, the large, modern technology park in a pine forest between Nice and Antibes, bills itself as "the Silicon Valley of France," and formerly staid Montpellier has become one of the liveliest cities in France, thanks to its computer, telecommunications, and medical technology businesses. These sectors are very vulnerable to economic fluctuations, however, and unfortunately the chronic business downturn of the 1990s gave Montpellier one of the highest unemployment rates in France.

Besides the more modern industries, Mediterranean France continues to support itself by its traditional occupations. The Côte d'Azur grows vast amounts of flowers for its perfume industry and the florist trade, and Provence is France's leading producer of fruit and rosé wines. Languedoc and Roussillon remain France's largest wine producer. Almost 10% of the work force there cultivates the land. While Marseille's traditional industries of shipping and heavy industry have declined since the War, it remains Southern Europe's main port, and its huge steel plants and petrochemical zones west of the city are major employers.

Politically, Mediterranean France is in stronger shape than it has been in centuries in relation to central government as a result of the move to decentralization. In 1982 the French government established regional governments in which several departments were grouped together to form larger administrative units with locally elected leadership. In the Mediterranean area two regional governments were created, Provence-Alpes-Côte d'Azur, comprising six departments with its capital in Marseille, and Languedoc-Roussillon with five departments and its capital in Montpellier. Paris still has most of the power, but decentralization has given the regions considerably more control over their own cultural and economic directions.

The wave of the economic future in both Mediterranean regions is toward the formation of economic mini-states capable of competing effectively in the European Union business environment in the "post-tourist" economy of the twenty-first century. In the Nice-Antibes area, the first building block is already in place with the Sophia-Antipolis complex, and plans are being drawn up to link the economy of the eastern Côte d'Azur with that of Northern Italy. In Languedoc, a high-tech axis between Montpellier and Nîmes was formed in the 1960s and has spread south to Perpignan. Plans for the future call for a link-up with the economies of Marseille and Aix, which have also become centers for high technology. A high-technology Age of the Troubadours may be in the offing for the twenty-first century.

Yet for all the changes, some for the better and some for the worse, the Mediterranean remains the Mediterranean. *Mare nostrum* is "our sea" not just for the Romans, but for anyone who has shared in the great, ancient culture born on these shores. If the coast has become annoyingly modern in places, all you need to do is go a short distance inland where vineyards and olive orchards fan out from little hilltop villages and the timeless quality of the Mediterranean remains.

LIFE AND ART

Any notions you might have about the supposed distinction between Life and Art will evaporate quickly as you stroll through a market in Mediterranean France, where the ramble itself becomes an aesthetic experience. The light of the region — "soft and tender, in spite of its brilliance," as Matisse termed it — gives an extraordinary luminosity to the colors of fruits and vegetables raising them to the level of artistic delight. Add the aesthetic pleasure of medieval houses or neoclassic arcades surrounding the market and the artistry of a local craftsman whose work you pause to admire, and you start to understand why, given a atmosphere such as this, this region has nourished so much artistic achievement over the past 2,000 years.

BUILDINGS OLD AND NEW

French people call their old buildings *vieilles pierres*, or "old stones," and in most places treat them somewhat solicitously, like feeble senior citizens of distinction. But not in Mediterranean France. Here the "old stones" are expected to pull their weight. They are kept in constant use as museums, of course, but also as sites for public events and performances, wine showrooms, tourist offices, and even, in the case of Perpignan's fourteenth-century maritime tribunal the Loge de la Mer, the most elegant fast-food outlet you'll ever see.

There have been four outstanding periods for architecture in Mediterranean France — Roman, medieval, the seventeenth and early eighteenth century, and modern times — corresponding to the region's moments of greatest prosperity. In each period, the society of the day left a vivid self-portrait in stone.

The Roman Period

In the arenas, temples, forums, baths, water systems, highways, and other vast public works projects the Romans built wherever they settled, they created an image of unshakable self-confidence, as was perfectly appropriate for the masters of the known world. By the first century AD, Provincia Romana Narbonensis, covering an

area equivalent to today's Mediterranean France, seemed to historian Pliny the Elder "more than a province, another Italy." You can find Roman remains intact in all parts of the region from Augustus's impressive Trophée des Alpes (Trophy of the Alps) overlooking Monaco to a 29-arch irrigation aqueduct watering vineyards in the foothills of the Pyrénées. But the place that really shows you what Pliny meant by "another Italy" is the area of the lower Rhône Valley in and around Nîmes, Arles, and Orange (see TAKE A ROMAN HOLIDAY, page 16 in TOP SPOTS). They have arenas, theaters, baths, aqueducts, residential neighborhoods, triumphal arches, temples — the works. The Romans were the

masters of stone construction, here you will see them at their best. Archaeology buffs may want to stop at Fréjus, an important port in the early days of the Empire. While none of its original buildings remain intact, the foundation stones of the old port and its 10,000-seat amphitheater and some sections of walls can be seen. Cimiez, the Roman town of Cemenelum in a park overlooking Nice, on the other hand, has a well preserved 5,000-seat theater still in use, extensive baths and other Roman vestiges and a Museum of Archaeology with exhibits on the Roman presence in the Maritime Alps. Emperor Augustus's 50-m-tall (160-ft) Trophée des Alpes (Trophy of the Alps) is perched high above Monaco on the Grande Corniche in La Turbie. It was built to

Place Richelme in Aix-en-Provence, where a food market has been held daily since the Middle Ages.

commemorate the final defeat of the Ligurians. There's no question who was the boss here.

The Romanesque Period

The region's second great period for architecture started in the tenth century and extended into the thirteenth, and the lovely churches, abbeys and cloisters built during this period are touching expressions of the deep religious faith of medieval society. The style is known as "Romanesque" because the architects were inspired by the Roman buildings they saw around them. Barrel vaults and rounded arches became characteristic features.

The Counts of Barcelona were important patrons of the burgeoning monastic movement, and thanks to them, Roussillon has an especially large number of Romanesque masterpieces. The most dramatically situated is the eleventh-century abbey of Saint-Martin-du-Canigou high on the slopes of Mont Canigou in the Pyrénées. The tenth-century abbey of Saint-Michel-de-Cuxa in nearby Prades has delightfully sculpted floral patterns on the capitals of its cloister, and the Priory of Serrabone is known for the vivid depiction of monsters from the Book of the Apocalypse on the capitals of its pink marble columns. The Cathedral at Elne has a large, handsome cloister built between the twelfth and fourteenth centuries whose sculptures show the evolution of the Southern Romanesque style, one with a peculiarly Southern sensuality quite distinct from the austere medieval styles one finds in the North. As cultural historian Fernand Benoît points out, "In the face of the abstract art of the North, the knowledge of Humanism, that is to say, of the human figure, is an essentially Mediterranean fact." This can be seen in the touching faces of the saints and angels, of the chosen people and especially of the damned, on the main portal of the church of Saint-Trophime at Arles.

Other fine examples of Romanesque art and architecture abound throughout Mediterranean France. They include the Abbey of Fontfroide near Narbonne, Saint-Guilhem-le-Désert north of Montpellier, the elaborately sculpted portals of the church of Saint-Gilles on the western edge of the Camargue, and the twelfth-century Cistercian abbeys of Sénanque, Silvacane and Le Thoronet, known as "The Three Sisters of Provence."

Neoclassic and Baroque Architecture

The worldly societies of the seventeenth and eighteenth centuries built cities with neoclassic and baroque flair. In the Quartier Mazarin of Aix-en-Provence, there are entire streets of honey-colored stone mansions, some with balconies supported by statues of giant muscle men known as *Atlantes*, and all with grand interior

staircases decorated with intricate wrought-iron railings in a style peculiar to Aix. The Pavilion de Vendôme is an especially elaborate summation of Aix's neoclassic characteristics. The leading sculptor of Atlantes and more importantly the greatest Southern architect of the period was Marseille-born Pierre Puget. He designed Marseille's elegant Vieille Charité, originally a large workhouse, now home to art museums and exhibition centers. In Vieux Montpellier, the old part of the city has many fine homes from the period, and in the surrounding countryside, there are several wildly fanciful residences of the period known as "Follies." Nearby Pézenas, which was the co-capital of Languedoc with

Montpellier in the seventeenth century, is a living museum of "Great Century" architecture. Here you can visit the Hôtel d'Alfonce, where Molière and his company used to perform, and Gély's barber shop (now the Tourist Office), where he used to gather material for his comedies by eavesdropping on the conversations of the nobles.

Nice developed a very Italian version of the baroque, and in a stroll through Old Nice, built almost entirely in this period, you will see many examples, including the Cathedral of Sainte-Réparate, whose interior is lavishly decorated with gilded plaster and marble, and the Lascaris Palace, with its sweeping main staircase and airy mythological paintings on the ceilings. Menton's Parvis Saint-Michel, the baroque main square of the old city, is a model of taste and discretion. Drive north from Menton into the Alpes-

Maritimes, and you will find exquisite baroque churches in Sospel, Breil-sur-Roya, and Saint-Martin-Vésubie.

Modern Era

Unlike the structures of the earlier periods, late twentieth century architecture is more likely to be built of concrete, steel, and glass than of limestone and marble. Unlike the serenely monolithic ensembles of the earlier styles, the modern approach is one of diversity. Instead of one universal style, you will find a variety of disparate personal styles, as is appropriate to the Age of Anxiety. Le Corbusier launched the Post-War period with the most controversial building of its time,

and the results were striking. Nîmes now has a large array of imaginative buildings and public spaces designed by Jean Nouvel, Martial Raysse, Philippe Starck, Sir Norman Foster, and Michel Wilmotte. In Montpellier, grandiose projects have been the order of the day. They include Claude Vasonti's bunker-like concert hall, the Corum, and Ricardo Bofill's Antigone, an expanse of residential and business structures that are monumental in their vastness and their updated neoclassic style.

The modern buildings of Montpellier and Nîmes may not please one and all. But this much is sure: they have made these cities more interesting to look at. Not many can make that claim.

L'Unité d'Habitation in Marseille. Built in the late 1940s, the cantilevered 17-story bare concrete and glass box was a self-contained living unit with duplex apartments, shops and schools all in the same building. It was the first of a projected six-building residential complex called La Cité Radieuse, but it stirred up such a such storm that Le Corbusier never found the financing to build the other five. In sunny Marseille, the objectors called it a crime to put people inside a concrete container sitting off the ground. They called it "*La Maison du Fada*," "The House of the Madman." Nevertheless, young architects loved it, and few buildings of the twentieth century have been more influential.

The most active cities for contemporary architecture in the 1980s and 1990s were Nîmes and Montpellier. Their mayors sought out top modern architects for major public works projects,

Other Monuments

The four major styles mentioned may be the most abundant in the region, but there are many unique, exciting buildings to be seen from other periods as well. For dramatic medieval fortresses go to Languedoc, where you'll find the huge walled city of Carcassonne and the sun-blasted Cathar fortress of Peyrepertuse, a "citadel of vertigo" sitting on a jagged cliff in Corbières. Along the coast in the Camargue and Languedoc there are medieval fortified churches, menacing structures designed to double as strongholds. In Avignon is the ultimate in fortified religious establishments, the fourteenth-century Papal

OPPOSITE: The Cloisters of Saint-Trophime in Arles, one of many Romanesque gems in Mediterranean France. ABOVE: Twentieth-century art in a fourteenth-century setting, a Botero exhibit at the Papal Palace in Avignon.

Palace, a vast walled ensemble of buildings and courtyards protected by battle towers over 50 m (160 ft) high. Gothic architecture is rare in the region. The most outstanding example is Narbonne's powerful Cathedral of Saint-Just, whose 41-m-tall (135-ft) nave is the third tallest in France. Renaissance buildings are rare too. Most are medieval castles that were converted into Renaissance palaces. The *châteaux* of Grignan, Gordes, and Cagnes-sur-Mer are good examples.

In the nineteenth century, a heavy, pompous Romanesque-Byzantine style developed in Marseille. Its prime examples are the basilica of Notre-Dame-de-la-Garde at the highest point in the city and the Cathédrale de la Major overlooking the main docks. For light pompous architecture, the Côte d'Azur's ultra-elaborate *belle époque* style can't be beat. It blossomed in the late nineteenth century, a time when the rich were not the slightest bit embarrassed about displaying their wealth. Landmarks of the style are Monte-Carlo's Grand Casino, Hôtel de Paris and Hôtel Hermitage, and Queen Victoria's sprawling Regina Palace in Cimiez. The *belle époque*'s last two landmarks were constructed just before World War I brought the period abruptly to an end: the Hôtel Negresco in Nice and the "wedding cake" to end all wedding cakes, the Hôtel Carlton in Cannes.

PAINTING

So powerful is the artistic charisma of Van Gogh, Cézanne, Matisse and Picasso that they throw the rest of the region's artists into the shadows. Travelers tend to follow "in the footsteps" of those famous four, along with perhaps a few other stars of the modern period such as Chagall and Dufy, and often miss out on exciting works by artists who are not so well-known. The many works of Matisse and Picasso in the region may be its most outstanding art treasures, but they are by no means the only ones. The museums of the region offer many happy surprises for those who look around — works by Charles Camoin or Paul Guigou, for example, excellent painters with whom most travelers are unacquainted. The churches and abbeys contain many art treasures from the earlier periods, often hiding in obscure corners.

Early Painting

The Popes of Avignon were the first to stimulate painting in the region by hiring distinguished Italian painters such as Simone Martini and Matteo Giovannetti to decorate the Papal Palace in the early fourteenth century, and luckily some of the many frescoes they and their teams of artists painted on the walls of the palace have survived. After the popes went back to Rome late in the century, art remained an important activity in Avignon, and in the fifteenth century, a full-fledged School of Avignon emerged. There are fine examples of this work at the Musée du Petit Palais near the Papal Palace, including an altarpiece by the most talented member of the school, Enguerrand Quarton. His masterpiece, *The Coronation of the Virgin*, dating from 1453, is in the Musée Municipal Pierre de Luxembourg across the Rhône in Villeneuve-lès-Avignon. I urge you to see this painting, for many reasons, including Quarton's unusual depiction of the Father and the Son as mirror images, but especially for his sensitivity to the clarity of Mediterranean light. The other great painting of this period is the triptych *The Burning Bush* at the Cathedral of Saint-Sauveur in Aix-en-Provence. It was painted in 1476 by Nicholas Froment under the patronage of "Good King" René, whose portrait can be seen in the left hand panel.

The other important movement in painting during the transition to the Renaissance in Mediterranean France was that of the late fifteenth- to mid-sixteenth-century School of Nice Primitives. Its leader was Ludovico Bréa, whose finely drawn figures and personal approach to light and shadow can be admired in his triptychs in the Franciscan church in Cimiez and Monaco's Cathedral. Bréa has been labeled "the Fra Angelico of Provence." The comparison is just in that the two artists share a gentle sensibility, but unfair to Ludovico Bréa in that it robs him of his individuality. Other works by Bréa and other School of Nice artists can be found in little churches in the Alpes-Maritimes north of Menton and in Biot and other hill towns between Nice and Antibes.

Baroque Era Painters

Hyacinthe Rigaud was the most successful portrait artist of Louis XIV's time. One of his three famous (and enormous) portraits of the Sun King can be seen in the main salon of the Hôtel Negresco in Nice. The Hyacinthe Rigaud Museum in Perpignan has a self-portrait of the benign-looking artist.

The great Southern-born painter of the late eighteenth century was Jean-Honoré Fragonard from Grasse. The Villa-Musée Fragonard has a large collection of his lighthearted engravings, rococo sketches, wash drawings, and paintings.

Nineteenth-century Realism

In 1854, Gustave Courbet, "The Father of French Realism," made a trip to Montpellier and worked in the Languedoc countryside. His painting *La Rencontre*, better known as "Bonjour, Monsieur Courbet," had an enormous influence on young Southern painters and awakened them to the power that could be achieved through meticulous analysis of the Mediterranean light.

Two painters who fell under that influence were Frédéric Bazille from Montpellier and Paul Guigou from the Vaucluse. Bazille became one of founders of Impressionism and painted outdoors with Renoir and Monet, but his career was cut short at the age of 29 when he died in the Franco-Prussian War. The Musée Fabre in Montpellier has nine of his sunny, vivacious early-period Impressionist paintings.

Paul Guigou was more traditional in style, but also an artist of exceptional sensitivity to the light of the South. His tender landscapes can be seen at the Musée des Beaux-Arts in Marseille and the Musée Granet in Aix. Guigou died at the age of 37.

Modern Art

The work done by painters in Mediterranean France from the late nineteenth century to the mid-twentieth century, and the influence it had on the rest of the art world can only be described as explosive. It started in the 1880s with the return of Paul Cézanne to his native Aix and the arrival of Vincent Van Gogh in Arles, and it continued with the arrival of Signac, Matisse, Derain, Renoir, Bonnard, Dufy, Picasso, Braque, Léger, Chagall, Cocteau, de Staël, and numerous others.

From Menton on the Italian border to Collioure and Céret in French Catalonia, there seems to be hardly a place along the coast where one of these artists did *not* work. It would take far more space than we have here to give this subject even a cursory treatment. The travel itineraries include information about these artists, where they painted, and where you can see their works. The principal modern art collections are at the Matisse and Chagall museums in Nice, the Cocteau Museum in Menton, the Fondation Maeght in Saint-Paul-de-Vence, the Picasso Museum in Antibes, the Cantini in Marseille, the Annonciade in Saint-Tropez, the Vasarely Foundation in Aix-en-Provence, the Réattu in Arles, the Fabre in Montpellier, the Hyacinthe Rigaud Museum in Perpignan, and the Museum of Modern Art in Céret.

As for Cézanne and Van Gogh, who are ultimately responsible for all this, they were not understood in their time by the people of Aix and Arles. Now they are, but more for their commercial than their artistic value. Posters, postcards, souvenir books, Van Gogh tee-shirts, Cézanne coffee mugs, et cetera, etc. It doesn't matter. The sunflowers and olive trees and starry nights that Van Gogh painted in the fields around Arles and Saint-Rémy are still there, as beautiful as ever — even better, in fact, because of what he showed us. The same could be said about Cézanne and his beloved Montagne Sainte-Victoire.

Little of their work can be found in the region — only one painting by Van Gogh (at the Musée

Angladon-Dubrujeaud in Avignon) and eight small paintings by Cézanne at the Musée Granet in Aix.

Contemporary Art

The history of art in Mediterranean France does not end with the passing of Matisse and Picasso. In the 1960s a group of artists called the New School of Nice or *Nouveaux Réalistes*, emerged, with Nice-born Yves Klein as their leader. They reacted against the French modern art establishment much the same way American Pop artists reacted against Abstract Expressionism, by basing much of their art on surprising and often comical treatment of everyday objects. The sculp-

tors Arman and Martial Raysse, also from Nice, were early partners of Klein, and their fellow Mediterranean artists César and Ben share their satirical bent. Their temple is MAMAC, Nice's Musée d'Art Moderne et d'Art Contemporain, which opened in 1990. It also has a large collection of American works from the 1960s on.

Other museums where contemporary art is on display are the Fondation Maeght, the Picasso Museum in Antibes, the Musée Cantini in Marseille, the Carré d'Art in Nîmes, and the Museum of Modern Art in Céret, where the Catalan and Languedocian side of the contemporary art world is represented by Tàpies, Viallat, Jean and Jacques Capdeville and others.

The Picasso Museum in Antibes is one of many museums in Mediterranean France where you can see works by outstanding artists who have lived and worked here.

The Côte d'Azur

EASTERN CÔTE D'AZUR

IF THERE'S ONE PLACE IN THE SOUTH that would seem to need no introduction, it's the eastern end of Mediterranean France, the fabled Côte d'Azur. We've been so bombarded with media coverage of the Cannes Film Festival, Monaco's princely family and the hype of glamour there in general, that it's easy to become jaded. But this place is full of surprises, and the first is that those clichés we've been fed about elephantine yachts draped with golden-tanned beauties and fabulous mansions overlooking the azure sea are all true — and more excessively true than we could have possibly imagined. Stroll along the yacht basin in Cannes or drive past the estates of Cap d'Antibes, and you'll be exposed to a level of sybaritic living that is staggering. It's hard to imagine as you gape at the cathedral of luxury, the Grand Casino of Monte-Carlo, that little more than a century ago, the Côte d'Azur was a poor, backward region, and the priceless real estate upon which the Grand Casino now stands was a rocky goat pasture owned by a Prince of Monaco who was practically down to his last franc.

In Côte d'Azur, the Inventing of the French Riviera, Mary Blume describes the area before the development of tourism as "a raised and spectacularly beautiful sea front strip which consisted of villages sharing poverty, brilliant sunshine and inaccessibility. A fringe, a liminal space, waiting to be invented."

What made it all possible was the arrival of the railroad in the 1860s. Suddenly it became easy to get to this isolated strip, and when Queen Victoria, Czar Nicholas II and the other crowned heads of Europe decided to make sunny Nice, Cannes and Monte-Carlo their winter headquarters, the rich and the well-to-do swept along in their wake. Modern mass tourism was born on the Côte d'Azur and quickly became its major source of income, as it remains to this day. This is no bagatelle we're talking about. Twenty-four million visitors spend 40 billion francs a year (roughly eight billion dollars) on their travels in this region.

The catchy term "Côte d'Azur" created by poet Stephen Liégeard in 1887 originally applied to the 60-km (38-mile) stretch of coast between Menton and Cannes, where belle époque tourism flourished, but in the twentieth century its has been broadened to cover the 200 km (125 miles) of coastline from Menton to Bandol and a good deal of countryside inland. On the coast, this adds another 140 km (87 miles) of lovely, twisting shore line to the west of Cannes along with many resort towns, including swinging Saint-Tropez, and the three delightful islands of the Îles d'Hyères. The big naval port of Toulon and the prestigious wine-growing area of Bandol are at the western end of the coast. Moving inland, the Côte d'Azur extends northward into the Maritime Alps (Alpes-Maritimes) and the Alps of Upper Provence (Alpes-de-Haute-

Provence). Exactly how far it goes into the mountains is open to debate, but for the purpose of our travels, it extends as far north as the "Lavender Alps" of Upper Provence, where fields of lavender stretch out as far as the eye can see. Digne-les-Bains, the lively main town, is the perfect base for exploring the area. It lies 152 km (95 miles) northwest of Nice and is easily reached by road or the colorful Train des Pignes, the "Pine Cone Train," up the Var River Valley.

Today's view of the Côte d'Azur takes account of the wide range of attractions it has to offer beyond the classic fleshpots of the coast. In summer, when the narrow, two-lane coast road is usually crowded, trips to the interior offer welcome relief.

Besides the "Lavender Alps," the beauties of nature include the Vallée des Merveilles (Valley of Marvels) in the Mercantour National Park of Alpes-Maritimes, where Stone Age shepherds carved enigmatic designs in the rocks, and the Grand Canyon du Verdon, the largest canyon in Europe, 700 m (2,500 ft) deep, where hiking, whitewater rafting, and horseback excursions are popular. The Côte d'Azur is peppered with fortified medieval hilltop villages, "perched villages," from the coastal highlands far up into the mountains. In one cluster where Matisse, Bonnard and Picasso and many other artists lived, you can now visit potters, glass blowers, weavers, sculptors, and other craftspeople at work in their studios. The Var district in the western Côte d'Azur is a vast sea of vineyards, producing Côtes de Provence and Bandol wines, and there is no end of wine-making châteaux to be visited.

Taking advantage of the whole Côte d'Azur can add a great deal of enjoyment to your trip. But let's face it, what draws us here is the coast and its reputation.

And that brings us to Nice.

The Grand Canyon of the Verdon River, one of the scenic treasures awaiting those who venture in from the coast.

NICE

Nice is *the* big city of the Côte d'Azur, the one place you can't avoid, and you shouldn't. It is everything the main city of an area should be — its capital, its commercial center, its transportation hub, and a fully functioning metropolis 365 days a year, the only one on this end of the coast. It is also one of the most delightful cities in Europe to visit, and the main reason is that Nice is a city made for walking. There are formal promenades such as the famed Promenade des Anglais along the grand sweep of the Baie des Anges (Bay of Angels) and the flowery, fountain-filled Promenade du Paillon through the center of the city. But the narrow, winding streets of Vieux Nice (Old Nice) present a different kind of walking experience. Italianate houses, baroque churches, lively markets and shops will reward you with a discovery a minute. Snacking on Nice's unique cuisine is an irresistible part of the fun.

Thanks to the sheltering crescent of high hills behind the city, Nice has fine weather the year round. In the spring, you can take a dip in the Mediterranean and be on a ski slope in the Alpes-Maritimes an hour later. Because of its mild winters, Nice has a high percentage of retirees. But young people choose to live here too, drawn by the University of Nice and job opportunities in tourism and high-technology. Along with the old Niçois families, who provide Nice with its distinctly Italian flair, the cross-section of young and old makes for an interesting mix. The verve of this city of 380,000 is such that despite the importance of tourism to its economy, it gives you the feeling that life would go on even if the three million tourists a year who visit it stopped coming.

While Nice delivers sun, sea, palm tree-lined promenades and high living to those who seek it, this city is also is treasure chest of art. You can find religious paintings by the early renaissance School of Nice Primitives, individual museums devoted to longtime residents Matisse and Chagall, and works by the artists of the contemporary New School of Nice. Nice has more museums genuinely worth visiting than any other city in the South of France.

BACKGROUND

The first known inhabitants of Nice were nomadic Stone Age hunters who stalked hippos and elephants in the area of the Port 400,000 years ago. They camped in caves at the foot of Mount Boron, where their bone-littered shelters were unearthed during a construction project in 1966 at Terra Amata just east of the Port. But permanent settlement did not come until 4,000 centuries later, in the fourth century BC, when the Greeks from Marseille established a port for their coastal shipping and built an acropolis on top of the Colline du Château (Castle Hill) overlooking the port and Baie des Anges. They named the town Nikaia, most likely in honor of Nike, the Goddess of Victory. The Romans preferred to set themselves up on the heights of Cimiez three kilometers (two miles) inland, where they established an army post on the Julian Way. After Augustus crushed the last independent Ligurian tribes in the Alps in 14 BC, they made Cemenelum the capital of the Alpes-Maritimes district. By the second century AD, it had grown to a city of 20,000, and extensive ruins remain from this period, including a 5,000-seat theater still in use.

The Italian flavor so conspicuous in Nice comes from its five centuries of rule by the House of Savoy. In 1388, Duke Amadeus VII, in need of a port for his landlocked Alpine duchy, took advantage of a split in the House of Anjou, Provence's rulers, and talked Jean Grimaldi, their governor in Nice, into betraying the County of Nice to Savoy. Except for occasional periods of French occupation, Nice would remain under Savoyard rule until 1860, when Napoléon III made an arrangement with the Italian minister Cavour that brought Nice and its county under French sovereignty, to the horror of Giuseppe Garibaldi, who yearned to see his native city become the western-most port of a unified Italy.

In 1763, Dr. Tobias Smollett, a British physician and novelist, spent the winter in Nice and wrote that it was as warm in December as London was in May, so the British upper classes started to come here to winter. By the time Nice became French a century later, there was already a well-established British colony and a Promenade des Anglais. With the arrival of the railroad in 1864, the well-to-do English started coming in numbers, and when Queen Victoria wintered in Cimiez in the 1890s, Nice's fortune in upscale tourism was made. *Belle époque* palaces sprouted from the Promenade des Anglais up to Queen Victoria's Regina Palace in Cimiez. In 1890, 22,000 people wintered in Nice. By 1910, there were more than 150,000 winter residents. The Russian nobles were the most extravagant of all. In 1912 they built Nice's Russian Orthodox Cathedral. But World War I put an abrupt end to the *belle époque* period and the Russian Revolution to its biggest spenders.

While The Jazz Age brought a resurgence of tourism to the Côte d'Azur in the 1920s, sunbathing came into vogue, and Nice lost its cachet because of its pebbly beaches. Towns down the coast with sandy beaches such as Juan-les-Pins and Cannes became more attractive to vacationers, who now started coming more in the summer than in the winter.

The beach of Nice and the city's landmark, the domed Hôtel Negresco.

In the post-World War II era, Nice has moved actively into high-tech, modern service industries, and business-related tourism with its mammoth new Acropolis convention center, and it is the second most visited city in France. The Promenade des Anglais has lost most of its *belle époque* palaces, but the landmark Negresco is still there — and Old Nice, the seventeenth- and eighteenth-century baroque section of town, a crime-ridden, to-be-avoided slum 20 years ago, has been renovated and is now one of the stellar attractions of the Côte d'Azur.

GENERAL INFORMATION

As everywhere in Mediterranean France, your first stop should be the **Tourist Office**, where you will find mountains of maps and booklets on hotels, camping grounds, restaurants and cultural attractions in French and English and well-informed personnel eager to help. Or, before you get there, E-MAIL them at otc@nice-coteazur.org, or visit their extensive WEB SITE www.nice-coteazur.org. There are four offices in Nice. One is at the Nice Airport (04 93 21 44 11; another is at Ferber, halfway between the airport and town on the Promenade des Anglais (04 93 83 32 64; another is at the SNCF, the train station on Avenue Thiers, between Boulevard Gambetta and Avenue Malaussena (04 93 87 07 07; and the fourth is at 5 promenade des Anglais (04 92 14 48 00. The Office de Tourisme arranges walking tours of Old Nice and *belle époque* Nice led by passionate and erudite guides.

The **Carte Musées Côte d'Azur** allows priority access (you don't have to wait in line) to 62 museums and monuments in Nice and the Alpes-Maritimes, including almost all the most important ones, for 70 francs for three days, 140 francs for seven days. You can purchase it at any of Nice's 15 municipal museums, at the Nice Office de Tourisme, or by mail from MAMAC, Promenade des Arts, 06300 Nice. For Nice only, the **Passe-Musées 7 Jours** authorizes one entry to each of the city's 15 municipal museums over a seven-day period for only 40 francs.

For a booklet on the moderately priced and inexpensive hotels of the Logis de France group (04 93 80 80 40, ask at the Tourist Office or pick it up at the information desk at the Gare Routière, the bus station, on the Esplanade du Paillon. There are about 100 Logis de France hotels in the Alpes-Maritimes, but not in Nice itself.

For airport information, contact **Nice-Côte d'Azur Airport** (04 93 21 30 30 WEB SITE www.pageszoom.com/aeroport-nice. For information on the *grandes lignes* (main lines) **train service** and regional Métrazur service between Saint-Raphaël and Menton call the Gare SNCF (main railway station) (08 36 35 35 35. Call Chemins de Fer de Provence (04 97 03 80 80 for the *Train des Pignes*.

The **bus station**, or Gare Routière (04 93 85 61 81 is on the Esplanade du Paillon. RCA (Rapides Côte d'Azur) has bus service along the coast and to hill towns inland: Cannes-Grasse (04 93 39 11 39, Monte Carlo-Menton (04 93 85 64 44. Navette Bus Aéroport-Riviera (04 97 00 07 00, is the airport bus service. For **taxis**, call (04 93 13 78 78.

Car rental agencies include Avis (04 93 21 42 78; Budget (04 93 21 36 50; EuropCar (04 93 21 36 44; Hertz (04 93 21 36 72; Thrifty (04 93 44 07 08. The Automobile Club de Nice et Côte d'Azur (04 93 87 18 17 is on Rue Massenet.

Guided **coach tours** to Monaco and the *corniches* of the Riviera and other day-trips are offered by Phocéens Cars (04 93 85 66 61 at 2 place

Masséna, and Santa Azur (04 93 85 46 81 at 11 avenue Jean Médecin.

Boat excursions to Monaco and points along the Riviera and to the Îles de Lérins are operated by Trans Côte d'Azur, Quai Lunel, on the west side of the port (04 92 00 42 30.

For **health emergencies**, contact SOS Médecins (04 93 85 01 01, or dial (15 for SAMU (mobile emergency medical service).

Little **Tourist Trains** (*Les Trains Touristiques de Nice*) (04 93 18 81 58 are a good way to get your bearing. They make a 40-minute circuit of the Old City, the Château and the Promenade des Anglais, leaving the Promenade des Anglais at the foot of the Jardin Albert Ier every half-hour from 10 AM to 7 PM in the summer, to 6 PM in the spring and fall, and to 5 PM in the winter (30 francs). Tourist

A wine festival in Cimiez, where the Romans settled on the hilltop overlooking Nice.

passes for unlimited rides on **Sunbus** (04 93 16 52 10, Nice's excellent bus system, cost 22 francs per day, 85 francs for five days, 110 francs per week.

FESTIVALS AND EVENTS

Carnaval is two weeks of parades with lavish floats, dancing in the streets, masked balls, theater, and the Battle of Flowers centered on Place Masséna, but spilling out everywhere into the city. It starts 12 days before Ash Wednesday and culminates in fireworks over the Baie des Anges the night of Shrove Tuesday (Mardi Gras).

The **Nice Jazz Festival** is another week of partying, this one up the hill in the Park of Cimiez, featuring top names in jazz, blues and R&B, with picnics, concerts in the Roman theater, and relaxed conversations between musicians and fans. Formerly called **La Grande Parade du Jazz**, it was Dizzy Gillespie's favorite festival, and I have warm memories of the time I spent with him and other musicians here. It takes place from early to mid-July.

WHAT TO SEE AND DO

The best place to start exploring Nice is on top of the **Colline du Château** (Castle Hill), the rock towering above the east end of the Promenade des Anglais. This is where the Greeks had their acropolis and the House of Savoy built the fortress that gave the hill its name. Unfortunately, Louis XIV had the fortress demolished during the War of the Spanish Succession in 1706 and the Dukes never got around to rebuilding it when they recovered the city. From the observation platform you can see the entire panorama of Nice. To the west is the blue and turquoise Baie des Anges with Nice's five and a half kilometers (three and a half miles) of pebbly beach and the palm-lined Promenade des Anglais and Quai des États-Unis running along it. Directly below the Château is Vieux Nice (Old Nice), the triangle of red-tiled roofs of baroque-era churches and houses between the foot of the Colline du Château, the Quai des États Unis, and the wide garden esplanade built over the bed of the Paillon River which cuts through the city. This is the boundary between seventeenth- and eighteenth- century Old Nice, with its narrow winding streets, and the nineteenth- and twentieth-century part which is laid out in a grid. The esplanade, which changes names a few times along its way, begins at the bay with the Jardin Albert 1er, followed by Espace Masséna, Promenade du Paillon and Promenade des Arts, where the new theater, modern art museum, and Acropolis convention center are located.

Looking down from the east side of the Château, you see Port Lympia, the inner harbor cut into the gap between the Château and Mount Boron, and the outer harbor where the ferries for

Corsica dock. Cupping the city is a natural amphitheater of steep hills and beyond them to the north, the Alpes-Maritimes, usually topped by snow. Few cities have been blessed with a natural setting as perfect as this.

To get up to the Château, there is an elevator at the end of Rue des Ponchettes, open 9 AM to 8:00 PM (10 AM to 6 PM in the winter), five francs round-trip. Or you can walk up the 300 steps.

Vieux Nice

Old Nice is a city-within-a-city, with narrow winding streets, bright baroque squares in pastels, rust and ochre, and visual surprises and tantalizing aromas at every turn. The only way to explore it is by foot, which is easy enough, since all of Vieux Nice has been made a pedestrian zone. The heart of the old city is **Cours Saleya**, a few minutes by foot down Rue des Ponchettes from the Château. The long rectangular courtyard was the promenade for Nice's high society in the eighteenth century, and now is the site of a flower market every morning except Mondays, when the antique and bric-a-brac dealers take over. The greenhouses of the Riviera are among Europe's main producers of roses, carnations and other cut flowers, so visitors to the **Cours Saleya Flower Market** are treated to a dazzling array of color and aroma all year round. Adjoining is a fruit and vegetable market, where the food stall of **Thérèse** is abuzz with activity. Customers are lined up for *soccas* (chickpea crepes) and *pissaladières* (fried-onion tarts), cooked and served sizzling hot by a crew of jovial and tireless *Niçoises*. They don't sell beverages, those you buy from **La Cambuse**, the café across the street. A cool glass of Côtes de Provence rosé washes these Niçois treats down very nicely.

A few steps away is the **Chapelle de la Miséricorde**, a 1740 baroque gem designed by Bernardo Vittone. It is open only for mass on Sunday mornings and by special arrangement with the Tourist Office, which organizes tours.

Those with a sweet tooth should pop into **Pâtisserie-Confiserie Auer**, at 7 rue Saint-François-de-Paule across from the Nice Opera House, to sample the delicious chocolates and candied-fruit that have made it an institution since 1820.

At No. 14 is the retail store of the olive oil mill **Alziari**, selling cured olives *à la Niçoise*, olive oil, lavender honey, and herbs. Just breathing in the sweet Provençal aromas is intoxicating.

From the Cours Saleya, take Rue Sainte-Réparate one block to the Rue de la Préfecture. At No. 17, photographer **Jean-Louis Martinetti** sells his exquisite postcards and posters of Nice. Across the street at No. 16 is the cavernous **Grandes Caves**

OPPOSITE: The Monday antiques market at the Cours Saleya. RIGHT: All of Old Nice has been converted to vehicle-free walking streets.

Caprioglio which has a huge selection of Provençal wines, including Château de Bellet and Château de Crémat from the tiny Bellet wine-producing area north of Nice. (There is very little wine produced in the eastern Côte d'Azur, unlike the rest of Mediterranean France, which produces vast quantities.)

Baroque **Sainte-Réparate Cathedral** on Place Rossetti is dedicated to Nice's patron saint, a 15-year-old virgin martyred in Palestine and whose body floated to Nice on a flower-decked boat towed by Angels (hence the name Baie des Anges). Also on Place Rossetti you can try the delicious homemade ice cream and sherbet at **Fenocchio**, in more than eighty flavors.

Palais Lascaris, at 15 rue Droite, is a Genoese-style mansion built by the Count of Ventimiglia in the seventeenth century. It has a grand balustraded staircase and richly decorated apartments with frescoes of mythological themes on the vaulted ceilings. Closed on Monday.

Continue up Rue Droite past artists' boutiques and vendors of savory food (see WHERE TO EAT, page 103) to **Place Garibaldi**, where the lively **Grand Café de Turin** takes up one corner of the handsome yellow-ochre arcaded square named for the Nice-born Italian patriot.

The Port

A few minutes by foot to the east of Place Garibaldi on Rue Cassini will take you to **Port Lympia**, the protected inner harbor used by fishing boats and pleasure craft and lined by seafood restaurants and cafés. For a fascinating visit to a traditional candied fruit, jelly, jam, and chocolate candy-making operation, stop in at Confiseries Florian's **Confiserie du Vieux Nice** (04 93 55 43 50 at 14 quai Papacino, on the west side of the port. There are free tours daily between 9 AM and noon and 2 PM and 6:30 PM, and at the end of the tour, you get to sample their delicacies. Taste the jellies made from fresh flowers — jasmine, violet, rose — they are amazing. Florian's main plant in Pont-du-Loup can also be visited daily (see THE GORGES OF THE LOUP RIVER, page 134).

On the lower slope of Mont Boron just to the east of the inner harbor, you will find **Terra Amata**, where nomadic Stone Age hunters' shelters were discovered in 1966 (see MUSEUMS, below). Continue around Port Lympia to the commercial port and the **Gare Maritime** (Maritime Station). It handles ferry service to Corsica and boat trips along the coast.

Place Masséna and the Promenade du Paillon

One block west of Place Garibaldi is the Promenade du Paillon, the flowery, fountain-dotted esplanade that divides Old Nice from the modern city. (Note the Gare Routière, the station from

which buses leave to all parts of the Côte d'Azur and Provence.) The central point of Nice straddling the esplanade is Place Masséna, a wide square framed by red-ochre Italianate buildings with vaulted arcades. Rue Masséna leads to a pleasant walking area of fashionable boutiques, bars and cafés, and ice-cream parlors.

The Promenade des Anglais

The Promenade des Anglais was begun in 1822 as a public works project funded by a wealthy English clergyman, Reverend Lewis Way. Originally a barely two-meter (six-foot)-wide footpath along the Baie des Anges called La Strada del Littorale, it was widened and renamed the Promenade des Anglais in 1844. In its *belle époque* heyday, the upper classes of all Europe strolled past its domed white wedding-cake palaces. Today a busy six-lane roadway disrupts the former leisurely pace, and most of the palaces have given way to modern high-

rises. A McDonald's and the crude Las Vegas-style Casino Ruhl further detract from the air of elegance. But reminders of grandeur remain — the **Musée Masséna** (see MUSEUMS, below), the nineteenth-century **Westminster** and **West End** hotels, and above all, the mythic 1912 **Hôtel Negresco** (see WHERE TO STAY, page 101), whose jolly pink and green dome has become as much a symbol of Nice as the Eiffel Tower is of Paris. Take a stroll through this splendid hotel even if you don't plan to check in. It is a registered National Historic Monument with more art treasures than many museums, including one of Hyacinthe Rigaud's famous full-figure portraits of Louis XIV showing off his legs, and the largest Aubusson carpet in the world. This is the hotel where the celebrities stay, and to see them and touch up with the *belle époque* ghosts, have a drink at the bar, unchanged in style since the day it opened. The Negresco's restaurant is also the finest in Nice (see WHERE TO EAT, page 103).

Museums

The **Musée d'Art Moderne et d'Art Contemporain (MAMAC)** (Museum of Modern and Contemporary Art) has an extensive collection of late twentieth-century art including De Kooning, Stella, Warhol, Haring, and particularly the New School of Nice — Arman, Martial Raysse and Yves Klein, with more than 20 of that Nice-born innovator's works. Go up to the roof for Klein's Garden of Eden installation and the fine view of the city. On Fridays at 9:30 PM, a weekly lighting of Klein's *Wall of Fire* takes place.

MAMAC's building, four massive gray marble towers linked by thick arched steel beams around a glassed-in core, sparked controversy when it opened in 1990. Designed by Yves Bayard and Henri Vidal, it forms an architectural unit with the

MAMAC, Nice's Museum of Modern and Contemporary Art, whose collection is as bold as its design.

The Côte d'Azur

hexagonal gray marble **Théâtre de Nice** across the **Esplanade des Arts**, an open walkway between the buildings lined with sculptures by Calder, Barry Flanagan, Marc de Suvero, and others. Looking out on the sculptures from the ground floor of the museum is the fashionable but quite affordable **Café des Arts**. The museum is closed Tuesdays.

The **Musée Masséna**, housed in the former mansion of Marshal Masséna's grandson, is Nice's historical museum. It has artifacts from the Roman era through the nineteenth century. The lavish Second Empire rooms are worth the visit in themselves. The museum is at 35 promenade des Anglais, near the Negresco, and is closed Mondays.

The **Musée des Beaux-Arts**, Nice's fine arts museum, is in an Italian Renaissance-style mansion with a grand formal staircase and winter garden and has works by Fragonard, Degas, Monet, Renoir, Sisley, Rodin, Braque, Picasso, Bonnard, and Van Dongen. There are also areas devoted to Nice's Van Loo family of Rococo painters and pioneering *belle époque* poster artist Jules Chéret, and there are numerous paintings, watercolors, drawings and prints by longtime Nice resident Raoul Dufy, including several of his airy scenes of the Côte d'Azur. It is at 33 avenue des Baumettes, a ten-minute walk west of the Negresco. The museum is closed Mondays.

The **Musée International d'Art Naïf** (International Museum of Naive Art) has 600 works by naive artists from all over the world from the eighteenth century to today in the Château Sainte-Hélène, the grand pink *belle époque* mansion built by François and Marie Blanc, Monte-Carlo casino bosses. The museum is on Avenue de Fabron in the Fabron district west of downtown Nice; closed on Tuesdays.

Opened in 1998, the beautiful new **Asian Arts Museum** is an elegant white marble and glass pavilion designed by Kenzo Tange that appears to be floating on the surface of the Phoenix Parc Floral de Nice's largest lake. It houses the most important Asian art collection in southern France — jade, bronze and celadon from China; gold, black, and brown lacquer work and ceramics from Japan; red and gray sandstone sculptures from India; and magnificent silk from the entire continent. It is at 405 promenade des Anglais opposite the Nice International Airport; closed Tuesdays.

The **Musée de Terra Amata**, built on the site of the shelters of nomadic Early Paleolithic Acheulean hunters who lived here 4,000 centuries ago, has true-to-life tableaus of their mode of living. The museum is at 25 boulevard Carnot near the northeastern corner of Port Lympia; closed Mondays.

Cimiez, the hill overlooking Nice where the Romans built their city of Cemenelum, is now home to an archaeological museum at the Roman

site, a monastery with important School of Nice art works, and two exciting modern art museums. To get to Cimiez by bus from downtown Nice, take the No. 17 bus from the Promenade du Paillon. As you climb the Boulevard de Cimiez you can't miss the sprawling white *belle époque* Regina Palace where Queen Victoria spent the last several winters of her life. She enjoyed riding around Nice in a little donkey cart and was loved by the *Niçois*, who erected a statue of her in front of the Regina Palace, which is now an apartment house. Henri Matisse also spent his last years at the Regina where he died in 1954. He is buried in the cemetery at Cimiez.

The **Musée Matisse** is a handsome red-ochre Italianate seventeenth-century villa set amid the Roman ruins of Cimiez's park at the crest of the Boulevard de Cimiez. The collection includes 236 of Matisse's drawings, 218 engravings, 59 sculptures including *Nus vus de Dos*, his four cast bronze studies of female nude backs done between 1909 and 1930, each one more abstract than its predecessor. It is on the far wall of the lobby. There are colored paper cutouts for the Chapel of the Rosary at Vence, 68 paintings, including *Portrait de Madame Matisse* (1905), *Nu au Fauteuil, Plante Verte* (1936–1937), and *Nature Morte aux Grenades* (1947), as well as many photos and items from the master's personal art collection. The museum is closed Tuesdays.

The main points of interest at the Roman archaeological site of **Cemenelum** are the **Baths**, the largest in all Gaul, which remind us how very advanced the Mediterranean peoples were then in comparison to Northerners, and the **Arena**, the 5,000-seat amphitheater used for combats of gladiators, which reminds us how bloodthirsty they were. The Arena is now used for concerts, including those of the superb Nice Jazz Festival. The **Musée d'Archéologie de Nice-Cimiez**, opened in 1989, contains objects from the Iron Age to the Middle Ages, and especially the Roman period at Cemenelum and in the Alpes-Maritimes. It is closed Mondays.

The **Franciscan Monastery of Cimiez**, also in the park, has a lovely cloister and three masterpieces of the School of Nice Primitives in its church of **Notre-Dame-de-l'Assomption** — a 1475 *Piéta* and a 1512 *Crucifixion* by Ludovico Bréa, and a *Deposition* by Ludovico and his younger brother Antonio.

Musée National Message Biblique Marc Chagall (Marc Chagall National Museum of the Biblical Message) features the 17 huge canvases of Chagall's happy ecumenical vision of the books of Genesis and Exodus, *The Biblical Message*, in glowing Chagallian blues, greens, yellows, purples, and reds. *The Song of Songs*, a group of six large red-toned paintings, is a touching love song to his wife Vava. Be sure not to miss the recital hall. It has the magnificent blue, blue, blue stained-glass windows of *The Creation*. The Chagall Museum is downhill from the park on Avenue Docteur Ménard, just to the west of Boulevard de Cimiez. The admission charge is 30 francs off-season, 38 francs in the summer. Closed Tuesdays.

Except for the Chagall Museum, the other museums mentioned are municipal museums, where the full-price entrance fee is 25 francs. All municipal museums are free on the first Sunday of each month. All Nice's museums except the MAMAC and the Matisse close for lunch, normally from noon to 2 PM. For information about the low-priced museum passes available, see GENERAL INFORMATION, page 95.

Russian Orthodox Cathedral

Funded by Czar Nicholas II and completed in 1912, five years before his overthrow, Nice's **Russian Orthodox Cathedral** is the largest Russian church outside Russia. It has five colorful glazed-tile onion domes and a splendid array of gold icons, well worth a visit. The cathedral is open daily but closed Sunday morning to sightseers. However, visitors who wish to attend a Russian mass are welcome. Mass starts at 10:30 AM and lasts about two and a half hours. It is a magnificent ceremony. The cathedral is at 17 boulevard du Tzarewich in a quiet residential district to the west of the railway station.

Phoenix Parc Floral de Nice

This seven-hectare (17-acre) park on the western end of the Promenade des Anglais, across from the Nice Côte d'Azur Airport, is home to the world's largest greenhouse, **Le Diamant Vert**, a vast four-sided pyramid that simultaneously controls seven different tropical climates, from steamy jungle to arid cactus garden, with fruit-bearing banana trees, royal palms, and an extraordinary collection of orchids. Open daily from 9 AM to 7 PM April to September, 9 AM to 5 PM October to March. Also in the park are three lakes, numerous specialized gardens, and the new Asian Arts Museum (see MUSEUMS, above).

Beaches

Nice has one of the most beautiful waterfronts you will ever see, but because its beaches are made of pebbles, many sunbathers prefer the sandy beaches of the towns to the west. I find the rustle of pebbles rolling in the waves very soothing as I soak up the sun on the less crowded beaches here, and a pair of plastic sandals solves the problem of walking on the hot stones. The large **Plage Publique des Ponchettes** on the Quai des États-Unis is a free public beach with freshwater showers. For an inexpensive day at the beach, pick up the makings of a picnic at the nearby Cours Saleya market. But if you want to be pampered, 15 private beaches along the Quai des États-Unis and

the Promenade des Anglais have restaurants and snack bars and rent mattresses and beach umbrellas. The fee for a changing room and mattress is 40 to 65 francs. I like the Hôtel Beau Rivage's **Restaurant de la Plage** (04 93 80 75 06, on Quai des États-Unis. It has a festive open-air grill, moderate to moderately expensive, and a modestly priced snack bar. Reed mats are put on the pebbles to make it easy for you to get to the water, and windsurfing, waterskiing, and parascending (flying behind a speed boat) are available. At night you can dine here under the stars. **Castel Plage** (04 93 85 22 66, at the eastern end of the Quai des États-Unis, is another beach I enjoy. This is where Nice's young artistic crowd goes.

WHERE TO STAY

A number of Nice's top hotels have undergone extensive renovations in the past couple of years, and the overall level of quality is very high. There are 188 classified hotels with a total of 9,000 rooms, the second greatest number in France after Paris. You should have no problem getting a room of your choice except during *Carnaval* or the month of July and the first three weeks of August, for which you should book well in advance. However, Nice is a big convention city, and there's always a possibility of your visit coinciding with one. So to be on the safe side, book ahead if you can. Many hotels reduce their prices off-season, and a number of them offer two nights for the price of one on weekends. The Tourist Office has a list.

Very Expensive

All the great names have stayed at the **Negresco****** (04 93 16 64 00 FAX 04 93 88 35 68 E-MAIL negresco @nicematin.fr, 37 promenade des Anglais, from Scott and Zelda Fitzgerald to Queen Elizabeth II, who must have felt right at home in the palatial

The Hotel Negresco, one of the domed "wedding cake" palaces which evoke the nineteenth-century heyday of the Promenade des Anglais.

surroundings. Her subject Paul McCartney wrote the lyrics to "The Fool on the Hill" here on Negresco stationery. The 150 rooms and suites are little museums in themselves, with antiques chosen by the owner, Madame Augier. There are two restaurants, the Chantecler, Nice's leading gourmet restaurant, and the excellent Rotonde for lighter fare (see WHERE TO EAT, below), and the bar is the most glamorous in town. The hotel's private beach is across the Promenade.

The **Palais Maeterlinck****** (04 92 00 72 00 FAX 04 92 04 18 10 E-MAIL maeterlinck@webstore.fr WEB SITE www.webstore.fr/maeterlinck, 30 boulevard Maurice-Maeterlinck, Cap de Nice, is splendidly isolated on a seaside cliff between Nice and Villefranche-sur-Mer. This cypress-studded estate of the famed Belgian playwright is now a classy hotel (26 rooms and suites) with a colonnaded pool, beach, and gourmet restaurant, La Mélisande.

Château des Ollières**** (04 92 15 77 99 FAX 04 92 15 77 98 E-MAIL ollieres@riviera-isp.com, 39 avenue des Baumettes, is the extravagant late nineteenth-century mansion of Prince Alexei Lobanov-Rostowski, built as a love nest for the prince and his French mistress and converted in 1990 into an opulent four-room, four-suite hotel that is the most expensive in Nice (3,300 francs a night for the magnificent Tower Apartment in high season). The hotel sits amid grand palms in a large private park a few steps west of the Musée des Beaux-Arts. Its collection of paintings and antiques is so rich that it could easily pass for an extension of the museum. The restaurant has three intimate dining rooms individually decorated in antiques, serving traditional French gastronomic cuisine (very expensive).

Expensive

The *grande dame* of Nice's hotels is the **West End****** (04 92 14 44 00 FAX 04 93 88 85 07 E-MAIL hotel-westend@hotel-westend.com WEB SITE www.hotel-westend.com, 31 promenade des Anglais, built in the 1840s and enlarged and renamed several times over the years. After a period of decline, this six-story, 126-room *belle époque* beauty has been fully renovated and is now a paragon of old-style elegance enhanced by all the latest comforts. It has a pretty restaurant fronting on the sea, a bar with live music at night, and a private beach, Le Blue Beach. The West End is a member of the Best Western group. The **Beau Rivage****** (04 93 80 80 70 FAX 04 93 80 55 77 E-MAIL nicebeaurivage@new-hotel.com WEB SITE www.new-hotel.com, 24 rue Saint-François-de-Paule, down the street from the Cours Saleya, is a fashionable address where Matisse, Chekhov, and Nietzche stayed. It has 120 elegant rooms and its own private beach a block away.

Built into a cliff of the Château's hill, **La Pérouse****** (04 93 62 34 63 FAX 04 93 62 59 41 E-MAIL lp@hroy.com, 11 quai Rauba-Capeu, is a 65-room

hotel with a cozy, private club atmosphere, a small rooftop pool and garden, intimate bar and restaurant, and a superb view of the Nice shore front and Baie des Anges. The **SAS Radisson****** (04 93 37 17 17 FAX 04 93 71 21 71 E-MAIL res@ncezh.rdsas.com, 223 promenade des Anglais, has 333 modern rooms, a big rooftop pool, piano lounge, and good buffet lunches. Jazz artists in town for the festival stay here. Another modern hotel, the **Méridien****** (04 93 82 25 25 FAX 04 93 16 08 90 WEB SITE www.lemeridien-hotels.com, 1 promenade des Anglais, has 314 deluxe, spacious rooms tastefully renovated with Mediterranean color schemes, four stories up from the ground-floor Casino Ruhl. When reserving, specify a room with a view of the sea or the Jardin Albert 1er. There is a rooftop pool, a health club, a beauty salon offering a range of massages and body and face care treatments, and a large airy restaurant, Le Colonial Café, featuring Pacific Rim cuisine.

At the lower end of the expensive category is the **Mercure Nice Promenade***** (04 93 82 30 88 FAX 04 93 82 18 20 E-MAIL mercureprom@francemultimedia.com WEB SITE www.hotel.coteazur.org/mercure-promenade, on the Promenade des Anglais, but with its entrance around the corner at 2 rue Halevy. It occupies the second and third floors of the same building as the Casino Ruhl and the Méridien, and its 122 attractive, comfortable, modern rooms have the same fine Mediterranean and Jardin Albert 1er views as the Méridien — but are little more than half as expensive.

Moderate

Nice offers many good choices in the moderate price category. The most imaginative is the **Windsor***** (04 93 88 59 35 FAX 04 93 88 94 57 E-MAIL windsor@webstore.fr, 11 rue Dalpozzo, a hotel with a Zen ambiance. It has an oriental lobby, a tropical garden with a small pool and recorded jungle bird calls, a gym, wood-paneled bar, and restaurant, and all 65 rooms are decorated by well-known contemporary artists (Room 23 has murals by that master of off-the-wall art Glen Baxter). The Windsor is three blocks in from the Promenade des Anglais.

Another of the Mercure chain's comfortable, modern, well-run hotels in Nice is the cheerful 43-room **Relais Mercure Marché aux Fleurs***** (04 93 85 74 19 FAX 04 93 13 90 94 E-MAIL h0962@accorhotel.com, 91 quai des États-Unis, fronting on the Baie des Anges, a few steps from the Cours Saleya market. The **Primotel Suisse***** (04 92 17 39 00 FAX 04 93 85 30 70 E-MAIL nice@hotels-primotel.com, 15 quai Rauba-Capeu, has 40 plain, modern rooms, half of them with the same marvelous Baie des Anges view as its more glamorous next-door neighbor La Pérouse.

For a hotel in a quiet setting with a view of the whole city, try the **Petit Palais*** (04 93 62 19 11 FAX 04 93 62 53 60 E-MAIL petitpalace@ provence-riviera.com, 10 avenue Emile-Bieckert in Cimiez. Actor-director Sacha Guitry's former mansion has 25 tasteful rooms and a lovely terrace overlooking all of Nice. It is convenient to the Chagall and Matisse Museums and Cimiez's Roman ruins. It is a member of the Best Western and Relais de Silence hotel groups. At the low end of this price category is the **Régence*** (04 93 87 75 08 FAX 04 93 82 41 31 E-MAIL HTLRegence @aol.com, 21 rue Masséna, with 40 neat, simple rooms at a top price of 380 francs. As in the more costly hotels, the rooms all have private baths or showers, television, and direct-dial phones. It is in the pedestrian shopping area west of Place Masséna.

Inexpensive

The **Dante*** (04 93 86 81 00 FAX 04 93 97 27 17, 12 rue Andrioli, is a friendly hotel with 30 spotlessly clean, renovated rooms 200 m (about 220 yards) from the Promenade des Anglais. At the **Acanthe*** (04 93 62 22 44 FAX 04 93 62 29 77, 2 rue Chauvain, you will find 50 cheerful, well-kept rooms, many with views of the Espace Masséna, and the warm Southern hospitality of owner Patrice Duchesne, a transplanted Northerner. Ask for one of the four round rooms overlooking the fountain. This is one of the best deals in town.

Camping

There are no camping grounds in Nice itself, but there are many in the outlying communities. Cagnes-sur-Mer just west of Nice Airport has 10 and Villeneuve-Loubet-Plage, the next town, has eleven. For a complete list of camping sites in the eastern Côte d'Azur and its backcountry, stop in at the Office de Tourisme in Nice, or any other tourist office in the area, and pick up the multilingual brochure *Les Campings Caravanings* published by the Comité Régional du Tourisme (CRT) Riviera-Côte d'Azur, or get it by contacting the CRT Riviera Côte d'Azur by phone, fax, or Internet (see TOURIST INFORMATION, page 363 in TRAVELERS' TIPS). The brochure lists each campsite's address, phone, fax, location, facilities (hot showers, laundromat, grocery store, etc.), and rates them for overall quality. But it does not give prices. At a highly rated camping grounds in this area, a site for a medium-sized car and caravan with two people rents for about 150 francs (plus about 30 francs per additional person). For a car and a two-person tent, it is 100 to 125 francs (depending the size of the tent), and it is about 70 francs for space for a two-person tent alone. (For more about camping, see BACKPACKING, page 39 in YOUR CHOICE).

The Côte d'Azur

The top site in Villeneuve-Loubet-Plage is **La Vieille Ferme** (04 93 33 41 44 FAX 04 93 33 37 28, at 296 boulevard des Groules (Route N7). It has a large indoor-outdoor pool in use 10 months of the year and is less than a mile from the beach. It is open all year. Another attractive, well-equipped camping grounds in Villeneuve-Loubet-Plage that is also open all year is **Parc des Maurettes** (04 93 20 91 91 FAX 04 93 73 77 20, 730 avenue du Docteur-Lefevbre, in a wooded setting a 15-minute walk from the beach. If you're driving, it's in back of the big Intermarché shopping center on N7. If you go by Métrazur train (a 15-minute ride from Nice, 30 francs round-trip), it's 400 m (about 440 yards) north of the Villeneuve-Loubet-Plage station.

WHERE TO EAT

Good food at all prices is easy to find in Nice, from the gourmet cuisine of the Negresco's Chantecler to the *Niçois* treats that you buy in the street — *socca* (chickpea crêpes), *pissaladière* (onion tart), *salade Niçoise*, and *pan bagnat* (*salade Niçoise* in a big roll). You can have a filling lunch of *pan bagnat*, beer or wine, and coffee for about 30 francs. If you still have room, try a *tourta de bléa* (or *tourte aux blettes*), a pie made of raisins, Swiss chard and pine nuts, an odd-sounding combination, but somehow it works. Vieux Nice has lots of little restaurants and stands specializing in fast food *à la Niçoise* such as this. Some of my favorites for *socca* are bustling **Thérèse** at the Cours Saleya market, **Nissa Socca** at 5 rue Sainte-Réparate, and in the evening

Al fresco dining is common virtually year-round in the balmy climate of Nice.

(not open in the day), the maestro of the specialty, **Pipo**, at 13 rue Bavastro near the Port. He makes *socca* just the way I like it — slightly crisp on the outside, soft but not mushy inside. A big plate of socca and a half bottle of rosé will run you about 40 francs.

La Fanny (04 93 80 70 63, at 2 rue Rossetti, serves savory Nice-style bistro fare in its cheerful dining room, which has a jolly cartoon poster of Pagnol's movie *Fanny* on the wall, or on the outdoor dining terrace facing Place Rossetti and Sainte-Réparate Cathedral. The copious three-course *menu* (fixed price meal) for 65 francs is a an exceptionally good deal, and the young staff are friendly, efficient, and full of life.

Merenda, a hole-in-the-wall with only 30 places at 4 rue de la Terrasse near the Cours Saleya, serves *beignets de fleurs de courgette* (zucchini blossom fritters), *potage au pistou* (vegetable soup), the *Niçois* cod fish specialty *stockfisch*, *daube* (Provençal stew), and *mesclun* (tender mixed salad greens). The chef is the very talented Dominique Le Stanc, who abandoned the gastronomic fast track in 1997, leaving his Michelin two-star restaurant the Chantecler to buy the little Merenda and devote himself to family cooking and a sane way of life. A meal will run you 150 to 210 francs (cash only, no credit cards). There's no phone, and they don't take reservations, so come early. Merenda is closed most of August.

For a full *Niçois* meal and an unforgettable evening, try **La Mère Barale** (04 93 89 17 94, at 39 rue Beaumont, seven blocks north of the Port. You sit at your table, and the irrepressible octogenarian Catherine-Hélène Barale starts dishing out her savory array of *Niçois* specialties — *pissaladière*, *socca*, *salade Niçoise*, a main course of *daube* (veal stew), *tourta de bléa* — more than you can possibly eat, all for 200 francs, wine included. The evening ends with the singing of "Nissa la Bella," led by Madame Barale, and a visit to her "museum" — an amazing memorabilia collection that includes two cars she drove in the 1930s. The restaurant is usually full, so be sure to reserve. Madame Barale accepts cash or French checks only, no credit cards. Closed the month of August.

Expensive

The **Chantecler** (04 93 16 64 00, at the Negresco is in a class by itself. In the glamorous Regency-style dining room fronting on the Baie des Anges, young chef Alain Llorca, one of the rising stars of Provençal Mediterranean cuisine, concocts Nice's finest gourmet cuisine, with an illustrious Michelin two-star rating. The Chantecler is expensive, but offers a three-course lunch *menu* for 290 francs, beverages included — a chance to sample the best of the region's cuisine at a more than reasonable price. If money's no object, try the 550-franc, six-course Menu de la Mer, with dainty scallops

sautéed to perfection, roast turbot Meunière, and truffle-laced lobster with gnocchi. Every taste is sublime. The wine list is correspondingly superb, featuring the fine local Bellet wines, Côtes de Provence, and Bandol.

At **Don Camillo** (04 93 85 67 95, 5 rue des Ponchettes, young chef Stéphane Viano serves upscale Italo-Niçois *cuisine de terroir* — risotto with wild boletus mushrooms, roast filet of *rouget* (red mullet), lamb baked in bread crust — and a good, reasonably priced selection of Provençal wines in his bright, pleasant restaurant near the Cours Saleya. The **Grand Pavois (Chez Michel)** (04 93 88 77 42, 11 avenue Meyerbeer, two blocks in from the Promenade des Anglais, makes the best *bouillabaisse* in town, along with a full range of lobster and fish dishes. *Loup de mer* (Mediterranean sea bass) baked in lemon or garlic wine sauce and flambéed in cognac at the table is an old family recipe. Veteran Côte d'Azur *restaurateur* Jacques Marquise and his vivacious wife Joianna, a Californian, maintain a relaxed ambiance in their flowery, rose-toned dining room, where most of the diners are regulars.

Another first-rate seafood house is **Dents de la Mer** (04 93 80 99 16, at 2 rue Saint-François-de-Paule, a colorful eatery on the Cours Saleya with an open terrace and a pirate ship dining room with aquariums built into the walls.

Moderate

La Rotonde (04 93 16 64 00, at the Hôtel Negresco, is a domed room decorated with brightly painted wooden merry-go-round horses, which serves French bistro cuisine and Nice specialties under the supervision of Alan Llorca. One of the most animated spots in town is the **Grand Café de Turin** (04 93 62 66 29, 5 place Garibaldi, where fresh shellfish is served under the arcades, open to 11 PM. If it is jammed, as it usually is, and you don't feel like waiting, try one of the smaller seafood restaurants under the arcades. The shellfish is just as fresh there. For solid brasserie fare, go to **Flo** (04 93 13 38 38, a member of the famed chain of that name, at 2–4 rue Sacha Guitry near Place Masséna. Here you eat in a former theater converted into a spectacular dining space where the kitchen is on stage. Late supper specials served after 11 PM include a fresh seafood platter and white wine for 99 francs. **La Zucca Magica** ("the magic pumpkin") (04 93 56 25 27, at 4bis quai Papacino on the Port Lympia, is what owner-chef Marco Folicaldi calls "a vegetable, egg, and cheese restaurant," and this genial Roman giant truly works magic with those everyday ingredients, transforming them into astonishing, original concoctions, with fresh improvisations at every meal. Just because this is a "vegetarian" restaurant, don't expect to cut down on calories. This is very rich cuisine. The restaurant is always full, and a lively atmosphere reigns in the jolly, pumpkin-festooned dining room. Reservations are essential.

NIGHTLIFE

For serious music, the **Opéra de Nice** (04 92 17 40 40, presents classical concerts, ballets, and a season of six operas. For information contact the Opéra de Nice at 4–6 rue Saint-François-de-Paule near the Cours Saleya market. Many concerts are held in churches. The Office of Tourism has a full schedule of programs. For a taste of the life in the fast lane, **Casino Ruhl** (04 93 87 95 87, 1 promenade des Anglais, offers slot machines, table games, a

rock island just east of the ferry boat harbor, with the entrance at 60 boulevard Franck Pilatte. By day it is a swimming club (a *plongeoir* is a diving platform) and casual lunch spot, by night in warm weather, a candlelit open-air terrace for drinks and refreshments, with a grand sea view and an amiable young team at the helm.

HOW TO GET THERE

At the large, modern **Nice-Côte d'Azur Airport**, there are 15 direct flights per day from London (British Airways, British Midland, Easyjet) and one direct flight a day from New York on Delta. There are more than 45 flights per day from Paris

Vegas-style floor show, and a disco. The **Bar des Oiseaux** (04 93 80 27 33, at 5 rue Saint-Vincent in Vieux Nice, is a lively jazz club and café-theater with birds flying around the room. **Tam-Tam Masséna** (04 93 80 21 60, 1 rue Desboutin (near Place Masséna), offers live Caribbean music in a tropical setting. **Chez Wayne** (04 93 13 46 99, 15 rue de la Préfecture in Vieux Nice, has rock music and British beer. **Frog** (04 93 85 85 65, at 3 rue Milton Robbins (near the Opéra de Nice), has rock music, Tex-Mex food, steak and ribs. **Le Bar** (04 93 87 80 25, 6 avenue de Suède (near the Méridien), is a musical lounge with a sophisticated but mellow ambiance that presents live middle-of-the-road pop. **La Douche** (04 93 62 81 31 E-MAIL ladouche@ wanadoo.fr, 34 Cours Saleya, has a congenial bar on the ground floor and an up-to-date cybercafé upstairs. The most unique bar in Nice is **Le Plongeoir** (04 93 89 27 97, perched high on a teeny

(Air France, AOM, and Air Liberté) and hundreds from 25 other airports in France and more than 50 airports in Europe, Africa, and the Middle East.

There is bus service every 20 minutes on the **Navette Bus Aeroport-Riviera** from the airport to Nice's Gare Routière (bus terminal), with stops along the Promenade des Anglais on its 15-minute route. The cost is 21 francs. If you want to take a **taxi**, be sure you have agreed on a price with the driver before you set off from the airport (the Tourist Office will tell you what a fair price to your destination should be). Most of Nice's taxi drivers are honest, but there are enough bad eggs to have given them a poor reputation.

Nice is also well-served by **SNCF**, the national rail service. It has four direct trains a day from Paris and five more with connections in Marseille

Longtime Nice resident Henri Matisse loved the red ochre façades of this city.

or Toulon. By high-speed trains (*trains à grande vitesse*, or *TGVs*), the trip from Paris takes six and a half hours. These trains also stop at the major cities along the coast. In addition, the SNCF runs a regional service for the Côte d'Azur called Métrazur that makes all the local stops between Saint-Raphaël and Menton, with trains approximately every half hour.

For international bus service, **Eurolines** runs coaches from London and other non-French European cities, and the regional bus company **Phocéens Cars** runs buses from main points in Provence and the Côte d'Azur. There is no bus service to Nice from Paris or other French cities out of the region. (For more information on plane, train and bus service, see GETTING THERE, page 361 in TRAVELERS' TIPS.)

Regionally, Nice's excellent train and bus service along the coast and inland make it the only practical base for exploring the eastern end of the Côte d'Azur. For those traveling by car, all roads in the area lead to and from Nice.

EXCURSIONS INLAND

There are fascinating excursions to be made in every direction from Nice, but many are in directions in which travelers often fail to look — inland. The few I have selected provide a sample of the variety available to those who can divert their gazes from the beguiling coast and cast them toward the mountains. These journeys are a ride on the *"Pine Cone Train"* to the Alpes-de-Haute-Provence and a trip to a "perched village" near Nice. See also page 126 for rambles in the magnificent and mysterious Vallée des Merveilles (Valley of Marvels) in the Alpes-Maritimes and the colorful villages of the Roya Valley.

THE *TRAIN DES PIGNES*, ANNOT, AND DIGNE-LES-BAINS

The *Pine Cone Train* (*Le Train des Pignes*) runs from Nice along the dramatic Var River Valley to Digne-les-Bains in the Alpes-de-Haute-Provence, a quiet refuge from the intensity of the coast. The train earned its nickname in the nineteenth century because it was so slow-moving that people could hop off and on to gather pine cones. The distance from Nice to Digne is 152 km (95 miles), and the trip takes three hours. You can get off at any of the colorful hill towns along the way to poke around or have lunch, then get on another train and continue your journey. On summer Sundays, you can take a marvelous old steam train that only runs on the section between Puget-Théniers and Annot. One place to get off and explore is **Entrevaux**, a

Entrevaux, a stop on the route of the *Train des Pignes* from Nice to the Alpes-de-Haute-Provence.

tiny town in the middle of nowhere with incongruously massive ramparts and fortifications running up a steep hill. This was once the frontier of France, and the fort and walls were built by Vauban to confront the Duchy of Savoy.

Annot is a gracious medieval walled town of 1,100 in a bright mountain valley with a broad main street shaded by large plane tree and strange caves in the hills where ancient troglodytes once lived.

Digne-les-Bains (population 17,000) is a lively spa town, a center of lavender and fruit growing, with first-rate restaurants and hotels. It is the perfect base for exploring the Alpes-de-Haute-Provence. Be sure to visit **Samten Dzong**, a touch of Shangri-La in Provence. This is the home of intrepid world traveler Alexandra David-Néel, the first Western woman to visit Tibet, who died here in 1969 at the age of 101. It is now a Tibetan meditation center which has been visited twice by the Dalai Lama.

General Information

The **Nice Tourist Office** (see GENERAL INFORMATION, page 95, under NICE) can help you with train schedules and information, but note that the *Train des Pignes* does not leave from the Gare SNCF. It is operated by **Chemins de Fer de Provence** (04 97 03 80 80 E-MAIL trainpigne@aol.com, and it leaves from the **Gare du Sud** at 4 rue Alfred Binet, a few blocks north of the Gare SNCF. This is where you buy your ticket. There are four trains a day. The Nice-Digne round-trip fare is 218 francs, Nice-Entrevaux 110 francs, 25% off for people 55 and older, 50% off for children 4 to 12 years of age.

The town of Annot has a particularly helpful **Tourist Office** (04 92 83 23 03, on the main square. At the **Digne-les-Bains Tourist Office** (04 92 36 62 62 FAX 04 92 32 27 24 E-MAIL info@ot-dignelesbains.fr WEB SITE www.ot-dignelesbains.fr, the large oval building at the Rond Point, the main traffic circle, the efficient team can probably tell you anything you'd care to know about the town or the surrounding area. They can inform you about hiking, horseback excursions, whitewater rafting, hang-gliding, and other outdoors activities in the Alpes-de-Haute-Provence.

Where to Stay and Eat

For a stay in a restful country town, Annot is the best choice, and the **Hôtel de l'Avenue**** (04 92 83 22 07 FAX 04 92 83 33 13, just off the main square, is pleasant and inexpensive, and the restaurant is good. In Digne-les-Bains, the **Hôtel Restaurant du Grand Paris****** (04 92 31 11 15 FAX 04 92 32 32 82, 19 boulevard Thiers, is a seventeenth-century monastery, now a charming hotel with 26 well-maintained rooms in the moderate to slightly expensive categories and the top restaurant in

town. Owner-chef Jean-Jacques Ricaud is noted for his mastery of lamb, pigeon, game, and other local ingredients. It is expensive. **Origan** (04 92 31 62 13, an easygoing restaurant at 6 rue Pied de Ville, features snails, lamb with truffle butter and foie gras, and other classic regional fare at moderate prices; it has tables on a pedestrian street in the summer. Origan also rents eight inexpensive rooms.

Twenty-five kilometers (15 miles) west of Digne in Château-Arnoux is **La Bonne Étape****** (04 92 64 00 09 FAX 04 92 64 37 36 E-MAIL bonneetape @relaischateaux.fr WEB SITE www.relaischateaux .ft/bonneetape, a former coach house, now a handsomely decorated Relais & Châteaux inn. It has 10 plush expensive rooms and eight suites, a pool, and a restaurant that is the gourmets' first choice in Upper Provence. Here you can savor subtle delights prepared by the renowned father and son team of Pierre and Jany Gleize — zucchini blossoms stuffed with vegetables, duck with lavender honey and lemon, Sisteron lamb, a remarkable assortment of local cheeses, frozen cream with lavender honey in its hive, and an exceptional wine list featuring the vintages of the South. La Bonne Étape is expensive.

THE PERCHED VILLAGE OF PEILLON

Peillon is one of the most dramatically perched of all "perched villages," 376 m (1,234 ft) up on the tip of a spur of rock overlooking the narrow valley of the Paillon River, its geometrical cluster of houses looking like the work of a Cubist painter. But the austerity is a façade. Once you get into the village, you find a charming square with a fountain, a medieval chapel with School of Nice frescoes, and flowers everywhere. Despite it being only 19 km (12 miles) from Nice, Peillon has managed to remain one of the most authentic of all the medieval villages. (See LAND IN AN EAGLE'S NEST, page 21 in TOP SPOTS).

Peillon is one of the 400 or so medieval "eagle's nest" villages in the Côte d'Azur and Provence region. They are built on the top of steep hills and surrounded by walls or by the outer walls of houses arranged to form ramparts encircling the town, as in the case of Peillon. Today, these places look quaint, but they are vivid reminders of how dangerous life was in the Middle Ages, when Saracen pirates or roving bands of marauders known as *les grandes compagnies* could appear at any moment. It gave the inhabitants daunting defensive positions, and most importantly, the chance to spot the brigands trying to sneak up on them before it was too late. Inside a perched village, the streets are steep and narrow, with steps cut into the rock in places to get from one level to the next, and

Villefranche-sur-Mer on the Corniches of the Riviera, one of the finest natural harbors in the Mediterranean.

alleys run underneath the houses. The local lord's castle was usually built at the highest point, but in many cases, a church replaced it in more peaceful times, as occurred in Peillon in the eighteenth century.

Where to Stay and Eat

For lunch or dinner, the clear choice is the flowery, olive tree-shaded terrace of the **Auberge de la Madone** (04 93 79 91 17 FAX 04 93 79 99 36, overlooking the valley at the foot of the village. The quality of the cooking, strictly seasonal and regional, matches the charm of the setting. But it is not cheap. Fixed-price *menus* start at 150 francs for a weekday lunch. This is a very popular spot, so book in advance.

The Auberge has 20 rooms, moderately priced, with cheerful Provençal decor, and is an extremely restful place to unwind in. It is closed from late October to late January except at Christmas and New Year.

How to Get There

To get there by car from Nice, head out of town from Place Masséna on Boulevard Jean-Jaurès and Boulevard Risso following the signs for Sospel, and follow D2204 and D21 to Peillon. The drive takes half an hour. The TRAM bus line runs three coaches a day from Nice's Gare Routière, in the early morning, at noon, and in the late afternoon. The price is 12 francs.

ALONG THE COAST

The **Corniches of the Riviera** are three parallel roads that run 32 km (20 miles) across the face of the mountainous coast between Nice and the Italian border. The two upper roads offer such spectacular views of the Mediterranean and the shore line that they would be worth driving for the scenery alone. But the *corniches* also offer several exciting towns to visit, and even have a small foreign country tucked into their craggy folds, the Principality of Monaco.

The **Grande Corniche**, the highest, was built in 1806 by Napoléon and runs along Via Julia Augusta, the Roman route from Genoa to Cimiez. It has quasi-aerial views of the coast and sea. From the **Moyenne (Middle) Corniche** you get the best views of the Villefranche-Beaulieu-Cap-Ferrat section, and it provides the only access to the "perched village" of Èze. The **Corniche Inférieure**, built by the Princes of Monaco in the eighteenth century, twists along the coast, where Monaco and most of the towns are situated (see CRUISE THE CORNICHES OF THE RIVIERA, page 13 in TOP SPOTS).

Tour operators in Nice offer daily bus excursions to the towns of the *corniches* (see GENERAL INFORMATION, page 95, under NICE), but if you can do it, I urge you to drive it yourself, to control your own pace and shift up and down from *corniche* to *corniche* at will.

The first town you come to is Villefranche seven kilometer (four miles) to the east of Nice, separated from it by Mont Boron.

VILLEFRANCHE-SUR-MER, BEAULIEU-SUR-MER, AND CAP-FERRAT

Villefranche-sur-Mer, its next-door neighbor Beaulieu, and the little Cap-Ferrat peninsula poking out into the sea form one of the most exclusive areas in France, with estates by the dozens, luxury hotels, classy restaurants, and yacht-filled harbors

shielded by steep olive-wooded hills. Incongruously, you will often find gun-sprouting warships in Villefranche, whose deepwater port is used by the French, British, and United States navies.

Since these towns form a unit, we have grouped their hotels and restaurants together to give you a better picture of the range that is available in the area.

BACKGROUND

Villefranche was founded at the beginning of the fourteenth century by the Count of Provence, Charles II of Anjou, as a free port, hence its name. Later in the century it fell into the hands of the Dukes of Savoy, who began fortifying Villefranche, one of the finest natural harbors in the Mediterranean, as their main naval base. Vauban so admired the citadel, built in 1560, that he talked Louis XIV into sparing it from demolition, a fate the château in Nice did not escape. Much of the harbor front and lower village date from the seventeenth and eighteenth century, when the Savoyard navy was a power to reckon with and was kept busy in wars against France.

In the 1920s, Jean Cocteau and his surrealist crowd stayed at the Welcome Hôtel on the water-front, where they wrote, painted, and composed music in the day and hobnobbed with sailors at night.

GENERAL INFORMATION

The **Villefranche Tourist Office (** 04 93 01 73 68, is at Place François-Binon on the Corniche Inférieure. The train and bus stations are to the east of the port overlooking the town beach. The **Saint-Jean-Cap-Ferrat Tourist Office (** 04 93 76 08 90, is at 59 avenue Denis-Séméria, the central street of the peninsula, and the **Beaulieu-sur-Mer Tourist Office (** 04 93 01 02 21, is at Place Georges-Clemenceau.

WHAT TO SEE AND DO

The Villefranche-sur-Mer **waterfront** is colorful, with little fishing boats in the water, houses painted in cheerful pink and pastel tones, busy cafés and restaurants, and a small public beach to the east of the port. The **old town** rises almost vertically from the shore, and if you have good legs, its winding old streets are fascinating to explore. It's so steep that in some places they've had to use stairs. Look for **Rue Obscure**, a street that tunnels under a row of houses in back of the harbor, parallel to the waterfront.

In 1957, Cocteau came back to Villefranche to portray the life of Saint Peter in frescoes and ceramics on the walls of the abandoned Chapelle Saint-Pierre. "It is beautifully done," noted Noel Coward in his diary. "Lovely craftsmanship and pale colors, but I had no idea all the apostles looked so like Jean Marais." Nearby in the **citadel** is a museum of the late sculptor Volti, a longtime resident and ardent admirer of the female form.

Cap-Ferrat is the small, wooded peninsula directly to your left as you look out from the waterfront of Villefranche. To drive there from Villefranche, take the Corniche Inférieure east out of town, then take the first right you come to, and you are there. Or you can take the local bus to the little port of Saint-Jean-Cap-Ferrat. The Cap-Ferrat peninsula has dozens of lavish estates, Somerset Maugham's Villa Mauresque among them, but most are hidden from view by high walls, and trying to catch a glimpse of the life-styles of the rich and famous is an exercise in frustration. But the **Villa Ephrussi de Rothschild**, the pink and white mansion constructed by

Baroness Rothschild in the early 1900s, is open to the public and displays her exquisite collection of eighteenth-century paintings, tapestries, and furniture. There are also seven hectares (17 acres) of gardens with views of Villefranche and Beaulieu which should not be missed. It is closed on Mondays.

The view from **Pointe de Saint-Hospice** on the east side of the peninsula takes in the Gulf of Saint-Hospice, Èze, Monaco and Cap-Martin, with the Alpes-Maritimes soaring up from the sea. The old fishing port of **Saint-Jean-Cap-Ferrat**, also on the east side, now bulges with yachts and sail-boats. It's a pleasant place to stop for a sandwich or a drink and watch the boats. If you want to take

a dip, there are several little beaches, including a sandy one — as sandy as they get on this end of the coast, anyway — the **Plage de Passable** on the west side of the peninsula.

Beaulieu, "beautiful place," so-named by Napoléon, lies immediately to the east of Cap-Ferrat on the Baie des Fourmis (Bay of Ants), which got its name from the cluster of black rocks in the water. This flowery town is shielded by a ridge of high hills, which gives it one of the gentlest winter climates in France (Beaulieu and Menton compete for bragging rights as to which is the warmest in winter). **Villa Kerylos** sits on a bluff overlooking the east end of the bay. It is a lavish reproduction of an ancient Greek estate with a number of authentic Greek mosaics, statues, amphorae and vases, and its magnificent setting gives it views of

OPPOSITE: Villa Kerylos in Beaulieu-sur-Mer.
ABOVE: Villa Ephrussi de Rothschild in Cap-Ferrat.

Cap-Ferrat, the Gulf of Saint-Hospice, and the "perched village" of Èze.

The villa is open afternoons only, closed Mondays and the month of November.

WHERE TO STAY

For these who want to indulge themselves, some of the ritziest hotels on the Côte d'Azur are found in these towns. But good choices are to be found in moderate and inexpensive hotels too.

Very Expensive
Grand Hôtel du Cap Ferrat**** (04 93 76 50 50 FAX 04 93 76 04 52 E-MAIL reseve@

27 supremely elegant, but restful rooms, a big heated seawater pool overlooking the Mediterranean, and a formal dining room fit for Lorenzo the Magnificent. Its next-door neighbor and fellow Relais & Châteaux member is **Le Métropole****** (04 93 01 00 08 FAX 04 93 01 18 51 E-MAIL metropole@relaischateaux.fr WEB SITE www.le-metropole.com, at 15 boulevard du Général-Leclerc, Beaulieu-sur-Mer. This sunny, cream-colored nineteenth-century Italianate palace has 35 rooms and five suites, supremely elegant also, with a large pool overlooking the sea, open all year, and a private beach. The dining room opens out onto a large dining terrace protected from the sun by a white canopy.

grandhotelcapferrat.com WEB SITE www .grandhotelcapferrat.com, sits right on the tip of Cap-Ferrat, in a six-hectare (15-acre) park with a funicular to its pool on the sea and 59 sumptuous rooms and suites. Perched above the yacht harbor of Saint-Jean-Cap-Ferrat is the **Voile d'Or****** (04 93 01 13 13 FAX 04 93 76 11 17 E-MAIL voiledor@ calva.net—a refined 50-room, five-suite hotel with a grand view toward Èze and Monaco. The smaller of its two pools is built into a rock shelf by the edge of the sea. It has the same marvelous view, and there's a bar serving lunch and refreshments.

La Réserve de Beaulieu**** (04 93 01 00 01 FAX 04 93 01 28 99 E-MAIL beaulieu@relaischateaux .fr WEB SITE www.relaischateaux.fr/beaulieu, at 5 boulevard du Général-Leclerc in Beaulieu, is a grand eggshell and white Florentine-style château, *pieds dans l'eau* ("feet in the water"), looking out at the eastern shore of Cap Ferrat and the sea. It has

You can go for lunch and enjoy the pool facilities at all four of these magnificent hotels.

Expensive
At the **Welcome***** (04 93 76 27 62 FAX 04 93 76 27 66 E-MAIL folder@welcomehotel.com WEB SITE www.welcomehotel.com, Quai Colbert, Villefranche-sur-Mer, you'll find 32 comfortable, freshly renovated rooms at this hotel directly on the port where Kiki de Montparnasse, Cocteau, and company holed up in the 1920s. It is a member of the Best Western group. In Saint-Jean-Cap-Ferrat, the **Brise Marine***** (04 93 76 04 36 FAX 04 93 76 11 49 E-MAIL bmarine@ nicematin.fr, at 58 avenue Jean-Mermoz, has 16 pleasant, spacious rooms, a quiet garden and a view of the gulf; it is convenient to the port and Pointe-Sainte-Hospice, but has no pool or restaurant.

Moderate

Comté de Nice*** (04 93 01 19 70 FAX 04 93 01 23 09 WEB SITE www.bestwestern.fr, 25 boulevard Marioni, Beaulieu-sur-Mer, is an attractive, modern 33-room hotel on a hill overlooking Cap-Ferrat. Be sure to ask for a room with a sea view. It is a Best Western member. **Clair Logis**** (04 93 76 04 57 FAX 04 93 76 11 85 WEB SITE www.hotel-clair-logis.fr, at 12 avenue Centrale, Saint-Jean-Cap-Ferrat, has 18 spacious rooms in a rambling Provençal house in a wooded park on a hill in the center of the little Cap-Ferrat peninsula, a short walk from the beach facing Villefranche. It has no restaurant. **Provençal**** (04 93 76 53 53 FAX 04 93 76 96 00 E-MAIL provencal@riviera.fr, at 4 avenue du Maréchal-Joffre in Villefranche, has 49 well-kept rooms, a restaurant, and a quiet garden setting on the hill above the citadel. Some rooms are in the inexpensive category.

Inexpensive

Costière* (04 93 76 03 89, on Avenue Albert 1ᵉʳ, Saint-Jean-Cap-Ferrat, has 15 neat, simple rooms, a garden, and pretty views from the center of the cape. **La Frégate** (04 93 76 04 51 FAX 04 93 76 14 93, at 11 avenue Denis Séméria, Saint-Jean-Cap-Ferrat, is a cozy little 10-room hotel with restaurant right on the port. *Demi-pension* (rate including breakfast and one meal) is required in season.

WHERE TO EAT

All four of the four-star hotels mentioned above have distinguished gastronomic restaurants. The restaurant of **La Réserve de Beaulieu** is among the highest-rated in the Côte d'Azur, with two Michelin stars. The **Grand Hôtel du Cap Ferrat** has one star. The **Voile d'Or** and the **Métropole** have had stars in the past and will undoubtedly have them again. All are very good, very elegant, and very expensive, and they all feature refined seafood dishes with Provençal accents.

On the Port de Plaisance in Saint-Jean-Cap-Ferrat, **Le Sloop** (04 93 01 48 63, serves imaginative seafood and pasta dishes at relatively modest prices, with a fixed-price *menu* at 155 francs. In Villefranche, **Carpe Diem** (04 93 76 27 20, on Place Amélie Pollanais, the little square next to the Welcome Hôtel, is a lively spot serving salads and Provençal standards, with a filling *plat du jour* always on the menu (moderate prices). In good weather, you dine outdoors on the square overlooking the fishing port. For good, hearty food at modest prices, go where the locals go: up the hill to **La Belle Époque** (04 93 01 96 22, a big, bustling, red-ochre *restaurant-glacier-bar-pizzeria* with a wide range of choices, from pizzas and salads to traditional regional cuisine. It fronts on Place de la Paix, the center of the eternal, non-tourist Villefranche-

sur-Mer, and has a dining terrace overlooking the town and the harbor.

HOW TO GET THERE

The Métrazur service has trains from Nice's Gare SNCF roughly every half hour in season, barely a five-minute trip to the area.

There is also frequent bus service from Nice's Gare Routière. If you are driving from Nice, you have two choices. You can come via the Corniche Inférieure, which you pick up by taking Boulevard Carnot (N98) east from Port Lympia and follow the coast around the base of Mont Boron to Villefranche, or, as I recommend, take the Moyenne Corniche (N7), which winds up behind Mont Boron and gives you marvelous high angle views of Villefranche and Cap-Ferrat before you descend to Villefranche via Avenue du Général Leclerc. To get onto the Moyenne Corniche from Nice, take Rue Barla, four blocks north of Port Lympia. You can get to Beaulieu by Métrazur train or by bus.

ÈZE

From Èze-Bord-de-Mer, the beach town three kilometers (two miles) east of Beaulieu on the Corniche Inférieure, you can drive up to the "perched village" of Èze, sitting a rocky spur 427 m (1,400 ft) above the sea. Èze is on the Moyenne (Middle) Corniche, and this is one of the few spots where there is an access road between *corniches*. Alternately, you can park your car at sea level and walk up the **Sentier Nietzsche** (Nietzsche's Path). This footpath that winds its way up to the village was the favorite promenade of the German philosopher when he vacationed here, and the philosopher is said to have thought out parts of *Thus Spoke Zarathustra* when he took his walks. You'll see as he did, that the views of the coast get more and more powerful as you ascend, and from the top they are nothing short of spectacular. On a clear day you can see Corsica 160 km (100 miles) away.

Èze is a typical medieval hilltop village in most ways, but unlike the others, which normally have a castle or a church at the top, this perched village is crowned by a garden of cactus.

BACKGROUND

Èze was originally a Celto-Ligurian *oppidum* which, due to its superb defensive and lookout position, was valued by the Greeks, Romans, Saracens, Counts of Provence, and various medieval lords after Èze fell under Savoyard rule in 1388. Èze used to have a castle at the top of the town, but Louis XIV demolished it in 1706 during

The Château de la Chèvre d'Or in the perched village of Èze is one of the Riviera's many supremely elegant hotels.

a war against Savoy. But the people don't seem to have held that against the French. As a monument in the village states, 100% of Èze's voters opted to join France in the County of Nice plebiscite of 1860.

GENERAL INFORMATION

The **Tourist Office** (04 93 41 26 00, is at Place du Général-de-Gaulle by the main gate of the village. Hikers can pick up a map called *Èze Randonnées* (Èze Rambles) which will point out the many footpaths in this rugged area.

WHAT TO SEE AND DO

There is a fourteenth-century **White Penitents' Chapel** with a strange thirteenth-century Catalan crucifix in which Christ is seen smiling. The highest point of the village has the **Jardin Exotique**, an exotic garden with dozens of varieties of cacti and succulents built around the ruins of the castle. Spring is the best time to see the cacti, as they put out their psychedelic yellow, orange, and blood-red blossoms then.

But the main thing to see is not *in* Èze, but *from* Èze: the utterly breathtaking view of the coast far — very far — below.

WHERE TO STAY

Èze has two exquisite small luxury hotels within the old village, the **Château Eza****** (04 93 41 12 24 FAX 04 93 41 16 64 E-MAIL chateza@webstore .com WEB SITE www.slh.com (for Small Luxury Hotels), and the **Château de la Chèvre d'Or****** (04 92 10 66 66 FAX 04 93 41 06 72 E-MAIL chevre@ relaischateaux.fr WEB SITE www.chevredor.com. Both have the famed breathtaking Riviera views. The Eza has five rooms and five suites. The Chèvre d'Or, a Relais & Châteaux member, has 22 rooms, eight suites, and a small pool overlooking the sea. Both hotels are very expensive. An inexpensive alternative on a hill above the village is the **Hermitage du Col d'Èze** ** (04 93 41 00 68 FAX 04 93 41 24 05, on the Grande Corniche. This cheerful 14-room Logis de France inn has a pool, sea and mountain views, and a good, moderately priced restaurant featuring regional cuisine. It is reached by taking D46 (Route du Col d'Èze) from the village. Another pleasant moderately priced Logis de France inn is the seven-room **Auberge des Deux Corniches**** (04 93 41 19 54 FAX 04 92 10 86 26, on D46 one kilometer (half a mile) from the village.

Camping

Les Romarins (04 93 01 81 64, on the Grande Corniche, is a wooded 50-place campsite with modest facilities (hot showers and a snack bar) and a magnificent panorama of the Alps, Cap-

Ferrat, and the sea. It is open from mid-April to the end of September. Be sure to reserve long in advance for the summer months.

WHERE TO EAT

At the **Château Eza**, the accent is on Provençal and Niçois cuisine, while the **Château de la Chèvre d'Or** features more classically French fare. Both are outstanding gourmet restaurants, and very expensive. **Le Troubadour** (04 93 41 19 03, in a charming old house at 4 rue de Brec at the start of the walking streets, serves refined Provençal fare with a special lunch *menu* at 125 francs. Reservations are required at all three restaurants.

HOW TO GET THERE

The Métrazur train stops at Èze-Bord-de-Mer. Seven buses a day from Nice's Gare Routière stop at Èze's

Place du Général-de-Gaulle and continue on to Monaco. By car, Èze can be reached directly from Nice by the Moyenne Corniche, or by the Corniche Inférieure to Èze-Bord-de-Mer and the access road up to the village, or by the Grande Corniche and D46 from Col d'Èze down to the village.

THE PRINCIPALITY OF MONACO

Though its once-beautiful skyline has become cluttered with modern banking, corporate, and condo high-rises, and its aura of refined idle-class debauchery — "a sunny place for shady people," Somerset Maugham called it — has all but evaporated, no visitor to the Côte d'Azur should think of bypassing Monaco. It remains the best place on the Riviera to get a taste of the way the crowned heads of Europe lived during the "banquet years" of the late nineteenth century, thanks to the Casino of Monte-Carlo and the other grandiose *belle*

époque buildings clustered around it. They were frequented by kings, princes, emperors, and legendary courtesans such as Caroline Otéro, "La Belle Otéro," whose perfect *poitrine* several Côte d'Azur hotels claim as the model for their domes. That ravishing creature was covered with jewels by the likes of King Edward VII, Czar Nicholas II, King Leopold II, King Alfonso XIII, and William K. Vanderbilt, but when she eventually went broke, "La Belle Otéro" took it in stride. She said, "What does one come to Monte-Carlo for if not to lose?"

Besides its casinos and *belle époque* attractions, Monaco has one of the world's largest exotic garden, the world's finest oceanographic museums, the oldest and second-most publicized ruling family in the world, public safety second to none, and a level of excellence in its hotels and cuisine that has set the standards for the world for more than

For the daily changing of the guard at the Prince's Palace in Monaco, be there by 11:55 AM.

a century. With its illustrious Opera, Ballet and Philharmonic Orchestra and a first-rate lineup of pop stars at the Salle des Étoiles, Monaco's cultural agenda is remarkably rich for a country with only 28,000 residents.

BACKGROUND

In 1297, Francesco ("the Clever") Grimaldi disguised himself as a monk, coaxed the guards into letting him into the palace, took out a sword and killed them, opened the gate to his associates and made himself master of Monaco. To this day, the Grimaldi coat of arms features two monks with swords in their hands.

tourism could no longer support the economy, he has focused on international banking and business tourism. At the same time, he has worked to maintain Monte-Carlo's image of glamour, a juggling act helped greatly by his 1956 marriage to the elegant Hollywood queen Grace Kelly.

In 1987, worried that the "Hong Kong of Europe" label was tarnishing Monte-Carlo's reputation for luxury, the Société des Bains de Mer (Sea Bathing Society), the major hotel, restaurant and casino-owning company in Monaco, embarked on an ambitious program to refurbish its image. They hired an up-and-coming young chef to run its flagship Louis XV Restaurant at Monte-Carlo's Hôtel de Paris and gave him *carte blanche* and a

In the mid-nineteenth century, after his citrus producing possessions of Roquebrune and Menton had broken away, and his remote little realm was threatened with bankruptcy, Prince Charles III took a plunge into casino gambling in the hope of reviving the economy. He built a gaming house on a goat-grazing rocky promontory called Spélugues and renamed it Monte-Carlo — Mount Charles. The railroad arrived a few years later, and with it the rich and demimonde from all over the world. Prince Charles's bet paid off so well that he exempted Monaco's residents from taxes in 1869, a status they have enjoyed ever since.

As Grimaldi rulers have been doing for seven centuries, Prince Rainier III, *"Le Patron"* ("the boss"), as his subjects call him, has redirected the economy of his little nation since coming to power in 1949. Aware that the gambling-based luxury

12-million-franc ($2.4-million) budget for renovations. In 1990, at the age of 33, Alain Ducasse became the youngest chef ever to win three Michelin stars, and he went on to become the most influential chef of the decade (food critics write about the "Generation Ducasse"). The Louis XV-Alain Ducasse has become one world's most venerated restaurants, and, haute cuisine being what it is in French culture, its success helped spark Monte-Carlo's return to star quality.

GENERAL INFORMATION

No visa is needed to enter Monaco from France. Monaco uses French currency, but has its own postal system and issues colorful stamps.

The Rock of Monaco, where the Prince's Palace, the cathedral and the Oceanographic Museum are located.

Monaco has its own telephone country code. From France, for instance, you dial 00-377, then the eight-digit Monaco number. From Monaco to France, dial 33, then the French number, dropping the initial zero. Locally, just dial the eight digit number.

The **Monaco Tourist Bureau** (92 16 61 66 E-MAIL dtc@monaco-congres.com WEBSITE www.monaco-congres.com, at 2A boulevard des Moulins, Monte-Carlo, offers superlative tourist literature and service. Pick up the map of Monaco's excellent, inexpensive public transportation system. If you are coming by private car, I suggest parking it (the big "P" indicates public parking) and getting around by foot, bus, and the numerous

ing circus acts in big top set up in the Espace Fontvieille exhibition center in February.

The **Monte-Carlo Open**, the first big clay-court tennis tournament of the year, is held at the Monte-Carlo Country Club in April.

The Formula 1 auto race, the **Grand Prix de Monaco**, whose course runs through the city streets, takes place the weekend of Ascension (40 days after Easter). The town is jammed, so unless you're a fan, I suggest you stay away.

The **Festival International des Feux d'Artifice** is a fireworks festival held several evenings in July and August, when the world's leading pyrotechnics specialists put on shows. Check with the Tourist Bureau for the exact dates.

public elevators that have been installed to take you from level to level in this steep town.

The **Gare SNCF** (train station) (93 10 60 01, at Place Sainte-Dévote, is centrally located between La Condamine and Monte-Carlo. The **Navettes Bus Aéroport-Riviera** (93 21 30 83 are the Airport-Riviera Shuttle Buses.

For helicopter trips between Nice Airport and Monaco (a seven-minute flight) and aerial tours of the region, contact **Heli Air Monaco** (92 05 00 50 or **Monacair** (92 05 60 70. For **taxis** call (93 30 71 63 or a 24-hour radio taxi (93 15 01 01.

In case of health emergencies, contact the **Princess Grace Hospital Center** (93 25 98 69.

FESTIVALS AND EVENTS

The **Monte-Carlo International Circus Festival** presents a selection of the world's most outstand-

WHAT TO SEE AND DO

With only 195 hectares (468 acres) — half as big as New York's Central Park, two percent of the size of Paris — Monaco is small enough to explore by foot. But to save time, take the No. 1 bus between Monaco ("the Rock," where the Palace and the Oceanographic Museum are) and Monte-Carlo, and to save leg muscles, the No. 2 to the Exotic Garden, high on a hill.

Small as it is, the Principality has six distinct areas. From west to east, they are **Fontvieille**, a new business district with a heliport, a new harbor, the football stadium, the Princess Grace Rose Garden (4,000 bushes of more than 150 varieties), and Prince Rainier's magnificent stamp and coin collection and his equally magnificent collection of 100 classic cars; the **Exotic Garden** on a hill overlooking the sea and coastline; **Le Rocher**, the

Rock of Monaco, a sheer-cliffed promontory on which the Prince's Palace, the cathedral, and the Oceanographic Museum sit; **La Condamine**, which has the train station, market, and yacht harbor; **Monte-Carlo**, where casinos and deluxe hotels abound; and **Larvotto**, with the public beach, the Monte-Carlo Sporting Club, and the big new Forum Grimaldi convention center. **Monte-Carlo Beach**, with the beach hotel and tennis courts, is in the neighboring French town of Roquebrune. The Monte-Carlo Golf Club is on Mont Agel 900 m (3,000 ft) above the sea in the neighboring French town of La Turbie.

La Condamine

La Condamine is the center of Monaco, where the port cuts a swath between the steep promontories of the Rock and Monte-Carlo. Multimillionaires keep their Onassis-sized yachts in the **harbor**, and you can ogle them from the promenade or a café along the Boulevard Albert 1er. The **railway station** is on the eastern edge of the district at Place Sainte-Dévote, and a colorful food and flower market is held mornings in and around the nineteenth-century **Marché de la Condamine** a few blocks in from the harbor.

Le Rocher (The Rock)

The Rock of Monaco lies immediately to the west of La Condamine. This is where the palace, the cathedral and the Oceanographic Museum are located. The **Prince's Palace (Palais Princier)** is a large rambling, cream-colored Renaissance building on a wide square where the main event of the day is the changing of the guard at 11:55 AM. The Palace's seventeenth-century Grand Apartments are sumptuous and house a fine collection of Napoléonic memorabilia, thanks to Prince Louis II's fascination with the Emperor.

The somber late nineteenth-century neo-Romanesque **cathedral** in the center of the Rock has several fine School of Nice paintings, including Ludovico Bréa's subtle 18-panel Saint Nicholas altarpiece, which demonstrates why he is known as "the Fra Angelico of Provence." To the left of the altar is the austere tomb of Princess Grace, touchingly decorated by bouquets from her admirers. High Mass is at 10 AM Sundays, and many concerts are scheduled in the cathedral.

The **Musée Océanographique** (Oceanographic Museum) atop the western face of the Rock was built in 1910 by Albert I, the Scientist Prince, for the collections he and his teams brought back from their pioneering oceanographic voyages in the early twentieth century. It has grown under the direction of Jacques-Yves Cousteau from 1957 to 1988 and François Doumenge since. It is one of the two sights you absolutely must see in Monaco (the other being the Grand Casino). The aquarium is one of the world's finest, with ninety large, bright,

modern tanks filled with 4,500 fish of 450 different species. The colors are dazzling, the movement hypnotic. This is a place you have to drag yourself away from. The upper floors contain scientific exhibits, including whale skeletons and a 13-m (43-ft) giant squid. There is a 60-franc entrance fee.

The Exotic Garden

The Jardin Exotique is a garden of cacti and succulents that grows up a protected rocky hillside overlooking La Condamine. In this warm, dry, windless microclimate, many of these strange plants do better than in their African and American homelands. There are Mexican candelabras

over 40 ft (12 m) tall, bigger than any in Mexico, and a 135-year-old *Echinocactus Grusonnii* sent back by Emperor Maximilian to Napoléon III. The garden is open daily and is most easily reached by the No. 2 bus from the Rock.

Monte-Carlo

The huge ornate *belle époque* **Casino** on the Place du Casino is the focus of everything in Monte-Carlo. Designed by Charles Garnier, the famed architect of the Paris Opéra, in the 1870s, it is visited by more than a million people a year, though only six to seven percent actually try their luck in the vast rococo gambling rooms where roulette, *chemin de fer*, blackjack, and baccarat are played. Finally yielding to popular demand several years ago, the Casino installed *machines à sous* (slot

OPPOSITE: The Café de Paris at the Place du Casino in Monte-Carlo. ABOVE: The Exotic Garden.

machines) off to one side in the Salle Blanche. To get into the gaming rooms, you must show your passport and pay a 50-franc fee. No tie is required for the first rooms, where the minimum stakes are low, but to enter the *salons privés*, the private rooms where stakes start at 100 francs, there is an additional 50-franc entrance fee, and men must wear jackets and ties. (There's an even more private room where stakes start at 50,000 francs, but you need to be known by the management to get in there.) Even if you don't gamble, it's a thrill to wander through these incredibly ornate rooms and watch the high-rollers scatter their chips on the tables, like being in a James Bond movie.

The **Opéra de Monte-Carlo** is located off main the lobby of the Grand Casino. You can't always get in to see it, but it doesn't hurt to ask. It is a smaller but more opulent version of Garnier's Opéra de Paris. In the summer, the private gambling rooms move down from the Grand Casino to the Sporting Club at the beach in Larvotto.

Sun Casino is the Las Vegas-style gaming house in the Grand Hôtel on the seafront of Monte-Carlo that brought the one-armed bandit to town in the 1970s. It also has craps, poker, punto banco and American roulette, and many people prefer its more easygoing American ambiance.

The **Café de Paris** on the Place du Casino has black jack, craps and an impressive array of slot machines, and here there are no entry fees or dress requirements. Its lively outdoor terrace is the best spot in town for the other popular game in Monte-Carlo, people-watching.

Across the square is the glittering **Hôtel de Paris**, where the *belle époque* high rollers stayed. Notice the small equestrian statue of Louis XIV in the lobby. The horse's right knee is shiny because rubbing it is said to bring good luck. Be sure to look into **Louis XV-Alain Ducasse Restaurant** to the right of the entrance. It is one of the most beautiful as well as one of the finest restaurants in the world (see WHERE TO EAT, below).

The **Musée National de Monaco** (Doll Museum), a short walk down the hill east of the Place du Casino at 17 avenue Princesse Grace, has a huge collection of minutely detailed nineteenth-century dolls, their furnishings and possessions, including printed books you'd need a magnifying glass to read. There are 80 automated figures with movements so human that they are eerie—Pierrot writing a letter, in particular. The museum is open daily.

WHERE TO STAY

Monaco has 2,500 hotel rooms, three-quarters of them in palaces or four-star hotels where prices run from 1,000 to more than 3,000 francs for a double. But there are a few comfortable, modestly priced rooms to be found here too.

Very Expensive

The glamorous **Hôtel de Paris****** (92 16 30 00 FAX 92 16 38 50 E-MAIL: hp@sbm.mc WEB SITE www.montecarloresort.com, on Monte-Carlo's Place du Casino, is where Edward VII and other *belle époque* high-rollers stayed. It has 160 supremely elegant rooms, 40 suites, and a deluxe health spa, **Les Thermes Marins de Monte-Carlo**, which has a gorgeous indoor-outdoor pool and a terrace overlooking the harbor, sauna, steam bath, and massage. Les Thermes offers *thalassothérapie* (seawater therapy), with programs tailored to the client's individual needs (slimming, stress control, stopping smoking); quite expensive.

The Hôtel de Paris's sister hotel, the Hermitage, in which the pool complex is actually located, shares this facility. The **Hermitage****** (92 16 40 00 FAX 92 16 38 52 E-MAIL hh@sbm.mc WEB SITE www.montecarloresort.com, on quiet Square Beaumarchais a few steps away from the Place du Casino, is a more discreetly elegant *belle époque* masterpiece. It has 215 rooms and 15 suites, many overlooking the harbor, a winter garden with a stained-glass cupola designed by Gustave Eiffel, and the lovely new Restaurant de la Mer opened in 1999, featuring the sea food of noted chef Joël Garault. This is my favorite hotel in Monaco.

The **Monte-Carlo Beach Hotel****** (04 93 28 66 66 FAX 04 93 78 14 18 E-MAIL bh@sbm.mc WEB SITE www.montecarloresort.com, Route du Beach, in the adjoining French town of Cap-Martin, is a 46-room art deco resort hotel on a lovely Mediterranean cove with a private beach, Olympic swimming pool, gourmet restaurant, rustic buffet-grill on a pier and snack bar. The 23 tennis courts of the Monte-Carlo Country Club are right up the hill. This is a very fashionable address, with designer Karl Lagerfeld the next-door neighbor. Remember, if you want to call this hotel, it is in France, not Monaco.

Expensive

The **Abela***** (92 05 90 00 FAX 92 05 91 67 E-MAIL abela-hotel@monte-carlo.mc, 23 avenue des Papalins, Fontvieille, is an up-to-date 192-room hotel and a member of the highly professional Abela chain. **Alexandra***** (93 50 63 13 FAX 92 16 06 48, at 35 boulevard Princesse Charlotte, Monte-Carlo, is a comfortable, modernized older hotel with 56 rooms, some in the moderate price category (under 650 francs), and a top rate of 870 francs.

Moderate

Hôtel de France** (93 30 24 64 FAX 92 16 13 34 E-MAIL hotel-france@monte-carlo.mc, 6 rue de la Turbie, has 26 simple rooms with showers. **Helvetia*** (93 30 21 71 FAX 92 16 70 51 E-MAIL hotel-helvetia@monte-carlo.mc WEB SITE www.monte-carlo.mc/helvetia, 1bis rue Grimaldi, has 25 modest rooms, 21 with a bath or shower, overlooking the pleasant Rue Princesse Caroline walking street. Both these hotels are in La Condamine.

WHERE TO EAT

One of the great restaurants in the world is the **Louis XV-Alain Ducasse** (92 16 30 01, in the Hôtel de Paris, where you will eat like a king, but healthier, on the sophisticated Provençal-Ligurian cuisine of Alain Ducasse and Franck Cerruti. Here amid the glowing Louis XV period decor, you may choose your wine from among the 250,000 bottles in the cellar. Plan on 1,200 to 1,500 francs à la carte for dinner, but there is a three-course lunch special on weekdays for just 500 francs, wine included.

The room only seats 50, so be sure to reserve well in advance. **Le Grill** (92 16 30 02, is the Hôtel de Paris's penthouse restaurant where you will dine overlooking the Casino and the sea and savor the bright Provençal offerings that have earned it one Michelin star. Expect to pay 600 to 800 francs for a meal.

Monaco's other Michelin-starred eatery is **La Coupole** (92 16 66 99, at the Hôtel Mirabeau, 1 avenue Princesse Grace, Monte-Carlo, featuring refined Mediterranean-Provençal cuisine. The fixed-price *menu* at 310 francs is an excellent value. The **Saint-Benoît** (93 25 02 34, at 10 avenue de la Costa, Monte-Carlo, is an excellent fish restaurant overlooking the port with prices less than half those of Le Grill. Still more modestly priced are the **Café de Paris** (92 16 20 20, on the Place du Casino, for brasserie food on a large, busy terrace in the heart of Monte-Carlo's action,

and **Pinocchio** (93 30 96 20, at 30 rue Comte Felix Gastaldi, Monaco-Ville, for fine Italian cuisine in the old city.

Sam's Place (93 50 89 33, at 1 avenue Henri Dunant, Monte-Carlo, is a low-key eatery, good for grilled fish or meat. **Le Texan** (93 30 34 54, at 4 rue Suffren Reymond, a popular spot up the street from the port in La Condamine, features Tex-Mex cuisine. On Avenue des Spélugues, to the east of the Place du Casino, a number of lively restaurants with outdoor dining terraces stay open late and offer good, solid Italian food at moderate prices. Among the best of them are **Rampoldi** (93 30 70 65, at 3 avenue des Spélugues; **Chérie's Café** (93 30 30 99, at 9 avenue des Spélugues; and

Giacomo (93 25 20 30, in the Galerie du Métropole at 17 avenue des Spélugues. Rampoldi and Giacomo stay open until midnight, Chérie's Café until 6 AM.

NIGHTLIFE

The fashionable disco of the principality is **Le Jimmy'z** (92 16 22 77, at the Monte-Carlo Sporting Club. **Le Cabaret** (92 16 36 36, the Casino de Monte-Carlo's nightclub, features the nubile beauties of Paris's famed Crazy Horse "art of the nude" review (jacket and tie required for men). **Stars and Bars** (93 50 95 95, at 6 quai Antoine 1er in La Condamine, has an American-style sports bar downstairs and a blues bar upstairs with live bands most nights. Here you'll find buffalo chicken

LEFT: The Casino of Monte-Carlo. RIGHT: A street in old Monaco.

wings, baked potato skins, burgers, draft beer by the bucket, and the occasional vocal by Prince Albert. There's also an outdoor terrace. This is the most informal place in town.

HOW TO GET THERE

From the Nice Airport, **Navettes Bus Aéroport-Riviera** (Airport-Riviera Shuttle Buses) depart every hour, and the 22-km (14-mile) trip takes 45 minutes. It costs 80 francs. **Heli Air Monaco** and **Monacair** have helicopter shuttles every 20 minutes from Nice Airport, a spectacular seven-minute trip, 400 francs one-way (which is slightly less than a taxi). There are **trains** from Nice's Gare SNCF train station every half hour in summer, somewhat less frequently off-season (a 15-minute trip). Travelers arriving by train will find themselves in the heart of Monaco at the Gare SNCF in La Condamine. There are frequent **regional buses** from the *gares routières* (bus stations) of Nice or Menton that stop at a number of places along the Corniche Inférieure in Monaco. Coming by **car**, Monaco is most easily reached by the Corniche Inférieure (N98), its main through street. For those who aren't daunted by the steep, twisting roads, D53 winds down from both the Grande Corniche (D2564) and the Moyenne Corniche (N7). By the Autoroute, it's only 25 minutes by car from the Nice Airport.

MENTON

The contrast is striking. While Monaco races into the twenty-first century, Menton is content to amble along in the nineteenth, which gives it its charm. This faded but still graceful Italianate seaside town of 29,000 (the same size as Monaco) on the frontier with Italy is known for its lemon trees, flower gardens, and high proportion of retirees — almost a third of the population. Lemon trees produce fruit the year round, and a colorful Lemon Festival (Fête du Citron) is held during Mardi Gras, with extravagant parade floats decorated in citrus fruits by the hundreds of thousands. Menton rivals Beaulieu as the warmest place on the Côte d'Azur.

BACKGROUND

Menton became a property of the Grimaldis of Monaco in 1346, and its citrus farming provided the bulk of the Principality's income until Menton and neighboring Roquebrune-Cap-Martin broke free of Monaco's rule in the great democratic upheaval of 1848. In 1860, the same year as Nice's plebiscite, Menton and Roquebrune-Cap-Martin voted to join France. Like Monaco, Menton (or "Mentone," as it was still known at the time) became a prosperous winter resort in the late nineteenth century, favored particularly by the English, as the large number of British-named hotels indicates. But they came for health reasons, not the high life, under the influence of Dr. J. Henry Bennet's best-seller, *Mentone and the Riviera as a Winter Retreat*, which promoted Menton's climate as a panacea against tuberculosis.

GENERAL INFORMATION

The **Tourist Office** (04 92 41 76 50 is at the Palais de l'Europe, 8 avenue Boyer on the Jardin Biovès. It can give you the dates of the **Chamber Music Festival** that is held in August and brochures on hotels, restaurants, and tourist attractions in and around Menton. It is open Monday to Saturday mornings and afternoons all year, and Sunday mornings from 10 AM to noon in the summer.

For train information call the **Gare SNCF** (08 36 35 35 35. The **Gare Routière** (04 93 35 93 50, or bus station, is on Route de Sospel. **Navigation de Menton** (04 93 35 51 72, a boat line based at Quai Napoléon III at the old port, runs boat trips around the harbor and along the Riviera coastline from the beginning of April to the end of October. Fares run from 60 to 90 francs depending on the itinerary. The **Little Tourist Train** makes a 35-minute circuit of the beachfront, the harbor, and the Old Town, leaving from the Promenade du Soleil bus stop, by the Bastion, from 10 AM to noon and from 2:15 PM to 7 PM between Easter and November 1, to 5 PM the rest of the year. From July 1 to the end of August there are trips in the evening from 8:30 PM to 11 PM.

WHAT TO SEE AND DO

The Vieille Ville is the pink and pastel old town winding up the steep hill overlooking the harbor, its narrow streets lined with tall Genoese-style houses from the seventeenth century. At the top is the **Parvis Saint-Michel**, a small baroque square paved with gray and white stones with a mosaic of the coat of arms of town's former owners, the Grimaldi family. Two baroque churches, the large **Église Saint-Michel**, and the **Chapelle des Pénitents Blancs**, and several mansions of the period front on the square. The concerts of the Chamber Music Festival are held here in August.

The **Promenade du Soleil** is a pleasant beachfront walk that meets the **Casino de Menton** at the intersection with the **Jardin Biovès**, the flowery, palm and lemon tree-lined main esplanade of the new (nineteenth century) town that runs diagonally inland from the shore.

The **Salle des Mariages**, the wedding hall in the Hôtel de Ville (City Hall) on Rue de la

A popular resort for affluent English people in nineteenth century, Menton retains a bit of the old *très British* charm.

République, has fanciful historical-mythological murals on the theme of love by the multi-talented Jean Cocteau. It is open weekdays. The **Musée Cocteau** is in a small fort on the Quai Napoléon III at the eastern end of the Promenade du Soleil built by Honoré II of Monaco in the seventeenth century. Here there are more love scenes by Cocteau in a series of paintings called *Innamorati* and an amusing animal series, *Animaux Fantastiques*. Admission is free. The museum is closed Tuesdays. The colorful **town market** is held daily across the street.

"My Town is a Garden" is Menton's motto, and this is no empty hype. Besides the Jardin Biovès in the center of town, two other gardens to see are

Jardin des Colombières and the **Jardin Botanique Exotique** in the luxurious Garavan section in the hills to the east of the old town. The former is a six-hectare (15-acre) garden designed by Ferdinand Bac, a jack-of-all-arts and illegitimate son of Napoléon III; it features Mediterranean vegetation growing in seemingly wild profusion. The garden is open daily. The Jardin Botanique Exotique, also known as Val Rahmeh, the name of the villa it surrounds, belongs to the Natural History Museum of Paris and has more than 700 varieties of plants, many from the Mediterranean, but others from tropical and subtropical areas as well. The gardens are terraced and offer lovely views of the sea and the town. The garden is closed Tuesdays. If you'd like a horticultural bonus, you can easily nip into Italy to visit the ravishing **Hanbury Gardens** at Mortola Inferiore, which is outside Ventimiglia, four kilometers (two and a half miles) to the east. It has 2,000 varieties of plants from all four corners of the world. Hanbury Gardens is closed Wednesdays.

WHERE TO STAY

After the overwhelmingly luxurious hotel scene in Monaco, Menton is quite a comedown, because most of its *belle époque* grand hotels have been converted into apartment buildings. Luckily, however, the recently and tastefully restored **Hôtel des Ambassadeurs****** (04 93 28 75 75 FAX 04 93 35 62 32, has resisted the trend. Located at 3 rue Partouneaux on a quiet corner of the Jardin Biovès, the hotel has an elegant but inviting lobby with blonde wood-paneled walls, a splendid main staircase with wrought iron balconies, and 49 spacious, supremely comfortable deluxe rooms. The prices are in the expensive category, but far lower than you would pay for accommodation of this quality in Monaco. Its Café Fiori is the best and most attractive restaurant in town (see WHERE TO EAT, below).

Prince de Galles*** (04 93 28 21 21 FAX 04 93 35 92 91, at 4 avenue de Gaulle, is a moderately priced seaside hotel with a homey, club-like atmosphere. It has 68 attractively modernized rooms, most of them with balconies overlooking the sea, a cordial bar decorated with marvelous old travel posters, a good Mediterranean-style restaurant, Le Petit Prince, and its own beach (pebbly, as are all Menton's beaches). The hotel attracts mainly a British clientele. It is a Best Western member. **Hôtel de Londres**** (04 93 35 74 62 FAX 04 93 41 77 78, at 15 avenue Carnot, is a modest, but pleasant little hotel with 21 neat rooms, and it is only 25 m (about 27 yards) from the beach; it is a Logis de France member.

WHERE TO EAT

Café Fiori at the Hôtel des Ambassadeurs (see above) is a bright, cheerfully elegant winter garden-style restaurant dotted with plants. It serves market-inspired Mediterranean-Provençale gourmet cuisine — ravioli stuffed with goat cheese from Gorbio, seafood risotto, lamb casserole, and subtly savory, elegantly presented fish and shellfish dishes. Prices are moderate to moderately expensive, depending on what you order. **Au Pistou** (04 93 57 45 89, at 9 quai Gordon Bennett, is a cozy restaurant with a big terrace overlooking the Old Port, serving the ubiquitous Provençal vegetable soup after which it is named, along with fresh local fish and a wide range of regional specialties. Prices are reasonable, with a daily fixed-price lunch *menu* at 88 francs. Closed Mondays. For a change of pace, **Le Darkoum** (04 93 35 44 88, at 23 rue Saint-Michel, serves couscous, tajine, and other well-prepared Moroccan classics. It is open daily.

NIGHTLIFE

The **Casino de Menton** (04 92 10 16 17, built in 1934 and operated by the Lucien Barrière Group, is Menton's only real entertainment center, offering the full range of games, including slot machines, and a floor show at the Club 06. It is open daily all year.

HOW TO GET THERE

To get to Menton, take the Corniche Inférieure from Monaco and follow it along the coastal lowland 16 km (10 miles) to the east. There is Métrazur train service from Nice every half hour in the summer and frequent coach service by the **Rapides Côte d'Azur** (RCA) bus line.

ROQUEBRUNE-CAP-MARTIN

The town of Roquebrune-Cap-Martin has two distinct parts. Cap-Martin is a cape with a sea-level community, Roquebrune is on a hill town

BACKGROUND

Roquebrune's castle, one of the oldest in France, was built at the end of the tenth century by Count Conrad I of Ventimiglia as a defense against Saracen pirates. Like most properties of value around here, it eventually fell into the hands of the Grimaldis, who owned it for several centuries and rebuilt it to make it suitable for artillery. Originally the whole village of Roquebrune was part of the castle, but in the fifteenth century, the keep at the top was isolated from the rest of the buildings, and the village became a separate entity.

overlooking it, reached by the Grande Corniche. Before returning to Nice via the Grande Corniche, you may want to take a swing through Cap-Martin, a little peninsula directly west of Menton. Cap-Martin is one of the rare verdant spots in the area, with woodlands and magnificent, flowery estates. The road along the east side of the cape offers expansive views of Menton and the Italian Riviera, and on the west side, there are footpaths through the pines and cypresses. The coastal path to the west, the Promenade Le Corbusier, named in honor of the architect, who drowned here in 1965, reveals dramatic vistas of Monaco, the steep hills behind it and the castle of Roquebrune.

The road through Cap-Martin leads you to the Grande Corniche (D2564). Follow it up into the bare, rocky hills overlooking the coast to the medieval village of Roquebrune, whose narrow streets, many of them vaulted, lead to the castle at the top.

GENERAL INFORMATION

The **Tourist Office** (04 93 35 62 87 is in the modern part of Roquebrune below the Grande Corniche at 20 avenue Paul-Doumer.

WHAT TO SEE AND DO

Despite its souvenir and crafts shops, old Roquebrune has managed to conserve its medieval character, and prowling its steep, winding cobblestone streets, staircases, and vaulted passageways is intriguing. Rue Moncollet leads to the top of the village, where you can't miss the **castle** with its massive walls 3.5 m (11.5 ft) thick. In the *donjon*,

The quiet life in Menton OPPOSITE, a haven for retired people. The mountain vistas, grassy valleys, and trails of Mercantour National Park ABOVE are only 50 km (30 miles) inland from Menton.

the castle's keep, the fully furnished and surprisingly small apartment of the medieval lord can be visited on the third floor. However cramped the lord of the castle may have felt in his quarters, the vast panorama from the fourth-floor artillery platform more than makes up for it — the red roofs of the old village, Cap-Martin, Monaco, the sea, and the mountains. Another sight to pause for is the 1,000-year-old olive tree just outside the village on the Route de Menton, 10 m (33 ft) around the middle.

Every August 5, a large religious procession takes place in the afternoon in which scenes from the Passion of Christ are reenacted at different places between the village and the Chapel of La

Pausa, fulfilling a vow villagers made to the Virgin in 1467 after being spared from the plague.

WHERE TO STAY

At Vistaero Point 1,000 ft (300 m) up on the Grande Corniche in Roquebrune, the **Vista Palace Hôtel****** (04 92 10 40 00 FAX 04 93 35 18 94 E-MAIL vistapalace@webstore.fr WEB SITE www.webstore .fr/vistapalace, has the most spectacular view of any hotel. All of Monaco is at your feet to the west, and Menton and the Italian Riviera in the other direction. Rooms in this elegantly modern hotel are expensive off-season and very expensive in-season, when standard doubles go for 2,400 francs. A much more modest choice is the 31-room **Westminster**** (04 93 35 00 68 FAX 04 93 28 88 50 E-MAIL westminster@ifrance.com WEB SITE www .westminster06.com, at 14 avenue Louis Laurens, Roquebrune, a Logis de France member. It offers a garden, sea views, a cozy atmosphere, and doubles at 400 francs.

WHERE TO EAT

Le Vistaero, the Vista Palace's gourmet restaurant, serves refined French and Mediterranean cuisine against a panoramic backdrop and at

appropriately lofty prices. In the pedestrian area of old Roquebrune, **Au Grand Inquisiteur** (04 93 35 05 37, at 18 rue du Château, is a fourteenth-century shepherd's house with a vaulted stone ceiling converted into a cozy rustic-chic dining room, serving imaginatively prepared specialties of this region (sea scallops roasted with thyme, rabbit with olives) and of the Southwest (foie gras, sweetbreads with truffles), with a satisfying fixed-price *menu* at 147 francs for lunch or dinner. Reservations are a must. The restaurant is very small. Closed Mondays and Tuesdays at lunch, and from November 1 to December 26.

LA TURBIE

Heading toward Nice on the Grande Corniche, the next town to the west of Roquebrune is La Turbie, seven and a half kilometers (four and a half miles) away, where you should stop for one more sensational panorama of the Riviera. Here you can see from Italy to the Esterel Mountains west of Cannes, and on most days Corsica across the sea. You can also visit the **Trophée des Alpes** (Trophy of the Alps), the 50-m-high (165-ft) monument erected in 6 BC to celebrate Emperor Augustus's final triumph over the last independent tribes of Ligurians in the Alps. Though mostly in ruins, four of its original columns remain standing.

EXCURSIONS INLAND

PERCHED VILLAGES

While you're on the eastern end of the *corniches*, there are three dramatically perched villages you may want to see. All of them are at the dead end of narrow valleys leading in from the coast. **Gorbio** sits on a particularly savage rocky site, but in contrast, the houses are richly landscaped with flowers, olive trees, and pines. It can be reached from Roquebrune by a narrow, twisting nine kilometers (five and a half miles) of back road through the hills, or from Menton on the equally twisting D23, a distance of 13 km (eight miles). At 750 m (2,450 ft), **Sainte-Agnès** is the highest of all the Côte d'Azur's villages. It is 13 km (eight miles) north of Menton on D22. **Castellar**, also the same distance from Menton on D24, is where the *GR-51*, the *Grande Randonnée* hiking trail "the Balcony of the Côte d'Azur," begins. There are buses from Menton's Gare Routière to all three of these villages.

Another route north from Menton, D2566 in the direction of Sospel, leads to the Roya Valley and the Vallée des Merveilles (Valley of Marvels).

THE VALLEY OF MARVELS

La Vallée des Merveilles carries its name for two reasons — the 100,000 designs scratched into its rocks by Bronze Age shepherds and the particularly magical quality of its scenery. In the summer, this bright mountain valley in the heart of the 70,000-hectare (173,000-acre) Mercantour National Park is carpeted in grass and wildflowers, and there is a chain of crystal-clear lakes running north and south along the nine kilometers (five and a half miles) of the valley. Tall peaks surround it, and rugged Mont Bégo, 2,872 m (9,423 ft) high, dominates the scene. The valley was a site of pilgrimage for the Ligurians, and strange ancient inscriptions in stone enhance its aura of mystery. There are shapes that can be made out in the pictures — human figures, spears, axes, heads of cattle, half moons — but also abstract designs whose meanings are unknown. Though the drawings are numerous, they are not easy to find, and first-time visitors are strongly advised to go accompanied by a professional guide. The valley can be visited safely from June through September; at other times the weather can be a problem.

There are no roads in the Vallée des Merveilles. It can reached only by walking, but approved off-road vehicles can take you right up to its entrances. The access tracks lead in from the parallel valleys on either side, the dramatic **Valley of the Vésubie**, "Little Switzerland," to the west on Route D2565 and the equally dramatic **Roya Valley** to the east on Route N204 near the Italian frontier. The principal towns for organizing trips into the Vallée des Merveilles are Saint-Martin-Vésubie to the west and Tende to the east. The **Bureau des Guides du Val des Merveilles** in Saint-Martin-Vésubie (04 93 03 31 32 or in Tende (04 93 04 77 73 can help you make your plans and arrange for a guide. For information about the park, contact **Parc National du Mercantour** (04 93 16 78 88 WEB SITE www .parcsnationaux-fr.com (the site of the National Parks of France, where you can find information about the Mercantour until its own web site is up and running), 23 rue d'Italie, 06000 Nice. In Nice, you can also get information from the **Comité Régional du Tourisme Riviera-Côte d'Azur** (04 93 37 78 78 WEB SITE www.crt-riviera.fr, 55 promenade des Anglais.

If you go up there from Menton, the Tourist Office on the Jardin Biovès can give you all the information you need.

THE ROYA VALLEY

For an excursion that combines history, art, architecture and colorful little hill villages with enchanting mountain scenery, explore the upper valley of the Roya River, in the easternmost corner of the French Maritime Alps, between Mercantour National Park and the Italian frontier. In fact, some of it was *in* Italy until 1947, when the French and the Italians adjusted their borders, and Mussolini's

former subjects in Tende and La Brigue suddenly found themselves citizens of the land of *Liberté, Égalité, Fraternité*.

From Nice or Menton, the route is the same as for the Valley of the Marvels, but instead of heading out into nature, one tours colorful hilltop villages known for their Italianate baroque architecture, the organs in their churches, and their painted chapels. Most churches have frescos, some quaint and primitive, others quite sophisticated. They date from the thirteenth to the seventeenth century and were designed to teach illiterate peasants about the life of Christ, the Virgin, the Last Judgment, and Saints Sebastian, Anthony and Rocco, the great protectors against the plague.

To drive to the Roya Valley from Nice, follow boulevards Jean-Jaurès and Risso out of town and continue 41 km (26 miles) on D2204 to **Sospel**, a picturesque Alpine town of 2,500, spanning the Roya's tributary the Bévéra. The two sides are linked by an eleventh-century bridge that was destroyed during World War II and rebuilt. This is the crossroads of the routes between Menton and the Vésubie Valley (to the west of the Mercantour) and between Nice and the Roya. Sospel has a mixture of medieval and baroque buildings, none of great individual distinction, but charming in the ensemble. The Cathedral of Saint-Michel has one of the seven superb organs in the Roya-Bévéra built by Tuscan and Lombard craftsmen in the eighteenth and nineteenth centuries. Concerts are held here in June and July.

Continue up the twisting mountain road to **Breil-sur-Roya**, a lively, even more picturesque town of some 2,000 souls, aside a big lake in the Roya River and with thousands of olive trees on its hills. Visit the huge eighteenth-century church of Sancta-Maria-in-Albis with a sumptuous baroque interior, including a magnificent sculpted wood organ loft and another superb organ. Concerts are also held here in June and July.

Saorge, 10 km (six miles) to the north on N204, is a striking village clinging to the side of a steep mountain amphitheater overlooking a wide bend in the Roya. A nineteenth-century visitor likened it to "a swallow's nest stuck to the wall of a house." Then it was a prosperous town of 3,000. Today Saorge has few more than a hundred inhabitants. The streets are a labyrinth of old stone staircases and narrow passages between houses, and there are arcades and big portals between sections of the town. The tall, ancient houses have as many as ten levels. The fifteenth-century houses have elaborately worked wooden doors and sculpted stone lintels, and the baroque church of Saint-Sauveur has an organ. For the best panorama of the town, go to the chapel of **La Madone del Poggio** just to the south. It is worth a visit in itself for its

The Marina Baie des Anges, a modern luxury apartment complex west of Nice.

six-story-high, striped Lombard-style bell tower and its late fifteenth-century frescos of the life of the Virgin attributed to School of Nice Primitive artist Giovanni Baleison.

A short detour east from the main road at **Saint Dalmas-de-Tende** takes you through the charming little village of **La Brigue**, whose church, the Collégiale Saint-Martin, has an organ and fine frescos. Continue on to the chapel of **Notre-Dame-des-Fontaines**, one of the highlights of the trip for its powerful series of 25 frescos depicting the life of Christ and the Last Judgment. This "Sistine Chapel of the Southern Alps" was painted by Giovanni Canavesio and Giovanni Baleison in the late fifteenth century (one mural is dated 1492).

The last stop on the trip is **Tende**. Like Saorge, its mass of multistory slate-roofed houses hugs the hills, but this is a much larger town, with 2,000 inhabitants, and much livelier. It is the principal jumping-off point for the Valley of the Marvels. The church of the Collégiale Notre-Dame-de-l'Assomption has one of the famous organs, and the ceiling of the sacristy is decorated with seventeenth-century frescoes.

As everywhere, these little towns are most animated on market days: Tuesdays in Breil-sur-Roya, Wednesdays in Tende, Thursdays in Sospel and La Brigue, Fridays in Saint Dalmas-de-Tende, and Saturdays in Saorge.

For information on the whole area, contact the **Association pour Le Développement Touristique de la Roya-Bévéra** (04 93 04 92 05 E-MAIL adtrb @nicematin.fr, Boulevard Rouvier, 06540 Breil-sur-Roya. For information on the specific localities,

contact their tourist offices: Breil-sur-Roya (04 93 04 99 76, La Brigue (04 93 04 36 07, Saorge (04 93 04 51 23, Saint Dalmas-de-Tende (04 93 04 76 39, Sospel (04 93 04 15 80, and Tende (04 93 04 73 71.

Where to Stay and Eat

You can make the trip in a day. Tende is only 82 km (50 miles) from Nice and 55 km (34 miles) from Menton, albeit over twisty mountain roads, but if you want to spend some time in the area, **Le Prieuré**** (04 93 04 75 70 FAX 04 93 04 71 58, in Saint Dalmas-de-Tende is your best bet for a neat, charming hotel in a lovely setting with a good restaurant. This former priory has 24 pleasant, airy, up-to-date rooms, and a pretty restaurant with a mountain-view patio that serves honest, attractively presented local and regional fare. Prices are in the inexpensive and low-moderate range. The **Logis de France** group (04 93 80 80 40, also has seven of its homey, well-kept hotel-restaurants in the Roya-Bévéra. They are in the inexpensive and low-moderate price range too.

HOW TO GET THERE

If you drive, take the scenic routes D2204 from Nice or D2566 from Menton and wind up the main road to Tende. On the return trip, take the N204 south through Breil-sur-Roya, direction Ventimiglia. The road soon becomes a straight shot to that Italian coastal town, where you can pick up the A8 Autoroute and drive on the superhighway to Menton, Nice, or any of the localities in between.

If you don't want to drive, the trains of the Nice-Cuneo line of the **SNCF** (08 36 35 35 35, leave Nice's Gare SNCF roughly every two hours and stop at Sospel, Breil-sur-Roya, Saorge, Saint Dalmas-de-Tende, La Brigue, and Tende.

CAGNES-SUR-MER

As you head west out of Nice on the Promenade des Anglais, just past the Nice-Côte d'Azur Airport you cross the wide, pebbly, usually dry bed of the Var River, the former frontier between France and the Duchy of Savoy. Immediately across the river starts the most artistically rewarding cluster of towns and villages in France — Cagnes-sur-Mer, Saint-Paul-de-Vence, Vence, Biot, and Vallauris. Renoir, Matisse, Picasso, Chagall, and Léger lived and worked here, and the area remains a prime *lieu* for artists, potters, glass blowers, weavers, sculptors and jewelry makers, many of whose workshops are open to the public. The first town you come to is Cagnes-sur-Mer.

Cagnes-sur-Mer, directly west of the Var River, is made up of three different parts: Cros-de-Cagnes on the coast, the modern town of Cagnes-Ville on the hill, and the walled medieval village of

Haut-de-Cagnes at the town's highest point. Driving along the N98 coast road from Nice, you will first pass through the cluttered sea-level beach and port area of Cros-de-Cagnes, where the Hippodrome de la Côte d'Azur, the race track, is located. You can go to daytime horse races here from December through March and evening races in July and August. For information call (04 93 20 30 30. But the main attractions in Cagnes-sur-Mer are to be found two kilometers (one and a quarter miles) in from the coast in hilltop Haut-de-Cagnes.

BACKGROUND

As in many places along this coast, the Grimaldi name figures heavily in this town's history. The Château Grimaldi was built as a fortress in 1309 by Rainier Grimaldi, Lord of Monaco and Admiral of France. A later member of this branch of the family, Henri Grimaldi, gained the favor of Cardinal Richelieu and Louis XIII by influencing his cousins in Monaco to ally themselves with France. The riches heaped upon Henri Grimaldi by France enabled him to transform the old fortress into an opulent Renaissance château in 1620 and financed several generations of notoriously high-living descendants until the people of Cagnes threw them out of town during the Revolution.

GENERAL INFORMATION

The **Tourist Office** (04 93 20 61 64, is on the hill in the modern part of town at 6 boulevard Maréchal Juin.

WHAT TO SEE AND DO

Enter the thirteenth-century main gate of **Haut-de-Cagnes** and wind your way up the steep streets to the castle at the top of the hill. The **Grimaldi Château and Museum** has a bright Renaissance patio and banquet hall contrasting with the heavy vaulted medieval rooms on the ground floor. On the second floor is the **Museum of Modern Mediterranean Art**, with paintings by Chagall, Dufy, Fujita, Kisling, and other artists who worked on the Côte d'Azur. The **Suzy Solidor Bequest**, also on the second floor, is a group of 40 portraits of the popular French musical star of the early twentieth century by well-known artists of the period, including Cocteau, Dufy, Picabia, and Marie Laurencin. The château-museum is closed Tuesdays and from mid-October to mid-November.

The **Musée Renoir** on Route des Collettes east of Haut-de-Cagnes is the house where Pierre-Auguste Renoir moved to in 1908 at the age of 67 in hopes that the Mediterranean climate would enable him to keep painting. Though assistants had to fix his brush between his crippled arthritic fingers, Renoir's 12 final years turned out to be among his most productive (the Musée d'Orsay's *Les Grandes Baigneuses* in Paris is an example), and ten canvases from this period are on display in the museum. Renoir also took up sculpture for the first time, by proxy, through a young sculptor who followed his instructions. His large bronze statue *Vénus Victrix* stands in the garden, amid flowers, lemon, orange, and olive trees. The museum is closed Tuesdays and from mid-October to mid-November 15.

WHERE TO STAY

The deluxe hotel is **Le Cagnard***** (04 93 20 73 21 FAX 04 93 22 06 39 E-MAIL lecagnard@csi.com WEB SITE www.le-cagnard.com, on Rue Pontis-Long in Haut-de-Cagnes. It is a fourteenth-century mansion within the town walls converted to a Relais & Châteaux hotel with 23 expensive rooms and four suites. For more modestly priced hotels, head down toward the race track, where **Le Tiercé***** (04 93 20 02 09 FAX 04 93 20 31 55 WEB SITE www .hotelchoice.comtravelweb.com (you can book through the web site), at the corner of Boulevard de la Plage and Boulevard Kennedy, offers 23 neat, modern, mid-priced rooms near the beach. The **Chantilly**** (04 93 20 25 50 FAX 04 92 02 82 63, has 18 simple rooms in the inexpensive range. It is at 31 rue de la Minoterie, behind the race track.

Camping

There are ten camping grounds in Cagnes-sur-Mer, eleven in the neighboring town of Villeneuve-Loubet-Plage, and numerous others in nearby communities. For information, ask at any local tourist office or contact **L'Hôtellerie de Plein Air des Alpes-Maritimes**, the trade association of camping grounds operators in the *département*. Their office is at La Vieille Ferme (04 93 33 41 44 FAX 04 93 33 37 28, at 296 boulevard des Groules (Route N7), Villeneuve-Loubet-Plage.

WHERE TO EAT

Le Cagnard has the most glamorous restaurant in town, serving inventive dishes such as John Dory with fresh pasta in octopus ink and lamb with fresh coconut, quite expensive. There is a lunch special at 290 francs, drinks included. Closed Thursdays at lunchtime. At **Josy-Jo** (04 93 20 68 76, at 4 place Planastel, Haut-de-Cagnes, you'll dine on fish or meat grilled on a wood fire served on the lively terrace by the Bandecchi family — delicious, but quite expensive. It is closed at lunch on Saturday, all day Sunday, and the first half of August. Le Cagnard and Josy-Jo both sport one Michelin star.

Renoir's studio at the Renoir Museum in Cagnes-sur-Mer, where the artist spent the last 12 years of his life.

La Bourride (04 93 31 07 75 is a small, elegant eatery in a pine grove facing the port at Cros-de-Cagnes with outstanding seafood, but at high prices (*menus* from 195 francs). It is a good place to try the savory Mediterranean fish stew after which it is named. Closed Wednesdays. Another exceptionally fine seafood restaurant is the Campo brothers' **La Réserve (Chez Loulou)** (04 93 31 00 17, just down the road at 91 boulevard de la Plage. It is very expensive too, with the lowest-priced *menu* at 220 francs. Closed Saturdays and lunch Sundays. For good, simply prepared fare at far more modest prices, go to **Tony's** (04 93 07 57 83, facing the fishing port at Cros-de-Cagnes. Here you can feast on grilled *loup de mer* (sea bass), grilled squid, *petite friture* (deep-fried whitebait), and good homemade pasta dishes. Closed Sunday nights and Mondays except in July and August.

All these restaurants are very popular. Be sure to reserve, especially in the summer.

HOW TO GET THERE

By train, take the Métrazur line to the station at Cagnes-sur-Mer, which is in the lowland part of town. There are frequent buses from the train station to Haut-de-Cagnes. There are also frequent buses from Nice's Gare Routière. Tour operators in Nice run daily tours excursions to Cagnes-sur-Mer, Saint-Paul-de-Vence, and the other artistic villages of this area (see GENERAL INFORMATION, page 95, under NICE). If you are driving, take the N98 coast road west from Nice, turn right onto D36 at the Hippodrome and drive two kilometers (one and a quarter miles) north to Haut-de-Cagnes. The old town is open to pedestrians only. So park you car at the underground parking area by the main gate (look for the big letter "P").

SAINT-PAUL-DE-VENCE

Built on the slopes of an especially graceful hill, Saint-Paul-de-Vence, seven kilometers (four miles) north of Cagnes-sur-Mer, is another medieval walled village that has had an exceptional involvement in the arts.

BACKGROUND

Saint-Paul-de-Vence was one of the fortified villages guarding Provence's frontier with Savoy, and it owes its sixteenth-century ramparts to King François I, who built them to ward off aggression by his perennial rival Emperor Charles V. The town declined in the nineteenth century, but became a favorite of artists such as Bonnard and Picasso in the 1920s and was adopted by film celebrities such as Yves Montand and Simone Signoret, who were married on the terrace of the Colombe d'Or, the hotel and restaurant the artists made their clubhouse.

GENERAL INFORMATION

The **Tourist Office** (04 93 32 86 95 is at 2 rue Grande, just inside the main gate of the walled village.

WHAT TO SEE AND DO

Inside the imposing fourteenth-century portal, the steep, narrow streets of the village are lined with handicrafts shops and souvenir boutiques, as this is a prime stop for tourist buses, especially in the summer. But no matter how crowded it gets, the view from the top of the sixteenth-century ramparts, with fields of flowers and orange groves in the valleys and the Alps towering in the distance, makes a visit worthwhile. The **church**, which dates from the early thirteenth century, but was largely redone in baroque style, has a rich treasury of twelfth- to fifteenth-century silver-work and a painting of Saint Catherine of Alexandria attributed to Tintoretto.

The **Colombe d'Or** has one of the finest personal art collections in France, with works by Bonnard, Picasso, Matisse, Dufy *et al*, which owner Paul Roux amassed as payment of artists' hotel and restaurant bills. You can see it for the price of a meal. The Colombe d'Or is opposite the main portal of the village.

One kilometer (half a mile) northeast of the village, idyllically set in a pine forest, is the museum of the **Fondation Maeght**. It was built in 1960 to house the dazzling collection of the husband and wife team of modern art dealers, Aimé and Marguerite Maeght. It is one of the museums I enjoy most in France. Sculptures by Calder, Arp, and Miró greet you as you cross the green lawn to the entrance, and inside architect Jose-Luis Sert's sweeping pavilion are paintings by Kandinsky, Matisse, Chagall, Braque, Léger, Bonnard, and de Staël. In a grassy inner courtyard you will find a cluster of Giacometti's lanky figures, and Miró has a playful sculpture garden all his own. Be aware that in the summer much of the permanent collection is loaned out or put in storage to make room for exhibits by contemporary artists. The museum is open daily but closed at lunch time off-season.

WHERE TO STAY

Expensive

The famous **Colombe d'Or***** (04 93 32 80 02 FAX 04 93 32 77 78 is on Place des Ormeaux, outside the main gate of the medieval village. It has 16 very attractive, expensive rooms and 10 very expensive suites, a lovely view of the countryside, a pool, and lots of modern art. Just west of town on the route to Colle-sur-Loup is the **Mas d'Artigny******

✆ 04 93 32 84 54 FAX 04 93 32 95 36 E-MAIL mas.artigny @wanadoo.fr WEB SITE www.slh.com/dartigny, with 55 deluxe rooms and 30 suites amid eight hectares (20 acres) of pines. It has a large swimming pool, two tennis courts, and small private pools with 25 of the living units.

Moderate

Le Hameau* ✆ 04 93 32 80 24 FAX 04 93 32 55 75, on Route de la Colle-sur-Loup, one kilometer (half a mile) from the village of Saint-Paul, is a lovely old Provençal farm converted into delightful 14-room, three-suite hotel that has all the modern facilities, but has managed to keep its old charm. It has a pool, 5,000 sq m (a bit over an acre) of grounds with flower gardens and an orange grove. At **Les Orangers*** ✆ 04 93 32 80 95 FAX 04 93 32 00 32, Chemin des Fumerates, Saint-Paul-de-Vence, you'll find 10 charming rooms and two suites in an orange grove, with fresh juice at breakfast. To get there from the village of Saint-Paul, take the Route de la Colle-sur-Loup for one kilometer (half a mile) and turn right onto Chemin des Fumerates. **Marc Hely*** ✆ 04 93 22 64 10 FAX 04 93 22 93 84 E-MAIL marchely@altavista.net WEB SITE www .nscfr/marchely, in a countrified setting on Route de Cagnes (D6) in La Colle-sur-Loup, has 15 tasteful modern rooms, a lovely garden, and swimming pool. It is a Relais du Silence member.

WHERE TO EAT

The food is reasonably good at the **Colombe d'Or**, but it is more for the beauty and vivacity of the myth-shrouded dining terrace overlooking the countryside than the quality of the cuisine that people have kept flocking decade after decade to this overpriced place. It is open daily for lunch and dinner. The **Mas d'Artigny** serves refined Provençal gourmet cuisine of markedly superior quality on its verandah restaurant with a grand panoramic view of the countryside, but the prices here are very high too. **La Couleur Pourpre** ✆ 04 93 32 60 14, at 7 rempart Ouest (the western rampart of the old town of Saint-Paul), is a restaurant of great charm in a narrow, ancient building on three levels with lots of stairs and big wooden beams, but despite its name, surprisingly little purple. It serves sunny, inventive Provençal fare, 195 francs for the fixed-price *menu* at lunch or dinner, or à la carte, and the ambiance is friendly and vivacious. Closed Tuesdays and Wednesday lunch out of season.

HOW TO GET THERE

There are frequent local buses from Cagnes-sur-Mer. By car, take D6 from Cagnes-sur-Mer to Saint-Paul-de-Vence via La Colle-sur-Loup, a distance of seven kilometers (four miles).

VENCE

Vence is a large walled medieval hill town of 15,000 on a plateau 10 km (six miles) from the Mediterranean with an open view of the sea and the mountains. It lies four kilometers (two and a half miles) north of Saint-Paul-de-Vence and is considerably less crowded than its neighbor. Its most noted attraction is Matisse's Chapelle du Rosaire.

BACKGROUND

Vence was founded by the Ligurians and later became an important Roman town. It was one

of the early centers of Christianity, and from the fourth century until the Revolution, its destiny was guided by a series of powerful bishops. The most remarkable of the bishops was Godeau in the seventeenth century, an ugly dwarf-like man, but a brilliant wit, poet, man of letters, and favorite of aristocratic ladies. Cardinal Richelieu made him the first member of the Académie Française. But Godeau renounced the worldly life at the age of 30, took holy orders and was appointed Bishop of Vence the following year. For the next 36 years of his life until his death in 1672, he devoted himself to improving the town, introducing the industries of tanning, perfume-making and pottery, and rebuilding the cathedral.

An installation by Miro in the sculpture garden of the Fondation Maeght in Saint-Paul-de-Vence.

GENERAL INFORMATION

The **Tourist Office** (04 93 58 06 38 is in the center of town at Place Grand-Jardin.

WHAT TO SEE AND DO

Matisse considered his decoration of the **Chapelle du Rosaire**, completed in 1951, the culmination of everything he had been striving to achieve. He designed the stained glass windows of the chapel simply and in three colors — lemon yellow for God and sunlight, grass green for vegetable life, and blue for the Mediterranean sea. His famous biblical figures on the walls are done in bold black outlines, baked into white ceramic tiles. The soft light from the windows gently colors the figures on the surrounding walls, creating an otherworldly effect. Matisse also designed the boldly patterned priests' robes, the paper cutouts of which can be seen at the Musée Matisse in Nice.

The Chapel is on Route D2210 about one kilometer (half a mile) north of town (the street is named Avenue des Poilus in town and changes to Avenue Henri Matisse as you approach the chapel). Watch carefully, because, the chapel is a little white box you could easily drive past without noticing. It is open Tuesdays and Thursdays from 10:00 AM to 11:30 AM and 2:30 PM to 5:30 PM all year and is also open Wednesdays, Fridays, and Saturdays from 2:30 PM to 5:30 PM in July and August and during French school vacations. It is closed from November 1 to December 15.

La Vieille Ville, the old part of Vence within the walls, has preserved its medieval character. If you enter the town on the west side by the fortified **Porte de Peyra**, you find yourself in the **Place du Peyra** where the Romans had their

Ferrière's superb Provençal cuisine. This Relais & Châteaux member is open from the beginning of April to the end of October. To reach it, take the D2 north two and a half kilometers (one and a half miles) in the direction of Coursegoules. **Villa Roseraie***** (04 93 58 02 20 FAX 04 93 58 99 31 E-MAIL rvilla5536@aol.fr is a peaceful 14-room country house with a pool in a garden setting at 128 avenue Henri Giraud (in the direction of Coursegoules, 400 m or 1,300 ft from the center of town). This Logis de France member is moderately priced, with some rooms in the expensive category in season, and has no restaurant. For a hotel and restaurant at the low end of the moderate price category, try the **Auberge des Seigneurs**** (04 93 58 04 24 FAX 04 93 24 08 01, on Place Frêne, a quaint old stone inn in La Vieille Ville with six pleasant rooms, serving hearty, moderately priced regional food.

The most important gastronomic address in these hills is unquestionably **Jacques Maximin** (04 93 58 90 75, at 689 Chemin de la Gaude, three kilometers (two miles) south of town on the Route de Cagnes (D236). Here you can savor the brilliant, original, unfailingly inventive cuisine of one of the true princes of the Mediterranean-Provençal school. Maître Maximin's 240-franc fixed-price *menu* is a remarkable value. More elaborate meals at 340 and 450 francs. Michelin gives Jacques Maximin a prestigious two-star rating. One must reserve well in advance.

How to Get There

There are frequent local buses from Saint-Paul-de-Vence, Cagnes-sur-Mer (where you can connect with the Métrazur train line) and Nice, and three or four shuttle buses a day from Nice Airport to Place Grand-Jardin. By car, take D2 from Saint-Paul-de-Vence, four kilometers (two and a half miles) away.

TOURRETTES-SUR-LOUP

The cliff-side village of Tourrettes-sur-Loup five kilometers (three miles) west of Vence became a virtual ghost town after World War II, but was brought back to life by the artisans who settled here. It is now one of the leading handicrafts villages of the Côte d'Azur and for its mixture of quality and ambiance, the one I like best. It is much less touristy than Saint-Paul-de-Vence and much more authentically artisanal. The countryside around Tourrettes is a major producer of violets, and during the Fête des Violettes in March, all the houses are decked with the flowers.

---

forum and there is now a pretty eighteenth century fountain. A market is held here every morning, and there are many crafts boutiques. The **cathedral** was built over several centuries from the Romanesque to the baroque periods, and there are even some Roman stones with Latin inscriptions to be seen. You may also visit the **tomb of Bishop Godeau**.

Where to Stay and Eat

The magnificent and very expensive **Château Saint-Martin****** (04 93 58 02 02 FAX 04 93 24 08 91 E-MAIL st-martin@webstore.fr WEB SITE www.chateau-st-martin.com, on Avenue des Templiers, is a former Knights Templar residence in a 13-hectare (32-acre) private park with panoramic views of Vence and the coast. Its 33 rooms and five suites are richly furnished with antiques, and its restaurant is known for chef Dominique

---

The eagle's nest village of Gourdon high above the gorges of the Loup River, a Saracen stronghold in the Middle Ages.

The Côte d'Azur

GENERAL INFORMATION

The **Tourist Office** (04 93 24 18 93 is on Place de la Libération, the main square.

WHAT TO SEE AND DO

The main attraction here is the **handicrafts workshops**. The town is especially noted for its weavers, but Tourrettes also has fine potters, jewelry-makers, wood-carvers and metal sculptors, and you can watch many of them as they work. Almost all are on Grande-Rue, the little horseshoe-shaped main street that follows the line of the town's cliff, entered by either of the gates on the main square. The fifteenth-century church has a School of Nice triptych, and the Chapelle Saint-Jean at the entrance to the village is decorated with charming naive frescoes done by Ralph Soupault in 1959.

HOW TO GET THERE

Tourrettes is on the bus line between Vence and Grasse. Ask at the Tourist Office in Vence for the schedule. By car, it is five kilometers (three miles) west of Vence on D2210.

FURTHER AFIELD

THE GORGES OF THE LOUP RIVER

West of Tourrettes-sur-Loup, the Loup River cuts a deep gorge into the Pre-Alps of Grasse, presenting a chance for a drive through some of the most spectacular scenery in the South of France. To explore the gorges of the Loup, you will need a car or some other form of self-locomotion, and though the distance is only 35 km (22 miles), you should figure on a good two hours to make this drive. The **Tourist Office** in Tourrettes-sur-Loup has information on the entire area.

Pont-du-Loup

In Pont-du-Loup, the next village west of Tourrettes-sur-Loup on Route D2210, you can tour the **Confiserie des Gorges du Loup** (04 93 59 32 91, the main factory of **Confiseries Florian**, created in 1949 to perpetuate traditional Provençal methods of candied fruit, jelly, and jam-making. Here you see every step of the process, from preparation of the fresh fruit for its various uses to the shaping of the final product, which you can taste and can buy in the gift shop. Be sure to try the amazing jellies made from fresh flowers — jasmine, violet, and rose. There are tours every day from 9 AM to noon and 2 PM to 6:30 PM. The Confiserie is easy to find. Just follow the Florian signs. They also have a branch in Nice (See WHAT TO SEE AND DO, page 95, under NICE).

Le Bar-sur-Loup

Le Bar-sur-Loup is a handsome hilltop village 16 km (10 miles) west of Tourrettes-sur-Loup on D2210 where Americans can pay homage to of one of the great heroes of their Revolution, Admiral Count François de Grasse, whose family seat this was. His naval blockade of Chesapeake Bay in 1781 prevented Lord Cornwallis and his Redcoats from escaping by sea, thus enabling Washington, Rochambeau, and Lafayette to close the trap at Yorktown, the turning point of the war. A life-size bronze of Admiral de Grasse is in the main square by the church.

At the **Église Saint-Jacques**, put a franc in the coin-operated timing device to light up the 14-panel **altarpiece** by School of Nice master Ludovico Bréa. On the rear wall of the church is the haunting *Danse Macabre*, a primitive work painted on a wood panel by an unknown fifteenth-century artist. It shows a death-figure firing arrows into the thighs of dancers to punish them for dancing during Lent, after which their little naked souls leave their bodies through their mouths. They are then weighed on a scale by Saint Michael who is seated at the foot of Christ, before being hurled into the mouth of a Hieronymus Bosch-like monster representing Hell.

For lunch, **L'Amiral** (04 93 09 44 00 is a bright, spacious restaurant in an eighteenth-century house on the Place du Château that once belonged to the admiral. It serves tasty regional fare with fixed-price *menus* from 100 francs.

There is a little **Tourist Office** (04 93 42 72 21 in the *donjon* (keep) of the château.

Le Bar-sur-Loup to Gourdon

Continuing the circuit, head north from Le Bar-sur-Loup to Pont-du-Loup and take D6 north along the crest of the dramatic **gorges of the Loup** where you will find a lovely waterfall a few kilometers farther along the road. At Bramafan, cross the river and wind southward on D3 for the best views of the deep gorge this little river has cut, especially dramatic from the eagle's nest village of **Gourdon**. This old Saracen stronghold sits on a rocky spur 500 m (1,640 ft) above the river, 765 m (2,510 ft) above sea level, and offers a vast panorama of the valley, the coast and the mountains. With its winding streets and restored houses, this perched village with only 300-year-round inhabitants has a wonderful atmosphere off-season. During the summer, however, it tends to get crowded with tourists and vendors selling carved olive-wood pieces, honey, and nougat.

The thirteenth-century **château** was built on the foundations of the original Saracen fortress, and architectural features of the original one were retained. There is a **Historical Museum** on the ground floor with a disturbing collection of ancient weapons and a prison with a torture table. Seven rooms on the second floor contain the **Museum of Naive Painting**, with a fine collection of naïve art by international artists from the period 1925 to 1970 and a portrait by Henri Rousseau. The château has three levels of terraced **gardens by Le Nôtre**, the designer of Versailles's gardens, and from the top level you get the same grand panorama as from the square by the church.

A cheerful, moderately priced lunch spot with a view is the **Taverne Provençale** at Place Église Grandure.

BIOT

Back on the coast road, you'll find Biot, a pleasant and remarkably tranquil old town in the heart of prime tourist country between Cagnes-sur-Mer and Antibes. Biot has been known since antiquity for its earthenware jars made from the rich local deposits of clay, and while a few potters carry on the tradition, the town was supplanted as the area's main ceramics producer in the nineteenth-century by the booming potteries of Vallauris. It is the glassblowers who now draw people to Biot.

GENERAL INFORMATION

The **Tourist Office** (04 93 65 05 85 is at Place de la Chapelle in the center of town.

WHAT TO SEE AND DO

At the **Verrerie de Biot** (04 93 65 03 00, you can watch master glass blowers at work, a magical process resulting in the tasteful vases, glasses, and pitchers in pale shades of blue, green, and purple bubble glass that you can buy at the retail shop. The Verrerie is open daily from 8 AM to 7 PM. It is southeast of the village, just off D4 on Chemin des Combes.

The **Musée Fernand Léger**, with its football field-sized (500 sq m or 600 sq yard) mosaic façade of sports scenes in primary reds, blues, yellows, and greens is one of Biot's major attractions. Léger lived and worked in Biot and bought the site in 1955 to create a sculpture garden, but died shortly thereafter. Madame Léger oversaw the construction of the museum, which opened in 1960 and was enlarged in 1989. It has 348 of Léger's paintings, ceramics, and tapestries featuring his chunky people at work and play in the industrial age and the world of the circus. The museum is closed Tuesdays. The museum is on Chemin du Val de Pôme, just down D4 from the Verrerie, and is clearly marked.

The **Église Sainte-Madeleine-Saint-Julien** has two School of Nice altarpieces, the eight-panel *Retable du Rosaire* (Virgin of the Rosary) attributed to Ludovoco Bréa and the four-panel *Ecce Homo* by Giovanni Canavesio.

The winding narrow streets and the colonnaded **Place des Arcades** have great charm, especially in the evening after the day-trippers have gone back to Nice or Cannes.

Marineland

The largest marine zoo in Europe is **Marineland** (04 93 33 49 49, attracting 1.2 million visitors per year. The show features porpoises, orcas, seals, and other trainable creatures of the sea. It is on the coast road in La Brague, four kilometers (two and a half miles) southeast of Biot.

Next to Marineland there is a permanent **fairground** with large water slides, a farm with animals of Provence, miniature golf, and a jungle walk filled with thousands of butterflies.

WHERE TO STAY

The **Galerie des Arcades*** (04 93 65 01 04 FAX 04 93 65 01 05 is the Brothier family's hotel in the arcades of old Biot, with 12 pleasant rooms at inexpensive to moderate prices, a restaurant (see WHERE TO EAT, below), and an interesting contemporary art gallery. This is a lively spot, combining, as their brochure puts it, French charm and *"une ambiance très Greenwich Village."*

Camping

There are 10 camping grounds in La Brague and 11 in neighboring Villeneuve-Loubet-Plage. For information, contact the Tourist Office in Biot, Villeneuve-Loubet, or Antibes, or contact the trade association of camping grounds operators in the *département*, **L'Hôtellerie de Plein Air des Alpes-Maritimes** (04 93 33 41 44 FAX 04 93 33 37 28, at La Vieille Ferme, 296 boulevard des Groules (Route N7), Villeneuve-Loubet-Plage.

The colorful Fernand Léger Museum in Biot.

The Côte d'Azur

WHERE TO EAT

Auberge du Jarrier (04 93 65 11 68, at 30 passage de la Bourgade, a charmingly rustic restaurant with a dining terrace with a grand panorama, serves what chef Brigitte Guignery calls "a woman's cuisine, based on herbs and vegetables." Wild boletus mushroom tart with a bouquet of crayfish, sea bass with local violet artichokes, filet of duckling with lavender honey, and roast pears and figs are some of her specialties. There is a fixed-price lunch *menu* at 170 francs, wine included — a very good price for cuisine of this quality. The restaurant rates one Michelin star. It is very

popular, so be sure to reserve. The easygoing **Bistro du Jarrier (** 04 93 65 11 68, next door at 28 passage de la Bourgade, serves simpler, less expensive versions of Madame Guignery's cuisine, with the same fine view as the mother house. The wines at both the Auberge and the Bistro are reasonably priced. Both eateries are closed Monday evenings and Tuesdays except in the summer, when they are open daily.

Terraillers (04 93 65 01 59, at 11 route du Chemin Neuf (D4) at the foot of the village, is a sixteenth-century pottery workshop, now an elegant restaurant featuring Claude Jacques's outstanding gourmet Provençal cuisine, which has earned one Michelin star. It has lunch *menus* starting at 220 francs, wine included; it is more costly in the evening. The wine is expensive too. Closed Wednesdays and Thursday at lunch in July and August and the month of November.

For good, solid food in a vivacious setting, I head for the restaurant of the **Galerie des Arcades** (see WHERE TO STAY, above), for *pistou, pieds de porc, tripes à la Niçoise* (vegetable soup, pigs' knuckles, and Nice-style tripe), and other Provençal specialties. The copious 160-franc *menu* is excellent value. Be sure to reserve, as the 15 tables are usually packed.

HOW TO GET THERE

To get to Biot by train, take the Métrazur line to La Brague on the coast where the station is located. There is a bus every hour from the station to Place des Arcades in Biot. To come by bus, there is also frequent local bus service along the coast road. If you are driving, take D4 from La Brague, four kilometers (two and a half miles) away.

VALLAURIS

Pottery has been made at Vallauris since the time of the Romans. In 1501, after the population had been wiped out by the plague, 70 Genoese families were brought in to repopulate the village, potters among them. These families reconstructed the town and laid it out in the checkerboard pattern we see today.

In 1946, Picasso, who was then living nearby in Golfe-Juan, met the potters Georges and Suzanne Ramié, who invited him to their studio, Madoura, in Vallauris. Picasso fell in love with the process, moved to Vallauris and started working with the Ramiés, turning out as many as 25 pieces a day. Picasso's work in ceramics brought Vallauris great fame. In 1952 he returned to Vallauris and painted the huge *War and Peace* fresco in an abandoned chapel.

Today Vallauris, two kilometers (one and a quarter miles) inland from Golfe-Juan, is a bland, semi-industrial town of 25,000 that makes a living from the mass production of ceramics. But you can find some independent potters here and many ceramics boutiques that carry the full gamut of quality from the sublime to the dreadful.

GENERAL INFORMATION

The **Tourist Office (** 04 93 63 82 58 is in the center of town on Square du 8 Mai 1945. To arrange visits to potters' workshops, contact **L'Association Vallaurienne d'Expansion Céramique (** 04 93 64 66 58, in the heart of town at 15 rue Sicard.

WHAT TO SEE AND DO

One of the few examples of Renaissance architecture in Provence, the **château** is a sixteenth-century priory of the Îles de Lérins monks that houses two museums. The **Musée National de la Guerre et de la Paix** (National Museum of War and Peace) is an abandoned chapel with Picasso's huge *War and Peace* fresco on its walls. On the left wall are the horrors of war, on the right the joys of peace, and on the rear the brotherhood of Man, with the four races shaking hands and holding the dove of peace aloft. The other museum is the **Musée Municipal de Céramique et d'Art Moderne**. It has a collection of droll Picasso ceramics and six rooms on the second floor devoted to Italian-born painter Alberto Magnelli (1888–1971), who worked most of his life in France.

You can see potters working at the **Musée de la Poterie** on Rue Sicard, or simply walk along Avenue Georges-Clemenceau, Rue du Plan, or Rue Sicard where you can find plenty of shops to drop

in on, or better, follow the program laid out for you by the Association Vallaurienne d'Expansion Céramique. Alain Ramié runs **Galerie Madoura** (04 93 64 66 39, where Picasso worked with Alain's parents George and Suzanne, and this studio has the exclusive right to sell reproductions of Picasso's pottery. It is on Avenue des Anciens Combattants d'Afrique du Nord.

HOW TO GET THERE

By local bus service, you can reach Vallauris from Place Charles de Gaulle in Antibes or from the Gare SNCF in Cannes, the train station there. If you are driving from Biot, take D504 west for eight kilometers (five miles), then turn left on D103 and continue two kilometers (just over a mile), then right (west) on D435 for the last two kilometers (just over a mile).

ANTIBES

Antibes is one of the oldest, most attractive port towns of the Côte d'Azur with a wide, sheltered harbor filled with yachts, ramparts along the sea front, and the star-shaped Fort Carré perched on a steep hill. Antibes, its ritzy peninsula of Cap d'Antibes, and its nightlife oasis of Juan-les-Pins all have good beaches. Antibes is famed for the many varieties of roses created here (one-third of all varieties sold in the world), though fewer and fewer are grown because of the high price of real estate. In addition, this growing metropolis of 70,000 has Sophia-Antipolis, the large new high technology complex in the hills nicknamed the "Silicon Valley of the Côte d'Azur." This blend of the very old and the very new makes Antibes, perhaps more than anywhere else, the epitome of today's South of France.

BACKGROUND

The name Antipolis, "the city opposite," was given to the town by the Greeks from Massalia who founded the port in the fifth century BC. But opposite what? Most scholars say Nice, but others say Corsica. In the civil war between Caesar and Pompey, Antibes sided with the winner and was rewarded with special status, prospering under Roman rule, unlike its mother city of Marseille which lost all. But the Visigoths and Ostrogoths reduced it to rubble after the fall of the empire, and plagues and Saracen pirates almost finished it off. By the year 1,000, the city was practically a ghost town. Under the Angevin Counts of Provence and local ownership by yet another branch of the Grimaldi family, Antibes returned to prosperity, particularly after 1388, when Nice defected to Savoy and Antibes became Provence's easternmost port. A century later it became the Kingdom of France's easternmost port, which was a mixed blessing, since the town was bombarded time and again by the navies of the Dukes of Savoy, Emperor Charles V, and the British.

GENERAL INFORMATION

The Antibes **Tourist Office** (04 92 90 53 00 E-MAIL tourismeajlp@pcse.fr WEB SITE www.guide-azur.com is at 11 place du Général-de-Gaulle in the center of town.

The **Gare SNCF** (08 36 35 35 35, the train station, is near the port on Avenue Robert-Soleau. The **Gare Routière** (04 93 34 37 60, the bus terminal, is located at Place Guynemer just east of Place du Général-de-Gaulle. For **taxis** call the Gare SNCF station

OPPOSITE: A pottery workshop in Vallauris. ABOVE: A beach full of youth at Antibes.

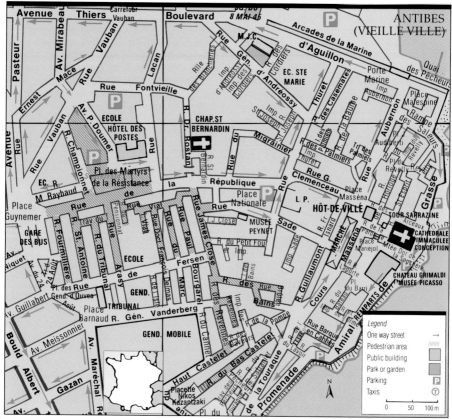

(04 93 67 67 67 or the one on Place du Général-de-Gaulle (04 93 34 03 47.

There are numerous auto rental agencies: **Avis** (04 93 34 65 15, **Budget** (04 93 34 36 84, **EuropCar** (04 93 34 79 79, **Thrifty Rent-a-Car** (04 93 67 66 94, **Hertz** (04 93 61 18 15, and **Midi Location** (04 93 34 48 00.

Antibes is one of Mediterranean France's most active pleasure-boat ports, and there are numerous companies that rent boats or take charters. It is also a Mecca for scuba divers, windsurfers, and would-be practitioners of these and other water-related sports. The Tourist Office has a long list of companies that rent sports equipment and offer training programs for beginners.

Le Petit Train, the little motorized tourist train, makes a 50-minute circuit of Antibes and Juan-les-Pins, leaving Place des Martyrs de la Résistance in downtown Antibes every hour on the hour from 10 AM to 11 PM in the summer. The fare is 30 francs.

WHAT TO SEE AND DO

La Vieille Ville is the walled old city centered on the medieval **Château Grimaldi** and **cathedral**, with mighty **ramparts** on the sea side that were designed by Vauban in the late seventeenth

century. The Greeks built here first, followed by the Romans and later the Grimaldis, who built their château in the twelfth century on top of Roman ruins. Its watch tower dates from medieval times too, as does the matching Saracen tower nearby, so-named because it was used to watch out for the pirates. As you wander about, look carefully at the stones of the buildings and you will see Latin inscriptions, sometimes upside-down, revealing how the successive masters of Antibes reworked the materials left by their predecessors.

Picasso left the mark of his genius in many places in Mediterranean France, but nowhere more powerfully than in the Château Grimaldi. In the autumn of 1946, he was living in Golfe-Juan, and desperately in need of a studio. Dor de la Souchère, the director of the modest local museum in the château, offered him the use of some empty rooms. This was during the early period of Picasso's relationship with Françoise Gilot, one of the most joyous periods of his life, as evident in *La Joie de Vivre*, his large painting of a voluptuous nymph dancing on the seashore, centaurs tooting flutes, and smiling goats prancing. Picasso departed Antibes after six months and left his enormous output of the period to the Château Grimaldi museum, and it became the core of the **Musée Picasso**. Two years later he added a dazzling selection of his ceramics from Vallauris. The museum later added Picasso prints from different periods and also acquired first-rate works by other twentieth-century artists — Léger, Ernst, Klein, Arman, Raysse, Alechinsky, César, Germaine Richier, and 10 works by Nicholas de Staël, including his last work, the huge, partially unfinished canvas *The Big Concert*, painted in Antibes in 1955 the week before he took his own life. The museum is closed on Tuesdays, major holidays, and from early November to early December.

Antibes's **Provençal market**, one of the best on the Côte d'Azur, is held every morning except Mondays in the open pavilion on the Cours Masséna and around it, outside the walls of the old city. **Veziano**, the *boulangerie-pâtisserie* at 2 rue de la Pompe near the market, makes deservedly famous *pissaladière*, the Nice-style onion tart.

The eastern Côte d'Azur is not wine country, but **Domaines Ott (** 04 92 93 12 00, one of the most prestigious makers of Côtes de Provence and Bandol wines, has a retail outlet in Antibes. For a preview of wine tasting visits to their vineyards in the Var, sample some of their distinctive wines. It is at 4 avenue Edmond Salvy.

CAP D'ANTIBES

Cap d'Antibes is the small peninsula that starts just to the south of Vauban's ramparts and extends some two and a half kilometers (about a mile and a half) into the sea, with the Baie des Anges to the east and Golfe-Juan to the west. This lovely cape is studded with majestic umbrella pines, covered with elegant estates and ringed by pretty beaches, one of which, La Garoupe, became the setting for the famous opening scene of Scott Fitzgerald's *Tender is the Night*. He and Zelda spent a good deal of time here in the 1920s visiting Gerald and Sara Murphy at their Cap d'Antibes estate, the Villa America. The novel's palatial hotel was modeled on the Hôtel du Cap. The views are marvelous from everywhere.

The **Jardin Thuret**, on Boulevard du Cap, is a botanical garden that has been introducing plants from other warm climates to the Côte d'Azur environment since 1857. Some 3,000 species of exotic trees and plants are represented in the four-hectare (10-acre) spread, including the eucalyptus, now very common on the Côte d'Azur, which the garden brought in from Australia. The Jardin Thuret is open weekdays and entrance is free.

The **Sanctuaire de la Garoupe** is a sailors' shrine with a large collection of marine ex-votos, naïve paintings that have been offered as thanks to Notre-Dame-de-Bon-Port (Our Lady of Safe Homecoming), the patron saint of sailors, for saving their lives in storms, shipwrecks, and other

accidents. On either the first or second Sunday of every July there is a solemn procession in which the gilded wooden statue of Notre-Dame-de-Bon-Port, brought down to the cathedral in Antibes a few days prior, is returned to the Sanctuary by the seamen. The **Musée Naval et Napoléonien**, a former gun battery, is a museum with a collection of Napoléonic memorabilia. It has a fine panorama of the Îles de Lérins.

WHERE TO STAY

Very Expensive

The **Hôtel du Cap****** **(** 04 93 61 39 01 FAX 04 93 67 76 04 E-MAIL edenrochotel@wanadoo.fr WEB SITE

www.edenroc-hotel.fr, at the tip of Cap d'Antibes, is a vast, sumptuous palace built in 1870 with acres of gardens and a private beach facing the Îles de Lérins. Masters of the universe come here to unwind. Your fellow guests will be the likes of Madonna, Arnold Schwarzenegger, Robert De Niro, and the Marvin Davises, who had $10 million in jewels with them until they were robbed in their limousine on the way to the Hôtel du Cap in 1992. It is one of the most expensive hotels in France, as is its gorgeous restaurant, the **Eden Roc**. No credit cards are accepted. Open April through October.

Expensive

La Garoupe*** **(** 04 92 93 33 33 FAX 04 93 67 61 87, at 60 chemin de la Garoupe in Cap d'Antibes, is a handsome 20-room hotel with a restaurant and

Trompe l'œil at the ultra-deluxe Hôtel du Cap on Cap d'Antibes.

pool overlooking the Plage de la Garoupe, open late March through the end of October.

Moderate

Mas Djoliba*** (04 93 34 02 48 FAX 04 93 34 05 81 E-MAIL info@hotel-pcastel-djoliba.com, at 29 avenue de Provence (the main road between Old Antibes and Juan-les-Pins), is a villa from the *années folles* of the 1920s in a quiet, woodsy setting with 13 attractive Provençal-style rooms and a pool. Open from the beginning of February to the end of October. **Royal***** (04 93 34 03 09 FAX 04 93 34 23 31 is an old-fashioned 38-room hotel situated south of the ramparts of Old Antibes at 16 boulevard du Maréchal Leclerc. No pool, but the beach

Its delicious *bouillabaisse*, generally rated the Côte d'Azur's best, and other impeccably fresh gourmet seafood dishes have earned the Sordello brothers a Michelin star. The dining terrace is delightful, with a magnificent view over the Baie des Anges. It is quite expensive (280 francs for the most modest fixed-price *menu*), but very popular, so reserve early. Closed Mondays at lunch in July and August, all day Monday the rest of the year. **Aux Vieux Murs** (04 93 34 06 73 is a sunny restaurant with vaulted ceilings built into the ramparts of old Antibes with a beautiful view of the port on Promenade Amiral de Grasse. It serves a delicious four-course Provençal *menu* with such choices as young rabbit pie, *pissaladière* made with fresh cod

of La Salis is nearby. The hotel has its own restaurant, the **Dauphine**. Open January 1 to the end of October and the Christmas period.

Auberge Provençale* (04 93 34 13 24 FAX 04 93 34 89 88, centrally situated at 61 place Nationale, two blocks from the market in downtown Antibes, has seven spotless rooms with baths and a good restaurant. **Relais du Postillon**** (04 93 34 20 77 FAX 04 93 34 61 24 WEB SITE www.relais-postillon, is a hotel-restaurant in a seventeenth-century post house at 8 rue Championnet in downtown Antibes. It has 15 pleasant, well-maintained rooms, some of them in the inexpensive category.

WHERE TO EAT

Le Bacon (04 93 61 50 02, at Cap Bacon on Cap d'Antibes, is my first choice for seafood in the area.

flakes, mixed fish casserole with *ratatouille* sauce, and stuffed saddle of lamb for a reasonable 200 francs. Closed Mondays. **Albert 1er** (04 93 34 33 54, at 46 boulevard Albert 1er near the Antibes beaches, is a lively brasserie much appreciated by its clientele of Antibes regulars for its fresh shellfish platters, grilled and cooked local fish, seafood paella, and the full panoply of brasserie fare at moderate prices. Closed Wednesdays.

JUAN-LES-PINS

Stretched out on the gentle curve of a fine sandy shore immediately to the west of Cap d'Antibes, Juan-les-Pins has something no other town on the Côte d'Azur can boast of: a jumping nightlife area. Cafés, bars, discos and pizzerias are jammed to all hours, which makes Juan-les-Pins a great place for the young.

BACKGROUND

It was here in 1921 that restaurateur Edouard Baudoin came up with the revolutionary idea of launching a summer season on the Riviera, which up until then had been strictly a winter vacation land. Millionaire Frank Jay Gould, son of the "Mephistopheles of Wall Street" Jay Gould, came up with the financing, and they built the first casino here. It was a great success, but a bitter one for Baudoin, because a few years later, Gould, true to his robber-baron genes, aced him out of it. But Baudoin has not been forgotten by Juan-les-Pins: the most prestigious street for nightlife, where the modern Eden-Casino is located, is named Boulevard Edouard-Baudoin. The vogue of sunbathing first caught on in Juan-les-Pins in the 1920s, and its pine-lined shore remains one of the best on the Côte d'Azur.

GENERAL INFORMATION

Tourist Office (04 92 90 53 05 is on the waterfront at 51 boulevard Charles-Guillaumont. Bikes and motorbikes can be rented from **Deux Roues Location** (04 93 61 33 24, at 33 boulevard Guillaumont, and **Holiday Bikes** (04 93 61 51 51 at 122 boulevard Wilson. For **taxis** call (04 93 61 14 08 or 04 93 61 09 39.

WHAT TO SEE AND DO

The action is basically the beach and the nightlife, but from the middle to the end of July, **Jazz à Juan**, one of Europe's premier jazz festivals, which started here in 1960, is held in the Pinède, the pine grove in the center of town. Information about the Jazz Festival can be obtained from the Tourist Office.

WHERE TO STAY

Juan-les-Pins is essentially a summer resort. Except as noted, the following hotels are open from April through October. If you are planning to stay for a week or more, a number of modern apartment complexes rent out furnished studios and apartments, which can be less expensive than hotels. The Tourist Office has a list.

Very Expensive

Juana**** (04 93 61 08 70 FAX 04 93 61 76 60, on Avenue Gallice is a deluxe 1930s resort with an easygoing ambiance. It has 45 rooms, a pool complex amid palms and flowers, and a private beach across the Pinède. **Belles Rives****** (04 93 61 02 79 FAX 04 93 67 43 51, on Boulevard Edouard-Baudoin, was the Fitzgeralds' favorite. This 41-room art deco hotel is directly on its own private beach and has

been beautifully restored to the way Scott and Zelda liked it.

Expensive

Beauséjour**** (04 93 61 07 82 FAX 04 93 61 86 78 is a handsome early twentieth-century mansion in a quiet residential neighborhood converted into a very comfortable, warmly elegant hotel. It has lovely grounds, with big cedars, ancient olive trees, flower gardens, and a secluded pool area. There are views of the sea, the gardens, or the pool from the balconies of all 30 rooms. The hotel is on Avenue Saramartel, a five-minute walk from the Pinède or the beach. It is a Best Western member.

Moderate

Pré Catelan** (04 93 61 05 11 FAX 04 93 67 83 11, at 22 avenue des Lauriers, is a pleasant 18-room hotel in a palm garden a few minutes walk from the beach. It is open all year.

WHERE TO EAT

La Terrasse at the Hôtel Juana is the leading gourmet table in the Antibes area, and chef Christian Morriset has earned two Michelin stars with his Provence-accented cuisine. Stuffed zucchini flowers, cannellonis of cuttlefish and clams in squid ink, rack of lamb baked in Vallauris clay, and *fruits rouges* (strawberries, raspberries, and wild strawberries) flavored with vanilla oil balsamic vinegar, are a few of the specialties he's known for. The 280 franc lunch *menu* is well worth the price. The restaurant is closed for lunch on Mondays and Wednesdays and Wednesdays at dinner off-season. The **Grill du Casino** (04 92 93 71 71, at the Eden-Casino, Boulevard Edouard-Baudoin, has an attractive dining terrace overlooking the beach, a good place for lunch. **Bijou Plage** (04 93 61 39 07, on Boulevard du Littoral, has a seafood restaurant on the beach with a tasty lunch *menu* at 100 francs. Neighboring **Moorea Plage** (04 93 61 58 68 has live Brazilian music and modestly priced food and is popular with the young professional crowd. In the heart of the nighttime entertainment district, both **Vesuvio** (04 93 61 21 47, at 3 avenue Galice, and **La Bodega** (04 93 61 07 52, on Rue Datheville, make good pizzas and other honest, uncomplicated fare.

NIGHTLIFE

Every night is Carnival in Rio at the main intersection of the nightlife area, as the Brazilian bands at the open-air Pam-Pam and Le Festival clubs fire salvos of samba across the street at each other. The **Pam-Pam** (04 93 61 11 05 is at 137 boulevard Wilson, **Le Festival** (04 93 61 04 62 at 146 boulevard

The sculpture garden of the Picasso Museum in Antibes.

The Côte d'Azur

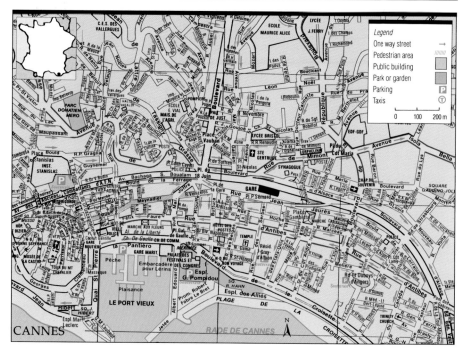

Legend

One way street	→
Pedestrian area	/////
Public building	
Park or garden	
Parking	P
Taxis	Ⓣ

0   100   200 m

CANNES

RADE DE CANNES

Wilson. The **Madison Piano Bar** (04 93 67 83 80, in the Hotel Beachotel, 6 avenue Alexandre III, features jazz. In the summer, the six discos and numerous bars are hopping until 3 AM or 4 AM. More adult-type pursuits, such as gambling your life's savings away, are focused on the **Eden Casino** (04 92 93 71 71, on Boulevard Edouard-Baudoin.

HOW TO GET THERE

There are several trains a day from Paris, Marseille, Toulon, and Italy that arrive at the Gare SNCF in Antibes. The local Métrazur train also makes frequent stops there. Buses from Cannes and Nice, including the Nice Airport shuttle bus, stop at Place du Général de Gaulle. All other buses stop at the Gare Routière. By car, Antibes is easily reached by the A8 *autoroute* or the N98 coast road. Access Juan-les-Pins by car from Antibes, taking Boulevard Wilson west from Place du Général-de-Gaulle, a five-minute drive. Juan-les-Pins has its own SNCF train station on Avenue de l'Esterel. There are also local buses along the coast.

GOLFE-JUAN

Golfe-Juan is an uninspiring little beach town that neighbors Juan-les-Pins to the west. It is known mainly as the place where Napoléon landed on March 1, 1815, after escaping from exile on Elba. This marked the beginning of the Hundred Days, when Napoléon rallied the country to his banner and led it to Waterloo. There is a suitably grave-

stone-like monument by the beach at the spot where the Emperor landed. This is where the Route Napoléon starts, the modern road that follows the trail Napoléon took to the north. Golfe-Juan is also the place where Robert Capa took the wonderful photograph of Picasso following Françoise Gilot on the beach holding a big umbrella over her head.

CANNES

In December 1834, Lord Brougham, the former Chancellor of the Exchequer and one of the best-connected men in England, was on his way to Italy for the winter, but his coach was stopped at the Var frontier by the Savoyard health authorities because of a cholera quarantine. Unable to proceed, Lord Brougham returned west along the coast until he came to a little fishing village in a magnificent natural setting with reeds (*cannes*) fringing its pretty harbor. He fell completely under the charm of the place, bought land and started building a villa. His upper-class friends came from England to visit and started building villas of their own. And so, by this twist of fate, Cannes was launched on its upscale trajectory. Gourmet restaurants, fine shops, and luxury hotels soon followed. The Prince of Wales gave his weighty stamp of approval. Grand Duke Michael of Russia financed the Cannes-Mandelieu golf club. The Hôtel Carlton went up in 1912 and became the touchstones of Cannes's aura of wealth and glamour.

On the level of permanent cultural attractions, Cannes is no Nice or Antibes. But it makes up for this lack by putting on festivals and conventions practically nonstop. The Cannes Film Festival in May is the most famous, and the hype it generates is a key factor in maintaining Cannes's image of glamour, but there are literally dozens of other trade shows and festivals, and even if they don't interest you directly, they keep the city's hotels, restaurants, casinos, and nightspots hopping most of the year. "Life is a Festival," Cannes says, and it means it.

BACKGROUND

The earliest traces of habitation in Cannes are from a Celto-Ligurian settlement on Mount Chevalier,

In 1939 the Cannes Film Festival tried to hold its first session, but was annulled by the outbreak of World War II. It resumed in 1946, and its success has been a big factor in Cannes's overall success in tourism. Cocteau, Bardot, Truffaut, Goddard, Belmondo, Deneuve, and Delon set a sophisticated European tone in the 1950s and 1960s, but from the 1970s on, the festival has tended to go more and more Hollywood. Today's pilgrims to Cannes are movie producers who flock to the festival in May and devote themselves to business pursuits with more-than-religious zeal. The Freudian quest for fame, power, riches, and the love of women reverberates everywhere, and people-watching on the Croisette, amusing the rest

the hill of the Suquet district overlooking the harbor. The Romans followed and set up a military post there, Castrum Marsellinum. In the eleventh century, the monks of Saint-Honorat, who owned Cannes, built the square tower you see on the highest point of the hill. It was needed to watch for Saracen pirates, for whom the monks' island monastery just off the coast was a juicy target. The monastery became very wealthy during the Middle Ages as one of France's most popular sites of pilgrimage. Ultimately the pirates and various foreign navies made life too difficult for the monks, and they abandoned the Island of Saint-Honorat, leaving the fisherfolk of Cannes to fend for themselves.

Lord Brougham introduced Cannes's new lifestyle and economy in the nineteenth century. But he also helped the local fishermen by getting his friend King Louis Philippe to clean up the harbor, which had become overgrown with reeds.

of the year, becomes more and more frenzied as the festival goes on, with all eyes darting about for a glimpse of a Star. But despite all the hype and the shlock — and unfortunately, more and more purse snatching and theft from vehicles in recent years — Cannes has somehow managed to maintain its image of class.

GENERAL INFORMATION

There are two **Tourist Offices**. The main one is at the central landmark of the city, the **Palais des Festivals** (locally known as *"Le Bunker"*) (04 93 39 24 53 E-MAIL semloimb@palais-festivals-com WEBSITE www.cannes-on-line-com. The other office is at the **Gare SNCF** (train station) (04 93 99 19 77.

Night on the Boulevard de la Croisette, where Cannes' palatial hotels, chic cafés and luxury shops and casinos are.

The staff will make hotel reservations for you, provide you with free local maps and brochures, and help you with festival bookings.

The Gare SNCF is centrally located on Rue Jean Jaurès, which parallels the Croisette five blocks in from the beach. For **train information** call (04 36 35 35 35 (main line trains or the local Métrazur line).

There is a **bus terminal** (04 93 39 31 37 at the Gare SNCF for buses to the neighboring hill towns such as Mougins, Grasse, and Vallauris. The **Gare Routière** bus station (04 93 39 11 39 by the Hôtel de Ville has buses that run along the coast. There you can also get the **bus to Nice-Côte d'Azur Airport** (04 93 39 11 39. For long-distance trips, the **CTM station** (04 93 39 79 40 across from the Palais des Festivals at Square Prosper Merimée has buses for Marseille, Aix, and Avignon.

Bus Azur is the city's bus line, and its terminus is by the Hôtel de Ville (04 93 39 18 71.

At the **Gare Maritime**, the maritime terminal next to the Palais des Festivals, you can get boats to the Îles de Lérins.

For **taxis**, call (04 92 99 27 27.

Car rental agencies include **Avis** (04 93 94 15 86, **Budget** (04 93 99 44 04, **Europcar** (04 93 06 26 30, and **Hertz** (04 93 99 09 44.

You can **rent bikes** at the Gare SNCF baggage counter (04 93 38 20 10. Bike, scooter, and motorcycle rental can also be found at **Azur Moto Location** (04 93 38 33 20, 10 rue Mimont; **Alliance Location** (04 93 38 62 62, 14 rue des Frères Pradignac; and **Holiday Bikes** (04 93 94 61 00, 16 rue du 14 Juillet.

Books in English can be found at the **Cannes English Bookshop** (04 93 99 40 08, at 11 rue Bivouac-Napoléon. This is the real thing, well-stocked with English-language fiction and nonfiction from the classics to the latest bestsellers.

In case of **medical emergencies**, dial (15 for the SAMU (mobile emergency medical service).

FESTIVALS AND EVENTS

Festivals, congresses, and large business gatherings keep Cannes active 40 weeks of the year. The biggest, the **Cannes Film Festival**, is held the second and third weeks of May. Other large entertainment industry gatherings are **MIDEM** for the music business in January, and **MIP-TV** in April and **MIPCOM** in October for television. Summer is very active for musical events, with **Nuits Musicales du Suquet**, a classical music festival in mid-July. Three dates to note in your travel agenda are July 14, August 15 and August 24, when Cannes stages three of its six **Pyromusical Evenings**, fabulous fireworks displays over the Croisette scored to music; the other three dates are variable, in July and August. In December, there is the **Cannes International Dance Festival**.

For schedules and details on these and Cannes's dozens of other festivals, congresses and performances, contact the Tourist Office.

WHAT TO SEE AND DO

Modern Cannes

There are two different Cannes, really, one old and one new. The one the whole world knows is the modern Cannes. It centers on the palm-lined **Boulevard de la Croisette** with its palatial hotels and cafés and luxury shops fronting on the long crescent of beach to the east of the Palais des Festivals, the dividing point. For beach lovers, the long sandy curve of the Croisette is lined with beach clubs, each with a restaurant, open for lunch only, except for special holiday nights (see WHERE TO EAT, below). The palatial hotels all have elegant beach clubs open to one and all, for a price. There are free public beaches in Cannes too, but only one small one in this costly part of town, in the seaside of the Palais des Festivals. (The best public beaches are at **Gazagnaire** on the east side of Pointe de la Croisette, which gets the best sun in the morning, and the **Plages du Midi** west of the Vieux Port, which gets it in the afternoon.)

The *"palaces,"* as the palatial hotels of the Croisette are called, play a large part in keeping the feeling of glamour alive in Cannes, and to get in touch with that glamour, you should visit the lobbies of these stunning establishments. Pause for a drink on the legendary terrace at the **Carlton** where the movie crowd gathers at Festival time, and in the evening stop at the lounge of the art deco **Martinez**, where you will find genial Jimmy McKissic entertaining at the piano. The serene **Majestic** and the ultramodern **Noga Hilton** are also well worth a visit.

Upscale **shopping** is a main activity in Cannes, whose Golden Triangle of luxury boutiques is comparable to Rodeo Drive in Beverly Hills or Rue du Faubourg Saint-Honoré in Paris. The shopping course runs from the mall of the Noga Hilton along the Croisette to the Galleries of the Gray-d'Albion and on to Rue d'Antibes, the city's main shopping street. Haute couture, men's fashions, shoes, jewelry, perfume, leather work, and other luxury products can all be found here, often with the words "and Cannes" added to London, New York, and Paris on the label.

But the greatest fun in this part of Cannes is **people-watching** along the Croisette, and that doesn't have to cost you a franc.

The natural setting could hardly be better — a mile-long crescent of sandy beach along the Croisette, the Îles de Lérins across the water in

---

Inhibitions evaporate on the beaches of southern France ABOVE, as here in Cannes. BELOW: The Old Port of Cannes, which Lord Braugham came upon by chance in December, 1834.

front of it, the rust-colored peaks of the Esterel range off to the right, and the amphitheater of hills shielding the city from behind. The bulky **Palais des Festivals** at the beginning of the Croisette is where the movie stars mount the famed red-carpeted steps in May. The Tourist Office is here too, along with the most active casino on the Côte d'Azur, the **Casino Croisette**.

Old Cannes

To the west of the Palais des Festivals lies the **Vieux Port** and **Le Suquet**, the old part of Cannes that existed before Lord Brougham first set foot here in 1834. A statue of the elegant gentleman surveys the old fishing port from the plane tree-shaded Allées de la Liberté, where the main activity is *pétanque*, Provençal bowling. In back of the **Hôtel de Ville** (City Hall) at the western end of the Allées, turn right on Rue Louis Blanc and walk two blocks to the place I love best in Cannes — the big pink stucco pavilion of the **Forville Market**. It bursts with the colors, flavors, and aromas of the region — roses, carnations, fresh fruit and vegetables, locally caught fish, olives, herbs from Provence. This is where you meet the real *Cannois*, the people of Cannes, a world apart from the high life of the Croisette. The market is open every morning except Mondays.

Behind the Hôtel de Ville you will also find **Rue Saint-Antoine**, which winds its way up Mont Chevalier to the **Suquet**, the old town built on the site of the Roman military camp. The narrow street is lined so solidly with eating places that it looks like one long restaurant that keeps changing cuisines. Some of the best food bargains in Cannes are to be found here (see WHERE TO EAT, below). Bear left at the top, and you will see the sixteenth-century church of **Notre-Dame de Bonne Espérance** where classical concerts are held in the summer. Nearby is the **Musée de la Castre**, a medieval castle, now an eclectic archaeological museum. Its square tower, the highest point in Cannes, is the one that was built by the monks of Saint-Honorat in the eleventh century to watch for the Saracen pirates. The panorama gives you views of the Esterel, the Îles de Lérins, the Riviera, the Vieux Port, the Palais des Festivals, the Croisette, and Cannes's hills. The view from the top of the Suquet is especially dramatic at night, when the palaces of the Croisette are illuminated.

If you go back to the Hôtel de Ville and go one block up Rue Louis Blanc then turn right onto **Rue Meynadier** you will find the liveliest food-shopping street in town. **Ceneri (La Ferme Savoyarde)** at No. 22 is the most respected cheese shop on the Côte d'Azur. For gifts, look into **Cannolive** at 16 rue Venizelos, the block that runs between Rue Meynadier and the railway station. It has a large, tasteful selection of Provençal fabrics, ceramics,

little saints, olive products, honey, and regional wines and liqueurs, including Lérina, a liqueur made from honey by the monks of Saint-Honorat Island.

WHERE TO STAY

Cannes is one of the top places in the world to indulge in lavish living, and rooms at the palatial hotels of the Croisette are staggeringly expensive. But there are plenty of modestly priced one- and two-star establishments among the 110 classified hotels, and out of season, the luxury hotels offer special rates. The Tourist Office will be happy to help you find a room you can afford and also make

your reservation for you. They will also inform you about the remarkably attractive six-day package rates offered by more than 60 hotels in Cannes, including practically all the ones mentioned below. Room rates are at least a third lower than normal, and continental breakfasts, a six-day pass to a beach club (mattress, parasol, locker, shower), museum passes, and a mini-cruise to the Îles de Lérins are included.

Very Expensive

There are four hotels on the Croisette known as "the palaces," and the term is no exaggeration. The marble bathrooms in these hotels are larger than most bedrooms in others, and taking a bath is a transcendental experience. These hotels are generally fully booked in high season, so reserve early. If you want a room at film festival time, you will have to book years in advance.

Since each one of the palatial hotels has its own distinct personality and all are at the pinnacle of quality and in the same price range, the choice of where to stay is mainly a matter of aesthetic taste. The **Carlton****** (04 93 06 40 06 FAX 04 93 06 40 25 E-MAIL cannes@interconti.com, at 58 boulevard de la Croisette, is a dazzling 1912 "wedding cake" with 310 luxurious, luminous rooms and 28 suites, and is the cornerstone of Cannes's *belle époque* period. In front of the hotel is the famous outdoor café, the Terrasse, where the movie moguls go to be seen. The **Majestic****** (04 92 98 77 00 FAX 04 93 38 97 90 E-MAIL majestic@lucienbarriere.com, at 14 boulevard de la Croisette, was built in 1926 in *belle époque* style, with 280 elegant rooms and 24 suites, beautifully renovated in 1999, a pool in a grassy lawn, and a piano lounge. An art deco hotel built in 1929, the **Martinez****** (04 92 98 73 00 FAX 04 93 39 67 82 E-MAIL martinez@concorde-hotels.com, at 73 boulevard de la Croisette, is nothing less than stunning. This is the largest hotel in Cannes, with 380 spacious, recently restored rooms and 24 suites. The **Noga Hilton****** (04 92 99 70 00 FAX 04 92 99 70 11 E-MAIL sales-cannes@hilton.com, at 50 boulevard de la Croisette, is an ultramodern 196-room, 33-suite hotel built in 1992 at a cost of $100 million on the site of the former Palais des Festivals. It has a piano lounge in its soaring white marble lobby, a modern rooftop pool, and a sun deck with magnificent sea and mountain views.

Expensive

The **Gray d'Albion****** (04 92 99 79 79 FAX 04 93 99 26 10 E-MAIL graydalbion@lucienbarriere.com, is an attractive modern 186-room hotel at 38 rue des Serbes, a few steps from the Croisette. It has a lively atmosphere, lots of shops, and its own beach.

Moderate

The **Splendid***** (04 93 99 53 11 FAX 04 93 99 55 02 E-MAIL hotel.splendid.cannes@wanadoo.fr, at 4 rue Felix Faure, fronting on the Allées de la Liberté, is a tastefully renovated 64-room *belle époque* beauty overlooking the port and the Palais des Festivals. It is also near the Forville market, and many rooms have kitchenettes, an advantage if you are staying for any length of time. Big rooms with a sea view and kitchenettes are in the expensive price range. I like this hotel very much and consider it the best deal in town. **Hôtel de Paris***** (04 93 38 30 89 FAX 04 93 39 04 61 E-MAIL reception@hotel-de-paris.com, at 34 boulevard de l'Alsace, is an elegant early twentieth-century hotel with 50 up-to-date rooms and a pool in its palm-lined courtyard. It's near the train station and about a 10-minute walk from the Croisette. **Villa de Olivier***** (04 93 39 53 28 FAX 04 93 39 55 85 E-MAIL

hptel-olivier-cannes@csi.com, at 5 rue Tambourinaires, is a charming old inn in the Suquet with 24 pleasant rooms and a swimming pool, convenient to the public beaches of the Plages du Midi.

Inexpensive

Albert 1er** (04 93 39 24 04 FAX 04 93 38 83 75 WEB SITE www.cannes-hotels.com, at 68 avenue de Grasse, has 11 cozy rooms with baths and is located in back of the Suquet. A number of inexpensive modern chain hotels are located out by the Cannes-La Bocca Aérodrome to the west of the city. **Campanile**** (04 93 48 69 41 FAX 04 93 90 40 42 WEB SITE www.cannes-hotels.com, has one of its well-run

hotels with 100 rooms right at the Aérodrome, and there is a **Climat de France**** (04 93 48 21 00 FAX 04 93 48 23 00 E MAIL societe.hoteliere.du.phare@wanadoo.fr., at 204 avenue Francis Tonner, with 129 bright, modern rooms at 230 to 360 francs. Both hotels at the airport have restaurants and pools.

Camping

The camping grounds most convenient to the city are to be found in the area of the Cannes-La Bocca Aérodrome. **Bellevue Caravaning** (04 93 47 28 97, near the beach at 67 avenue Maurice Chevalier in La Bocca, is open from April to mid-October. **Le Grand Saule** (04 93 90 55 10, at 24 boulevard Jean Moulin in Le Cannet, is open from April 1 to October 15. **Le Ranch** (04 93 46 00 11, on Chemin Saint-Joseph-l'Aubarède in Le Cannet, is open all year. For more information, contact the Tourist Office.

WHERE TO EAT

There is a heavy concentration of expensive gourmet restaurants in Cannes, but there are plenty of good reasonably priced eateries too, especially in

LEFT: One of the lively cafés near the Old Port in Cannes. ABOVE: One of Cannes' "palaces," the Majestic.

the Suquet. Note too that a number of top gourmet restaurants have introduced fixed-price lunch *menus* that give you a chance to sample the *haute cuisine* of the region at affordable prices.

Very Expensive

Christian Willer's refined Provençal cuisine at the airy **Palme d'Or** (04 92 98 74 14, in the Hôtel Martinez, has made this one of the most illustrious restaurants in Southern France, with two Michelin stars. You can sample it for as little as 295 francs, wine included, thanks to the weekday lunch special. Otherwise it is much more expensive. Closed Mondays and Tuesdays, except Tuesday dinner in season. **La Belle Otéro** (04 92 99 51

10, with the same lofty Michelin two-star rating, features Francis Chauveau's delicate touch with regional cuisine. It is at Carlton Casino Club, a deluxe English-style gaming club on the seventh floor of the Carlton Hotel. There is a fixed-price lunch *menu* at 290 francs, wine and coffee included. Otherwise *menus* start at 410 francs (wine not included). The restaurant is open daily in the summer, closed Sundays, Mondays, and Tuesdays at lunch off-season.

The other two "palaces" also have excellent restaurants. The Majestic's gorgeous **Villa des Lys** (04 92 98 77 00 offers a refined *cuisine de terroir* that has earned young chef Bruno Oger a Michelin star. Though not up to that exalted gastronomic level, **La Scala** (04 92 99 70 00, at the Noga Hilton, serves savory Italo-Provençal specialties on its flowery mezzanine terrace directly overlooking the Croisette and the sea.

Expensive/Moderate

A cluster of three good restaurants of different styles can be found on the lower end of Suquet's restaurant row, at prices that are moderate to expensive, depending on what you order. **L'Échiquier** (04 93 39 77 79, at 14 rue Saint-Antoine, serves traditional French cuisine in a cozy atmosphere. The **Maschou** (04 93 39 62 21, at 15 rue Saint-Antoine, serves charcoal grilled meats and fish in a candlelight setting. The **Mesclun** (04 93 99 45 19, at 16 rue Saint-Antoine, is noted for creative Provençal cuisine served in a refined, traditional French dining room. Down the hill on the Vieux Port, **Gaston et Gastounette** (04 93 39 47 92, at 6 quai Saint-Pierre, is a lively, folksy eatery serving fish, *bouillabaisse*, and other honestly prepared Provençal fare. For vegetarian cuisine of exceptionally high quality, head for **Montagard** (04 93 39 98 38, at 6 rue du Maréchal-Joffre, where chef Jean Montagard, a real artist, extracts the maximum flavor from the products he brings back daily from the Marché Forville — mostly vegetables, some fish, but no meat. The restaurant is closed Sundays and (like the market) Mondays.

For lunch in a spectacular setting, you can't top the beach restaurants along the Croisette. Here, as you savor your *coquilles Saint-Jacques* (sea scallops) and sip a cool glass of rosé, you gaze out at the Îles de Lérins, the Esterel hills, the boats in the water, and visual delights on the beach. All the "palaces" have beach restaurants. Those of the **Martinez** and the **Carlton** are chic, and the food is very good. The **Plage Ondine** near the Palais des Festivals generally gets the best ratings for cuisine, and the **Plage Gray d'Albion** is also quite good. These eateries are not cheap. Figure on 250 francs minimum for a very simple lunch. The **Miramar** and **Lido** beach restaurants are less expensive and serve tasty, filling lunches for about 200 francs, wine included.

Inexpensive

La Cave (04 93 99 79 87, at 9 boulevard de la République, serves *légumes farcis, beignet de fleurs de courgette, rougets grillés* (stuffed vegetables, deep-fried zucchini blossoms, and grilled mullet), and the whole range of Provençal dishes. The restaurant is very popular, and service can be slow. **La Brouette de Grand-Mère** (04 93 39 12 10, 9 rue d'Oran, off Rue d'Antibes, is an old-style bistro that serves rabbit, beef stew, and other homey fare. **La Moule Rit** (04 93 39 19 99, at 13 rue du Suquet, has mussels, fries, and beer. At **Taverne de Lucullus** (04 93 39 32 74, at 4 place du Marché Forville on the south side of the market pavilion, you'll find a grand selection of *tapas* and a hearty regional *menu* for 48 francs. This is a colorful spot, bursting with good Provençal cheer, patronized mainly by vendors from the market. It is open from 5 AM to 4 PM and is closed Mondays.

NIGHTLIFE

As elsewhere along the Côte d'Azur, nightlife centers on the casinos. In Cannes there are two. The **Casino Croisette** in the building of the Palais des Festivals is the busiest on the Côte d'Azur, attracting up to 10,000 players a day to its tables and machines at the height of the season. Most people play *machines à sous*, the slot machines. The **Carlton Casino Club** on the seventh floor of the Hôtel Carlton is a more discreet, elegant English club-like casino for traditional games. No special dress code is required to play the slot machines, but to enter any of the gambling rooms, gentlemen must wear jackets and ties, and everyone must show a passport, or an identity card of a European Union member country.

To dance the night away, go to **Le Jane's Club** (04 92 99 79 59, at the Hôtel Gray d'Albion, which is open from 10:30 PM to dawn, or to **Le Jimmy'z de Regine** (04 93 68 00 07, at the Casino Croisette, which carries on from 11 PM to dawn. **Cat Corner** (04 93 39 31 31, at 22 rue Macé, is the hot discotheque at the moment, open from 10 PM to dawn. **La Chunga** (04 93 94 11 29, at 72 boulevard de la Croisette, is a lively café with recorded rock music that rocks from 8:30 PM to dawn. Across the street at the **Amiral Lounge** of the Martinez, versatile Jimmy McKissic settles down at the piano at 10 PM.

HOW TO GET THERE

To come by plane, you fly to the Nice-Côte d'Azur Airport and take the airport bus to Cannes. The Airport-Riviera Navette Bus leaves every hour and takes 45 minutes. The fare is 70 francs. There are four direct trains a day from Paris and five more with connections at Marseille or Toulon, and the local Métrazur train stops at Cannes's Gare SNCF. By bus, there are numerous coaches serving the coast road and the hill towns of the interior. Coming by car you can take the A8 *autoroute*, the N98 along the coast, or the N85 from the Alpes-de-Haute-Provence.

THE ÎLES DE LÉRINS

For a delightful excursion from Cannes, take a boat ride to the Îles de Lérins, the two islands just off the coast, where you can swim, visit the fortress where the mysterious "The Man in the Iron Mask" was kept prisoner, stroll through the pine- and eucalyptus-covered hills, or simply enjoy the change of pace. The good restaurants on the islands are fairly expensive, so you may want to buy the ingredients for a picnic on Rue Meynadier or at the Forville Market before you leave. This is strictly a day trip. There are no hotels on the islands.

There are frequent boats from the Gare Maritime in Cannes. The 15-minute round trip to Île Sainte-Marguerite costs 40 francs, the 30-minute round trip to Saint-Honorat 45 francs.

ÎLE SAINTE-MARGUERITE

The closer and larger of the two islands, Île Sainte-Marguerite, is three kilometers (two miles) long and one kilometer (two-thirds of a mile) wide. It offers a number of nature walks through the hills, and there are groves of giant eucalyptus on the southeastern side. **Fort Sainte-Marguerite** (also called Fort Royal or Fort Vauban), is a sixteenth-century fortress on a steep cliff, guarding the narrow passage between the island and Pointe Croisette. From this vantage point you will have another dramatic view of Cannes. Enter the **Musée de la Mer** in the fort to visit the cell of "The Man in the Iron Mask" (*Masque de Fer*), who was kept here from 1687 to 1698, then transferred to the Bastille, where he died in 1703. Scores of theories continue to circulate about the identity of this man who got on the wrong side of Louis XIV. Was he Louis's illegitimate older brother? Was he Louis's wife Maria Theresa's African page boy and lover? To this day his identity remains a mystery. The one thing we do know is that the mask was velvet, not iron. The museum also has items salvaged from ancient shipwrecks, including ones from a first century BC Roman vessel and a tenth century AD Arab wreck. The museum is closed on Tuesdays.

For lunch on Île Sainte-Marguerite, **La Guérite** (04 93 43 49 30, serves good seafood dishes at fairly steep prices (figure on 200 francs, drinks included). To get there, follow the sign for the *Sentier Botanique*, the botanical trail that leads up the hill from the ferry pier. **L'Escale** (04 93 43 49 25, on the main path from the pier to the fortress, also serves good seafood specialties at similarly high prices.

ÎLE SAINT-HONORAT

The smaller island, Île Saint-Honorat, is 1,500 m (about one mile) long and 400 m (1,300 ft) wide. It is owned by the Cistercian order, which has a monastery and farm fields, but they allow you to walk about the island freely. They will also sell you a bottle of Lérina, the delicious liqueur they make from honey.

The original monastery was founded at the end of the fourth century by Saint Honorat, one of the pioneers of the monastic movement in France. During the Middle Ages, it grew wealthy from revenue from pilgrims and extended its holdings to the mainland. At one time the Monastery of Saint Honorat owned Cannes, Mougins, and Vallaurius. Incessant raids by pirates and foreign navies eventually led to the monastery's abandon-

The Carlton, where movie moguls gather on its famed terrace during the Cannes Film Festival.

ment, but the Cistercians of the Abbey of Sénanque brought it back to life in 1869.

Be sure to visit the eleventh-century fortified **monastery** built on a little point of land surrounded by water on three sides. The only entrance is a doorway cut into the wall four meters (13 ft) above the ground. It looks bizarre, but it had its purpose — to protect the monks from Saracen raiders. They would climb to the door by ladder, then pull the ladder inside and slam the door.

MOUGINS

Mougins, one of the former properties of the monks of Saint Honorat, is a hill town built around a

medieval bell tower seven kilometers (four and a half miles) north of Cannes. All the land around here used to be covered by olive groves and fields of roses. Some remain, but residential development has gobbled up much of it. The town itself has kept the atmosphere of a Provençal village, and its little houses are decked with flowers. So a visit here may come as a welcome relief to the high-intensity life at the shore. It is also one of the prime spots to explore the gastronomy of the region, made world-famous by chef Roger Vergé and his Moulin de Mougins. But Mr. Vergé is by no means alone. This little town is loaded with good eating places.

The **Tourist Office** (04 93 75 87 67 is at 15 avenue Jean-Charles Mallet.

WHAT TO SEE AND DO

Roger Vergé and his staff hold Provençal **cooking classes** designed for amateur chefs in small groups, 15 maximum, at **L'École du Moulin** in a specially-designed kitchen upstairs at L'Amandier, Mr. Vergé's restaurant in the village. The two-and-a-half-hour sessions are built around one theme or one *menu*. Classes are held Tuesdays through Saturdays, 300 francs per session, 1,350 francs for a series of five. You must reserve

48 hours in advance. For information or bookings, contact the school at (04 93 75 35 70 or FAX 04 93 90 18 55 E-MAIL mougins@ relaischateaux.fr WEB SITE www.relaischateaux.fr/mougins, or write to them at Restaurant l'Amandier, 06250 Mougins.

For a taste of the Côte d'Azur when it was the playground of *only* the rich, visit the **Musée de l'Automobiliste** (04 93 69 27 80, which has a large fleet of magnificent antique cars — Bugattis, Hispano-Suzas, Rolls Royces, and old racing cars, with 70 on display at one time. It is five kilometers (three miles) east of Mougins at the Nord de Breguières parking area on the A8 *autoroute*. The museum is open from 10 AM to 7 PM April through September, to 6 PM the rest of the year.

WHERE TO EAT

The famous **Moulin de Mougins** (04 93 75 78 24, is an elegant old mill in the Quartier Notre-Dame-de-Vie in the countryside outside the village. It remains a highly prized destination for the well-healed gourmet. But to make his cuisine more available to people of ordinary means, Mr. Vergé has introduced a sumptuous three-course Mediterranean-Provençal lunch *menu* at 250 francs. In town, Madame Vergé oversees the running of the **Restaurant l'Amandier** (04 93 90 00 91, at Place du Commandant Lamay, a café-restaurant with specials of the day such as *bouillabaisse* or *brochettes* of lamb, and wine by the *pichet*. Fixed-price *menus* start at 140 francs.

Another favorite of mine is **Feu Follet** (04 93 90 57 78, Place de la Mairie, Jean-Paul Battaglia's restaurant by the fountain in the heart of the old village. On the sunny, fun-filled terrace, waitresses in Provençal dress will bring you fresh pasta, fish, lamb, and bright little regional wines at reasonable prices. The fixed-price lunch *menu* is 128 francs. A few doors away is the **Bistrot de Mougins** (04 93 75 78 34, a warm, cheerful eatery in vaulted stone dining space offing a surprisingly large array of bright Provençal *entrées* (first courses) and *plats* (main courses) for such a small restaurant, and an astute selection of regional wines. For meals and wine of this quality, the prices are very reasonable, with a weekday lunch *menu* at 125 francs.

HOW TO GET THERE

There is regular bus service from the Gare SNCF in Cannes. Take the RCA bus No. 60. You can get a bus schedule there or from the Tourist Office. If you are driving from Cannes, take Boulevard Carnot north, then bear left onto Avenue de Campon (the *autoroute* connector), which is Route N285. You pass under the *autoroute*, then follow the signs to Mougins.

GRASSE

Sitting high on a limestone plateau overlooking flower fields 17 km (11 miles) north of Cannes, Grasse is the perfume capital of the world, and most visitors come here to see how its most famous product is made and to buy some right at the source. Grasse is a large, rather cluttered-looking town of 42,000 and the hardest place in southern France to find your way around in. The streets are a maze. But if you have the time and the patience to explore it, many surprises are in store.

BACKGROUND

The perfume industry was introduced in the sixteenth century by the Queen of France, Catherine de Medici, who encouraged the Grasse's traditional glove-making industry to perfume its gloves, as was done in refined circles in Italy. With the Revolution, elegant gloves went out of fashion, and the companies simply switched to perfume alone. They perfected the techniques for extracting the essence of a flower's scent, the base element for perfume, and the sweet smells of some thirty factories continue to bring success to the area today.

GENERAL INFORMATION

The **Tourist Office** (04 93 36 66 66 is at 22 cours Honoré-Cresp, the large public promenade at the lower end of the Vieille Ville, the old part of town.

FESTIVALS AND EVENTS

There is a **rose festival** the third week of May and a **jasmine festival** the first Sunday in August. Check with the tourist office for information.

WHAT TO SEE AND DO

To see the old part of Grasse, the **Vieille Ville**, start at the Place de la Foux, and descend the double set of steps with a fountain in the middle to wend your way to the long, narrow **Place aux Aires**. Try to get here in the morning, when the **market** is held daily except Mondays, and you will be plunged into the spirit of old Provence. There is a fountain in the square and on the north side, a tall, handsome arcaded mansion, the **Hôtel Isnard**, built in 1781. The **Cathedral of Notre-Dame-du-Puy**, started in the Romanesque style and elaborated with Gothic and baroque elements, should not be missed. The main points of interest there are three early paintings by Rubens, *Christ Crowned with Thorns*, *The Crucifixion* and *Saint Helena*, and one of Fragonard's rare ventures into religious art,

his *Washing of the Feet*. There is also a touchingly sincere School of Nice triptych of Saint Honorat, Saint Clement, and Saint Laurent attributed to Ludovico Bréa.

At the **Musée de l'Art et de l'Histoire de Provence** (Museum of Provençal Art and History), a handsome eighteenth-century residence at 2 rue Mirabeau built by Count Mirabeau's sister Louise, there is an excellent collection of pottery from Biot and Vallauris and earthenware from Moustiers, Apt, and Castellet along with rooms furnished in the styles of Louis XIII, Louis XIV, and Louis XV. The museum is closed Mondays and Tuesdays, the month of November, and the first week of December.

The **Musée de la Parfumerie** nearby at 8 place du Cours, an elegant, terraced promenade, has many exhibits illustrating the history and manufacturing processes of perfumes from antiquity to the present. It is also closed Mondays and Tuesdays, the month of November, and the first week of December.

The **Musée de la Marine** (Naval Museum) around the corner on Boulevard du Jeu-de-Ballon has five rooms of exhibits relating mainly to the career of Admiral de Grasse, including a model of his flagship, *La Ville de Paris*, on which he received Generals Washington, Rochambeau and Lafayette in Chesapeake Bay during the Yorktown campaign. This museum is closed on Sundays and during the month of November.

The **Villa-Musée Fragonard** at 23 boulevard Fragonard is the seventeenth-century mansion of Jean-Honoré Fragonard, the darling of Louis XVI's court, in which the Grasse native took refuge in 1791 to escape the fate met by many of his aristocratic clients. The museum has an extensive collection of his sketches, engravings, wash drawings, oils, and five well-executed copies of a lighthearted series of panels called *Le Progrès de l'Amour dans le Cœur d'Une Jeune Fille* (The Progress of Love in the Heart of a Girl) which he painted for Madame du Barry (the originals are in the Frick Museum in New York). The museum keeps the same hours as the Musée de l'Art et de l'Histoire de Provence.

The most popular tourist attraction in Grasse is the **perfume factories**, and the three largest and most prestigious, Fragonard, Galimard, and Molinard offer free tours. Here you can see how the fragrances are extracted from the vast quantities of roses, mimosa, lavender, and jasmine grown in the region (it takes six tons of rose petals to make one quart of essence) and how the master perfume makers exercise their ancient craft. Naturally, each tour ends in the gift shop. **Fragonard** (04 93 36 44 65 WEB SITE www.fragonard.com, is at 20 boulevard Fragonard near the Musée Fragonard.

Picking flowers in the perfume capital, Grasse.

Galimard (04 93 09 20 00 WEB SITE www
.galimard.com, is at 73 route de Cannes. **Molinard**
(04 93 36 03 91 WEB SITE www.molinard-parfums
.com, is at 60 boulevard Victor-Hugo. They are
open all day in the summer from 9 AM to 6:30 PM
or 7 PM. In the winter they close from noon to 2 PM
and in the evening at 6 PM.

Not surprisingly, Grasse is one of the Côte
d'Azur's best spots for gardens. **Princess
Pauline's Garden**, constructed by Napoléon's
sister Pauline Borghese on a high point overlooking the town, offers a fine panorama of Grasse
and the coast. In the Saint-François district, the
sumptuous gardens designed by **Viscount
Charles de Noailles** in the 1930s have been

reopened to the public after extensive restoration. Guided visits are given on Fridays or by
special arrangement with the Tourist Office.

An interesting detour in the vicinity is to the
Huilerie de la Brague (04 93 77 23 03, an olive oil
mill in Opio, seven kilometers (four miles) east of
Grasse. To get there take D2085 to Châteauneuf
de Grasse, then D3 to Opio. It is at the bottom of
the valley at 2 route de Châteauneuf. This ancient
mill, some of whose walls date from the fifteenth
century, has been in the same family for six generations, and during the harvest season from
November through March, visitors can observe
the manufacturing process, from the washing of
the olives, to the crushing by huge stone wheels,
to the various methods used to prepare the oil and
the paste. Besides its high-quality olive oil and
every other olive product imaginable, the mill's
excellent gift shop sells a wide range of other
Provençal products, including honey, jams and
jellies, and Provençal fabrics.

WHERE TO STAY

In the city center, **Hôtel des Parfums***** (04 92
42 35 35 FAX 04 93 36 35 48 E-MAIL jcastiastier@
nicematin.fr., offers tranquillity, a swimming
pool, and 71 pleasant, moderately priced rooms.
It is on Boulevard Eugène-Charabot near Place
de la Foux in the upper part of Grasse. The **Hôtel
du Panorama**** (04 93 36 80 80 FAX 04 93 36 92
04, is at 2 cours Honoré-Cresp, convenient to
the Fragonard Museum. It has 36 comfortable
modern rooms in the inexpensive and moderate price ranges, all with balconies and fine
views.

South of the city, **Bastide Saint-Antoine******
(04 93 70 94 94 FAX 04 93 70 94 95 E-MAIL info@
jacques-chibois.com WEB SITE www.jacques-
chibois.com, at 48 avenue Henri-Dunant, off Boulevard du Maréchal-Leclerc, is Grasse's most elegant address. The deluxe 11-room inn is famed
chef Jacques Chibois's lovingly converted eighteenth-century country manor house, opened in
1998. It is in a large private park with ancient olive trees, gardens, quiet shaded terraces, a *pétanque*
court, and a swimming pool. The biggest attraction of all: Jacques Chibois's cuisine (see WHERE
TO EAT, below). Room rates are in the 1,000-to
1,200-franc range.

Also to the south of the city is the **Relais
Mercure**** (04 93 70 70 70 FAX 04 93 70 46 31, a
cheerful contemporary-style inn in a countrified

setting with 65 neat, attractive rooms done in Provençal colors, along with a restaurant, a coffee shop, and a pool. Prices are moderate. It is on Rue Martine Carole in the Quartier Saint-Claude, just off Route N85, a few hundred yards north of the big McDonald's at the corner of N85 and Boulevard Marcel Pagnol.

WHERE TO EAT

Oddly, for a town that has made its living off the olfactory senses, Grasse has not been noted for gourmet cooking — not until 1996, that is, when Jacques Chibois, the longtime master of the ovens at the Royal Gray in Cannes, opened his own

(cabbage stuffed with meat and vegetables), on a charming outdoor terrace. Prices are moderate.

HOW TO GET THERE

There are frequent buses from the Gare SNCF in Cannes. If you are driving, take Route N85 north from Mougins.

FURTHER AFIELD

GRAND CANYON DU VERDON

While not nearly as gigantic as its namesake on the Colorado, the Grand Canyon du Verdon is

restaurant here. The **Bastide Saint-Antoine** (see WHERE TO STAY, above) instantly became one of the Côte d'Azur's top gourmet addresses. Maître Chibois serves his dazzling Provençal concoctions in the lovely dining room or at tables shaded with big white parasols on the terrace overlooking the olive grove. There is a weekday lunch *menu* at 240 francs, otherwise at 490 and 560 francs. The restaurant has two Michelin stars.

Amphitryon (04 93 36 58 73, at 16 boulevard Victor-Hugo, at the bottom of Cours Honoré-Cresp. Here you can feast on duck, wild mushroom ravioli, *foie gras*, fisherman's stew with red wine, and hot apple tart loaded with cinnamon and nuts. *Menus* start at 122 francs. There is an excellent, reasonably priced selection of wines. **Maître Boscq** (04 93 36 45 76, at 13 rue de la Fontette, in the heart of La Vieille Ville, features Grasse specialties such as garlic soup, snails with basil sauce, and *fassum grassois*

the largest gorge in Europe, 21 km (13 miles) long, with widths varying from 200 to 1,500 m (650 to 5,000 ft) and depths from 250 to 700 m (800 to 2,500 ft) cut by the green waters of the Verdon River into the white limestone plateau of Haute-Provence. Remarkably, this vast natural wonder was unknown to the world until the early twentieth century, when Edouard-Alfred Martel, the explorer, mountain climber and father of speleology in France, began surveying the gorges in 1905.

The key town for the Grand Canyon du Verdon is **Castellane**, 63 km (40 miles) north of Grasse on the Route Napoléon, N85. It sits on the north bank of the Verdon River a few miles east of the start of the Grand Canyon du Verdon.

Views of the village of Aiguines in the Grand Canyon du Verdon.

General Information

Stop at the **Tourist Office (** 04 92 83 61 14, on Rue Nationale in downtown Castellane, and they will provide all the information you need on hotels, camping grounds and sports facilities, and detailed maps for hikers indicating emergency phones and shelters on the trails through the canyon.

Boats and canoes can be rented at Pont du Galetas at the west end of the canyon where the Verdon River empties into big Lac de Sainte-Croix. For **river rafting**, contact Verdon Animation Nature. They have offices at La Palud-sur-Verdon **(** 04 92 77 30 15 and in Moustiers **(** 04 92 74 66 94. A number of stables in the area offer **horseback tours**. Information on all sports in the area is provided by the **Comité Départemental du Tourisme des Alpes-de-Haute-Provence (** 04 92 31 57 29 FAX 04 92 32 24 94 E-MAIL CDTL04@wanadoo.fr WEB SITE www.alpes-haute-provence.com, 19 rue du Docteur-Honorat, BP 170, 04005 Digne-les-Bains.

In the summer, the Castellane Tourist Office runs a shuttle bus two or three times as a day to the Grand Canyon, dropping people off at the start of the various hiking trails and picking them up later in the day. On Tuesdays, there is a guided tour (in French) that makes a circuit of the Grand Canyon and gives the customers two hours in Moustiers-Sainte-Marie for lunch and visiting the pottery studios.

You can make a day trip from the coast (see HOW TO GET THERE, below), but it is a very long day. I strongly recommend that you spend a night up here to give yourself enough time to really experience the area.

What to See and Do

There are two roads for touring the Grand Canyon by car, the **Corniche Sublime** along the southern rim and **Route des Crêtes** (Ridge Road) along the northern rim. Both sides are very dramatic, with perspectives that take your breath away. But if you only have the time see one side, I recommend the Corniche Sublime, because the best hotels and restaurants are on that side. From Castellane take D952 for 12 km (seven and a half miles) to Pont-de-Soleils and turn left onto D955 south, which will lead you around to D71, which is the Corniche Sublime. The most vertiginous points along this drive are the **Balcons de la Mescla**, a sheer drop 230 m (750 ft) to the Mescla, where the raging waters of the Artuby meet the equally fast-flowing waters of the Verdon. Further along is the **Falaise des Cavaliers** (the Knights' Cliff), the start of a three kilometers (two miles) stretch of gorge with depths ranging from 250 to 400 m (800 to 1,300 ft). For motorists, walkers and bikers, the *corniches* along the rim of the cliffs offer sensational views, while hikers, horseback riders, and whitewater rafters can enjoy their sports thousands of feet below. Hiking trails are well-marked,

but very rugged, and only experienced hikers with good boots and emergency supplies should consider it. At the western end of the Grand Canyon, is the large **Lac de Sainte-Croix**, an artificial lake covering 2,500 hectares (6,000 acres), where swimming and sailing are popular.

Where to Stay and Eat

My favorite place in this area is unquestionably the **Château de Trigance***** **(** 04 94 76 91 18 FAX 04 94 85 68 99 E-MAIL trigance@relaischateaux.fr WEB SITE www.relaischateaux.fr/trigance, in Trigance, an eleventh-century castle with round towers and crenellated battlements on a hill above its tiny village, eight kilometers (five miles) south of the Grand Canyon. It has been beautifully converted into 10-room Relais & Châteaux hotel and restaurant where you can enjoy tranquillity and dine like a lord on fine Provençal cooking in its vaulted stone dining hall decorated with medieval

pennants and armor. Rooms are 600 to 900 francs. *Demi-pension* (breakfast and one meal are included in the price of the room) is 580 to 730 francs per person. The Trigance is open from late March to late November.

Le Vieil Amandier** (04 94 76 92 92 FAX 04 94 85 68 65, also in Trigance, is a pleasant 12-room Logis de France inn down the hill from the château and half the price. It is open from the beginning of April to the beginning of November. The **Hôtel-Restaurant du Grand Canyon**** (04 94 76 91 31 FAX 04 94 76 92 29, is at the Falaises des Cavaliers in Aiguines, 39 km (24 miles) west of Castellane on D71. This modern hotel is the only one directly on the Grand Canyon. It is built at the top of the cliffs 275 m (900 ft) up with a dining terrace extending out over the edge — a sensational place to have lunch, at moderate prices. It has 16 moderately priced rooms, and there are footpaths into the canyon, hang-gliding, rock-climbing, horseback riding, canoeing, and rafting nearby. Open from the beginning of May to mid-October. A Logis de France member.

Camping

The area around the Grand Canyon du Verdon and the Lac de Sainte-Croix is a magnet for campers. Castellane has 14 camping grounds with 1,571 individual places, La Palud-sur-Verdon on the north side of the Canyon has seven grounds with 82 places, and there are numerous others. The best bet is to inquire at the Tourist office in Castellane.

How to Get There

Castellane can be reached by bus daily from the *gare routières* in Nice, Cagnes-sur-Mer, or

Moustiers-Sainte-Marie at the western end of the Grand Canyon du Verdon, one of France's most creative centers for ceramics.

The Côte d'Azur

Grasse by the **VFD** bus company. For informa tion call VFD in Grenoble (04 76 47 77 77 or check with the Tourist Offices in any of those towns. **Santa Azur** also offers day trips by bus from Nice (04 93 85 46 81.

If you are driving, the best way to get to the Grand Canyon du Verdon from the coast is on N85, the **Route Napoléon**. This is the route, a shepherd's path in his day, that the fallen Emperor took with his little column of supporters after landing at Golfe-Juan on March 1, 1815. It is marked with plaques in the shape of an eagle, a reference to Napoléon's boast, "The eagle will fly from bell tower to bell tower to the towers of the Notre-Dame de Paris." The route was inaugurated in 1932, and it starts at the gravestone-like monument in Golfe-Juan where he landed, follows the N7 to Cannes, skirts the city (too many royalists), and heads north to Mougins and Grasse on N85. North of Grasse, Napoléon made his way through barren, rocky terrain into the mountains. The route, now a well-surfaced secondary highway, winds up through appropriately ominous countryside, with the Alpes-de-Haute-Provence in the distance. The Route Napoléon continues all the way up to Grenoble in the Alps, but for our purpose, we only go as far as Castellane, the eastern gateway to the Grand Canyon.

MOUSTIERS-SAINTE-MARIE

At the western end of the canyon is one of Europe's most renowned ceramics centers, Moustiers-Sainte-Marie, an attractive village in a craggy mountain setting with a waterfall pouring down from the rocks above it, and a long iron chain with a star in the middle strung between two peaks above the town. A knight from the area taken prisoner during the Crusades swore to put the chain there if he ever saw Moustiers again, and this is the fulfillment of his vow. The town became an important ceramics center in the seventeenth century thanks to a secret glaze given to it by a monk from Faenza in Italy, from which came the word *faïence*, fine glazed earthenware with colorful designs. The **Musée de la Faïence** has a large selection of the white tableware with delicate blue or yellow decorations that made Moustiers famous.

This is a very creative little town, and a number of workshops sell their handmade ceramics. If you are thinking of buying, be sure the piece has the label of the Moustiers-Sainte-Marie artisans association stamped on it. **J&V Fine** (04 92 74 61 96, on Place de l'Église, the Fine family's workshop, is noted for its classical and original designs, with everything made and decorated by hand (closed January and February). Other outstanding *ateliers de faïence* are **Lallier** (04 92 74 66 41, in the village, and **Soleil** (04 92 74 63 05, on

Chemin Marcel Provence. There are more than a dozen workshops in Moustiers, and watching the potters at work is a delightful experience, whether you decide to buy something or not.

The **Tourist Office** (04 92 74 67 84 WEB SITE www.ville-moustiers-sainte-marie.fr/is in the town hall, the Mairie.

Where to Stay and Eat

Bastide de Moustiers**** (04 92 70 47 47 FAX 04 92 70 47 48 E-MAIL bastide@i2m.fr WEB SITE www .bastide-moustiers.i2m.fr, is a big seventeenth-century stone house with a sun-bleached red tile roof on a four-hectare (10 acre) spread. In a splendid country setting protected by a sturdy rock ridge just south of town, it has flower, vegetable, and medicinal herb gardens and a heated outdoor swimming pool. Combining the latest in creature comforts with real old-time charm, the 11 rooms and one suite are all individually decorated in refined Provençal style and furnished in antiques, reflecting the individual taste of the owner, master chef Alain Ducasse. The rooms are expensive — 1,300 to 1,700 francs in high season (May through September), 200 francs less the rest of the year. The superb restaurant offers a *menu* of the day featuring vegetables fresh from the Bastide's gardens, foodstuffs from the local area, and wines from Alain Ducasse's personal stock. Crispy green salads right from the garden, spit-roasted haunch of rabbit from the farm next door, grilled pigeon from the Alpes-de-Haute-Provence, Sisteron lamb roasted in the big fireplace, cheeses from the nearby Valensole Plateau — these are the kinds of food featured here. Set *menus*, which are all that are offered (no à la carte) run 215 francs for lunch, 285 francs for dinner. The hotel is open all year, the restaurant from the first week of March to the first week of January; it is a Relais & Châteaux member.

Near the Bastide de Moustiers, in the same open countryside with a fine view of the village and its two craggy hills, is **La Ferme Rose**** (04 92 74 69 47 FAX 04 92 74 60 76, a delightful seven-room inn. Owner Kako Vagh has decorated it in a highly personal style, mingling furniture and objects from the 1950s with old paintings, *faïence* from Moustiers, and a marble-topped bar from a grand old brasserie in Marseille. The rooms are bright and airy, priced from 390 to 450 francs. Kako will arrange boating trips in the gorges of the Verdon and on the Lac de Sainte-Croix. There is no restaurant, but a big breakfast is served (48 francs), and brunch on demand.

Two comfortable, moderately priced inns are the 22-room **Colombier**** (04 92 74 66 02 FAX 04 92 77 66 70 WEB SITE www.le-colombier.com, on Route de Castellane just outside town, which has no restaurant and is open from mid-February to mid-December, and the 16-room **Bonne**

Auberge** ℂ 04 92 74 66 18 FAX 04 92 74 65 11, in town, which has a restaurant and is open from mid-February to mid-November and during the Christmas–New Years vacation period.

For elegant dining in the Village, **Les Santons** ℂ 04 92 74 66 48, on Place de l'Église, is a top gourmet restaurant with specialties — fresh noodles with foie gras and truffles, turbot with artichokes, and roast pigeon casserole with sausage — created by chef André Abert, a native of the area, whose delicate touch has earned him one Michelin star. This is a cozy place with a vine-covered dining terrace with a fine view of the valley, very expensive, but very popular, so be sure to make reservations.

Camping

There are eight camping grounds in Moustiers with a total of 762 places. For information, contact the Tourist Office.

How to Get There

There is regular bus service between Castellane and Moustiers only one day a week, on Saturday. You really need a car up here.

CANNES TO FRÉJUS

From Cannes to Fréjus, there are 42 km (28 miles) of remarkably varied coast line. The drive starts with a grand sweep of sandy beach as you head west from Cannes on N98 — the **Plages du Midi**, the **Plages de la Bocca**, and the beach of **La Napoule** dominated by a bizarre gothic castle built in the 1920s by Henry Clews, a rich American

eccentric and self-styled sculptor, overlooking the gentle curve of the Gulf of Napoule. Then you arrive at the **Massif de l'Esterel**, a craggy range of rust-red volcanic rock 19 km (12 miles) long by 11 km (seven miles) wide that looms to the west of La Napoule, and here starts a lovely, winding drive along tiny turquoise bays niched into sheer-cliffed inlets where the blue of the sea contrasts boldly with the red of the rock.

At the resort town of **Le Trayas** eight kilometers (five miles) west of La Napoule, you enter the **Var**, the western part of the Côte d'Azur. Continuing along the Esterel Corniche (N98), the lofty observation points at **Pic de Cap Roux** (452 m or 1,484 ft) at Le Trayas and the **Sémaphore du Dramont**, the lighthouse near Agay, offer grand panoramas of the sea and the mountains. The beach towns of **Miramar**, **Anthéor**, **Agay** and others lie along this road, and in summer, the traffic can be murder. It is 22 km (14 miles) from Le Trayas to Fréjus.

FRÉJUS AND SAINT-RAPHAËL

The name Fréjus is derived from "Forum Julii," "The Forum of Julius." It was founded as a naval port by Julius Caesar in 49 BC and became an important base under his nephew Octavius. The light, fast galleys that carried the day against Antony and Cleopatra at Actium in 31 BC were built here. During the first and second centuries AD the town boomed and is believed to have reached a population of 40,000, about the same as today. It was an active naval and commercial port with an aqueduct, baths, an arena, and all the other accouterments of a prosperous Roman city. But in the declining years of the Empire and afterwards, the harbor was neglected, and silt from the Argens River started filling the Roman port.

Fréjus was an important early center of Christianity, and in the fourth century, became the see of a bishop. Like the other towns along this coast, Fréjus was invaded time and again by Saracen pirates, who reduced it to rubble in the tenth century. In the twentieth century, the development of the Fréjus Plage and neighboring Saint-Raphaël beach resorts have brought the area back to prosperity as a vacation spot for the French middle classes. But the area has not abandoned its military roots. Fréjus is the home of the French Navy's largest air base.

Fréjus is one of the larger towns of the Var with 41,500 inhabitants, and urban sprawl has linked it with Saint-Raphaël, a town of 26,500 to the east, a key place for rail and bus connections (see HOW TO GET THERE, below).

A shepherd moving his sheep to pasture in the Alpes-de-Haute-Provence.

GENERAL INFORMATION

The **Tourist Office** in Fréjus is near the cathedral at 325 rue Jean-Jaurès (04 94 51 83 83. Saint-Raphaël has its own Tourist Office (04 94 19 52 52 by the train station at Place de la Gare. For information about train schedules, contact the Gare SNCF station (08 36 35 35 35 in Saint-Raphaël. For bus information, get in touch with **Sodétrav** (04 94 95 24 82 at the Gare Routière bus station, Square Docteur-Régis, Saint-Raphaël, just up the street from the train station. There are frequent trains and buses between downtown Fréjus and downtown Saint-Raphaël, a distance of three kilometers (two miles).

WHAT TO SEE AND DO

While not nearly as impressive or well-preserved as the Roman ruins of Cimiez and certainly not those of Nîmes or Arles, **La Ville Romaine** (The Roman City) merits a visit. The **arena**, some of whose walls and vaulted passageways remain, seated 10,000 and is now used for occasional bullfights and rock concerts. There are bases of stone walls that outline the **Roman port**, now filled in and grassed over. Adjoining the Roman City to the south is the **Quartier Episcopal**, where the **cathedral** has a late fourth- or early fifth-century octagonal **baptistery** that is one of the oldest Christian structures in France. In the cathedral, don't miss the *Retable de Sainte-Marguerite*, a mid-fifteenth-century altarpiece painted on wood by School of Nice artist Jacques Durandi. There is also a handsome two-story cloister from the thirteenth century to the side of the cathedral, and upstairs is the interesting **Archaeological Museum**, with a perfectly preserved Roman mosaic tile floor, a double-faced marble bust of Hermes, and other statuettes in marble and bronze that were unearthed at Forum Julii.

WHERE TO STAY AND EAT

A peaceful hotel near the Ville Romaine and the Quartier Episcopal is **L'Aréna***** (04 94 17 09 40 FAX 04 94 52 01 52 E-MAIL info@arena-hotel.com WEB SITE www.arena-hotel.com, at 139 rue du Général-de-Gaulle, a red-ochre manor with 22 bright, very comfortable rooms in Provençal decor overlooking the garden and the pool, with rates in the moderate range. It has one of the area's best restaurants, with a gastronomic repertoire that changes according to the season, with fresh seafood and Provençal market *menus* always featured, at very fair prices. The outdoor dining terrace in the flowery garden near the pool is delightful. In the Quartier Episcopal, the **Auberge du Vieux Four**** (04 94 51 56 38 FAX 04 94 53 64 50, at 57 rue

Grisolle, has eight cozy, inexpensive rooms and a rustic-style restaurant offering a full range of well-prepared classic French fare at moderate to expensive prices.

For a hotel right on the beach, take a look at the **Excelsior***** (04 94 95 02 42 FAX 04 94 95 33 82 E-MAIL info@excelsior-hotel.com, on the Promenade René-Coty in Saint-Raphaël, with its street entrance at 193 boulevard Félix-Martin. It has 36 bright rooms that open onto the main beach and the Gulf of Fréjus, with room rates on the lower end of the expensive range. For a Provençal lunch by the sea, try **L'Orangerie** (04 94 83 10 50, on Promenade René-Coty on the beach in Saint-Raphaël, where you will feast on stuffed *sardines à la Niçoise*, *bourride* (fish soup), and fillet of lamb with rosemary-flavored gnocchi, at moderately expensive prices. An inexpensive restaurant with a lively dining terrace is **L'Équipe** (04 94 51 12 62, at 10 boulevard Gallieni in Fréjus Plage. It is noted for its deserts. Try the *crème brûlée* (custard tipped with caramelized sugar), on menus everywhere, but especially delicious here.

Camping

There are 24 camping grounds with more than 7,000 places in Fréjus and the neighboring beach town of Saint-Aygulf. The largest is **Camping de Saint-Aygulf** (04 94 17 62 49 FAX 04 94 81 03 16, at 270 avenue Salvarelli in Saint-Aygulf, open April to the end of October. It has 1,100 places. **Holiday Green** (04 94 40 88 20 FAX 04 94 51 49 59, on the Route des Combattants en Afrique du Nord in Fréjus, is a plush camping ground with 690 places in wooded terrain with a huge swimming pool six kilometers (four miles) from the beach. It caters to a mainly British clientele and is open from late March to mid-October. For the summer, you must book long in advance. For a full list of camping grounds in this area, contact the Tourist Office of Fréjus or Saint-Raphaël. The Comité Départemental du Tourisme du Var publishes a free list of 250 camping grounds throughout the Var (see TOURIST INFORMATION, page 363 in TRAVELERS' TIPS).

HOW TO GET THERE

Fréjus and Saint-Raphaël are both stops on the main SNCF train line. Saint-Raphaël is the western terminus of the Métrazur line, the local train service that stops at all the towns along the coast between Saint-Raphaël and Menton. To the west of Saint-Raphaël and Fréjus, the rail line swings inland north of the Massif des Maures, and there are no train stations along the coast for the next 93 km (58 miles) until the line rejoins the coast at Toulon.

Transportation to and from the coastal towns in between Fréjus–Saint-Raphaël and Toulon is by the buses of Sodétrav (Société Départemental des Transports du Var) (04 94 12 55 00, whose headquarters is in Hyères, and whose schedules can be obtained by contacting them directly or by checking with local tourist offices or bus stations.

Coming from the east by car, take N98, the coast road, or N7 from La Napoule to Fréjus. From the west, you can take the A8 *autoroute*, the N7, or the N98.

FRÉJUS TO SAINT-TROPEZ

As you leave Fréjus, the N98 runs through a string of beach towns sprinkled along a pretty 19-km (12-mile) stretch of undulating coast, with the cork-oak- and pine-wooded hills of the **Massif des Maures** inland. It takes you to **Sainte-Maxime** on the Gulf of Saint-Tropez. This is a middle-class family resort where female sunbathers wear not only the bottoms of their bathing suits, but often the tops, while across the gulf shimmers the town that invented toplessness, Sainte-Maxime's polar opposite, Saint-Tropez.

SAINT-TROPEZ

Guy de Maupassant discovered Saint-Tropez while cruising the Côte d'Azur in 1887 in his sailboat *Bel Ami* and described it as "one of those charming and simple daughters of the sea, those nice little modest towns, bred in the water like shellfish, that produce sailors."

A few years later, painter Paul Signac fell under its spell and settled here, which influenced his friends, Matisse, Bonnard, and other artists to come (Matisse painted his seminal *Luxe, Calme et Volupté* in Saint-Tropez). By the 1930s, when Colette joined the small army of writers and artists in residence, Saint-Tropez had become "Montparnasse on the Sea."

In 1955, Brigitte Bardot and Roger Vadim blew the town's mildly bohemian image wide open with their film *Et Dieu créa la femme* (*And God Created Woman*), and Saint-Tropez became France's epitome of fashionable sun-baked sex. "Saint-Trop" introduced the Bikini in the 1950s and the first topless sunbathing in public at Tahiti Beach 20 years later. For those seeking action, there's still more of that here in the summer than anywhere else on the coast, except perhaps Juan-les-Pins, but at a level of chic incomparably higher. Insufferable or amusing? That's for you to decide. Saint-Tropez is the acid test.

After the throngs go back to Paris and Frankfurt and Brussels and Tokyo and Los Angeles at the end of the summer, Saint-Tropez becomes the peaceful, utterly charming little town that the native *Tropépeziens* and *Tropépeziennes* love, and they settle into a quiet Provençal life until the next wave hits the shore.

Saint-Tropez is the name of a peninsula as well as the famous port town, and we will be exploring this land of vineyards and quaint villages too. But first, we will plunge into the belly of the beast.

It is reached by Route D98, a five-kilometer-long (three-mile) branch of the coastal road N98 that dead ends at the port of Saint-Tropez.

BACKGROUND

Athenopolis to the Greeks, Heraclea to the Romans, Saint-Tropez takes its name from Torpes, a Christian martyr whose body floated in on a boat. According to legend, Torpes was a Roman centurion during the reign of Nero who declared his

Christianity and was beheaded. The headless body was set adrift from Pisa in a boat with a cock and a dog put there to devour it, but out of respect for the holy martyr, they kept their appetites in check. The saint's body was preserved by the locals but disappeared during the Saracen raids in the eighth century.

The port of Saint-Tropez prospered under the Counts of Provence, but its wealth and isolated position made it a tempting target for pirates and the navies of England and Spain, and for centuries the people of Saint-Tropez resisted one raid after another.

Admiral Pierre-André de Suffren, known as the Bailli (Bailiff), was Saint-Tropez's eighteenth-century hero. He fought the English in the Indian Ocean and in the Caribbean during the American

Tahiti Beach, in Saint Tropez, still swinging after all these years.

Revolution, and his image in bronze surveys the port. In August 1944, the Germans blew up most of the buildings on the port side of Saint-Tropez before surrendering to the invading Allies. The charming pink and ochre houses that now line the quays are mostly reproductions.

GENERAL INFORMATION

Saint-Tropez's main **Tourist Office** (04 94 97 45 21 E-MAIL tourisme@nova.fr WEB SITE www.nova .fr/saint-tropez, on the port at Quai Jean-Jaurès, is open all year. The highly professional staff can help with any inquiries. They have a reservation service that will book rooms for you in hotels and advise you about residences with furnished rooms and apartments (*meublés*), which can cost much less than hotels for longer stays.

The **Gare Routière** (bus station) is on the Avenue du Général-de-Gaulle at the entrance to town. All **bus service** to Saint-Tropez is by **Sodétrav** (04 94 12 55 00 (main number) or 04 94 97 88 51 (local number, in season).

Car rental agencies include **Avis** (04 94 97 03 10, Avenue du 8 Mai 1945; **Europcar** (04 94 97 15 41, Résidence du Port; **Hertz** (04 94 55 83 00, Rue de la Poste; **Sixt** (04 94 55 40 40, Résidence du Port.

With the volume of traffic in the summer, bikes or motor scooters make a lot of sense. They can be rented at: **Établissements Mas-Louis** (04 94 97 00 60, at 5 rue Joseph-Quaranta, down from the Place des Lices; **Sixt** (04 94 55 40 40, Résidence du Port; and **Yamaha Espace 83** (04 94 55 80 00, at 2 avenue du Général-Leclerc.

The **taxi stand** (04 94 97 05 27 is in front of the Annonciade Museum on the Port.

Boat services are provided by **TMR** (04 94 95 17 46, which has regular summer service between Saint-Raphaël and Saint-Tropez (50 minutes), and **MMG** (04 94 96 51 00, which has regular summer service between Sainte-Maxime and Saint-Tropez (20 minutes). **TMG Bateaux Verts** (04 94 54 14 14 charters boats for excursions, parties, and fishing trips.

In case of a medical emergency, the **Saint-Tropez Hospital** (04 94 79 47 30 or 04 94 97 65 65 is located on Avenue Foch.

FESTIVALS AND EVENTS

There are two local celebrations known as *bravades* every year, and the people here take them very much to heart. The **Bravade de Saint-Torpes** dates from the Middle Ages and is religious in origin, commemorating the arrival of the body of Saint Torpes in the boat. It takes place on May 16, 17 and 18, and the whole town celebrates it with parades and religious ceremonies. The **Bravade**

The port of Saint-Tropez is the prettiest on the Côte d'Azur.

des Espagnols on June 15 honors a heroic defense the people of Saint-Tropez put up against the Spanish fleet in 1637, with parades in fanciful red, white, and blue sailors' uniforms. There is much firing of noisy muskets at both celebrations.

The last event of the season is the **Nioulargue**, a sailing event that started as a friendly challenge between two skippers in 1981 and now attracts hundreds of classic and modern racing vessels of all sizes from all over the world, including a number of America's Cup boats and their famous captains. It is usually held the last week of September or the first week of October.

WHAT TO SEE AND DO

The Port

The port of Saint-Tropez is the prettiest on the Côte d'Azur and in summer the liveliest. The harbor is packed with elephantine motor yachts moored with their sterns to the dock. In the evening, onlookers stand and gawk at the wealthy owners and their guests taking cocktails on the deck and supping in their open cabins, much like the courtiers at Versailles did when Louis XIV dined on a platform to allow his lessers to watch. As at Cannes during the film festival, all eyes are constantly darting around for celebrities (who never show up). In the past few years, Saint-Tropez has financed a major redevelopment of the port, making it one of the most technically up-to-date yacht harbors in the Mediterranean. It has also spruced up the waterfront for strollers and café-goers. It is animated in the morning, swarming in the late afternoon and evening, and when the discos get going, rocking until the wee hours.

For the best people-watching in this part of town go to the **Café de Paris** near the statue of the Bailli de Suffren. The century-old **Sénéquier** remains popular too, with its three-legged red tables and excellent *tarte tropézienne*, a tart filled with confectioners cream. Unlike Nice, Cannes and the other ports along the Côte d'Azur, which face south and east and get their best sun in the morning, the port of Saint-Tropez is on a hook of land that faces north and west and gets its most direct sun in the late afternoon.

The extraordinary quality of Saint-Tropez's light has attracted many painters, as you will see at the **Musée de l'Annonciade** on the west side of the port, a sixteenth-century chapel converted into a museum to house the art collection of industrialist Georges Grammont. Mainly Pointilist, Nabi and Fauve, the collection includes Matisse's *La Gitane*, Bonnard's *Nue Devant la Cheminée*, and works by Seurat, Vuillard, Dufy, Vlaminck, Derain, Braque, Manguin, and Maillol, and there are a number of paintings of Saint-Tropez. Two evocative scenes of the town are Signac's rosy pointillist

Vue de Saint-Tropez Coucher du Soleil au Bois de Pins of 1896 and Charles Camoin's 1939 *Place des Lices*, with village men playing *pétanque* under the plane trees on the sun-dappled town square. The museum is open from 10 AM to noon and 3 PM to 7 PM from June through September, from 2 PM to 6 PM the rest of the year. It is closed Tuesdays and the month of November.

Place des Lices

At the Place des Lices, a five-minute stroll from the port up Rue Georges-Clemenceau, you'll see the sons and grandsons of Camoin's players pitching *boules* on the same spot. The tree-shaded, bare-earthed place des Lices (*lices* means lists, where

the jousts were held in the Middle Ages) is the heart of Saint-Tropez and my favorite part of the town. It is the best place to learn the rules and strategies of the Provençal bowling game of *pétanque*, as the *Tropéziens* are an amiable bunch, glad to elucidate the fine points of the game. The food market is held here on Tuesday and Saturday morning, the clothing and bric-a-brac market on Saturday.

Saint-Tropez is fine town for **shopping**, and its two supremely stylish general stores are near the Place des Lices. **Fred Prysquel** at 34 boulevard Louis-Blanc has the best in pottery, home furnishings, shoes, and men's clothing with a real flair. The impeccable **Galeries Tropéziennes** at 56 rue Gambetta has espadrilles, wicker baskets, yard goods, and everything for the house and pool. **Rondini** at 16 rue Georges-Clemenceau down the street from the Place des Lices has been making top-quality, extremely comfortable leather sandals for three generations, and at pretty **Place de la Garonne** one block away, you'll find several classy couturiers' boutiques.

Old Saint-Tropez

The **Quartier de la Ponche** is the old section of town with narrow, cobbled boutique- and restaurant-lined streets interspersed with tiny squares that wind up the hill from the port to the Citadel's park. A sixteenth-century hilltop fortress, the **Citadel** has a commanding view in all directions from the roof of its *donjon* (keep) — the port, the gulf, the Maures, the Esterel, and even the Alps after an air-clearing blast of the Mistral. Its **Musée Naval** has scale models of ships from the days of the Greeks and the Romans and celebrates the exploits of Saint-Tropez's local hero the Bailli de Suffren. There are also exhibits on the Allied landings in August 1944 at Saint-Tropez and the Côte d'Azur.

The Beaches

There are some small beaches to either side of the port, but the main beaches lie to the east. The **Plage des Salins** is three kilometers (two miles) straight east of town on the Route des Salins, and **Tabu Plage** and **Tahiti Plage**, scandalous in their day and still very sexy, are about the same distance to the southeast, reached by the Route de Tahiti. But the best beaches are along the **Plage de Pampelonne**, a five-kilometer (three-mile) sweep of fine sand that actually lies in the neighboring town of Ramatuelle. It is reached by the Route des Plages (D93). There are some 30 beach clubs here where you can rent mattresses, umbrellas and windsurfing equipment, and have lunch or refreshments at their restaurants and snack bars.

If you want to spend a day surrounded by people who look like they stepped out of the pages of *Town and Country* magazine, head for the ultra-chic **Club 55 (** 04 94 79 80 14, which started as an informal canteen for the cast and crew of *And God Created Woman* in 1955 (hence the name). It is on the Plage de Pampelonne directly to the left of the Allied Landing memorial at the foot of Boulevard Patch, the connector road from D93. Those who like vulgar displays of the flesh (and who doesn't?) should check out the **Voile Rouge (** 04 94 79 84 34, a 10-minute walk up the beach toward town. There you will find beefy guys with ponytails and bulging babes of *Penthouse* proportions undulating to loud thumping music.

The best food at the beach is at **Kaï Largo (** 04 94 79 82 14, Nioulargo Beach, Boulevard Patch, a laid-back place with a mock-colonial ambiance with big overhead fans, and cheerful waiters and waitress in whites and bare feet. It serves savory Vietnamese cuisine, mainly seafood — large shrimp with garlic, black pepper and coriander,

or *daurade* (sea bream) with sweet spices baked in a banana leaf, for example.

Topless sunbathing is the norm on these beaches. Nude sunbathing is officially prohibited, but there are isolated beaches north of the Plage des Salins and from Cap Camarat at the southern end of the Plage de Pampelonne to La Croix-Valmer where sunbathing in the altogether is legally tolerated and commonly practiced.

WHERE TO STAY

Saint-Tropez and the Saint-Tropez Peninsula have the greatest concentration of elegant small hotels in the South of France. There are 10 in the four-

star (luxury) category, with double rooms running 1,200 to 4,000 francs in season, suites up to 5,500 francs, and another 24 are three-star (very comfortable) establishments, with doubles generally in the 600 to 1,200-franc range.

The following selection is for the town of Saint-Tropez only. For accommodations in the surrounding area, consult the listings for the SAINT-TROPEZ PENINSULA (see page 165).

Very Expensive

As you drive into Saint-Tropez on D98, look on the left for the **Résidence de la Pinède****** **(** 04 94 55 91 00 FAX 04 94 97 73 64 E-MAIL pinede@webstore .fr WEB SITE www.webstore.fr/la-pinede, at Plage de la Bouillabaisse. This gorgeous 38-room, four-

OPPOSITE: Saint-Tropez has fascinating old back streets to explore. ABOVE: On Pampelonne Beach.

suite Relais & Châteaux establishment, traditional in decor, is the town's only luxury hotel right on the water, *pieds dans l'eau*, as they say. Every room has a balcony overlooking the sea. Open Easter through mid-October. **Le Byblos****** (04 94 56 68 00 FAX 04 94 56 68 01 E-MAIL saint-tropez@ byblos.com WEB SITE www.byblos .com, on Avenue Paul-Signac, is a simulated Mediterranean village built around a large pool on the hillside of the citadel with a generous view of the town and the gulf. Its 50 individually decorated rooms and 48 duplex suites are all gorgeous. Ursula Andress's favorite, room 245, has a circular Jacuzzi in the loft bedroom and a private sunning terrace (yours for 4,200 francs). Open April through mid-October. The **Bastide de Saint-Tropez****** (04 94 97 58 16 FAX 04 94 97 21 71 E-MAIL bst@wanadoo.fr WEB SITE www.bastide-saint-tropez.com, on Route des Carrels, is a refined country estate in a lovely garden setting with 18 elegant rooms and eight suites. Closed the month of January. The **Château de la Messardière******** (04 94 56 76 00 FAX 94 56 76 01 E-MAIL hotel@messardiere.com WEB SITE www .messardiere.com, on Route de Tahiti is a medieval-style nineteenth-century *château* on a hilltop between Saint-Tropez and the beaches with the most spectacular views of any hotel in the area, a large circular swimming pool, and 82 plush rooms and six suites. It is open late March to the end of October.

Expensive

Sube** (04 94 97 30 04 FAX 04 94 54 89 08 WEB SITE www.nova.fr/sube, on Quai de Suffren, has 30 bright rooms and a big ship's bar and lounge overlooking the port. It is open all year. Centrally located at the top of La Ponche facing the park of the Citadel, **Hôtel le Baron**** (04 94 97 06 57 FAX 04 94 97 58 72, 23 rue de l'Aioli, is a friendly 11-room hotel and restaurant that is open all year round.

Moderate

Two small, spotless, hostelries a short walk from the Place des Lices are **Lou Cagnard**** (04 94 97 04 24 FAX 04 94 97 09 44, on Avenue Paul-Roussel, with 19 pleasant, newly renovated rooms on a quiet garden, and **Le Colombier**** (04 94 97 05 31 FAX 04 94 97 32 57, on the Impasse des Conquettes, with 13 rooms in a town house with a flowery courtyard. Both are open all year, but no credit cards are accepted.

Inexpensive

You have come to the wrong place.

WHERE TO EAT

You will have no trouble finding good food in Saint-Tropez. At **Leï Mouscardins** (04 94 97

29 00, at the Tour du Portalet near the port owner chef Laurent Tarridec, a native of Brittany, serves up the specialties that have made him one of the grand masters of Mediterranean cuisine. His starter of light batter-fried sardines with aromatic leaves and a puree of sweet peppers, followed by a main course of *brandade de morue* (salt cod purée) with garlic oil and meat juices is an unbeatable combination, particularly when accompanied by a fine bottle of Côtes de Provence. This is a Michelin one-star restaurant, quite expensive, but for the quality of the cuisine, service and ambiance, the 260-franc lunch special, wine included, is a very good deal. It is open mid-February to mid-November and over the Christmas vacation period.

For elegant dining on the water, the Provençal-Mediterranean restaurant of **La Pinède** is tops. It also boasts one Michelin star. The **Byblos**, the **Bastide de Saint-Tropez**, and the **Château de la Messardière** all have excellent gourmet restaurants too, all serving refined Provençal cuisine. Just down the street from the Place des Lices, enterprising chef Christophe Leroy has **La Table du Marché** (04 94 97 85 20, 38 rue Clemenceau, a contemporary bistro-style restaurant that is one of the most popular in the area. Expensive, but not ruinous, if you choose carefully.

The **Café des Arts** (04 94 97 02 25, on the Place des Lices has a lively terrace, usually packed at meal time, where you dine on well-prepared, medium-priced local specialties, but the real treat is ogling your chic fellow diners and watching the *pétanque* players on the tree-shaded place. **Hôtel le Baron** has a friendly restaurant on the front porch looking up at the Citadel, also offering well-prepared, medium-priced local specialties. It is open all year. The **Auberge des Maures** (04 94 97 01 50, on rue de Boutin, a tiny alley off 43 rue Allard, has solid food at modest prices in a tree-shaded courtyard. Open April through the end of October.

NIGHTLIFE

The disco-to-be-seen-at for suave adults has long been the **Caves du Roy** (04 94 97 16 02, at the Byblos, but lately the **VIP Room** (04 94 97 14 70 has emerged as a chic alternative for a sophisticated night on the town. It is at the Résidence du Nouveau Port, to the west of the main harbor. The Beautiful People, mostly young (of course), go to dance at the **Papagayo** ("Le Gayo") (04 94 97 76 70, a Saint-Tropez institution, on Rue du 11 Novembre 1918 on the west side of the port. The music begins at 10:30 PM, the disco starts filling up around midnight, is throbbing by 2 AM, and blasts on into the wee hours, as long as the dancers keep going. On busy nights you'll need "*un look*" to get in. Study the chosen to find out what works. For men of all ages, clip-on pony tails are highly recommended. Downstairs at the **Bodega du Papagayo** there's live salsa music from 10:30 PM to about 3 AM, after which you can repair to the **Bodeggita de la Havana** next door for Cuban food, drinks and music. **L'Octave** (04 94 97 22 56, at Place de la Garonne to the east of the Port, is an attractive lounge with an eclectic range of jazz and other live music nightly.

HOW TO GET THERE

There is no train to Saint-Tropez, so if you're not driving, your choices are bus, boat, air shuttle service from Nice Airport in the summer, private helicopter or private plane, and a few flights from Switzerland and Germany in summer. All bus services from other coastal towns of the Var are provided by **Sodétrav** (04 94 12 55 00 (main number) or 04 94 97 88 51 (local number, in season). If you are arriving in the region via the Toulon-Hyères Airport, Sodétrav will take you to Saint-Tropez (see GENERAL INFORMATION, page 160).

By bus from the Nice Airport, **Beltrame** (04 94 83 87 63 has four trips a day to Saint-Raphaël, a one-hour ride, and you can take the Sodétrav bus from there to Saint-Tropez.

There is regular boat service from Sainte-Maxime and Saint-Raphaël in the summer (see GENERAL INFORMATION, page 160).

For information about Air Saint-Tropez's five shuttle flights per day from Nice in the summer, contact the local airstrip, the **Aérodrome de la Môle** (04 94 49 57 29, at La Môle, 16 km (10 miles) west of town. They can also tell you about private planes, helicopters, and scheduled flights from a few points in Switzerland and Germany in the summer.

THE SAINT-TROPEZ PENINSULA

Besides its beaches, the hilly, 20-km (12-mile) square Saint-Tropez Peninsula has magnificent umbrella pines, vineyards, several interesting old villages to explore and outstanding choices of hotels and restaurants.

GENERAL INFORMATION

The **Maison du Tourisme Golfe de Saint-Tropez Pays des Maures** (04 93 43 42 10 FAX 04 94 43 42 78 E-MAIL semgst@franceplus.com WEB SITE www .franceplus.com/golfe.de.st-tropez, is located in a little house of its own at the Carrefour de la Foux, the big intersection of the Saint-Tropez Peninsula, in Gassin, five kilometers (three miles) from the town of Saint-Tropez. This office furnishes superb travel information on the Saint-Tropez

Peninsula, the Maures hills to the northwest, and the Maures coast to the west. They will also book accommodations for you. Their **hotel reservation desk** has a separate number (04 94 43 40 70 FAX 04 94 43 42 77.

WHAT TO SEE AND DO

Port Grimaud, a mini-Venice where boats tie up in front of the houses, was built in 1968 but has aged, as architect François Spoerry intended, to look like a Mediterranean fishing village that has been there forever. It is very pleasant to stroll along the canals and stop for a *pastis* in one if the cafés. To get there from Saint-Tropez go north on D98

and N98 about seven kilometers (four and a half miles). It is nestled in the crook of the Gulf of Saint-Tropez.

A colorful old perched village on a plateau overlooking Pampelonne Beach, **Ramatuelle** was occupied by Saracen pirates in the ninth century, until they were finally dislodged by Count William I of Provence in 972. There is an important **jazz festival** (04 94 79 26 04 in the middle of July. To get here, take Route D93, the Route des Plages, south from Saint-Tropez for six kilometers (three and three quarter miles), then D61 west.

Moulins de Paillas is the peninsula's highest point. From 326 m (1,070 ft), you can see all the way from the Îles d'Hyères to the Italian Riviera a distance of more than a 160 km (100 miles). To get there from Ramatuelle, take the D89 for four kilometers (two and a half miles) to the north.

The pretty hill town of **Gassin** can be reached by driving through rolling vineyards and is two and a half kilometers (about a mile and a half) away from Moulins de Paillas on D89. A number of outstanding winemakers are here (see WINE TASTING, below).

A café on the port in Saint-Tropez.

WINE TASTING

Driving through the Saint-Tropez Peninsula, you will see vineyards practically everywhere. This is prime Côtes de Provence wine country, and you have the perfect opportunity to start learning about the region's vintages in Gassin. **Château Minuty** (04 94 56 12 09 is the most distinguished winemaker of the peninsula, and one of only 23 wine-making estates of the Côtes de Provence area to be designated a *cru classé*, an extremely prestigious rating. The Côtes de Provence area is especially noted for its delicate, dry rosés, and Château Minuty excels in them. But it also makes outstanding whites and, what is relatively rare in this area, a deep-colored, flavorful red, *Cuvée de l'Oratoire*. Château Minuty is set in a magnificent valley in the hills overlooking the Gulf of Saint-Tropez with tall plane trees, palms and rose bushes around its handsome Second Empire château. It is on the Route de Ramatuelle in Gassin. Open Monday to Friday, 9 AM to noon and 2 PM to 6:30 PM, year round.

Also on the Route de Ramatuelle is **Château Barbeyrolles** (04 94 56 33 58, a small vineyard with a 12 hectares (29 acres) of vines whose diaphanous and delicately flavorful *Pétale de Rose* ("Rose Petal") rosé, made by Régine Sumeire, one of the rare female winemakers, is highly prized by the *sommeliers* and wine connoisseurs and of the area. Château Barbeyrolles is open daily all year, from 9 AM to 7 PM from April 1 to October 1, and to 5 PM the rest of the year.

The oldest of the Saint-Tropez Peninsula's vineyards is **Domaines Bertaud-Belieu**, again on the Route de Ramatuelle (04 94 56 16 83, a 50-hectare (120-acre) spread that was owned by the Charterhouse of La Verne monastery in the Middle Ages. It produces 300,000 bottles of wine a year, rosé, white, and red. It is open daily in season, weekdays only off-season.

WHERE TO STAY

Very Expensive

La Giraglia**** (04 94 56 31 33 FAX 04 94 56 33 77 is a pretty ensemble of Provençal-style houses integrated into the "little Venice" of Port Grimaud, right on the beach with a big swimming pool looking across the bay at Saint-Tropez and 49 extremely comfortable rooms. Open late April to the end of September.

Expensive

La Ferme d'Augustin*** (04 94 55 97 00 FAX 04 94 97 40 30 E-MAIL vallet.ferme.augustin@wanadoo.fr WEB SITE www.nova.fr/augistin/index-f.htm, Plage de Tahiti, Ramatuelle, is a 46-room inn situated in a park full of flowers about 90 m (100 yards)

from Tahiti Beach with its own restaurant. It is a Relais du Silence member, open Easter to October. The **Hostellerie le Baou***** (04 94 79 20 48 FAX 04 94 79 28 36, Avenue Gustave-Etienne, Ramatuelle, sits on the edge of an this ancient perched village and has 41 tasteful rooms with balconies and terraces overlooking the sea. Open March 1 through November 15. **Les Bergerettes***** (04 94 97 40 22 FAX 04 94 97 37 55, Route des Plages, Ramatuelle, is a 29-room Provençal-style villa shaded by umbrella pines on six hectares (15 acres) of rolling woodlands overlooking vineyards and Pampelonne Beach. Open April to October. Though primarily a restaurant (see WHERE TO EAT, below), **Les Moulins** (04 94 97 17 22 FAX 04 94 97 72 70 WEB SITE www.nova.fr/christophe-leroy, a delightful country inn on the Route des Plages, Ramatuelle, rents five very comfortable bedrooms decorated in elegantly rustic Provençal style. The big old stone house sits amid kitchen gardens, grassy lawns, and tall trees, a 500-m (about 550-yard) walk from Pampelonne Beach. It is open March through mid-November and the Christmas–New Year vacation period.

Camping

There are numerous camping grounds on the Saint-Tropez Peninsula. The closest to Saint-Tropez on the Plage de Pampelonne and the most cramped for space are the 500-place **Toison d'Or** (04 94 79 83 54 and the 700-place **Kon Tiki** (04 94 55 96 96 next door, both open from Easter to the end of October. They are right on the beach and always full July and August. The campsites at the other end of Pampelonne Beach are less cramped. **Les Tournels** (04 94 55 90 90, with 900 places on a pine-covered hill on the road to the Cap Camarat lighthouse, is very pleasant and is open all year. In Gassin, **Camping Moulin de la Verdagne** (04 94 79 78 21, with 150 emplacements in the middle of vineyards, is open in season. You must reserve long in advance for July and August at any of these campsites. For a full list of camping grounds and assistance, contact the **Maison du Tourisme Golfe de Saint-Tropez Pays des Maures** (see GENERAL INFORMATION, above).

WHERE TO EAT

One of the best restaurants and perhaps the most charming of all in the area is Christophe Leroy's **Les Moulins** (see above), where you dine on iced potato soup with truffles, spit-roasted milk-fed lamb with truffle-laced potato cake, and other refined traditional French and Provençal gastronomic specialties in the big whitewashed stone-walled dining room with its cozy fireplace or

ABOVE: Along the Route Napoléon north of Grasse. BELOW: Mercantour National Park in the Maritime Alps.

outside in the delightful garden in fine weather. It is expensive. For a change of pace, try **Port Diffa** (04 94 56 29 07, for *couscous, tagine* (a spicy meat stew), and other Moroccan dishes prepared and served to perfection on a cheerful terrace overlooking the boat-filled Giscle River at Cogolin Plage on the Gulf of Saint-Tropez. It is at Les-Trois-Ponts-sur-la-Giscle on Route N98 just south of Port Grimaud, immediately to the east of the big Carrefour de la Foux traffic circle. A meal here will run you about 200 francs.

HOW TO GET THERE

Sodétrav runs the occasional local bus between the towns of the Saint-Tropez Peninsula, but to explore the area, you need a car or some other individual transport. Bikes or mopeds can be rented in Saint-Tropez (see GENERAL INFORMATION, page 160, under SAINT-TROPEZ). For reasonably presentable individuals, hitchhiking is a viable alternative.

FURTHER AFIELD

Some travelers in southern France find that what they like most about the area are the sophisticated pleasures of the Côte d'Azur. If you are one of them, you will not want to budge from the Saint-Tropez Peninsula. But for those who tire of hot sand, bare flesh and voluptuous living, or who simply want to see some other, quite different places, two refreshing jaunts to the north may be in order.

THE MASSIF DES MAURES

The Maures is a strange place, a solitary island of crystalline rock covered by pine, cork-oak, and chestnut forests in an area that is otherwise limestone covered by vineyards. Along with Corsica, Sardinia and the Balearic Islands, this range of low, rounded mountains, which runs 64 km (40 miles) long by 32 km (20 miles) wide between Fréjus and Hyères, is a remnant of a primitive land mass called Tyrrhenia that once covered practically all the western Mediterranean basin. It lies directly north of the Saint-Tropez Peninsula.

For more than two centuries, these hills were occupied by Saracen pirates. They were descendants of Moorish warriors defeated by Charles Martel at Poitiers in AD 732 who established themselves here. They used it as a land base to raid towns in Provence until Count William of Provence finally drove them out in 973.

The name Maures is not derived from Moors, however, but from the Provençal word *maouro* meaning dark, because of the dense forests that used to cover the area. The forest is not as dense as it used to be, because of fires in the late 1980s. Much of it has grown back as scrub. But there are

still plenty of cork-oaks, which are used to make corks for bottles, a technique taught to the natives by the Saracens, and the chestnuts are used to make the delicious candies known as *marrons glacés*. The foothills are covered with vineyards, and practically every village has its cooperative and estates producing wines of all levels from *vins de table* to *AOC* Côtes de Provence.

General Information

Tourist Offices with information on the Maures are in **Grimaud** (04 94 43 26 98, at 1 boulevard des Aliziers, and **La Garde-Freinet** (04 94 43 67 41, 1 place Neuve.

What to See and Do

A swing through some interesting towns in the Maures starts at Grimaud, five kilometers (three miles) north of the big traffic circle of the Carrefour de la Foux. The name Grimaud derives from Grimaldi, another branch of the enterprising Genoese family that made such a mark along this coast. This Grimaldi was a knight who came to help Count William chase out the Saracens.

Grimaud is a lively town of 3,300 that has managed to keep its medieval look. The town has good handicrafts workshops and boutiques centering around arcaded Rue des Templiers. From the impressive ruins of a castle at the top of the hill there is a grand vista of the Maures and the Gulf of Saint-Tropez. There is an outstanding Provençal gastronomic restaurant, **Les Santons** (04 94 43 21 02 (Michelin one-star, quite expensive), and a good, modestly priced café-restaurant, **Café de France** (04 94 43 20 05, with a dining terrace outside its vine-covered old house on Place Neuve. On your way to Collobrières, 20 km (12.5 miles) west of Grimaud on woodsy Route D14, keep an eye out for the sign for the **Chartreuse de la Verne** on the left six kilometers (three and three quarter miles) before you reach Collobrières. Take the narrow winding access road through the cork-oaks, pines and chestnuts to the Chartreuse (Charterhouse) de la Verne, a monastery founded in the twelfth century and expanded several times over the centuries. In the Middle Ages, it established the vineyards that now cover the Saint-Tropez Peninsula. The impressive buildings date mainly from the seventeenth and eighteenth centuries. They were abandoned during the Revolution and are in a semi-ruined state. But the Bethlehem monastic community, which moved here in 1983, is renovating them little by little. It is closed Tuesdays, October, and main religious holidays. There are splendid views of the mountains.

The pretty, shaded village of **Collobrières** is the *marron glacé* capital, and the **Confiserie Azuréenne** on Boulevard Koenig makes a delicious version of the chestnut candies and other mouth-watering treats, such as jellies made from roses, violets, rosemary, and (of course) chestnuts. There is also good local wine at the **Cave des Vigernons**, and for lunch, **La Petite Fontaine** (04 94 48 00 12 on Place de la République, the main square, serves tasty Provençal home cooking at modest prices.

From Collobrières, drive north on the wooded mountain roads through the attractive village of **Notre-Dame-des-Anges** and continue east to **La Garde-Freinet**, the Saracens' chief stronghold until Count William expelled them. The village, which lies 10 km (six miles) north of Grimaud on D558, has also kept its medieval atmosphere. It makes corks and its own brand of *marrons glacés*, Marrons de Luc. From town you can hike past chestnut trees dating back almost to the time of the Saracens to the hilltop ruins of their fortress, a climb of about half an hour. There you can see what a perfect vantage point this was to watch for ships along the coast. When the lookout spotted a prize, he would signal the pirate ships waiting in the Gulf of Saint-Tropez, and the chase was on. Looking north, you will see the wide, vineyard-covered plain of the central Var.

How to Get There

There is little public transportation the Maures. Sodétrav has a daily bus from Le Lavandou to Cogolin, Grimaud and La Garde-Freinet, but there is no bus service from Saint-Tropez. You need a car or a scooter to get around here.

THE HEART OF THE VAR

North of the Maures you descend into the flat semiarid central plain of the Var where the Aurelian Way ran in Roman times and the big east–west roads run today — the bland, but speedy A8 *autoroute* and good old Nationale 7 (N7) celebrated in Charles Trenet's song. This is the oldest wine-making region in France, dating from the arrival of the Greeks. Rosé, its specialty, is sometimes thought of as a recently created wine, but in fact the ancient Greeks and Egyptians made it, and in the fifteenth century, Good King René, who governed this area as Count of Provence, was a great fan of rosé.

General Information

Tourist Offices are located at 21 avenue Gambetta in **Les Arcs-sur-Argens** (04 94 73 37 30; at Place d'Entrechaux in **Lorgues** (04 94 73 92 37; and at 3 rue des Ormeaux in **Le Thoronet** (04 94 60 10 94.

What to See and Do

In **Les Arcs-sur-Argens**, the medieval quarter of **Le Parage** is dominated by the ruins of the castle of the Villeneuve family, with its beautifully restored **watch tower**. In the **church** is a 16-panel **altarpiece** of the Virgin and Child surrounded by Provençal saints by Ludovico Bréa, and an odd *crèche animée*, a mechanical crib, with a decor of the old village of Les Arcs. Four kilometers (two and a half miles) to the east of Les Arcs is the **Chapelle Sainte-Roseline** (Saint Roseline's Chapel), on the site of the Charterhouse of which Saint Roseline, a member of the Villeneuve family, was prioress from 1300 to 1328. The body of the saint lies in a remarkably well-preserved state in a shrine to the right of the nave. There is a handsome early baroque altarpiece and several interesting modern pieces, including a large mosaic by Chagall on the life of Saint Roseline.

The **Abbaye du Thoronet** is a Romanesque gem built in the late twelfth century on land do-

nated by Raimond Bérenger III, the Count of Barcelona and Provence. It lies near **Lorgues**, 28 km (17.5 miles) west of Les Arcs via D10 and D562. This is the oldest and smallest of the "Three Sisters of Provence," exquisite Cistercian abbeys all built within a few years of one another. The other two are Silvacane north of Aix and Sénanque near Gordes in the Lubéron (see GORDES, page 235 under THE LUBÉRON). The code of the order called for simplicity and disdain of all decoration, something the architecture certainly reflects. But the loveliness of the natural settings (an isolated niche amid wooded hills in this case) and the stone they are made of (here a slightly reddish stone from the Esterel) soften the severity of the design. Because of that and of many pleasing design details — such as the fountain in the little vaulted hexagonal pavilion in Le Thoronet's cloister — each of the three "sisters" has its own personality. Open all year.

Wine Tasting

The center of the Var is a rich wine-growing area, producing predominantly rosés. Long stigmatized as a wine that was not serious, rosé has gained respect over the past few decades as winemakers

Restaurant signs in the northern Var announce that the wild boar has arrived.

of the area worked to improve quality, and in 1977 they succeeded in earning their *Appellation d'Origine Contrôlée* (*AOC*). There are 18,000 hectares (43,000 acres) under cultivation in *AOC* Côtes de Provence-approved vines. Seventy-five percent of the production is rosé, and the dry, light rosés of the Côtes de Provence now account for 40% of France's *AOC* rosé wine. Good reds and whites are also made. Do not hesitate to give them a try.

The **Maison des Vins des Côtes de Provence** (04 94 99 50 10, a large, attractive information center on Route N7 in Les Arcs, is operated by the wine growers' association. Its wine tasting cellar is open daily from 10 AM to 7 PM, to 8 PM between July and September, and there is a Provençal restaurant where special care is given to matching the cuisine and the wine. The Maison des Vins will help you map out a wine route. It is open every day except Monday.

A magnificent wine estate that extends a big welcome to visitors is **Château de Berne** (04 94 60 48 88 WEB SITE www.chateau-berne.fr, in Lorgues. Besides the daily tours of its grand *caves*, it has a wine school, a 19-room inn that offers cultural and gastronomic tours in the region, a large swimming pool, and tennis courts. Another visitor-friendly vineyard is **Château de Saint Martin** (04 94 73 02 01, in Taradeau, between Lorgues and Les Arcs, a 100-hectare (240-acre) spread where wine has been made since the days of the Romans. It has a handsome eighteenth-century mansion with a colorful fifteenth-century cellar, offers numerous food and wine tasting sessions, and 10 times a day it puts on a sound-and-light show about the history of wine in Provence, with sound tracks in French and English.

Other outstanding winemakers with picturesque *châteaux* to visit are **Château de Selle** (04 94 99 50 30 in Taradeau (one of Domaines Ott's three vineyards in the Var, all marvelous); **Château Sainte-Roseline** (04 94 72 32 57, a medieval convent in Les Arcs; and the fourteenth-century **Domaine de Castel Roubine** (04 94 73 71 55 in Lorgues. All these vineyards make first-rate reds, whites, and rosés.

Where to Stay and Eat

Compared to the Saint-Tropez Peninsula, excellent choices in hotels and restaurants in this area are few and far between. Because most of the best restaurants in this area are in hotels, we deal with food and lodging together.

As you move in from the coast, you will notice that the cuisine changes, with more emphasis on lamb as the main course and a greater use of truffles in the cooking. That magical root may be the most unique food ingredient native to Provence, but there are no ifs or buts about where to try it: **Bruno** (04 94 73 92 19 in Lorgues, three kilometers (two miles) south of town on the road to Les Arcs. Hefty

Clément Bruno's truffle-laced cuisine has made it a prized stop on every gastronome's Southern itinerary. The pigeon pie with foie gras and truffles is much in demand. Prices are far from low here, but for quality and originality, Bruno's 300-franc fixed-price *menu* is more than fair. Bruno is very popular, so reserve. Bruno also rents four rooms in the expensive price range.

The **Logis du Guetteur***** (04 94 99 51 10 FAX 04 94 99 51 29 E-MAIL le.logis.du.guetteur@wanadoo .fr, at Place du Château in Les Arcs, is a picturesque hotel-restaurant in the fortress of the medieval village with a swimming pool and 10 very comfortable rooms at the low end of the expensive category. *Demi-pension* is required in season (that is, breakfast and one other meal included in the price of the room), 580 francs per person. The excellent restaurant features regional dishes with plenty of truffles.

Bastide du Calalou*** (04 94 70 17 91 FAX 04 94 70 50 11 E-MAIL bastide.du.calilou@wanadoo .com, in Moissac-Bellevue further north near Aups, is a delightful 35-room country resort on an old estate amid olive groves, with a swimming pool, tennis courts and fine Provençal restaurant, open mid-March to the end of October and the Christmas vacation period. *Demi-pension* is required in season, 550 francs per person on average. For nonguests who want to dine here, it has a fine Provençal restaurant with fixed-price *menus* at 135 and 250 francs. It lies only 28 km (18 miles) south of the western end of the Grand Canyon du Verdon, which makes it a perfect base for exploring that natural wonder, see GRAND CANYON DU VERDON, page 153).

Two other attractive mini-resorts in the Var countryside are the more elegant, more expensive 16-room **Hostellerie des Gorges de Pennafort***** (04 94 76 66 51 FAX 04 94 76 67 23, in Callas, north of Draguignan, which boasts one of the best restaurants in the Var (Michelin one-star), and the charming, modestly priced 24-room **L'Orée du Bois**** (04 98 11 12 40 FAX 04 98 11 12 53, in the Sainte-Roseline quarter of Le Muy, just east of Les Arcs, where doubles go for 410 francs in high season, with *demi-pension* at 375 francs.

Two moderately priced little country inns I heartily recommend for their charm and tasty regional food are **Lou Calen***** (04 94 04 60 40 FAX 04 94 04 76 64, 1 Cours Gambetta in Cotignac, which is 23 km (14 miles) west of Lorgues, and the **Auberge du Vieux Fox**** (04 94 80 71 69 FAX 04 94 80 78 38, on the Place de l'Église in Fox-Amphoux, 10 km (six miles) north of Cotignac.

CAMPING

On the outskirts of Les Arcs, **Camping L'Eau Vive** (04 94 47 40 66 FAX 04 94 47 43 27 is open from March to the beginning of November, but it is near the *autoroute* and somewhat noisy. For a small quiet

site, head north to **Camping des Prés** on the Route de Tourtour at Aups (04 94 70 00 93 FAX 04 94 70 14 41. It is open all year. Also at Aups are **Camping Saint-Lazare** (04 94 70 12 86 FAX 04 94 70 01 55 and **International Camping** (04 94 70 06 80 FAX 04 94 70 10 51 on the road to Fox-Amphoux, both open from April to the end of September. For a more information on camping, contact the local Tourist Office.

How to Get There

Les Arcs is on the main SNCF line. By *TGV* (high-speed train), the trip takes about six hours from Paris with connections at Marseille or Toulon. From Saint-Raphaël or Fréjus it is a trip of half an hour. For train information in the Var call (04 94 91 50 50.

    Rapides Varois (04 94 47 05 05 has a few buses a day between Les Arcs and Lorgues and a few other towns, and there are a few other small bus lines whose schedules you can get at the Tourist Office at Les Arcs, but frankly, unless you have all kinds of time to waste, you need a car to get around here.

THE SAINT-TROPEZ PENINSULA TO TOULON

The town of La Croix-Valmer at the western edge of the Saint-Tropez Peninsula is where Emperor Constantine is said to have had his vision of the cross (*In hoc signo vinces*), and there is a stone cross commemorating the event. It is also the start of the Corniche des Maures, Route D559, which hugs the ins and outs of the seaside cliffs along a verdant stretch of coast running 20 km (12.5 miles) between La Croix-Valmer and Bormes-les-Mimosas. A new turquoise bay is revealed at every turn, and across the water sit the Îles d'Hyères. Most of the little towns along the Corniche des Maures have preserved a good deal of their natural beauty, Le Rayol on the coast, for example, and Bormes-les-Mimosas, a hill town as flowery as its name. But sadly, some have buried it in concrete. The once-charming port of Le Lavandou is an example of that.

GENERAL INFORMATION

The **Tourist Office** at Bormes-les-Mimosas (04 94 71 15 17 is at Place Gambetta. At Le Lavandou (04 94 71 00 61, it is at Quai Gabriel Péri.

WHAT TO SEE AND DO

At Le Rayol in the middle of the *corniche*, the **Domaine du Rayol** (04 94 05 32 50 is a *belle époque* estate by the sea that had fallen into ruin, but to conserve its rich plantings was taken over by the Conservatoire du Littoral in 1989 to be turned into a botanical garden. It is still partly abandoned,

which adds to its poetry. There are tours seven times a day from July to September and less often the rest of the year.

WINE TASTING

La Londe-les-Maures, between Bormes-les-Mimosas and Hyères, has only one distinction, but what a delightful distinction to have: it makes some of the best Côtes de Provence wines. Three of the top châteaux are **Domaine du Galoupet** (04 94 66 40 07, **Domaine Saint-André-de-Figuière** (04 94 66 92 10, and **Clos Mireille** (04 94 66 80 26, one of Domaines Ott's superlative vineyards. You can visit their *caves* daily except Sunday.

WHERE TO STAY

Les Roches**** (04 94 71 05 07 FAX 04 94 71 08 40 E-MAIL lesroches@europost.org, at 1 avenue des Trois-Dauphins in Aiguebelle, four and a half kilometers (three miles) east of Le Lavandou, has everything a seaside luxury hotel should have — a pool and private beach, gardens, 40 deluxe rooms with big terraces with view of the sea and the Îles d'Hyères, and a fine gourmet restaurant. It is very expensive, a Relais & Châteaux member, and open Easter to mid-October. In the moderate price category, the **Palmiers***** (04 94 64 81 94 FAX 04 94 64 93 61 E-MAIL les.palmiers@wanadoo.fr is a quiet

OPPOSITE: Porquerolles, the main island of the Îles de Hyères TOP. The ferry between the Giens Peninsula and the Îles de Hyères BOTTOM. The harbor of Porquerolles seen from Fort Sainte-Agathe ABOVE.

country hotel a five-minute walk from the sea with 21 pleasant rooms; *demi-pension* is required in season, open January 1 to November 15. It is on Chemin du Petit Fort in Cabasson, eight kilometers (five miles) west of Le Lavandou on Cap de Brégançon. The **Paradis**** (04 94 01 32 62 FAX 04 94 01 32 60 is an unassuming paradise in a big, flower-filled hillside garden with 20 neat, cheerful, inexpensive rooms and sea views. It is on Mont-des-Roses in Bormes-les-Mimosas. Open April through the end of September.

Camping

There's only one camping grounds right on the beach, **Camping du Domaine de la Favière** (04 94 71 03 12 FAX 04 94 15 18 67, at the Plage de la Favière in Bormes-les-Mimosas, two kilometers (one mile) west of Le Lavandou on Route D559. It has 1,200 places on 25 hectares (60 acres) of pine groves on a fine sand beach. To be sure of getting a place in the summer, you should book a good

six months in advance. Open mid-March to the end of October. **Camping Manjastre** (04 94 71 03 28 FAX 04 94 71 63 62, Route de Cogolin (N98), Bormes-les-Mimosas, and the following camping grounds in towns along the Maures coast are less than half a mile from the beach: **Parc-Camping de Pramousquier** (04 94 05 83 95 FAX 04 94 05 75 04 in Pramousquier, eight kilometers (five miles) east of Le Lavandou, and two sites in Cavalaire-sur-Mer — **Camping de la Baie** (04 94 64 08 15 FAX 04 94 64 66 10, on Boulevard Pasteur, and **Camping la Pinède** (04 94 94 11 14 FAX 04 94 64 19 25, on Chemin des Mannes. They are open from March to mid or late October. Reserve as early as possible for midsummer.

WHERE TO EAT

In Bormes-les-Mimosas, at the **Tonnelle des Délices** (04 94 71 34 84, Alain Gigant carries on the tradition of his mentor Guy Gedda, the recently

Ages, the town moved up onto Castéou hill for the protection of the castle built there by the Lords of Fos. Hyères is the ancestor of all modern Côte d'Azur resorts. It was the first town the upper-class English started coming to in Mediterranean France, as early as the late eighteenth century. With nineteenth-century regulars like Queen Victoria and Robert Louis Stevenson, it became the place to be in the winter until the center of luxury tourism shifted to Nice, Cannes, and Monte-Carlo at the end of the century. Today Hyères is the center of a prosperous fruit, vegetable, and wine growing area.

GENERAL INFORMATION

The **Tourist Office (** 04 94 65 18 55 is at Rotonde Jean-Salusse, Avenue de Belgique, in modern Hyères just below the old city.

Toulon-Hyères Airport (04 94 00 83 83, the main airport for this part of the coast is in Hyères.

The **SNCF (** 08 36 35 35 35 has train service to Toulon and points west; there is no train service east from Hyères. **Sodétrav Bus Line (** 04 94 12 55 00 is at Place Joffre.

Ferries leave from **Hyères-Plage** (the Port of Hyères) and the port of **La Tour Fondue** on the Giens Peninsula, the main ports for access to the Îles d'Hyères. See HOW TO GET THERE, page 178, under ÎLES D'HYÈRES.

WHAT TO SEE AND DO

Place Massillon is the heart of **La Vieille Ville**, the medieval part of town, and a lively market is held there daily. The ruins of the twelfth-century **Tour Saint-Blaise** can be seen in the park up the hill. Nearby in the park is a showplace of modern architecture, the austere **Villa de Noailles**, also known as the Château Saint-Bernard, built by Robert Mallet-Stevens in 1924 for the patron of Surrealist artists, Charles de Noailles. The villa has been renovated by the city and is used as an exhibition center. It has grand panoramas of the sea and the islands. South of La Vieille Ville are the **Jardins Olbius-Riquier**, one of the finest gardens on the Côte d'Azur, six and a half hectares (16 acres) planted with many species of palms, cacti and other exotic plants, with a pond for aquatic birds.

The flat, narrow **Giens Peninsula** extends seven kilometers (four miles) south of the **Toulon-Hyères Airport**. From ancient times, sea salt was harvested in salt pans here, but that activity was recently abandoned. There are good sandy beaches along the east coast of the peninsula, leading to the cute little hill town of **Giens** at the tip. This hill was an island as recently as Roman

retired "the Pope of Provençale Cuisine," featuring savory specialties of the Midi at moderate to expensive prices. It is at Place Gambetta.

HOW TO GET THERE

There are no trains. All these towns are serviced by the buses of Sodétrav that run between Toulon and Saint-Raphaël. For information call **Sodétrav (** 04 94 12 55 00 in Hyères. By car, the towns are all on Route D559.

HYÈRES

Hyères is a pleasant little city of 48,000 on a well-sheltered slope overlooking the sea with lots of flowers and palm trees. It is one if the oldest settlements on the coast. It started as a trading post called Olbia set up by the Greeks from Marseille on the shore at Almanarre, which later became the Roman port of Pomponiana. In the Middle

Plage Notre-Dame, Porquerolles's largest beach.

times, and like the Îles d'Hyères, is geologically part of the Massif des Maures. At the end of the road is **La Tour Fondue**, where ferries leave for Porquerolles.

WHERE TO STAY AND EAT

The best hotel is in Hyères proper is the **Mercure***** (04 94 65 03 04 FAX 04 94 35 58 20, at 19 avenue Thomas, a few blocks south of the center of town. This is a friendly, attractive modern hotel with 84 spacious, well-appointed rooms, palm trees, a grassy lawn, a swimming pool, and a grill. Room and food prices are moderate. For more ambitious eating, try the **Jardins de Bacchus** (04 94 65 77 63, nearby at 32 avenue Gambetta, or **La Colombe** (04 94 65 02 15, two and a half kilometers (about a mile and a half) west of town on N98 (Ancienne Route de Toulon), both serving well-tempered Provençal fare at moderate prices.

In the tiny village of Giens at the tip of the peninsula, the hotel of choice is **Le Provençal** (04 94 58 20 09 FAX 04 94 58 95 44 E-MAIL Hotel .Residence.le.Provencal@wanadoo.fr, a hostelry of great charm on a hilltop overlooking the sea and the island of Porquerolles. Most of the 41 comfortable rooms have a balcony with the great view, as does the restaurant's dining terrace. The hotel has a luxuriant two-hectare (five-acre) private park with big umbrella pines, flowering bushes, flower gardens, a tennis court, and at the seaside a long saltwater pool. In the summer, there are barbecues in the park. The restaurant serves savory Provençal cuisine, and the dessert buffet offers an amazing variety of mouth-watering treats. Room prices vary according to the view. The top price for a double room with a sea view in season (July and August) is 680 francs. Rooms fronting on the village are much less expensive, as are all rooms off season. Restaurant prices are moderate. Open April 1 to the end of October. It is a Best Western member.

Camping

There are more than 30 camping grounds in Hyères and the Giens Peninsula. Three sites close to the beach are **Domaine du Ceinturon** (04 94 66 32 65, at the Plage d'Ayguade near the airport, and **Clair de Lune** (04 94 58 20 19 and **La Réserve** (04 94 58 90 16, on the beach at La Madrague in Giens. For a complete list, contact the Hyères Tourist Office (see GENERAL INFORMATION, above).

HOW TO GET THERE

There are 12 flights a day from Paris to Toulon-Hyères Airport on TAT and AOM, and numerous connections to other cities in France and Europe, including Amsterdam, through the air hub of Clermont-Ferrand. There are nine train connec-

tions a day from Paris to the Gare SNCF in Hyères, changing trains at either Marseille or Toulon, a trip of six to seven hours depending on the connection. By bus, Phocéens Cars connects Hyères with the main places of the Côte d'Azur and Provence, including Marseille, Aix, Saint-Tropez, Saint-Raphaël, Nice, etc., and Sodétrav links it with all the stops along the coast between Toulon and Saint-Raphaël. By private car, there are numerous routes from the east, west and north.

THE ÎLES D'HYÈRES

The three islands one sees from Hyères and the Corniche des Maures are the Îles d'Hyères: Port-Cros, Porquerolles, Levant. They are also known as the "Îles d'Or" — the Golden Isles — because of the glow given off in certain light by mica in their rocks. The islands have been fought over by everyone from the ancient Ligurians, Greeks and Romans, the monks from Saint-Honorat, the Saracens, French, Turks, Spanish, and the English down to the Germans and the Americans in World War II.

Much of the land on these islands is now protected, and nonresidents are not allowed to bring cars.

GENERAL INFORMATION

Porquerolles has its own **Tourist Office** (04 94 58 33 76 at the ferry dock on the island. For information about Port-Cros and Île du Levant, call or go to the Hyères Tourist Office (04 94 65 18 55, at Rotonde Jean-Salusse. They can provide information about boating and scuba diving, popular on all three islands.

For information about the nature reserve on the Île de Port-Cros, contact **Parc National de Port-Cros** (04 94 12 82 30 FAX 04 94 12 82 31 E-MAIL pnpc @wanadoo.fr WEB SITE www.parcsnationaux-fr.com, at Castel Sainte-Claire, Rue Sainte-Claire, 83400 Hyères. They will provide a list of dive clubs in and convenient to Port-Cros.

For information about **Héliopolis**, the nudist colony on the Île du Levant, contact the Tourist Office in Hyères or write to the Association des Amis de l'Île du Levant, 203bis rue Saint-Martin, 75003 Paris, for a brochure in French, English, German, and Italian.

ÎLE DE PORQUEROLLES

In 1971 the French Government, showing admirable foresight, bought most of the western Island of Porquerolles, the largest of the three, to preserve it in its natural state. Otherwise it might well be bristling with condos today. The hills are covered with pine, eucalyptus and underbrush of many shades of green, and 200 hectares (about

500 acres) of vineyards. Environmental controls on this wooded island of seven and a half by two kilometers (four and a half by one and a quarter miles) are very strict. Since forest fires are a real menace, no smoking is allowed except in the town, with fines ranging up to 5,000 francs. The town of **Porquerolles** is the very image of the small Mediterranean port, with its little **Fort Sainte-Agathe** on the hill, red-roofed houses around the boat-filled harbor, palm trees, and sunshine practically every day.

In short, Porquerolles is a paradise. But it's a paradise that is easy to get to, and in the summer, ferry-load after ferry-load of nature-lovers pour onto the island: 10,000 to 15,000 visitors per day

My first choice on the Mediterranean coast to unwind in is the **Mas du Langoustier****** (04 94 58 30 09 FAX 04 94 58 36 02 E-MAIL langoustier @compuserve.com WEB SITE www.langoustier .com, a rambling pink-ochre hotel with 48 very spacious and comfortable rooms and three suites on a remote point amid 40 hectares (96 acres) of eucalyptus, parasol pines and vineyards, over-looking a lovely cove with a tiny old fortress on a hill. It positively exudes serenity. Chef Joël Guillet gets the most savory tastes out of stuffed zucchini blossoms, gently sautéed cuttlefish served with a purée of melted peppers, pigeon roasted in eucalyptus honey and licorice, and other remarkable Provençal concoctions. The fixed-price *menu* at

join the 3,500 summer residents (the winter population is 400) to roam the countryside and seek out the dozens of little sandy beaches that ring the shore. Nevertheless, if you only have time for one boat trip on your travels through southern France, I recommend that it be to Porquerolles. Even if you only have a short time on the island, try to take the approximately two-and-a-half-kilometer (about one-and-a-half-mile) walk across the middle of the island from the port to the lighthouse (*phare*), the high point on the south side of the island, which has magnificent views in all directions. Allow about 90 minutes from the port and back.

Where to Stay and Eat

Most hotels on Porquerolles require *demi-pension* (breakfast and one meal included in the price of the room) in season. Hotel restaurants are open to the general public.

330 francs includes wine from Mas's fine vineyard. The hotel is expensive, in the 1,000 to 1,900-franc range for a double, depending on the month and type of room. The Mas is open from the beginning of May to the middle of October.

The moderately priced **Auberge des Glycines**** (04 94 58 30 36 FAX 04 94 58 35 22 is a pretty inn on Place d'Armes, Porquerolles's main square. It has 12 tastefully decorated rooms, a shaded patio, and fresh, tasty Mediterranean cuisine. Open mid-February to the end of the year.

The inexpensive **Sainte-Anne**** (04 94 58 30 04 FAX 04 94 58 32 26, also on Place d'Armes, is a friendly, old-fashioned family-style hotel with 13 rooms and a restaurant with hearty, uncomplicated fare. Open early February to mid-November.

Mas du Langoustier, a supremely restful resort hotel on Porquerolles.

ÎLE DE PORT-CROS

The whole of the middle island of Port-Cros is a nature reserve, the **Parc National de Port-Cros**, with well-marked botanical trails to follow. The reserve includes a 1,800-hectare (4,320-acre) underwater park around the island too, where divers and snorkelers armed with plastic-coated maps follow nature trials leading through a marvelous variety of sea plants and colorful fish you can swim close to, because they are used to people who come with no lethal intentions. The place to stay on Port-Cros is **Le Manoir*** (04 94 05 90 52 FAX 04 94 05 90 89, an old-fashioned

23 room **Brise Marine*** (04 94 05 91 15. There are three little camping grounds, eight guesthouses, rental apartments, bungalows, restaurants, shops, and water sports facilities. For information, see GENERAL INFORMATION, above.

HOW TO GET THERE

There is regular **ferry service** to the Îles d'Hyères from six ports along the coast: Cavalaire-sur-Mer, Le Lavandou, Port-de-Miramar, Hyères-Plage near the Toulon-Hyères Airport, La Tour Fondue at the tip of the Giens Peninsula, and Toulon.

The **TLV** line runs boats to Porquerolles from La Tour Fondue (04 94 58 21 81 every half hour in

20-room hotel that is run like a family resort from the last century. When the dinner bell rings, the meal is served, and if you miss it, you're out of luck. *Demi-pension* is required, with rates from 860 to 1,100 francs per person. Open early May to early October.

ÎLE DU LEVANT

The Île du Levant, the easternmost island, is most famous for **Héliopolis**, the original French *naturiste* (the preferred term for nudist) gathering place, founded in 1931. It is very casual, not formal enough to be called a colony. On a day trip, just go, and where you notice that people aren't wearing clothes, you can take yours off too. Cameras are strongly discouraged. There are three hotels on the island, the 18-room **Héliotel*** (04 94 05 90 63, the 15-room **Gaëtan*** (04 94 05 91 78, and the

the summer, at 80 francs for the 20 minute ride. TLV also runs boats to Port-Cros and Île du Levant from Hyères-Plage (Port d'Hyères) (04 94 57 44 07 and offers all-day trips to the three islands from both ports in the summer.

Vedettes Îles d'Or (04 94 71 01 02 has boats from Cavalaire-sur-Mer, Le Lavandou and Port-de-Miramar to Porquerolles, Levant, and Port-Cros. Three companies in Toulon offer circuits of the three islands, **SNRTM** (04 94 06 52 56, **Transmed 2000** (04 94 92 96 82, and **Bateliers de la Rade** (04 94 46 24 65.

TOULON

If there's one place that doesn't fit the Côte d'Azur's image, it's Toulon, a big navy and proletarian city singularly lacking in architectural merit. Much of its downtown was leveled by bombing in World

War II, and the city was rebuilt helter-skelter, with no thought for aesthetics. It now has more than 400,000 inhabitants in the metropolitan area, 167,000 in the inner city.

Yet for all its apparent drawbacks, this is not a place you should bypass. It has a magnificent natural harbor, the largest in the Mediterranean. It also has some very interesting museums. And who knows, after overindulging in *le luxe* in Saint-Tropez, a blast of relatively gritty reality may be refreshing.

Toulon lies 18 km (11 miles) west of Hyères.

BACKGROUND

Like the other main towns and cities of the coast, Toulon was founded by the Greeks from Marseille, who called it Telonion. Under the Romans, who called it Telo Martus, it became important because of a rich purple dye, much prized by the Roman upper classes, extracted from conches living in its waters.

Despite its superb natural harbor, Toulon didn't become a military port until the sixteenth century, after France absorbed Provence. In the seventeenth century, Louis XIV made this his main naval port and set Vauban to strengthening its defenses, which had plenty of chances to prove their worth in Louis's bellicose reign. It was during this period that slaves were used to row the infamous royal galleys. These men were common criminals, political prisoners, or prisoners of war, 54 slaves to a galley, hefting 15-m-long (50-ft) oars. People amused themselves by watching the galley slaves at the Vieille Darse (the old port). This punishment was abolished in 1748 and was replaced by the *bagne*, the equally infamous system of prison camps from which Victor Hugo had Jean Valjean escape in *Les Misérables*.

During the French Revolution, Toulon's royalists turned the city over to the British in 1793, and in the campaign to retake it, Napoléon, then a 23-year-old artillery officer, first made a name for himself. In the fall of that year, he led a six-week siege of a seemingly impregnable complex of British forts known as "Little Gibraltar" in La Seyne on the west side of the harbor and dislodged the British. In appreciation, the Convention promoted him to brigadier general.

In the nineteenth century, as the French built their colonial empire, their main naval base of Toulon grew rapidly and became almost exclusively a naval town.

In World War II, when the Germans occupied southern France, the French Navy scuttled its own fleet in Toulon harbor in December 1942, sending 60 ships to the bottom to prevent their falling into German hands. Toulon was liberated from the Nazis in August 1944.

GENERAL INFORMATION

The **Tourist Office** (04 94 18 53 00 is at 8 avenue Colbert. For flight information, call **Toulon-Hyères Airport** at (04 94 00 83 83. For information concerning the **Airport shuttle bus** call (04 94 12 55 12.

The train station, **Gare SNCF** (08 36 35 35 35, is on Avenue Toesca. The bus station is next to the train station. **Sodétrav** (04 94 12 55 00 serves Hyères and the coastal towns to the east, including Saint-Tropez, and **Phocéens Cars** at the same phone number serves Cannes and Nice; **Littoral Cars** (04 94 74 01 35 and **Société Varoise de Transports** (04 42 70 28 00 serve towns to the west; **Transvar** (04 94 28 93 28 and **Autocars Blanc** (04 94 69 08 28 serve towns to the north. For information on the web of bus lines that cover the area, contact the Tourist Office.

For 24-hour **taxi** service, call (04 94 93 51 51.

Transports Maritimes Toulonnais (TMT) (04 94 23 25 36, **Bateliers de la Rade** (04 94 46 24 65, **Vedette Alain** (04 94 46 29 89 offer boat tours of the harbor. All are open all year. For boat tours to the Îles d'Hyères **SNRTM** (04 94 62 41 14, **Transmed 2000** (04 94 92 95 88, or Bateliers de la Rade.

In case of health emergencies, call the **SAMU** (15 or **SOS Médecins** (04 91 31 33 33.

WHAT TO SEE AND DO

Several companies offer boat rides around the **harbor** (see above), very impressive when the aircraft carrier *Clemenceau* and other big French warships are in port. The harbor has two parts, **La Petite Rade**, the perfectly sheltered inner harbor, and **La Grande Rade**, the larger outer harbor, which is also well-protected by the Saint-Mandrier Peninsula.

On the waterfront **Quai Stalingrad**, look out for the **Atlantes**, the colossal twin muscle-men sculpted in the seventeenth century by Pierre Puget, said to have been modeled on suffering galley slaves, and themselves the models for the many Atlantes straining to hold up balconies in Aix and elsewhere in Provence. At the west end of Quai Stalingrad, the **Musée Naval** has an excellent collection of scale models of ships, figureheads by disciples of Puget, statues of admirals by Puget himself, paintings and drawings of old Toulon, including scenes of its notorious *bagne*. Closed Tuesday.

La Vieille Ville is the one part of Toulon that escaped the World War II bombings. A little section of the rough old sailor-bar district remains. It is so pungently realistic with its flophouses, neon

---

The port of Porquerolles.

signs, and street-walkers that you'd swear you had walked onto the set of a 1930s waterfront movie. Take **Rue d'Alger**, leading inland from Quai Stalingrad, to reach it. Get there fast, before the urban developers beat you to it.

You can also take the *téléphérique*, the cable car, up to **Mont Faron** for one of the best panoramas on the Côte d'Azur (which is saying a lot). From a height of 584 m (1,917 ft), it takes in all of Toulon, the huge harbor and roadstead, Cap Sicié to the west, and the mountains in back of the city. The **Musée-Mémorial du Débarquement en Provence** near the top of the *téléphérique* is a modern museum with electronic displays, films, and memorabilia relating to the Allied landing on the cost of Provence in August 1944. Closed Mondays.

West of Toulon is **La Seyne**, a promontory with good views of Toulon and the harbor from **Fort Balaguier**. The fort has a **museum** with Napoléon memorabilia, naval models, and artifacts made by prisoners in the *bagne*. Closed Mondays and Tuesdays.

Farther out on this peninsula is **Cap Sicié**, from which there are views along the coast from the Îles d'Hyères to the Calanques de Marseille 32 km (20 miles) away. The view is best from the hilltop church of **Notre-Dame-du-Mai**, 358 m (1,175 ft) high. The church is a place of pilgrimage for sailors and contains a number of ex-voto artworks.

WHERE TO STAY

On the slope of Mont Faron overlooking downtown Toulon, **New Hôtel Tour Blanche***** (04 94 24 41 57 FAX 94 22 42 25 E-MAIL toulontourblanche @newhotel.com, Avenue de Vence (at the foot of the *téléphérique*), has views of the harbor from all 91 comfortable, moderately priced modern rooms and the restaurant terrace, and there is a pool and a *pétanque* surface. In the center of the city, the best hotel is the **Mercure Toulon Centre Congrès***** (04 98 00 81 00 FAX 04 94 41 57 57 E-MAIL info@ hoteldupalais.com, on Place Bessange facing the Palais des Congrès. It caters mainly to a business clientele, but its 148 spotless modern rooms decorated in soothing pastels, its airy Provençal restaurant, **La Table de l'Amiral**, and its location one block from the port's waterfront promenade make it a suitable choice for the individual traveler. **Dauphiné**** (04 94 92 20 28 FAX 94 62 16 69, 10 rue Berthelot, is a well-maintained older hotel with 57 inexpensive rooms on the edge of La Vieille Ville. It has no restaurant.

Immediately to the east of downtown Toulon lies the pleasant beach area of Le Mourillon on Toulon's wide outer harbor with the Porquerolles islands in the distance. Here, **La Corniche***** (04 94 41 35 12 FAX 04 94 41 24 58 WEB SITE WWW .bestwestern.com, at 1 Littoral Frédéric Mistral, Corniche du Mourillon, is a friendly hotel with

23 comfortable rooms attractively decorated in Provençal style and a particularly fine restaurant overlooking the charming little fishing port of Saint-Louis, a few steps from the beach. The hotel is a Best Western member; moderately priced.

The most elegant hostelry in Toulon is **Hôtel les Bastidières** (04 94 36 14 73 FAX 04 94 42 49 75, at 2371 avenue de la Résistance, in quiet Cap Brun, one kilometer (half a mile) east of the Mourillon beaches. This handsome Mediterranean mansion has a beautifully landscaped private park dotted with palms and spectacular pines, a large pool in a secluded area amid lush flowers and exotic trees, and five very spacious deluxe rooms with huge, antique Provençal-decorated bathrooms. Room prices are at the low end of the expensive range. No credit cards are accepted. There is no restaurant.

Camping

The camping grounds in the Toulon are mainly at La Seyne-sur-Mer on the west side of the port. **Camping Beauregard** (04 94 20 56 35, only 300 m (1,000 ft) from the beach in La Garde, is open all year. For a complete list of camping grounds in the area, contact the Tourist Office.

WHERE TO EAT

At **La Chamade** (04 94 92 28 58, at 25 rue de la Comédie, two blocks north of the Place des Armes, you may savor noted chef Francis Bonneau's starter of warm foie gras with pears and spiced caramel, a main course of sautéed fresh sea scallops with Bandol wine sauce and green lentils, and a dessert of roasted figs served with almond-milk sherbet — or whatever else happens to be on that day's fixed-price *menu* — all for only 185 francs, remarkably low for a Michelin one-star gourmet restaurant. La Chamade's superb Côtes de Provence wines are correspondingly gentle in price.

In its handsome dining room overlooking little Port Saint-Louis or on the lush tropical garden patio, **La Corniche** at the Hôtel Corniche at Mourillon beach serves the refined Provençal fare of chef Anne Bodin, noted for her truffle-laced prawns, sea bass roasted in wild herbs, and such original specialties as braised veal kidneys and tender green cabbage with licorice-flavored gravy. Prices are very reasonable (the fixed-price lunch *menu* is 135 francs, drinks included).

Les Terraces at the New Hôtel Tour Blanche features grilled shrimp and fish and good regional cuisine at reasonable prices, and the high-angle view of the harbor is magnificent.

HOW TO GET THERE

There are 12 flights a day from Paris to Toulon-Hyères Airport and four direct trains a day from

Paris, a five-hour trip, along with another half-dozen trains with connections at Marseille, which adds a half-hour to an hour to the trip. The trains continue on to Saint-Raphaël, Cannes, and Nice. By bus, several lines connect Toulon with the other towns and cities of the Côte d'Azur and Provence (see GENERAL INFORMATION, above). By car, Toulon is easily reached by highway.

TO BANDOL

On the western shore of Cap Sicié, 12 km (seven and a half miles) directly west of Toulon, starts a sports-oriented stretch of beach towns and there are some interesting little islands owned by the late *pastis* baron Paul Ricard.

GENERAL INFORMATION

Tourist Offices in the area are the following: **Six-Fours** (04 94 07 02 21, Plage de Bonnegrâce, the main beach; **Sanary** (04 94 74 01 04, Jardins de Ville, the beachfront promenade; **Bandol** (04 94 29 41 35, Allées Alfred Vivien, by the pleasure port. These Tourist Offices can supply information on hotels, camping, bicycle rental, and sports. A couple of places where you can rent bikes in Bandol are **Hookipa Sport** (04 94 29 53 15 and **Gallia Sports** (04 94 29 60 33. There are **ferries** to the Île de Bendor every half hour from the Port of Bandol in the summer, an eight-minutes ride. There is a **market** every morning on Place de la Liberté in the center of Bandol.

WHAT TO SEE AND DO

The **Île des Embiez** off Le Brusc has an oceano-graphic park and a sports center, and the **Île de Bendor** off Bandol offers scuba diving, a marine museum, an art gallery and a wine and liqueur exposition. The stretch of coast from Le Brusc through Six-Fours-les-Plages to **Sanary-sur-Mer** is one of the leading spots for windsurfing in France. Sanary and Bandol are active pleasure-boat ports. **Bandol** is famed for its wine (see WINE TASTING, below).

The pretty port town of Sanary has an exceptional past. In the 1930s it became a main place of refuge for German writers and artists fleeing Hitler's Germany — Thomas Mann, Franz Werfel, Lion Feuchtwanger, Arthur Koestler, and Berthold Brecht among them. After the fall of France in 1940, a number of them were smuggled to the United States via Marseille by resourceful American undercover agent Varian Fry and his operatives, who saved a long list of European intellectuals from the Nazis.

In **La Cadière-d'Azur**, a charming medieval hilltop village in the heart of Bandol wine country, noted chef René Bérard, a native of the village,

and his English-speaking staff offer a four-day "Passport to Provence" **cooking course** at the beautiful Hostellerie Bérard. For information, see SPECIAL INTERESTS, page 60 in YOUR CHOICE.

WINE TASTING

Bandol is one of the most prestigious wine regions of southern France, noted especially for its vigorous reds. It was one of the South's pioneers in the movement from low-quality, high-quantity inexpensive wines to high-quality expensive ones. In Bandol's case, this was a return to high quality, because its wines had enjoyed a great reputation during the *Ancien Régime* (it was Louis XV's favorite wine). Because they traveled well by sea, Bandol wines were prized all over the world. After the phylloxera epidemic wiped out the vineyards in the 1870s, however, for practical and marketing reasons, the growers replanted their fields in higher-yield grapes than the Mourvèdre traditionally used to make Bandol. The long road back to quality started in the 1920s. It was pursued in the 1930s by a small group of visionaries who went back to the traditional vines. Their efforts were rewarded with an *AOC* for Bandol in 1941.

The vineyards of Bandol extend over an area of 2,700 hectares (6,500 acres) though only half of it is planted with the Mourvèdre, Grenache, and Cinsaut grapes used to make the wine. They include the coastal towns of Bandol and Sanary, and inland the attractive medieval perched villages of Le Castellet and La Cadière-d'Azur and the market town of Le Beausset, gently hilly countryside to drive through with vineyards practically everywhere. The winemakers are especially easygoing and enjoyable to visit.

Domaine Tempier (04 94 98 70 21, in Plan-du-Castellet north of Bandol, has long been recognized as one of the area's finest producers. Lucien Peyraud, the late patriarch of the family, led the movement to quality wines in the 1930s, with the support of his spirited wife Lucie, née Tempier, a famous cook and one of the most beloved individuals in the South of France. Their sons Jean-Marie and François now run the vineyard. It can be visited weekdays except at lunchtime and Saturday mornings. Closed Saturday afternoon and Sunday.

Other top producers of Bandol are Comte de Saint-Victor's **Château de Pibarnon** (04 94 90 12 73 in La Cadière-d'Azur, **Domaine de Terre-Brune** (04 94 74 01 30 in Ollioules, and Domaines Ott's **Château Romassan** (04 94 98 71 91 in Le Castellet. But these are by no means the only producers of fine Bandol wines. For information on the wines and more vineyards to visit, contact the **Association de Vins de Bandol** (04 94 90 29 59 in Le Beausset.

WHERE TO STAY

There are plenty of hotels to chose from. Bandol has 23, Sanary-sur-Mer has 11, Six-Fours has seven, and there are others in the hill towns just in from the coast.

Hostellerie Bérard*** (04 94 90 11 43 FAX 04 94 90 01 94 E-MAIL berard@hotel-berard.com WEB SITE www.hotel-berard.com is a charming 40-room inn in the authentically Provençal hill village of La Cadière-d'Azur in an ensemble of three pretty stone buildings overlooking the prestigious vineyards of Bandol, with a good swimming pool, a health club, an exceptionally good restaurant (see WHERE TO EAT, below), and courses in Provençal cuisine (see SPECIAL INTERESTS, page 60 in YOUR CHOICE). Room prices are in the bottom half of the expensive category, about 800 francs on the average.

Perched by the sea on the Île de Bendor, seven minutes by boat from Bandol, the château-like 55-room Délos Palais*** (04 94 32 22 23 FAX 04 94 32 41 44 E-MAIL ethebaulte@hoteldelos.com WEB SITE www.hoteldelos.com is an ideal spot for watersports enthusiasts. It is a Relais de Silence member, and rates are expensive. In Sanary I like the Hôtel de la Tour** (04 94 74 10 10 FAX 04 94 74 69 49, Quai du Général-de-Gaulle, a charming, old-fashioned 24-room hotel on the pretty port with a flowery terrace restaurant, moderately priced both for rooms and food. Thomas Mann lived here in the late 1930s after he left Nazi Germany.

Camping

In Sanary, the main camping grounds are Les Girelles (04 94 74 13 18 and Le Mogador (04 94 74 10 58. In Bandol it is Vallonge (04 94 29 49 55. They are open from Easter to the end of September.

WHERE TO EAT

In the elegant country dining room of the Hostellerie Bérard (see WHERE TO STAY, above), chef René Bérard serves raviolis of cèpes (wild boletus mushrooms) with truffle-laced vinaigrette, râble (saddle of hare) with olives, rack of lamb with tapenade (black-olive paste), and other refined Provençal specialties that have made him the leading chef on this end of the Côte d'Azur. The presentation is exquisite, the service relaxed and thoroughly professional, and the prices are in the expensive (but not too expensive) range, with a weekday lunch menus at 160 francs and a dinner menu at 290 francs.

Auberge du Port (04 94 29 42 63, at 9 Allée Jean-Moulin in Bandol, is a very good strictly-seafood restaurant right on the waterfront with menus from 120 to 250 francs. In Sanary, the Relais de la Poste (04 94 74 22 20, on Place de la Poste, is another fine, if rather formal, restaurant for seafood — the rockfish soup with rouille (rust-colored garlic mayonnaise) and croutons is superb — and they also have excellent meat and fowl dishes. Fixed-price menus range from 120 francs for a weekday lunch, wine included, on up to 345 francs. In Six-Fours-les-Plages, Le Saint-Pierre (Chez Marcel) (04 94 34 02 52, at the little port of Le Brusc facing the Île des Embiez, offers copious servings of delicious, absolutely fresh seafood on a shaded dining terrace, with fixed-price menus from 95 francs (weekdays only) to 198 francs. The excellent bouillabaisse costs 195 francs. The service is very easygoing and friendly.

HOW TO GET THERE

Bandol and Ollioules (near Sanary) are stops on the main SNCF train line. Sanary and Six-Fours can be reached by regular bus service from Toulon.

MASSIF DE LA SAINTE-BAUME

Continuing inland from the Bandol wine area, you come to one of the most mysterious places in southern France, the Massif de la Sainte-Baume and Saint-Maximin-la-Sainte-Baume.

Baoumo is Provençal for cave, and La Sainte-Baume is the cave where Mary Magdalene is said to have spent the last 33 years of her life in prayer. The cave, now converted into a chapel, is on the slope of Saint-Pilon, a mountain in the heavily wooded Massif de la Sainte-Baume about 40 km (25 miles) north of the Bandol wine country. It has been an important place of pilgrimage since the Middle Ages. For the legend of how Mary Magdalene came to France, see LES SAINTES-MARIES-DE-LA-MER, page 268 under THE CAMARGUE. On July 21 and 22 and on Christmas Eve a midnight mass is celebrated in the chapel. The cave is reached by a not-too-difficult 30-minute hike on well-marked paths up Saint-Pilon from either the village of Plan-d'Aups-Sainte-Baume on D80 or the Carrefour des Chênes at the intersection of D80 and D95. Real hikers can continue another three-quarters of an hour to the top of Saint-Pilon, 994 m (3,260 ft) high with a panoramic view of the Mediterranean, Montagne Sainte-Victoire, and Mont Ventoux. The north slope of the mountain has a cool, damp Northern European microclimate. Maples, beeches and lime trees grow here amid a dense, leafy underbrush of ivy, yew, holly, and privet. On the southern side of Saint-Pilon, there is a complete change of ecology, with only Mediterranean plants and trees.

Long before Mary Magdalene's time, even before the Greeks, Sainte-Baume was a place of pilgrimage. Ligurians came to pray to fertility goddesses. All civilizations have considered it holy.

To this day, though the Var has as rapacious a bunch of real estate predators as can be found anywhere, this area has been left free of commercial exploitation, in contrast to much of the Var's coast.

Two hotels stand on either side of Saint-Pilon, both are elegant eighteenth-century country houses with outstanding restaurants. **Domaine de Châteauneuf****** (04 94 78 90 06 FAX 04 94 78 63 30 E-MAIL chateauneufhotel@opengolfclub.com WEB SITE www.opengolfclub.com/ch9/, to the north in Nans-les-Pins, is a very expensive 22-room, eight-suite hotel on the grounds of its own 18-hole golf course; it has three tennis courts, two swimming pools, and a helicopter landing pad. **Relais de la Magdeleine****** (04 42 32 20 16 FAX 04 42 32 02 26, to the south of Saint-Pilon in Gémenos, is a 24-room hotel exquisitely furnished in antiques, serenely situated in its own woodsy park, with room and restaurant prices in the expensive range. It has a pool, and there is golf, tennis, and horseback riding nearby. Also in Gémenos is **Le Parc**** (04 42 32 20 38 FAX 04 42 32 10 26, Vallée Saint-Pons, a pleasant, moderately priced 11-room hotel and restaurant in a tranquil setting. There is also a **hostel for pilgrims** (04 42 04 50 21, at Plan-d'Aups-Sainte-Baume.

For information on this area, contact the **Gémenos Tourist Office** (04 42 32 18 44.

To get to this area from Bandol wine country, take N8 northwest from Le Beausset to Gémenos, 28 km (17.5 miles), then wind up little D2 another 12 km (7.5 miles) to Plan-d'Aups-Sainte-Baume.

SAINT-MAXIMIN-LA-SAINTE-BAUME

Saint-Maximin-la-Sainte-Baume, 20 km (12.5 miles) north of La Sainte-Baume, is a depressing town that looks like some dusty forgotten corner of Mexico. Bulging up like a whale on the surface of the ocean, visible for miles around, is the **Basilica of Saint-Maximin**. Millions of pilgrims have come over the centuries, including such notables as Louis XIV. What brought them are relics claimed to be those of Mary Magdalene. Her remains were said to have been hidden in the eighth century to prevent them from falling into the hands of the Saracens, but disappeared. In the thirteenth century Charles of Anjou, Count of Provence and brother of King Louis IX (Saint Louis), launched a search for the missing relics, and lo and behold, in 1279 they were found. Charles built a crypt that was elaborated over the next two and a half centuries into the largest Gothic church in Provence. A cranium said to be Mary Magdalene's is on display in a gold reliquary in the crypt. The crypt also contains relics of Saint Maximinus and Saint Suedonius, two of her companions on the boat to the Camargue. The relics of Mary Magdalene are taken out for a procession on her feast day, July 22.

The basilica has one of the largest and finest pipe organs in France, built in 1773, with almost 3,000 pipes. They were saved from being melted down for guns during the Revolution by Lucien Bonaparte, Napoléon's clever younger brother, who was in charge of the warehouse the basilica had been converted to. He saved it, the story goes, by having *La Marseillaise* played on it at critical moments.

The adjoining **Ancien Couvent Royal** (Old Royal Convent), started at the same time as the basilica and finished in the fifteenth century, has a large cloister with 32 bays.

There are organ recitals at the basilica on 4 PM Sundays in the summer. Orchestral concerts of religious music are held in the cloister of the Ancien Couvent Royal and in the basilica in July and August.

For information, contact the **Tourist Office** (04 94 59 84 59, at the Hôtel de Ville (Town Hall).

Opened in 1999, **L'Hôtellerie du Couvent Royal** (04 94 86 55 66 FAX 04 94 59 82 82 E-MAIL couvent-st-maximin@dial.oleane.com offers 29 former monks' cells attractively converted to up-to-date hotel rooms, with a top rate of 350 francs for a double. The convent's vaulted Gothic refectory has become the **Restaurant du Couvent Royal**, serving chef Philippe Gouby's gastronomic Provençal cuisine. Fixed-price *menus* range from a simple three-course meal keyed to what's fresh in the market for 110 francs (mineral water, wine, and coffee included) to a veritable royal feast for 260 francs. Reservations required. There is also a wine bar, **Les Dix Vins**, that serves Provençal-style *tapas* — all you'd need for a satisfying lunch — and a great selection of regional aperitifs and wines.

By car, Saint-Maximin can be reached by D80 and N560 from Plan-d'Aups 20 km (12.5 miles) to the south, and it is about 40 km (25 miles) east of Aix-en-Provence on the A8 *autoroute* and roughly the same distance from Marseille. Three bus lines come here from Marseille and Aix, **Phocéens Cars** (04 93 85 66 61, **Blanc** (04 94 69 08 28, and **Lombard** (04 94 78 00 32. Phocéens's buses also come from Nice, Fréjus-Saint-Raphaël and other points east, and Blanc has two buses a day from Toulon.

Provence

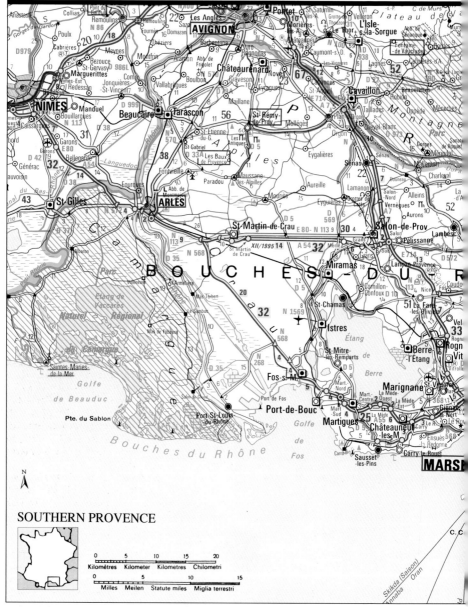

SOUTHERN PROVENCE

PEOPLE GET MISTY-EYED when they talk about Provence. And why not? It is the heart of historical Provincia Romana with legendary cities such as Arles, Nîmes, Avignon, Aix, and Marseille. It has mountains and vineyard-covered valleys, a great river flowing the length of it and a dramatic coastline from the soaring cliffs of Cassis and the Calanques of Marseille to the moody wetlands of the Camargue. In Provence, there is a fine equilibrium between the beauty of nature, the riches of culture, and the pleasures of the flesh. There are music, dance, and theater festivals galore in the

summer and cuisine, wine, and lodging of the highest order all year round.

In the Côte d'Azur, the coastline is the focus of everything. But in Provence, although the coast is certainly important, the axis is its river, the Rhône. The towns and cities of Orange, Avignon, Tarascon, Beaucaire, and Arles are on it, and Marseille, though it fronts on the Mediterranean, owes its development as a great port to its position near the mouth of the Rhône. The Rhône Valley has been the main route between the North and the South from the times of the Greeks and Romans

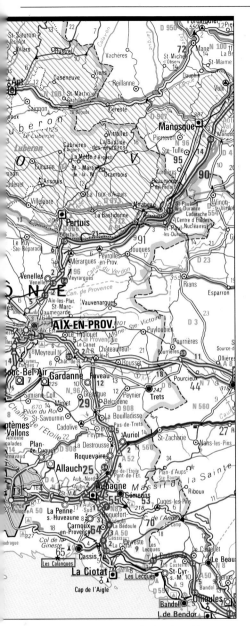

country, and the Roman towns of Orange and Vaison-la-Romaine.

Readers who have been following our east to west itinerary through the Côte d'Azur may continue with the sections that follow: CASSIS, below, MARSEILLE, page 190, and AIX-EN-PROVENCE, page 202.

The distances between places are short. It takes half an hour to drive each leg of the Nîmes-Arles-Avignon triangle, half an hour from Marseille to Aix, and it is only 160 km (100 miles) from the Drôme Provençale in the north to Marseille in the south.

BANDOL TO CASSIS

From Bandol, take the coast road D559 west toward Marseille through **Les Lecques**, the last town of the Côte d'Azur, and enter Provence at **La Ciotat**. This town, half beach resort, half shipyard, is where the Lumière brothers shot the first motion picture in 1895. They filmed a head-on scene of a train entering La Ciotat station, and when they projected it in a theater, the audience panicked and ran out. It is also the town where the rules for the Provençal bowling game of *pétanque* were devised.

Following the curve of the shore, drive through the center of La Ciotat, turn right onto Route D141 and climb to the 13-km (eight-mile) **Route des Crêtes** (Ridge Road) along the cliffs of Cap Canaille. It is 399 m (1,310 ft) down to the sea from its highest point at **Grande Tête**—the loftiest cliff in France. The view from the headland just east of Cassis, with vineyards running down steep slopes to the shore, sailboats on the sparkling sea, and the little port in the crook of the bay is a marvelous mental postcard.

Be warned, though: if it's windy and you're driving a light car, the gusts on the Route des Crêtes can be dangerous. As an alternative, stay on D559, the main road inland from La Ciotat to Cassis.

CASSIS

Few small ports in the Mediterranean could compete with Cassis in a beauty contest. The harbor is filled with boats and lined with cafés, villagers play *pétanque* on a tree-shaded square, and its town beach pokes out into the sea on a finger of land. But what makes Cassis unique is the grandeur of the high ridge in the background and the mighty cliffs of Cap Canaille to the east—not close enough to overwhelm it, as the Maritime Alps do the little ports east of Nice, but framing the town perfectly.

What also makes Cassis unique is its wine.

GENERAL INFORMATION

The **Tourist Office** (04 42 01 71 17 E-MAIL omt-cassis@enprovence.com WEB SITE www.cassis

to our days. The main north–south rail line runs through the Rhône corridor, as does the Autoroute du Soleil, the six-lane highway most cars and trucks use, carrying southern fruit, vegetables, and wine to the cold north and armies of northern vacationers to the sunny south.

Travelers driving down from the north will enter Mediterranean France in the sunny olive-, truffle- and wine-growing region south of the Drôme River nicknamed "La Drôme Provençale," or directly south of it, the Vaucluse, home of the papal city of Avignon, the Côtes du Rhône wine

.enprovence.com, on Place Baragnon, one block in from the *pétanque*-playing square in the port, offers information on restaurants, accommodations, sports facilities and excursions, and a list of 14 Cassis vineyards that can be visited.

WHAT TO SEE AND DO

Cassis is the most popular and most convenient place for visiting the **Calanques de Marseille**. This is a string of dramatic fjords (*calanques*) with sheer white limestone cliffs and amazingly translucent turquoise and blue water that filigrees the coastline for 17 km (11 miles) to the west of Cassis. Most lie within the city limits of Marseille, hence the name. Boats run frequently from the port of Cassis to the *calanques* daily all summer. The 45-minute trip to the three closest ones, **Port-Miou, Port-Pin**, and **En-Vau** is well worth the price of 50 francs. Boat trips are also available to more remote *calanques*. Excursions to eight *calanques*, including the especially dramatic **Sugiton, Morgiou,** and **Sormiou,** cost 90 francs.

Calanques can also be explored from the land. From Cassis, drive to Port-Miou, the boat-lined *calanque* west of town, and park in the lot, where you will find a clearly marked trail to the next *calanque,* Port-Pin, with a pretty little beach. Allow one hour round-trip for the hike. For En-Vau, the prettiest, allow two and a half hours.

WINE TASTING

Cassis is one of South's most prestigious winemaking areas. Its dry whites are the only beverage the *Marseillais* would think of drinking with *bouillabaisse* (not be confused, by the way, with black-currant *cassis* liqueur from Burgundy used to make *kirs*). The most beautiful of Cassis's vineyards to visit is the **Clos Sainte-Magdeleine** (04 42 01 70 28, which has a handsome mansion overlooking the sea and 12 hectares (28 acres) of vines running up to the Cap Canaille cliffs. The proprietors, Monsieur and Madame Sack, will be happy to let you taste their excellent whites and rosés. **Domaine du Bagnol** (04 42 01 78 05, another outstanding Cassis vineyard, also makes reds as well as whites and rosés.

WHERE TO STAY AND EAT

Les Roches Blanches**** (04 42 01 09 30 04 FAX 42 01 94 23 WEB SITE www.provencetourism.com is a luxurious 24-room hotel on a verdant point of land halfway between the port and the *calanques* on the Route des Calanques, with a magnificent view of the sea and Cap Canaille, gardens descending to the shore, and a lovely pool overlooking the blue, blue water. The rooms are expensive, as is the restaurant. Open mid-February to mid-November.

The most charming place to stay and to eat at in Cassis is **Le Jardin d'Émile**** (04 42 01 80 55 FAX 04 42 01 80 70, one kilometer (half a mile) west of town on the Plage du Bestouan. The old red-ochre house has seven small, but delightful Provençal-style rooms, some with beamed ceilings, at 550 to 650 francs. The hotel is well-kept and has all the modern comforts including soundproofing and air conditioning. The restaurant serves fresh, creative Mediterranean cuisine, and the garden dining terrace amid ancient olive trees, figs, pines, and cypress could not be more relaxing. There is a weekday lunch *menu* at 98 francs and one for 195 francs in the evening. The young staff is very friendly. Closed the last

half of November and the second and third weeks of January.

Another charming red-ochre hotel, but without a restaurant, is the **Cassitel** ** (04 42 01 83 44 FAX 04 42 01 96 31, centrally located at Place George Clemenceau. Its 32 attractive, moderately priced rooms have views either of the open sea, the old port, or the village. It is open all year. The neighboring **Liautaud**** (04 42 01 75 37 FAX 04 42 01 12 08, at Place George-Clemenceau, is a pleasant, moderately priced 35-room hotel fronting on the port. It has no restaurant. Open from February 1 to the end of November. Another hotel at the beach is **Plage du Bestouan***** (04 42 01 05 70

The *calanques* of Marseille LEFT, the chain of dazzling white limestone fjords between Cassis and Marseille, are most easily reached by boat from Cassis. The Route des Crêtes ABOVE between La Ciotat and Cassis has the highest seaside cliffs in France.

FAX 04 42 01 34 82 WEB SITE www.cassis.enprovence
.com/hotelbestouan, modern, with 29 well-
equipped moderately priced to slightly expensive
rooms overlooking the little strand after which
the hotel is named. Open April 1 to the end of
October.

The leading gastronomic restaurant in Cassis
is **La Presqu'île (** 04 42 01 03 77, two kilometers
(one and a quarter miles) from town on the road
to Port-Miou, offering impeccably prepared seafood served in a garden with a magnificent view
of the sea and Cap Canaille. It is expensive. Open
early March to mid-November.

Camping

Les Cigales (04 42 01 07 34 FAX 04 42 01 34 18 is a
250-place camping ground on three shaded hectares (eight and a half acres) on the Route de Marseille, D559, one kilometer from the port of Cassis;
open March 15 to November 15. It is one of the
closest camping sites to Marseille, which is 22 km
(13.5 miles) away.

HOW TO GET THERE

There are trains every hour from the Gare Saint-
Charles in Marseille. However, the train station
in Cassis is located three kilometers (two miles)
from town. Buses operated by the SCAC line also
run every hour from Marseille, from either the Gare
Saint-Charles or Place Castellane, and drop you
at the Casino in Cassis, which is a short walk to
the port. By car, Cassis is 23 km (14 miles) from
downtown Marseille on D559 and four kilometers
(two and a half miles) from the A50 *autoroute* between Marseille and Toulon.

MARSEILLE

Marseille is the most surprising city in Mediterranean France, and the most astonishing discovery
many visitors make is that they can walk about
freely with little danger of being robbed or gunned
down in the street. Unfortunately, most people's
image of Marseille is right out of *The French Connection*, where the hit man shoots his victim, coolly
breaks off a chunk of the dead man's *baguette*, and
saunters off up the street munching it. But in fact,
though the noxious influence of the Mafia has
indeed been strong, Marseille, which is France's
second city with 800,000 people, ranks well below
Paris in crimes against persons and only ninth
among French cities. Compared to any American
big city, its crime rate is laughably low. Except in
one or two rough neighborhoods you have no
reason to visit anyway, the ordinary precautions
one would take in any big city are all that are needed.

What does Marseille have going for it other
than safe streets? Plenty: a spectacular natural
setting, Greek island weather kept bright by the

mistral, the ever-lively Vieux Port and fascinating urban corners to explore, a panoply of cultural
attractions, and easy access to the beach-studded
coast and islands. Marseille also has one of the
most exciting cuisines of France, starting with *bouillabaisse*. To this should be added the cuisines of
the immigrant populations of Italians, Armenians,
Greeks, Turks, Spaniards, North Africans, West
Africans, Vietnamese, Thai and Chinese, all represented in substantial numbers. The nightlife is
active too, mainly in the many clubs, discos, bars
and cafés around the Vieux Port, and in recent years
Marseille has become the most vibrant city in
France for popular music and the fine arts.

To learn to appreciate this city, give yourself
time and poke around. Marseille will reward you
in unexpected ways.

BACKGROUND

Marseille is the oldest city in France, founded in
the seventh century BC by Greek sea traders from
Phocaea in Asia Minor who named it Massalia.
They brought the olive tree and the secret of wine-
making and set up trading posts along the coast
and up the Rhône. Marseille prospered for centuries until it made the mistake of going against Julius
Caesar in 49 BC, and he and his successors cut
Marseille out of the profits for the rest of the Pax
Romana. A thousand years later, the Crusades to
the Holy Land, which started in 1095, brought
Marseille fully back to life, when it became their
main port. Despite wars, plagues and frequent
pirate raids, it continued to prosper, particularly
after Provence joined the Kingdom of France. The
discovery of America and the opening up of the
ocean route to Asia via the Cape of Good Hope,
which gave the Atlantic ports the advantage in
world trade, undermined Marseille's dominance.
In 1720, a plague that came in on a merchant ship
from Syria killed more than half the population
of 90,000. But by the time of the Revolution, the
city had grown to its pre-plague level, and the
economy was doing well.

Habitually at odds with all central governments, Marseille welcomed the Revolution. In
1792, a company of 500 volunteer soldiers from
Marseille stirred people with their singing of a
new song called "The War Song of the Army of
the Rhine," and it became known as the "*La
Marseillaise.*"

In the 1830s, Marseille became the gateway to
France's developing colonial empire in North and
Equatorial Africa, and a period of fabulous prosperity ensued, especially after the opening of the
Suez Canal in 1867, linking the Mediterranean with
the Far East. Locally manufactured products such
as soap added to the city's affluence. Prosperity
continued until the Great Depression of the 1930s
and the disaster of World War II, in which Marseille

was heavily bombed by the Allies. On top of that, German occupation forces dynamited a large part of the Panier, the immigrant neighborhood on the west side of the Vieux Port, which was a hotbed of *Résistance* activity.

The collapse of the French colonial empire in the 1950s and 1960s brought further economic disaster to the city. Though the Port of Marseille remains one of Europe's largest ports for cargo, and a million passengers a year still pass through it, its economic vitality is nowhere near what it once was. Marseille still makes a lot of soap (20% of the household soap sold in France), but the giant steel mills built in Fos-sur-Mer have failed to deliver the economic stimulus hoped for. High-tech

cultural tours by passionate, well-informed guides, some in English. A 15-day tourist pass to all the museums in the city can be purchased here or in the museums for 50 francs.

The following phone numbers may be useful: **Marseille-Provence International Airport (** 04 42 14 14 14, at Marignane; Gare Saint-Charles, the **SNCF train station (** 08 36 35 35 35; the bus station, **Gare Routière (** 04 91 08 16 40, Place Victor-Hugo, in back of the train station.

For taxis, contact **Marseille Taxi (** 04 91 02 20 20, **Taxis Phocéens (** 04 91 06 15 15, or **Eurotaxis** (multilingual) **(** 04 91 97 12 12.

Car rental agencies include **Avis (** 04 91 08 41 80; **Budget (** 04 91 64 40 03; **EuropCar (** 04 91 49 67

and clothing manufacture hold promise, and Marseille has belatedly awakened to fact that is has a big future in cultural tourism. This was sparked by the chance discovery in 1967 of the ancient Greek port of Massalia, which gave the *Marseillais* a new sense of the city's archaeological riches. In 1999, Marseille celebrated the 2,600th anniversary of its founding.

GENERAL INFORMATION

The **Tourist Office (** 04 91 13 89 00 E-MAIL destination-marseille@wanadoo.fr WEB SITE www. destination-marseille.com is easy to find at 4 La Canebière, Marseille's main street that starts at the Vieux Port. It is open daily, until 8 PM in summer. There is also a small office at the Gare Saint-Charles, the railway station. The Tourist Office offers excellent brochures; practical assistance, and

28; **Hertz (** 04 91 79 22 06; **Rent-a-Car (** 04 91 50 01 20; and **Thrifty (** 04 91 05 92 18.

The bus and subway lines of the local RTM are modern and simple to use.

Little **Tourist Trains** from the Quai des Belges to Notre-Dame-de-la-Garde or the Panier run frequently all summer, 30 francs. (The No. 60 city bus also runs between the Vieux Port and Notre-Dame-de-la-Garde.)

Tour boats (*navettes*) to the Château d'If run every hour in the summer from the Quai des Belges, 45 francs. There are also trips to the *calanques* of Marseille at 100 francs and up, depending on the length of the trip.

In case of medical emergencies, contact **SOS Médecins (** 04 91 52 91 52.

The Palais Longchamp, where Marseille's Museum of Fine Arts and Museum of Natural History are located.

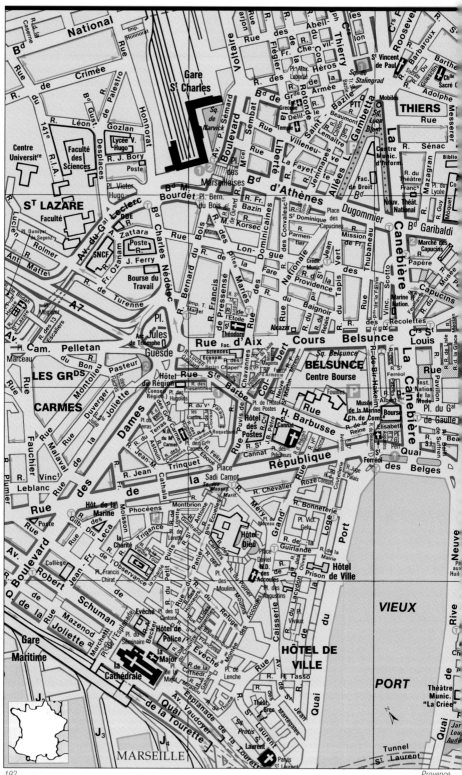

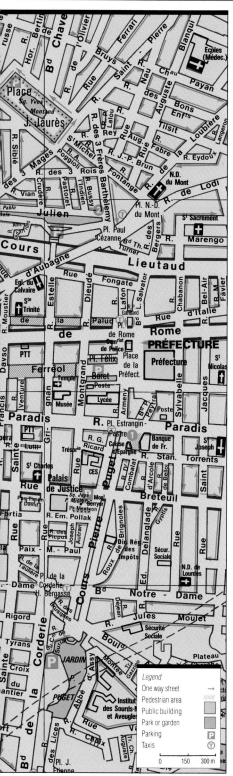

FESTIVALS AND EVENTS

La Fête de la Chandeleur is a religious event that dates from the eleventh century. Every February 2 at 6 AM, pilgrims gather at the Basilica of Saint-Victor to join the annual procession in which the ancient statue of the Black Virgin is carried through the streets to bless the city and the sea. Some 50,000 people. The feast is called *La Chandeleur* because of the green candles the pilgrims carry.

La Fête de Saint Eloi takes place on the third Sunday of June in Château Gombert, a northern nook of the city that has retained its old-time village feeling. Saint Eloi is the patron saint of goldsmiths and blacksmiths, and the festival celebrates the handicrafts of yore, particularly those having to do with the horse. There are parades around the village square — people in Provençal garb, fife and drum corps, and lots of horses.

Le Festival de Marseille is a lively festival of contemporary music, dance, theater, and art held over the whole month of July, with most performances taking place at the elegant seventeenth-century Vieille Charité cultural center. The music is a mix of Mediterranean, Oriental, hip-hop, and rap, reflecting the city's mosaic of races, cultures, and religions. Some of the world's most original choreographers present their work here.

La Fiesta des Suds ("Suds" meaning "Souths" in French) has been bringing the music, art, and food of the sunny parts of the world to Marseille since 1992 — from Andalusia to Cuba to Argentina, the Near East, Brazil, and Senegal. It is held in October at the Docks des Suds, a huge space by the Port de la Joliette with a theater that seats 3,000.

La Foire aux Santons de Marseille, the most important fair for creators of Provençal "little saints," clay statuettes originally made for Christmas crèches, started in 1803, when three *santon* makers showed their works. Today it attracts about 40 of the top practitioners and runs from the last week of November to end of the year. They display their products in booths set up along the Allées de Meihan near the Église Saint-Vincent-de-Paul.

WHAT TO SEE AND DO

Vieux Port

The focal point of the city is the Vieux Port (Old Port), a long natural harbor indented into the city and surrounded by hills. It was Marseille's main port until the mid-nineteenth century, when the large-scale shipping activities were shifted to the new port of La Joliette to the west. The Vieux Port is now filled with pleasure and fishing boats, and a funny little ferry boat crosses it from the **Hôtel de Ville** to the **Place aux Huiles**. Don't miss the open-air **fish market** held every morning on the **Quai des Belges** at the foot of Marseille's main street, **La Canebière**. Here fishermen's wives sell their husbands' catch of the previous night. It is a very animated scene. Walk over to the **Jardin des Vestiges**, where Greek and Roman ruins unearthed in 1967 during excavations for a commercial center have been preserved in a garden setting as an archaeological site (it is two minutes from the port, at the back of Église Saint-Ferréol). There are walls dating from the second century BC, and the shape of Lacydon, the ancient port, is clear. The modern **Musée d'Histoire de Marseille**, which fronts on it, has scale models of the port as it was in antiquity and ancient artifacts including the remains of a Roman ship. It is open from noon to 7 PM, closed Sundays.

In the nineteenth century, when the port of Marseille was bursting with activity, the cafés that lined La Canebière were where the traders did all their business. Napoléon III considered this undignified and had a splendid Bourse built for them. The traders never used it. They stayed in their coffee shops and kept doing business Marseille style. All the old cafés and grand hotels are closed now, and La Canebière has lost its luster. In 1994, the city opened **Espace Mode**, a new fashion institute, museum, and exhibition space, in a grand nineteenth-century building at 11 la Canebière remodeled by architect Jean-Michel Wilmotte. Its goals were to help revitalize Marseille's fashion industry and to help bring La Canebière back to life. The street hasn't come around yet, but on the fashion front, Espace Mode has been a smashing success. The museum has an outstanding collection of French fashions from

the days of Coco Chanel to Jean-Paul Gaultier, beautifully displayed, and puts on major retrospectives devoted to individual designers. It has also helped many young local fashion designers develop their talents and show their work. It is open from noon to 7 PM, closed Monday and holidays.

On the east side of the Vieux Port, to your left as you look out to the sea, along the **Quai de Rive Neuve** and the pedestrian streets in back of it, there are dozens of restaurants and cafés on the streets intersecting at **Place Thiars** and on the long, wide, Italian-looking square, the **Cours d'Estienne d'Orves**. This square used to be covered by a dominatingly ugly above-ground parking

garage, but a campaign by local business people succeeded in having it torn down. Suddenly the Vieux Port shed its rough sailor ambiance and became a bright, cheerful, safe, but still colorful, place for tourists to relax and enjoy the many outdoor cafés and restaurants on the Cours. Take a look at **Les Arcenaulx**, a big stone loft building that was part of the seventeenth-century arsenal complex, and is now an attractive modern bookstore with a restaurant. Its owner, publisher Jeanne Laffitte, led the campaign to renovate the square.

The **Musée Cantini**, Marseille's museum of twentieth-century art, is nearby at 19 rue Grignan. Its permanent collection is particularly strong on surrealism and contemporary paintings and sculptures, with works by César, Arman, Alechinsky, Hartung, Bacon, Balthus, Tàpies, Viallat, and others. It is open from 11 AM to 6 PM June through

September, 10 AM to 5 PM the rest of the year, closed Monday and holidays.

Notre-Dame-de-la-Garde

From the highest point in the city on a hill to the east of the Vieux Port, "La Bonne Mère," the huge gilded statue of the Virgin on top of the basilica of Notre-Dame-de-la-Garde, casts her protective gaze over the city and acts as a beacon to sailors out at sea. The basilica's observation point is the best place for visitors to get the geographical sense of Marseille — the Vieux Port, the islands, the *corniches*, and the mountains.

The basilica itself is lugubrious mid-nine-teenth-century neo-Byzantine structure designed

Château d'If

As the Statue of Liberty is to New York, the Château d'If is to Marseille. No trip would be complete without a boat ride to it. The sixteenth-century fortress, most famous as the prison of Dumas's fictional Count of Monte Cristo, sits on a barren white limestone island surveying the roadstead of Marseille. The trip including a visit to the château takes an hour and a half.

Vieille Charité and the Panier

The Vieille Charité is a beautifully restored seven-teenth-century neoclassical gem designed by Mar-seille architect and sculptor Pierre Puget, who de-serves to be much better known than he is. The

by Espérandieu, who also built the Cathedral of the Major on the other side of the Vieux Port. It is filled with votive offerings, including ex-voto paintings given by sailors saved from shipwrecks.

Down the hill is the fortress-like eleventh-century **Basilica of Saint-Victor**. Its deep, vaulted **crypt** is the remains of the first monastery in France, built by Saint Cassien in the fifth century. *La Chandeleur*, an all-night vigil with green candles and a procession of the Black Madonna of Saint-Victor, is held on February 2. The bishop blesses the *navettes de Saint-Victor*, biscuits in the shape of little boats like the one that, legend has it, car-ried Mary Magdalene, Lazarus, and their fellow saints to Provence. They are made from a secret recipe in a 1781 oven by the **Four des Navettes** at 136 rue Sainte up the street from the Basilica. The tasty orange-flavored *navettes* are sold the year round.

former workhouse has three levels of arcaded walkways and wraps around a courtyard with an elegant oval-domed chapel in the middle. The com-plex is used for expositions and houses a **Museum of Mediterranean Archaeology**, with a rich Egyp-tian collection, and a new **Museum of African, Oceanic, and Amerindian Art (MAAOA)**. They are open from 11 AM to 6 PM June through Septem-ber, 10 AM to 5 PM the rest of the year, closed Mon-day and holidays. To get there from the Vieux Port, you follow narrow, twisting, colorful, formerly sinister streets of the **Panier**, a quarter that has hosted wave after wave of immigrants. In the twentieth century, they were Armenians, Italians, and now North Africans. Gentrification is well under way.

OPPOSITE: The Château d'If, where Dumas's Count of Monte Cristo was imprisoned. ABOVE: The island fortress of the Château d'If and the Frioul Islands in the roadstead of Marseille.

Other Sights

The **Palais Longchamp** is a twin-winged wedding-cake palace with a huge, ornate fountain in the middle built by Espérandieu in the 1860s to celebrate the arrival of the water from the Durance via Montrichier's Canal de Marseille. The **Musée des Beaux-Arts** is in the west wing of the palace and has works by Marseille natives Pierre Puget and Honoré Daumier, Paul Guigou from the Vaucluse and Gustave Courbet, his mentor. It is open from 11 AM to 6 PM June through September, 10 AM to 5 PM the rest of the year, closed Monday and holidays. The **Musée d'Histoire Naturelle** is in the east wing of the building, and there is a shady park and a small zoo. It is a the

On an esplanade with fountains and trees, pedestrian **Cours Julien** on the hill north of the Vieux Port is lined with antique and curiosity shops, fascinating for browsing in the daytime, and its cafés, restaurants, and little theaters and cabarets make for lively evenings. You can walk up the hill or go by Métro. The stop is Cours Julien.

The **Unité d'Habitation**, Le Corbusier's 17-story concrete and glass building cantilevered on sculptural concrete pillars, is one of modern architecture's most controversial landmarks. It is a self-contained living unit for 1,600 people with a shopping center, elementary school, hotel, and recreational areas built into it. Le Corbusier

northern end of Boulevard Longchamp. To get there from the Vieux Port, take the No. 80 bus up the Canebière or the Métro to Longchamp-Cinq-Avenues.

Across the street from the Palais Longchamp is the **Musée Grobet-Labadié**, the handsome mansion at 140 boulevard Longchamp built in 1873 by a Marseille merchant named Alexandre Labadié. In 1919 the family gave the house and its contents to the city as a museum. It has an eclectic collection of paintings, drawings, sculpture, furniture, tapestries, carpets, and *faïence* (fine glazed earthenware) mainly from the eighteenth and nineteenth centuries, much of it collected by the Labadiés and son-in-law Louis Grobet, another astute judge of artistic quality. The house, its decor, and its collection reveal how the *haute bourgeoisie* — a family of great taste in this instance — lived in the glory days of Marseille.

planned six of them for his Cité Radieuse, but only this one, completed in 1952, went up. It is at 280 boulevard Michelet, just over one and a half kilometers (one mile) east of the Vieux Port, on the No. 21 bus line. The stop is called "Corbusier."

The **Musée des Arts et Traditions Populaires**, a museum devoted to the area's popular arts and traditions, has fully furnished nineteenth-century rooms, pottery, kitchenware, china, traditional costumes, and a fine collection of *santons*, the handmade "little saints." The museum is in the Provençal estate house of Julien Pignol, a disciple of Mistral, at 5 place des Héros in **Château Gombert**, one of the 111 villages that make up Marseille that has best retained its small-town identity. The museum is open from 2:30 PM to 6:30 PM, closed Tuesday. To get there, take the Métro to La Rose and the No. 5S or 5T bus to Château Gombert.

The Corniche

Corniche Président J.F. Kennedy starts just past the **Parc du Pharo**, the lighthouse park on the east side of the mouth of the Vieux Port, and winds eastward for five kilometers (three miles) along the shore. Look for the big **Monument aux Morts d'Orient** on your right. Park there if you can and walk down to the **Vallon des Auffes**, a tiny *calanque* (fjord surrounded by rocky cliffs) in the city that is an active fishing port, very colorful, and with restaurants. You can swim off the rocks at the entrance to the Vallon des Auffes or at the beach club of the **Restaurant de la Corniche Bistrot Plage** a few steps west of the monument, overlooking the Château d'If. Farther east on the

corniche, you come to the **Plage du Prado**, the main public beach, and the château and large grassy park of the **Parc Borély**. The No. 83 bus from the Vieux Port follows the Corniche Kennedy to the beaches.

The **Musée de la Faïence** is in the Château Pastré, an impressive nineteenth-century *bastide* (rural manor house) in the 115-hectare (276-acre) Parc du Montradon in the eastern suburb of that name. It brings together the collections of pottery and *faïence* (fine glazed earthenware) formerly at three museums (the Beaux-Arts, the Cantini, and the archeology collection of the nearby Château Borély), along with important new acquisitions. There are approximately 1,500 pieces covering 7,000 years of history from the Neolithic era to the present. Items come from all over the world, but the collection is particularly strong in *faïence* and porcelain from Marseille, an impor-

tant center in the seventeenth and eighteenth centuries, and other localities in Provence. To get there by bus, take the No. 19 line to the Montradon-Pastré stop.

The Calanques de Marseille

Follow the coast road another six kilometers (four miles) past the Rond Point du Prado traffic circle eastward to **Cap Croisette**, and you will see why the Greeks liked it here. The burning white rock islands just off the cape are more typically Cycladic than most of the Cyclades. The road ends at **Callelongue**, a little port at the start of the *calanques* of Marseille (reached by the No. 19 bus from Place Castellane, then the No. 20 bus from La Madrague de Montredon eastward from the Plage du Prado). From here hikers can set off into the limestone hills called the **Marseilleveyre** along the *calanques*. Trails lead to Cassis about 17 km (11 miles) away.

The dramatic **Calanque de Sormiou** can be reached by car, but in the summer only if you know people there or a have a reservation at one of its restaurants (see WHERE TO EAT, page 199).

WHERE TO STAY

There are good hotels at all prices, and the Tourist Office will help you find one. Ask about the two-nights-for-the-price-of-one weekend program that many Marseille hotels take part in. Because the city is so spread-out geographically, we deal separately with hotels in downtown Marseille and ones along the *corniche*.

Downtown Hotels

In the expensive category, the **Mercure Beauvau Vieux Port****** (04 91 54 91 00 FAX 04 91 54 15 76 E-MAIL h1293@accor-hotel.com WEB SITE www.accorhotel.com, at 4 rue Beauvau, is a handsome old antique-furnished 71-room hotel at the most central of all possible locations, the foot of La Canebière fronting on the Vieux Port. At the other end of the Vieux Port is the **Sofitel Vieux Port****** (04 91 15 59 00 FAX 04 91 15 59 50 E-MAIL h0542 WEB SITE www.accorhotel.com, Boulevard Charles-Livon, a modern 127-room hotel by the Parc du Pharo, beautifully renovated in Provençal style, with a panoramic view of the city from the mouth of the port. Half the rooms have the grand view, as does the restaurant, Les Trois Forts, which serves talented chef Dominique Frérard's refined Provençal cuisine. The hotel has a swimming pool.

In moderate price range, the **Résidence du Vieux-Port***** (04 91 91 91 22 FAX 04 91 55 60 88 E-MAIL hotel.residence@wanadoo.fr, at 18 quai du

---

OPPOSITE: Le Vallon des Auffes, a tiny fishing port in Marseille. ABOVE: L'Évêché, the eighteenth-century bishop's palace of the Cathédrale de la Major.

Port, is a Marseille institution with a spectacular view of the boat-filled old port and the Notre-Dame-de-la-Garde from all 45 of its spacious, attractive, well-maintained rooms. Leave the curtains of the sliding glass doors open when you go to sleep and wake up to the grand picture-postcard panorama of Marseille in the morning. Service is friendly and efficient. A short walk from the Vieux Port, the **Mercure Eurocentre***** (04 91 39 20 00 FAX 04 91 56 24 57 E-MAIL h1148@accor-hotel.com, Rue Neuve-Saint-Martin overlooking the Jardin des Vestiges, has 199 tasteful modern rooms, a bright, helpful young team at the front desk, and a fine restaurant, L'Oursinade. **Hôtel Saint-Ferréol***** (04 91 33 12 21 FAX 04 91 54 29 97,

at 19 rue Pisançon, three blocks from the Vieux Port, has 20 attractive rooms, each decorated with the works of one artist — Cézanne, Van Gogh, or Gauguin — with big marble bathrooms, a pleasant lounge and coffee room, and warm personal service. Some rooms have Jacuzzis.

At the low end of the moderate price range is the recently opened **Hermès**** (04 91 90 34 51 FAX 04 91 91 14 44, at 2 rue Bonneterie, just around the corner from the Résidence du Vieux Port, both owned and managed by genial Alain Paulain. It has 28 small, but bright, cheerful, spotlessly clean rooms, all with shower or bath, telephone and television. The rooms on the top floor have patios with fine views of the Vieux Port. Standard doubles go for 350 francs, patio rooms for 395 francs.

In the inexpensive range, **Chambres d'Hôtes Gilles et Pia Schaufelberger** (04 91 90 29 02 E-MAIL schaufel@wanadoo.fr, at 2 rue Saint-Laurent, are

two impeccable bed-and-breakfast rooms rented by a marvelous couple in their spacious apartment overlooking the Vieux Port. At 300 francs, breakfast included, this is a steal.

The Corniche

Le Petit Nice**** (04 91 59 25 92 FAX 04 91 59 28 08 E-MAIL passedat@relaischateaux.fr WEB SITE www.relaischateaux.fr/passedat, 160 Corniche Kennedy at the little Anse Madlormé *calanque*, is the Passédat family's delightful 13-room, two-suite mansion, splendidly perched on a shelf of rock on the sea. This is one of my favorite hotels anywhere. It's like being on a luxurious yacht. It is a Relais & Châteaux member, and ranges from expensive to very expensive. In the moderately priced category, the **New Hotel Bompard***** (04 91 52 10 93 FAX 04 91 31 02 14 E-MAIL marseillebompard@new-hotel.com WEB SITE www.new-hotel.com, is perched high above the *corniche* at 2 rue Flots-Bleu off Boulevard Bompard in its own peaceful park with a swimming pool. But be sure to get a room with a view. For people 35 and under who can do without the maximum in creature comforts, a laid-back guest house called **La Cigale et la Fourmi** (The Cicada and the Ant) (/FAX 04 91 40 05 12 is at 19 rue Théophile Boudier in the eastern suburb of Mazargues, near the *calanques* and within walking distance of the sea. It has 10 neat, pleasant rooms with sofa beds, running water and cooking areas. Rates run from 60 to 140 francs per person, depending on season and location of room. The owner has a boat and a kayak and offers trips to the *calanques*.

Camping

As of this writing there are no camping grounds operating within the city limits of Marseille. The closest ones are **Les Cigales** in Cassis (see WHERE TO STAY AND EAT, page 190, under CASSIS) or **La Verdière** (04 91 65 59 98 FAX 04 91 51 89 13, a 66-place site in Septèmes-les-Vallons, 10 km (six miles) north of Marseille on N8 in the directions of Aix. It is open all year.

WHERE TO EAT

The Vieux Port

There's no need to leave the Vieux Port for your *bouillabaisse*, because the hefty Minguella brothers

dishes inspired by the fresh products in the market, artistically presented. The ambiance is calm, with the tables well-spaced for privacy both in stylish modern dining room and on the outdoor terrace—a rarity in Marseille's restaurants. Closed Sundays and lunch Mondays. **Les Arcenaulx** (04 91 59 80 30, at 25 cours d'Estienne d'Orves, is a classy modern restaurant in a large bookstore and art gallery that once was an arsenal. It serves regional cuisine. Closed Saturday lunch and Sunday. **Les Mets de Provence** (04 91 33 35 38, 18 quai Rive Neuve, is a rustic-style restaurant on the second floor overlooking the Vieux Port serving the famed Provençal *menu* created by chef Maurice Brun, a full evening of

make a magnificent one and serve it to perfection at the **Miramar** (04 91 91 10 40, at 12 quai du Port. It is expensive, but well worth it, and dining on the terrace with its expansive view of the harbor is a pleasure in itself. Besides its famous *bouillabaisse*, the Miramar serves a wide range of fish and shellfish specialties, all impeccably fresh. Your fish is brought to the table for you to inspect it before it goes to the kitchen for cooking. Unlike many fish restaurants, the Miramar has excellent and very imaginative desserts. The restaurant richly merits the Michelin star it has long sported. Reservations are essential. Closed Sundays, the first three weeks of August, and the first half of January.

L'Entracte (04 91 33 50 20, at 23 place Thiars, the cute little square in the pedestrian area to the east of the Vieux Port, serves Marseille-accented *nouvelle cuisine* — imaginative, refined

feasting for 295 francs plus wine. Closed Sundays and Monday lunch.

In the moderate price range, **Bar de la Marine** (04 91 54 95 42, at 15 quai de Rive Neuve, serves hearty food and drinks in a bar modeled after the one in Marcel Pagnol's *Marius* or at tables on the port, near the place where the ferry crosses from the Place aux Huiles to the Hôtel de Ville (City Hall). **L'Oliveraie** (04 91 33 34 41, at 10 place aux Huiles, has the atmosphere of an old-fashioned Provençal bistro in its vaulted dining room strictly devoted, as its name indicates, to the olive-oil based Mediterranean diet. Closed Saturday lunch, Sundays, and the month of August. **L'Atelier** (04 91 33 55 00, at 18 place aux Huiles, is an art gallery

OPPOSITE: The relics of fifth-century Saint Jean Cassien in the crypt of the Basilica of Saint-Victor. ABOVE: Fort Saint-Nicolas guards the entrance to Marseille's Vieux Port.

and lunch spot with a cozy club-like ambiance. It serves light Provençal main courses and excellent desserts. Closed Saturday dinner, Sundays, and the month of August. **Bistro Gambas** (04 91 33 26 44, at 29 place aux Huiles, serves grilled shrimp, curries, and *ratatouille*. Closed Saturday lunch and Sundays.

The Panier

The **Panier des Arts** (04 91 56 02 32 at 3 rue des Petits-Puits, serves savory Provençal bistro meals at reasonable prices, down the street from the Vieille Charité. **L'Art et les Thés** (04 91 56 01 39 is a pleasant tea room in the courtyard of the Vieille Charité, serving light lunches. At **Chez Etienne** (no phone), 39 rue de Lorette, Etienne Cassaro, a legendary figure in the Panier, makes the best pizzas in Marseille.

The Corniche

At **Passédat**, the superb restaurant of the **Petit Nice Hôtel**, the father-and-son team of Jean-Paul and Gérald Passédat come up with the astonishing Provençal-Marseillais inventions that have made them a legend and earned them their two Michelin stars. It is expensive, but a real gastronomic thrill. A 400-franc lunch *menu* is offered on weekdays, beverage included. In good weather you dine on the terrace overlooking the sea. For succulent seafood and lots of atmosphere, a colorful old eatery that I enjoy enormously is **Chez Fonfon** (04 91 52 14 38 in the tiny *calanque* the Vallon des Auffes. Prices are moderate to expensive.

The *Calanques*

L'Escale (04 91 73 16 78, at 2 boulevard Alexandre Delabre, at the entrance to the port of Les Goudes, is run by a former fisherman and serves high-quality, impeccably fresh seafood, with a marvelous view of the little fishing port and the open sea. **La Grotte** (04 91 73 17 79 is at the Calanque de Callelongue in Les Goudes, where the coast road dead-ends at Cap Croisette. It serves good seafood and pizzas in a pleasant garden at moderate prices (closed evenings October to May, except Saturday). **Le Lunch** (04 91 25 05 37, at the Calanque de Sormiou, serves excellent seafood on a terrace overlooking this remote, dramatic *calanque*. It is expensive (figure on 200 francs for a full lunch, a more if can't resist the eminently drinkable chilled white wine from Cassis). After lunch you can enjoy a walk or a swim. You could easily spend a whole day here.

In the summer, the road to Sormiou is closed to all cars except those of residents or people who have booked a table at a restaurant. So be sure to book ahead. In summer, there's a free shuttle bus from the stop called "Cayolle" on the No. 23 bus line. It runs between 7:30 AM and 7 PM and leaves when the coach is full.

NIGHTLIFE

For highbrow entertainment, Marseille has the **Opéra Municipal** (04 91 55 00 70, which puts on an ambitious season of operas and classical music in its handsome art deco opera house; the **Ballet National de Marseille** (04 91 71 03 03, directed by Marie-Claude Pietragalla; and a prestigious French national theater, the **Théâtre National Marseille la Criée** (04 91 54 70 54. The Tourist Office can provide information on their programs.

For lighter entertainment, **Le Trolley-Bus** (04 91 54 30 45, at 24 quai de Rive Neuve, has four vaulted cellars, three with jazz, rock and Latino music, the last an art gallery and wine bar; open Thursday, Friday and Saturday from 11 PM. **Le Pelle Mêle** (04 91 54 85 26, at 45 cours d'Estienne d'Orves, has live jazz. **Le Bar de la Marine** (04 91 54 95 42, at 15 quai de Rive Neuve, has a warm Pagnol-like ambiance and is a relaxed place to have

a drink on the Vieux Port. For a taste of Marseille in its Golden Age, try the last of the grand pre-War cafés, **Café Parisien** (04 91 90 05 77, at 1 place Sadi Carnot. **Il Caffe** (04 91 42 02 19 at 63 cours Julien, is a popular watering place. **O'Stop** (04 91 33 85 34, at 1 place de l'Opéra, directly across the street from the opera house, has a lively *clientèle* of night creatures. Open all night.

How to Get There

There is one flight per hour on average from Paris's Orly Airport to Marseille-Provence International Airport from 6:30 AM to 9:55 PM on Air France domestic or AOM. From London there are three flights a day on British Airways. There are shuttle buses (*navettes*) every 20 minutes from the airport to Gare Saint-Charles, Marseille's railway station. The ride takes 25 minutes and costs 42 francs. By train from Paris's Gare de Lyon, there are 11 *TGVs*

(high-speed trains) a day from Paris, a four-hour and 25-minute trip. There are also train connections to most other southern cities.

Eurolines has a bus service to Marseille from London and most other major European cities. **Phocéens Cars** and other companies have buses between Marseille and the main towns of the Côte d'Azur, Provence, and Languedoc.

By car, the A7 *autoroute* down the Rhône Valley leads directly to its terminus in Marseille, and numerous highways lead to the city from the east. Driving in Marseille can be confusing. I suggest parking your car at the big underground garage at the Cours d'Estienne d'Orves near the Vieux Port and exploring the downtown on foot, Little Tourist Train and local bus, and save the car for trips to the outlying areas.

The port of Martigues west of Marseille, whose special light made it a favorite subject of Provençal painters.

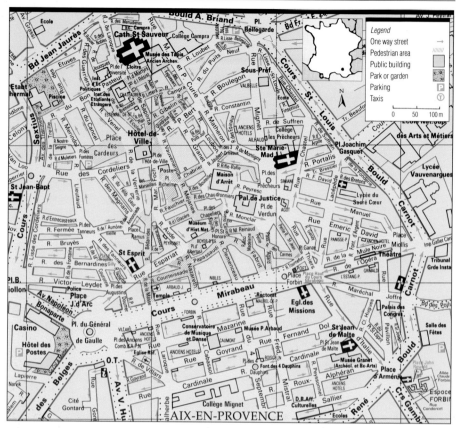

AIX-EN-PROVENCE

AIX-EN-PROVENCE

The old Provençal capital of Aix lies only half an hour inland from Marseille, but you would be hard pressed to find two cities more different than these — Marseille, the big, flamboyant nineteenth-century port in a dramatic sun-bleached setting, teeming with immigrant masses and fanatical fans of the Olympique de Marseille football (soccer) team, and Aix, the calm, aristocratic, tree-shaded, very French (Caucasian, that is) city of modest size with gurgling fountains and honey-colored seventeenth-century neoclassic mansions. Aix doesn't even have a football team.

This is an old city with young people. Almost one-third of its 170,000 residents are students at its university's faculties of law and letters (the more modern subjects such as science and medicine are taught in Marseille). But far from closing itself off from the modern world, Aix has moved into computer and high-tech industries, and in the past 40 years its population has doubled. Most of the growth has taken place in the bland new suburbs that ring the city, leaving the elegant old center intact. Aix is modest in size, but large in cultural attractions, a nice combination. Not surprisingly, Aix

comes out tops in the public opinion polls rating the cities French people would most like to live in.

BACKGROUND

The first settlement at Aix was on the plateau of Entremont north of the present city, where the Celtic-Ligurian Salyen tribe established an *oppidum*. They traded with the Greeks from the sixth century BC and were much influenced by them artistically. But the Greeks and the Saylens had a falling-out in the second century BC, and the Greeks asked the Romans for help. Consul Caius Sextius and his legions destroyed Entremont in 124 BC and cleared the Celtic-Ligurians out, but the Romans stayed and set up a colony at the hot springs on the plain below. They called it Aquae Sextiae (the waters of Sextius), the origin of the name Aix. With its key position at the intersection of the roads from Rome to Spain and from upper Provence to Marseille, Aix flourished during the Pax Romana. But it was reduced to rubble and all but deserted during the barbarian invasions.

Under the Church, which made it a bishopric, and the Counts of Provence, who made it their

Aix's daily food market at the Place Richelme.

capital, Aix recovered from the Dark Ages, and a rich, artistic court life developed under the Angevin dynasty. The University of Aix was founded in 1409, and the last Angevin Count of Provence, "Good King" René, a lover of poetry, music, art and good living, had the most sophisticated court in Europe in the mid-fifteenth century.

When the Angevin line died out in the late fifteenth century, Provence passed under the rule of the King of France. Aix remained the regional capital under a viceroy and the Parliament of Aix. In the seventeenth century, an extremely rich period for Aix, the elegant Quartier Mazarin went up, under the aegis of Archbishop Michel Mazarin, the Cardinal's brother. Prosperity continued until the French Revolution, in which one of its native sons, the scandalous Count Mirabeau, played an early role, but he died in 1791 of apparently natural causes before the guillotine could get him. Aristocratic Aix took the full brunt of the Revolution. Nobles and clergy were killed by the thousands, and Aix lost its position as a capital, reduced to a mere sub-prefecture in the new Bouches-du-Rhône *département*, of which proletarian Marseille became the capital. While Marseille boomed in the nineteenth century, Aix stagnated. By World War I its population had dropped to 30,000.

Only since World War II has Aix has fully recovered its morale and become the universally admired city it is today.

GENERAL INFORMATION

Aix's large **Tourist Office** (04 42 16 11 61 E-MAIL aixtour@aix.pacwan.net, WEB SITE www.aixenprovencetourism.com is at 2 place du Général-de-Gaulle, the main traffic circle at the Fontaine de la Rotonde. That's the big wedding cake of a fountain with the three Graces on top, naked boys riding swans, and jets of water shooting every which way. The Tourist Office's highly professional staff will help you with all reservations and provide excellent maps and documents in all major languages. They also offer guided tours of Vieil Aix (Old Aix), the Quartier Mazarin, and "Cézanne Country."

For airport information, contact **Marseille-Provence International Airport** (04 42 89 09 74. For train service, contact the **SNCF** (08 36 35 35 35. The bus station, **Gare Routière**, can be reached at (04 42 27 17 91.

For taxis, call **Bornes** (04 42 26 29 30, **Mirabeau** (04 42 21 61 61, or **Taxi-Radio Aixois** (6 AM to 8 PM) (04 42 27 71 11 or (night) (04 42 26 29 30.

Car rental agencies include **Avis** (04 42 21 64 16 (also rents bikes and scooters), **Budget** (04 42 38 37 36, **EuropCar** (04 42 27 83 00, **Hertz** (04 42 27 91 32, and **Lubrano** (04 42 26 72 70 (also rents

scooters, open Sundays). Bike rental is available at **Cycle Naddeo** (04 42 21 06 93 and **Cycles Zammit** (04 42 26 72 70.

The **CAP** bus company (04 42 97 52 10 offers day trips to Cassis and the *calanques*, Les Baux-de-Provence, the Lubéron, and other places in Provence.

In case of medical emergency, call the **Hospital** (*Centre Hospitalier*) (42 33 50 00 or **SOS Médecins** (04 42 26 24 00.

FESTIVALS AND EVENTS

The **Festival d'Art Lyrique et de Musique**, generally known as the **Festival d'Aix**, is an opera

and classical music festival that takes place in July. It is one of France's oldest and most prestigious festivals, created in 1948. After a period of experimentation in which it lost some of its following, it has returned to its Mozartian roots. For information, contact the Tourist Office.

WHAT TO SEE AND DO

Aix is a compact city with almost everything of interest within walking distance of the Fontaine de la Rotonde and the adjoining Cours Mirabeau. **Fontaine de la Rotonde** is the most un-Aix-like of Aix's many fountains, foisted upon the city by Napoléon III and his heavy-handed public works czar, Baron Haussmann (the pained looks on the faces of the lions around the base seem to mirror the feelings of the Aixois, disdainful and slightly embarrassed).

Vieil Aix, the medieval city where the cathedral and markets are, lies directly to the north of the Cours, and the aristocratic seventeenth-century Quartier Mazarin (for which the Cours was built in 1651 as the carriage promenade) to the south.

Cours Mirabeau

The broad, café-lined street of the Cours Mirabeau is sheltered by majestic old plane trees in four parallel rows, giving one the feeling of being inside a great cathedral, but more ethereal because of the sunlight filtering in through the canopy of leaves. And better yet, in this cathedral you can have a drink.

The cafés, shops, and restaurants are all on the north side. At No. 55, notice the sign for Cézanne's father's hat business, Chapellerie du Cours Mirabeau. The south side is lined by honey-colored limestone *hôtels particuliers* (private mansions), most now banks or public buildings. The **King René Fountain** is at one end, the Fontaine de la Rotonde at the other, and between them, amid the four auto lanes that run the Cours's four-block length, there are two other fountains — squat, lumpy brutes caked with moss and sprouting weeds that are much loved by the Aixois. One is called "**Moussue**" (mossy) or "**Fontaine Chaude**," because the water is hot, and the other is **Neuf Canons** (Nine Canons). At the top of the Cours is the King René Fountain with a nineteenth-century statue of the "Good King" holding a bunch of Muscat grapes, and facing it is "Les 2 G," **Les Deux Garçons**, one of the most famous cafés in

France. For many travelers, their happiest memory of southern France will be of lingering over a drink at one of the cafés on the Cours Mirabeau watching the bright-looking, mostly young people of Aix parade by.

Vieil Aix

To explore Old Aix start at the mossy fountain and walk up Rue Clemenceau to little Place Saint-Honoré, where the elegant seventeenth-century Hôtel Boyer d'Eguilles at 6 rue Espariat is now the **Musée d'Histoire Naturelle** and has a famous collection of Provençal dinosaur eggs. It is open daily from 10 AM to noon and 1 PM to 5 PM. At nearby **Place d'Albertas** with its three-winged *hôtel particulier* and fountain (one of supposedly 200 in Aix), turn right and follow rues Aude and Maréchal-Foch to **Place Richelme**, where a **food market** has been held every morning since the Middle Ages. The **Hôtel de Ville**, an Italian baroque building with handsome wrought-iron balconies and gates, is in the next square, along with the **flower market** and the **Tour de l'Horloge**, an elaborate clock tower built in 1510 on the foundations of a Roman gate. The large, open **Place des Cardeurs** is popular with students because of the numerous modestly priced cafés and eating places on it.

Saint-Sauveur Cathedral was built piecemeal from the twelfth to the seventeenth centuries, but incorporates elements that are even older. On the front wall facing little **Place de l'Université**, you can see sections of Roman, Romanesque, and Gothic stonework side by side. This spot was also the crossroads of the highways that made Aix important in the days of Provincia Romana — the Aurelian Way (the street in front of the cathedral) and the Decumanus Way to the Mediterranean (now Rue du Bon Pasteur).

Inside the cathedral is Nicolas Froment's gentle **triptych of** *The Burning Bush*, with portraits of King René (to whom the painting was long attributed) and Queen Jeanne at prayer on the side panels, one of the finest works in the South of France. The main panel presents a mystical vision of the Virgin and Child in the middle of Moses's burning bush. (As of this writing, the triptych is under restoration and is shown to the public only on Tuesdays between 3 PM and 5 PM; inquire at the Tourist Office about any changes in the hours of viewing.) The main door of the church secretes another masterpiece: carved walnut figures of the **Four Prophets** by early sixteenth-century Provençal sculptor Jean Guiramand. Again you must get the guardian to open the protective panel. In the **Baptistry**, which dates from the fourth or fifth century, six of the

OPPOSITE: A café on Aix's elegant Cours Mirabeau. ABOVE: The Tour de l'Horloge, built in 1510, in the ancient Vieil Aix section of Aix-en-Provence.

eight Corinthian columns are from the Roman forum that formerly stood on this site. The little **cloister** dates from the twelfth century. Some Festival d'Aix concerts are held here, but operas and other big events are presented in the courtyard of the adjoining **Palais de l'Archevêché**, the grand seventeenth- and eighteenth-century archbishops' palace. Upstairs the excellent **Musée des Tapisseries** has seventeen delightful Beauvais tapestries from that period, including nine based on Don Quixote. It is open 10 AM to noon and 2 PM to 6 PM, closed Tuesday.

L'Établissement Thermal, the eighteenth-century baths on the site of Caius Sextius's 122 BC baths west of the cathedral, reopened in 1999 after

a long period of renovation as **Thermes Sextius** (04 42 23 81 81 FAX 04 42 95 11 33 E-MAIL thermes .sextius@wanadoo.fr, a bright, modern facility offering a multitude hydrotherapy cures, mud baths, and massages.

Across the Cours Sextius on Rue Celony in its own park is the **Pavillon Vendôme**, one of the epitomes of Aix's particular neoclassic style, with twin Atlantes, colossal sculpted bodybuilders, straining to hold up the central balcony. Open 10 AM to noon and 2 PM to 6 PM, closed Tuesday.

Two lively markets are held on the east side of Vieil Aix on Tuesday, Thursday, and Saturday mornings. A **Provençal market** is held at Place des Prêcheurs near the Église de la Madeleine and an **antiques and *brocante* (bric-a-brac) market** at the adjoining **Place de Verdun**. Chocolate lovers can satisfy their craving at the **Puyricard** chocolate factory's retail outlet nearby at 7 rue Rifle-Rafle.

Quartier Mazarin

The Quartier Mazarin is the six-block grid, starting on the south side of the Cours Mirabeau and running down to the Boulevard du Roi-René, that Archbishop Mazarin laid out in the mid-seventeenth century. Over the following century, a remarkable concentration of elegant *hôtels particuliers* went up. At 38 cours Mirabeau is the **Hôtel Maurel de Pontevès**, now a courthouse, eight windows wide and three-stories high with colossal twin Atlantes from Pierre Puget's studio in Toulon straining on either side of the front door to support a fancy wrought-iron balcony. Go inside and admire more fancy wrought iron, much prized in Aix, on the staircase.

Hôtel de Caumont, now the **Darius Milhaud Music School**, at 3 rue Joseph-Cabassol (named for the banking partner of Cézanne's father) was designed by Robert de Cotte, the architect of the chapel at Versailles. It too has handsome wrought-iron exterior balconies and a great sweeping stairway in the main hall, all open and airy, with delicate wrought-iron balustrades.

About the **Fontaine des Quatre Dauphins** at the intersection of Rue Cardinale and Rue du Quatre Septembre writer M.F.K. Fisher says, "Four of the merriest dolphins ever carved by man spout into the graceful basin under its stone needle, topped by a stone pine cone, and it seems unlikely that anyone can pass by this exquisite whole without feeling reassured in some firm way."

The **Musée Granet** just down Rue Cardinale from the Fontaine des Quatre Dauphins at Place Saint-Jean-de-Malte has eight small paintings by

Cézanne. Among them are *Bathsheba* from his impressionist period, *Portrait of Madame Cézanne* from his middle period, and *Baigneuses* and one of his scenes of Montagne Sainte-Victoire from his so-called synthetic period, 1886 to 1906, when he planted the seeds that would soon grow into Cubism. The paintings are on loan to the museum by the French Government. To the eternal shame of Aix, the Aixois scorned Cézanne as the dilettante son of a rich banker and nobody bought his work. The feeling was mutual. Cézanne never painted a single picture of his native city.

Be sure to go down to the basement of the museum to see the Celto-Ligurian sculptures from the archaeological digs at Entremont. The grim-

faced heads of warriors are particularly fascinating. The Greek stylistic influence is clear, but they have personalities of their own that are disturbingly real. The museum is open from 10 AM to noon and 2 PM to 6 PM, closed Tuesdays.

As you walk around the Quartier Mazarin, keep an eye out for Aix's most famous food product, the little flat biscuits made from almonds, honey and melon called *calissons d'Aix*. **Maison Béchard** at 12 cours Mirabeau, **Confiserie Brémond** at 16 rue d'Italie, and **Léonard Parli** at 33 avenue Victor-Hugo make delicious *calissons*. They are especially tasty when eaten fresh.

Aix is also known for its *santons de Provence* (little saints), the sculpted figures of Provençal country people used in Christmas crèches. **Paul Fouque** at 65 cours Gambetta is the acknowledged master of this craft. *Santons* by **Simone Jouglas** are sold at Au Petit Bonheur, a crafts shop at

16bis rue d'Italie. It also carries pottery from Moustiers and cheerful yellow bowls from Aubagne.

WINE TASTING

The principal wine of the area is **Coteaux d'Aix-en-Provence**, known mainly for its light, dry rosés, but also making some reds and whites. The **Syndicat Général des Coteaux d'Aix-en-Provence** (04 42 23 57 14, the producers' association, furnishes information on the *appellation* and a list of vineyards you can visit. Their office is at the Maison des Agriculteurs on 22 avenue Henri-Pontier, up the hill from the north side of Vieil Aix.

To the northeast of Montagne Sainte-Victoire in Rians, **Château Vignelaure** (04 94 37 21 10 is a top producer of the Coteaux d'Aix-en-Provence *appellation* with a large cellar open to the public daily and a modern art gallery with works by Miró, Hartung, Arman, César, and others. Two other Coteaux d'Aix-en-Provence vineyards of the highest quality that are gorgeous old *châteaux* to visit are **Château de Fonscolombe** (04 42 61 89 62 and **Château la Coste** (04 42 61 89 98, north of Aix in **Le Puy-Sainte-Réparade** by the Durance River.

One of the most prestigious wine-growing areas in southern France lies just off the road from Aix to Saint-Victoire on D58. **Palette**, around the village of Meyreuil, is a minuscule *AOC* with only two vineyards. Long-respected **Château Simone** (04 42 66 92 58 makes richly scented deep purple reds, along with whites and rosés. **Château Crémade** (04 42 66 92 66, the other Palette vineyard, is also highly appreciated by wine connoisseurs.

AROUND AIX

Montagne Sainte-Victoire and "Cézanne Country"

The Tourist Office has designed a walking tour called "In the Footsteps of Cézanne" and pointing out all the places in Aix that were important in Cézanne's life — L'Église de la Madeleine where he was baptized, the school where he and his boyhood friend Émile Zola were classmates, Les Deux Garçons where they drank. But as a grown man, Cézanne had a hostile relationship with his native city and spent as little time in town as possible, preferring to be in the studio in his home on the outskirts of Aix or in the countryside now thought of as "Cézanne Country." Route D17 to the east of Aix is a lovely tree-lined road well marked with "Route Cézanne" signs and leading to **Le Tholonet**, **Château Noir** and the **Bibemus Quarries**, all of which he painted many times, through red-earth countryside dotted with scrub pines. Above looms fabled **Montagne Sainte-**

OPPOSITE: Two of the estimated 200 fountains in Aix.
ABOVE: A butcher shop in Aix.

Victoire, named for the victory of Marius over the Teutons in 102 BC, lying 15 km (9 miles) east of Aix. This massive, elongated ridge of limestone with myriad planes and ever-changing patterns is a natural kaleidoscope that endlessly fascinated the painter who Renoir called "the master of all of us." Cézanne painted it about sixty times. Shame on anyone who visits Aix without making the effort to see Montagne Sainte-Victoire.

Outdoors-types who can handle the 945-m (3,100-ft) hike up Montagne Sainte-Victoire will be rewarded with a vast panorama from the **Croix de Provence** at the top. The hike normally takes three to four hours round-trip. The trail starts at **Les Cabassols** on Route D10 on the north side of

the mountain near the **Château de Vauvenargues**, where Picasso is buried.

Vasarely Foundation

The Vasarely Foundation on Avenue Marcel-Pagnol in Jas-de-Bouffan, four kilometers (two and a half miles) west of town, is a vast space created by the Hungarian-born optical art pioneer to display his "architectural" environments — ensembles of murals, wall hangings, and large paintings among which the spectator wanders and "feels" the artist's bold manipulations of color and geometric patterns. The building itself is a work of op-art, made up of 16 juxtaposed hexagons punctuated by large geometric figures of circles within squares, creating a vibration in the eyes of the beholder. Open Monday through Friday from 10 AM to 1 PM and 7 PM, Saturday and Sunday from 10 AM to 7 PM.

Cézanne's Studio, Entremont, and Puyricard

North of Vieil Aix, **Cézanne's Studio** in the last house he lived in has been lovingly restored to the way he left it when he died in 1906, complete with apples and bottles and a statue of Cupid he used in still-lives. The house is set in a wooded garden on a hillside overlooking the city at 9 avenue Paul Cézanne, about 500 m (550 yards) north of the Cathedral Saint-Sauveur via Avenue Pasteur. It is open daily from 10 AM to noon and 2:30 PM to 6 PM, 2 PM to 5 PM in the winter.

Continue out Avenue Paul-Cézanne and you will come to the **Oppidum d'Entremont**, a four-hectare (10-acre) field of ruins on a plateau north

of the city, which was the thriving Celto-Ligurian community the Romans destroyed in 124 BC. The artifacts from here, powerful and well worth seeing, are attractively displayed in the Musée Granet in Aix. Unless you are an archaeology buff, this site its likely to be disappointing. It is two and a half kilometers (about a mile and a half) north of Aix on D14. Open 9 AM to noon and 2 PM to 6 PM, closed Tuesdays and national holidays.

A few kilometers north on D14 in Puyricard, you can visit the **Chocolaterie Puyricard** factory and watch their yummy candies being made. Better yet, you can taste them. Open weekdays.

How to Get There

There are local buses to Montagne Sainte-Victoire, Cézanne's Studio, the Oppidum d'Entremont, and Puyricard. Ask for bus schedules at the Tourist Office. If you are driving from the center of Aix, to get to Montagne Sainte-Victoire, take Boulevard des Poilus and Route D17 east. For Cézanne's Studio, the Oppidum d'Entremont, and Puyricard head north on Avenue Pasteur, and the signs will lead you to your destinations.

WHERE TO STAY

There are 75 hotels in Aix and environs and many furnished flats. The Tourist Office helps visitors find accommodations.

Expensive

The **Villa Gallici****** (04 42 23 29 23 FAX 04 42 96 30 45 E-MAIL villaGallici@wanadoo.fr WEB SITE

21 15 83, is in a large wooded park on the plateau of Entremont overlooking the city. It has a tennis court, swimming pool, and respected restaurant. Its 18 rooms are spacious, medieval in decor, with heavy wooden furniture, beamed ceilings and wrought iron grills, and there are isolated bungalows on the grounds. It is in Celony, three kilometers (two miles) northwest of Aix on the N7.

Moderate

The **Mercure Paul Cézanne***** (04 42 26 34 73 FAX 04 42 27 20 95, at 40 avenue Victor-Hugo, a few minutes walk from the Cours Mirabeau, is a charming antique-furnished hotel with 55 comfortable rooms, big modern bathrooms, and use

www.villaGallici.com, at 18bis avenue Violettes, a short walk from the cathedral, is one of the loveliest hotels in southern France. All 17 rooms have canopied beds, and the use of Provençal fabrics is delightful. It is set in a secluded private park on a hillside above town, and its pool and gardens have a flavor of ancient Rome. No restaurant, but the neighboring Clos de la Violette, the best in town, caters the hotel. The **Grand Hôtel Mercure Roi René****** (04 42 37 61 00 FAX 04 42 37 61 11 E-MAIL h1169@accor.hotels.com WEB SITE www.mercure .com/hotelweb/f/11/1169@ht, at 24 boulevard Roi-René, is on the southern edge of the Quartier Mazarin, a five-minute stroll from the Cours Mirabeau. It has 134 tasteful, modern sound-insulated rooms, a small pool in the interior garden, an indoor garage, a restaurant, and efficient service.

For those who, like Cézanne, crave privacy, the **Mas d'Entremont****** (04 42 23 45 32 FAX 04 42

of the pool at the Grand Hôtel Mercure Roi René right down the street. There is no restaurant, but the hotel serves a copious buffet breakfast, and there is room service from neighboring restaurants between 6 PM and 10 PM. It is my favorite place to stay in downtown Aix. The **Hôtel des Augustins***** (04 42 27 28 59 FAX 04 42 26 74 87, 3 rue Masse, a few steps from the Cours, is a fifteenth-century convent with a soaring stone-walled entrance hall and 29 large, attractive rooms. Martin Luther holed up here with his Augustinian brothers after being excommunicated in Rome by the pope. The hotel has no restaurant, but there are many a few steps away.

For a charming little country inn outside Aix, you can't beat the Bergès family's **Relais Sainte-Victoire***** (04 42 66 94 98 FAX 04 42 66 85 96, in

OPPOSITE AND ABOVE: The striking Vasarely Foundation in the Jas-de-Bouffan suburb of Aix.

Beaurecueil, 10 km (six miles) to the east of the city in an exquisite setting at the foot of Montagne Sainte-Victoire. It has 10 spacious rooms in cheerful Provençal decor, some with patios on the large private park, and a swimming pool. It also has one of the best restaurants in the Aix area (see WHERE TO EAT, below).

Inexpensive

The **Hôtel Cardinal**** (04 42 38 32 30 FAX 04 42 26 39 05 occupies two eighteenth-century townhouses at 22 and 24 rue Cardinale in the Quartier Mazarin. It has a warm ambiance and attentive personnel, 24 quaint, cozy rooms, and seven suites with kitchenettes in the moderate price range. There are three modern **Campanile**** hotels and motels in and around Aix, spotless and good for a family. The closest to the center of town is the 60-room motel on Route de Valcros in the Jas de Bouffan section and can be reached at (04 42 59 40 73 FAX 04 42 59 03 47 WEB SITE www.campanille.fr. Rooms go for 285 francs. The **Hôtel des Arts*** (04 42 38 11 77 FAX 04 42 26 77 31, at 69 boulevard Carnot, is a modest, well-kept hotel on the fringe of Vieil Aix. **Hôtel Paul*** (04 42 23 23 89 FAX 04 42 63 17 80 E-MAIL paul@wanadoo.fr, 10 avenue Pasteur, about 200 m (nearly 220 yards) north of the cathedral, has 24 neat, simple rooms (all with showers), a quiet garden in the back, and a youthful clientele.

Camping

The largest camping ground and the closest to town is the **Chantecler**(04 42 26 12 98 on the Route de Nice in Val Saint-André five kilometers (three miles) from Aix, reached by Cours Gambetta from the center of the city. It has 250 to 300 places on its well-shaded eight hectares (20 acres) of land, a clear view of Montagne Sainte-Victoire, and is open all year. You must reserve early for the period from May to the end of August. A smaller camping grounds, **Arc-en-Ciel** (04 42 26 14 28 is nearby at Pont des Trois-Sautets, also on the Route de Nice, open mid-March to October 1.

WHERE TO EAT

Expensive

The **Clos de la Violette** (04 42 23 30 71, an elegant restaurant in a discreet garden setting at 10 avenue Violette, features the cuisine of one of the top chefs in southern France, Jean-Marc Banzo, noted for his truffle specialties, stuffed vegetables, roast pigeon, roast *rouget* (red mullet) with an herb and bacon stuffing, and other refined Provençal creations that have earned his restaurant a prestigious Michelin two-star rating. Fixed-price *menus* run 250 and 550 francs. It is closed on Sundays and on Mondays at lunch. Reservations are essential.

Amphitryon (04 42 26 54 10, at 2 rue Paul-Doumer, just around the corner of the Cours Mirabeau, is a stylish, but relaxed restaurant with three intimate dining rooms and a pretty courtyard, delightful in the summer, featuring talented chef Bruno Ungaro's savory, strictly regional cuisine. The three-course market-inspired *Retour du marché* and the four-course gastronomic *Menu de chez nous* offer great variety, top quality ingredients prepared with finesse, and attractive presentation, and are real bargains at 155 and 235 francs. Closed Sundays and Mondays at lunch.

Out in the country at the **Relais Sainte-Victoire** in Beaurecueil at the foot of Cézanne's mythic mountain (see WHERE TO STAY, above), chef René Bergé brings his sunny Provençal touch to fish arriving directly from the Vieux Port de Marseille, lamb from the Alpes-de-Provence, and vegetables from the Durance, and there is a fine selection of local and regional wines. The restaurant has one Michelin star. Closed Friday at lunch, Sunday at dinner, and Mondays.

Moderate

The **Bistro Latin** (04 42 38 22 88, at 18 rue de la Couronne in Vieil Aix, is just what its name indicates: a lively eatery serving hearty Provençal fare. I like everything about it. The tasty three-course lunch *menu du marché*, keyed to the fresh products in the market that morning, is a remarkable value at 75 francs, and young owner Gilles Holtz keeps the ambiance relaxed and friendly. There is a good, reasonably priced selection of regional wines. The vaulted yellow cave downstairs is more roomy than the ground floor dining room and just as convivial. Closed Sundays and Monday lunchtime. The **Cour de Rohan** (04 42 96 18 15, at 10 rue Vauvenargues on the Place de l'Hôtel de Ville, is an airy tea room with a courtyard and large open fireplace serving light lunchs. For solid brasserie fare in the heart of the Provençal and bric-a-brac markets, try the busy **Brasserie la Madeleine** (04 42 38 28 02, at 41 place des Prêcheurs.

Inexpensive

La Brocherie (04 42 38 33 21, at 5 rue Fernand-Dol, two blocks from the Cours Mirabeau in the Quartier Mazarin, serves fish and meats grilled on a wood fire in a big open fireplace in the spacious dining room, and there's an open-air dining terrace in back. The restaurant also serves a wide range of typically Provençal dishes. Lunch *menus* start at 59 francs. Low prices are also to be found at bistros and cafés on the Place des Cardeurs, where the clientele is mostly students. **Hacienda** (04 42 27 00 35, at 7 rue Mérindol on a tiny tree-shaded square at the lower end of the Place des Cardeurs, serves a good fixed-price lunch of hors d'œuvres, hot main course, quarter-carafe of wine, and dessert for 62 francs. **Dolce Vita** (04

42 96 45 22, on Place des Martyrs, the square in front of the Archbishop's Palace serves *carpaccio* (razor-thin slices of raw beef or salmon seasoned with herbs and olive oil) and salads. It is open in the summer only. The best pizza in town is at **Pizzeria Capri** (No phone), a hole-in-the-wall takeout counter on Rue Fabrot, just above the Cours Mirabeau.

Cafés

The famous **Les Deux Garçons**, "Les 2 G" (pronounced lay-duh-jhay), at 53 cours Mirabeau, dates from 1792 and was named for the two waiters named Guérin and Guion who bought it in 1840. You can sip where Cézanne, Zola, Picasso,

having a good time. If you study the menu carefully, as they do, and stick to the wine in carafes, you can eat here surprisingly cheaply, given the location and ambiance, for 70 to 100 francs.

NIGHTLIFE

The best fun is hanging out on the Cours. But if you like to gamble, Aix has a **Casino** (04 42 26 30 33, near the Fontaine de la Rotonde. For jazz, **Le Scat Club** (04 42 23 00 23, on Rue de la Verrerie, gets big name artists from time to time, as does **Hot Brass** (04 42 21 05 57 on Chemin de la Plaine des Verguetiers. The top disco as of this writing is **Le Mistral** (04 42 38 16 49 at 3 rue Frédéric

Cendrars, Milhaud, Piaf, Churchill, Mauriac, Sartre, and many other famous clients sipped before you, either on its regally situated terrace near the Fontaine du Roi René or in its grand gilt-framed-mirrored salons inside. Unfortunately, such is its fame that Les 2 G's tables are often deluged with tourists.

For a somewhat less opulent, yet very attractive old café with a more indigenous crowd at the tables, take a look at the **Café de Grillon**, just down the street at 49 cours Mirabeau. University students and other young French-speaking people gather here for spirited discussions on the big L-shaped terrace or in the atmospheric interior, where the cigarette smoke's not too offensive because of the very high ceiling. At the **Café du Cours** at 45 cours Mirabeau there are live bands in the evening, and the music spills out onto the terrace where the tables are packed with students

Mistral. But this can change rapidly. For the latest update, ask a hip-looking student.

HOW TO GET THERE

The closest airport to Aix is Marseille-Provence. There are buses from the airport to Aix's Gare Routière every 45 minutes, a 30-minute ride that costs 43 francs. To come by train, you have to connect at Marseille. Aix's train station is centrally located, a five-minute walk to the Rotonde. By bus, there are frequent connections from Avignon, Marseille and Nice. By car it is 80 km (50 miles) from Avignon by the N7 or the A7 and A8 *autoroutes*, 176 km (110 miles) from Nice by the A8, and 31 km (19 miles) from Marseille by the N8 or the A51. If you arrive by car, I suggest that

Cézanne's beloved Montagne Sainte-Victoire east of Aix.

you park at the municipal parking garage (marked by a big "P") at either the casino, which is convenient to the Tourist Office and the Cours Mirabeau, or at Place des Cardeurs in the heart of Old Aix.

AVIGNON

The hulking Papal Palace and the medieval ramparts that encircle Avignon make this city on a bend in the Rhône a dramatic sight from any approach. In the Middle Ages, when the walls were ringed by deep moats, the effect would have been even more potent.

Avignon today is a city of 100,000, with most of its residents living in modern neighborhoods outside the five-kilometer (three-mile) circle of ramparts. Inside the walls, old Avignon is quiet, even somber, off-season. But in July and early August when the Festival d'Avignon attracts outstanding theater troupes, dance companies and orchestras from all over the world, it becomes the most animated city in France. Crowded, yes. But exciting. Full of life. Musicians in the broad square in front of the Papal Palace, buskers on the Place de l'Horloge. Avignon in July gives a sense of what it must have been like to be at a medieval fair.

Avignon is also the capital of the Vaucluse, an area made up mostly of the Comtat Venaissin, the lands that belonged to the popes of Avignon in the Middle Ages and did not become French until 1791. It is bounded by France's largest river, the swift-flowing Rhône on the west, the Durance on the south and the east, and by Provence's protective ring of mountains, the Dauphiné Alps, in the north. The whole area is easily explored from Avignon.

BACKGROUND

The Rocher des Doms, a steep spur of rock overlooking the Rhône is a natural fortress that has made Avignon attractive to settlers since prehistoric times. Traces of habitation go back to 4000 BC. The town had a name, Avenio, and was the capital of the Gallic Cavares tribe by the time the Greeks from Marseille established a river port and trading post there in the fifth century BC. Avignon flourished under the Romans, but was destroyed by successive waves of invaders that swept up and down the Rhône, Germanic tribes, the Saracens, the Franks, and the Burgundians, until peace was reestablished by the Counts of Toulouse and Barcelona in the twelfth century.

In 1309, Pope Clement V (1305–1314), a Frenchman, fed up with Rome at a time when Italy was in virtual anarchy, accepted King Philip the Fair's offer of protection and moved to the Church-owned Comtat Venaissin, apparently viewing it as a temporary relocation. A pious man, Clement V

lived in rural monasteries in the Comtat. His more worldly successor John XIII (1316–1334), a former bishop of Avignon, moved back into his old bishop's palace in Avignon and set up his court there. His successor Benedict XII (1334–1342) felt that the seat of the Roman Catholic Church needed more impressive quarters and built what is now known as the Old Palace. Clement VI (1342–1352) added the even more impressive New Palace. He also bought Avignon from Queen Jeanne of Naples, the Countess of Provence, in 1348. The vast wealth of the Church stimulated the arts, but also attracted all sorts of scoundrels and *débauchés*. Petrarch, who worked for a cardinal in Avignon, called the City of the Popes "a sinkhole of vice." In 1376, Saint

Catherine of Siena convinced Pope Gregory XI to move back to Rome. But when he died the next year, cardinals loyal to the King of France elected a pope in Avignon and cardinals in Rome elected another one there. They promptly excommunicated one another, and the Great Schism was on. It was a period of unparalleled venality in the Church, with the rival popes in Rome and Avignon outdoing one another to market pardons for sins. This went on until 1409, when the last antipope in Avignon, Benedict XIII, lost favor with the French king and had to leave town. The Church of Rome regained its uncontested title to Avignon and the Comtat Venaissin and held it until the French Revolution, when the former papal holdings became one of the richest and most intriguing parts of the patrimony of France.

A fountain of flowers in front of the Palais de Papes.

GENERAL INFORMATION

The **Avignon Tourist Office** is at 41 cours Jean-Jaurès (04 32 74 32 74 E-MAIL information@ot-avignon.fr WEB SITE www.avignon-toursime.com, a short walk up the main street from the railway station. The staff is helpful and well-informed and has mountains of intriguing brochures about Avignon, trips on the Rhône, and excursions into the Vaucluse. They can also help you with Festival of Avignon reservations.

The **Comité Départemental du Tourisme de Vaucluse** (04 90 80 47 00 E-MAIL info@provenceguide.com WEB SITE www.provenceguide.com, at 12 rue Collège de la Croix, can advise you about itineraries and accommodations in the Vaucluse.

The **Avignon-Caumont Airport** (04 90 81 51 51 is eight kilometers (five miles) east of town on the N7. The **Marseille-Provence International Airport** (04 42 14 14 14 is 75 km (47 miles) away.

The railway station, **Gare SNCF** (08 36 35 35 35, is on Boulevard Saint-Roch, outside the main gate of the city, the Porte de la République.

The bus station, **Gare Routière**, is on Boulevard Saint-Roch near the train station. For information on **regional buses** call (04 90 82 07 35. The international bus lines **Eurolines** (04 90 85 27 60 and **Iberbus** (04 90 86 88 67 also stop here. **City buses** and buses for Villeneuve-lès-Avignon leave from the main Post Office and Place Pie. For information call (04 90 85 44 93.

Car rental agents include **Avis** (04 90 87 17 75, **Budget** (04 90 27 94 95, **Europcar** (04 90 14 40 80, and **Hertz** (04 90 82 37 67. Bike rental is offered by **Masson** (04 90 82 32 19, Place Pie; **Vélomania** (04 90 82 06 98, 1 avenue de l'Amelier; and **Dopieralski** (04 90 86 32 49, 80 rue Guillaume Puy. For **24 hour radio taxis**, Place Pie, call (04 90 82 20 20.

There are **boat trips** on the Rhône you can board at the **Quai de l'Oulle**. The **Bateau Bus** (boat bus) makes six round-trips a day between Avignon and Villeneuve in July and August. The *Delphin* (04 90 85 62 25 makes a one-hour-and-fifteen-minute cruise around Avignon and Villeneuve, leaving at 3 PM daily. The boat restaurant *Miréio* (04 90 85 62 25 offers daily lunch or dinner cruises on the Rhône all year.

The little **Tourist Train** makes a circuit of the old town from March to the beginning of October. It leaves every half-hour from the Tourist Office and the square in front of the Papal Palace.

Lieutaud Voyages (04 90 86 36 75 offers full-day and half-day bus tour trips to Roman Provence, the Camargue, the Lubéron, Les Baux,

The twelfth-century Pont Saint-Bénézet, exalted in the song *Sur le Pont d'Avignon*, and the fourteenth-century Papal Palace of Avignon.

and the Alpes and wine roads. They leave from the Cours de la Gare by the railway station.

The **Comité Interprofessionnel des Vins des Côtes du Rhône** (04 90 27 24 00 FAX 04 90 27 24 13 E-MAIL france@vivarhone.com WEB SITE www.vins-rhone.com, at 6 rue des Trois Faucons, two blocks from the main Tourist Office, offers a free booklet laying out seven different Côtes du Rhône wine routes with the names and addresses of *caves* that can be visited.

In case of medical emergencies, call the **SAMU** (emergency medical service) at (15 or **SOS Médecins** (04 90 82 65 00.

FESTIVALS AND EVENTS

The **Festival d'Avignon**, created by Jean Vilar in 1947, is held from early July to early August and puts on 300 theatrical, dance, and musical events in 12 locations including the Grand Cour of the Papal Palace. One hundred thousand spectators attend. Most plays are in French. For information, contact the Festival d'Avignon office (04 90 14 14 14 WEB SITE www.festival-avignon.com, at Hospice Saint-Louis, 20 rue Portail Bocquier, 84000 Avignon. Book well in advance for the main events. The **Festival Off** (01 48 05 01 19 (a Paris number) is a spin-off from the main festival offering productions by new and avant-garde theater companies, often more original than those of its older brother. The Festival Off has no permanent address in Avignon. Their mailing address is: Avignon Public Off, BP 5, 75521 Paris Cedex 11.

WHAT TO SEE AND DO

Everything you will want to see in Avignon is within walking distance. If you arrive by train, you are 10 minutes from the center of town. If you are traveling by car, park near the train station on the south side of the city, just outside the peripheral road that skirts the ramparts. Cours Jean-Jaurès, the main street, takes you from the station to the heart of town. Just past the Tourist Office at 41 cours Jean-Jaurès, the street changes its name to Rue de la République and leads to tree-shaded, café-lined **Place de l'Horloge**, the main square of Avignon for more than 2,000 years. This was the site of the Roman forum when the town was called Avenio. There are no traces left of the Romans, but you can admire the fifteenth-century **Gothic clock tower** after which the place is named and two handsome nineteenth-century neoclassical buildings, the **Hôtel de Ville** and the **theater**.

A few steps farther is the larger **Place du Palais**, dominated by the vast bulk and relentless austerity of the fourteenth-century crenellated fortress-cum-palace the **Palais des Papes**, one of the best-preserved structures of the medieval period. Its 50-m-tall (160-ft) battle towers are a striking reminder of the insecurity of those times, for even so exalted a personage as a pope. The **Cour d'Honneur** inside the main portal becomes the main stage for theatrical and dance performances during the Festival.

Inside, the Papal Palace is as austere and imposing as it is on the outside. The rooms are vast, most of the walls bare stone. In the days of the popes, they were covered with frescoes or hung with rich tapestries, and every corner of the palace was lavishly furnished. While there are a few frescoes by Simone Martini and Matteo Giovanetti, and the papal bed chamber has fanciful blue walls and a ceiling with hundreds of painted birds, little else remains. In the vast banquet hall four huge eighteenth-century Gobelins tapestries hint at its former sumptuousness, and the museum has plans to create virtual reality imagery to show visitors exactly how it looked when the popes lived here. From April 1 to November 1, the Papal Palace is open daily from at 9 AM to 7 PM, to 9 PM in July, to 8 PM in August and September, and 9:30 AM to 5:45 PM the rest of the year.

The **Musée du Petit Palais** is a fourteenth-century cardinal's mansion at the north end of the Place du Palais that houses an excellent collection of medieval and early Renaissance painting and sculpture from Italy and the School of Avignon. Some artists represented here are Taddeo Gaddi, Paolo Veneziano, Botticelli and Ghirlandajo, and there is a fifteenth-century School of Avignon altarpiece by Enguerrand Quarton, whose masterpiece, the *Coronation of the Virgin*, is worth a trip across the Rhône to Villeneuve-lès-Avignon to see. The Petit Palais is open from 9:30 AM to noon and 2 PM to 6 PM, closed Tuesday.

The **Rocher des Doms**, now a park, was the original settlement of Avignon. The panorama from the observation point at the top is tremendous — the Papal Palace and all of Old Avignon, the Rhône, the Pont d'Avignon, Villeneuve-lès-Avignon across the river with its Tower of Philippe-le-Bel, Charterhouse of the Val de la Bénédiction, and mighty Fort Saint-André dominating the whole valley, while to the northeast, Mont Ventoux commands the horizon.

The **Musée Calvet** reopened its doors in 1996 after a long and successful renovation of an elegant eighteenth-century mansion, which houses an eclectic array of paintings, sculptures, and decorative arts of very high quality. Among its treasures are a stunning collection of French and Avignon paintings from the sixteenth to the nineteenth century (including Joseph Vernet, Hubert Robert, David, Géricault, Corot, Daumier, and Toulouse-Lautrec), Greek, Etruscan, Roman and Greco-Roman sculpture and reliefs, and a huge collection of prehistoric artifacts from local sites. The museum is at 65 rue Joseph Vernet. It is open from 10 AM to 1 PM and 2 PM to 6 PM.

Pont Saint-Bénezet, the famous bridge of the song *Sur le Pont d'Avignon*, was completed in 1190 and spanned 900 m (2,925 ft) between Avignon and the Île de la Barthelasse. It was built, legend has it, because angels commanded a shepherd boy named Bénezet to construct a bridge across the Rhône at this spot, and to prove it was Heaven's wish, gave him the strength to lift an impossibly heavy stone. A brotherhood formed to build the bridge, raised the money and completed the project in eleven years. The bridge is narrow, suitable only for pedestrians and horses. Originally it had 22 arches, but by the seventeenth century, after it had been broken by floods and repaired time and again, the

century. The museum is open Wednesday through Sunday from 1 PM to 6 PM, to 7 PM in the summer.

Avignon is a fascinating city to stroll in, with many corners to explore. **Rue des Teinturiers**, the cloth dyers' street, is a tree-shaded, cobblestone alley that runs alongside one of the little fingers of the Sorgue. A few mossy waterwheels the dyers used in the nineteenth century to rinse their fabrics remain in place. Petrarch's beloved Laura, who died in the plague of 1348, was buried by the Sorgue at the Convent of the Cordeliers, whose bell tower remains. At the **Chapelle des Pénitents Gris** (Grey Penitents Chapel), proceed deep into the interior to see a strange altarpiece, a large gilded

city abandoned it. Only four arches remain, along with its little Romanesque chapel. The bridge can be visited daily from 9 AM to 7 PM April through the end of September, 9:30 AM to 5:30 PM the rest of the year.

The **Musée Angladon-Dubrujeaud** houses the collection of Jean and Paulette Angladon-Dubrujeaud, heirs to the illustrious late nineteenth- and early twentieth-century collector Jacques Doucet, presented as they wished it in their own mansion at 5 rue Laboureur, two blocks from the Tourist Office. The artworks include paintings by Daumier, Manet, Degas, Sisley, Cézanne, Modigliani, and the only Van Gogh painting in Provence, *Wagons de Chemin de Fer*, painted in Arles in August, 1888. The canvases are hung as they were when the couple lived here, in a series of salons furnished superbly with pieces from the Middle Ages to the eighteenth

bas-relief sunburst, a seventeenth-century work from Peru.

Les Halles, the town's lively covered food market is at Place Pie, between Rue des Teinturiers and Place de l'Horloge, open Tuesday through Sunday mornings. This is the best place to find the makings for picnics, and there are modestly priced restaurants around it.

WHERE TO STAY

For a population area of modest size, Avignon and the localities in its immediate vicinity boast an extraordinary number of good hotels in all categories.

In the Papal Palace, the Chapel of Saint-Jean LEFT, decorated in 1346 by Matteo Giovanetti, and RIGHT a contemporary art exhibit of works by Botero.

Expensive

La Mirande**** (04 90 85 93 93 FAX 04 90 86 26 85 E-MAIL mirande@la-mirande.fr WEB SITE www.la-mirande, at 4 place Amirande, is a splendid seventeenth-century mansion in back of the Palais des Papes, meticulously restored and converted into an exquisite, aristocratic 20-room hotel, the most expensive in the Avignon area. The **Hôtel d'Europe****** (04 90 14 76 76 FAX 04 90 85 43 66 E-MAIL reservations@hotel-d-europe.fr WEB SITE www.hotel-d-europe.fr, at 12 place Crillon, is a sixteenth-century nobleman's home that has been a luxury hotel since the eighteenth century and has hosted the likes of Napoléon and the Brownings. There are Aubusson tapestries in the public rooms and 47 guest rooms furnished with antiques. The Europe and the Mirande are lovely places to visit and have tea. The **Auberge de Cassagne******(04 90 31 04 18 FAX 04 90 32 25 09 E-MAIL cassagne@wanadoo.fr WEB SITE www.valrugues-cassagne.com, at 450 allée de Cassagne in the suburb of Pontet, is an old Provençal estate with 19 deluxe guest rooms, a beautiful garden, a pool, and tennis courts. It is five kilometers (three miles) northeast of the city via Route N7 and is a Relais de Silence member.

Moderate

Mercure Cité des Papes***(04 90 86 22 45 FAX 04 90 27 39 31, 1 rue Jean-Vilar, is an attractive, modern 61-room hotel that is as centrally located as a hotel can be — right next to the Palais des Papes, with rooms overlooking the Place de l'Horloge. With its marvelous panorama of the Palais des Papes and the Place du Palais, the penthouse breakfast room is an exhilarating spot to start off the day. Its sister hotel, the **Mercure Palais des Papes*****(04 90 85 91 23 FAX 04 90 85 32 40 is in the Quartier de la Balance, down the hill from the Petit Palais. It has 87 attractive, modern rooms in a quiet neighborhood, a five-minute walk from the Place de l'Horloge. For a more rural hotel experience, **La Ferme*** (04 90 82 57 53 FAX 04 90 27 15 47, is a 20-room inn amid woods and farm fields, with a swimming pool and a very good restaurant. It is at Chemin des Bois on the Île de la Barthelasse, an island in the middle of the Rhône, reached by the Pont Edouard Daladier. It is moderately priced in summer, inexpensive off-season.

Inexpensive

Médiéval*(04 90 86 11 06 FAX 04 90 82 08 64, 15 rue Petite Saunerie, has 35 rooms, spacious but somewhat somber, in a seventeenth-century townhouse near the Palais des Papes. The **Angleterre*** (04 90 86 34 31 FAX 04 90 86 86 74, at 29 boulevard Raspail, a short walk from the train station, is a Logis de France member with 40 simple rooms.

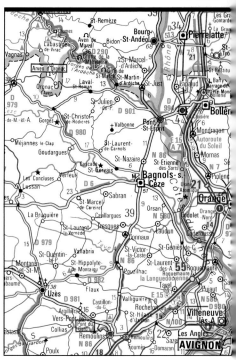

The 15 room **Mignon***(04 90 82 17 30 FAX 04 90 85 78 46 is a pleasant, modest hotel centrally located at 12 rue Joseph-Vernet.

Camping

The camping grounds are on the Île de la Barthelasse, easily reached by the Pont Edouard Daladier. The **Camping Municipal Saint Bénezet** (04 90 82 63 50 FAX 04 90 85 22 12 and the **Bagatelle** (04 90 86 30 39 FAX 04 90 27 16 23 are attractive sites with views of the Papal Palace and the Pont d'Avignon. The Camping Municipal has 300 places and is open from March 1 to October 31. Bagatelle has 238 places and is open all year. Also on the island, but less well-situated, are the 195-place **Parc des Libertés** (04 90 85 17 73 FAX 04 90 86 36 62 open June 15 to September 15, and the 100-place **Deux-Rhônes** (04 90 85 49 70 FAX 04 90 85 91 75 open all year.

WHERE TO EAT

Expensive

For a creative gourmet dining experience in a unique aesthetic setting, try **Christian Étienne** (04 90 86 16 50, at 10 rue de Mons, to the right of the Papal Palace. Amid the bold contemporary art decor of his thirteenth- and fourteenth-century townhouses, chef Christian Étienne reinterprets traditional Provençal cuisine with dishes such as roast *rougets* (red mullet) with melted apples and garlic, or fennel sherbet with saffron sauce.

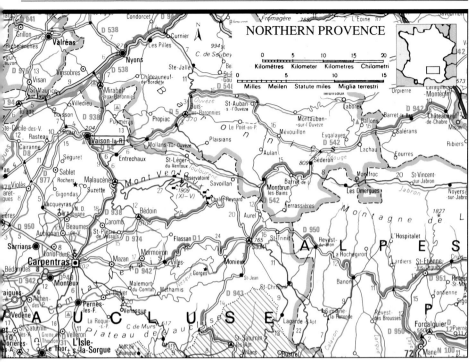

NORTHERN PROVENCE

There's a lunch *menu* at 170 francs on weekdays, but otherwise it is very expensive. Like Christian Étienne, the restaurants of all three expensive hotels mentioned above rate one prestigious Michelin star. **La Vieille Fontaine** at the Hôtel d'Europe is known for its exquisite *coquilles Saint-Jacques* (sea scallops) and roast baby lamb, while at **La Mirande** you can dine on lobster ravioli and roast squab with pistachio butter, and at the **Auberge de Cassagne** Provençal classics are featured: stuffed zucchinis and tomatoes, *rougets* with fresh lime and fennel sauce, breaded strips of lamb, and young rabbit with *légumes farcis*.

In an unpromising location upstairs on a main shopping street, **Hiély-Lucullus ℂ** 04 90 86 17 07, at 5 rue de la République, is an Avignon institution that raises hearty traditional regional cooking to gourmet level. The gratin of mussels and spinach, lobster stew, and *râble de lapereau farci de son foie avec sauce poivrade* (young rabbit stuffed with its liver, served with pepper sauce) are delicious, and regional wines are available by the carafe. There are fixed-price *menus* from 160 francs. I find the relaxed ambiance of Hiély-Lucullus very appealing. The wine of preference at all these top restaurants is, naturally, Châteauneuf-du-Pape.

Moderate

La Fourchette ℂ 04 90 85 20 93, at 17 rue Racine near the Place de l'Horloge, is a relaxed eatery with cheerful Provençal decor serving savory regional food at reasonable prices. Fixed-price *menus* start at 100 francs. It is very popular, so reserve in advance. **Cuisine de Reine ℂ** 04 90 85 78 03 83, at Rue Joseph-Vernet, serves sophisticated traditional French and Provençal cooking and an exceptional selection of wines in glamorous settings, in its spacious art deco dining rooms, or in its 100-place outdoor dining area under a huge white canopy in the arcaded courtyard of the Cloître des Arts, a cluster of classy boutiques and eating places in an elegant old cloister. Closed Sundays except in July. **L'Épicerie ℂ** 04 90 82 74 22, at 10 place Saint-Pierre, is a charming little restaurant seating 30 diners in its cozy interior decorated like an old-time grocery store, adding 50 places on the secluded square in front of the elaborately sculpted Gothic Église Saint-Pierre in fine weather — very romantic in the evening. The cuisine is traditional French and Provençal, with fine three-course fixed-price *menus* at 138 francs. Open April to October, closed Sundays at lunch.

In Provence, where the vegetable is king in most leading chefs' cuisine, oddly enough, you don't find many vegetarian restaurants. **Terre de Saveurs ℂ** 04 90 86 68 72, at 1 rue Saint-Michel, more than makes up for this lack with its subtle, strictly organic, gourmet Provençal vegetarian fare that attracts as many non-vegetarian as vegetarian customers. The restaurant is decorated in the best Provençal taste, and the ambiance and service are exemplary. It also has one of the most astutely chosen wine lists in town.

Inexpensive

At **Le Jujubier (** 04 90 86 64 08, at 24 rue des Lices, two vivacious ladies named Marylin and Marie-Christine prepare and serve Provençal soups, salads, *bœuf des mariniers* (Rhône River boatman's beef stew), *tian de morue* (gratin of codfish baked in an earthenware dish), and other local specialties in their cheerful high-ceilinged space decorated with a big mural of a spreading *jujubier* (a jujube tree). Open for lunch only Monday through Friday except during the Festival, when it is open daily for lunch and dinner.

Wooloomooloo (04 90 85 28 44, at 16 rue des Teinturiers, is a cavernous former printing plant converted into a wildly theatrical eatery decorated with leftover printing presses and Orientalia, lit by hundreds of candles, and run by a mellow young team, serving a sprightly mix of Pacific Rim and Mediterranean dishes such as codfish empanadas, tajines, ginger grilled duckling, pineapple grilled with brown rum and sesame. It is open daily for lunch and dinner all year. Down the street at the **Tache d'Encre (** 04 90 85 81 03, at 22 rue des Teinturiers, you'll find simple, nourishing fare in a big rustic barn of a restaurant that has live pop groups on weekends in the summer. Bustling **Tapalocas (** 04 90 82 56 84, at 10 rue Galante, just down the street from Place de l'Horloge, serves two dozen varieties of tasty Spanish *tapas* at 12 francs per serving and modestly priced wine and beer. It is open daily all year from noon to 1:30 AM.

NIGHTLIFE

Outside the Festival period, this is not an exciting city for nightlife. But one place to look for it is at **La Manutention (** 04 90 82 65 36, at 4 rue des Escaliers Sainte-Anne, behind the Cathedral of Notre-Dame-des-Doms, a big old loft building converted into a movie theater, bar, and restaurant complex where jazz concerts are often held. The mirrored, high-ceilinged **Grand Café (** 04 90 86 86 77 is an *in* spot for drinks or dinner. It is open daily until midnight. Otherwise, head for the **Rue des Teinturiers**, where a young crowd gravitates to its bars and inexpensive restaurants like Wooloomooloo and the Tache d'Encre (see above), especially during Festival time, when impromptu bodegas tend to spring up.

HOW TO GET THERE

There are three flights a day from Paris to Avignon-Caumont Airport on Air France and about a dozen high-speed *TGV* trains, a trip of three hours and 20 minutes. There are also frequent trains from Nîmes, Arles, Montpellier, Marseille, and other main southern cities. Eurolines has buses from London and other European cities, and a number of regional bus lines service Avignon. The only direct public transportation between Aix and Avignon is by bus. By car, take the A7 *autoroute* down the Rhône Valley from the north or up from Marseille 95 km (59 miles) to the south. From Aix take the A8 and the A7. The distance is 80 km (50 miles).

VILLENEUVE-LÈS-AVIGNON

Avignon is the City of Popes, Villeneuve-lès-Avignon the City of Cardinals. It lies directly across the Rhône from Avignon and was easily reached in the Middle Ages by the Pont Saint-Bénezet to the Île de la Barthelasse, then a short bridge over

the western branch of the river to Villeneuve. In the fourteenth century, cardinals crossed the bridge and set up their residences in Villeneuve to maintain a bit of independence from the popes. Villeneuve was in France, Avignon in the Holy Roman Empire.

GENERAL INFORMATION

The **Tourist Office (** 04 90 25 61 33 is at 1 place Charles-David and is open all year.

WHAT TO SEE AND DO

The **Tour Philippe-le-Bel** was part of the French fortifications at the Villeneuve end of the bridge, and in the late fourteenth century, formidable **Fort Saint-André** went up on Villeneuve's highest hill. There are panoramas of Avignon from both places.

On the hill below Fort Saint-André are the moody ruins of a huge Carthusian monastery, the **Chartreuse du Val de Bénédiction**, founded in 1356. It became an important way-station on the medieval pilgrimage route to Compostela. Concerts are held here in the summer.

A few **cardinals' residences** remain on Rue de la République. The finest, that of Pierre de Luxembourg, is now the **Musée Municipal**. It houses one of the great paintings of the medieval period, the *Coronation of the Virgin* by Enguerrand Quarton (sometimes spelled Charanton). Quarton was a native of Picardie, but worked for years in Aix and Avignon and became fascinated by the Mediterranean light. This brilliantly luminous, hard-edged

work looks like it could have been painted in the 1980s instead of 1453, when it was. On the theological level, an unusual feature is that God the Father and God the Son, seen placing a crown on the head of the Virgin, are represented as twins. Among many other works to see in this rich collection are a remarkable fourteenth-century Virgin painted on sculpted ivory, and a death mask of Jeanne de Laval, the second wife of Good King René. Open from 10 AM to 12:30 PM and 3 PM to 7:30 PM from the April 1 to the end of September, 10 AM to noon and 2 PM to 5 PM the rest of the year. Closed the month of February and national holidays.

WHERE TO STAY AND EAT

The **Hostellerie le Prieuré****** (04 90 15 90 15 FAX 04 90 25 45 39 E-MAIL leprieure@relaischateaux.fr WEB SITE www.relaischateau.fr/leprieure, at 7 place du

Chapitre, is a fourteenth-century priory in the Cardinals' District with 26 antique-furnished rooms and 10 apartments, lush gardens, a pool, and tennis court. The rooms are expensive, as is its excellent Provençal restaurant, which rates one Michelin star. The hotel is a Relais & Châteaux member. **La Magnaneraie****** (04 90 25 11 11 FAX 04 90 25 46 37 E-MAIL magnaneraie@gulliver.fr WEB SITE www.avignon-et-provence.com/la-magnaneraie is an elegant fifteenth-century cardinal's residence on the heights of Villeneuve at Camp de Bataille. It has a large swimming pool and sun deck, tennis court, and 26 very comfortable rooms, some in the moderate price range, most of them expensive. Its lovely garden restaurant serves noted chef Gérard Prayal's Provençal cuisine. **L'Atelier**** (04 90 25 01 84 FAX 04 90 25 80 06 is a charming, moderately priced small hotel in a sixteenth-century house at 5 rue Foire in the center of Villeneuve-lès-Avignon.

Camping
Camping Municipal de la Laune (04 90 25 76 06 is a spacious, well-shaded camping ground with a pool, on Chemin Saint-Honoré, near Fort Saint-André.

HOW TO GET THERE

To get to Villeneuve-lès-Avignon by bus, take the No. 10 from the Avignon train station (Gare SNCF), Place Pie, or from Porte de l'Oulle on the Avignon end of the Pont Edouard Daladier. It leaves every half-hour. Driving, take the Pont Edouard Daladier across the Rhône and the Île de la Barthelasse and go right on the opposite side of the river on Avenue Gabriel-Péri to get to the center of Villeneuve.

CHÂTEAUNEUF-DU-PAPE

This hilly town 18 km (11 miles) north of the Papal City is where the popes of Avignon chose to establish their vineyards. With the tower of a castle built by wine-loving John XXII in 1316 overlooking it, Châteauneuf-du-Pape continues to produce southern France's most prestigious wine. The vineyards are unusual. They are covered by a thick bed of *galets*, rounded stones deposited by the Rhône in the Ice Age, that heat up in the sunlight and stay warm at night, making the vines feel good so that the grapes make especially delicious wines.

GENERAL INFORMATION

The **Tourist Office** (04 90 83 71 08 is at Place du Portail in the center of town. It will provide a map and a list of wine estates and their visiting hours.

OPPOSITE: Villeneuve-lès-Avignon, with Fort Saint-André on top of the hill. ABOVE: Working in the vineyards at Châteauneuf-du-Pape.

WINE TASTING

Châteauneuf-du-Pape wines belong to the over-all family of Côtes du Rhône wines. This family of wines is grown on both sides of the Rhône River, and the ones grown in the areas south of the Drôme River are known as Côtes du Rhône Méridionales (southern Côtes du Rhône). The wines are pre-dominantly reds. Generally speaking, they are lighter, clearer, and more fruity in the northern areas — the Drôme, the Papal Enclave, and the northern part of the Gard — and more full-bodied and earthy in the Vaucluse, where other famous wine villages such as Gigondas and Vacqueyras

are located, and where Châteauneuf-du-Pape makes the deepest-hued, most robust reds of all.

The system of *Appellation d'Origine Contrôlée* (*AOC*) began here. In 1923, the winegrowers of Châteauneuf-du-Pape agreed on a rigid set of standards governing every aspect of the growing of the grapes and the making of the wine, an idea that spread to other wine regions. Thirteen kinds of grapes are blended to make red Châteauneuf-du-Pape, and each vineyard has its own secret recipe. Reds account for 95% of the production. The remaining five percent are whites, normally made from six varieties of grapes. The reds should be kept three to five years for full maturation. The whites can be drunk in the first two years.

The most beautiful wine château to visit and among the most highly respected is **Château la Nerthe (** 04 90 83 70 11, an elegant mansion in a tree-shaded park that was taken by the Nazis as

their regional HQ during World War II. Its big, atmospheric cellar is open weekdays from 8 AM to noon and 2 PM to 6 PM. Other prestigious estates one can visit are **Domaine du Vieux Télégraphe (** 04 90 33 00 31, **Clos des Papes (** 04 90 83 70 13, and **Château de Mont Redon (** 04 90 83 72 75. The wines of Châteauneuf-du-Pape tend to be quite expensive, especially those of glamorous estates such as these. Much more affordable Châteauneuf-du-Pape, but of very high quality, is made by the **Domaine de Nalys (** 04 90 83 72 52, an up-to-date operation that spurns glamour and tries to keep prices down. They were among the first to market whites, in the 1960s. They are on the Route de Courthezon (D92) east of town.

In general, the cellars are open weekdays and by appointment only on Saturdays.

WHERE TO STAY AND EAT

The **Hostellerie des Fines Roches****** **(** 04 90 83 70 23 FAX 04 90 83 78 42 E-MAIL finesroches@ enprovence.com is an ivy-covered mock-medieval château on a hill, reached by a private road through its vineyards. It has seven antique-furnished guest rooms all with views of Avignon and the Rhône Valley. It also boasts one of the area's top restaurants, featuring chef Philippe Estevenin's gastronomic Provençal fare and local wines. It is expensive. The **Verger des Papes (** 04 90 83 50 40 is a casual eating place by the ruins of the fourteenth-century Château des Papes with a large open terrace and grand panoramic view, serving hearty Provençal cuisine — *escargots*, *daube*, *bourride* (snails, beef stew, fish stew) — at moderate prices.

HOW TO GET THERE

By car, Châteauneuf-du-Pape is 18 km (11 miles) north of Avignon on N7 and D17. There are three buses a day from Avignon's Gare Routière.

ORANGE

This bustling town of 30,000 lies 28 km (18 miles) north of Avignon and six kilometers (four miles) east of the Rhône. It is a main distribution center for the area's big peach, pear and apple orchards, market gardens, and vineyards and is home to a military airbase and a Foreign Legion post. But to the world, it owes its fame to its Roman Arc de Triomphe and especially its huge Roman Théâtre Antique, still in regular use after almost 2,000 years.

BACKGROUND

Orange's name has nothing to do with the fruit or the color. It comes from Arausio, its Celtic-Liguarian name. With the support of Octavius, veterans of Caesar's Second Gallic Legion colonized the town in 35 BC, and their patron's largesse continued when he became Augustus in 27 BC. Orange prospered under the Pax Romana until 412, when it was sacked by the Visigoths.

In the twelfth century, the town gained the status of an independent principality under the rule of the troubadour-prince Raimbaut of Orange. In 1530, through a complicated series of marriages, the Dutch branch of the German house of Nassau came into possession of Orange. Its leader, William the Silent, began the Netherlands' war of independence against Spain, and he made Orange a bastion of Protestantism during the Wars of Religion. It became a refuge for dissenters persecuted in arch-Catholic Avignon and the Comtat Venaissin. In 1713, after the War of the Spanish Succession, Orange's Dutch rulers ceded the principality to France. They kept the name of the House of Orange, however, which they had adopted, and it remains the name of the Dutch royal family to this day.

GENERAL INFORMATION

The **Tourist Office** (04 90 34 70 88 is opposite the Théâtre Antique at Cours Aristide-Briand.

The train station, **Gare SNCF** (08 36 35 35 35, is on Avenue Frédéric-Mistral.

The bus station, **Gare Routière** (04 90 34 15 59, is nearby on Avenue Frédéric-Mistral.

FESTIVALS AND EVENTS

Since 1902, Orange's Théâtre Antique has been the site of one of Europe's most important opera and orchestral music festivals, **Les Chorégies d'Orange** (04 90 34 24 24, held in July and early August. By writing, contact Chorégies d'Orange, BP 205, 81017 Orange. The box office is at the Théâtre Antique.

WHAT TO SEE AND DO

The **Théâtre Antique**, built in the first century AD, is the best preserved Roman theater anywhere. Its huge brick scenic backdrop stands 38 m (125 ft) high and is 103 m (338 ft) wide. In Roman times it was decorated with 76 columns in three tiers with dozens of statues in niches. Only a few columns and one statue remain, that of Augustus striking a suitably imperial pose. The auditorium's steep semicircle of stone risers can seat up to 10,000. The acoustics are excellent, but if you go to a performance, be sure to bring cushions. The stone slabs are a killer.

The theater can be visited daily except Christmas, New Years, and May Day. The best overall view is from the high hill in back of the auditorium, the **Parc de la Colline Saint-Eutrope**. This

is where the Princes of Orange had their castle. It was demolished in 1672 by the Count of Grignan, Madame de Sévigné's son-in-law, during one of Louis XIV's many wars.

The **Arc de Triomphe** from 20 BC is also well preserved. It has a vivid bas-relief of the Second Gallic Legion doing battle against the Gauls on the top central panel, naval emblems and other decorative elements, and handsome Corinthian columns. At 22 m (72 ft) high and 21 m (68 ft) wide, it is the third largest Roman triumphal arch standing.

Harmas is the museum and botanical garden of Jean Henri Fabre (1823–1915), a world-renowned entomologist from the area, who spent the last 36 years of his life at his big farm near Orange amassing a vast collection of butterflies, insects, shells, fossils, and minerals and painted a series of 700 astonishingly lifelike watercolors of mushrooms of the Vaucluse. Harmas is in **Sérignan-du-Comtat**, eight kilometers (five miles) northeast of Orange on the N7 and D976. It is open from 9 AM to 11:30 AM and 2 PM to 6 PM, to 4 PM in the winter; closed Tuesday, the month of October, and national holidays.

WHERE TO STAY AND EAT

Hôtel Arène* (04 90 11 40 40 FAX 04 90 11 40 45, at Place de Langes, has 30 large, pleasant, moderately priced rooms on a quiet square in Old Orange, and is a Relais du Silence and Logis de France member. For truffle omelets, guinea fowl, zucchini blossoms, and other Provençal treats, try **Le Parvis** (04 90 34 82 00, at 3 cours Pourtoules, where you dine on the shaded terrace or in the wooden-beamed dining room. The three-course fixed-price *menu* at 98 francs is an excellent value.

Camping

Camping is at **Le Jonquier** (04 90 34 49 48, on Rue Alexis-Carrel northwest of the city, open April to the end of September.

HOW TO GET THERE

The *TGV* (high-speed train) now stops at Orange, and there are frequent trains from Avignon. By bus, there are connections with Avignon, Carpentras, Séguret, and Vaison-la-Romaine. The tourist office and bus stations have the schedules. If you are driving, Orange is reached by the A7 *autoroute* from the north or the south and the A8 from Nîmes, Montpellier, and the southwest, and there are good direct roads from Carpentras and Vaison-la-Romaine.

The statue of Emperor Augustus, the town's patron, at the first century AD Théâtre Antique in Orange.

SUZE-LA-ROUSSE AND LA DRÔME PROVENÇALE

North of Orange lies a sunny wedge of land known as "La Drôme Provençale." It is shielded from frigid northern air by the mountains of the Dauphiné, making it the northernmost area in France where the olive tree will grow, thus Mediterranean in climate. It is also is an important truffle-producing area and makes Côtes du Rhône and Coteaux du Tricastin wines. This area lies in the *département* of the Drôme, which is north of the current political boundaries of Provence, but is climatically and historically Provençal. As it is a bit off the main tourist track, it offers the traveler a chance to discover this "admirable land of happy hills and light," as Jean Giono called it, in a relatively untrammeled state.

Suze-la-Rousse, 20 km (12.5 miles) directly north of Orange, is an important town for students of wine — literally, because it is the home of the **Université du Vin (** 04 75 97 21 30 FAX 04 75 98 24 20 E-MAIL universite.du.vin@wanadoo.fr. This respected institute founded in 1978 offers a full range of courses about wine, from professional programs for wine-makers and *sommeliers* to weekend wine tasting sessions for the serious amateur. To contact them by mail, write: Université du Vin, Le Château, 26790 Suze-la-Rousse (Drôme).

The university is housed in the **Château de Suze**, a twelfth-century castle, once the property of the Princes of Orange, which dominates the pretty village and the vine-covered countryside from a hill in the center. It was remodeled in the sixteenth century and has an elegant arcaded Renaissance courtyard and richly painted and stuccoed Renaissance and baroque rooms. The architecture of the château makes it worth visiting in its own right, and the university's state-of-the-art wine tasting laboratory in a former chapel is a marvel of function and beauty. The château and its **tour office (** 04 75 04 81 44 are open from 9:30 AM to 11:30 AM and 2:30 PM to 5:30 PM, 6 PM in the summer, every day in July and August, closed Tuesdays and Wednesday mornings the rest of the year.

There is a **reception office (** 04 75 04 81 44 in the château. The town's **Tourist Office** 04 75 04 81 41 is in the village below.

HOW TO GET THERE

Suze-la-Rousse is easily reached by car from Orange, a lovely drive on D11 and D117. Traveling through this part of the country is particularly enjoyable, because grape-growers have the happy custom of planting rose bushes at the ends of their rows of vines. There is no public transportation to Suze-la-Rousse.

GRIGNAN

Grignan is a graceful old northern Provençal town built around the handsome hilltop château of the powerful Adhémar family. As in Suze-la-Rousse, the château was a medieval stronghold first and was expanded and turned into a Renaissance showplace in the sixteenth century. It owes its everlasting fame to Madame de Sévigné, whose letters to her daughter written in the late seventeenth century and published in 1726 became popular thanks to her sharp observations of the life of her period. Her daughter was the wife of the Count of Grignan, the Viceroy of Provence, and Madame de Sévigné loved Grignan, spent a good deal of time here, and died at the château. It was looted and badly damaged during the Revolution, but heirs of the Adhémar family restored it early in the twentieth century.

GENERAL INFORMATION

The **Tourist Office (** 04 75 46 56 75 is next to the château.

The **Caveau des Coteaux du Tricastin (** 04 75 46 56 96, next door to the Tourist Office, has wines of all the producers of the *appellation* and makes them available for free tasting, and it sells them at the same price as the vineyards themselves. Knowledgeable personnel are there to help you with your choices and direct you to vineyards you may want to visit.

WHAT TO SEE AND DO

In the richly furnished and decorated 25-room **Château de Grignan**, the main attraction is Madame de Sévigné's apartments, restored to the style of her period with Louis XIII and Louis XIV furniture and Aubusson tapestries of mythological scenes. Classical music **concerts** are held at the château in the summer, and there are fine views of Mont Ventoux to the southeast. The château can be visited daily from 9:30 AM to 11:30 PM and 2 PM to 5:30 PM (6 PM in the summer), and it is closed Tuesdays from November to March.

WHERE TO STAY AND EAT

For deluxe lodging in Grignan, the **Manoir de la Roseraie***** **(** 04 75 46 58 15 FAX 04 75 46 91 55 E-MAIL roserie.hotel@wanadoo.fr, on the Route de Valréas, is an elegant mansion in a large private park with a beautiful pool and a view of the château. It has 17 spacious, tastefully decorated rooms in the expensive range, and a gourmet restaurant.

For an inexpensive lunch of lamb and fresh vegetables or other simple, savory Northern Provençal fare, seek out **L'Eau à la Bouche (** 04 75 46

57 37, a flowery little restaurant on Rue Saint-Louis in the heart of the old village.

For a real country experience and a chance to get to know Coteaux du Tricastin wines, the **Domaine Saint-Luc*** (04 75 98 11 51 FAX 04 75 98 19 22 rents six comfortable guest rooms, all with private baths, including one deluxe room with a Jacuzzi, in Eliane and Ludovic Cornillon's big eighteenth-century farmhouse. For dinner, guests feast on local farm products and sample the Domaine Saint-Luc's prize-winning wines. A double room costs 400 francs, 600 francs for the deluxe one, breakfast included, and dinner is 150 francs. There is a pool in the oak grove. Reserve early. It is in La Baume-de-Transit halfway between Grignan and Suze-la-Rousse.

Camping

Grignan has two camping grounds, **Les Truffières** (04 75 46 93 62, which has 35 places, a restaurant, bar, washing machines and a pool, and the 30-place **Grignan Municipal** (04 75 46 50 06. Both are open from April 1 to the end of October.

HOW TO GET THERE

For those motoring down from Northern Europe, the closest exit to Grignan from the A7 *autoroute* is Montélimar-Sud, which is about a six-hour drive from Paris. That's where I get off when I'm heading for my little retreat in the Vaucluse, and for anyone who's not in hurry, I recommend leaving the A7 at this point and taking the well-maintained secondary roads through the lovely olive groves and vineyards of La Drôme Provençale and the Vaucluse. This is a much more pleasant way of getting into the mood of Provence than driving past the Centrale Nucléaire du Tricastin, the huge nuclear power plant you will see if you keep driving south on the *autoroute*.

Grignan is 18 km (11 miles) east of the *autoroute* on D541.

There are five buses a day to Grignan on the Teste bus company's regular route between Montélimar and Nyons.

VALRÉAS AND THE PAPAL ENCLAVE

The Papal Enclave is an anomaly of history, a little island of land acquired by the popes of Avignon and owned by the Papacy until 1791; it is now part of the Vaucluse, but lies within the borders of the Drôme. Valréas is the chief town of the Papal Enclave. It has a handsome, mostly eighteenth-century **Hôtel de Ville** and a jewel of a Romanesque church, the twelfth-century **Église de Notre-Dame-de-Nazareth**.

On June 23 Valréas enacts the medieval pageant of the **Nuit du Petit Saint-Jean** in which a four-year-old boy is crowned Little Saint John, blesses the crowd in a procession, and protects the town for the rest of the year.

Market days are Wednesday mornings at Place du Cardinal Maury and Saturdays at the war memorial. On Wednesdays in November, there is a truffle market.

The **Tourist Office** (04 90 35 04 71 is at Place Aristide-Briand, Valréas.

WINE TASTING

The Papal Enclave is prime Côtes du Rhône wine country, and there are outstanding wine cooperatives in Valréas and Visan, nine kilometers (five and a half miles) to the south. Two exceptional individual wine makers in the Papal Enclave are **Domaine du Val des Rois** (04 90 35 04 35 and **Domaine de la Prévosse** (04 90 35 05 87, in Valréas.

HOW TO GET THERE

The Teste line's Montélimar-Nyons buses stop at Valréas five times a day in either direction, and Cars Mery has five buses a day from Avignon's Gare Routière via Orange, a trip of one hour and thirty minutes. By car, Valréas is nine kilometers (five and a half miles) east of Grignan and 14 km (nine miles) west of Nyons on D541, and 35 km (22 miles) northeast of Orange on D976.

NYONS

Nyons is the olive capital of La Drôme Provençale. Chef Alain Ducasse calls the black olives of Nyons the best in the world, and in 1994, "the Black Pearl," as it is known here, and the olive oil of Nyons were the first to be awarded an *AOC* in this newly created agricultural *appellation contrôlée* category.

Lest you think this is some quaint little business, the Cooperative du Nyonsais has 260,000 trees and presses 65,000 tons of olive oil per year. And there are private producers as well. From late November to late February, the oil mills are in full swing, and the public is invited to watch the process.

But all is not olives in Nyons. Truffles ("black diamonds"), fruit jams and jellies, and honey are also important products of the region, and this town of 6,500 is the center of it all.

GENERAL INFORMATION

The **Tourist Office** (04 75 26 10 35 is on the broad main square of town, Place de la Libération.

FESTIVALS AND EVENTS

Les Olivades, the big olive festival, takes place the second Sunday in July.

WHAT TO SEE AND DO

To savor cured olives of all kinds and olive preparations such as *tapenade* — a purée of black olives flavored with herbs of Provence and capers, which is also made in a green olive version — or *anchoïde*, made with anchovies, vinegar and olive oil, there are three excellent choices in town. The bright, modern **Cooperative du Nyonsais** at Place Olivier de Serres, a few blocks from Place de la Libération, offers the full range of products, including their *AOC* olive oil, as well as wines of the region that you can buy by the glass, by the bottle, or *en vrac*, in 28-liter (nearly 30-quart) plastic containers. **Moulin Ramade** on the Impasse du Moulin off Avenue Paul Laurens is another distinguished mill. The colorful **Vieux Moulin**, by the Pont Roman, is part mill, part shop, and part museum of traditional processing techniques. It has been owned and operated by the Autrand family since 1725, and genial owner Jean-Pierre Autrand will show you the operation. During pressing season from November to February, you can watch the process at all three mills.

The town has a medieval section, the **Quartier des Forts**, an arcaded old square, **Place Docteur Bourdongle**, and a fourteenth-century donkey-back bridge called the **Pont Roman** over the River Eygues. Nyons has a busy **market** Thursday mornings on Place de la Libération, one of the best in Provence. For marvelous cheeses from the nearby mountains, **La Halle aux Fromages** on Place de la Libération is open Tuesday through Sunday, with a delicious selection of breads to go with them.

WHERE TO STAY AND EAT

The **Auberge du Vieux Village***** (04 75 26 12 89 FAX 04 75 26 38 10, on the Route de Gap three kilometers (two miles) east of town in the village of Aubres, is a charming 22-room country inn with rustic decor, modern bathrooms and balconies overlooking a peaceful valley, a swimming pool, gym, and restaurant. Prices are moderate. A Logis de France member. **La Picholine***** (04 75 26 06 21 FAX 04 75 26 40 72, on the Promenade de la Perrière, one kilometer from Nyons via the Promenade des Anglais, has 16 attractive, moderately priced rooms, a big pool, and a garden shaded with ancient olive trees, a restaurant, and a view of the town from its hillside. A Logis de France member. For a hotel on the main square in town, try the **Colombet**** (04 75 26 03 66 FAX 04 75 26 42 37, at 55 place de la Libération, with 25 pleasant rooms and a cheerful restaurant, with room and food prices inexpensive to moderate.

For restaurants, my top choice in town is **Le Petit Caveau** (04 75 26 20 21, at 9 rue Victor-Hugo,

for its offbeat culinary combinations, such as lamb with honey and linden-blossom tea, or stuffed rabbit with *tapenade*, and good local wines. The prices are moderate, with fixed-price *menus* starting at 110 francs. Another fine restaurant with lots of culinary surprises and moderate prices is **La Charrette Bleue** (04 75 27 72 33 in Condorcet, seven kilometers (four miles) to the east of town on the Route de Gap.

Camping

There are two camping grounds in Nyons. The deluxe **Camping des Clos** (04 75 26 29 90, on the Route de Gap, open all year, has 150 places and a pool. The **Camping Municipal de Nyons** (04 75 26 22 39, on the Promenade de la Digue near the center of town, is a more modest grounds with 97 places and no pool, open April through early November. There are a dozen camping grounds in nearby communities. For information contact the Nyons Tourist Office.

HOW TO GET THERE

Lieutaud Voyages has three buses a day from Avignon via Vaison-la-Romaine. By car, Nyons is 14 km (nine miles) east of Valréas and 16 km (10 miles) north of Vaison-la-Romaine on D938, a pretty drive through peach orchards, vineyards, and rolling hills. It can also be reached by the D976 and D94 from Orange, a distance of 42 km (29 miles).

VAISON-LA-ROMAINE

Vaison-la-Romaine is three towns in one. As its name indicates, Provence's Roman heritage figures strongly in one of them, but you will also have a restored medieval town and a lively "modern" one to explore. Attractively situated at the foot of Mont Ventoux, this town of 7,000 is the commercial and cultural hub of the upper Vaucluse. The good selection of hotels and restaurants in and around Vaison make it the best base for exploring the northern reaches of Provence.

BACKGROUND

The earliest inhabitants were Bronze Age Ligurians, conquered in the fourth century BC by the Celtic Voconces tribe, who set up their capital at Vaison. In 123 BC, the same year the Romans established Aix, they defeated the Voconces and took over Vasio Vocontiorum, as they called it. As Rome integrated Provence into its economy, especially after Caesar's defeat of Massalia in 49 BC, the Roman landowners of Vaison became rich on wine, fruit and vegetables, the area's most important products to this day, and Vaison became a thriving town of least 10,000 inhabitants.

As the Empire collapsed, the Church took the lead in Vaison's direction, installing a bishop as early as the fifth century. In 1125, the great lords of the South, Counts Alphonse of Toulouse and Raimond Bérenger III of Barcelona, agreed to settle their claims in Provence, with Toulouse getting the lands north of the Durance. When the Count built Vaison's château on the hill to the south of the Ouvèze River, people started to build their houses on the slope below the castle for protection, and Haute Ville, the medieval city, developed. In the next century, because of his support of the Cathars during the Albigensian Crusade, the Count of Toulouse was stripped his lands, and in 1274, King Philip III of France and his uncle Count Charles of Provence gave Toulouse's lands in Provence to the pope. As part of the Papal Comtat Venaissin, comprising most of the present *département* of the Vaucluse, Vaison remained a possession of the Church until the Revolution.

In the eighteenth and nineteenth centuries, people abandoned the Haute Ville and moved the town back across the river to its modern site between the Roman and medieval cities.

GENERAL INFORMATION

The **Tourist Office** (04 90 36 02 11 is on Place du Chanoine Sautel between the Roman sites of Puymin and La Villasse. It also handles tourist information for Séguret and the Mont Ventoux area.

FESTIVALS AND EVENTS

In July Vaison has its **Festival d'Été** (summer festival), with music, dance, and theater performances at the Roman theater practically every night. For information, get in touch with the Tourist Office.

WHAT TO SEE AND DO

To either side of the **Place du Chanoine Sautel**, named in honor of the abbot who led the excavations, lie 12 hectares (30 acres) of **Roman archaeological sites**, open daily except Christmas and New Years Day. The **Puymin** quarter lies to the east on a slope planted with cypress and oaks and contains foundations of villas and copies of statues found during excavations. The originals can be seen in the **Museum** in the middle of the site, which also has delightful mosaics of birds and flowers. The **water cistern** is on the eastern edge, and to the north there is a 6,000-seat **Roman Theater** where concerts of the summer festival are held.

At **La Villasse** to the west of the Place Sautel are the central shopping streets of the Roman city, the baths, the House of the Silver Bust (where a silver bust on display in the museum was found)

and the Dolphin House, the luxurious villas of wealthy Roman families of the first century AD.

The excavations date from 1907, when Abbé Sautel began his digs. In 1924 Vaison added "la-Romaine" to its name.

A few steps to the west of La Villasse is the former **Cathedral of Notre-Dame-de-Nazareth**, a Romanesque church built mainly in the twelfth and thirteenth centuries, but containing elements from earlier Christian churches and even a Roman temple that stood on the site. It has an unusual cloister from the eleventh and twelfth centuries with groups of three small arches supported by double rows of pillars, with large vaulted arches above.

A short walk along Avenue Jules-Ferry takes you to the heart of the "modern" town, centering on pleasant café and restaurant-lined Place Montfort. The **market** there Tuesday mornings is very festive. Cross the **Roman Bridge** over the Ouvèze River. During the flood in 1992, this 2,000-year-old structure withstood 1,000 tons per square meter of water pressure, with the raging waters washing over the top of it. Up the hill is the **Haute Ville**, where the houses and churches date mainly from the thirteenth to the sixteenth century. Since World War II, Haute Ville has been restored and massively gentrified, and its narrow cobble stone streets, tiny squares with fountains, and shops of crafts people are very pleasant to explore. The hike up the hill to the **Château of the**

An AD 43 portrait of Emperor Claudius in the museum at Vaison-la-Romaine, excavated from the ruins in the Roman quarter of Puymin.

Counts of Toulouse is quite a workout. Only part of the shell of the *donjon* (keep) remains, but there is a superb panorama of Mont Ventoux, the Barronies range, and the Valley of the Ouvèze.

WHERE TO STAY AND EAT

The **Beffroi***** (04 90 36 04 71 FAX 04 90 36 24 78 E-MAIL lebeffroi@wanadoo.fr WEB SITE www .chateauxethotels.com, in Haute Ville, the medieval part of town, has 22 antique-furnished rooms in adjoining sixteenth- and seventeenth-century residences with a garden overlooking the modern and Roman towns, and there's a swimming pool. Doubles in the moderately expensive. **Logis du Château**** (04 90 36 09 98 FAX 04 90 36 10 95, in Les Hauts de Vaison above Haute Ville, is an attractive, medium-priced 45-room modern hotel with a pool, tennis court, and panoramic view. Both hotels have perfectly good restaurants. **L'Évêché** (04 90 36 13 46 FAX 04 90 36 32 43 WEB SITE www.avignon-et-provence.com, Rue de l'Évêché, in the Haute Ville, a beautifully restored seventeenth-century bishop's house where Aude and Jean-Loup Verdier rent four lovely rooms (*chambres d'hôte*) for 400 to 440 francs for two people, breakfast included. Breakfast is served on the terrace overlooking the medieval city, modern Vaison, and the Roman ruins.

The top restaurant in town is the **Moulin à Huile** (04 90 36 20 67, a medieval olive oil mill on Quai Maréchal-Foch by the Pont Romain where noted chef Robert Bardot and his acolytes serve grilled *rougets* (red mullet) with *pistou* (Provençal pesto sauce); roast pigeon and local almonds with honey caramel; large shrimps with young spinach, garlic, and nutmeg; and *millefeuille* (puff pastry) with vanilla cream. In fine weather dine on the patio overlooking the Ouvèze with Mont Ventoux in the distance. This is a Michelin one-star restaurant and expensive.

Brin d'Olivier (04 90 28 74 79, at 4 rue Ventoux, is a cheerful Provençal restaurant one block from the river in "modern" Vaison, serving tasty tuna lasagna with basil, *bourride* (Mediterranean fish stew), pigeon with honey and spices, and other well-prepared regional fare. There is a three-course weekday lunch *menu* at 80 francs, from 130 to 350 francs otherwise, or à la carte.

At **Auberge de la Bartavelle** (04 90 36 02 16, at Place Sus Auze, near Place Montfort, you can feast on the full range of local and regional specialties, plus some from the Southwest, such as *foie gras* and *magret de canard* (breast of fattened duck). The dining room has bright Provençal decor, and there is a pleasant dining porch fronting on the little square. Prices are moderate.

Le Bateleur (04 90 36 28 04, at Place Aubanel near the Roman bridge, serves honorable Provençale fare at moderate prices.

In the countryside just west of Vaison in Saint-Marcellin, **Auberge d'Anaïs** (/FAX 04 90 36 20 06 WEB SITE www.members.aol.com/anais2006 is a friendly inn amid vineyards and olive trees with a clear view of Mont Ventoux. It rents five pleasant rooms at 310 francs for a double, breakfast included, and has a very good restaurant that attracts a faithful local clientele for its simple three-course *menu du jour*, which changes daily, at 56 francs, or more elaborate *menus* at 89, 160, and 160 francs. Savory local and regional specialties such as roast guinea fowl with basil, *gambas* (large prawns) grilled with dill, rabbit *à la Provençale*, and grilled *entrecôte* (rib steak) with green pepper or Roquefort sauce are served in the cheerful whitewashed dining room or on the shaded terrace by the pool with a grand view of the vineyards and the mountain.

Restaurant Saint-Hubert (04 90 46 00 05, in Entrechaux, a few kilometers farther along the road in the direction of Ventoux, is a big, lively country eatery, good at any time of the year, but especially noted for its game dishes during hunting season (it is named for the patron saint of hunters). The *civet de sanglier*, a stew of wild boar hunted on the slopes of Ventoux, and a fine red wine from the Dentelles de Montmirail (see WINE TASTING, page 129, under SÉGURET AND THE DENTELLES DE MONTMIRAIL) makes a marvelous combination.

Camping

There are two camping grounds in Vaison-la-Romaine, both open from Easter to the end of October. They are the 55-place **Camping du Théâtre Romain** (04 90 28 78 66, across the street from the Roman theater, and the somewhat larger **Carpe Diem** (04 90 36 02 02, which is 800 m (half a mile) from the center of town on the Route de Saint-Marcellin. For other camping grounds in the surrounding countryside, contact the Tourist Office.

HOW TO GET THERE

There are three buses a day from Avignon and Orange, two from Carpentras, and two from Nyons. The Tourist Office can give you the schedules. By car, it is 27 km (17 miles) northeast of Orange on D975, 16 km (10 miles) south of Nyons on D938, and 27 km (17 miles) north of Carpentras, also on D938.

MONT VENTOUX

"The Giant of Provence," Mont Ventoux, looms over Vaison-la-Romaine, only 18 km (11 miles) from the domed peak of the mountain. Bald at the top, it looks perpetually snow-covered. But in fact, what you see in the summer are fields of light-colored stones. There is snow only in the winter, normally at altitudes above 1,200 m (4,000 ft), and skiing is generally possible from December to March. The mountain is 1,912 m (6,265 ft) high.

Francesco Petrarch, the poet and pioneer of Humanist thinking, who has been called "the first modern poet" and "the first modern man," lived for many years in Provence and climbed Mont Ventoux in 1336. For this he has been called "the first mountain climber," in that he is the first individual on record to climb a mountain just for the pleasure of it.

As you climb to the top, you pass from Mediterranean vegetation to pine forests to bare pebbles above the tree line. The view from the top is vast — the Cévennes, Montagne Sainte-Victoire, Marseille, and the Mediterranean — and on a very clear day, you can see all the way down to Mont Canigou in the Pyrénées. The best time to be up here is at dusk, to see the lights coming on in towns all over Provence and the beacons lighting up along the coast. The clearest visibility is right after a *mistral*. But a word of warning: the mountain is not called *Ventoux* for nothing. In fact, the early inhabitants of the area believed that the god of the wind lived here and that Ventoux was the source of the *mistrals*. If it is windy below, it will be very uncomfortable, even unbearable on the top.

HOW TO GET THERE

To get to Mont Ventoux, take D938 from Vaison-la-Romaine to Malaucène, then D974 along the north slope 21 km (13 miles) to the observation point at the Col des Tempêtes. There are no organized tours to Mont Ventoux from Vaison-la-Romaine, but you can hire a taxi (04 90 36 00 04 for the trip for about 300 francs.

SÉGURET AND THE DENTELLES DE MONTMIRAIL

The Dentelles de Montmirail is a chain of limestone hills topped by a jagged filigree of white rock that looks something like lace (*dentelles*) from a distance. They run 16 km (10 miles) north–south from just below Vaison-la-Romaine on their northern end to Beaumes-de-Venise on the south. Few of the peaks top 400 m (1,300 ft), but their cragginess makes them impressive. They are a favorite place of rock climbers. Flat and gently rolling vineyards lie to the west, lovely with the Dentelles as a backdrop. This is some of the finest wine country in the South, and the wines of Gigondas, Vacqueyras, and Beaumes-de-Venise have gained international renown.

Séguret, 10 km (six miles) south of Vaison on D23, is a charming town of 714 inhabitants that clings to the western face of the Dentelles and looks like Bethlehem in a Christmas crib—which is just

what it becomes in December, a living *crèche* with townspeople in costume, when it puts one of the most colorful Christmas pageants in Provence. The village is closed to cars. Its narrow pedestrian streets are lined with upscale shops, winding up to the top of the hill, and there are good restaurants (see WHERE TO EAT, below).

Continue south from Séguret on the road that hugs the craggy Dentelles on your left, past the medieval-looking villages of **Sablet**, **Gigondas**, and **Vacqueyras**, with vineyards everywhere a grape vine will take root.

Beaumes-de-Venise (*beaume* is the word for cellar in Provençal and "Venise" is a contraction of Venaissin) at the southern end of the Dentelles

has an unusual Romanesque chapel, **Notre-Dame-d'Aubune**, sitting atop a lonely hill outside town. Its tall, square bell tower has windows, cornices, and moldings treated with classical motifs.

GENERAL INFORMATION

The **Tourist Office** (04 90 62 94 39 in Beaumes-de-Venise is on Cours Jean-Jaurès.

WINE TASTING

There are outstanding **wine cooperatives** in Roaix-Séguret, Sablet, Gigondas, Vacqueyras, and Beaumes-de-Venise. Besides table wine, the Beaumes-de-Venise cooperative also sells its delicious Muscat de Beaumes-de-Venise, a sweet

The fountain of the medieval village of Séguret in the Dentelles de Montmirail.

apéritif wine. Some outstanding individual producers whose cellars you can visit are: **Domaine de la Monardière** (04 90 65 87 20, in Vacqueyras, which makes wines of the Vacqueyras and Côtes du Rhône *appellations*; **Château de Montmirail** (04 90 65 86 72, also in Vacqueyras, which makes Vacqueyras, Gigondas, and Côtes du Rhône *AOC* wines; **Domaine du Pesquier** (04 90 65 86 16, in Gigondas, making *AOC* Gigondas wines; **Domaine Raspail-Ay** (04 90 65 83 01, in Gigondas, making *AOC* Gigondas. For an especially beautiful drive through the Dentelles de Montmirail wine country, take the road from Beaumes-de-Venise in the direction of Malaucène and follow the signs for the **Château Redortier** (04 90 62 96 43, in

mine is **Le Mesclun** (04 90 46 93 43, a very good medium-priced restaurant on Rue Poternes in the village, serving seasonal specialties and delicious house Côtes du Rhône from the Roaix-Séguret cooperative. In summer, they offer a healthy "hiker's lunch" (*déjeuner du randonneur*) for 90 francs. In good weather, dine on the terrace overlooking the vineyards. Off-season, ask for a table by the window. It is very popular, so reserve in the morning. Open mid-April through October.

Domaine de Cabasse*** (04 90 46 91 12 FAX 04 90 46 94 01 E-MAIL cabasse@avignon.pacwan.net, on Route de Sablet outside the village of Séguret, is a peaceful 11-room inn on the grounds of a working vineyard at the foot of the Dentelles, with

Suzette. Motor 15 minutes up into the hills to the de Menthon family's vineyard that nestles amid white limestone crags at the top of the Dentelles. The château itself is not fancy, but it makes outstanding Gigondas and Beaumes-de-Venise Côtes du Rhône wines, and the view is spectacular.

WHERE TO STAY AND EAT

In Séguret, **La Table du Comtat***** (90 46 91 49 FAX 04 90 46 94 27, at the top of the old village with a marvelous view of the plain, is the deluxe address of the Dentelles. It has eight tasteful, moderately expensive rooms, a pool, and a gourmet restaurant that features the inventive Provençal cuisine of chef Franck Gomez, excellent, but expensive, with *menus* starting at 165 francs for a weekday lunch, a 450-franc *menu* in the evening. It is open late March to November. A favorite of

a pool and a restaurant. The top priced double rooms are 650 francs.

Domaine de la Ponche (04 90 65 85 21 FAX 04 90 65 85 23, in Vacqueyras, is a sturdy seventeenth-century *bastide* with a red tile roof and jolly round tower, a large garden and swimming pool amid cypress and olive trees, and vineyards all around. It rents six spacious rooms decorated in authentic Provençal style with antique furniture and all the modern comforts. Rooms run 600 to 1,200 francs in high season (May through mid-October), about a third less the rest of the year. The restaurant is first-rate. Quail on a bed of salad, grilled sea bass on a bed of zucchini, gratin of strawberries with Muscat de Beaumes-de-Venise, pigeon cooked in Rasteau (a local sweet wine), and figs marinated in Vacqueyras wine are a few of talented chef Jean-Pierre Onimus's specialties, which change regularly with the seasons. The superb, reasonably priced selection of wines from Vacqueyras and the surrounding villages makes this the best place to sample these smooth, yet robust and remarkably flavorful Côtes du Rhône wines of the Dentelles de Montmirail. There is a three-course weekday lunch *menu* at 95 francs, a more elaborate one a 135 francs. The feast in the evening goes for 190 francs. Meals are served in the tree-shaded garden in fine weather. La Ponche lies two kilometers (a little over a mile) north of the village of Vacqueyras, well-marked on a little side road off Route D8.

On the Route de Vaison in Vacqueyras, **Le Pradet** (04 90 65 81 00 FAX 04 90 65 80 27 is a comfortable, tastefully decorated modern motel with 20 spotless rooms at moderate prices. No

restaurant, but breakfast is served in your room or on the terrace.

In a quiet, tree-shaded setting in the Dentelles on Route de Vacqueyras in Montmirail, the **Montmirail** *** (04 90 65 84 01 FAX 04 90 65 81 50, has 45 comfortable, moderately priced rooms, a restaurant, and a pool. **La Treille** (04 90 65 03 77, Route D3, Suzette, in the heart of the Dentelles de Montmirail, is a rambling red-tile-roofed Provençal stone house high on a hill with a splendid panorama of the vineyards, the tiny village, and surrounding peaks. Owners Caty and Jérôme Challier have restored and decorated it with exquisite taste, and they rent two guest rooms (*chambres d'hôte*) at 400 francs a night for two people, breakfast included, and two fully equipped apartments suitable for four people, 500 francs a night for the larger one, 400 francs for the smaller one. This place is a little paradise.

Camping

Camping Municipal Roquefigueur (04 90 62 95 07 is an attractive, shaded site with 40 places on the Route de Lafare at the entrance to Beaumes-de-Venise. It is next to the town swimming pool. Open April 1 to the end of October.

CARPENTRAS

All roads in the middle of the Comtat lead through Carpentras. Since you are bound to get lost trying to find your way through it, the signs being amazingly hard to follow, you may as well stop and look around. It is a big, busy town of 26,000, the hub of the central Vaucluse. Carpentras was the administrative center of the papal Comtat Venaissin from 1320 until the French Revolution, and it had an important place in Jewish history in France. From 1342 onward, Jews were offered special protection here, as in other localities in the Comtat, where quarters called *"carrières"* (from the Provençal word meaning street) were set aside for them. After the expulsion of the Jews from the Kingdom of France in the late Middle Ages, the papal properties of Avignon and the Comtat became their only safe haven on the territory that is now France.

This was not all done out of Christian charity, however. Along with the special protection came some very special taxes.

GENERAL INFORMATION

The **Tourist Office** (04 90 63 57 88 is at 170 Allée Jean-Jaurès across from the marketplace.

There is a fair in mid-July, **Corso de Nuit**, with theater, song and folk arts.

WHAT TO SEE AND DO

The **Porte Juive** (Jewish Portal), built in the 1470s, is the richly decorated Gothic Flamboyant south door of **Saint-Siffrien Cathedral**. It was given its nickname at the end of the fifteenth century, when Jews entered it to be baptized as Christians in order to escape discrimination and persecution, which were widespread despite the "special protection." Construction of the cathedral itself was started in 1404 and completed in 1519. Its interior is elaborately decorated, and there is a glorious gilded wood baroque altarpiece by the sculptor Jacques Bernus, a native of the area, whose work can also be seen in the **local museum**.

The **synagogue**, the oldest in France, was first built in the fifteenth century, but was rebuilt in the eighteenth century and has the look of that period — full-blown baroque. Some fourteenth-

OPPOSITE: The Dentelles de Montmirail, where some of southern France's best wines come from. ABOVE: Medieval washbasin in Séguret.

century ritual baths remain. It fronts on the Place de la Mairie and is open weekdays from 10 AM to 5 PM, closed to the public on Saturdays, Sundays, and Jewish holidays.

There is a large **market** Friday mornings extending from Les Halles in the heart of the old city out to the long, plane tree-shaded Allée Jean-Jaurès. It is one of the best and most colorful in all of Provence.

Carpentras is famed for its *berlingots*, a caramel sweet. The **Confiserie Villeneuve-Hardy** makes a particularly delicious version. They can be found at 288 avenue Notre-Dame-de-Santé.

WHERE TO STAY AND EAT

Le Fiacre** (04 90 63 03 15 FAX 04 90 60 49 73, 153 rue Vigne, is a little hotel of great charm with 20 inexpensive to moderately priced rooms right in the heart of the old town. It has no restaurant. Oddly, for a town that has one of the best food markets is France, Carpentras has surprising few really fine restaurants. The best bet is probably still **Le Vert Galant** (04 90 67 15 50, formerly the area's finest, lately taken over by a new chef, Michel Castelain, respected for his delicate and inventive Provençal touch at his previous restaurants. Prices are moderate to expensive, with the least expensive *menu* at 110 francs. It is at 12 rue Clapies, near Les Halles, the town's covered market. Somewhat less expensive, **Atelier de Pierre** (04 90 60 75 00, at 30 place de l'Horloge, near Les Halles, is an established restaurant that serves good dependable, market-based fare. **Le Marijo** (04 90 60 42 65, at 73 rue Raspail in the heart of the old town, is a cheerful little rustic-style bistro with savory Provençal home cooking that changes daily with the products coming fresh to the market, served with *pichets* of Côtes du Ventoux wine. Servings are generous and prices are modest — 65 francs for a lunch *menu*, 88 and 120 francs for a big dinner.

Camping

There are no camping grounds in Carpentras itself, but a number of attractive ones in the countryside nearby. **Camping le Ventoux** (04 90 69 70 94 is a deluxe site at Mazan, seven kilometers (four miles) east of town. It has 49 places and a pool; open all year. **Camping le Brégoux** (04 90 62 62 50 is another upscale site with 197 places in Aubignan, five kilometers (three miles) north of town, open March 15 to the end of October. **Camping le Bouquier** (04 90 62 40 28, is a modest 35-place site, open from March 15 to the end of October. It is in Caromb, five kilometers (four miles) northeast of town.

A moss-covered waterwheel in the antiques-shoppers paradise of L'Isle-sur-la-Sorgue.

HOW TO GET THERE

Carpentras is the transportation hub of the central Vaucluse. There are bus connections ever hour from Avignon, less frequently from the other directions. For schedules, contact the Tourist Office. If you are driving, the main roads are D942 from Avignon 25 km (16 miles) away, D950 from Orange 23 km (14 miles) away, and D938 from Vaison-la-Romaine to the north and L'Isle-sur-la-Sorgue and Cavaillon to the south.

L'ISLE-SUR-LA-SORGUE

As you drive south from Carpentras, you will see that the Sorgue River branches out into little fingers and irrigation canals, some dating from the time of the popes, that wend their way to the Ouvèze and the Rhône. One branch filled the moat that encircled the ramparts of Avignon. The water of the Sorgue is cool. It creates a microclimate very different from that of most of Provence — moist and green, with market gardens rather than vineyards — one of the richest vegetable growing areas in France. Long rows of old cypresses protect the fields from the *mistral*.

L'Isle-sur-la-Sorgue is called "the Venice of Provence," but looks more like a canal town in northern Europe — shady streets, cafés alongside canals, mossy waterwheels, relics of the town's once-thriving silk industry, all in Manet-like tones of dark green. This is a graceful, sophisticated town of 13,000 with many art galleries and antique shops, delightful to visit any time, but bursting with activity on Saturdays and Sundays, and to a lesser extent Mondays, when the big weekly antiques market is held. More than 110 antiques dealers display their wares at the **Village des Antiquaires de la Gare**, a huge rambling wooden shed near the train station, and another 30 at the **Quai de la Gare**. At Easter and on August 15, dealers come from all over Europe for the big **antiques auctions**.

Besides the antiques dealers, numerous bric-a-brac dealers display their wares at table set up near the canals in center of town for the *brocante* (flea market) on Saturdays and Sundays. Sunday morning is the liveliest time of all, because there is also a colorful Provençal market along the canals, winding into the center of town.

The **Tourist Office** (04 90 38 04 78 is on the central square, Place de l'Église.

WHERE TO EAT

La Prévôté 04 90 38 57 29 is a rustically elegant restaurant at 4 rue Jean-Jacques-Rousseau directly behind the church, where salmon

cannelloni with fresh goat cheese, duckling lacquered with lavender honey, and saddle of rabbit stuffed with olives are a few of the specialties that earned young chef Roland Mercier his Michelin one-star rating. The weekday lunch *menu* is 135 francs, dinners run 230 and 320 francs. **La Guinguette** (04 90 38 10 61, at Le Partage-des-Eaux, is an old-fashioned café-dance hall with an outdoor terrace under the plane trees by the edge of the Sorgue with fresh, tasty Provençal *menus* starting at 85 francs. **Le Caveau de la Tour de l'Isle** (04 90 20 70 25, at 12 rue de la République, is a delightful wine-shop-cum-wine-bar with a superb selection of Southern French wines; it also serves light lunches.

development of lyric poetry, a virtuous lady, attainable only in flights of verse.

Unfortunately, the tranquillity that once attracted the poet is shattered in the summer, when tens of thousands of tourists ride into the valley every day and are bombarded with tacky souvenirs. Come here off-season if at all possible. The **Tourist Office** (04 90 20 32 22 is on Chemin de la Fontaine, the walkway leading to the fountain.

WHAT TO SEE AND DO

From a clear, perpetually self-renewing pool at the foot of a 200-m (650-ft) rock cliff in a narrow valley in the Vaucluse Plateau, the cool water

HOW TO GET THERE

L'Isle-sur-la-Sorgue is 17 km (10.5 miles) from Carpentras on D938, and 26 km (16 miles) from Avignon on N100. There are buses from Avignon practically every hour.

FONTAINE-DE-VAUCLUSE

The Fontaine-de-Vaucluse is a mysterious natural fountain in a valley 10 km (six miles) east of L'Isle-sur-la-Sorgue that is the source of the Sorgue River. The Latin *vallis clausa* (closed valley) is the origin of the name Vaucluse.

Petrarch lived here for 16 years and sat by the river writing sonnets about Laura de Noves, a young woman he first saw at church in Avignon on April 6, 1327. He was overwhelmed by her beauty, but she was married and, luckily for the

of the **Fontaine-de-Vaucluse** rushes downhill with impressive force to form the Sorgue River. The source of this water is a mystery that has defied all attempts to locate it. Commander Cousteau failed in three separate explorations, as did a series of costly high-tech probes in the early 1980s.

Le Monde Souterrain de Norbert Casteret (the Underground World of Norbert Casteret) is a collection of rock formations brought together by the renowned speleologist from his thirty years of explorations under the earth, with stalagmites and stalactites, subterranean rivers and waterfalls that have been imaginatively reconstructed in caves, and there are audiovisual displays on the attempts to find the source of the Fontaine. Open from February 1 to November 15, daily in June, July and August, closed Tuesdays the rest of the year. The hours are 10 PM to 6 PM.

Next door is the big waterwheel and machinery of **Vallis Clausa**, a paper mill that demonstrates how paper was made in the fifteenth century. It has an attractive gift shop. Next to it, the **Musée du Santon** has a collection of more than a thousand Provençal "little saints" and exhibitions on how the statuettes are made.

The **Musée de la Résistance** is devoted to France during World War II, with absorbing displays on the collaborationist Pétain government and on the *Résistance*, which was very active in the town of Fontaine-de-Vaucluse and in the nearby Lubéron. Open daily except Tuesdays from 10 AM to noon and 2 PM to 6 PM from Easter to All Saints Day and on weekends only the rest of the year.

WHERE TO STAY AND EAT

Two fine restaurants with dining terraces overlooking the river and lunch *menus* at less than 100 francs are **Le Parc (** 04 90 20 31 57 and **L'Hostellerie du Château (** 04 90 20 31 54.

Camping

There are good camping grounds in the area of Fontaine-de-Vaucluse. **Camping Municipal les Prés (** 04 90 20 32 38 is a pleasant 42-place site in town, open all year. **Camping La Coutelière (** 90 20 33 97, in Cagnes two and a half kilometers (about a mile and a half) south of town on the banks of the Sorgue, has 80 places and is open mid-March to the end of October. It has a pool and tennis court.

HOW TO GET THERE

Fontaine-de-Vaucluse is 33 km (21 miles) east of Avignon, seven kilometers (four miles) east of L'Isle-sur-la-Sorgue. There are eight buses a day from L'Isle-sur-la-Sorgue and four from Avignon.

THE LUBÉRON

The Lubéron is a discreet rural retreat of chic Parisians that became famous in the English-speaking world when Peter Mayle's tongue-in-cheek narrative of his adventures renovating his house in the area, *A Year in Provence*, became a bestseller in 1989. The British arrived, much to the annoyance of the Northerners who had been there before Mr. Mayle.

The Lubéron comprises the wooded range of the Montagne du Lubéron and a lovely farm valley with the little Coulon River flowing through it. The Lubéron starts about 25 km (15 miles) east of Avignon and runs east–west some 50 km (30 miles), with Route N100 running straight down the middle. On the north it is bounded by the Vaucluse Plateau and the south by the Durance

River. Much of the Lubéron is part of a 130,000 hectare (312,000 acre) natural preserve, the Parc Naturel Régional du Lubéron, created in 1977, with 51 towns and villages included in it.

The most interesting towns to visit are in the western half of the Lubéron—Gordes, Roussillon, Bonnieux, Lacoste, and Oppède-le-Vieux. Lovers of the great outdoors should head for the eastern half, where there are plenty of hiking trails and campsites through this heavily forested part of the Montagne du Lubéron. The Lubéron is a restful area with few sites of real cultural importance, a nice breather for those who have overdone it in Aix or Avignon. But a word of warning: accommodations are limited. If you want to stay here in

summer, you must book months in advance. For assistance, contact the Comité Départemental du Tourisme de Vaucluse in Avignon (see GENERAL INFORMATION, page 214, under AVIGNON).

Since the area is close to Avignon and to Aix, which lies directly to the south, day-trips can be made from either city by coach or private vehicle.

GORDES

The hilltop town of Gordes, whose dramatic profile has been seen on many a travel poster, was the first town in the Lubéron to undergo full-scale gentrification in the 1960s, thanks to the support of Minister of Culture André Malraux. There are

OPPOSITE: Fontaine-de-Vaucluse, site of the mysterious source of the Sorgue River, and where the poet Petrarch lived. ABOVE: Gordes, the most luxurious town in the chic Lubéron.

good **crafts shops**, and for those who want to stay in the Lubéron, Gordes has the most hotels and restaurants. But they are expensive.

The **Tourist Office** (04 90 72 02 75 is in the château.

What to See and Do

The **château** dominates the town, an eleventh-century fortress replaced in the sixteenth century by a Renaissance palace. Inside there is a magnificent Renaissance fireplace.

Dry-masonry huts called *bories*, igloos made of flat stones, abound in the area around Gordes. They look prehistoric, but most date from the seventeenth century or later. Some were shep-

herds' huts, others apparently refuges from town in times of plague. There is a heavily promoted **Village of Bories** off Route D2 a few kilometers outside of Gordes. If you are traveling with kids, they can have fun romping from *borie* to *borie*. But for adults this pseudo-historical tourist-trap is not worth the 30 francs. With 3,000 *bories* in the area, you can see all you want as you drive around.

Dramatically set in a deep, narrow valley three kilometers (two miles) north of Gordes, the **Abbaye de Sénanque** is the most beautiful of the twelfth-century Cistercian abbeys known as the "Three Sisters of Provence." All were built on the same pattern, but unlike its uncompromisingly austere sisters of Le Thoronet and Silvacane, Sénanque has allowed a slight touch of roundness to creep into its design. Without diminishing its purity in the least, the bay of the church adds an appealing softness to the overall effect.

Sénanque is a working monastery occupied by a Cistercian monastic community, and part of the complex is reserved to them, but the original twelfth-century parts are open to the public. They include the scriptorium, where the monks copied manuscripts, the only room that was heated; the chapter house; the church, with its purity; the cloister; and the refectory. The buildings have been kept in exactly the state they were in when they were built 800 years ago. Sénanque is especially attractive in July when the field of lavender in front of it is in flower.

The abbey is open to visitors from 10 AM to noon and 2 PM to 6 PM March through October except on Sunday mornings, and open afternoons only the rest of the year. Mass is open to the public on Sunday at 9 AM and on weekdays at 11:55 AM.

Silvacane, Sénanque's sister abbey in Provence, lies on the south bank of the Durance, about halfway between Gordes and Aix. In summer it is the site of the prestigious International Piano Festival of La Roque d'Anthéron. The third sister abbey, Le Thoronet in the Var is described on page 169.

Saint-Pantaléon five kilometers (three miles) south of Gordes on D104, is the smallest community in Provence, with a surface of 78 hectares (190 acres). The core of its tiny Romanesque **Church of Saint-Pantaléon** dates from the fifth century. Little **sarcophagi** are cut into the rock outcropping upon which the church is built, put there for children who died before being baptized. The child would be laid in a sarcophagus, a Mass would be said, the child would be considered to have come back to life long enough to be baptized, then to have died again in a state of grace. The church is kept locked. To see it, get the key from the innkeeper down the street.

The village of **Roussillon** 10 kilometers (six miles) east of Gordes is so-named because of the reddish color (*rousse*) of the earth of the sheer-cliffed plateau it sits on. The material is ochre. It was mined by the people of the area and used as pigment for paint, bringing prosperity to the village until synthetic pigments came along. This is a quiet village noted mainly for its tranquillity and unusual site. It was also the place where Samuel Beckett spent the dark years of the World War II Occupation and served as a courier for the *Résistance*. The **Tourist Office** (04 90 05 60 25 is at Place de la Poste.

Where to Stay and Eat

On the expensive side, the **Bastide de Gordes****** (04 90 72 12 12 FAX 04 90 72 05 20 E-MAIL bastide-gordes@avignon.pacwan.net WEB SITE www

ABOVE: A café in Gordes. RIGHT: The Abbey of Sénanque near Gordes, one of the exquisite twelfth-century Cistercian monasteries known as "The Three Sisters of Provence."

.provenceguide.com, in Gordes, is a noble Renaissance residence on the hillside of town, now a refined 30-room hotel with a pool cut into the rock and a grand view of the Lubéron. **Les Bories****** (04 90 72 00 51 FAX 04 90 72 01 22 E-MAIL lesbories @aol.com WEB SITE www.euhotels.com/lesbories, on the Route de Sénanque just outside Gordes, is a picturesque hotel on eight hectares (20 acres) of private park, with some of its 18 deluxe rooms in authentic *bories*, indoor and outdoor pools, a tennis court, and a view of Gordes. The restaurant is one of the Lubéron's finest, serving refined Provençal fare. It has one Michelin star.

A Relais & Châteaux member, **Mas des Herbes Blanches****** (04 90 05 79 79 FAX 04 90 05 71 96

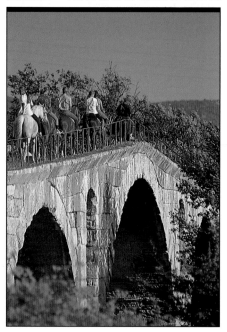

E-MAIL masherbes@wanadoo.fr WEB SITE www .integra.fr/relaischateaux/masherbes, Route des Murs in Joucas, eight kilometers (five miles) east of Gordes, is an elegant country house in the middle of 10 hectares (24 acres) of sweet-smelling *garrigue* (wild herbs, flowers and grasses) with 19 pretty guest rooms. There's a pool, tennis court, and one of the Lubéron's top restaurants, serving brochettes of grilled prawns with rosemary, slices of young pigeon breast with *tapenade*, and other sophisticated Provençal cuisine. It has one Michelin star.

The **Ferme de la Huppe** (04 90 72 12 25 FAX 04 90 72 01 83 E-MAIL gerald.konings@wanadoo.fr, five kilometers (three miles) east of Gordes on D2, is an eighteenth-century farm with nine charming, moderately priced guest rooms, swimming pool, and an expensive restaurant that serves some of the area's best Provençal country cuisine.

Auberge de Carcarille** (04 90 72 02 63 FAX 04 90 72 05 74 E-MAIL carcaril@clubwanadoo.fr is an 11-room inn in the countryside in Les Gervais, four kilometers (two and a half miles) south of Gordes on D2. It has a swimming pool and peaceful location, and its rooms are less than 400 francs — remarkable for the quality and the location (a Logis de France member).

CAMPING

Camping des Sources (04 90 72 12 48 is a well-shaded 100-place site with a swimming pool two kilometers (bit over a mile) from Gordes on the Route de Murs. It is open from March 15 to the end of October.

How to Get There

There are three buses to Gordes from Cavaillon every day except Sunday, with frequent bus connections between Cavaillon and Avignon. By car, Gordes can be reached via N100, the road through the center of the Lubéron, and D2. Coming from Fontaine-de-Vaucluse, take D100 through the hills, a distance of 16 km (10 miles).

THE COLORADO DE RUSTREL

For more ochre and plenty of it, drive east to **Rustrel**, about 20 km (12.5 miles) past Roussillon, and follow the signs for the *carrières d'ocre*, the ochre quarries. Known as the Colorado de Rustrel, this 15-sq-km (10-sq-mile) expanse of open-pit mines was exploited between 1871 and 1930, when it was abandoned. The wind and the rain have sculpted strange natural forms, and the 22 shades of color, from bright yellows to deep reds, are truly amazing. For the best color for photographs, come in the late afternoon.

APT

Plunked square in the middle of the valley, Apt is the commercial center of the Lubéron with a population of 11,500. It has been famed for centuries for its candied fruit, as beautiful as they are sweet. Madame de Sévigné loved them. The **Aptunion** candied-fruit factory skillfully follows the old tradition, and you can watch them at work in the Quartier Salignan, two kilometers (a little over a mile) out of the center of town on the Route d'Avignon. Aptunion is especially noted for its magic with cherries. They also sell nougat, *calissons*, unusual jams and jellies, and fruits preserved in alcohol, all at low factory prices.

Apt is also the gateway to the nearby **Parc Naturel Régional du Lubéron** (Lubéron Regional Nature Park), and the **Maison du Parc** (04 90 04 42 00 E-MAIL pnr.Lubéron@wanadoo.fr has an information center and exhibits on the plants and wildlife of the Lubéron. They publish the brochure

20 promenades et Randonnées dans le Parc Naturel Régional du Lubéron (20 Walks and Rambles in the Lubéron Regional Nature Park) that suggests walking, bicycling, and horseback itineraries. It is at Place Jean-Jaurès in the heart of the old town.

For ambiance and quality, Apt's Saturday morning **market** that winds through the town from Place de la Bouquerie to Place de la Mairie is one of the most authentic in all of Provence. If you find yourself anywhere near Apt on a Saturday, it is well worth the effort to get here for it.

The **Tourist Office** (04 90 74 03 18 for the Pays d'Apt (Apt Country) is located at 20 avenue Philippe-de-Girard at the entrance to the old part of town.

Where to Stay and Eat

There are clean, comfortable, moderately priced little inns scattered throughout this part of the

Lubéron, most with pools and tennis courts, and there are even a few inexpensive ones. Logis de France has more than 20 member hotels in the Lubéron. **Lou Caleu**** (04 90 75 28 88 FAX 04 90 75 25 49, in Saint-Martin-de-Castillon east of Apt near the Colorado de Rustrel is an example, with 16 tasteful rooms, a restaurant serving French and Provençal dishes, pool, and tennis court.

CAMPING

There are two camping sites in Apt, the modest 75-place **Camping Municipal les Cèdres** (04 90 74 14 61, 300 m (about 330 yards) outside of town on the Route de Rustrel, open February 15 to November 15, and the more luxurious 100-place **Camping du Lubéron** (04 90 04 85 40, on the Route

The Pont Julien across the Coulon River OPPOSITE on the Roman Empire's Domitian Way, leading to the ochre-toned village of Roussillon ABOVE.

de Saignon, open from Easter to the end of September 30. For a list of sites in more remote areas, contact the Tourist Office.

How to Get There

There are five buses a day from Avignon, a trip of somewhat over an hour, depending on the route the bus takes. For details, contact the Tourist Office. By car, take N100 from Avignon.

LE GRAND LUBÉRON

The Lubéron range stretches out from east to west "like a big blue whale," as writer Jean Giono described it. To the southeast of Apt, the tallest and most heavily forested part of it centers on the **Mourre Nègre**, at 1,125 m (3,700 ft) the highest point in the range, with a tall telecommunications tower at the top. Hikers will find a vast panoramic view, with humpbacked Mont Ventoux looming to the north and Montagne Saint-Victoire, a white whale, to the south.

Fort de Buoux south from Apt is another high point hikers will enjoy climbing to. Here you will find the hilltop ruins of a medieval fortress destroyed in the seventeenth century by Louis XIV because it had become a Protestant stronghold. It was the successor to Roman and Ligurian fortresses, whose stones can be seen among the ruins. There is a view of the narrow valley of the Aigue Brun, the stream that separates the Grand Lubéron from the Petit Lubéron.

Where to Stay

The **Auberge des Seguins** (04 90 74 16 37 FAX 04 90 74 16 37, reached by D113 up the hill from the town of Buoux, is a Logis de France inn with 28 rooms in a colorful complex of rustic stone houses built into the hillside below the fort. It has a swimming pool and a restaurant serving hearty meals featuring fresh local products, such as trout from the mountain streams, and something that is extremely rare in these parts — low prices. Rooms go for 230 to 290 francs *demi-pension*, and a meal will cost you about 120 francs.

LE PETIT LUBÉRON

The southwestern part of valley is known as the "Le Petit Lubéron" to the French, and as "Peter Mayle country" to the rest of the world. Like much of rural France, this area lost population in the great migration to the cities in the late nineteenth and early twentieth centuries, to the point that many of these villages were virtual ghost towns by the end of World War II. But in the late 1950s artists, craftsmen, and *Le Tout-Paris* discovered the

The dramatically hued cliffs of the village of Roussillon in the Lubéron, where ochre for paints was once mined.

Lubéron, and it became fashionable to buy an old house here and fix it up, particularly in the affluent 1970s and 1980s. Anti-snob snobs may sneer at the palpable chic of these villages, but if it weren't for gentrification, most would be ghost towns today.

The most picturesque spots in the Petit Lubéron are the perched villages of **Bonnieux**, **Lacoste**, **Ménerbes**, and **Oppède-le-Vieux**, which are pleasant to stroll in. The **Marquis de Sade's Château** on the hilltop in Lacoste may be interesting to visit some day, but at the snail's pace its private restoration project is moving, it will be years before it is ready. This is the place where the divine Marquis orchestrated the monster debauch during the winter of 1774–1775 that landed him in the Bastille for 12 years. The book he wrote in prison, *The 120 Days of Sodom*, made him a household name. The château was destroyed during the Revolution and is closed to the public.

At the **Musée de la Boulangerie** (04 90 75 90 28, at 12 rue de la République in Bonnieux, you can see the ancient process of bread-making in a wood-burning stove built in 1844 and study the history of the staff of life. Open 10 AM to noon and 3 PM to 6:30 PM June through September, except Tuesdays; open weekends September through May; closed January and February. The **Tourist Office** (04 90 75 91 90 is at Place Carnot.

Where to Stay and Eat

Hostellerie du Prieuré*** (04 90 75 80 78 FAX 04 90 75 96 00 is a seventeenth-century priory at the foot of the ramparts of the village of Bonnieux with a pretty garden, 10 antique-furnished rooms, a big fireplace, good country cooking, and moderate prices. **Le Fournil** (04 90 75 83 62, at 5 place Carnot, is a pretty restaurant in the heart of the village of Bonnieux with a dining terrace by the fountain, serving bright fixed-price lunch *menus* at 90 francs.

CAMPING

The modest **Camping Municipal du Vallon** (04 90 75 86 14, on Route de Ménerbes, is open from March 15 to November 15.

How to Get There

There are three buses a day from Avignon to Bonnieux, a one-hour ride, and three from Apt, a 20-minute ride. By car, Bonnieux can be reached by N100 and D36 from Avignon, or by a number of possible roads from Aix, which is about 40 km (25 miles) to the south.

AVIGNON TO NÎMES

In the heyday of the Roman Empire, Nîmes was one of the key cities of Provincia Romana, the link between the road to Rome and the road to Spain, and it has retained the most impressive architectural ensemble from that period of any city in France. This Roman heritage links Nîmes closely with the Roman cities of Provence — Orange, Vaison-la-Romaine, Saint-Rémy, and Arles. So, for reasons of historical and cultural continuity as well as the ease of visiting Nîmes from Avignon or Arles, short drives or train rides away, we include Nîmes and its surrounding area in our itinerary of Provence, even though it lies west of the Rhône in the modern political region of Languedoc-Roussillon rather than Provence-Alpes-Côte d'Azur.

Using Avignon as our starting point, we head for the Pont du Gard, the famous bridge of Nîmes's aqueduct system. It sits 26 km (16 miles) straight west of Avignon via Route N100.

The Pont du Gard aqueduct bridge, a masterpiece of Roman engineering, provided the water for the city of Nîmes.

PONT DU GARD

The Pont du Gard is one of the engineering masterpieces of classical antiquity. Built under Claudius or Nero in the middle of the first century AD, this beautifully preserved aqueduct bridge, the highest the Romans ever built, spans a gorge over the Gardon (or Gard) River about 20 km (12.5 miles) northeast of Nîmes. It is part of a 50-km-long (30-mile) system that brought water down to the city from the source of the Eure River in the hills near Uzès. The bridge is 275 m (900 ft) long and 49 m (160 ft) high with three tiers of rounded arches that are wide on the bottom and middle levels and narrow on the upper level. Visitors are free to cross the lower level of the bridge on foot, but to walk across the top level, they must join a guided group. The river is suitable for swimming. The best time is at sundown.

This is a very popular monument, visited by 1,250,000 people a year. To enhance their experience, two large modern visitors' centers, one on each side of the river, opened in summer 2000. They have four restaurants featuring a variety of regional cuisine, shops selling artifacts, books and souvenirs, and a permanent exhibition on the history of the aqueduct, including films. The buildings have been designed so that neither of the low-lying structures is in the same line of sight as the Pont du Gard. The 165 hectares (400 acres) of park land are also being redeveloped to provide tree-shaded parking areas, nature paths through nearly 20 hectares (49 acres) of olive tress, *garrigue*, Mediterranean gardens and wooded hills, and neat picnic and swimming areas, and the Pont du Gard will be illuminated at night.

Where to Stay and Eat

The **Vieux Castillon****** (04 66 37 61 61 FAX 04 66 37 28 17 E-MAIL vieux.castillon@wanadoo.fr WEB SITE www.relaischateaux.fr/vieuxcastillon, in Castillon-du-Gard, is a luxurious 33-room Relais & Châteaux hotel with tennis courts and a large swimming pool in a tiny medieval village perched on a rock near the Pont du Gard. The rooms are very expensive (925 to 1,625 francs), as is the restaurant, which rates one Michelin star. But costly as it is, the 280-franc lunch *menu* is a good value for its superb truffle-laced Provençal cuisine and lovely setting. It is four kilometers (two and a half miles) north of the Pont du Gard on Route D228. It is closed early January through the first half of February.

Bégude Saint Pierre***(04 66 63 63 63 FAX 04 66 22 73 73 E-MAIL begudesaintpierre@wanadoo.fr WEB SITE www.vaucluse.enprovence.com/ WELCOME/Begude, on D981 in Les Coudou-

lières, just east of the Pont du Gard, was originally a seventeenth-century *bégude*—a farm that served as a post road inn, later just a farm, and is now back to being an inn — and a thoroughly delightful one at that. Plunk in the middle of 14 hectares (34 acres) of vineyards, woods and *garrigue*, it has 28 spacious rooms decorated in Souliado fabrics and antiques, with all the modern amenities, at double room rates from 350 to 680 francs. There is a lovely swimming pool. The restaurant, open to the public as well as hotel guests, serves fine regional cuisine — *tapenade* (olive paste), *bourride* (fish stew), *médaillon de taureau poêlé aux Costières de Nîmes* (the center cut of a Camargue bull steak, sautéed in Costières de Nîmes wine) — in a relaxed ambiance, with fixed-price *menus* at 170 and 350 francs. Open all year.

Colombier* (04 66 37 05 28 FAX 04 77 37 35 75, Avenue du Pont-du-Gard in Remoulins, is a cozy 10-room Logis de France hotel-restaurant in a quiet garden setting, open daily all year. It is one kilometer (half a mile) east of the aqueduct on D981. Open all year.

Another ensemble of old stone buildings converted into a lovely inn is the **Hostellerie le Castellas*****(04 66 22 88 88 FAX 04 66 22 84 28, on Grand'rue, the tiny main street of Collias, seven kilometers (four miles) west of the Pont du Gard. This friendly hotel has 17 artistically renovated rooms, a pool and flowery garden, and a restaurant with savory regional cuisine. Rooms run 500 to 800 francs, fixed-price *menus* 180 and 389 francs, with a lunch special at 140 francs. Open mid-March through the New Year vacation period. Collias, reached by D981 and D112, is a sweet little village, once a haven for hippies, where you can rent kayaks and paddle on the river.

CAMPING

Camping International des Gorges du Gardon (04 66 22 81 81, Chemin de la Barque Vieille, is a large, well-shaded camping ground with 180 places, a snack bar and swimming pool, on the bank of the river by the Pont du Gard, open March 15 to October 15. Reserve long in advance. The more deluxe **Camping le Barralet** (04 66 22 84 52, is in Collias, seven kilometers (four miles) to the west along the river. It has 90 places and is open from Easter to the end of September.

How to Get There

There are six buses per day from Avignon, 10 from Nîmes and Uzès. For schedules, check with the Tourist Office. By car, it is 26 km (16 miles) from Avignon via N100 to Remoulins and D981 to the Pont du Gard. From Nîmes, it is 23 km (14 miles) via N86 to Remoulins and D981.

The middle and top arches of the Pont du Gard.

UZÈS

"O, little Uzès! If you were in Umbria, tourists would run from Paris to see you!" wrote André Gide. Uzès is an aristocratic hill town of exceptional charm, the seat of the Dukes of Uzès, the highest-ranking noble family of France in the seventeenth century. It sits on a little plateau 15 km (nine miles) northwest of the Pont du Gard above treeless countryside covered with scrub brush, wild herbs, and grasses known as *garrigue*. Rosemary, thyme, sage, lavender, iris, and orchids are among the plants that create its powerful aroma. The scents in the spring make it an especially pleasurable time to visit.

GENERAL INFORMATION

The **Tourist Office** (04 66 22 68 88 WEB SITE www.otuzes@wanadoo.fr, is in the former Chapelle des Capucins on Place Albert 1er. The **bus station** (04 66 22 00 58 is on Avenue de la Libération, by the large public parking area at the western entrance to the old town.

WHAT TO SEE AND DO

The main square is the **Place aux Herbes**, tree-shaded and framed by arcaded houses. The **weekly market** centers here and spills out all over town. It is one of the liveliest, most colorful, best-provisioned of all Provençal markets. There are oysters from Bouzigues, sausages from Arles, cheeses from Haute-Provence and the Cévennes, wine from the Rhône Valley, lavender honey, and a fine selection of regional crafts and fabrics. If you have time for only one market on your trip, this is the one I would recommend. It is held on Saturday mornings.

The **Palace of the Dukes of Uzès** began as a fortress in the eleventh century, and new sections were added regularly up to the time of Louis XV. As a result, it is a living catalogue of French château architecture. It can be visited from 9:30 AM to noon and 2:30 PM to 6 PM from April 1 to the end of September and closes at nightfall the rest of the year. Seventeenth-century **Cathédrale Saint-Théodorit** has an imposing organ from the period of Louis XIV that is played at the **Nuits Musicales d'Uzès**, the classical music festival in July (for information, call the Tourist Office). The twelfth-century **Tour Fenestrelle** is a rounded Lombard-style campanile of six stories with many windows, the only one of its kind in France, and the sole remains of the medieval cathedral destroyed by the Protestants in the Wars of Religion. The **Municipal Museum** in the former Episcopal Palace next to cathedral has a collection of André Gide memorabilia; his family was from Uzès, and he spent a good deal of time here (open mornings and afternoons in the summer, afternoons and weekends the rest of the year). Another literary great with links to Uzès was Jean Racine. His family sent him here as a youngster in hopes that he would forget the theater. He is said to have meditated at the **Pavillon Racine**, a belvedere near the cathedral that overlooks a wide expanse of *garrigue*. Young Jean enjoyed Uzès and wrote to his friends in Paris, "Our nights are more beautiful than your days." But the first chance he had, he went back to Paris.

WHERE TO STAY AND EAT

The **Hôtel d'Entraigues***** (04 66 22 32 68 FAX 04 66 22 57 01 E-MAIL hotel.entraigues.agoult@wanadoo.fr, at 8 rue de la Calade, is a fifteenth-century mansion across from the Archbishop's Palace with 17 restful rooms, swimming pool and the best restaurant in town, the **Jardins de Castille**. Room and food prices are moderate. For an elegant château in the country, try the **Hôtel Marie d'Agoult***** (04 66 22 14 48 FAX 04 66 22 56 10 E-MAIL hotel.entraigues.agoult@wanadoo.fr, in Arpaillargues, five kilometers (three miles) west of Uzès on D982. This seventeenth-century manor house has 29 tastefully decorated rooms, a swimming pool and tennis courts, a large private park, and a fine restaurant with a 145-franc lunch *menu*. Rooms are in the 600 to 1,000 franc range. A Relais du Silence member, it is open late March to late

ABOVE: The twelfth-century Tour Fenestrelle in Uzès. OPPOSITE: A back street in Uzès, one of the most elegant towns in southern France, and one of the most pleasant to stroll in.

October. Both hotels are operated by owners Gérard and Isabelle Savry.

Another good place to eat in the area is the charming, rustic **Auberge Saint-Maximin** (04 66 22 26 41, in the village of Saint-Maximin, five and a half kilometers (three and a half miles) from Uzès on D891, the road to Pont du Gard. It serves flavorful country cooking at modest prices.

Camping

The **Camping Municipal du Val de l'Eure** (04 66 22 11 79 has 70 places by the river with the municipal pool and tennis courts nearby; open June 15 to September 15. It is on the road to Bagnols-sur-Cèze (D982), 500 m (about a third of a mile) from the center of Uzès. The 50-place **Camping la Paillote** (04 66 22 38 55 is just up the road in Quartier Grezac. It has a pool and is open from March 20 to October 20. **Camping le Moulin Neuf** (04 66 22 17 21, three and a half kilometers (two miles) north of town on the road to Saint-Quentin-la-Poterie, is a spacious 131-place site in the *garrigue* with a swimming pool and tennis courts, open April 1 to the end of September. There are several others in the vicinity. The Tourist Office has a list.

HOW TO GET THERE

There are 10 buses a day from Nîmes. If you are driving, Nîmes is 25 km (16 miles) to the south on D979.

NÎMES

After decades of slumbering on its Roman laurels, this city of 140,000 known as "the Rome of France" woke up in the 1980s and embarked on an adventure in modern architecture. The result is an array of public buildings and monuments by famous modern artists, designers and architects such as Jean Nouvel, Philippe Starck, and Martial Raysse. Sir Norman Foster's elegant art exhibition center and library the Carré d'Art, which opened in 1993, faces the Maison Carrée, built at the start of the first century AD. Unlike the provocatively ultramodern Centre Georges Pompidou built in Paris in the 1970s, which many people still consider an affront to good taste, the new buildings in Nîmes counterpoint rather than clash with the city's architectural heritage.

Incongruously, Nîmes is also the bullfighting capital of France. Only Madrid and Seville have more *corridas* than Nîmes.

BACKGROUND

Nemausus was the name of a water spirit worshipped by the Ligurian Volcae Arecomici tribe. He lived in the spring that is now part of the Jardin de la Fontaine, around which the tribe settled. In 121 BC, the Romans took control of the area, and with its key position on the road between Italy and Spain, the town of Nemausus started to grow. When the original spring proved too small for the Romans' large water needs, they built the aqueduct of which the Pont du Gard is part to bring water down from the Eure River near Uzès, providing 44 million gallons a day. Nîmes grew to a population of more than 20,000 and became one of the most prosperous cities in Gaul.

After the fall of Rome, Nîmes was overrun by the Visigoths, Saracens, and Franks before coming under the rule of the Counts of Toulouse.

As supporters of the Cathars, Nîmes suffered during the Albigensian Crusade, and as one of the principal cities of Protestantism, it was caught up for centuries in ravages of the Wars of Religion. Nevertheless, under the direction of its Protestant bourgeois, a prosperous cloth manufacturing industry developed. In the seventeenth century, they invented a new way to make sturdy fabric from Egyptian cotton that they dyed blue and sold to be made into shepherd's capes, skirts for farm women, and workers' clothes. It sold well in Europe and eventually made its way to America, where, in 1848, a San Francisco clothing manufacturer named Levi Straus started using it to make sturdy pants for gold miners. The label on the shipment from France said "*de Nîmes*." The Americans called it "denim." In the late twentieth century,

OPPOSITE: The Palace of the Dukes of Uzès. A café on the Place aux Herbes in Nîmes ABOVE.

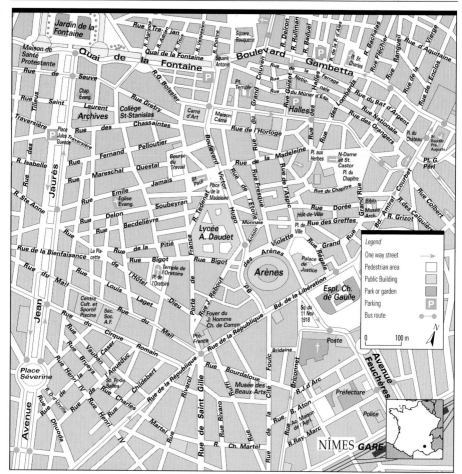

when every young person in the world was wearing the product it invented, "The Rome of France" joined the modern world and transformed itself into one of the economic and cultural centers of the new South.

GENERAL INFORMATION

The city of Nîmes has two **Tourist Offices**. The main one is on 6 rue Auguste (04 66 67 29 11 E-MAIL tourisme.nimes@compuserve.com WEB SITE www.ot.nimes.fr, near the Maison Carrée. The other is at the Gare SNCF (04 66 84 18 13. They have excellent free brochures in several languages, including English, and a particularly helpful staff who will make hotel reservations for you in Nîmes and the surrounding area. They also run guided tours of the city in English.

For more information about the Département du Gard, contact the **Comité Départemental du Tourisme du Gard** (04 66 36 96 30 FAX 04 66 36 13 14 E-MAIL cdtgard@imaginet.fr, at 3 place des Arènes.

The **Nîmes-Arles-Camargue Airport** can be reached at (04 66 70 06 88. The train terminal, **Gare SNCF** (04 66 70 40 40 or 08 36 35 35 35, is on Boulevard du Sergent Triaire, a ten-minute walk east of the Arena. The bus terminal, **Gare Routière** (04 66 29 52 00, is on Rue Sainte-Felicité, behind the train station.

For **taxis**, call (04 66 29 93 33 or 04 66 29 40 11. **Bike rental** is available at the baggage room of the train station. Car rental agencies include **ADA Location** (04 66 84 25 60, 6bis avenue du Général-Leclerc; **Avis** (04 66 29 05 33, 1800 avenue du Maréchal-Juin; **Europcar** (04 66 21 31 35, 1 rue de la République; **Hertz** (04 66 76 25 91, 39 boulevard Gambetta; and **Rent-a-Car** (04 66 62 30 40, 14 avenue Georges-Pompidou.

In case of medical emergency, contact the **SAMU** (15 (mobile emergency service).

FESTIVALS AND EVENTS

Nîmes has three major **bullfighting** festivals a year. In February, there is the **Feria du Carnaval**. In May, the **Feria de Pentecôte** (Pentecost) is a five-day festival. In the third week of September, **Feria des Vendanges** coincides with the harvest festival.

Bullfighting is pursued with a passion in the area from the lower Rhône Valley to Spain. Two styles are practiced, Spanish style, with its pomp and colorful costumes, where the bulls are killed in the ring, and Provençal style, *à la cocarde*, where nimble young men in white try to pluck a rosette from between the horns of the bull without getting gored, and the bulls are not put to death. Nîmes is the capital of *la tauromachie*, as Spanish-style bullfighting is known. But most people who go to the *ferias* are not *aficionados*. They go to party. They dance in the streets, frolic all night and drink wine at *bodegas*, informal bars that spring up everywhere. The meat of the bulls killed in the ring is sold to butchers and can be eaten in restaurants, the ultimate homage or the ultimate insult, depending on your point of view.

From the second week of July to the third week of August, **L'Été de Nîmes**, the summer cultural festival, puts on an ambitious program of dance, classical folk, pop and rock music, and street performances.

WHAT TO SEE AND DO

Les Arènes, Nîmes's 24,000-seat arena, is the best preserved of the 70 Romans amphitheaters in the world. Like the Roman theater in Orange, it owes its survival to the fact that it was converted into a fortress in the Middle Ages, and it later became a walled village. In the days of Provincia Romana, the arena was used for combats of gladiators and animals. In hot weather, it was covered by a huge awning. The holes for its support poles can be seen in the rock of the upper façade. Now it is converted to a 7,000-seat indoor theater from October to April by covering it with a huge translucent textile membrane and heating the interior space. Otherwise the arena is open-air and is used for pop, rock, and classical music concerts, operas, circuses, and bullfights. It can be visited from 9 AM to 7 PM in the summer, 9 AM to noon and 2 PM to 5:30 PM the rest of the year.

One block from the Arènes, in the café-lined **Place du Marché**, look at the fountain designed by Martial Raysse of a life-sized crocodile in chains, the emblem of the city, commemorating the defeat of Antony and Cleopatra by Octavius in Egypt. **G. Courtois**, the Pâtissier-Confiseur-Glacier-Salon de Thé at 8 place du Marché near the fountain, is a good spot to pause for a delicious pastry or chocolates and coffee.

The **Maison Carrée**, the central landmark of the city, was built in AD 5 and is the best preserved of all Roman temples. Though *"carrée"* is French for "square," it is a rectangle, 26 m (85 ft) long by 15 m (50 ft) wide. Until the late Middle Ages, the term *carrée* was used to describe any figure with four right angles. It stands 17 m (56 ft) high, has 32 perfect Corinthian columns supporting its roof and sits on a pedestal 15 steps high. The Maison Carrée looks like the vastly larger Madeleine in Paris, for which it served as a model. It is open from 9 AM to 7 PM in the summer, to 5:30 PM the rest of the year.

Directly across the square is the **Carré d'Art**, Norman Foster's homage to the Maison Carrée. The cool, airy, classically ordered glass and steel pavilion opened in 1993 and is the city's major art exhibition center, contemporary art museum, and art library. It is open from 11 AM to 6 PM, closed Monday.

One block up Boulevard Alphonse-Daudet, named for the Nîmes-born author, is Martial Raysse's 1989 assembly of fountains and sculptures at **Place d'Assas**, which interprets the story of water in Nîmes with elegance and a modern sense of humor.

The nearby **Jardin de la Fontaine** is the eighteenth-century reworking of Nîmes's original *raison d'être*, the spring of Nemausus, turned into an ornate public garden with canals lined with stone balustrades, statuary, and shade trees. To the left of the spring are the ruins of the so-called Temple of Diana, which was more likely the library of the Roman sanctuary. It was destroyed during the Wars of Religion. Brides and grooms traditionally have their pictures taken in the Jardin de la Fontaine. On a Saturday in June, as you look around, you can see half a dozen festively dressed wedding parties striking poses at the same time.

Take the stone staircase up the wooded hill overlooking the garden and follow the paths to the top of Mont Cavalier, 114 m (374 ft) high, where the **Tour Magne** stands. The ruins of this octagonal tower stand 30 m (almost 100 ft) tall. The Romans built it in 15 BC as a watch tower, as a visible symbol of Roman domination that could be seen

Nîmes's AD 5 Maison Carrée and its 1993 Carré d'Art, a library and art exhibition center.

from far away, and as a marker for the imperial sanctuary encircling the spring of Nemausus at the foot of the hill. The panorama from the top of Mont Cavalier is the best in the city.

Museums

The **Musée du Vieux Nîmes** (Museum of Old Nîmes), housed in the seventeenth-century former bishop's palace, is the city's most interesting museum, covering the history of Nîmes and its surrounding area from the Middle Ages to the present, including the tragic Wars of Religion. It has a fascinating collection of textile patterns from the nineteenth century and furniture from the seventeenth century on. The museum puts on two special exhibits per year, always worth seeing. It is on the Place aux Herbes, near the cathedral.

The **Musée Archéologique** (Archaeological Museum) has a rich collection of statues, ceramics, and other finds from Gallo-Roman antiquity through the Middle Ages, with an outstanding collection of ancient coins. It is in a large seventeenth-century Jesuit school at 13bis boulevard Amiral-Courbet on the east side of town. The **Natural History Museum** is also located here.

The **Musée des Beaux-Arts** illustrates different schools of painting from the Renaissance through the nineteenth century, mainly French, German and Dutch, and some from Italy and Spain, and there is a huge, magnificent Roman mosaic, *The Marriage of Admète*, on the ground floor. The museum is on Rue de la Cité Foulc to the south of the Arènes.

The **Musée d'Art Contemporain** at the Carré d'Art puts on ambitious exhibitions of contemporary art in its vast, airy galleries. Its permanent collection has works by Claude Vialat, Arman, César, Gerhard Richter, and other contemporary artists.

The museums are open from 11 AM to 6 PM, closed on Monday.

WINE TASTING

Costières de Nîmes, formerly known as Costières du Gard, is a one of the new *appellations* of Languedoc that has made great strides in improving quality. Its vineyards cover a large area of pebbly ground between the hills north of Nîmes and the edge of the Camargue. They make dry rosés and some whites, and are building a good reputation for their reds, which are similar to Côtes du Rhône, but less expensive.

At the **Château de la Tuilerie** (04 66 70 07 52, on Route de Saint-Gilles next to the Golf de Campagne golf course, you can sample the wines from their own estate and those of many other producers of Costières de Nîmes in their Jardins des Vins boutique. It is open Monday through Saturday.

WHERE TO STAY

Expensive

Imperator Concorde**** (04 66 21 90 30 FAX 04 66 67 70 25 E-MAIL hotel.imperator@wanadoo.com WEB SITE www.concorde-hotel.com, Quai de la Fontaine, is a lovely old mansion on the Jardin de la Fontaine with 62 rooms decorated in Provençal style.

Moderate

The **New Hôtel la Baume***** (04 66 76 28 42 FAX 04 66 76 28 45 info@newhotel.com WEB SITE www.newhotel.com, 21 rue Nationale, is a grand, tastefully modernized, seventeenth-century mansion in the heart of old Nîmes with 33 comfortable rooms. The **Royal***** (04 66 58 28 27 FAX 04 66 58 28 28, 31 boulevard Alphonse-Daudet, is a 31-room art deco hotel with lots of atmosphere and favored by artists. **Clarine Plazza**** (04 66 76

16 20 FAX 04 66 67 65 99 WEB SITE www.leplazza.fr, 10 rue Roussy, is a favorite of bullfighting aficionados, with 28 rooms in 1930s style. It's near the arena.

Inexpensive
The **Lisita**** (04 66 67 66 20 FAX 04 66 76 22 30, 2bis boulevard des Arènes, is a less expensive hotel favored by fans of the *corrida* and 24 of its rooms have private bath. Just up the street, the 17-room **Amphithéâtre**** (04 66 67 28 51 FAX 04 66 67 07 79, at 4 rue des Arènes, is a friendly hotel, and with a top price of 260 francs, a very good value for the money.

Camping
Camping du Domaine de la Bastide (04 66 38 09 21 is an attractive 240-place site five kilometers (three miles) south of Nîmes on the Route de Générac near the Costières stadium. It is open all year. There are eleven other camping grounds in

the vicinity of Nîmes and several others further afield. Ask for a list at the Tourist Office.

WHERE TO EAT
For wildly inventive gourmet dishes, such as a floating island of truffles on a sauce of wild mushrooms or *fricassée* of quail and sweetbreads with licorice, head out to Chef Michel Kayser's restaurant **Alexandre** (04 66 70 08 99, nine kilometers (six miles) from the center of town in Garons. This Michelin one-star establishment has an outstanding list of Costières de Nîmes wines. It is expensive. At the Imperator Concorde, **L'Enclos de la Fontaine** is one of the city's top restaurants, and its flowery dining terrace is a good, though expensive, place to try *brandade de morue*, the garlic-flavored codfish dish that is a specialty of Nîmes.

The Roman arena in Nîmes is used regularly for bullfights, circuses, and pop concerts.

A place I enjoy greatly is **Le P'tit Bec** (04 66 38 05 83, at 87bis rue de la République, a pretty little garden restaurant with tasty, moderately priced regional fare and a good choice of Languedoc wines with *menus* starting at 90 francs for lunch, 130 francs for a *menu du terroir*. The *cabillaud à l'infusion d'estragon* (fresh codfish in tarragon sauce) is excellent here. So is the Camargue bull meat steak with olives and anchovies. A friendly little bistro with tasty regional fare, somewhat less expensive, is the **Chapon Fin** (04 66 67 34 73, at 3 place du Château, just behind the church of Saint Paul. *Brandade de morue*, free-range chicken roasted with honey and spices, and veal stew with zucchini a few of the dishes featured.

For tasty *tapas* and other inexpensive Spanish specialties in a warm *bodega* setting, try **La Casa Don Miguel** (04 66 76 07 09 at 18 rue de l'Horloge, near the Maison Carrée.

The best spots for people-watching are at **La Grande Bourse** and **La Petite Bourse**, colorful old cafés at the angle of Boulevard Victor Hugo and Boulevard des Arènes, across from Les Arènes.

HOW TO GET THERE

Air France has six flights a day from Orly to Nîmes-Arles-Camargue Airport, eight kilometers (five miles) south of the city. There are eight *TGV*s (high-speed trains) from Paris, a four-and-a-half-hour trip, and many trains from Avignon and Arles (a 20-minute trip from each), from Montpellier and points south, and Carcassonne and points west. There is **international bus service** from Spain on Iberbus (04 66 29 50 62 and from many places in Europe on Eurolines (08 36 69 52 52, and frequent **regional bus service** to and from Uzès, Pont du Gard, Aigues-Mortes, La Grande Motte, and other towns of the Languedoc coast. All bus service is from the **Gare Routière** (04 66 29 52 00. By car, Nîmes is easily reached by a web of highways converging from every direction, including the A9, La Languedocienne, the through route from the north that branches off from the A7 at Orange and continues south to Spain.

BEAUCAIRE

In the days of the Roman Empire, Beaucaire was a key point on the route between Rome and Spain. Twenty-four kilometers (15 miles) east of Nîmes on the west bank of the Rhône, it was the port where you crossed the river to or from Tarascon on the other side. The Roman road stayed in use long after the collapse of Empire, and in the Middle Ages, strategically situated Beaucaire became the site of a huge, tremendously colorful fair to which as many as 300,000 traders and merchants came

from all over Europe during the month of July to do business and have fun. Streets were named for the products they specialized in — wool, cotton, silk, jewelry, weapons, saddles. Traders in foodstuffs had their stands by the river, and the fairground spread out across the plain between the river and the castle. There were troubadours, jugglers, clowns, acrobats, and performing animal acts. It remained active from the thirteenth century to the nineteenth century, when the railroad made it obsolete.

Beaucaire was also a key military position for the Kingdom of France on the Rhône, which was the border with Provence in the Middle Ages. For centuries, two mighty castles, France's Château de Beaucaire and Provence's Château de Tarascon menaced each other across the Rhône. The Count of Provence was a vassal of the Holy Roman Emperor, and boatmen still referred to the two banks of the river as "Kingdom" and "Empire" as late as the nineteenth century.

GENERAL INFORMATION

The **Tourist Office (** 04 66 59 26 57 E-MAIL beaucaire @mnet.fr is at 24 cours Gambetta.

WHAT TO SEE AND DO

The **Château de Beaucaire** was built in the eleventh century by the Count of Toulouse and dismantled in the seventeenth century by Richelieu, and only the outer shell of remains. But it is impressive nevertheless, and its panoramic view of Tarascon, the Rhône Valley, and the Alpilles is exceptional. The Château de Beaucaire puts on a medieval costume show called **Les Aigles de Beaucaire (** 04 66 59 58 33 (The Eagles of Beaucaire) with free-flying eagles, vultures and falcons every afternoon from Easter to the end of October at 3, 4, 5 and 6 PM. It costs 35 francs for adults, 20 francs for children under 13. For information call. If you are traveling with children, this is one of the most

unique and exciting events you can take them to. But it is a thrill for people of any age.

Beaucaire is also the place where the **Canal du Rhône à Sète** begins, the boat canal that cuts to the west of the Camargue and connects the Rhône River with the Canal du Midi. Those who fantasize about cruising the canals of southern France may want to look at the houseboats. Companies that rent them in Beaucaire are: **Camargue Plaisance (** 04 67 50 77 00 and **Nautic (** 04 67 94 78 93 at Quai du Général-de-Gaulle, and **Connoisseur Cruisers (** 04 66 59 46 08 E-MAIL connoisseur @wanadoo.fr WEB SITE www.connoisseur-cruiser.co.uk, at 14 quai de la Paix.

WHERE TO STAY AND EAT

Les Doctrinaires*** **(** 04 66 59 23 70 FAX 04 66 59 22 26 WEB SITE www.archimix.com-web-doctrinaires,

The Eagles of Beaucaire, a medieval birds of prey show at the Château de Beaucaire on the Rhône.

is a splendid seventeenth-century residence of the Doctrinaire religious order tastefully converted into a hotel with 34 very comfortable rooms at moderate rates. Its respected gastronomic restaurant, **Le Saint-Roman**, has a grand, vaulted dining room and a pretty courtyard terrace, with fixed-price *menus* at 98 and 240 francs, wine included. It is centrally located on Quai du Général-de-Gaulle. Another very good hotel-restaurant here is **Le Robinson*** (04 66 59 21 32 FAX 04 66 59 00 03, in a quiet country setting northwest of town on the Route de Remoulins (D986). It has 30 pretty Provençal-style rooms, a warm family atmosphere, a tennis court, a swimming pool, and an excellent, reasonably priced restaurant that serves some

of the best *gardiane de toro* (Camargue bull stew) you will find anywhere. This is a Logis de France hotel that fully lives up to the motto, "hotel-keeping with a human face." Double rooms run 300 to 350 francs. Open daily the year round, except the month of February.

Camping

Camping le Rhodanien (04 66 59 25 50 is a well-equipped site with a swimming pool on the fairground, the Champ de Foire, by the river. It has 100 places and is open from March 20 to October 20.

HOW TO GET THERE

There are regularly schedules buses from Nîmes and Avignon, and frequent service from Tarascon just across the bridge. By car, from Nîmes take

D999, a distance of 24 km (15 miles), or from Avignon N570, which connects with D970 to Tarascon, where you cross the bridge to Beaucaire. It is 24 km (15 miles) too.

TARASCON

Massive Tarascon Castle on the east bank of Rhône halfway between Avignon and Arles is the very image of the medieval storybook castle. The town's name comes from the Tarasque, a legendary man-eating monster tamed by Saint Martha, Mary Magdalene's sister. Its name is also associated with Tartarin de Tarascon, the Provençal braggart hunter-warrior hero of Alphonse Daudet's mock epic novel.

GENERAL INFORMATION

The **Tourist Office** (04 90 91 03 52 is at 59 rue des Halles, in back of the Church of Saint Martha.

WHAT TO SEE AND DO

The **Château de Tarascon**, begun in the twelfth century and completed in the fifteenth, was the alternate principal residence of Good King René. Its mighty exterior walls soar to 150 ft (45 m) above the river, and from the upper battlements, there is a grand panorama of the lower Rhône Valley. Inside you will find a marvelous collection of eighteenth-century ceramic apothecary jars, elaborate painted wood ceilings and a dramatic series of seventeenth-century tapestries on the life of Scipio Africanus. It is open from 9 AM to 7 PM in the summer, from 9 AM to noon and 2 PM to 5 PM the rest of the year.

The mostly fourteenth-century **Église Sainte-Marthe**, across the street from the château, has a sarcophagus that supposedly contains the remains of the saint.

La Maison de Tartarin is a reconstruction of the home of Daudet's fictional hero, including the wildly overgrown exotic garden in which Tartarin wove overblown tales of his exotic adventures. The people of Tarascon hated the book when it came out, feeling that Daudet, a native of Nîmes, had ridiculed their town. Now, since it keeps their town on the tourist map (like Cézanne in Aix, Van Gogh in Arles), they love it. The Maison de Tartarin is at 55bis boulevard Itam, open from 9:30 AM to noon and 2 PM to 7 PM in the summer; it closes at 5 PM off-season.

HOW TO GET THERE

There is frequent regular bus service from Nîmes, Arles and Avignon, some 25 km (16 miles) away, and from Beaucaire directly across the bridge.

ARLES

With its sun-baked hues and terracotta tiled roofs and its spot on a wide bend of the lower Rhône, Arles is the Provençal city par excellence. Though half the size of Nîmes, it is even more loaded with historical attractions, having been a great Roman port, the capital of Provincia Romana, the seat of a Christian archbishopric from the third century, even the capital of the Roman Empire for a moment in the early fifth century, and the most important center of Christianity in southern France throughout the Middle Ages. For more than a thousand years, thanks to its strategic position near the mouth of the Rhône halfway between Italy and Spain, Arles was the crossroads of Western civilization. Much of its interest today comes from that glorious millennium.

As if all that weren't enough, the ghost of Vincent Van Gogh hovers over Arles too.

BACKGROUND

In the sixth century BC the Greeks from Marseille established a Rhône port and trading post in a marshy place they called "Arlate" — "the town in the swamp." Arles broke from the mother city and sided with Julius Caesar in his civil war against Pompey, and when Caesar triumphed in 49 BC, Arles was rewarded with a large part of Marseille's shipping business. Its position at the junction of the Rhône and the Aurelian Way made Arles a natural center for trading. From the beginning of the Pax Romana well into the Middle Ages, with periodic interruptions by the barbarians, Franks and Saracens, Arles was the most important and prosperous city in the region. Its markets drew traders from all over Europe and the Middle East.

Christianity established itself early in Arles. Saint Trophime became the first bishop early in the third century, and Emperor Constantine called the first council of bishops at his palace in Arles in AD 314. The Church of Saint-Trophime was begun at the beginning of the seventh century, and the monastery of Montmajour became one of the most powerful in Europe. Arles's necropolis of Les Alyscamps was the most revered in Christendom. Being buried there was a virtual guarantee of getting into heaven.

The reemergence of Marseille as the main port during the Crusades and establishment of Aix as the political capital by the Counts of Provence sent Arles into a slow, steady decline. Its geographic position kept the barge traffic alive, but in the nineteenth century, the railroad came down the Rhône and took away the most profitable north–south traffic.

Culturally, Arles became the capital of Frédéric Mistral and the Félibrige movement, which re-vived the Occitan language and the region's pride in its culture. When Mistral won the Nobel Prize for Literature in 1904, he invested his prize money in establishing the Muséon Arlaten, museum of Provençal folk arts and traditions.

In the twentieth century Arles has made itself a crossroads once more, not of empires or kingdoms, but of its own local area, and has become prosperous from agriculture and tourism.

GENERAL INFORMATION

There are two **Tourist Offices** in Arles. The main office (04 90 18 41 20 is on the Esplanade Charles de Gaulle, on the south side of Boulevard des Lices,

the main street of Arles. The other Tourist Office (04 90 49 36 90 is at the railway station, the Gare SNCF on Avenue Paulin-Talabot. These offices sell a pass to all museums in Arles, all of which are open daily except national holidays. The pass costs 40 francs They also offer a two-hour Van Gogh walking tour Tuesdays and Fridays, leaving at 5 PM from the main Tourist Office.

The **Nîmes-Garons Airport** can be reached at (04 66 70 06 88. The train station, **Gare SNCF** (04 90 82 50 50 or 08 36 35 35 35, is on the north side of town on Avenue Paulin Talabot. The bus terminal, **Gare Routière** (04 90 49 38 01, is just across from the train station. The city bus line is **STAR** (04 90 96 87 47, 16 boulevard Georges-Clemenceau.

OPPOSITE: A bird handler at the medieval show at Beaucaire. ABOVE: The twelfth-century Romanesque façade of Arles's Church of Saint-Trophime.

For **taxis**, call (04 90 96 90 03, 04 90 49 69 59, or 04 90 93 31 16.

Car rental agencies include **Arles Auto Service** (04 90 96 82 82, at 84 avenue de Stalingrad; **Avis** (04 90 96 82 42, on Avenue Talabot; **EuropCar** (04 90 93 23 24, at 2bis avenue Victor-Hugo; and **Hertz** (04 90 96 75 23, at 4 avenue Victor-Hugo. Bicycle rental is available at the **Gare SNCF baggage counter** (04 90 96 43 94, or **Collavoli** (04 90 96 03 77, at 15 rue du Pont.

Bus tours of Arles and the region are available through **Arles Voyages** (04 90 96 88 73, at 12 boulevard Georges-Clemenceau.

In case of medical emergency, contact the **SMUR** (mobile emergency service) (15; or **Centre Hospitalier** (the hospital) (04 90 49 29 29.

FESTIVALS AND EVENTS

The **Feria Pascale** (Easter Fair), with bullfighting and related activities, is held on Easter Saturday, Sunday, and Monday.

The **Fête des Gardians**, a rodeo of Camargue cowboys, takes place towards the beginning of May.

The Festival of Tradition, **Fête d'Arles**, features a parade with more than 1,000 people in period dress, with music, song, and dance. At the same time there is **La Course Royale de la Cocarde d'Or**, which is the running of the bulls and Provençal bullfighting. It all takes place the last weekend of June and first week of July.

Rencontres Internationales de la Photographie is a major international photography exhibition with seminars. It is held during the month of July.

The Rice Harvest Festival, **Prémices du Riz**, is held in mid-September, with bullfighting on the second Sunday of that month.

Much music and literature has been inspired by the beauty of the women of Arles. They are typically tall and proud of carriage with pale skin and dark eyes and hair. In their traditional long dress with lace shawl and cap that they wear at festivals, they make a fiery and elegant appearance.

WHAT TO SEE AND DO

Les Arènes, Arles's first century AD Roman arena, is slightly larger than Nîmes's, but less well preserved. Most of the stonework of the upper level was removed for other uses over the years. Luckily, as in Nîmes, the coliseum was converted into a fortress during the Middle Ages and a village built inside. Otherwise, there would have been a good deal less of it standing today. Like the arena of Nîmes, it hosts bullfights, concerts, and other events. It has a seating capacity of up to 12,000 in its 34 rows of bleachers. It can be visited daily from

9 AM to 12:30 PM and 2 PM to 7 PM, May through September, shorter hours in different months the rest of the year.

Only one small section of Arles's 25 BC Roman **Théâtre Antique** remains, but in its day it was larger than that of Orange, with a capacity of over 12,000, and more elaborately decorated. In the summer it is equipped with wooden risers for theatrical productions.

The main portal of the **Church of Saint-Trophime**, beautifully restored in the early 1990s, is one of the masterpieces of Provençal Romanesque sculpture. On the tympanum, a stern Christ oversees the Last Judgment surrounded by the symbols of the four Evangelists. To the left,

the saved are being welcomed into Heaven by an angel (we know they are good because they have their clothes on) and to the right the damned (no clothes on) are being dragged to Hell in chains by a devil, a pitiful scene that must have struck fear into the beholders' hearts when it was created in the twelfth century.

The capitals of its little pillars of the **Cloister of Saint-Trophime** are decorated with sculptures of biblical scenes and the pillars themselves with the lives of saints and apostles. The north and east arcades of the cloister are twelfth-century Romanesque, the south and west fourteenth-century Gothic.

The **Muséon Arlaten** (Museum of Arles, in Provençal), founded by Mistral, has a large, well-displayed collection of Provençal folk arts, farm and craftsmen's tools, and interesting historical documents, such as warrants to arrest nobles and seize their property during the French Revolution. Open from 9 AM to noon and 2 PM to 7 PM June through August, afternoons only the rest of the year. Closed Monday.

The **Musée Réattu** has 57 Picasso drawings donated by the artist in 1972 in appreciation for the many *corridas* he enjoyed attending in Arles. Most date from 1971 and deal with such favorite motifs as the artist and his model, harlequins, and monsters. The museum also has paintings, drawings and watercolors by Gauguin, Vlaminck, Dufy, Marquet, and Vasarely, sculptures by Germaine Richier, César, and Pol Bury, and a large photography collection, including prints by Lartigue, Karsh, and Man Ray. Open daily, 9 AM to 12:30 PM

Les Alyscamps (Elysian fields) was a Roman, then early Christian necropolis. Its long alleyway lined with great trees and a double row of stone sarcophagi leads to the ruins of the twelfth-century **Church of Saint-Honorat**. In the Middle Ages, when it was an important place of pilgrimage, there were sarcophagi by the thousands. Most have disappeared, but fortunately, the Musée de l'Arles Antique has some good examples. Les Alyscamps has long been a favorite scene for artists. Van Gogh and Gauguin painted side by side here during a period of relative harmony. Open daily, the same hours as Roman arena.

From any of these places, you are likely to end up on the **Boulevard des Lices**, the main street of

and 2 PM to 7 PM, May to September, with somewhat shorter hours in different months the rest of the year.

Espace Van Gogh, a cultural center, is a former hospital where Van Gogh stayed during the winter of 1888–1889 after he cut off part of his ear. The wide central courtyard's flower garden has been planted to match his famous painting. The space is now used for art exhibits.

From the welter of tee-shirts and postcards and other Van Gogh memorabilia on sale by souvenir hawkers in Arles, you would think he was their local sports hero. But Arles snubbed and rejected the troubled Van Gogh and never bought any of the 200 paintings and 100 drawings he did in the incredibly productive 15 months he spent here. The two houses he lived in, which would have been worth millions in any currency as tourist attractions, were destroyed by Allied bombs in 1944.

Arles, which is fine. It has wide sidewalks shaded by big plane trees and numerous cafés in lining the north side for you to relax and refresh yourself in. If you are here on Saturday morning, this is where the **market** is held.

Arles's spacious modern **Musée de l'Arles Antique** (Museum of Ancient Arles), opened in 1995, brings together the large collections of the **Musée d'Art Païen** (Museum of Pagan Art) and the **Musée d'Art Chrétien** (Museum of Christian Art) that were previously housed in two colorful, but very cramped, decommissioned baroque churches. With 3,000 sq m (28,000 sq ft) of exhibition space, Arles now can display many

OPPOSITE: A photography exhibit at the Van Gogh Foundation, part of the annual Rencontres Internationales de la Photographie. ABOVE: The restaurant-lined Place du Forum in Arles, where modestly priced food can be found.

fine pieces it previously had to keep in storage. Most of the works of art from the Roman period — sculptures, mosaics, and sarcophagi — were created in Arles and its region. They include the exquisite mosaic *The Rape of Europa*, a statue of *Orpheus*, and a copy of the *Venus of Arles*, a statue found in digs at the Roman Theater that is now in the Louvre. There is a remarkable collection of third- to fifth-century Christian sarcophagi carved with scenes from the Old and New Testaments and touching images of the deceased in white marble. Open daily from 9 AM to 12:30 PM and 2 PM to 7 PM, May through September, shorter hours in different months the rest of the year.

WHERE TO STAY

Expensive

Nord-Pinus**** (04 90 93 44 44 FAX 04 90 93 34 00 E-MAIL infor@nordpinus.com WEB SITE www.nord-pinus.com, on the lively Place du Forum, is a legendary hotel where Picasso, Cocteau, Piaf, and Montand were frequent guests and where matadors like to stay during the *corridas*. The atmospheric lobby and bar, worth visiting just for a look, are decorated with wrought iron, classic bullfighting posters, and a remarkable collection of contemporary art. All 25 deluxe rooms are individually decorated in imaginative mixtures of the old and the ultra-new. Double rooms are in the 850- to 1,000-franc range, suites 1,700 francs. The Nord-Pinus also has a good restaurant (see WHERE TO EAT, below).

The **Jules-César****** (04 90 93 43 20 FAX 04 90 93 33 47 E-MAIL julescesar@calva.net WEB SITE www.relaischateaux.fr/julescesar is a seventeenth-century Carmelite convent, now a traditionally deluxe 50-room, five-suite Relais & Châteaux hotel with gardens, a swimming pool, and two good restaurants (see WHERE TO EAT, below). It is at 9 boulevard des Lices. At the lower end of the expensive category, with some rooms in the moderate price range, is **D'Arlatan***** (04 90 93 56 66 FAX 04 90 49 68 45 E-MAIL hotel-arlatan@prov-net.fr WEB SITE www.arlatan@provnet.fr, at 26 rue Sauvage, a quiet side street near the Place du Forum. The former residence of the Counts d'Arlatan de Beaumont, it is a 34-room hotel of authentic charm with an interior garden and private garage.

All rooms in these hotels are air-conditioned — a very important feature in the height of summer. This city gets *very* hot.

Moderate

Calendal** (04 90 96 11 89 FAX 04 90 96 05 84, at 22 place du Docteur-Pomme, a quiet alcove near the arena and the Roman theater, is a true Provençal *hôtel de charme* with a cheerful, inviting lobby

and a friendly staff in it; 27 neat, attractive, air-conditioned rooms decorated in Provençal fabrics, with up-to-date bathrooms; and a lovely tree-shaded garden where breakfast or light meals are served in good weather.

Inexpensive

The **Musée**** (04 90 93 88 88 FAX 04 90 49 98 15 is a pleasant hotel with 20 renovated, air-conditioned rooms and a quiet patio at 11 rue Grand-Prieuré, across from the Musée Réattu. **Le Cloître**** (04 90 96 29 50 FAX 04 90 96 02 88, at 18 rue du Cloître, is a friendly, well-maintained old 30-room hotel on a side street by the Cloister of Saint-Trophime. No air-conditioning.

Camping

Camping City (04 90 93 08 86, a 100-place camping grounds at 67 route de Crau about two kilometers (one and a half miles) south of town is open March through the end of September. **Les Rosiers** (04 90 96 02 12 at Pont-de-Crau, also with 100 places, is open from mid-March through mid-October. Other nearby campsites are the 70-place **Le Gardian** (04 90 98 46 51 and the 81-place **La Bienheureuse** (04 90 98 35 64, both on Route N113 in Raphèle-les-Arles about eight kilometers (five miles) to the southeast of the city, both open all year.

WHERE TO EAT

Expensive

For gourmet Provençal cuisine in *Grand Siècle* surroundings, there's the elegant **Restaurant Lou Marquès** in the Hôtel Jules-César (see WHERE TO STAY, above), with *menus* at 150 and 420 francs (wine included). For a more casual dining experience at the Jules-César, the pretty **Restaurant du Cloître** serves light Provençal lunch *menus* at 105 francs and wine by the *carafe*. I enjoy the atmospheric **Brasserie du Nord-Pinus** (see WHERE TO STAY, above), whose cuisine is under the direction of Jean-André Charial of the Oustaù de Baumanière (see LES BAUX-DE-PROVENCE, page 262). It offers bright Provençal *menus* at 130 francs (wine included) for lunch, 180 francs for dinner, with wine from Mr. Charial's Château Romanin by the *carafe*. At **L'Olivier** (04 90 49 64 88, 1bis rue Réattu, you can sample the cuisine of another resourceful Provençal master chef, Jean-Louis Vidal, in a delightful sixteenth-century stone house with a glassed-over interior garden. With a lively terrace overlooking the Place du Forum, **Le Vaccarès** (04 90 96 06 17 serves savory Camargue-Arles cuisine and an outstanding selection of Côtes du Rhône wines. The lunch *menu* at 98 francs is an excellent value. Entrance on Rue Favorin around the corner from the Place.

Moderate

Right downstairs from Le Vaccarès, the **Café Van Gogh** (04 90 49 83 30, at 11 place du Forum, is a lively café-brasserie that is an exact reproduction of Van Gogh's *Café de la Nuit*, lit just the way he saw it in 1888. Plenty of tourists eat here, of course, and the prices are slightly high, but this is no tourist trap. The food is good — there's a fine selection of salads — and the atmosphere is marvelous, especially at night. **L'Escaladou** (04 90 96 70 43, at 23 rue Porte de Laure overlooking the Roman theater, is an authentically Provençal restaurant where a mainly local clientele feasts on *bouillabaisse* and other regional specialties. This is the perfect place to try *aïoli*, a heaping platter of boiled

and steak *tartare*. It attracts a mellow young crowd. **Poisson Banane** (04 90 96 02 58, a lively spot at 6 rue du Forum, serves Caribbean-flavored dishes at very affordable prices. On the shaded terrace of **Le Grillon** (04 90 96 70 97, at Rond Point des Arènes facing the Arena, you can choose from a wide array of salads, omelets, and other light fare, and in the evening, well-prepared Provençal home cooking.

For a pleasant lunch or dinner on the water, try **Acqua Café** (06 08 45 91 66, a converted barge permanently docked at the Halte Fluviale on Quai Saint-Pierre in Trinquetaille on the west bank of the Rhône, with a fine view of Arles directly across the river. It serves salads and local

salted codfish, snails, and vegetables served with the garlic mayonnaise after which the dish is named — delicious. **La Paillote** (04 90 96 33 15, at 28 rue du Docteur-Fanton, is a flowery little restaurant with a cozy rustic ambiance where talented chef Jean-Claude Tell serves his *papillote de poisson fumé* (smoked fish baked in parchment paper), *encornets* (little Mediterranean squid) sautéed in chopped parsley and garlic and flamed in anisette, roast lamb with parmesan eggplant, and other refined regional fare at remarkably reasonable prices, with a fixed-price *menu* at 96 francs, and a fine selection of regional wines at similarly friendly prices.

Inexpensive

Vitamine (04 90 93 77 36, at 16 rue du Docteur-Fanton, is a laid-back little eatery offering 50 different salads, pasta, cold cut and cheese platters,

specialties such as *petits farcis* (stuffed vegetables) and the ever-popular *brandade de morue* (mousse of salt cod with olive oil), with a fixed-price *menu* at 89 francs, or *à la carte* (closed all day Sunday, and Saturdays, and Mondays at lunch). You can get there easily by foot or by car via the Pont de Trinquetaille.

NIGHTLIFE

The cafés along the Boulevard des Lices cater to the tourists trade, and therefore are the most expensive in town. For livelier, less expensive cafés, go to the **Place du Forum**, where the Poisson Banane and the Café Van Gogh are, and colorful **Place Voltaire** north of the arena, where live jazz or pop music is played Wednesday nights.

Preparing for a bullfight in the first century AD Roman arena in Arles.

HOW TO GET THERE

The closest international airport is Marseille-Provence 65 km (40 miles) away. The closest domestic airport is Nîmes-Arles-Camargue 23 km (14 miles) away, to which there are four regular flights a day from Orly in Paris. By train, there is frequent service from Paris, a trip of about four and a half hours. There is also frequent train service from Avignon or Nîmes, a 20-minute ride, and from Aix, Marseille, and Montpellier. **Les Cars de Camargue** (04 90 96 36 25 provide daily bus connections with Nîmes, Aix, Marseille, and Les Saintes-Maries-de-la-Mer. **Les Cars Verts** (04 90 93 74 90 provide service between Arles and Avignon, Nîmes Airport, Aix, Marseille, and the Camargue. Driving from Paris by the *autoroutes*, take A7 to Orange, A9 to Nîmes, and A54 to Arles.

THE ALPILLES

From the outskirts of Arles as you look across the flat plain to the northeast, you see a chain of mountains off in the distance—at least, that's what it appears to be. But in fact, it's an illusion. The craggy white limestone peaks are mere hills, few of which reach even 300 m (985 ft), and they are closer to Arles than they look. They start only 10 km (six miles) away. This chain of would-be mountains is known as the Alpilles (pronounced aahl-pee), or "Alpettes" in English. Yet small as they are, these mini-Alps exercise a powerful appeal. They are indelibly associated with Alphonse Daudet, whose famous windmill is in Fontvieille and whose hero Tartarin de Tarascon hunted in these hills, and Van Gogh spent a year at the asylum in Saint-Rémy. "Saint-Rem" is every bit as chic as "Saint-Trop," and the Alpilles is an *in* place for celebrities and international princesses. There are chic wines here too—*AOC* Baux-de-Provence.

ABBAYE DE MONTMAJOUR

The first sight that greets you as you head northeast from Arles on D17, the road to Fontvieille, is the brooding ruins of the Benedictine **Abbey of Montmajour**, founded in the tenth century and a power in the Middle Ages. Its monks drained the swamps to create farm land, and with their revenues from agriculture and from pilgrims, Montmajour rose to national influence. After a period of decline in the seventeenth century, new constructions were undertaken in the late eighteenth century, but when the abbot, Cardinal Rohan, was implicated in the scandal of Marie Antoinette's necklace (1785), Louis XVI closed the abbey.

The medieval church, cloister and other early structures of the abbey have been restored and can be visited. The baroque wing has been left to the elements. The abbey offers a panoramic view of the Alpilles, the plain of the Crau, Arles, and the Cévennes.

The **Chapelle Sainte-Croix**, a twelfth-century Romanesque gem, sits on a field to the right of the road 200 m (about 220 yards) to the north of the abbey. Like Saint-Pantaléon near Gordes, it has child-sized sarcophagi hewn out of the slab of stone it rests on.

FONTVIEILLE

The **Moulin de Daudet**, the windmill made famous by Daudet's delightful collection of Provençal stories, *Lettres de Mon Moulin (Letters from My Windmill)*, is in Fontvieille, five kilometers (three miles) north of Arles. It is one of the South's most popular attractions for French tourists. Daudet did not live or write in the mill. He stayed at the home of friends when he came to Fontvieille, and the stories were written in Paris. But he loved the country around the mill and often meditated on the hillside. A small **Daudet Museum** has been installed in the mill with phonographs, documents, and memorabilia. It is open daily from 9 AM to noon and 2 PM to 7 PM April through September, to 5 PM the rest of the year. Closed the month of January.

The **Tourist Office** (04 90 54 67 49 is at 5 rue Marcel-Honorat in the center of Fontvieille.

Where to Stay and Eat

At the **Auberge la Regalido****** (04 90 54 60 22 FAX 04 90 54 64 29 E-MAIL regalido@relaischateaux.fr WEB SITE www.relaischateaux.fr/regalido, on Rue Frédéric Mistral in the center of Fontvieille, Jean-Pierre Michel, representing the sixth generation of chefs in his family, serves savory dishes of the Alpilles in the flowery terrace of his ancient former olive oil mill. There is a light lunch *menu* at 170 francs, beverages included, and more elaborate ones at 270 and 450 francs. This delightful restaurant, a favorite of mine, richly merits its Michelin star. The inn has 15 tranquil rooms tastefully decorated *à la Provençale*, expensive. A Relais & Châteaux member. Closed the month of January and the first half of February.

LES BAUX-DE-PROVENCE

This desolate, foreboding valley surrounded by barren white rocky crags is believed to have inspired Dante's description of Hell. It lies 10 km (eight miles) east of Fontvieille.

The name of Les Baux derives from the Provençal *li baus*—the rocks. The rocks turned out to have a valuable mineral in them, and rich deposits of it were discovered in 1821. The ore, used to make aluminum, was named after Les Baux — "bauxite."

High above the valley is the uninhabited **Upper Town**, the medieval seat of the powerful lords of Baux. This town had a violent history, particularly under Raymond of Turenne, "The Scourge of Provence," who delighted in making prisoners jump to their deaths off the sheer cliffs. The Upper Town may have been abandoned by residents, but certainly not by tourists, who swarm over the place in July and August, nor by merchants who service their craving for arts and crafts items and souvenirs. There is plenty of mass-produced junk, but also a good deal of high-quality handicrafts for sale in the better boutiques. The views from Les Baux are sensational in all directions — Arles and the Camargue, the Rhône Valley, Mont Ventoux,

sive, with fixed-price *menus* at 495 and 750 francs. But if you feel like a major splurge, this is the place to do it. Closed January and February. The **Cabro d'Or****** (04 90 54 33 21 FAX 04 90 54 38 88 E-MAIL cabro@relaischateaux.fr WEB SITE WWW .relaischateaux.fr/cabro, the Oustaù's sister inn a few kilometers away, is a delightfully soothing 30-room hotel amid flower gardens and cypresses, with a pool and tennis courts, and an outstanding restaurant. It is expensive, but far less than the Oustaù. Closed mid-November to mid-December. Both establishments are Relais & Châteaux members.

Auberge de la Benvengudo*** (04 90 54 32 54 FAX 04 90 54 42 58, a charming old inn nestled

Aix, and the Lubéron. For good photography, go early in the morning or late in the afternoon; at midday the intense sun burns everything out.

You will find the **Tourist Office** (04 90 54 34 39 at the Hôtel de Manville, a sixteenth-century mansion also housing the town hall and a contemporary art museum. It is halfway up the hill from the parking lot.

Where to Stay and Eat

The **Oustaù de Baumanière****** (04 90 54 33 07 FAX 04 90 54 40 46 E-MAIL oustau@relaischateaux.fr WEB SITE www.relaischateaux.fr/oustau, is a 500-year-old farm in the wild beauty of the Val d'Enfer at the foot of Les Baux, with 13 superb rooms and nine suites, and a lovely pool. Under the direction of owner-chef Jean-André Charial, it has one of the great restaurants of southern France, with two Michelin stars. It is very expen-

in the Vallon de l'Arcoule, the valley at the foot of the village, has 20 very comfortable rooms decorated *à la Provençale* with all the modern comforts and huge bathrooms. Features include a swimming pool, tennis courts, a flowery garden, and a very friendly ambiance. Rooms are moderately expensive, 620 to 750 francs. The 10-room **Hostellerie de la Reine Jeanne**** (04 90 54 32 06 FAX 04 90 54 32 33 is an inexpensive hotel on Grande Rue at the entrance of the Upper Town with striking views of the ruins of the château and the valley. *Demi-pension* (one meal a day in addition to breakfast) is obligatory in the summer, but the prices are modest and the food is good, making it very popular. One must reserve well in advance.

Two views of Les Baux-de-Provence, a town with a particularly violent history.

How to Get There

Bus service is minimal. There are two buses per day each from Arles, Avignon, and Saint-Rémy. The best way to explore the Alpilles is by car, which you can rent in Avignon or Arles. If you are biker who doesn't mind climbing a few hills, you could rent in bikes Arles or Saint-Rémy. By car, Les Baux is nine kilometers (five and a half miles) northeast of Fontvieille on D17 and D78.

SAINT-RÉMY-DE-PROVENCE

Saint-Rémy is the liveliest town in the Alpilles, the crossroads of the area, with an outstanding Provençal market, lots of festivals and important Roman and pre-Roman ruins to tour. It is also remembered as one of the key places in Van Gogh's troubled life.

General Information

The **Tourist Office** (04 90 92 05 22 is at Place Jean-Jaurès, about 90 m (100 yards) south of town via Avenue Durand-Maillane or Avenue Pasteur. It provides good maps, brochures and advice about what to do in Saint-Rémy and the Alpilles, including itineraries of places painted by Van Gogh. It also runs guided tours in English and several other languages.

Bike rental is available at **Florélia** (04 90 92 10 88, 35 avenue de la Libération, and horseback riding at the **Club Hippique des Antiques** (04 90 92 30 55, on Rue Astier.

Festivals and Events

Saint-Rémy is a town of many festivals and events, a dozen a month in the summer — music, sports, bulls, goats, horses — a rural version of Monaco or Cannes. The main ones are the **Fête de la Transhumance**, the shepherds' festival, on Pentecost Monday in late May or in June, in which thousands of sheep are driven through the streets. **Organa**, an international festival of organ music, is held from July to September. From August 13 to 15, **Feria**, a festival of bullfights and farm-related events, is held. It culminates with the Carreto Ramado, a procession featuring 50 horses and a huge carriage laden with flowers and farm products.

What to See and Do

Two beautifully preserved Roman memorials called **Les Antiques** are located an easy walk south of the Tourist Office on D5, the road to Les Baux. The more unusual one is the **Mausoleum**, so-called after what it was long thought to be. But in fact it is a memorial to Emperor Augustus's two favorite grandsons, and their statues can de seen inside the circle of columns in the uppermost level of the

18-m (60-ft) white stone tower. There are fine bas-reliefs of hunting and battle scenes on the lower level. The second of the Antiques is a **commemorative arch**, also from Augustus's reign.

Glanum, across the road, is an extensive archaeological site that has been under excavation since 1921. It is named for a Celtic-Ligurian tribe called the Glani, and evidence of three different civilizations, one on top of the other, has been unearthed — Celtic-Ligurian, Greek, and Roman. The site is open daily from 10 AM to noon and 2 PM to 7 PM.

Also across the road from Les Antiques and through a grove of olive trees is the former **Monastery of Saint-Paul-de-Mausole**, the mental hospital where Van Gogh had himself committed in May 1889 to try to tame his self-destructive demons. He spent a full year here and painted twisted olive trees, cypresses, hay fields and starry nights, 150 paintings and drawings in all. In the alleyway leading into the hospital he painted his famous irises the day after his arrival. The monastery dates from the twelfth century and has a charming little cloister and Romanesque church you should not overlook.

Sculptures and mosaics excavated from Glanum are on display at the **Archaeological Museum** at the fifteenth-century Hôtel de Sade on Place Favier in the heart of old Saint-Rémy, open daily from 10 AM to noon and 2 PM to 5 PM. Nearby, the **Église Saint-Martin** has a magnificent organ with 5,000 stops that is used for the Organa concert series.

The colorful **Vieille Ville** (Old Town) of this community of 9,400 lies within a small circular boulevard planted with old plane trees that occupies the space where the medieval walls formerly stood. Different stretches of it are called Boulevard Victor-Hugo, Mirabeau, Gambetta, and Marceau, and they are lined with cafés, restaurants, and boutiques. Victor-Hugo and Mirabeau are the liveliest parts. In the Old Town, numerous houses remain from the fifteenth and sixteenth centuries (Nostradamus was born here in 1503), and the winding old streets are delightful to stroll.

A large Provençal **market** is held in the main squares of the Old Town Wednesday mornings, and a smaller one Saturday mornings.

Wine Tasting

The towns of the Alpilles make wines of the Baux-de-Provence *appellation*. They produce mainly light, dry rosés, but their reds have gained a great deal of respect in recent years. A few of the prestigious vineyards you can visit are: **Château Romanin** (04 90 92 45 87, in Saint-Rémy, with huge wine caves cut into the rock near the ruins of a castle; **Domaine des Terres Blanches** (04 90 95 91 66, also in Saint-Rémy; and **Mas de la Dame** (04 90 54 32 24, in Les Baux.

OPPOSITE and PAGE 266: Saint-Rémy-de-Provence is the liveliest town in the Alpilles for festivals and special events.

Where to Stay and Eat

For the height of discreetly elegant living, the **Château des Alpilles****** (04 90 92 03 33 FAX 04 90 92 45 17 E-MAIL chateaualpilles@wanadoo.fr WEB SITE www.wanadoo.fr is a nineteenth-century mansion in a large private park shaded by huge trees with 22 very spacious, deluxe rooms, tennis courts and a pool, a fine Provençal restaurant, and a grill by the pool. It lies two kilometers (one mile) west of town on D31. **Hostellerie du Vallon de Valrugues****** (04 90 92 04 40 FAX 04 90 92 44 01 E-MAIL vallon.valrugues@wanadoo.fr WEB SITE www.valrugues-cassagne.com, on Chemin Canto Cigalo, is a 42-room, 10-suite luxury hotel with a large pool, tennis courts, a golf driving range and putting green, and a respected gourmet restaurant. It is a Relais de Silence member. Both of these hotels are expensive.

For a pleasant little country hotel with moderate rates, try **Canto Cigalo**** (04 90 92 14 28 FAX 04 90 92 24 48, also on Chemin Canto Cigalo, with 20 pretty rooms at 275 to 340 francs. **Villa Glanum**** (04 90 92 03 50 FAX 04 90 92 00 08 E-MAIL vglanum@strascom.fr, is a cheerful cluster of low Provençal buildings in an olive grove with 28 comfortable, moderately priced rooms and a swimming pool. It is at 46 avenue Vincent-Van Gogh, two kilometers (one mile) out of town on the road to Les Baux, near the Glanum archeological site, Les Antiques, and the Monastery of Saint-Paul-de-Mausole. Also in the moderate price range is the **Auberge de la Reine Jeanne**** (04 90 92 15 33 FAX 04 90 92 49 65, a comfortable, convivial 10-room inn in a seventeenth-century house at 12 boulevard Mirabeau in the heart of old Saint-Rémy.

For lunch or dinner, **L'Orangerie Chabert** (04 90 92 05 95, a courtly restaurant in a big townhouse at 16 boulevard Victor-Hugo, has a spacious back yard patio, delightful at lunch or dinner, and the cuisine is outstanding. *Aubergines provençales*, filet of *rascasse* (Mediterranean rockfish) *au pistou* (with pesto sauce), grilled sea bass, and filet of beef with wild morel mushrooms are a few of the specialties. There are fixed-price *menus* from 107 to 210 francs. Closed Mondays and lunch Tuesdays. Just down the street is the trendy **Bistrot des Alpilles** (04 90 92 09 17, at 15 boulevard Mirabeau, with a *terrasse* on the boulevard in the summer. It serves tasty local dishes such as roast lamb or *brandade de morue* (Provençal-style codfish), with a lunch *menu* at 75 francs. Closed Sundays.

Just off Boulevard Mirabeau at 13 avenue de la Libération (the road to Cavaillon) is a classy little restaurant called **La Source** (04 90 92 44 71, serving stuffed zucchini blossoms, *daube de toro* (stew made from Camargue bulls), filets of *rouget* (red mullet) with olive purée, *noisettes d'agneau* (center cuts of lamb) laced with truffles, and other regional dishes, refined in the cooking and the

presentation. Meals are served in the quiet backyard garden in the summer. Fixed-price *menus* start at 95 francs. Closed Mondays, except holidays. **Le Pistou** (04 90 92 59 56, on the Route d'Avignon, one block from Boulevard Mirabeau, is a cozy, old-fashioned bistro-style eatery serving a wide array of savory Provençal dishes, from *soupe au pistou* (vegetable and bean soup with basil), to leg of Alpilles lamb with garlic sauce, to *bouillabaisse*. There's a 99-franc weekday lunch *menu*, 135 francs otherwise. The *bouillabaisse* is 195 francs and must be ordered a day in advance. The ambiance is easygoing, both in the quaint dining room and on the tree-shaded *terrasse*. Closed Thursdays out of season.

CAMPING
Le Mas de Nicolas (Camping Municipal) (04 90 92 27 05, on Avenue Théodore-Aubanel, is a well-shaded deluxe camping ground with 140 places, a pool and view of the Alpilles, open from March 15 to the end of October. The 105-place **Camping Pegomas** (04 90 92 01 21, Route de Noves, also has a pool, open March 1 to the end of October.

How to Get There

There is frequent daily bus service to Saint-Rémy from Avignon, and some daily service from Arles, Tarascon and Aix, but little from Les Baux. All buses stop at Place de la République, the large square across from the Église Saint-Martin. For bus schedules, contact the Tourist Office. By car, it is nine and a half kilometers (six miles) north of Les Baux

ABOVE: Provençal horsewoman.

on D5, 24 km (15 miles) northeast of Arles via Les Baux, and 19 km (12 miles) south of Avignon on D571.

THE CAMARGUE

The Camargue is the wide, flat delta of the Rhône, made up of salt marshes and mud flats, lagoons with flamingos, long sandy beaches, rice and wheat fields, and grasslands for cattle and horses herded by Camargue cowboys called *gardians*, and is the scene of big Gypsy pilgrimages. It is one of the most haunting places in all of France.

The delta starts below Arles, where the Rhône forks: the Grand Rhône flowing to the southeast and the Petit Rhône to the southwest. In the winter of 1993–1994, dikes along the Petit Rhône gave way, and 24,280 hectares (60,000 acres) of Camargue ranch and farmland ended up under water, causing $10 million in property damage and havoc for the wildlife.

At the center of the Camargue is the 13,500 hectare (32,500 acre) Réserve Nationale de Camargue, established in 1927, one of the oldest national wildlife preserves in France. Essentially consisting of the Étang de Vaccarès (Pond of Vaccarès) and the marshlands along its shores, it is closed to the public, but its bird life can be observed from the road around its periphery and from the Digue de la Mer (sea dike) that runs between the Étang and the Mediterranean. There are more than 400 species of birds, and the pink flamingo is the symbol of the Réserve. In summer, there can be as many as 300,000 flamingos in residence.

Surrounding the Réserve is the 85,000-hectare (204,000-acre) Parc Naturel Régional de Camargue (Camargue Regional Nature Park). This is mainly privately owned land covered by environmental controls to protect the flora and fauna, and there are plenty of trails that allow you to explore it. Besides the wetlands, here you will also find rice and wheat fields, small vineyards and ranches known as *manades* that breed bulls for bullfighting *à la cocarde* (where they don't get killed) and the little white wild horses of the Camargue that aren't really wild any more, policed by the *gardians*. There are extensive salt pans at Salin de Giraud on the east side of the Camargue where the Grand Rhône flows into the Mediterranean and on the west side at the Salins du Midi near Aigues-Mortes. These are diked-off marshes where salt is evaporated from sea water, and mountains of it wait to be carted away.

LES SAINTES-MARIES-DE-LA-MER

The Camargue has only one real town, Les Saintes-Maries-de-la-Mer, whose large Romanesque church can be seen across the flatlands from miles around.

Background

The reason this little town of 2,000 has so impressive a church is the Provençal legend of the Boat of Bethany. According to this early medieval legend, Mary Magdalene, her brother Lazarus (he who was raised from the dead), her sister Martha, two other Marys (Mary Jacobé, the Virgin's sister, and Mary Salomé, the mother of the apostles James and John), their Black servant Sara, and Maximinus and Sedonius were set adrift in a boat from Jerusalem by Jews and washed up on the shore at Les Saintes-Maries-de-la-Mer in about AD 40. Mary Magdalene retired to the hills of La Sainte-Baume and became a hermit, and Lazarus, Martha, Maximinus and Sedonius proceeded inland to spread the Word. The two other Marys and Sara stayed in Les Saintes-Maries-de-la-Mer, tended the shrine they built to the Virgin, and when they died were buried there. Their tombs became a place of pilgrimage, and in the ninth century, the original shrine was replaced by a fortified church incorporated into the ramparts that the Archbishop of Arles ordered built to protect the town from Saracen pirates. Unfortunately for him, he was kidnapped from the construction site by the Saracens and died in their custody. In the twelfth century, the ninth-century church was replaced by the larger fortified church we see today.

There is no evidence that authenticates the legend of the Boat of Bethany. Furthermore, the participation of Mary Magdalene in this voyage seems to have been based on the confusion in the medieval mind between the identities of Mary of Bethany, who was the sister of Lazarus and Martha, and Mary Magdalene, who was not. Nevertheless, the worship of all the Saints Mary continues to this day at the places associated with them in Provence, and the Gypsies have adopted Saint Sara as their patron saint.

General Information

The Saintes-Maries-de-la-Mer **Tourist Office** (04 90 97 82 55 E-MAIL saintes-maries@enprovence.com WEB SITE www.saintes-maries-de-la-mer.com is at 5 avenue Van Gogh, near the town beach.

The **Fondation du Parc Naturel Régional de Camargue** (04 90 97 86 32, Centre de Pont du Gau, 13460 Ginès, Les Saintes-Maries-de-la-Mer, provides information about the nature reserve. At the **Parc Ornithologique du Pont du Gau** (04 90 97 82 62, Route D570, 13460 Les Saintes-Maries-de-la-Mer, you'll find information about birds and a short nature trail with blinds for bird-watching. Another wildlife information center is located at **La Capelière** on Route D36B on the east side of the Étang de Vaccarès. It has one and a half kilometers (one mile) of nature trails with observation points.

Bikes can be rented in Les Saintes-Maries-de-la-Mer at **Vélo Saintois** (04 90 97 74 56, Rue de la

République, or **Le Vélociste** (04 90 97 83 26, at 1 place des Remparts.

For information on renting horses, see the section on EXCURSIONS that follows.

Binoculars are highly recommended in the Camargue, and mosquito repellent is a must. The phrase used to ask for it is, *"de la crème anti-moustique, s'il vous plaît."*

Festivals and Events

There are two annual pilgrimages to Les Saintes-Maries-de-la-Mer, one in May the other in October. They are officially dedicated to the two Marys, (Jacobé and Salomé) and there are elaborate processions in their honor, but the Gypsies' homage

fortress, which it became when pirates invaded. Inside the somber building there is a well that provided water during sieges, a chapel with the relics of the two Saint Marys, a model of the boat that supposedly brought the saints to Provence, and in the crypt, relics of Saint Sara and the black statue that the Gypsies carry in the procession in May. For a small charge, you can climb the 53 steps to the roof for a splendid panorama of the Camargue and the sea.

For those who get swept up in the mystique of the Camargue, a trip down the street to the **Musée Baroncelli** on Rue Victor-Hugo is in order. Marquis Folco de Baroncelli, born in 1869 of a wealthy Florentine family in Avignon, became a *gardian* in

to Saint Sara on May 24 is the highlight of the year. Gypsies come from all over Europe, and though there are plenty of tourists among the 25,000 people who attend, the fête has a real Gypsy flavor. There is Gypsy music everywhere, and in the afternoon, they carry the effigy of Saint Sara from the church to the sea. The pilgrimage continues on May 25, and on the 26th, the *gardians* put on a celebration in honor of Marquis Baroncelli, a popular figure in the culture of the Camargue, with parades, cattle-branding, and horse races. In the fall, there is a smaller pilgrimage in honor of Mary Salomé on the Sunday closest to October 22.

What to See and Do

Like other medieval churches along this coast, **L'Église des Saintes-Maries** has thick stone walls, tiny windows, and the brutal look of a crenellated

the Camargue as a young man and, inspired by Mistral, devoted his long life to reviving the Camargue's traditions and developing it for ranching and agriculture. There are interesting displays on local history and archaeology from the days of the Romans onward, on the animal and plant life of the delta, and on the life of the extraordinary Marquis Baroncelli himself. It is open from 10 AM to noon and 2 PM to 6 PM, closed Tuesday from October to May.

The **Musée Camarguais** (04 90 97 10 82 is a huge nineteenth-century barn on the main road between Arles and Les Saintes-Maries-de-la-Mer that has been imaginatively converted into a museum of the Camargue's geology, history and culture, with a special emphasis on farm and ranch life. There is a three-and-a-half-kilometer (two-

The church of Les Saintes-Maries-de-la-Mer, fortified to defend against Saracen pirates.

mile) Camargue farm trail. It is on Route D570 at Mas du Pont de Rousty nearly halfway between Arles and Les Saintes-Maries-de-la-Mer. It is open from 9:15 AM to 6:45 PM June through August, 10 AM to 4:15 PM the rest of the year. Closed Tuesday.

EXCURSIONS

There are more than 50 stables and dude ranches in and around the Camargue where horses can be rented. Some simply send you off with a guide, but many of the big *manades* — ranches that raise bulls for the ring — offer demonstrations of cattle roping and branding, stunt riding, and bullfighting *à la cocarde*, along with **horseback excursions** into the Camargue. One of these is the 600-hectare (1,500-acre) **Domaine Paul Ricard (** 04 90 97 10 60, a dude ranch and experimental farm in Méjanes on the north side of the Étang de Vaccarès. They have exhibitions of bull roping and branding (Sundays and holidays from Easter through mid-July), a narrow-gauge train that takes you along the edge of the Étang de Vaccarès, and bullfights on July 14. Their rates for renting a horse are 200 francs for a half-day, 320 francs for a full day. For information on other stables and *manades*, contact the Tourist Office in Les Saintes-Maries-de-la-Mer or the **Association Camarguaise de Tourisme Equestre (** 04 90 97 86 27, Centre de Ginès.

La Digue de la Mer is a dike built in the nineteenth century between L'Étang de Vaccarès and the sea. It runs 20 km (12.5 miles) eastward from Les Saintes-Maries-de-la-Mer to connect with the road to Salin de Giraud, the next town. The roadway on top of the dike has been closed to vehicular traffic for several years, but it is open to people on foot, bicycle, or horseback — a boon to nature lovers.

The *Tiki III* **excursion boat (** 04 90 97 81 68 makes four trips per day up the Petit Rhône in July and August, less often the rest of the year. The trip takes 75 minutes and allows you to observe the cattle and horses and wildlife along the shore. It costs 58 francs. The pier is at the mouth of the Petit Rhône west of Les Saintes-Maries-de-la-Mer.

THE BEACHES

The Camargue has 60 km (40 miles) of fine sand beaches, much favored by *naturistes* and other sun-worshipers. The **Plage de Beauduc** has two rustic restaurants, **Chez Juju et Manu** and **Chez Marc et Mireille**, good for fresh grilled fish, moderate to expensive. The large **Plage de Piémanson** beach, also known as the **Plage d'Arles**, on the east side of the Camargue has lifeguards in July and August, as does the East Beach of Les Saintes-Maries-de-la-Mer. The main nudist beach is four kilometers (two and a half miles) east of Les Saintes-Maries-

de-la-Mer at **Pertuis de la Comtesse** near the Gacholle lighthouse. Nudists and non-nudists coexist on the **Plage de Piémanson**, and there is a small nudist stretch at **Le Golue** on the Salin de Giraud beach.

WHERE TO STAY AND EAT

Many people prefer to camp or rent flats, *gîtes*, or cottages in the Camargue, but there is no dearth of hotels, including five four-star establishments, 20 with three stars, and 22 with two stars.

The most luxurious is the **Mas de la Fouque****** **(** 04 90 97 81 02 FAX 04 90 97 96 84 E-MAIL masdelafouque@francemarket.com WEB SITE

www.masdelafouque.com, on Route du Bac du Sauvage, off D38, four kilometers (two and a half miles) west of Les Saintes-Maries-de-la-Mer. Serenity is guaranteed at this 13-room luxury resort in a private park deep in the Camargue, with swimming pool, tennis courts, golf practice holes, and regional food. Very expensive. In the same area as the Mas de la Fouque, **L'Estelle****** **(** 04 90 97 89 01 FAX 04 90 97 80 36 estelle@wanadoo.fr WEB SITE www.hotelestelle.com is an attractive modern ensemble of bungalows with 17 rooms, tennis court, pool and horses, with room rates in the expensive range.

The **Lou Mas du Juge (** 04 66 73 51 45 FAX 04 66 73 51 42 is an easygoing inn with seven cheerful, moderately priced rooms, and you can rent horses. The excellent, but expensive, restaurant specializes in seafood and the Camargue specialty *bœuf gardian*, bull meat stewed in red wine. It is on D85 in the Quartier Pin-Fourcat northwest of town. The **Pont de Gau**** (04 90 97 81 53 FAX 04 90 97 98 54, on Route D570 (the main road to Arles) five kilometers (three miles) north of Les Saintes-Maries-de-la-Mer, is a good Camargue-style restaurant with moderate prices that rents nine pleasant guest rooms at 265 francs. The **Longo Mai**** (04 90 97 21 91 FAX 04 90 97 22 92, in Le Sambuc, has 16 rooms in the inexpensive and moderate range, hearty regional food, and horses for rent. It is 24 km (15 miles) south of Arles via D36, on the west bank of the Rhône.

For the tops in Camargue cuisine in downtown Les Saintes-Maries-de-la-Mer, try **Hippocampe** (04 90 97 80 91, on Rue Camille-Pelletan, or **Brûleur**

How to Get There

Les Cars de Camargue has five buses a day from Arles in the summer, leaving from 24 boulevard Clemenceau or from the Gare Routière. In Les Saintes-Maries-de-la-Mer, the stop is at the intersection of Rue Emile-Ripet and Avenue d'Arles at the entrance to town (get there a half-hour early to be sure of a seat). In the summer, there are daily buses from Nîmes and a few buses per week from Montpellier. Tour operators run excursions from Arles (Arles Voyages) and Avignon (Lieutaud Voyages). For schedules, contact the Tourist Office.

de Loups (04 90 97 83 31, on Avenue Gilbert-Leroy, which has a terrace overlooking the sea. Both offer good value. Be sure to try the *tellines*, tiny succulent shellfish served as hors d'œuvres. Two inexpensive restaurants for good local fare are **Lou Cardelino** (04 90 97 96 23, at 25 rue Frédéric-Mistral, and **Lou Félibre** (04 90 97 82 18, at 17 place de l'Église.

Camping
La Brise (04 90 97 84 67 is a huge camping ground by the beach on the east side of town, open all year. It has 1,200 camping places on its 44 hectares (106 acres), a large swimming pool and a wading pool for little children. **Le Clos du Rhône** (04 90 97 85 99, two kilometers (a little over a mile) from town on D38, is a comfortable site with 450 places and a pool, open Easter through the end of September.

Driving from Arles to Les Saintes-Maries-de-la-Mer, take the bridge across the Rhône (Pont de Trinquetaille) and follow the Route de Camargue (D570) all the way. It is 38 km (14 miles) from Arles. To get to the east side of the Camargue (Le Sambuc, the Plage d'Arles), branch off to the left from D570 onto D36 two and a half kilometers (about a mile and a half) south of the bridge, and take D36 south, parallel to the Grand Rhône.

Alternatively, take D35 south from Arles along the west side of the Rhône and take the little ferry, the Bac de Barcarin, across the river. But be aware that in the summer, there can be a long wait for the ferry.

OPPOSITE: The monastery of Saint-Paul-de-Mausole in Saint-Rémy, where Van Gogh spent an astonishingly productive year. ABOVE: Exploring the Camargue by horseback. Don't forget your mosquito repellent.

Languedoc

THE LANGUEDOC OF HISTORY, the huge medieval realm of the powerful Counts of Toulouse, was the cradle of Occitan culture, the land of troubadours, courtly love, and religious toleration that was crushed by the Albigensian Crusade. Today's Languedoc covers only half the territory of old. When the new administrative regions were drawn up in 1981, Languedoc's historical capital of Toulouse was made the capital of another region, Midi-Pyrénées, and Montpellier was made the capital of modern-day Languedoc, with culturally Catalan Roussillon tacked on to form the region of Languedoc-Roussillon. As a result, Languedoc and Roussillon tend to get lumped together in people's minds the way Alsace and Lorraine used to be. But in fact, they are every bit as different as Alsace is from Lorraine, or as Provence is from the Côte d'Azur.

Languedoc is the only part of France named for a language. The language of Oc was suppressed by the Edict of Villers-Cotterêts in 1539, which established French as the state language. Southerners still resent the high-handed treatment they have received from Paris over the centuries, but the Félibrige movement in the nineteenth century set the area on the recovery of its cultural identity, and the economic rise of Montpellier and the Modern South since the 1960s has made the South — Montpellier especially — a very attractive place to young people. The cultural inferiority complex of the past has evaporated. Paris is no longer seen as the only place where one can do important things. Now even the casual traveler will find many a bright young ex-*Parisien* who has chosen to live in Languedoc, for the ease of living and for the career opportunities in the dynamic new South.

All this modernity enlivens Languedoc and improves creature comforts, but it also creates the seemingly inevitable curses that go along with it — urban sprawl, commercial centers, *hypermarchés* (super supermarkets), and fast-food chains killing the special ambiance of a place and defacing once-lovely coastal areas.

Nevertheless, compared to Provence and especially to the Côte d'Azur, Languedoc is a fresh place for the traveler to explore. There are wide open spaces, magnificent medieval abbeys and fortresses, interesting cities and surprising art treasures, 160 km (100 miles) of sandy beaches on the Golfe du Lion from the Camargue south to Argelès-Plage, and practically all Mediterranean Languedoc makes wine. Finally, for the budget-minded traveler Languedoc is noticeably easier on the wallet and credit card than its more established neighboring tourist centers to the east.

Readers who have been following our itinerary through Provence will approach Languedoc from Arles or the Camargue. Travelers driving from the north on the A9 *autoroute (la Languedocienne)* should exit at Nîmes. It is actually in Languedoc, though for historical and archaeological reasons we have included it in our look Provence (see AVIGNON TO NÎMES, page 243, and NÎMES, page 249). Visitors can either explore this "Rome of France" or head south to Saint-Gilles on the Languedoc fringe of the Camargue.

SAINT-GILLES

BACKGROUND

Saint-Gilles, three kilometers (two miles) west of the Petit Rhône, is named for another saint who

washed up on these shores, this one in the eighth century. The tomb of Saint Gilles at the abbey he founded became an important place of pilgrimage in the Middle Ages, and in the twelfth century the modest original church was replaced by a much more magnificent one.

It was an incident at Saint-Gilles that set off the Albigensian Crusade. In 1208 the papal legate Pierre de Castelnou was murdered at the door of the church by a follower of the Count of Toulouse, and Pope Innocent III seized on this rash act as his pretext for unleashing a crusade to crush the Cathars.

OPPOSITE: Celebrating Saint Louis, the king who established a permanent French presence on the Mediterranean coast at Aigues-Mortes. ABOVE: The old choir of the twelfth-century church of Saint-Gilles.

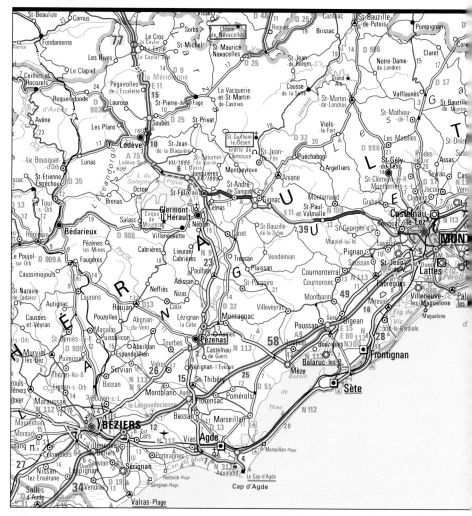

GENERAL INFORMATION

The **Tourist Office** (04 66 87 33 75 is at 1 place Frédéric-Mistral.

WHAT TO SEE AND DO

The splendid western façade of the **Église Saint-Gilles** has three Romanesque arched doorways with decorative columns and stone sculptures depicting the life of Christ. The ensemble dates from the same period as the tympanum of Saint-Trophime and is similar in style. The sculptures were the first to represent the Passion of Christ in full. For the best light, come in the late afternoon. Unfortunately, the Wars of Religion and the Revolution destroyed the rest of the building.

The town of Saint-Gilles is on the Canal du Rhône à Sète, and you can rent houseboats or take cruises. For **houseboat rental**, contact Blue Line (04 66 87 22 66, at 2 quai du Canal.

WHERE TO STAY AND EAT

For *petite friture* (fried whitebait), *rougets grillés* (grilled red mullet), *entrecôte gardianne* (steak from Camargue bulls), and other local dishes, stop in at the restaurant of **Hôtel le Cours**** (04 66 87 31 93 FAX 04 66 87 31 83, at 10 avenue Griffeuille. The lunch *menu* weekdays is 52 francs, the top-priced *menu* 150 francs, and there's a good selection of regional wines. It is also a homey, moderately priced Logis de France hotel with 34 nicely modernized rooms.

HOW TO GET THERE

There are frequent buses from Arles and Nîmes. By car, Saint-Gilles is 16 km (10 miles) west of Arles

EASTERN LANGUEDOC

on N572, 23 km (14 miles) north of Les Saintes-Maries-de-la-Mer on D570 and D37, and 19 km (12 miles) south of Nîmes on D42.

AIGUES-MORTES

The walled town of Aigues-Mortes ("dead waters" in Occitan) on the western edge of the Camargue was the Kingdom of France's first foothold on the Mediterranean coast. King Louis IX (Saint Louis) bought the land from the monks of the Abbey of Psalmody in 1240 and had a port built for Crusaders on their way to the Holy Land. By the mid-fourteenth century, Aigues-Mortes was a thriving town of 15,000. But its port silted up and eventually went dry and the fortunes of the town with it. The town now finds itself five kilometers (three miles) from the Mediterranean, and its population is one-third that of its glory days. But what remains from that period is very impressive.

GENERAL INFORMATION

The **Tourist Office** (04 66 53 73 00 is at Porte de la Gardette, to the left just inside the gate.

WHAT TO SEE AND DO

High **crenellated stone ramparts**, completely intact, surround the town, with ten gates and fifteen round towers interspersed. The 500-m (1,640-ft) **southwestern wall**, where the medieval docks used to be, is especially formidable. So is the massively thick, 40-m-tall (130-ft) circular **Tour Constance**. It was used as a political prison from the late Middle Ages to Napoléon's time. Protestant leaders spent long years of incarceration here during the Wars of Religion. From the top of the tower, there is a grand panorama: the town with its Roman-style grid pattern, the Camargue and the Salins de Midi salt pans to the east, the bulky resort of La Grande-Motte to the south and the Cévennes Mountains to the northwest.

Behind the stern walls, the town is surprisingly pleasant to stroll in, especially on Wednesday and Sunday mornings, which are the **market days**, and there are good crafts shops.

Le Pescalune (04 66 53 79 47, a converted barge, makes a two-and-a-half-hour circuit of the canals of the western Camargue, passing through wildlife areas, ranches, salt pans, and vineyards. It leaves the pier by the Tour de Constance daily at 10:30 AM and 3 PM in the summer. *Îles de Stel* (04 66 53 60 70, another converted barge, also makes daily cruises at 10:30 AM and 3 PM between April and October that include a 20-minute stop at a ranch to watch the Camargue cowboys at work.

WINE TASTING

Listel's **Domaine de Jarras** (04 66 51 17 00, on D979 between Aigues-Mortes and Le Grau-du-Roi, offers free tasting of its pale amber *vin des sables*, wine made from grapes that grow in the sand, a real thirst-quencher on a hot summer day. It is open daily all year.

WHERE TO STAY AND EAT

Les Arcades*** (04 66 53 81 13 FAX 04 66 53 75 46 E-MAIL info@les-arcades.fr, WEB SITE www.les-arcades.fr, at 23 boulevard Gambetta, is a handsome hotel in a sixteenth-century mansion in the heart of the walled city that has nine spacious, very comfortable, Provençal-style rooms furnished with antiques, and a rooftop terrace with a small pool. It has a very good restaurant offering sophisticated treatment of local and regional farm, ranch, and sea products in its stone-walled, beamed-ceilinged dining room. Room prices are moderate, the restaurant expensive. Another attractive, very comfortable, beautifully furnished hotel inside the walls is **Les Templiers***** (04 66 53 66 56 FAX 04 66 53 69 61, at 21 rue de la République, a seventeenth-century mansion with 10 guest rooms in the 550 to 800 franc range. The **Saint-Louis***** (04 66 53 72 68 FAX 04 66 53 75 92 E-MAIL saintlouis@wanadoo.fr is a tastefully furnished 22-room hotel with a quiet patio at 10 rue Amiral-Courbet near Place Saint-Louis. Its rooms are moderate in price. The **Croisades**** (04 66 53 67 85 FAX 04 66 53 72 95 is a pleasant newer hotel with 14 rooms in the 240 to 300 franc range. It is outside the walls of the town at 2 rue du Port, to the west of the maritime channel.

meters north of Aigues-Mortes on D46 in Saint Laurent d'Aigouze. It is a 100-place site with a pool and restaurant open April 1 to the end of October. **Camping Bellevue** (04 66 88 63 75 in Aimargues is open all year. This is an attractive, shaded area with 180 places and a pool, about 12 km (seven and a half miles) north of Aigues-Mortes on D979. Otherwise, head for La Grande-Motte or Port-Camargue on the coast.

HOW TO GET THERE

There are numerous buses daily from Arles, Nîmes, and Montpellier. Driving, Aigues-Mortes is 48 km (30 miles) from Arles by D570/D58 through the

The **Camargue** (04 66 53 86 88, at 19 rue de la République, is a family-style eatery under the trees serving local fare at moderate prices — fresh shellfish, grilled lamb chops, *gardiane* stew from the meat of Camargue bulls, and *vin des sables* (wine grown in the sands), a local specialty (see WINE TASTING, above).

Camping

Camping **La Petite Camargue** (04 66 53 98 98, in the Quartier Le Mole is a deluxe 420-place site with a swimming pool, tennis courts and restaurant, open from Easter to the end of September. **Camping de Port Vieil** (04 66 88 15 42 is a few kilo-

Camargue, 37 km (23 miles) from Nîmes by N113 and D979, and 29 km (18 miles) from Montpellier by D66 and D22.

LA GRANDE-MOTTE, LE GRAU-DU-ROI, AND PORT-CAMARGUE

Developed in the late 1960s as part of the de Gaulle government's master plan to create affordable vacation places for French families, La Grande-Motte (which literally means "the big lump") was the first of many modern beach and marina complexes to be built on this coast. Its cluster of bloated white concrete pyramids rises up out of nowhere on the flatlands to the west of the Camargue. It now accommodates 100,000 vacationers in the summer. You may not like La Grande-Motte's looks, but it does have a certain quirky flare, which is more than can be said for most of the *habitation à loyer*

ABOVE: The completely walled Crusaders' port town of Aigues-Mortes, where the Mediterranean once lapped at its walls. OPPOSITE: Italian flag throwers at the Feast of Saint Louis at Aigues-Mortes.

modéré or *HLM* (middle-income housing) vacation complexes farther down the coast. And with so many French people with vacation money to spend, you can be sure there is good eating in these parts.

The resort development has spread eastward to the neighboring old fishing port of Le Grau-du-Roi and spawned a new marina, Port-Camargue, now the largest yacht harbor in Europe, with 4,500 berths. If you like to look at big sailboats, this is definitely the place.

Le Grau-du-Roi and Port-Camargue are in *département* of the Gard, a rich agricultural and wine-producing region that stretches from here up into the Cévennes, and at **La Maison Méditerranéenne des Vins et des Produits Régionaux**

stretch of open sandy beach where no construction is allowed, very popular with people from Montpellier a mere 10 km (six miles) away. Continue south along the beach past the turnoff to Montpellier and drive through the old resort town of Palavas-les-Flots across the bridge to **Maguelone**, where a big fortified former cathedral from the twelfth century sits alone in the middle of nowhere, the sole survivor of another important Languedoc town left high and dry, not by the sea like Aigues-Mortes, but by the Church of Rome, when the pope transferred the bishopric to up-and-coming Montpellier in the sixteenth century. The church is austere on the outside, but inside its great rounded Romanesque vaults soften the aus-

du Gard (04 66 53 07 52 you can sample its fresh and preserved fruit, honey, olive oil, Costières de Nîmes wines, crafts products and fabrics. The shop is on Route de l'Espiguette east of Port-Camargue and is open daily all year.

For an excursion into the dunes, drive another seven kilometers (four miles) east to the lighthouse, **Le Phare de l'Espiguette**. Those with the urge to shed their clothes may do so. *Naturistes* and wearers of bathing suits mingle unabashedly on this beach.

The **Tourist Office** in Grande-Motte (04 67 56 42 00 is on Place de la Mairie; in Le Grau-du-Roi/Port-Camargue (04 66 51 67 70, at 30 rue Rédarès.

La Grande-Motte to Montpellier

Heading west from La Grande-Motte on D59, the shore road to Palavas-les-Flots, neighboring **Carnon-Plage** has an eight-kilometer (five-mile)

terity. It can be visited any day, but is best appreciated during the many concerts of religious choral music they have in the summer. The acoustics are perfect. The church fronts on the coastal lagoon where you often see flamingos and other waterfowl. In the summer Maguelone can be a problem for people with sensitive noses. The stagnant water in the area gives off a stench of rotten eggs.

WHERE TO STAY AND EAT

There are dozens of resort hotels on all levels of price and quality in these towns. My top choice as both a hotel and a restaurant is **Le Spinaker***** (04 66 53 36 37 FAX 04 66 53 17 47 E-MAIL spinaker @wanadoo.fr, at Pointe de la Presqu'île in Port-Camargue. It has 21 bright, cheerful rooms opening onto private sun terraces, with a garden and swimming pool, and it fronts on the vast pleasure boat port. The restaurant serves Jean-Pierre Cazals's savory specialties such as roast fillets of red mullet in olive oil and fillet of Camargue *toro* with anchovies and nuts. The restaurant is expensive, the hotel in the moderate category. It is open from April to the beginning of October.

Another good restaurant in Port-Camargue, though not very atmospheric, is **L'Amarette** (04 66 51 47 63, at the Centre Commercial Camargue 2000, for fresh shellfish and fish dishes, somewhat expensive. It is closed in December and January. In Le Grau-du-Roi, **Le Palangre** (04 66 51 76 30, at 56 quai Charles-de-Gaulle, is a pleasant restaurant with outdoor tables on the old port serving excellent grilled meat and fish at modest prices.

The other gourmet restaurant in this area, one of the most distinguished in Languedoc, is **Restaurant Alexandre** (04 67 56 63 63, in La Grande-Motte, serving the sophisticated regional cuisine of Michel Alexandre. Here you can treat yourself to a little *bouillabaisse* as an appetizer, fresh cod with *tapenade* (black olive paste), or pork baked with juniper berries and Provençal vegetables, and an outstanding regional wine list. Alexandre is on the Esplanade de la Capitanerie in front of the casino.

For information on other hotels in the area and help with reservations, the Tourist Offices will be happy to be of service.

Camping

This is an active area for camping. Port-Camargue has 13 camping grounds on the beach along the Route de l'Espiguette including the deluxe 1,440-place **Camping Élysée Résidence** (04 66 53 54 00, which has a swimming pool, and the more modestly equipped **Camping de l'Espiguette** (04 66 51 43 92, which has 2,250 places. La Grande-Motte has seven camping grounds with 1,511 places. For details, contact the Tourist Offices.

HOW TO GET THERE

There are frequent buses from Montpellier and Nîmes. Driving, take the same roads as for Aigues-Mortes.

MONTPELLIER

Like Nîmes, Montpellier is a city that woke up after a long period of somnolence. In this case the awakening started earlier, in the 1960s, when IBM moved to Montpellier and other high-tech companies followed suit, the prestigious university acting as a magnet. At the same time, a large influx of *pieds noirs* — former French colonists from Algeria who had to resettle because of the Algerian war of independence — brought a new wealth and a productive new population to the area.

Montpellier's bold contemporary architecture reflects its late twentieth-century dynamism.

This is a city that takes itself very seriously. It has even created its own grandiose vocabulary for the areas of economic activity (or *pôles* as they like to call them) it is focusing on: Pôle Agropolis (agricultural technology for hot climates), Pôle Héliopolis (tourism, culture, festivals, and leisure activities), Pôle Antenna (communications), Pôle Euromédecine (medicine and medical technology), and Pôle Informatique (computers). Montpellier's overall term for itself is "Le Surdoué" ("the highly gifted one").

This is a young persons' city. Of its 220,000 inhabitants, 60,000 are students.

BACKGROUND

Montpellier is a relatively new city for this part of the world. It celebrated its 1,000th birthday in 1985. Created by the Lords of Guilhem and originally a dependency of Maguelone, it benefited from its proximity to three important roads and had access to the Mediterranean by the then-navigable Lez River. From the beginning, Montpellier's merchants imported herbs and spices from the Middle East, including medicinal plants, and the town quickly became one of the main conduits in Europe for the medical secrets of the Arabs and Jews, then far ahead of the West. By the eleventh century, Montpellier had fortifications with

OPPOSITE: La Grande-Motte, the first modern resort complex built on the Languedoc coast.
ABOVE: A charming *Languedocienne*.

25 towers. The line of its walls had the shape of a shield, or *écusson*, a term by which Old Montpellier is still known.

In 1204 the marriage of King Pedro of Aragon and Marie of Montpellier, the daughter of Guilhem VIII, brought the town into the Catalan sphere, and it prospered for a century and a half under the Kingdoms of Aragon and Majorca. Montpellier's University was founded in the early thirteenth century and, thanks to its Arab and Jewish contacts, became one of Europe's leading medical schools (Rabelais studied medicine there in 1530). In 1349 King Philip VI of France bought Montpellier, and it became France's main Mediterranean port. In the fifteenth century Jacques

Cœur, the fabulously wealthy financial advisor to King Charles VII, set up his southern headquarters here. The city's thriving sea trade collapsed, however, when Provence was annexed by France in 1481, and Marseille took over the bulk of the shipping. As a Protestant stronghold during the Wars of Religion and Richelieu's and Louis XIII's invasions, Montpellier took a terrible beating. But somehow its cloth manufacturers and traders survived, evidence of which can be seen in the 50 or so mansions from the seventeenth and eighteenth century in the Écusson district.

Though the Lez River silted up long ago, Montpellier has not given up on being a Mediterranean port. One of Mayor Freche's dreams is the Port-Marianne project, which, among massive urban renewal, envisions a link from the foot of

The Promenade du Peyrou on the heights overlooking Montpellier.

the Antigone Center via a widened Lez River to the sea at Palavas-les-Flots some 10 km (six miles) away.

GENERAL INFORMATION

The Montpellier's main **Tourist Office** (04 67 60 60 60 WEB SITE www.ville.montpellier.fr is in the Pavillon, the glass oval in the Passage du Tourisme at the north end of the Place de la Comédie. There are other offices at: 78 rue de Pirée (04 67 22 06 16, to the right of D66, the connector road from the *autoroute* as you approach Antigone from the east; at Rond Point des Prés d'Arènes (04 67 22 08 80, at the southern approach from the *autoroute;* and at the railway station, the Gare SNCF (04 67 92 90 03. The Tourist Office makes bookings for hotels and country guest houses, runs cultural tours, sells tickets for festivals and shows, exchanges currency, sells regional products, and offers an array of free booklets, including one on the old mansions in the Écusson that are open to visitors. It provides literature and verbal assistance in several languages.

For travel information on the areas in the hills above Montpellier and along the shore in the Hérault *département*, contact the **Maison de Tourisme de l'Hérault** (04 67 67 71 71 E-MAIL cdt @cdt-herault.fr WEB SITE www.herault-en-Languedoc.com, BP 3067, Avenue des Moulins, 34034 Montpellier. It is located three and a half kilometers (two miles) west of downtown Montpellier at the Rond-Point d'Alco.

Montpellier Méditerranée International Airport can be reached at (04 67 20 85 00. There is **shuttle bus** service (04 67 06 03 67 between the airport and the city once an hour, a 15-minute ride. The train station, **Gare SNCF** (08 36 35 35 35, is at Place Auguste-Gilbert. The bus station, **Gare Routière** (04 67 92 01 43, is attached to the train station and fronts on Place du Bicentenaire. **Sodéthré** (04 67 42 15 15, the agency overseeing bus transportation in the Hérault *département*, also provides information on buses, but they only speak French. Non-French-speakers should contact the Tourist Office.

For taxis, contact **Radio Taxis**, Gare SNCF (24 hours) (04 67 58 74 82; **TRAM Taxi** (04 67 92 04 55; or **Taxi Radio 2000** (04 67 03 45 45.

Car rental agencies include **Avis** (04 67 92 92 00; **Budget** (04 67 20 07 34; **Europcar** (04 67 99 82 00; and **Hertz** (04 67 58 65 18. **Bike rental** is available at the reception desk of the Gare SNCF.

Courriers du Midi runs day trips in the summer to Marseille, Arles and the Alpilles, the Camargue, the Gorges du Tarn, Saint-Guilhem-le-Désert, the Canal du Midi and other places. For information and reservations, contact the Tourist Office or Courriers du Midi (04 67 06 03 67.

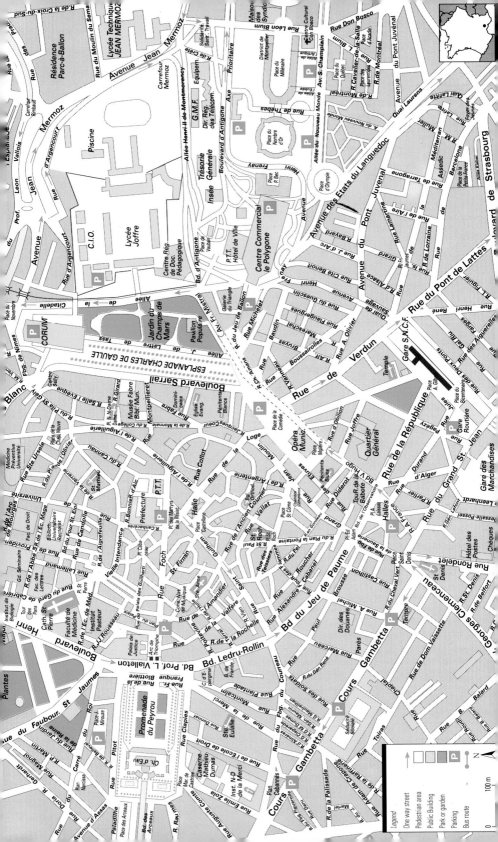

In case of medical emergencies, contact **SOS Médecins** (04 67 03 30 30.

FESTIVALS AND EVENTS

Printemps des Comédiens is a French and European theater festival held in early to mid-June. The **Festival International Montpellier Danse**, a tremendous event featuring all kinds of dance with top companies from all over the world, takes place in late June and early July. The **Festival de Radio France**, running from mid-July to mid-August, presents leading French and international ensembles performing opera, symphonies, chamber music and jazz at the cathedral, Opéra Comédie, Corum, Château d'O, and other sites in an around town. For details, see FESTIVE FOLLIES, page 18 in TOP SPOTS.

WHAT TO SEE AND DO

Named for the nineteenth-century opera house at the south end of the square, **Place de la Comédie** is the social center of the city and the link between the boldly modern areas of Polygone and Antigone to the east and discreet old Écusson to the west. The place itself is wide and lined with large cafés, with several rows of tables spreading out into the square, and the pretty **Fountain of the Three Graces** is in the middle. The tree-shaded Esplanade branches off its northern end, and many of the streets that run off the place are walking streets.

Vieux Montpellier

Head up into the **Écusson** district to explore one street after another lined with seventeenth- and eighteenth-century mansions, about 50 still standing, in Vieux Montpellier. Especially noteworthy are the **Hôtel des Trésoriers de France**, originally Jacques Cœur's mansion, updated in the seventeenth century, at 5 rue des Trésoriers-de-France, the elegant **Hôtel de Varennes** at 2 place Pétrarque (named for the poet, who studied at the university from 1316 to 1319) and **Hôtel des Trésoriers de la Bourse** at 4 rue des Trésoriers-de-la-Bourse, designed by the city's leading early eighteenth-century architect, Jean Giral. The work of a later Giral, Jean-Antoine, can be admired up the hill in the **Promenade du Peyrou**, on the other side of the big **Arc de Triomphe** dedicated to Louis XIV. This is a gem of a park on a plateau overlooking the city, marred only by an equestrian statue of the Sun King that is pompous even by his standards.

Jean-Antoine Giral's masterpiece is the **Château d'Eau** at the far end of the park, a hexagonal pavilion of classical proportions designed to mask the reservoir for water arriving from the 800-m-long (2,600-ft), 22-m-tall (72-ft) **Aqueduc**

Saint-Clement, longer but lower than the Pont du Gard after which it was patterned. The Promenade du Peyrou is a pleasant spot for a picnic with views of the Cévennes, the Mediterranean and, on days when the *tramontane* wind has cleared the air, Mont Canigou in the Pyrénées.

The **Musée Fabre** has an outstanding collection of nineteenth-century French paintings, especially strong on Courbet and Bazille, also three Delacroix and works by David, Ingres, and Géricault. The most important works were donated Alfred Bruyas, a would-be painter whose hobby was having his portrait painted—32 times in all. Nineteen likenesses of the sad-eyed narcissist with a bright red beard are on display at the Fabre, including four by Gustave Courbet, the father of French realism. One is *La Rencontre*, nicknamed "Bonjour Monsieur Courbet," in which the black-bearded painter is seen taking a stroll in the Languedoc countryside, where he happens to run into a red-bearded gentleman

(guess who). The museum also has nine paintings by Montpellier-born Frédéric Bazille, one of the founders of Impressionism, who painted side by side with Renoir and Monet, but was killed at 29 in the Franco-Prussian War. His *La Vue du Village* and *Les Remparts d'Aigues-Mortes* are drenched in the sunlight of Languedoc. There is also a gentle Berthe Morisot portrait, *L'Éte*, from the Impressionist period, and from the twentieth century, there are lesser works by Matisse, Bonnard, Delaunay, Dufy and de Staël, the bright, lively *Les Joutes à Sète* by François Desnoyer, and a charming landscape of Collioure by André Lhote. The museum also puts on major temporary exhibitions, such as a recent one on American Abstract Expressionists. The Musée Fabre is on the east side of the Écusson on Boulevard Bonne Nouvelle, fronting on the Esplanade. It is open from 9 AM to 5:30 PM Tuesday through Friday, 9:30 AM to 5 PM Saturday and Sunday, and closed Monday.

Modern Montpellier

Modern Montpellier, built in the 1980s and 1990s, starts on the east side of the Place de la Comédie with the **Polygone** business center, dominated by the multi-terraced pyramid of the Sofitel hotel. To Polygone's east is **Antigone**, architect Ricardo Bofill's vast, grandiose neo-neoclassical business and residential complex that is starting to soften a bit with age as trees grow in and human beings make their presence known, but still has a cold, Mussolini-like quality, except for the section down by the Lez River, where a graceful row of **restaurants** fronts on the stream. Another star of the modern architectural lineup is the **Corum**, a huge dark brown, bunker-like complex of concert and assembly halls designed by Claude Vasonti at the far end of the esplanade. Overall, Montpellier's new architecture is too stark for my taste, but it

Place de la Comédie, Montpellier's café-lined main square, a popular spot for this university town's 60,000 students.

may age well—and it sure has made the city more interesting to look at than it was 20 years ago.

The *Folies* of Montpellier

In the early eighteenth century, the rich of Montpellier built extravagant summer residences known as *folies* (follies) in the countryside around the city. The city has now gobbled up most of that countryside, but about 30 of them remain, and some have been restored and furnished in the style of the period and can be visited. **Château de la Mogère**, designed by Jean Giral, and **Château de Flauguergues** in the style of an Italian villa, lie to the east of the city and have been well maintained. **Château de la Mosson**, which lies to the west, was

once the most sumptuous of them all, but only its handsome shell remains standing today. It is well worth visiting, however, for its grand and magnificently melancholy park. **Château d'O** to the northwest of the city is used in the summer for festival performances. Its park is decorated with statues from Mosson. Check with the Tourist Office for visiting hours and ask for their brochure on the *folies* that can be visited.

WINE TASTING

The Hérault is the largest wine-making *département* in France.

In the past it was known mainly for plonk, but as the demand for such low-grade wine dried up in the decades following World War II, wine makers here moved more and more into quality wines. **Coteaux du Languedoc**, an *appellation*

contrôlée since 1985, is the most widely produced *AOC* wine, with 50,000 hectares (120,000 acres) planted in its approved vines, producing 45 million liters per year. It is a rising star in the firmament of French wines. Included are 12 different *terroirs*, specific wine-growing areas whose names are added to the *appellation* on the label. It extends over a large area from the southern edge of the Costières de Nîmes area to the northern edge of the Corbières and produces mostly robust reds, some rosés, and a little white—**Picpoul de Pinet**, excellent with shellfish.

This is a vast wine lake to plunge into, and one way to do it without drowning in confusion would be to visit the big, modern wine information center, the **Maison des Coteaux du Languedoc** (04 67 06 04 44 WEB SITE www.coteaux-Languedoc.com, in the seventeenth-century Mas de Saporta in Lattes just south of Montpellier's city limits. It has a huge wine shop and wine tasting room, and the **Restaurant des Cuisiniers Vignerons** (04 67 06 88 66, serves 70 different Coteaux du Languedoc sold by the glass to accompany the sunny Mediterranean cuisine of distinguished chef David Moreno. The center also helps people lay out an itinerary for visits to vineyards.

The **Syndicat des Producteurs de Vins de Pays d'Oc** (04 67 06 82 20 WEB SITE www.vindepaysdoc.com has an office in another building in the complex with information on *vin de pays* producers. Most wines produced in Languedoc and Roussillon are not the prestigious *AOCs*, but modestly labeled *vins de pays* (local wine). Do not let this discourage you. These wines can be remarkably good. The wines are generally labeled either *vin de pays d'Oc* or *vin de pays* from a specific locality. Wines made from a single variety of grape —Cabernet Sauvignon, Merlot, Syrah, Sauvignon, and Chardonnay in particular — are becoming increasingly popular.

The Mas de Saporta is less than fifteen minutes by car from the heart of Montpellier. It is immediately south of the Montpellier Sud (south) exit of the *autoroute*, or on Route de Palavas if you are coming from town. There are signs pointing the way.

Other *AOC* wine areas in the Hérault are **Faugères** to the north of Béziers, **Saint-Chinian** to the northwest, and part of the large Minervois area to the west of Béziers. The apéritif wines **Muscat de Lunel**, **Muscat de Frontignan**, **Muscat de Mireval**, and **Muscat de Saint-Jean de Minervois** are also made in the Hérault, and **Noilly-Prat** is located in Marseillan.

The **Club des Grands Vins de Châteaux du Languedoc**, a group of eight high-quality vineyards from the magnificent Abbaye de Valmagne near the Bassin de Thau down to the Château de Lastours in the Corbières, sets up wine tasting tours of their châteaux. This is strictly first class. A three-day tour with all hotels, meals, and ground transport included costs 3,480 francs, four days 4,415 francs. For information, contact Jean Viennet (04 67 28 15 61 FAX 04 67 28 19 75, Château de Raissac, Route de Murviel, 34500 Béziers.

WHERE TO STAY

Montpellier has 4,960 hotel rooms, an oversupply for a city of its moderate size, which puts the traveler in a good bargaining position. Rates are lower in Montpellier (and Languedoc generally) than they are to the east of the Rhône for hotels of comparable quality. If you are driving, call your hotel first for specific directions. Because of the one-way streets, finding places can be difficult in this city.

Expensive

Holiday Inn-Métropole**** (04 67 58 11 22 FAX 04 67 92 13 02 E-MAIL hicbmontepllier@wanadoo.fr, 3 rue Clos René, between the railway station and the Place de la Comédie, is the palatial hotel of the city with 81 luxurious rooms and rates in the 700 to 900 franc range. To the north of the city, **Le Jardin des Sens****** (04 67 79 63 38 FAX 04 67 72 13 05 WEB SITE www.integra.fr/relaischateaux/, at 11 avenue Saint-Lazare, has 14 stunning, deluxe modern rooms in the 750 to 1,300 franc range, but is best known for its restaurant, one of France's finest (see WHERE TO EAT, below).

Moderate

Le Guilhem*** (04 67 52 90 90 FAX 04 67 60 67 67, E-MAIL hotel-le-guilhem@mnet.fr, at 18 rue Jean-Jacques Rousseau near the Promenade du Peyrou and the cathedral in Vieux Montpellier, is a former seventeenth-century coach inn with a great deal of character. Its 33 comfy, well-equipped rooms are furnished with antiques, and it has a large terrace overlooking a garden area in the rear. Doubles run 350 to 470 francs. The multilingual staff could not be more friendly and helpful. This is a genuine *hôtel de charme* and a Best Western member. **New Hôtel du Midi***** (04 67 92 69 61 FAX 04 67 92 73 63 E-MAIL montpelliermidi@new-hotel.com WEB SITE www.new-hotel.com, at 22 boulevard Victor Hugo, has 47 tastefully modernized rooms in a *belle époque*-style building on a corner of the Place de la Comédie, with doubles at 460 francs. For a delightful hotel in a lush private park slightly outside of town, try the **Demeure des Brousses***** (04 67 65 77 66 FAX 04 67 22 22 17 E-MAIL demeure-des-brousses@epicuria.fr WEB SITE www.epicuria.fr/demeure-des-brousses/, an eighteenth-century estate on the Route de Vauguières, four kilometers (two and a half miles) southeast of the city by D21 and D172, toward the airport. It has 17 rooms in the 600-franc range.

At more moderate prices, **Les Arceaux**** (04 67 92 03 03 FAX 04 67 92 05 09, at 33 boulevard des Arceaux by the Aqueduct, has 18 rooms at 250 to 320 francs. **Palais**** (04 67 60 47 38 FAX 04 67 60 40 23, at 3 rue du Palais, is nicely situated in the Écusson and has 26 pleasant rooms in the 230- to 360-franc range. The plain **Campanile** chain WEB SITE www.campanille.fr has four of its cheerful, modern motels on the outskirts of town with rooms at 270 francs. They are the 82-room **Montpellier-Est**** (04 67 64 85 85 FAX 04 67 22 19 25, in the ZAC (commercial zone) du Millénaire, 1083 rue Henri-Becquerel; the 46-room **Montpellier-Nord**** (04 67 04 45 25 FAX 04 67 41 22 80, Centre Commercial Carrefour, Route de Ganges, Saint-Clément-de-

Rivière; the 59-room **Montpellier-Sud**** (04 67 58 79 80 FAX 04 67 92 51 81, Avenue du Mas d'Argelliers (Route N113); the 50-room **Montpellier-Ouest**** (04 67 47 99 77 FAX 04 67 47 99 15, Parc d'Activités la Peyrière, off Route N116, in Saint-Jean-de-Védas.

Camping

The closest camping grounds are in Lattes directly south of the city, which has eight sites ranging from the deluxe 302-place **Eden Camping** (04 67 15 11 05, open June 1 to the end of September, to the modest 78-place **Le Camarguais** (04 67 15 10 07, which is open all year. Both are on the Route de Palavas. For information contact the Tourist Office.

OPPOSITE: *Pétanque* players in Montpellier. ABOVE: Antigone, Montpellier's vast modern business and residential complex.

Where to Eat

As with hotels, Montpellier has a good selection of restaurants, starting with the Pourcel brothers' contemporarily elegant **Jardin des Sens** (04 67 79 63 38, the finest restaurant in Languedoc. Here you can feast on little squid (*encornets*) stuffed with *ratatouille*, fried oysters from Bouzigues, lamb with its sweetbreads, bitter chocolate soufflé, and a great selection of regional wines. This is a two-Michelin-star restaurant, quite expensive, with a weekday lunch *menu* at 240 francs. You must reserve in advance. It is at 11 avenue Saint-Lazare off Avenue de Nîmes (N113) to the north of the city.

For an exciting dining experience in the heart of Old Montpellier, try **Isadora** 04 67 66 25 23, at 6 rue du Petit-Scel just off Rue Foch, for the best in contemporary Languedoc-style *nouvelle cuisine*, either in the vaulted thirteenth-century stone dining room or on the shaded terrace on Place Saint Anne in fine weather. Among the many choices are *foie gras* of duck marinated in Muscat de Beaumes-de-Venise (a sweet wine from Provence), breast of guinea fowl cooked in Blanquette de Limoux (a sparkling wine from Languedoc), fillets of *sandre* (a delicious perch-like fish), and lamb with goat cheese and tarragon gravy. There are fine, reasonably priced Languedoc wines also. Meal prices are also very reasonable for food of such quality, with *menus* at 130, 160, and 260 francs.

Another respected gourmet restaurant is **Le Chandelier** (04 67 15 34 38, at 267 rue Léon Blum in Antigone, for traditional French cuisine. Prices here are a bit more expensive.

A place I enjoy greatly is **Le Ménestrel** (04 67 60 62 51, a big thirteenth-century grain warehouse with a vaulted ceiling that offers excellent regional fare, with *menus* from 90 to 150 francs. It is on Place de la Préfecture in Vieux Montpellier. Reservations are a must.

For modestly priced restaurants of all nations, try **Place de la Chapelle Neuve**, at the junction of Rue de l'Aiguillerie and Rue des Écoles Laïques, a few blocks west of the Corum. **Le Vieil Écu** (04 67 66 39 44 and **Chez Marceau** (04 67 66 08 09, offer hearty regional fare, and **Le Grillardin** (04 67 66 24 33 serves fish and meat grilled on a wood fire. The crowd is young and the ambiance cheerful at the restaurants clustered around the cute little tree-shaded square. Another spot for good, inexpensive restaurants in Old Montpellier is the area around **Place Saint-Roch**, by the church of that name. **Le Bouchon Saint-Roch** (04 67 60 94 18 has an outdoor dining terrace on quiet Rue du Plan d'Agde where tasty regional home cooking is served, with fixed-price *menus* from 50 to 98 francs. Around the corner at 20 rue du Petit Saint-Jean, **La Posada** (04 67 66 21 25 is a cozy little restaurant with bright Provençal decor and an outdoor terrace that serves local specialties, paella, and a huge array of grilled fish and meat dishes at remarkably low prices, with an appetizing three-course fixed-price *menu* at 48 francs. Wine prices are similarly affordable — 40 francs for a full liter of *vin de pays* by the pitcher, 80 francs for a bottle of Domaine de l'Hortus, a distinguished *AOC* Coteaux du Languedoc.

Nightlife

The venerable **Café Riche** and other big cafés of the **Place de la Comédie** spread out their tables on the wide, animated square in the summer and stay open late. If you prefer a cozier ambiance, walk down the Place toward the opera house, staying the right, turn right at its rear corner, and walk up Rue du Cygne to little **Place Saint-Côme** or **Place Saint-Roch** just up the street, where you will find a number of easygoing cafés and restaurants. Nearby **Place Jean-Jaurès** has a concentration of currently "in" bistros, such as **La Crypte** and **Le Mex**.

For good live music, you have to leave the center of town. **Mimi-la-Sardine** (04 67 99 67 77, a lively club with rock, jazz, and sounds from Languedoc, Cuba, Brazil, and all over the world, is at 694 Chemin des Cauquilloux in the northeastern suburb of Castelnau-le-Lez, off N113, the route to Nîmes. **Le Sax'aphone** (04 67 58 80 90, presents good jazz, blues, boogie, and salsa groups. It is at 24 rue Ernest Michel, south of the city center.

HOW TO GET THERE

There are 13 flights per day from Paris on Air France and six flights per day from Paris on Air Liberté. Air Liberté and Air Littoral also have flights from many other French cities. British Airways has one direct flight daily from London, but all other international flights connect through other French airports, mainly those of Paris and Nice. There are 10 *TGV*s (high-speed trains) a day from Paris, a four hour and 15 minute ride, and frequent trains from Perpignan, Avignon, Nîmes, Carcassonne, Marseille, with stops in between. There is good regional bus service in the depart-

GENERAL INFORMATION

If you have not already furnished yourself with the excellent travel brochures of the Maison de Tourisme de l'Hérault in Montpellier (see GENERAL INFORMATION, page 282, under MONTPELLIER), there is a **Centre d'Accueil (** 04 67 57 58 83, or welcome center, for this area at Place Général-Claparède in Gignac, about 10 km (six miles) south of Saint-Guilhem-le-Désert. The **Saint-Guilhem-le-Désert Tourist Office (** 04 67 57 44 33 is at the *Mairie* (town hall). In Saint-Martin-de-Londres, the little **Tourist Office (** 04 67 55 09 59 is open in the summer. Otherwise go to the **Tourist Office** at Ganges **(** 04

ment of the Hérault on Sodéthré, with frequent service to Aigues-Mortes, Béziers and the towns of the coast, and some service to towns in the hills north of Montpellier. The Tourist Office can give you the schedules. By car, Montpellier is easily reached by the A9 *autoroute* from the north or the south.

THE HÉRAULT RIVER VALLEY

Short drives north or west of Montpellier take you into the wide open countryside in the foothills of the Cévennes. Vineyards are practically everywhere, fragrances of the wild herbs, flowers, and grasses known as *garrigue*, long stretches of road lined by poplars, just like in the old French movies — and there is little traffic compared to the roads of Provence and especially the Côte d'Azur. It is worth renting a car, even for a day's outing.

67 73 66 40, 19 km (12 miles) to the north. It also has information on the Gorges of the Vis and the Cirque de Navacelles.

SAINT-GUILHEM-LE-DÉSERT

In the foothills of the Cévennes, Saint-Guilhem-le-Désert is less than an hour's drive west of Montpellier. It is a picturesque medieval village at the entrance of the dramatic gorges of the Hérault River, built around its Romanesque abbey. Its founder Guilhem was a warrior and trusted confidant of Charlemagne who gave up wealth and power and retired to this secluded spot to lead a life of prayer and austerity. A **festival of religious music** is held in the village throughout the summer.

OPPOSITE: Fishing is important in the lower Hérault River. ABOVE: A bridge over the Vis River in the foothills of the Cévennes.

Canoë Saint-Guilhem (04 67 57 44 99, by the river in Saint-Guilhem-le-Désert rents boats for rides down the rushing Hérault River and arranges guided hikes to upland sites. Other companies that rent boats here are **Rapido** (04 67 55 75 75, and **Kayapune** (04 67 57 30 25. You can also visit the **Grotte de Clamouse** near the river just south of Saint-Guilhem-le-Désert, an impressive cave with a labyrinth of vast galleries and tortured stalagmites coaxed out of the limestone by the action of water. It is open all year.

SAINT-MARTIN-DE-LONDRES

Thirty-six kilometers (22 miles) east of Saint-Guilhem-le-Désert lies Saint-Martin-de-Londres, a lovely medieval town with an eleventh-century **church** built by the monks of Saint-Guilhem. The ensemble is a classified historical site. This is also a good starting point for hikes into the *garrigue*-covered countryside or to climb or hang-glide from **Pic Saint-Loup**, the 658-m (2,160-ft) peak rising sharply to the east. The name Londres, by the way, has nothing to do with the one in England. It is strictly of local origin.

Another attraction of the area is the **Grotte des Demoiselles**, 17 km (11 miles) north of Saint-Martin-de-Londres on D896. It has vast galleries 50 m (165 ft) high and astounding stalagmites and stalactites, including the *Virgin and Child*, a limestone statue sculpted by water.

THE GORGES OF THE VIS AND THE CIRQUE DE NAVACELLES

The pleasant little tree-shaded town of **Ganges**, a former silk-manufacturing center eight kilometers (five miles) north of the Grotte des Demoiselles, is the starting point for an excursion to the west on D25 along the picturesque Gorges of the Vis to the even more picturesque Cirque de Navacelles. This is a gigantic crater cut deep into the limestone by an abandoned course of the Vis River. It zeros in on a perfect circle of flat farmland at the bottom with an island of limestone in the middle. This is one of many bizarre topographical features of this area that look like messages to extraterrestrial civilizations. The view from the top is extremely impressive, and for hikers the descent into the valley makes for an exhilarating outing.

WINE TASTING

Mas de Daumas Gassac (04 67 57 71 28, in Aniane, is a vineyard that sold its first wine little more than 20 years ago, in 1978, and became a star three years later, when its deep, flavorful reds were hailed by *Gault-Millau Magazine*. They have been getting rave reviews from the wine critics ever since. The vineyard now makes highly praised whites and

rosés as well. Their wine is a *vin de pays de l'Hérault* that sells at the prices of top Bordeaux wines — ten times the standard price of *vin de pays* from Languedoc. The special soil and microclimate of the vineyard, unusual choices of vine stocks, careful attention to the winemaking process, and owner Aimé Guibert's astute sense of publicity have made this little miracle possible. Open daily except Sunday from 10 AM to noon and 2 PM to 6 PM.

In Montpeyroux on Route D141 west of the Grotte de Clamouse, **Domaine d'Aupilhac** (04 67 96 61 19 and **Les Vignerons de Montpeyroux** (04 67 96 61 08 make highly praised Coteaux du Languedoc. You must call ahead to arrange a

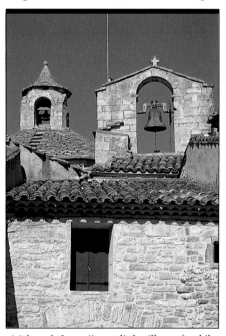

visit here. In Jonquières, a little village a few kilometers farther to the west on D141, Olivier Jullien, a passionately dedicated young oenologist who is a native of the area, operates **Mas Juillen** (04 67 96 60 04, a cluster of tiny Coteaux du Languedoc vineyards. Juillen is committed to expressing the character of each of his little parcels of land in the wine he makes. His two blends of red and two blends of white are all richly flavorful, and each one is truly unique. Mas Jullien is open daily, from 10 AM to noon and 2 PM to 6 PM in the summer, afternoons only off-season.

The Pic Saint-Loup area east of Saint-Martin-de-Londres is another outstanding Coteaux du

OPPOSITE TOP: The valley of the Vis. OPPOSITE BOTTOM and ABOVE: Medieval Saint-Martin-de-Londres.

Languedoc area. Top winemakers to visit here are **Mas Bruguière** (04 67 55 20 97, open daily from 5 PM to 8:30 PM; **Château la Roque** (04 67 55 34 47, open daily except Sunday from 9 AM to noon and 4 PM to 6 PM; and **Domaine de l'Hortus** (04 67 55 31 20, open weekdays from 5 PM to 8 PM and Saturdays from 9 AM to 8 PM and closed Sundays.

WHERE TO STAY AND EAT

The best bet for accommodation in the Saint-Guilhem-le-Désert area (and there are not a whole lot of choices out here) is the lovely **Ostalaria Cardabela** (04 67 88 62 62 FAX 04 67 88 62 82, at 10 place de la Fontaine in the tiny village of Saint-Saturnin-de-Lucian, about 10 km (6 miles) to the west of Saint-Guilhem-le-Désert. The *cardabela*, after which the inn is named, is a large thistle with a sunflower-like center that grows on the Larzac plateau. It symbolizes the sun to the local people, who fix the flower on their doors. That sunny spirit infuses the inn's seven spacious rooms, modernized in the finest of taste, enhancing the charm of the venerable stone townhouse. Room prices are moderate. The inn is open from the beginning of March to the beginning on November.

For a real culinary treat, go to the **Mimosa** (04 67 96 67 96, in next village of Saint-Guiraud, whose owners, David and Brigit Pugh, also created the Ostalaria Cardabela. The restaurant is a favorite of wine connoisseurs because of David Pugh's exceptional knowledge of the wines of the region, knowledge he is most generous about sharing. They also rave about Brigit Pugh's imaginative cooking, inspired by what's fresh in the market and in her own garden that day. Like the inn, the Mimosa is open from March to the beginning of November. It is closed Mondays and Sunday nights except in July and August. The fixed-price lunch *menu* is 190 francs, the dinner *menu* 290 francs. Reservations required. Mimosa is on Route D130 in Saint-Guiraud.

The **Hostellerie Saint-Benôit**** (04 67 57 71 63 FAX 04 67 57 47 10 E-MAIL hostelleriest-benoit @wanadoo.fr, in Aniane, six kilometers (four miles) south of Saint-Guilhem-le-Désert, is a pleasant 30-room Logis de France inn with a pool and a good restaurant; closed from the beginning of January to mid-February. Rooms are in the moderate price range, and fixed-price *menus* start at 99 francs.

The finest food in Saint-Martin-de-Londres area is to be found at the Rousset family's **Les Muscardins** (04 67 55 75 90, an old stone barn tastefully converted into a contemporary-style restaurant at 19 route des Cévennes in the heart of the old village. It is expensive, but on week-

days you can benefit from the 145-franc lunch, an extraordinary value, featuring such dishes as roasted half-salted cod with clam raviolis in squid ink, sautéed stuffed squid and seafood cannelloni with herbs, or rabbit baked in a crust of herb bread — using strictly regional products, according to the season — and served with a superb assortment of local and regional wines. Talented young Thierry Rousset is the chef, his charming wife Cyrille manages the dining room, and his father Georges is the sommelier. The restaurant is closed Mondays and Tuesdays.

The most beautiful hotel in the Gorges of the Vis is the **Château de Madières***** (04 67 73 84 03 FAX 04 67 73 55 71 E-MAIL madieres@wanadoo.fr, in Madières, 20 km (over twelve miles) southwest of Ganges on D24. Built within the walls of a fourteenth-century fortress on a remote hillside overlooking the gorge, this thoroughly comfortable 10-room Relais du Silence hotel has a large pool and fitness center and serves fine regional cuisine

in magnificent vaulted dining rooms. It is expensive. Open late March to early November.

For an inexpensive hotel near the Cirque de Navacelles, try to get into the five-room **Auberge de la Cascade**** (04 67 81 50 95 FAX 04 67 81 53 45. It is open from March to December. Another inexpensive option is the 14-room **Gorges de la Vis*** (04 67 73 85 05, in Gornies on D25, the road between Ganges and the Cirque de Navacelles. It has a restaurant that serves hearty regional fare.

Camping

Camping de la Muse (04 67 57 92 97, on Chemin de la Muse in Gignac, has a pool, tennis court, food shop and bar, and 61 places, open June to September. The well-equipped 36-place **Camping du Pont** (04 67 57 52 40 on Boulevard du Moulin in Gignac is open all year. In the Saint-Martin-de-Londres area, **Camping Pic Saint-Loup** (04 67 55 00 53, on the Route du Pic Saint-Loup, has 80 places, a pool, miniature golf, restaurant, food shop and bar, open April 1 to the end of September. There are no camping grounds near the Cirque de Navacelles, but if you ask their permission, farmers will generally let you camp on their land for a night.

HOW TO GET THERE

There is frequent daily bus service to Gignac, Saint-Martin-de-Londres, and Ganges, but to see the countryside around them, you need a car. Gignac is 30 km (19 miles) west of Montpellier on N109 and Saint-Guilhem 10 km (six miles) farther on D32 and D27 via Aniane. To Saint-Martin-de-Londres 27 km (17 miles) north of Montpellier, take the Route de Ganges (D986). Ganges is 46 km (19 miles) from Montpellier.

The Cirque de Navacelles, a spectacular crater carved into the limestone of the Grands Causses plateau by a former course of the Vis River.

THE GORGES OF THE TARN

One of the most satisfying drives in all of France is through the Gorges of the Tarn in the heart of the Cévennes. While they're not quite as dramatically deep or wide as the Grand Canyon of the Verdon in the Alpes-de-Haute-Provence, these gorges make up for their relatively modest proportions with their long expanses of flat tan limestone cliffs rising straight up from the Tarn, and with the river itself, which is visible at almost all points as you drive along gorge (as it is not in the Verdon), with lovely farms in a few places on the far side of the stream. This is natural beauty on a human scale — but it's plenty impressive, don't worry about that. Point Sublime, one of the main viewing points, is 400 m (1,300 feet) above the Tarn, and the view extends 16 km (10 miles) down the river's canyon.

To make a circuit of the Gorges of the Tarn from Montpellier, you will need two days at the minimum to have enough time to appreciate it (you could easily spend a week in this area). Starting from Montpellier, take the D986 (Route de Ganges) past Saint-Martin-de-Londres to Ganges, a distance of 45 km (28 miles), and follow the same route along the Hérault River up into the 960-sq-km (600 sq-mile) **Cévennes National Park**, where privately owned farms and little villages are part of the park, amid the public lands. The population is small, however. The *département* of the Lozère, in which most of the park is located, is the least populated in France. Wind up the lovely wooded road (still the D986) toward Espérou. **Mont Aigoual** (1,567 m or 5,145 ft), the largest mountain in the southern Cévennes, looms off to the right only 10 km (six miles) away. If the weather is clear, drive up the mountain to take in the immense panorama from the observation platform at the top. It extends from the neighboring Causses plateau and the Cévennes Mountains all the way south to the Pyrénées, northeast to Mont Ventoux and the Alpes-de-Provence, and east to the Mediterranean.

Rejoining D986, head now for **Meyrueis**, 112 km (70 miles) from Montpellier, a congenial town with several good hotels and restaurants in case you want to spend the night. Here you switch to Route D996 to follow the Gorges de la Jonte to the Tarn River at Le Rozier, pausing at the **Belvédère des Vautours** (Belvedere of the Vultures) in Le Truel to observe the great birds up close in their native habitat (open daily, mid-March to mid-November). Turn right on D907 at **Le Rozier** and follow the **Gorges of the Tarn** (for optimum viewing from a car, it's best to drive the gorges in this generally west-to-east direction, the gorges being to the right of the road). Almost immediately you find yourself in the most spectacular parts of the

gorge — the sheer-cliffed bend in the river called the **Cirque des Baumes**, overlooked by lofty **Point Sublime** and **Les Détroits**, the narrow straits between a long set of sheer cliffs. At **La Malène**, park in the lot of the **Bateliers de la Malène** and let the boatmen take you on a one-hour descent through the eight-kilometer (five-mile) straits. The water is calm, the boatmen are thoroughly professional, so there's nothing to fear, and at the end of the trip, they will drive you back to your car. It is expensive, though — 412 francs for a four-passenger boat.

This western half of the gorges is certainly the most dramatic, but there are lovely views along all 57 km (36 miles) of the gorges to Florac on the eastern end. **Sainte-Enimie**, a charming medieval village in the middle, is a good place to pause for lunch or refreshments, and for people who are trained and in good condition, this is a place to rent canoes and kayaks for jaunts on the river.

Besides the Gorges of the Tarn, there are also spectacular stalactite- and stalagmite-filled caves to explore in this area, most notably **L'Aven Armand**, which has a gigantic central gallery that Paris's Notre-Dame Cathedral could easily fit into, and **La Grotte de Dargilan**, the biggest cave in the Cévennes, both of them close to Meyrueis.

From Florac, head down the **Corniche des Cévennes** (D9), a drive almost as exciting as the Gorges of the Tarn. Here we enter country described by Robert Louis Stevenson in his 1879 book *Travels with a Donkey in the Cévennes*, which ended at **Saint-Jean-du-Gard**, 67 km (33 miles) to the south of Florac. This is a starting point for hikers who want to follow in Stevenson's footsteps. The *Train à Vapeur des Cévennes*, an old-fashioned steam train, makes the 13-km (eight-mile) run between Saint-Jean-du-Gard and **Anduze** three times a day in the summer. From Anduze you can either return to Montpellier via Saint-Hippolyte and Ganges, or head over to Nîmes. If you complete the whole circuit to Montpellier, you will have driven 320 km (200 miles).

WHERE TO STAY AND EAT

There are several good hotel-restaurants in the graceful town of Meyrueis and lovely castle-hotels on the Tarn in Le Rozier and La Malène.

Château d'Ayres*** (04 66 45 60 10 FAX 04 66 45 62 26, in a large private park in the rolling countryside outside Meyrueis, is an elegant eighteenth-century manorial residence on the site of a twelfth-century Benedictine monastery with 25 spacious, comfortable rooms, a pool, a tennis court, and a restaurant serving refined regional dishes. *Demi-pension* (room, breakfast, and one meal) is required in high season, about 600 francs per person. This Relais du Silence member is open

La Malène, the point of departure for a boat ride through the gorges of the Tarn River.

Easter to November 15. **Hotel Family**** (04 66 45 60 02 FAX 04 66 45 66 54, in downtown Meyrueis, has 48 neat, simple rooms with all the modern comforts, a spacious restaurant serving the excellent Lozère family-style cooking of owner-chef Didier Julian, and a little pool in the hotel's garden. *Demi-pension* is about 250 francs per person. A Logis de France member, it is open Easter to November 1.

Hôtel de la Muse et du Rozier*** (05 65 62 60 01 FAX 05 65 62 63 88 E-MAIL info@hotel-delamuse.com WEB SITE www.hotel-delamuse.com is a handsome manor house across the river from Le Rozier in Peryeleau, in the Aveyron. It has 38 tastefully modernized, very comfortable rooms,

a pool, a restaurant, and a quiet park overlooking the Tarn. *Demi-pension* is 420 to 620 francs. It is open Easter to early November. **Manoir de Montesquiou***** (04 66 48 51 12 FAX 04 66 48 50 47, the impressive fifteenth-century manor of the Montesquiou family in the little riverside village of Malène, is now a warm, inviting hotel with a vaulted dining room and flowery dining terrace, and 12 attractive rooms, with *demi-pension* at 440 to 630 francs. Open Easter to the end of October. **Château de la Caze****** (04 66 48 51 01 FAX 04 66 48 55 75 E-MAIL chateau.de.la.caze@wanadoo.fr, the most glamorous of them all, is a 500-year-old fortress-castle with storybook towers and round turrets in an isolated private park directly on the Tarn. It has seven antique-filled rooms in the old castle and six decorated in tasteful contemporary Provençal style in a new building — all of them spacious and very comfortable — and a big swim-

ming pool. The restaurant serves owner-chef Jean-Paul Lecroq's refined regional gourmet cuisine. *Demi-pension* costs 515 to 690 francs. Open April 1 to the middle of November.

All these hotels have good restaurants open to the public, with lunches in the moderate price range. For further information about this area contact: **Comité Départemental du Tourisme de la Lozère** (04 66 65 60 00 FAX 04 66 49 27 96 E-MAIL CDT.Lozere@wanadoo.fr, 14 boulevard Henri-Bourillon, BP 4, 48001 Mende Cedex; **Parc National des Cévennes** (04 66 49 53 00 WEB SITE www.bsi.fr/pnc; the **Tourist Offices** of Meyrueis (04 66 45 60 33, Sainte-Enimie (04 66 48 53 44, Florac (04 66 45 01 14, or Anduze (04 66 61 98 17.

THE BASSIN DE THAU

The Languedoc shore is one nearly unbroken sandy beach extending 160 km (100 miles) along the Gulf of Lion from the Camargue down into Roussillon, to the start of the rocky Côte Vermeille. Directly to the back of it are big saltwater lagoons called *étangs* or *bassins*. These lagoons were once open bays, but were sealed in by sands washed down by the Rhône over the centuries. Access to the sea is kept open by a few narrow channels that are constantly dredged. The sanding-up of the shore line has been a curse because it has ruined once-busy sea ports, but also a blessing, because the beaches attract tourists and the lagoons are rich breeding grounds for shellfish.

The largest of these lagoons, the Bassin de Thau, lies 30 km (19 miles) southwest of Montpellier. It is known throughout France for the mussels and oysters of Bouzigues.

GENERAL INFORMATION

There are Tourist Offices in **Balaruc-les-Bains** (04 67 48 50 07, at 6 avenue du Port; **Marseillan** 04 67 21 82 43, on the port; and **Mèze** (04 67 43 93 08, Rue Massaloup.

WHAT TO SEE AND DO

The Bassin de Thau is 20 km (12.5 miles) long by four kilometers (one and a quarter miles) wide, and as you look out over the water, you see row after row of rectangular platforms that look like they are floating in the air. They are frames for the nets in which the shellfish are raised and are supported by stilts in the water. This is France's largest shellfish breeding ground. The towns of the Bassin de Thau — **Mèze**, **Marseillan**, and several others — produce a quarter of France's oysters and mussels, all marketed under the name of the little town of **Bouzigues**. Fresh, inexpensive seafood can be found there and in simple eateries all around the Bassin de Thau.

The **Musée de l'Étang de Thau** (04 67 78 33 57, on the port in Bouzigues, has a videotape program showing the whole process of mussel and oyster farming, or *conchyliculture* as they call it. The program is in French, but for non-French speakers, the visuals are easy to follow, and there are displays of the tools of the trade. It is open daily from 10 AM to noon and 2 PM to 6 PM, closed November to February.

WINE TASTING

One visit you are sure to enjoy if you like either wine or medieval architecture and you will rave about if you like both is to the **Abbaye de Valmagne** (04 67 78 06 09, eight kilometers (five miles) north of Mèze on D161. The huge church of the defunct abbey is one of the rare examples of Gothic architecture in the South, and it now serves as a spectacular cellar for Abbaye de Valmagne wines, a prestigious *AOC* Coteaux du Languedoc grown on land first planted in vines by monks in the twelfth century. The abbey is open daily mornings and afternoons from June 15 to September 30, afternoons only out of season.

The village of Pinet lies 10 km (six miles) west of Mèze on D18E, and dry white **Picpoul de Pinet** of high quality can be tasted at **Les Vignerons de Pinet** (04 67 77 03 10, in Pinet, and **Hugues de Beauvignac** (04 67 77 01 59, in the next-door town of Pomérols. The *cave* of the Vignerons de Pinet is open daily except Sunday, but you must call ahead to visit the Abbaye de Valmagne or Hugues de Beauvignac.

Noilly-Prat (04 67 77 20 15 is on the port in Marseillan, and you can tour their big apéritif-making plant every day except Sunday.

WHERE TO STAY AND EAT

Côte Bleue*** (04 67 78 31 42 FAX 04 67 78 35 49, on the port in Bouzigues, is a comfortable 32-room hotel with a swimming pool and one of the Bassin de Thau's top sea food restaurants. Rooms are moderately priced, the restaurant expensive. Closed January. **La Palourdière** (04 67 43 79 19 is a rustic family-style eatery run by a shellfish producer with very fresh seafood at modest prices. Reserve in advance, because it is

always full. It is about two kilometers (just over a mile) south of Bouzigues on the little road that runs alongside the Bassin de Thau. Open from April to October.

Fronting on the colorful small-boat port of Marseillan, the **Château du Port**** (04 67 77 65 65 FAX 04 67 77 67 98, is a *belle époque* mansion with lots of character and 16 spacious rooms at moderate prices. The **Restaurant du Château du Port** (04 67 77 31 67, next to the hotel, is a cheerful eatery serving solid family-style cooking, fresh shellfish, and local seafood dishes at modest prices. The terrace overlooking the port is very relaxing.

OPPOSITE: A farm on the south bank of the Tarn and a pool in the sparkling river. ABOVE: Frames for oyster culture in the Bassin de Thau, the coastal lagoon that is France's leading shellfish producer.

There are two fine gourmet restaurants in Marseillan. **La Table d'Emilie** (04 67 77 63 59, at 8 place Couverte near the market, in a thirteenth-century stone house with vaulted stone dining room and a pretty garden, serves inventive regional cuisine at moderate to expensive prices. Try the Bouzigues oysters in Noilly apéritif wine from the local Noilly-Prat winery and the *montgolfière de Saint-Jacques, crevettes et pétoncles* (a hot air balloon-shaped melange of succulent sea scallops, shrimps, and tiny Mediterranean clams baked in a light crust). At **Chez Philippe** (04 67 01 70 62, manager Philippe Marquet and chef Sébastien Demeulle, who put the restaurant Pile ou Face on the map in Paris, have scored again in this town with their strictly fresh local products cooked to perfection. Specialties such as poached egg and oysters in aspic, sauté of pork with coco beans and lemon grass, their grand array of ingenious seafood dishes, astute choice of wines, and remarkably reasonable prices (a single *menu* at 110 francs) have made their restaurant the most sought-after in the area. So reserve well in advance. It is open for dinner only. The stylish yellow townhouse is located at 20 rue de Suffren near the port. There is a lovely pine-shaded dining terrace.

In Florensac, six kilometers (four miles) to the north of Marseillan in the heart of Picpoul de Pinet wine country, **Léonce** (04 67 77 03 05 FAX 04 67 77 88 89, at 2 place de la République, is one of the finest restaurants in Languedoc. Jean-Claude Fabre, in the third generation of chefs in his family, serves *supions* (cuttlefish) braised in balsamic vinegar, sea bass with wild morel mushrooms, pigeon thigh stuffed with giblets and roast pigeon breast, a sublime extra-bitter chocolate in citrus fruit sauce, among many unique specialties, and there is a marvelous selection of wines from Languedoc and Roussillon at very fair prices. For a Michelin one-star restaurant, the prices are modest. There is a weekday lunch *menu* at 150 francs, and the dinner *menu* is 340 francs. Léonce also rents 10 inexpensive rooms.

Camping

Camping Beau Rivage (04 67 43 81 48, in Mèze, is a well-equipped camping ground with 234 places, a restaurant, bar, and pool by the edge of the Bassin de Thau on N113. It is open from the beginning of April to the middle of October. In Bouzigues, the more modestly equipped **Camping Lou Labech** (04 67 78 30 38, on Chemin du Stade by the edge of the Bassin, has 40 places and is open from the beginning of July to the end of September. Balaruc-le-Vieux and its resort suburb of Balaruc-les-Bains have five camping sites. For information, contact the Tourist Office at Balaruc-les-Bains.

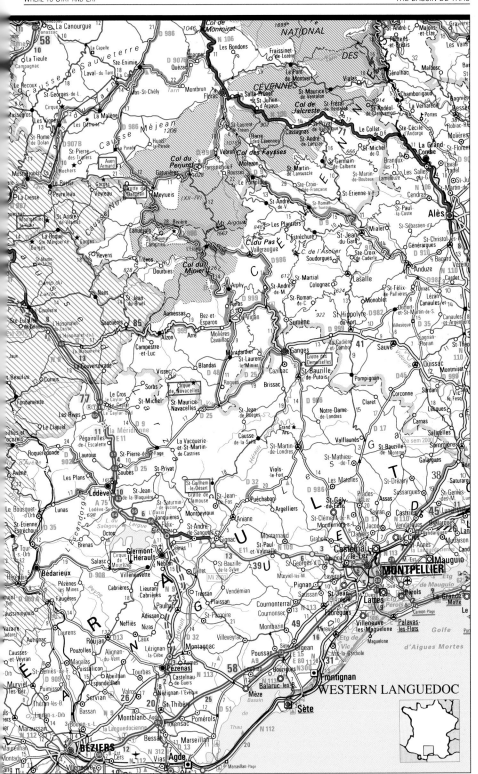

HOW TO GET THERE

There are more than a dozen buses a day from Montpellier to Mèze, Bouzigues, and other main towns of the Bassin de Thau. The trip takes less than half an hour by express bus from Montpellier to Bouzigues, ten minutes longer on the local bus. The easiest way to get there by car from Montpellier is by N113, which goes directly to Bouzigues and Mèze. This is a very rural area, and the best way to explore it is by car or bike.

SÈTE

Sète calls itself "the Venice of Languedoc," and unlike most would-be Venices, Sète delivers. This is not the touristy Venice of the Piazza San Marco, though. More the workaday Venice of, say, the Stazione Marittima. Sète is a real port, part rough and tumble but with picturesque spots too, like the wide Canal de Sète leading to the Vieux Port, where the houses are all painted in different shades of pastel.

Sète, then called "Cette," was created in the late seventeenth century as the port for the Mediterranean end of the Canal du Midi. Now a city of 42,000 and the largest French fishing port on the Mediterranean, it sits on the thin isthmus of Onglous between the Bassin de Thau and the sea with a complex of canals that link the two bodies of water. Its houses run up the slopes of Mont Saint-Clair, the only high ground for miles around.

Adding to Sète's Italianate flavor is its large population of descendants of Calabrian fishermen who emigrated here in the early twentieth century. Of the 2,000 families in Sète that support themselves on fishing, the majority are of Italian descent. *Tielle*, the local squid and tomato pie, is of Italian origin.

GENERAL INFORMATION

The **Tourist Office (** 04 67 74 71 71 is at 60 Grande Rue Mario-Roustan, the main street paralleling the west side of the Canal de Sète. This is a very well-run office with excellent maps and brochures.

The **Gare SNCF (** 04 67 46 51 00, the train station, is on the Quai Maréchal-Joffre. The bus station, **Gare Routière** and **La Sétoise bus service (** 04 67 74 18 77, are at Quai de la Résistance.

Taxis can be had at the Gare SNCF **(** 04 67 48 62 98; at Quai de Lattre-de-Tassigny **(** 04 67 74 05 61; Taxis Sétois **(** 04 67 53 24 14; and Claris Valérie **(** 04 67 74 01 89.

Car Rental agencies are: **Europcar (** 04 67 51 69 90, 23 quai Noel-Guignon; **Languedoc Location (** 04 67 43 34 34, Place de la Gare; **Wallgren (** 04 67 74 85 67, 11 quai de la République.

Société Nautique (04 67 74 98 97, at the Môle Saint-Louis, rents sail boats and windsurfers and organizes scuba-diving trips.

Sète Croisières (04 67 46 00 10, at the Quai de la Marine, offers frequent tours of the port and Bassin de Thau daily in season, cruises to Aigues-Mortes twice a week and a cruise on the Canal du Midi on Sundays. They also run two fishing trips per morning and offer night fishing twice a week.

Sète Croisières also operates **little tourist trains** from the Quai de la Marine that take you around the town and the port and up Mont Saint-Clair.

Should health emergencies arise, the **Hôpital Générale (** 04 67 46 57 57 is on Boulevard Camille-Blanc.

FESTIVALS AND EVENTS

Hardly a day goes by without some festival or special event. The main ones are the **Festival de Saint-Pierre** the first weekend of July and the **Fête de Saint-Louis** around the August 25. They feature nautical jousting, a sport in which youngsters stand on the elongated prows of competing galleys and try to knock each other into the water with big sticks, like Punch and Judy.

WHAT TO SEE AND DO

Walk along the **Môle Saint-Louis**, the sea wall that protects the Vieux Port and has the training base for France's America's Cup challengers at the far end of it. From here you get the best view of the busy port, the Venice-like Canal de Sète with pastel houses and the town rising up Mont Saint-Clair.

Calling a peak of 175 m (575 ft) a mountain might seem presumptuous, but if it happens to be the only elevation whatsoever for dozens of miles around, as **Mont Saint-Clair** is, you can get away with it. From its observation platform at the top, "the Venice of Languedoc" lies at your feet and grand vistas spread out before you: the Mediterranean, the beaches and beach towns up and down the shore, the Bassin de Thau, vineyards, Montpellier, and the foothills of the Cévennes.

Sète is the birthplace of the great modern poet Paul Valéry, who is buried in the Cimetière Marin, the Sailors' Cemetery, overlooking the Mediterranean on the slope of Mont Saint-Clair, about

WINE TASTING

Fortant de France (04 67 46 70 23, Robert Skalli's big, gleaming modern blending and bottling plant for single-variety *vins de pays* is a trend setter in winemaking and marketing in Languedoc. There is free wine tasting and a modern art gallery. It is at 278 avenue Maréchal-Juin, on the north side of the port; open Monday to Friday all year.

WHERE TO STAY

The glamorous *belle époque* **Grand Hôtel***** (04 67 74 71 77 FAX 04 67 74 29 27 WEB SITE www.epicuria.fr

which he wrote some of his most famous lines. The modern **Musée Paul Valéry** directly above the cemetery has a room devoted to the life and work of the poet, who was a talented artist as well. The museum also has exhibits on the history of Sète, an interesting modern art collection, and a room devoted to songwriter Georges Brassens, who also wrote about his native Sète. It is closed Tuesdays.

Georges Brassens is buried in the Cimetière Le Py on Boulevard Camille-Blanc facing the Bassin de Thau. **L'Espace Brassens** at 67 boulevard Camille-Blanc has more exhibits on this modern troubadour. It is closed Mondays.

The **Plage de la Corniche** is a 20-km (12.5-mile) strip of fine sandy, non-built-up Mediterranean beach that runs south from Sète to Cap d'Agde along the narrow isthmus between the Bassin de Thau and the sea.

has a delightful atrium winter garden four stories high and 43 very comfortable guest rooms. Here you can experience *le luxe* at a maximum double room rate of only 610 francs. It is at 17 quai Maréchal-de-Lattre at the junction of two main canals. For a charming and peaceful modern hotel overlooking the sea, **Les Terrasses du Lido***** (04 67 51 39 60 FAX 04 67 51 28 90, on the *corniche* at the Rond-Point Europe, has nine very comfortable, moderately priced rooms, a pool, and a very good restaurant (see WHERE TO EAT). **Le Saint-Clair**** (04 67 51 27 67, at 9 avenue du Tennis la Corniche, a quiet side street 200 m (about 220 yards) from the beach, is a modern hotel with 10 pleasant, inexpensive rooms, a pool, and a garden. Its rooms range from 200 to 350 francs. **Les Sables d'Or****

A water-jousting contest in the harbor of Sète, "the Venice of Languedoc." Sète is France's largest fishing port on the Mediterranean.

(04 67 53 09 98 FAX 04 67 51 56 06, also on the *corniche* at Place Edouard-Herriot, has 30 attractive modern rooms with a top rate of 320 francs.

Camping

Camping in Sète is at the deluxe 986-place **Le Castellas** (04 67 51 63 00, Plage de la Corniche, at the beach seven kilometers (four miles) south of the town on N112, open mid-May to the end of September, or the modest **Le Philippe** (04 67 53 08 64, at 6 boulevard Joliot-Curie by the Plage de la Corniche on the south side of Mont Saint-Clair, open April to the end of September. The adjoining beach area to the south, **Marseillan Plage**, has a vast complex of 22 camping grounds offering almost 4,500 places. For information contact the Tourist Office of Mèze, Sète, or Cap d'Agde.

WHERE TO EAT

Palangrotte (04 67 74 80 35, at 1 rampe Paul-Valéry (Quai de la Marine) near the Tourist Office, is a highly respected seafood restaurant, famed for its fresh shellfish platters, Sète's style of *bourride de baudroie* (monkfish stew), and *bouillabaisse*. Fixed-price *menus* start at 110 francs. Open daily, closed Sunday night and Mondays except in July and August. Reservations are recommended. Another fine place for fresh shellfish, *bourride, bouillabaisse,* and specialties such as *lasagne de homard aux cèpes* (lobster lasagna with boletus mushrooms) is the restaurant of **Les Terrasses du Lido** on the *corniche* overlooking the sea (see WHERE TO STAY, above). It is expensive. For inexpensive fish and shellfish in a bustling workaday ambiance, try **Chante-Mer** (04 67 46 01 75, or the **Hostal** (04 67 74 33 96, on the Promenade J.B. Marty overlooking the modern Criée aux Poissons, the wholesale fish market, and the Vieux Port. To sample the best in *tielles*, the local squid pie, go to **Paradiso** (04 67 74 26 48, at 11 quai de la Résistance.

HOW TO GET THERE

Sète is 30 minutes from Montpellier Airport. By rail it is half an hour from Montpellier or Béziers, and there are frequent buses from both those cities. By car, Sète is reached by the A9 *autoroute* and N300 to the shore or more colorfully by N112, the shore road from Montpellier to Béziers.

AGDE AND CAP D'AGDE

Agde, at the southern end of the Bassin de Thau, is the second oldest city in France after Marseille, founded 2,500 years ago by the Phocean Greeks. They called it *Agathé*, "the beautiful one." It became a prosperous colony trading in wine and olive oil, and it remained an important port until the late Middle Ages when Montpellier and Aigues-Mortes and later Sète took its business away. Today it is a somber-looking town of 20,000 at the junction of the Hérault River and the Canal du Midi dominated by a large twelfth-century fortified church made of black lava, the former **Cathedral of Saint-Étienne**. But this town's not nearly as somber as it might appear at first glance, and the resort community of Cap d'Agde is all bright and new.

GENERAL INFORMATION

The **Agde Tourist Office** (04 67 94 29 68 is at 1 place Molière; **Cap d'Agde Tourist Office** (04 67 01 04

04 E-MAIL contact@capdagde.com WEB SITE www .capdagde.com, is at the main traffic circle at the park-like entrance of the resort.

WHAT TO SEE AND DO

Agde is known as "the Black Pearl of Languedoc" because much of the **old town** is built of lava from the nearby extinct volcano, Mont Saint-Loup. Its web of twisting old streets lined with cafés, restaurants, and boutiques is lively and makes for pleasant strolling, as does the riverfront. **Bateaux du Soleil** (04 67 94 08 79, at 7 quai du Chapitre in front of the cathedral, offers all-day cruises on the cool, tree-shaded Canal du Midi from April through October and add half-day cruises in the summer.

The **Musée Agathois** on Rue de la Fraternité near the town market has numerous amphoræ from the ancient Greek port and other archaeological finds and an eclectic collection of models of ships, ex-voto (thanksgiving) paintings, costumes, apothecary jars and other interesting exhibits. It is open daily from 10 AM to noon and 2 PM to 6 PM, closed Tuesday.

Mont Saint-Loup is a few kilometers east of Agde. An easy walk to its 111-m (365-ft) peak gives you an excellent 365 degree panorama of the Bassin de Thau, the Mediterranean, Cap d'Agde, Agde, and the Cévennes.

Cap d'Agde on the coast five kilometers (three miles) east of Agde at the foot of Mont Saint-Loup, is a modern resort complex developed entirely since 1970. It is a neatly laid-out development

plorations of the harbor of Agde. The most important piece is an exquisite Hellenistic bronze statue of a nude youth, Ephèbe, found in the Hérault River in 1964. The museum is closed Tuesdays.

To get naked yourself, go to the *naturiste* **quarter**, which occupies the beach on the north side of the resort. This is a complete nudist community with a nudist hotel, a nudist bank, nudist camping grounds, restaurants, supermarkets, and apartment complexes, and on a typical midsummer day 25,000 to 30,000 nudists can be found on the beach here. The office (04 67 26 00 26 is at the Rond-Point du Bagnas, open in season. Otherwise contact the Cap d'Agde Tourist Office.

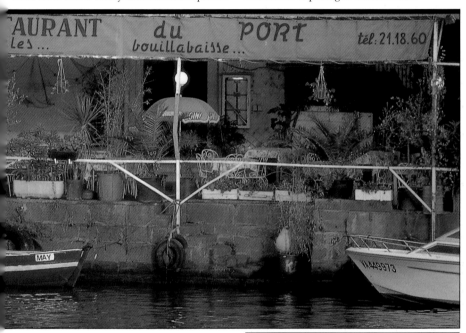

with curving drives and rows of red-ochre bungalows. If you blink your eyes, you might think you were in California. The resort is built around a yacht harbor with docks for 2,260 boats, and there are numerous sailing and windsurfing schools. Cap d'Agde boasts of some of the best sports facilities in Europe, including the **Cap d'Agde Club International de Tennis** (04 67 01 03 60 FAX 04 67 26 77 18, the largest tennis training center in Europe, with 40 courts. **Golf du Cap d'Agde** (04 67 26 54 40 is one of the best courses in Mediterranean France, and the **Centre Nautique du Cap d'Agde** (04 67 01 46 46, at Plage Richelieu Est, gives all levels of sailing instruction. There are also ten schools that teach **scuba diving**.

The **Musée de l'Ephèbe**, a museum of underwater archaeology, has a number of objects from Greek antiquity found in underwater ex-

WHERE TO STAY AND EAT

There are 35 hotels, most very modern, and dozens of modern rental apartment complexes (*résidences de tourisme*) — in Agde and Cap d'Agde, and the Cap d'Agde Tourist Office will book them for you. **La Tamarissière***** (04 67 94 20 87 FAX 04 67 21 38 40 E-MAIL hotellatamarissiere @wanadoo.fr., at 21 quai Théophile-Cornu at the mouth of the Hérault River in Agde, four kilometers (two and a half miles) from the center of town on D32E, is a very comfortable 27-room hotel in a peaceful waterfront setting with a flowery garden and pool, and it has one of the most distinguished restaurants in the Hérault. Seafood is Chef Nicholas Albano's specialty, and I

The waterfront of Agde at the eastern end of the Canal du Midi, on which boats can travel across France from the Mediterranean to the Atlantic.

recommend the grilled *loup de mer* (sea bass) or the flavorful *coquilles Saint-Jacques* (sea scallops). Fixed-price *menus* run from 165 to 390 francs and rooms are in the 600 to 700 area. For an unusual hotel, look into **La Galiote**** (04 67 94 45 58 FAX 04 67 94 14 33, at 5 place Jean-Jaurès in Agde, a former residence of the bishops of Agde, next to the cathedral. It has 16 moderately priced rooms, all furnished with antiques, some of them overlooking the Hérault River. It also has a cozy bar and an attractive, moderately priced restaurant. The hotel is run by a friendly Scandinavian couple.

In Cap d'Agde, **Le Manhattan** (04 67 26 21 54, right on the waterfront at 31 quai Jean-Miquel, has

a perfect view of the pleasure boat port from the open-air deck or the air-conditioned dining room. It serves excellent fresh shellfish platters and fish and seafood dishes, and owners Betty and Momo Khalkhal provide a warm welcome. **Le Capaô Beach** (04 67 26 68 00, in the middle of Richelieu Beach, is the perfect spot for a light lunch or early dinner (it closes at 9:30 PM) after a day at the beach, as you gaze out at the Mediterranean and the island of Brescou. After a period of decline, **Les 3 Sergents** (04 67 26 73 13, on Avenue des Sergents, is under new ownership, working hard to reclaim its position as Cap d'Agde's leading restaurant. The menu is based on fresh seafood.

Camping

There is a vast array of camping facilities, nudist and non-nudist, in the area. There are 20 camping grounds in Agde and Cap d'Agde and 27

in Vias, Agde's neighbor to the west. Between them they have several thousand camp places, most of them on or near the beach. For information on camping in Agde or Cap d'Agde, contact their tourist offices. Vias has its own Tourist Office (04 67 21 68 78, on Boulevard de la Liberté.

HOW TO GET THERE

There are seven trains a day to Agde from Paris via Montpellier, a five-and-a-half-hour trip. From Sète or Béziers, it is a fifteen-minute train ride. If you are driving, Agde and Cap d'Agde lie 20 km (12.5 miles) south of Sète by the coast road (N112), and Agde is eight kilometers (five miles) south of the A9 *autoroute*.

PÉZENAS

Pézenas is a tangle of seventeenth-century streets so storybook-perfect that they are often used as a location for *Three Musketeers*-era movies. It was an important place in the career of Molière, and there are many reminders of his presence here. It is 22 km (14 miles) north of Agde.

BACKGROUND

In the seventeenth century, Pézenas was the co-capital of Languedoc with Montpellier, and it was bursting with social activity when the Estates General were in session. From 1650 to 1656, Molière enjoyed the patronage of Prince Armand de Bourbon-Conti, the Governor of Languedoc, and Pézenas became his base during that part of his thirteen-year, self-imposed exile in the provinces. Molière enjoyed spending time in the shop of his friend Gély the barber, where he eavesdropped on the dialogue of the nobles.

GENERAL INFORMATION

The **Tourist Office** (04 67 98 36 40 E-MAIL ot.pezenas @wanadoo.fr is on Place Gambetta in the former barbershop of Gély. Be sure to pick up their excellent brochure on the historical buildings of the town, laid out as a walking tour. It is available in English (10 francs).

WHAT TO SEE AND DO

Pézenas today is a quiet town of 7,600, except when it comes alive for its **Mirandela des Arts et Été du Pays de Pézenas**, a festival of music, dance, and art exhibitions that goes on all summer. But even off-season, Vieux Pézenas is well worth a visit to stroll through its perfectly preserved *Grand Siècle* streets. The **Musée de Vulliod-Saint-Germain** is a beautifully preserved sixteenth-century mansion with a fine collection of period furniture, Aubusson tapestries, and exhibits on Molière. It is open from 10 AM to noon and 2 PM to 5 PM, closed Mondays off-season. **Hôtel d'Alfonce**, where Molière's company performed in 1655 and 1656, is open to the public daily from mid-June to mid-September.

Be sure to try the local specialty, *petits pâtés de Pézenas*, little tubular pies filled with meat, brown sugar, suet, and lemon rind, a sort of mincemeat pie. They were supposedly introduced by Lord Clive in 1768 during a leave he was taking from India. **Aux Palais des Délices**, the Quatrefages family's pastry shop at 1 rue Conti, is the grand master of this savory specialty.

WHERE TO STAY AND EAT

Oddly, downtown Pézenas does not have much to offer in the way of hotels and restaurants, but if you head out to the **Hostellerie de Saint-Alban***** (04 67 98 11 38 FAX 04 67 98 91 63, five kilometers (three miles) south of Pézenas at 31 route d'Agde in the village of **Nézignan-l'Évêque**, you will find a handsome nineteenth-century mansion with a large swimming pool, tennis court, peaceful, shaded grounds, restaurant, and 14 tasteful rooms. Double rooms run 390 to 530 francs at this Relais du Silence member. **Genieys**** (04 67 98 13 99 FAX 04 67 98 04 80, at 9 avenue Aristide-Briand in Pézenas, is a 28-room Logis de France inn, a bit outside the old part of Pézenas, but a comfortable, inexpensive place. **Le Pré Saint-Jean** (04 67 98 15 31, at 18 avenue du Maréchal-Leclerc, near the Place

du 14 Juillet, is a friendly restaurant offering solid regional cuisine (grilled tuna with garlic sauce and *ratatouille*, rack of lamb roasted with herbs) at moderate prices. For the best gourmet cuisine in the area, **Léonce** in Florensac is only 10 km (six miles) south of Pézenas (see WHERE TO STAY AND EAT, page 298, under THE BASSIN DE THAU).

HOW TO GET THERE

Pézenas is 20 km (12 miles) inland from the Bassin de Thau. There are frequent buses from Agde, Béziers, Sète, and Montpellier. By car it is 10 km (six miles) north of the A9 *autoroute*.

BÉZIERS

Unlike Pézenas, which reflects its time, not its place, in Béziers you know exactly where you are: in the South. Its central esplanade, the **Allées Paul-Riquet**, 600 m (almost 2,000 ft) long, shaded by four rows of huge plane trees and punctuated by outdoor cafés, has the look of Las Ramblas in Barcelona, though on a smaller and far mellower scale. Here you start to sense that you are approaching Spain, only 121 km (75 miles) away.

When it comes to bullfighting, "The French Seville," as it likes to be known, is outdone only by

OPPOSITE: The old Languedoc capital of Pézenas has a wealth of elaborate mansions from the seventeenth century, when Molière spent several years there. ABOVE: At the Feria in Béziers in August, the whole town comes alive for the big annual bullfighting event.

Nîmes and Arles in number of *corridas* in a French city. For rugby too — a sport in which Béziers has long been a top international competitor — the fans' passion for the home team is ferocious.

With 70,000 people, Béziers is the Hérault's second largest city, and it is the leading city for wine in this hugely productive wine-growing *département*.

BACKGROUND

During the Pax Romana, Béziers was a wealthy wine-producing colony and a main stop on the Domitian Way. In 1209, it became the tragic scene of the first military action of the Albigensian

Crusade, when the Northern army laid siege to the city. "Nearly twenty thousand were put to the sword, regardless of age and sex," papal legate Arnaud Aumary reported to the pope.

In the seventeenth century, Béziers native Pierre-Paul Riquet's brilliant engineering feat, the Canal du Midi, spurred major growth in the local wine trade and farm exports, and the city finally came back fully from the utter devastation of the Crusade. The Canal du Midi was the greatest engineering feat of its time — a 245-km-long (153-mile) canal linking the Atlantic and the Mediterranean via the Garonne. It has 64 sets of locks, seven bridges that take the canal over natural obstacles and a tunnel under the Ensérune plateau. The brainchild of Baron Riquet (1604–1680), it was begun in 1666 and took 10,000 to 12,000 workers 14 years to complete it. The strain wiped out Riquet physically and financially in the pro-

cess. But the result, which Riquet did not live to see, was a tremendous boon to the economy of the region. Rail and highway transport eventually took away the cargo hauling business, and today *le tourisme fluvial* (floating tourism) accounts for all the traffic, with houseboats and cruise barges plying the peaceful, tree-shaded ribbon of water.

Like the canal, Béziers is a peaceful, tree-shaded little city, pretty, but not terribly exciting except at festival time.

GENERAL INFORMATION

The **Tourist Office** (04 67 28 05 97 is at the Palais des Congrès, 20 avenue Saint-Saëns, two blocks east of the Allées Paul-Riquet. It has good travel literature on the city and the surrounding area, and there is a wine information center, **Béziers-Oenopole** (04 67 76 20 20, with a large display of local wines, abundant documents about vineyards to visit, and a wine bar to sample their wares.

For airport information, call **Béziers-Vias Airport** (04 67 90 99 10. The train station, **Gare SNCF**, can be reached at (08 36 35 35 35; the bus station, **Gare Routière** at (04 67 28 36 41; and **taxis** at (04 67 35 00 85.

Car rental agencies are **Avis** (04 67 28 65 44, **Budget** (04 67 49 38 81, **Europcar** (04 67 62 09 89, **Hertz** (04 67 62 82 00, **Locabest** (04 67 76 41 00, and **Wallgren** (04 67 76 57 46.

For boating on the Canal du Midi, contact **Port Neuf** (04 67 76 26 38.

In case of medical emergencies, contact the **Centre Hospitalier** (04 67 35 70 35 in the ZAC Montimarin, or the **SMUR** (15.

FESTIVALS AND EVENTS

In July the **Festival de Béziers** puts on an all-star program of classical, pop music and jazz, and in the first two weeks of August this normally tranquil city goes wild during the **Feria**, the big bullfighting festival. For details contact the Tourist Office.

WHAT TO SEE AND DO

The fortified **Cathedral of Saint Nazaire** sits on a steep hill above the River Orb. The best view is from below, on the south bank of the river by the end of the Pont Vieux. This is a blocky church, not graceful at all, but impressive, even intimidating — a reflection of the mentality of the Church at the end of the thirteenth century when it built this cathedral to replace the one destroyed in the Albigensian Crusade. Inside, other than a

The thirteenth-century Gothic Cathedral of Saint Nazaire in Béziers, built to replace the earlier one destroyed in the Albigensian Crusade.

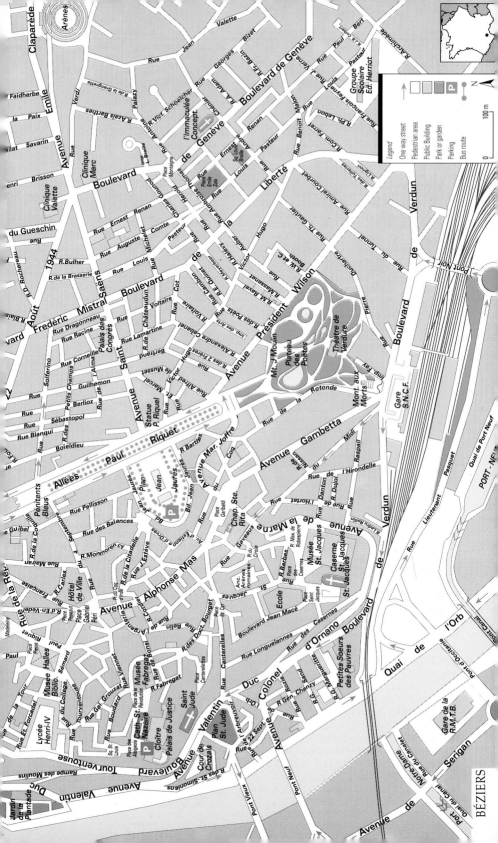

number of handsome stained-glass windows, the church has little to recommend it. But the view from its belvedere has a great deal to offer — the river, a vine-covered plain across which the table-top plateau of Ensérune stands out clearly to the southwest.

The **Musée des Beaux-Arts** near the rear of the cathedral has a heterogeneous collection of European paintings and sculpture from the fif-teenth century to the present, including works by Delacroix, Géricault, Corot, Dufy, Soutine, de Chirico, and Utrillo. It is open daily except Sun-day morning and Monday from 9 AM to noon and 2 PM to 6 PM.

But the most enjoyable thing in Béziers is ob-serving real life along the colorful promenade and in the cafés of the **Allées Paul-Riquet**. The best day to visit Béziers is Friday, when the Allées Paul-Riquet fills up with flowers, and the whole center of the city transforms itself into a vast open mar-ket. Regional food merchants take over Place David-d'Angers, clothes dealers the big Champ de Mars, and bric-a-brac stands spread out in all directions.

The most spectacular locks on the Canal du Midi are the **Écluses de Fonséranes**, better known as the **Neuf Écluses** (Nine Locks), in Béziers's western suburb of Fonséranes. It is reached by D113 and D9 south in the direction of Narbonne. This staircase-like series of nine locks was designed to overcome a 25-m (82-ft) drop in level. A modern water slope parallel to it has replaced the old locks.

Béziers Croisières (04 67 49 08 23 offers daily lunch cruises from Béziers on the Canal du Midi in the summer. **Les Bateaux du Soleil** (04 67 94 08 79, based in Agde, runs half-day lunch cruises from Béziers on Sundays.

Small boats can be rented all along the canal for little rides, and a number of companies rent houseboats for cruises. **Rives de France** (04 67 37 14 60, in Colombiers near Ensérune, has modern houseboats that sleep four, six and eight people, no permits required.

recently renovated little hotel with 10 neat, clean, inexpensive rooms. The Imperator and the Champ de Mars both have garages, important in this town, because parking is a real headache.

WHERE TO STAY

The **Château de Lignan***** (04 67 37 91 47 FAX 04 67 37 99 25, in Lignan-sur-Orb, seven kilometers (about four miles) north of Béziers via D19, is the most attractive hotel in the area. This handsome eighteenth-century château, now an elegant 49-room hotel, sits in a large private park with the Orb River flowing through it. It has a swimming pool, *hammam* (Turkish bath), Jacuzzi, and a gour-met restaurant. Double rooms are 600 to 800 francs. The most stylish downtown hotel is the 45-room **Imperator***** (04 67 49 02 25 FAX 04 67 28 92 30, moderately priced and ideally situated at 28 Allées Paul-Riquet. **Champ de Mars**** (04 67 28 35 53 FAX 04 67 28 61 42, at 17 rue de Metz, is a cheerful,

Camping

You can camp by the Canal du Midi at the 75-place **Berges du Canal** (04 67 39 36 09, a few kilometers east of Béziers in Villeneuve, open all year. The beach town of **Sérignan-Plage** has 17 camping grounds with 4,000 places, and **Valras-Plage** has eight with 1,400 places. They are both about 15 km (nine miles) southeast of Béziers. For information, contact the Tourist Office of Sérignan (04 67 32 42 21 or Valras-Plage (04 67 32 36 04.

WHERE TO EAT

L'Ambassade (04 67 76 06 24, a colorful, friendly, restaurant decorated with frescos of the Roman

countryside, serves a variety of sumptuous *menus de terroir* designed by talented chef Patrick Orly to present the best regional cuisine the Béziers area has to offer. The 130-franc *Menu Approche*, for instance, might include (depending on the season) a starter of tuna *tartare* with sardine marinade, a main course of saddle of hare with wild mushrooms, and one of the house's many desserts. With the more ambitions *Menu Decouverte* at 170 francs, your main course might be the sublime duo of cuttlefish and red mullet, and there will be a dazzling array of cheeses. An even more ambitious *menu* is offered at 330 francs, and to accompany them all, there is a marvelous choice of regional wines. L'Ambassade is at 22 boulevard de Verdun facing the railway station. Another fine restaurant is **Le Jardin (** 04 67 36 41 31, at 37 avenue Jean-Moulin, near the bus station, offering a delicious three-course lunch special of oyster casserole, salmon, and *dorade* (sea bream) with flavored rice,

and homemade sherbet at 135 francs. At the **Bistrot des Halles (** 04 67 28 30 46, at 3 rue Porte Olivier (Place de la Madeleine), you will find simple, tasty dishes such as platters of shellfish, fried mussels, smoked salmon, and *pot-au-feu* (beef simmered with vegetables), with fixed-price *menus* at 78 and 124 francs, wine included.

HOW TO GET THERE

There are four flights a day from Paris to Béziers-Vias Airport. Béziers is on the main line from Paris to Barcelona, and there are several trains a day, via Montpellier, Sète, and Agde. There are also frequent bus connections from Montpellier, the towns of the Bassin de Thau, and Pézenas. By car, Béziers is on the A9 *autoroute* and several other main national (N) and *départemental* (D) routes.

The bridge carrying the Canal du Midi over the River Orb at Béziers.

THE OPPIDUM D'ENSÉRUNE

The **Oppidum d'Ensérune** is a tabletop plateau that rises 120 m (394 ft) above the flat plains 13 km (eight miles) southwest of Béziers. The oppidum was a settlement of the Greeks from Marseille dating from the fourth century BC. A natural fortress, it quickly grew into a sizable town (estimates run up to 10,000), peopled mainly by newly emigrated Gauls. The Oppidum d'Ensérune was destroyed in the third century BC, most likely by Hannibal, but was rebuilt by the Romans when they established their colony at Narbonne. When the Pax Romana

Extraterrestrials must be scratching their heads over this message.

For tourist information, stop at the **Syndicat d'Initiative (** 04 67 37 14 12, 17 avenue d'Espignan, Nissan-lez-Ensérune. The oppidum is reached by N113 from Béziers to the town of Nissan-lez-Ensérune and D162E to the site.

WHERE TO STAY

In the village of Montady on Route D11 overlooking the Étang de Montady, the **Castrum de Montadino (** 04 67 90 66 02 FAX 04 67 90 51 25 E-MAIL aflim@mnet.fr is an ancient watch tower, chapel, and chapter house with three spacious two-bed-

made life on the lowlands safe, the impractical hilltop was abandoned forever.

Extensive ruins of dwellings have been excavated, and since it was an important necropolis for several centuries, digs have yielded many fine ceramic pieces. They are on display in the **museum** on the site, open daily in the summer, closed Tuesdays off-season.

There are panoramas from the oppidum's four observation points of the Cévennes, Béziers, the coastal plain, the Canal du Midi, which runs just south of the oppidum, and Mont Canigou off in the distance. Looking toward Béziers, on the plain just below the oppidum is the curious **Étang de Montady**, a huge former marsh that was drained and turned into a farm field by an order of monks in the thirteenth century. It is shaped like a gigantic pie chart with dozens of narrow wedges of many different shades zeroing in on a disk in the center.

room duplex flats (*gîtes*) and five bed and breakfasts (*chambres d'hôtes*), tastefully converted with all the modern conveniences, and a pool in the garden. The flats are rented by the week, 2,800 francs in July and August, less in the off-season, and the bed and breakfasts go for 350 for either single or double occupancy. Proprietors Jean-Luc and Sarah Pujol are a bright, knowledgeable young couple, fluent in English (Sarah *is* English, in fact). This is an ideal spot to settle down and explore the region.

For a bite to eat while admiring the Étang de Montady, **Restaurant de la Tour (** 04 67 90 50 73, 4 rue des Remparts at the top of the village of Montady, offers spectacular views from its dining terrace.

OPPOSITE: The Canal du Midi, once a vital cargo route, is now used almost exclusively by pleasure craft. ABOVE: The archaeological museum at the Oppidum d'Ensérune has displays dating from the Greek settlement in the fourth century BC.

NARBONNE

At first glance, only Narbonne's powerful cathedral, one of the three loftiest in France, testifies to this city's former importance in the world. But even with that, it is hard to imagine that this pleasant inland city of 47,000 with a secondary branch of the Canal du Midi flowing through it was once a booming Mediterranean port, the capital of Provincia Romana Narbonensis, and the most important city west of Rome itself.

BACKGROUND

Founded by the Romans in 118 BC as their first full-fledged colony between Italy and Spain, Colonia Narbon Martius quickly became a major port and transportation center on the Domitian Way. In 45 BC, Julius Caesar rewarded veterans of his Tenth Legion with properties there, and in 27 BC, it became the capital of Provincia Gallia Narbonensis, ranking with Lyon as the most populous city in Gaul. At the collapse of the Roman Empire, the Visigoths took Narbonne and made it their capital. One warring race after another followed — the Franks, the Saracens, the Franks again under Pépin the Short. Stability returned with the reign of Charlemagne, and under its powerful viscounts and archbishops, Narbonne steered clear of the Cathars and prospered as a port and center of commerce in the early Middle Ages, greatly aided by a productive Jewish colony welcomed by the city.

But in the fourteenth century, everything went wrong: the plague, invasion by the English during the Hundred Years War, the expulsion of the Jews by the Kingdom of France, the silting up of Narbonne's harbor due to a shift in the course of the Aude River and the closing of the Étang de Bages — Narbonne's passage to the sea — by sand bars. Like Aigues-Mortes, Montpellier and other towns along this coast, Narbonne was left high and dry.

With the bulwark of its economy gone, Narbonne faded from the world scene. Its cathedral was never finished. The Canal de la Robine, its connection to the Canal du Midi, was blocked from completion for a century by powerful interests in Béziers and did not reach Narbonne until three years before the French Revolution, by which time, only a few thousand inhabitants remained.

Only in the twentieth century, after the vineyards recovered from the phylloxera epidemic, did Narbonne start to come back, and in the period since World War II it has done very well. It is the main distribution center for the huge wine-growing areas of the Aude, and with its strategic rail and highway connections, has made itself a main transshipment center for manufactured goods. In recent years, it has attracted manufacturing to its modern suburbs as well. Since World War II, Narbonne has edged out Carcassonne as the most populous city in the department of the Aude.

GENERAL INFORMATION

The **Tourist Office (** 04 68 65 15 60 E-MAIL tourisme @mairie-narbonne.fr WEB SITE www.mairie-narbonne.fr is at Place Salengro near the front of the cathedral.

The train station, **Gare SNCF (** 08 36 35 35 35, is on Avenue Carnot, to the north of the center of the city. For **bus information**: call the Tourist Office. Intercity buses stop at the bus station, which is by the Gare SNCF.

Car rental are **ADA (** 04 68 42 44 81, **Avis (** 04 68 32 43 36, **Budget (** 04 68 90 74 64, **Europcar (** 04 68 32 34 54, **Spanghero (** 04 68 32 04 65.

WHAT TO SEE AND DO

The **Cathedral of Saint-Just** is Narbonne's claim to architectural fame. The only Gothic cathedral in Languedoc, it was begun in the thirteenth century after the Albigensian Crusades as a manifestation of the power of the Church, but the completion of the cathedral was blocked by a law suit by the City of Narbonne in 1340, preventing the Church from knocking down a section of the city walls, and the cathedral was never finished. Nevertheless, truncated as its nave is, it boasts of the third highest vault of any Gothic cathedral in France, 41 m (135 ft) in height, surpassed by one meter (just over three feet) by the cathedral of Amiens, and by seven meters (23 ft) by Beauvais cathedral. This is fortress-like Southern Gothic, massive and sturdy, not the lacy flamboyant style so familiar in the North. Its flying buttresses are block-like, not flutelike. The **Treasury**, a subterranean vault reached by a small door between the cathedral and the Chapel of the Annunciation, contains a strange early sixteenth-century Flemish tapestry on the Creation and part of an allegory on prosperity and adversity. It also has a fine collection of illuminated manuscripts and silver religious vessels. It is open daily from 9 AM to 6 PM in July and August, from 9 AM to noon and 2 PM to 6 PM the rest of the year.

The fourteenth-century gothic **cloister**, which has marvelously gruesome gargoyles, connects the cathedral and the **Passage de l'Ancre**, the medieval alley between the two buildings of the **Archbishops' Palace**, the **Palais Vieux** (Old Palace) on the side next to the cathedral and the **Palais**

Narbonne's graceful walkway along the Canal de la Robine and its soaring Southern Gothic Cathedral of Saint-Just.

Neuf (New Palace) across the passage. In the **Cour de la Madeleine** of the Palais Vieux stands the bell tower of the long-disappeared Church of Saint-Théorodat, its ninth-century rectilinear austerity contrasting with the maze of flying buttresses on the cathedral beyond.

The excellent **Musée Archéologique** is in the Palais Vieux, but is entered through the courtyard of the Palais Neuf. Unfortunately, all Narbonne's Roman buildings were torn down over the centuries and their stones recycled into other buildings, but pieces of them have survived and are displayed here. They include bas-reliefs from triumphal arches and sarcophagi, and there are models of Roman Narbonne. The museum also has artifacts

from as far back as the Paleolithic era. It is open daily from 9:30 AM to 12:15 PM and 2 PM to 6 PM, May to September, closed Mondays in the winter, and national holidays.

The larger Palais Neuf, dating mainly from the fourteenth century, contains the sumptuous apartments of the archbishops, redone in the seventeenth and eighteenth centuries, that now house the **Musée d'Art et d'Histoire**. Most of the art collection belonged to the archbishops. There are interesting paintings by Pieter Brueghel the Younger, Canaletto, and Salvatore Rosa, a large number of Montpellier apothecary jars, and an outstanding collection of ceramic tableware from Montpellier, Marseille, and Moustiers from the golden age of French *faïence* (glazed, painted earthenware) in the eighteenth century. It keeps the same hours as the Musée Archéologique.

If you are willing to walk up the 179 steps to the top of the massive thirteenth-century **Donjon Gilles Aycelin**, you will be rewarded with an excellent view of the cathedral, the red tile-roofed city, the hills of the Clape, the Corbières, and the Pyrénées. It is open daily from 10 AM to 6 PM in the July and August, from 10 AM to noon and 2 PM to 5 PM the rest of the year.

Wedged in between the Palais Vieux and the Palais Neuf on the Place de l'Hôtel de Ville is the nineteenth-century neo-Gothic **Hôtel de Ville** (town hall) designed by Viollet-le-Duc.

Narbonne is a very pleasant city to stroll in, especially along the plane tree-shaded park on both sides of the **Canal de la Robine**. The **Pont des Marchands** just below the Hôtel de Ville is lined with little shops. Just south of the canal on the Cours Mirabeau is the **Halles de Narbonne**, a big cast-iron, stone, and mostly glass pavilion from the year 1900 that is one of the most attractive and highest quality covered markets in all of France. There are plenty of cafés where you can have an inexpensive lunch and sample the wine of the region.

Excursions

In July and August, **Le Coche d'Eau** (04 68 90 63 98 or 04 68 49 12 40 (out-of-season), runs passenger barge cruises down the Canal de la Robine and out into the Étang de Bages et the Étang de Sigean, ending up at Port-la-Nouvelle on the Golfe du Lion. The boat leaves the Cours Mirabeau at 9:30 AM Monday, Wednesday, Friday, and Sunday, and arrives at Port-la-Nouvelle at 5:30 PM. The fare is 120 francs for adults plus 20 francs for the return trip to Narbonne by bus, 60 francs for children plus 10 francs for the bus. Food and drink prices on the boat are reasonable. More localized trips lasting two or three hours are also available on most days. Check at the Tourist Office.

You can **rent houseboats** and cruise on the Canal du Midi, or if you have ten days to spare, cruise up through the Camargue via the Canal du Rhône à Sète and turn the boat in at Beaucaire. **Connoisseur Cruises** (04 68 65 14 55, at 7 quai d'Alsace can arrange this.

Weekends and holidays from July through September, the *Autorail Touristique du Minervois* (04 68 27 05 94 WEB SITE www.multimedia.com/autor, makes trips from Narbonne to Bize-Minervois 20 km (12.5 miles) away, with stops at Sallèles de l'Aude to tour **Amphoralis**, a pottery museum on the site of a large Gallo-Roman pottery center, at the highly respected **Oulibo olive oil cooperative** at Cabezac to taste regional foods, and at Bize to see a seventeenth-century **textile mill** created by Colbert. The train leaves Narbonne at 2:30 PM and gets back at 7 PM. The fare is 56 francs. The station in Narbonne is on Rue Paul-Vieu near the Gendarmerie.

AROUND NARBONNE

Narbonne is the gateway to the *département* of the Aude. The Corbières starts immediately to the southwest, and the Minervois and Carcassonne are less than an hour's drive to the west. But there are some unusual drives to be made in the vicinity of Narbonne itself too.

Montagne de la Clape and Gruissan

The Montagne de la Clape is valuable wine country, and the growers cultivate little parcels far up into the piney hills between Narbonne and the coast 12 km (seven and a half miles) away. Its high-

est peak, 214 m (700 ft) **Pech Redon**, towers over the lagoons and flat vineyard-covered plains. Among the most distinguished makers of *AOC* Coteaux du Languedoc la Clape and the most picturesque to visit, with a truly magnificent *cave*, is **Château Pech-Céleyran** (04 68 33 50 04 WEB SITE www.logassist.fr / pech-celeyran, in Salles d'Aude at the northern end of La Clape, owned by the Count of Saint-Exupéry, a cousin of *The Little Prince's* author.

Domaine de l'Hospitalet (04 68 45 34 47 WEB SITE www.Nice.accommodation.hospitalet.com, founded in 1561, sits amid 1,000 hectares (2,400 acres) of vines, pines, olive trees and *garrigue* on hills in the heart of La Clape overlooking the Mediterranean; it is reached by D186 from Narbonne. It has a huge subterranean wine cellar, 16 small museums (winemaking, flora, fauna, minerals, fossils, classic cars), a crafts

village with potters, straw weavers, artisanal food producers, and papermakers, a 22-room inn, seven *gîtes*, a swimming pool, and a very good restaurant, the **Auberge des Vignes** (04 68 45 28 50, supervised by distinguished chef David Moreno.

Elegant **Château Pech Redon** (04 68 90 41 22 is on the southern end of the range, off D32, the road to Gruissan. These marvelous wines, little-known overseas, are well-worth making the effort to discover. They come in whites and rosés, but are best-known for their smooth, dark, spicy reds.

The fishing village of Gruissan on the Mediterranean side of La Clape, inhabited since the

dawn of history, has managed to retain much of its charm. Its little ochre-roofed houses form concentric circles around the hilltop ruins of its **Tour Barberousse**. Amid the bland modern beach resorts that have sprung up along the Languedoc coast in the past 20 years, this old village is a gem. Flamingos can often be seen wading in the **Étang de Gruissan**. There is no problem finding good seafood here. Two tried-and-true choices are **L'Estagnol** (04 68 49 01 27, with a terrace overlooking the Étang, and **La Marée** (04 68 49 16 26, in the heart of the village. Both are moderately priced.

On June 29 Gruissan celebrates the **Fête de Saint-Pierre** (Feast of Saint Peter) with vespers, blessing of the fishing fleet, wreaths of flowers

Narbonne's Archbishops' Palace LEFT, covered food market CENTER, and a quiet downtown street RIGHT.

cast into the water to commemorate sailors lost at sea, and at night there is a popular ball.

The **Tourist Office (** 04 68 49 03 25, in Gruissan is at Boulevard du Pech Maynaud. To get to La Clape and Gruissan from Narbonne, take D32, the Route de Gruissan. Gruissan is 17 km (11 miles) from Narbonne.

La Réserve Africaine de Sigean

The African Reserve of Sigean **(** 04 68 48 20 20 WEB SITE www.pageszoom.com/reserve-sigean has more than 3,500 animals living in nature on its 300-hectare (720-acre) simulated African range. There is a six-kilometer (four-mile) drive through the African savanna where you can see families

of lions and elephants, rhinos, giraffes, zebras, monkeys, ostriches — 157 species in all. The park attracts over 300,000 visitors a year. It is opens at 9 AM daily all year. The cost is 99 francs for adults, 78 francs for children four to 14 years old. A sure-fire attraction if you are traveling with kids. It is 15 km (nine miles) south of Narbonne via N9.

L'Abbaye de Fontfroide

The large, beautifully restored Abbey of Fontfroide **(** 04 68 45 11 08, a 14-km (nine-mile) drive south-west of Narbonne, is an oasis of greenery amid the parched limestone hills of the Corbières. Set in a little wooded valley with cypresses all around it, the place has a distinctly Tuscan air. The abbey was founded by Benedictines at the end of the eleventh century and prospered immediately. It affiliated itself with the Cistercians in 1146. Fontfroide became a bastion of Catholic orthodoxy against the Cathar movement. In fact, the murder of one of its monks, papal legate Pierre de Castelnau at Saint-Gilles in 1208, set off the Albigensian Crusade.

The abbey's main buildings, made of pink and ochre sandstone from the Corbières, date from the twelfth and thirteenth centuries — the church with its 18-m (60-ft) barrel-vaulted nave, the lovely cloister with double rows of marble columns and

capitals sculpted in floral motifs, along with the **chapter hall**, **refectory**, **kitchen**, **dormitory**, and **cellars**. The abbey owned vast farms and vineyards, with 30,000 hectares (72,000 acres) of land under cultivation and a flock of 20,000 sheep, and was a power in the region. One of its members became Benedict XII, Pope of Avignon from 1334 to 1342. From the fifteenth century on, the abbey declined, and it was abandoned in 1791. In the late nineteenth century, Cistercians from Sénanque tried to revive it, but gave up in 1901. Luckily, a philanthropic family of the area, the Fayets, bought the deteriorating abbey in 1908 and started its tasteful restoration. There is a **rose garden** with more than 3,000 bushes. Concerts are held at the abbey from June through September. Open all year.

The gourmet restaurant La Bergerie de Fontfroide and the bistro Les Cuisiniers Vignerons are on the left as you enter the grounds of the abbey (see WHERE TO STAY AND EAT, below).

WINE TASTING

Narbonne is the commercial center of a huge winemaking area with *appellations* that include Corbières, Minervois, La Clape, and Fitou along with non-*AOC* wine sold mostly as *Vin de Pays d'Oc*. In the past this area was known almost exclusively for the cheap table wine it produced for the French working man (with the exception of Fitou, an *AOC* since 1948), but it has made giant steps in quality in the past 20 years, and today is one of the most dynamic wine-growing areas in France. The large modern **Palais du Vin (** 04 68 41 47 20 E-MAIL palais.duvin@wanadoo.fr, just south of central Narbonne on the Route de Perpignan (N9), represents 2,500 wine makers and offers free wine tasting, literature and help on planning wine routes. It is open daily.

Serious students of wine should take a run out to Lézignan-Corbières, 20 km (12.5 miles) west of Narbonne on Route N113 to visit the **Musée de la Vigne et du Vin (** 04 68 27 07 57. It is a large nineteenth-century winemaking estate that was converted into a museum in 1973 with old tools and machinery, a big vat for crushing grapes by feet, wagons, storage cellars, and the family's home. There is free wine tasting and abundant literature. It is at 3 rue Turgot opposite the Lézignan-Corbières railway station. Open daily all year.

WHERE TO STAY AND EAT

Downtown Narbonne

La Résidence* (** 04 68 32 19 41 FAX 04 68 65 51 82, at 6 rue 1er Mai, a pretty nineteenth-century town house on a quiet street in the center of the city, has 26 tasteful rooms at moderate rates, with 420 francs the top price for a double. The big pink **Grand**

Hôtel de la Dorade** (04 68 32 65 95 FAX 04 68 65 81 62 E-MAIL investor.europa@laposte.fr, at 44 rue Jean-Jaurès overlooking the Canal de la Robine in the heart of the city, is a Narbonne institution, founded in 1648. It has 30 comfortable, modernized rooms at 300 francs tops for a double. Its **Villa Romaine** restaurant serves good regional food at honest prices. At the **Hôtel de France** (04 68 32 09 75 FAX 04 68 65 50 30, at 6 rue Rossini near the market, you will find 11 neat, inexpensive rooms. All the in-town hotels mentioned have garages.

The top restaurant in town is **La Table Saint-Crescent** (04 68 41 37 37, at the Palais du Vin (see WINE TASTING, above). Among chef Claude Giraud's best-known specialties are crème froide de coco

Around Narbonne

The most glamorous and expensive hotel in the Narbonne area is the **Château de Villefalse** (04 68 48 54 29 FAX 04 68 48 34 37, in Sigean, 16 km (10 miles) to the south of the city. It is a luxurious health-oriented resort in a nineteenth-century mansion in the middle of a vineyard with 15 sumptuous rooms and suites with canopy beds and 10 modern duplex suites in a new annex, a large pool, tennis courts, and a state-of-the-art fitness center. Room rates are in the expensive category. It also has a first-rate restaurant serving gourmet cuisine of the region.

Relais du Val d'Orbieu (04 68 27 10 27 FAX 04 68 27 52 44, just outside the village of Ornaisons,

cassoulet (a cold cream soup made of cassoulet beans and olives), écrivisses (freshwater crayfish) and black olives served with shellfish-flavored risotto, and roasted guinea fowl with a light mustard sauce. Prices are very reasonable for a gourmet restaurant with a Michelin star. The three-course weekday lunch menu goes for 100 francs, others for 148 and 248 francs. Corbières and Limoux wines are featured. Closed Sunday nights and Mondays. Reservations are a must.

Alsace (04 68 32 01 86, at 2 boulevard Carnot across the street from the train station, serves excellent fish and shellfish dishes, with a lunch special weekdays at 98 francs. Closed Tuesdays.

L'Estangol (04 68 65 09 27, at 5bis rue Marceau near the beautiful 100-year-old town market, is a good, lively, reasonably priced brasserie popular with Narbonnais and Narbonnaises of all walks of life.

14 km (nine miles) west of Narbonne by N113, is a delightful country inn with gardens, a large pool, tennis court, two hectares (five acres) of land, a restaurant, and 20 spacious rooms at moderate to slightly expensive rates.

David Moreno, one of the top chefs of Languedoc, has two eating places on the grounds of the magnificent Abbaye de Fontfroide, 14 km (nine miles) southeast of the city (see AROUND NARBONNE, above). At the gastronomic restaurant **La Bergerie de Fontfroide (David Moreno)** (04 68 41 68 06, you may sample refined Corbières cuisine de terroir in an unforgettable setting, either in the tastefully converted medieval stone shepherd's barn, very airy with its vaulted ceiling and picture windows,

OPPOSITE: The African Reserve of Sigean has 3,500 animals living in natural habitats. ABOVE: The Promenade des Barques in Narbonne, for cruises on the Canal de la Robine and the coastal lagoons.

or on the lovely garden terrace surrounded by olive trees. Tomato and shrimp gaspacho, fricassee of *fèves* (broad beans) with truffles, or peppers with anchovies are a few of the starters. The cardamom roasted duckling and the rack of lamb in its own juice flavored with thyme are popular main courses. The desserts are astounding, and the array of regional wines could hardly be improved upon. Fixed-price *menus* run 170 and 350 francs. This is a Michelin one-star restaurant, much in demand. You must reserve. La Bergerie is open for dinner only.

For lunch, **Les Cuisiniers Vignerons**, a bistro in the same building, offers tasty fixed-price lunches ranging from 84 francs (on weekdays) to

78-place **Camping Grange Neuve** (04 68 48 58 70, on the Route Réserve Africaine, open all year.

HOW TO GET THERE

The Béziers-Agde Airport is 36 km (22 miles) to the north and has four flights a day from Paris. Narbonne is a main railway interchange, where the line between Paris and Barcelona connects with the line between Narbonne to Toulouse, and there are frequent train connections with Montpellier, Béziers, Carcassonne, Perpignan and other cities of the area. Courriers du Midi has a regular bus line to Narbonne via Pézenas and Béziers, continuing on to Perpignan. However there is very

140 francs, or à la carte — the ideal place to eat while visiting the abbey.

Both restaurants are open from March 1 to the end of November, closed Mondays except in July and August.

Camping

The camping grounds of the region are mainly at the beach. There are three at Narbonne Plage: the deluxe **Camping Municipal La Falaise** (04 68 49 80 77, with 380 places; **Camping le Soleil d'Oc** (04 68 49 86 21, with 208 places; and the large 808 place **Camping Municipal Côtes des Roses** (04 68 49 83 65, on the Route de Gruissan. They are open from April to the end of September, very crowded in midsummer. In Gruissan, **Camping les Ayguades** (04 68 49 81 59 has 361 places and is open from March 1 to the end of October. At Sigean, the best equipped camping ground is the

little bus service between different parts of the Aude. To get around, you need your own transportation. Coming by car, Narbonne is at the junction of the area's two main thruways, the north–south A9 and the east–west A61.

THE CORBIÈRES

If we were to think of Languedoc as a living organism, its brain would be Montpellier, its stomach the Carcassonne to Castelnaudary *cassoulet* belt, its sex glands presumably Cap d'Agde, and its heart and soul the Corbières. This sun-blasted range of rugged limestone hills in the center of the Aude *département*, famed for its potent red wines, is also a land of savage beauty with historical sites that are unbelievably dramatic — the "citadels of vertigo," the cliff-top fortresses, that were the last refuges of the Cathars during the

Albigensian Crusade, where the "perfects" serenely, even cheerfully, plunged into the bonfires rather than give up their faith.

The hills of the Corbières start immediately to the southwest of Narbonne. They are bounded on the east by the narrow plain along the Gulf of Lion that runs 50 km (30 miles) south from Narbonne to Salses. On the south, the border is formed by the Agly River and the Fenouillèdes, foothills of the Pyrénées. The western and northern borders are defined by the Aude River, which flows north from the Pyrénées to Carcassonne, then elbows eastward to the Mediterranean above Narbonne, with the Canal du Midi, the *Autoroute des Deux Mers*, and N113 running along its valley.

In the Corbières, we have scenery, wine, history, and adventure — the chance to drive, ride bikes or horses, or hike miles and miles along *garrigue*-scented backcountry roads without seeing another car or person and explore magnificent sites only serious travelers get to. It is an area yet to be corrupted by mass tourism, perhaps because the spirit of the Cathars lives on. However, since there are so few tourists, there are also few tourist facilities. Hotels, restaurants and — be warned — service stations are few and far between. If you are exploring the Corbières by car, keep your eye on the fuel gauge and tank up frequently.

Most travelers dip into the Corbières from the cities on three of its corners — Narbonne on the northeast, Carcassonne on the northwest, and Perpignan on the southeast. Narbonne has a good range of hotels and restaurants, and Carcassonne and Perpignan offer creature comforts that should please even the most sybaritic of softies.

CHÂTEAU DE LASTOURS

A good start exploring the Corbières is the Château de Lastours (04 68 48 29 17 www.epicuria.fr/chateau-lastours, in Portel-des-Corbières, a few kilometers to the west of the African Reserve of Sigean via D611A. It is one of the region's most highly rated vineyards, making a wide range of wines, from robust aged *AOC* Corbières reds and bright *blanc de blancs* to this year's pale pink *vin gris*, a lifesaver when served chilled in the ovenlike summers around here. Besides its award-winning wines, the Château deserves high praise for its farsighted employment policy of providing work at fair pay in a stable community framework for mentally handicapped people, enabling them to lead independent lives. The village has become a cultural center for the area with concerts and art exhibitions the year round, and racing teams train for the Paris to Dakar cross-Sahara auto race in the 600 hectares (1,400 acres) of canyons and *garrigue* that surround the château's 160 hectares (385 acres) of vines. There is a good, attractive, moderately priced restaurant, **La Bergerie**.

According to Corbières folk wisdom, vines must "suffer" to produce grapes that make good wine. If there ever was a place for that, it is this arid, rocky, sun-blasted terrain swept often by the *tramontane*, a wind that can blow for days at a time. Only two things will grow here, the fragrant tangle of scrub brush, rosemary, thyme, lavender and wild flowers known as *garrigue* for one, and the grape vine for the other. Science has yet to resolve the mystery of how the flavors and aromas of other plants in the vicinity get into the grape, but they do it somehow, and the proof is found in the wine.

DURBAN AND THE EASTERN CORBIÈRES

The old fortified village of Durban-Corbières lies 12 km (seven and a half miles) west of Portel-des-Corbières via D611. Part of its fourteenth-century ramparts remains, as does one wall of its eleventh-century **Château des Seigneurs de Durban** on the hill in the center of town, very impressive nonetheless.

For wine, drive down to the **Cave Pilote de Villeneuve-les-Corbières** (04 68 45 91 59, four kilometers (two and a half miles) south of Durban on D611. This pioneering cooperative with 50 member vineyards was formed in 1948 to experiment and improve quality, and has become one of the region's most consistent producers of fine wines. They make five blends of Fitou reds, Corbières reds, whites and rosés, Muscat de Rivesaltes, and *vin de pays*. The *cave* is open daily in the summer from 10 AM to 12:30 PM and 2 PM to 5 PM. Off-season it's open from 8:15 AM to noon and 2 PM to 6 PM.

For cuisine, head for the **Auberge du Vieux Puits** (04 68 44 07 37, in the village of Fontjoncouse, where ingenious young chef Gilles Goujon creates dishes that exude the subtle flavors of the fresh herbs, plants, meats, fruit and vegetables of his native Corbières and points South, with fish from the nearby Mediterranean. Try his half-salted cod cooked with *calçotade* (little native onions) and *piquillo* (mild Spanish peppers), or in hunting season, one of the wild game dishes that are featured, washed down by a fine Corbières wine from the rich cellar. Gilles's charming wife Marie-Christine Goujon manages the attractive dining room, done in soothing pale yellow and light ochre tones. The fixed-price weekday lunch *menu* is 165 francs, at other times the *menu* is 320 francs. This is a Michelin one-star restaurant. Reserve a table as long as possible in advance. People come from Narbonne, Carcassonne, and all over the region to eat here.

To get to Fontjoncouse from Durban, take D611 to the north 11 km (seven miles) and then turn east on D123.

The sun-blasted hills of the Corbières, a land of wine, history, adventure, and savage beauty.

VILLEROUGE-TERMENÈS

As usual around here, this village in the heart of the Corbières is dominated by a medieval castle. What's unusual about Villerouge-Termenès is the big **medieval pageant** it puts on in the summer. The pageant is based on the tragic story of Guilhem Bélibaste, the last of the Cathar "perfects," burned at the stake here in 1321. It is held every Saturday in midsummer, and there are **medieval-style feasts**. For information and schedules, contact Festival Médiéval (04 68 70 06 24.

The eagle's nest Cathar fortress of **Termes** is 13 km (eight miles) west of town via D613 and D40. Its setting overlooking the Gorges of the Terminet is dramatic, but the fortress itself is in a state of utter ruin. Be careful if you decide to climb up there: the terrain is very rough and is considered dangerous. The fortress of Termes resisted the army and siege engines of Simon de Montfort for four months in 1210, but finally fell because of lack of water. It is one of the so-called "Five Sons of Carcassonne," (see THE CATHAR FORTRESSES, page 328).

What little lodging there is in the area is in *chambres d'hôtes* (bed and breakfasts) and *gîtes* (country cottages). For information, call **ADHCO** (04 68 42 77 00, in the nearby village of Mouthoumet. In the pretty village of Davejean seven kilometers (four miles) south of Villerouge-Termenès, **Madame Tavard** (04 68 70 01 85 rents two pleasant *chambres d'hôtes* with private baths, at 160 francs for a double, breakfast included, and meals are 60 francs. The nearest hotel and camping grounds are in Lagrasse, 13 km (eight miles) to the north.

The direct route from Durban-Corbières to Villerouge-Termenès is via the small but perfectly adequate D40, a distance of 20 km (12.5 miles) due west from Durban. The better choice from the gastronomic point of view would be to take the parallel roads a few miles to the north (D323 to D613) via Fontjoncouse, with a stop for lunch at the Auberge du Vieux Puits (see above).

LAGRASSE

The **Abbey of Lagrasse** in Lagrasse on Route D3 in north-central Corbières is even older than the Abbey of Fontfroide. Founded by Charlemagne himself around the year 800, it became rich thanks to gifts and privileges, and by the twelfth century owned lands as far afield as Béziers and Toulouse. Between them, the Abbeys of Lagrasse and Fontfroide owned most of the Corbières. In the fourteenth century, the Black Plague and the Black Prince Edward put an abrupt end to the prosperity. In the seventeenth century, the Saint-Maur order took over the abbey and restored it spiritually and financially, but during the revolution, it

was split in two and sold off. While it is no match architecturally for Fontfroide, the Abbey of Lagrasse has handsome buildings from both its prosperous times, and the village has two ancient bridges, one a "donkey back" from the twelfth century, the ruins of its ramparts, old houses, and a good market. The abbey can be visited daily from 10 AM to 12:30 PM and 2:30 PM to 6:30 PM in summer, from 2 PM to 5 PM the rest of the year.

The **Tourist Office** (04 68 43 11 56 is at 6 boulevard de la Promenade.

The **Auberge Saint-Hubert** (04 68 43 15 22 FAX 04 68 43 16 56, at 9 boulevard de la Promenade, has seven clean, pleasant, inexpensive rooms and a modestly priced restaurant serving regional fare. It is a Logis de France member. The **Auberge des Trois Grâces** (04 68 43 18 17, at 5 rue du Quai, rents three modest rooms at inexpensive rates.

Camping Boucocers Bachandres (04 68 43 10 05 is an attractive site with 40 places a few kilometers south of town, open from the beginning of March to the end of October.

To get to Lagrasse from Narbonne, take N113 west to Lézignan-Corbières (where you can visit the Musée de la Vigne et du Vin, see WINE TASTING, page 316, under NARBONNE) and D611 and D212 southwest to Lagrasse, 38 km (24 miles) in total. From Villerouge-Termenès, access Villerouge-Termenès, take D613, D23, and D3 to the north, a distance of 13 km (eight miles).

CARCASSONNE

Carcassonne is the largest medieval fortress city in Europe. Its twin rings of tall, massive crenellated walls measure three kilometers (nearly two miles) in circumference, and there are 52 mighty towers. It is one of the Old Continent's most unforgettable sights. Legend has it that when Edward the Black Prince arrived with his army in 1355, he took one look at the fortress and decided to move on (after sacking and burning the unwalled lower town first, naturally). Until the advent of the canon, it was considered impregnable. Hence its nickname, the "Maiden of Languedoc."

La Cité, as the walled city on the hill is called, looks down on the flat, grid-patterned Ville Basse —the Lower Town—on the left bank of the Aude. The Lower Town dates from the thirteenth century and prospered after the opening of the Canal du Midi, which runs through it. Today virtually all of Carcassonne's 43,500 people live in the Lower Town. It is the center of the area's wine trade, agroindustries and light manufacturing, and is the capital of the Aude department. Fewer than 100 people actually live year-round in the Cité.

The medieval Cité is particularly dramatic on summer nights, when it is illuminated, and even more so on July 14, when there is a tremendous fireworks display.

BACKGROUND

The earliest inhabitants of Carcassonne were Iberians whose traces date from the sixth century BC. They were supplanted by Germanic Volcae Tectosages in the fourth century BC. The Romans took it over and built their first fortress here in 122 BC, the year after they conquered Vaison-la-Romaine and established Aix-en-Provence and four years before they founded their colony at Narbonne. Their objective was to control the pass between the Montagne Noire and the Corbières, the strategic bottleneck on the only trade route between the Atlantic to the Mediterranean.

But all this changed abruptly in the early thirteenth century, when 24 year-old Viscount Raymond Roger Trencavel stepped forward to defend the many Cathars in his domains, defying Pope Innocent III. In August, 1209, after the fall of Béziers, Simon de Montfort and his army laid siege to Carcassonne. Violating a safe conduct for negotiations, de Montfort took Raymond Roger prisoner, and Carcassonne surrendered. Three months later, Raymond Roger died in his cell, and Simon de Montfort became Viscount of Carcassonne. After de Montfort was killed at the siege of Toulouse in 1218, his son Amaury was unable to maintain control of the lands and turned Carcassonne over to King Louis VIII in

Carcasso, as the Romans called their new oppidum, prospered for five centuries under the Pax Romana.

In the middle of the fifth century, as the Empire crumbled, the Visigoths overran Languedoc and Spain. They held Carcassonne until the Saracens swept up from Spain in 725, took it and renamed it Karkashuna. In 759, Pépin the Short, the King of the Franks and father of Charlemagne, descended from the North and chased them back to Spain. After the breakup of Charlemagne's empire, the Trencavel family ruled Carcassonne as vassals of the Counts Toulouse, and it became a thriving merchant town. Being Viscounts of Albi, Béziers and Nîmes in addition from 1082 to 1209, the Trencavels became very rich, and their court in Carcassonne was one of the brightest of the Age of the Troubadours.

1223. From then on, except when the Wehrmacht took it over during World War II, it has been under French rule.

Though there are some parts of Roman walls and extensive sections built by the Visigoths, most of what we see today dates from the thirteenth and fourteenth centuries, when Saint Louis, Philip the Bold, and Philip the Fair made the Cité a paragon of medieval defensive architecture. But the development of artillery made all medieval fortifications obsolete. When the Treaty of the Pyrénées in 1659 made the Pyrénées the frontier between France and Spain, Carcassonne lost its strategic importance. The Cité deteriorated, and by the time of the Revolution had became a virtual ghost town, with the whole social and economic life taking place in the Lower Town, where, thanks to the

The elegant Hôtel de la Cité within the walls of the medieval city of Carcassonne.

Canal du Midi, the linen and wine trades were booming. By the 1830s, all the roofs of the fortress had caved in and the walls had become dangerously dilapidated, and the government ordered it to be demolished. But local archaeologist Jean-Pierre Cros-Mayrevieille, writer Prosper Mérimée, then Inspector of Public Monuments, and architectural restorer Viollet-le-Duc mounted a successful campaign to save it.

About 30% of the Cité as it stands today, mainly the roofs and upper levels, is the work of Viollet-le-Duc. It has been controversial right from the start. Too medieval storybook romantic say the purists, especially the treatment of the roofs and turrets. The original roofs, it seems, were red tile, not slate. Such inaccuracies are easy to forgive, though, when you consider that if it hadn't been for those men, La Cité de Carcassonne would no longer exist. It was just in the nick of time that they managed to convince the Louis Philippe government to save it. Some of the demolition work had already begun.

GENERAL INFORMATION

The main **Tourist Office** (04 68 10 24 35 is at 15 boulevard Camille-Pelletan at Square Gambetta in the Lower Town. A sub-office in the Cité (04 68 10 24 36, just inside the Porte Narbonnaise, is open from Easter through November. For information about hiking, horseback riding, sports, and accommodations in other parts of the Aude, contact the **Comité Départemental du Tourisme de l'Aude** (04 68 11 66 00 FAX 04 68 11 66 01 E-MAIL Cdt.aude .Pays.cathare@wanadoo.fr, Conseil Général de l'Aude, Plateau de Grazailles, 11855 Carcassonne Cedex 09.

For airport information, contact **Carcassonne-De Salvaza Airport** (04 68 71 96 46. The train station, **Gare SNCF** (08 36 35 35 35, is at the northern end of Rue Maréchal-Joffre. The bus station, **Gare Routière** (04 68 25 12 74, is on Boulevard de Varsovie on the west side of town. For **taxis**, call (04 68 71 50 50.

Car rental agencies in town are **ADA** (04 68 11 71 92, **Avis** (04 68 25 05 84, **Budget** (04 68 72 31 31, **Europcar** (04 68 25 05 09, **Hertz** (04 68 25 41 26, and **MLS** (04 68 47 70 00.

Bicycle rental is available at the baggage room of the **Gare SNCF** (04 68 71 79 14 or **Fun Sports** (04 68 71 67 06, 14 rue J. Monet.

In case of **health emergencies** contact **SAMU** (15 or the **Hospital Center** (04 68 24 24 24 on Route Saint-Hilaire.

Le Petit Train de la Cité tourist train makes a 20-minute circuit of the Cité from May 1 to September 30.

Carcassonne, Europe's largest medieval fortress city, was saved from demolition in the early nineteenth century by pioneering landmark conservationists.

FESTIVALS AND EVENTS

The **Festival de la Cité** is a month-long program of music, theater, and dance events held during the month of July. On the **July 14** there is a spectacular fireworks display. During the first two weeks of August, **Les Médiévales**, a grand costume pageant, takes over the city. For more information contact the Tourist Office.

WHAT TO SEE AND DO

The view of the **Cité** standing out against the skyline can't help but impress even the most jaded of travelers. But for a full appreciation of the massive stone walls and 52 towers and the ingenuity of their design, I suggest taking the *Petit Train de la Cité*'s 20-minute **circuit of the walls**, which leaves from the main gate, the Porte Narbonnaise. The trip will take you through the *lices* (the lists), the fortress's most effective defensive feature. This is a wide, barren space between the outer and inner rings of walls in which any attacker who managed to make it over the outer wall would have no place to hide from the projectiles rained down on him by defenders atop the inner wall. In times when the city was not under attack, the *lices* were used for jousting. About 500 m (nearly 550 yards) to the right of the Porte Narbonnaise you will see a section of wall dating from late Roman Empire (fourth century AD), identifiable by its small gray stones broken by courses of red bricks, in contrast to the large rectangular stones of the medieval period. If you have the time to explore the walls on foot, all the better.

The **Porte Narbonnaise** is so-named because it faces east toward Narbonne. Built at the most vulnerable point of the fortress, it has two massive round bastions flanking a drawbridge and a portal, which was barred in the old days by a heavy chain and two iron portcullises. It dates from the time of Philip the Bold and was the only entrance wide enough for a carriage. Inside the gate, the narrow, cobblestone main street, **Rue Cros-Mayrevieille**, picturesque, but overloaded with souvenir shops, leads directly to the **Château Comtal**. This nine-towered castle was built by the Counts of Trencavel in the twelfth century and is surrounded by mighty walls and a moat of its own. The château is open daily from 9 AM to 7:30 PM in July and August, shorter hours off-season. The château is visited by guided tour only, and it is well worth taking, even if you don't speak French. It leads you through the **Lapidary Museum**, which has sculptures and carved stones from the Roman and medieval periods, out through courtyards and up along the top of the walls of the city, which adjoin the château's walls at one point. The view of the Cité and the countryside is spectacular from here.

The **Basilique de Saint-Nazaire** (Basilica of Saint Nazaire) started as a Romanesque cathedral, built between 1096 and 1130, and a barrel-vaulted nave supported by two side aisles with semi-circular vaults remain from that period, but the transept and choir are Gothic, built after the Albigensian Crusade. So is the church's most glorious feature, its fourteenth-century rose windows. Simon de Montfort's tombstone can also be seen in the church, but his body was removed from the cathedral in 1224 and buried in the North to prevent desecration. The basilica lost its cathedral status in 1803 when the bishopric was transferred to the Lower Town, where the church of Saint Michel became the cathedral.

The **Lower Town**, or "New Town" (it's only 800 years old) was laid out in a grid pattern by Louis IX in the mid-thirteenth century (like Aigues-Mortes, built at the same time), and the utter regularity of the streets gives it a feeling of monotony. This is, however, the place where practically all Carcassonne's 43,500 people live, a commercial and transportation hub (for train, bus, and canal traffic), and the capital of the Aude *département*, where there are good hotels and restaurants (generally much less expensive than in the Cité), a lively market on Tuesdays, Thursdays, and Saturdays, and a number of handsome seventeenth- and eighteenth-century mansions to visit, aided by a free map you can pick up from the main Tourist Office, which is also down here.

Carcassonne is one of three cities famous for *cassoulet*, a rich, very filling casserole of white beans and preserved meats baked in an earthenware pot called a *cassole*. The other two cities are Castelnaudary and Toulouse. All use as their base the white beans (*haricots blancs*) grown in the Lauragais countryside surrounding Castelnaudary. Essentially the differences among them reside in the meats used — various combinations of goose or duck parts conserved in their own grease, sausages, mutton, lamb, or pork. In Carcassonne's style, you will find mutton, and sometimes partridge during the hunting season. A war of words has raged for centuries over which of the three styles is the superior. This is a debate I steer clear of. They are all delicious when prepared well. So let your own taste be your guide. But you certainly should give *cassoulet* a try in either Carcassonne or Castelnaudary, or, if you have an enormous appetite, make a comparison in both towns.

WHERE TO STAY

The Carcassonne area has more fine hotels than any other part of the Aude.

In the Cité, the elegant address is the **Hôtel de la Cité****** (04 68 71 98 71 FAX 04 68 71 50 15 WEB SITE www.orient-expresshotels.com, at Place de

l'Église, a Gothic-style former episcopal palace transformed into an exquisite hotel with 60 rooms fully furnished with antiques and equipped with modern bathrooms in gray marble. There is a small swimming pool, a lovely French garden looking out at the ramparts, and an outstanding restaurant, Le Barbacane (see WHERE TO EAT, below). The hotel was acquired by the Orient Express luxury hotel group in 1997 and treated to $5-million overhaul, completed in 1999. Rooms run 1,350 to 1,900 francs. **Hôtel du Donjon***** (04 68 71 08 80 FAX 04 68 25 06 60 E-MAIL hotel.donjon.best.western @wanadoo.fr WEB SITE www.hotel-donjon.fr, at 2 rue Comte-Roger, is a tasteful, pleasant and very comfortable 36-room hotel in a medieval residence

with rooms in the 400 to 500 franc range. It is a Best Western member. **Les Remparts**** (04 68 71 27 72 FAX 04 68 72 73 26, at 3 place du Grand Puits, is the best choice in the lower price range, with 18 rooms at 330 francs. All these hotels have garages for guests' cars.

My choice, however, because I like a bit more space around me, is the **Mercure le Vicomté***** (04 68 71 45 45 FAX 04 68 71 11 45 E-MAIL .mercure.Carcassonne@wanadoo.fr, at 18 rue Camille Saint-Saëns, outside the walls of the Cité, a five-minute walk from the Porte Narbonnaise. This relaxing hotel has 61 attractive, modern rooms at a top price of 495 francs, a good-sized garden with a pool, and a poolside lunch patio with a marvelous view of the Cité.

In the Lower Town, the finest hotel is the **Montségur***** (04 68 25 31 41 FAX 04 68 47 13 22 E-MAIL Montsegur@wanadoo.fr, at 27 Allée Iéna, a nineteenth-century townhouse furnished with antiques, with 21 very comfortable moderately priced rooms. The **Royal Hôtel**** (04 68 25 19 12 FAX 04 68 47 33 01, at 22 boulevard Jean-Jaurès, has 24 neat rooms equipped with showers. Rooms run 220 to 270 francs. Up the street at 27 boulevard Jean-Jaurès, the **Central**** (04 68 25 03 84 FAX 04 68 72 46 41 has 16 clean, recently renovated rooms at the remarkably low rates of 140 to 200 francs for a double.

On the outskirts of the city, the **Domaine d'Auriac******(04 68 25 72 22 FAX 04 68 47 35 54 E-MAIL auriac@relaischateaux.fr WEB SITE www .relaischateaux.fr/auriac, is a gorgeous 24-room Relais & Châteaux inn in a country mansion set in

from March 1 to early October. For a full list, contact the Tourist Office.

WHERE TO EAT

The **Barbacane** at the Hôtel de la Cité (see above) is a dining room worthy of a medieval banquet. Here you may sample the subtle specialties of young chef Franck Putelat, a rising culinary star (one Michelin star at his previous restaurant, the Bastide de Saint-Tropez). A few of his mouthwatering inventions are carpaccio of duck *foie gras* with and its homemade *magret* (breast of fattened duck) served with hazelnut-flavored lentils, pan-fried shrimp scampi with orange

a 300-year-old park with ancient cedars, magnolias and flower gardens, a pool, tennis court, a private 18-hole golf course, and one of the area's best restaurants. Rooms here go for 600 to 1,600 francs in the summer, 500 to 1,000 francs off-season. It is on the Route de Saint-Hilaire, four kilometers (two and a half miles) southwest of the Cité.

Camping

The Carcassonne Tourist Office guide to lodging and restaurants lists seven camping grounds within an eight kilometers (five mile) radius of Carcassonne and five more within a 28 km (17.5 mile) radius. The closest to the Cité is **Camping de la Cité** (04 68 25 11 77, a few kilometers to the south on the Route de Saint-Hilaire, a well-equipped 200-place site with a restaurant, bar, food shop, swimming pool, and tennis court. It is open

butter sauce in a puff pastry, spit-roasted chicken rubbed with vanilla, and river bass (*sandre*) poached with chicory and served with melted shallots, wild *girolle* mushrooms and toasted almonds. The wine, cheeses, and desserts are all on the same lofty level — but so, of course, are the prices: *menus* at 350 and 470 francs, wine not included.

For cuisine and prices on a more earthbound level, the hotel has created a lively brasserie, **Chez Saskia**, also under the culinary direction of Franck Putelat, where you can find attractive three-course *menus* for as little as 80 francs, *cassoulet maison* at the same price, and wine similarly affordable, including wine by the glass or by *pichet*. In the summer, the hotel opens its lovely garden bistro,

OPPOSITE: Languedoc farmer. ABOVE: The grape harvest in Languedoc, where winemakers have greatly improved quality in the past few decades.

Le Jardin de l'Évêque, with a small but tempting range of starters, hot dishes (grilled tuna, skewer of scampi, thyme-flavored fillet of lamb), and desserts at similarly affordable prices, and there are inexpensive children's *menus* at both places.

Also in the Cité, the **Brasserie le Donjon** at the hotel of the same name (see above) is a good moderately priced restaurant that makes very fine *cassoulet*. It is one of the few places in the Cité open for lunch every day, and except for Sunday nights from November through March, it is open for dinner daily too.

In the Lower Town, talented young chef Didier Faugeras has made a name for himself at his restaurant **Le Languedoc** (04 68 25 22 17, at 32 Allée d'Iéna, across the street from his parents' hotel, Le Montségur. Here you will find an excellent *cassoulet* also, along with other cuisine of the region and original creations.

Out of town, the restaurant of the **Domaine d'Auriac** sports a Michelin star, thanks to owner-chef Bernard Rigaudis's *foie gras, cassoulet*, knuckle of veal in Chardonnay wine from Limoux, and cinnamon ice cream with a warm pear and almond tart, among numerous culinary delights. Fixed-price *menus* start at 250 francs.

At the **Château Saint-Martin "Logis de Trencavel"** (04 68 71 09 53, a sixteenth-century château in a wooded park, noted chef Jean-Claude Rodriguez makes a classic *cassoulet* that is highly esteemed by Carcassonne natives. The cost of the dish, a meal in itself, is 95 francs. Sea bass with a mousse of scallops and sole with tarragon are other specialties of the house. Fixed-price *menus* run 165 and 295 francs, and there is a fine selection of Corbières and Minervois wines. The Château Saint-Martin is in the hamlet of Montredon, four kilometers (two and a half miles) northeast of town.

How to Get There

There are three flights a day on weekdays from Paris's Orly Airport and one each on Saturday and Sunday on Air Liberté (08 03 80 58 05, along with several high-speed *TGV* trains daily from Paris via Montpellier (six and a half hours) and via Toulouse or Bordeaux (seven hours). There are trains from Montpellier about every hour, a one-and-a-half-hour ride, as well as from Narbonne. Occasional local trains run down the Aude River Valley to Limoux, Quillan, and Perpignan. Regional bus service is minimal in the Aude, except between the main cities. Driving to Carcassonne, the fastest way is by the A61 *autoroute* from Narbonne or Toulouse. If you are coming from Lagrasse, take D3 west through the dramatic gorge of the Alsou and on to Carcassonne, 35 km (22 miles) away. To get to the Cité by bus from the Lower Town, take the No. 4 local bus.

CASTELNAUDARY

Cassoulet lovers may want to make a pilgrimage to Castelnaudary, acknowledged by one and all as the birthplace of the dish. The basic ingredient, white beans known as *lingots*, are grown here. Their virtue is that they remain firm while at the same time becoming saturated with the juices of the meat as they bake in the clay pot.

Castelnaudary is a low-key provincial town of 11,000 with many fine seventeenth-and eighteenth-century homes, and its Grand Bassin, formed by a series of four locks on the Canal du Midi, is an important center for canal boating.

General Information

The **Tourist Office** (04 68 23 05 73 is at Place de la République. For train information, contact the **SNCF** (08 36 35 35 35. Houseboat rental can be arranged through **Crown Blue Line** (04 68 94 52 72 FAX 04 68 94 52 73 WEB SITE www.crown-blueline.com, **Le Saint-Roch** (04 68 23 49 40 or 06 62 03 49 40, or **Croisières Cathy** (06 09 33 15 96; all are at Le Grand Bassin, 11400 Castelnaudary.

Where to Stay and Eat

You can hardly go wrong finding a good *cassoulet* in this town. But one I can recommend is at the restaurant of the **Hôtel du Centre et du Lauragais** ** (04 68 23 25 95 FAX 04 68 94 01 66. Here it is made with *confit de canard* (duck parts conserved in their own grease). A regional *menu* of warm salad with poultry livers, *cassoulet*, a green salad, and desert will run you 120 francs. The hotel also has 16 neat, spacious, recently renovated rooms with at a top price of 220 francs. It is at 31 cours de la République. Another pleasant place to stay is the modern **Hôtel du Canal** ** (04 68 94 05 05 FAX 04 68 94 05 06, at 2ter Avenue Vidal on the bank of the Canal du Midi. It has 33 spacious, well-kept, inexpensive rooms. There is no restaurant.

About halfway between Carcassonne and Castelnaudary, there is another restaurant whose Castelnaudary-style *cassoulet* I can heartily recommend: **Aux Deux Acacias** (04 68 94 24 67, on N113 in Villepinte. Like the Hôtel du Centre et du Lauragais, it is a member of very serious Grande Confrérie du Cassoulet de Castelnaudary, whose members swear "to defend, for all my life and beyond, the quality and the glory of the great Cassoulet of Castelnaudary, until my head falls into Your grand Cassole."

How to Get There

Castelnaudary is 37 km (23 miles) west of Carcassonne on N113.

LIMOUX

Limoux is a delightful old hill town south of Carcassonne famed for its sparkling white Blanquette-de-Limoux wines, like champagne, but with its own unique taste. The so-called *méthode champenoise*, the method for putting bubbles in wine, was developed in Limoux in the sixteenth century, well before it made it up to Champagne.

Limoux's wide boulevards are lined with large plane trees, and pretty **Place de la République** has arcaded buildings around it and a fountain in the middle. There is a good **regional market** on

de Limoux labeled Blaners. They also make several highly rated varietal *vins de pays d'Oc*. They are on Avenue du Mauzac (D118) as you enter Limoux from the north. Open daily from June to the end of August, closed weekends the rest of the year.

WHERE TO STAY AND EAT

The handsome 19-room **Grand Hôtel Moderne et Pigeon***** (04 68 31 00 25 FAX 04 68 31 12 43 E-MAIL modpig@cbhouse.fr WEB SITE www.chez .com/modpig/endex-htm, at 1 place Général-Leclerc, was built as a nunnery, then became a private mansion, then a bank before it was turned

this square and on the Promenade du Tivoli on Friday morning.

This is a town that likes to have fun. In a tradition from the Middle Ages, **Carnaval** (Carnival) lasts from January through March, when it is celebrated every Saturday and Sunday with three frolics on the Place de la République at 11 AM, 5 PM, and 10 PM.

The **Tourist Office** (04 68 31 11 82 is on the Promenade du Tivoli.

WINE TASTING

Blanquette de Limoux is clean, bright, easy-to-drink champagne-like wine. **Caves du Sieur d'Arques** (04 68 74 63 46 makes excellent Blanquette de Limoux and the slightly less bubbly Crémant de Limoux, both wines in degrees of dryness up to extra-brut. Try the Blanquette

it to a hotel at the beginning of the twentieth century. Rooms here are in the moderate range. It has a solid, old-fashioned dining room that features *canard à la Limouxine* — a local duck dish prepared with saffron — and has an excellent cellar of local wines. For lunch, my favorite place is the **Maison de la Blanquette** (04 68 31 01 63, on the Promenade du Tivoli, a wine shop in the front and a bright, cheerful, very good restaurant in the rear. It serves hearty local dishes such as *fricassée*, Limoux's own *cassoulet*-like dish made with white beans, but substituting pork for goose or duck. Fixed-price *menus* run from 65 to 200 francs, wine included. It is owned by the Caves du Sieur d'Arques, the big local wine cooperative.

Limoux, where the secret of putting bubbles in wine was discovered, and is still very much in use.

HOW TO GET THERE

Limoux is 25 km (16 miles) south of Carcassonne on D118.

THE CATHAR FORTRESSES

The sheer-cliffed hilltop forts of Puilaurens, Peyrepertuse, Quéribus, Aguilar, and Termes had been built in the eleventh century by Catalan lords to defend themselves against the Trencavels, but eventually fell into the hands of Trencavel allies who put them at the disposal of the Cathars in their time of need. The Treaty of Corbeil between France and Spain in 1258 after the defeat of the Cathars gave these "citadels of vertigo" to France, and Puilaurens became France's southernmost stronghold. The vestiges we see at Puilaurens and the other fortresses in this group date mainly from the late thirteenth century, when France reinforced them to protect its new southern border with Spain.

After the Treaty of the Pyrénées in 1659, which pushed the frontier down to the Pyrénées, these fortresses lost their military purpose, and the sites were eventually abandoned.

Known as the "Five Sons of Carcassonne," four of the fortresses are described below. The fifth of the "Five Sons," the fortress of Termes, is in the middle of the Corbières near Villerouge-Termenès (see page 320).

PUILAURENS

The fortress of Puilaurens 43 km (27 miles) south of Limoux, one of the "Five Sons of Carcassonne," as the Albigensian Crusaders called these hilltop forts, became, along with Montségur to the west, the principal refuges of the Cathars after the Battle of Muret in 1213. Puilaurens sits on a sheer peak dominating its valley and can be seen from afar. It is the one Cathar fortress that the Albigensian Crusaders failed to take.

What to See and Do

From the parking area, a steep walled pathway zigzags up to the remarkably well-preserved fortress. Its large *donjon* (keep), four round towers, and high walls with their crenels and merlons are fully intact, everything bleached as white as the great lump of limestone it sits upon. There are sheer cliffs virtually the whole way around. From the top, 697 m (2,300 ft) high, you can see Mont Canigou, the mythic mountain of the Catalan nation, snowcapped most of the year. Do not try to climb to these ruins without sturdy hiking shoes.

Where to Stay and Eat

The **Hostellerie du Grand Duc**** (04 68 20 55 02 FAX 04 68 20 61 22, five kilometers (three miles) south of Puilaurens on D22 in Gincla, is a handsome old manor house in a quiet, woodsy setting that is an inn of exceptional charm with nine lovely rooms at 350 francs tops. It has a moderately priced restaurant with food of high quality. In the summer meals are served on the outdoor terrace, off-season in the cozy dining room with a fireplace and wood-beamed ceiling. This Logis de France member is open April 1 to November 15.

How to Get There

Puilaurens is 68 km (42 miles) south of Carcassonne. To get there, head down the Aude River Valley on D118 to Quillan, then take D117 southeast for 17 km (11 miles) along the narrow, twisting road through the Défilé de Pierre-Lys, a narrow steep-cliffed gorge along the Aude River. As you emerge from the gorge, turn right (south) at Lapradelle onto D22 and wind up two kilometers (one and a quarter miles) to the parking lot of the fortress.

PEYREPERTUSE

Peyrepertuse is the most dramatic of the Cathar strongholds and the largest purely military fortress in Languedoc, with outer walls measuring two and a half kilometers (over one and a half miles) around. The massive bleached stone ruins are perched high on a sheer rock outcrop with breathtaking views of the Corbières from a height of almost 800 m (2,600 ft). The ruins themselves and the panorama of the rugged Corbières countryside make Peyrepertuse one of the most spectacular sites in all of Mediterranean France.

Peyrepertuse fell to the Northerners in 1240. Like the rest of the fortresses in the southern Corbières, it lost its military importance after Roussillon became French, and was finally abandoned in 1789.

Access by road is from the village of **Duilhac-sous-Peyrepertuse**. Drive to the parking lot at the base, and hike up the rocky path a grueling 15 to 20 minutes to the **Lower Fortress**, built on the site of the original medieval fortress (though recent

finds of pottery shards place the site's earliest occupation at the time of the Romans). Continue upward to the newer sections built under Louis IX and his successors in the late thirteenth century: the *donjon* (keep), the **lower courtyard**, and climbing upward to the pinnacle 30 m (100 ft) above the courtyard, the round towers and crenellated walls of **Château Saint-Georges** with its vast panorama of the Corbières, the Château of Quéribus, and the Mediterranean in the distance.

Wine Tasting

The little **Domaine du Trillol** (04 68 45 01 13, with 11 hectares (26 acres) below Peyrepertuse in Rouffiac-des-Corbières, open daily.

Where to Stay and Eat

The **Auberge du Vieux Moulin** (04 68 45 02 17 FAX 04 66 45 02 18, at 14 rue de la Fontaine, is a quaint old inn in Duilhac-sous-Peyrepertuse. It has 14 rooms with bath or shower at 220 francs and offers light lunch *menus* at 48 francs, copious full meals at 88 and 120 francs, in the rustic dining room or on the tree-shaded dining patio.

How to Get There

The quick way from Puilaurens or Gincla to Peyrepertuse is to go north on D22 to D117 and eastward on that.

OPPOSITE: Olive trees were brought to Mediterranean France by the Greeks in the seventh century BC. ABOVE: The fortress of Quéribus, one of the "Five Sons of Carcassonne," Cathar strongholds in the southern Corbières during the Albigensian Crusade.

The **scenic route**, which adds 24 km (about 15 miles) to your trip — all twists and turns — offers the chance to see some very different scenery — gray granite stone of the Pyrénées, primeval forests, and innumerable little streams, a contrast to the parched white limestone of the Corbières. It loops around to the south on D22 through the hilly back country of the Fenouillèdes, a small range north of the Pyrénées. From Sournia, the only real town of this area, a 10-km (six-mile) detour to the south on D619 takes you to the 1,026-m (3,365-ft) **Pic du Baou**, which has a magnificent vista of Mont Canigou, the Conflent and Prades, with a huge field of yellow flowers in the foreground if you go in the spring. Heading north on D619, pause at Ansignan to admire the 168-m (550-ft), 29-arch **aqueduct** of an irrigation system built by the Romans that is still watering the vineyards to this day. Then proceed to Saint-Paul-de-Fenouillet a few kilometers away.

At Saint Paul-de-Fenouillet, reached by either D619 or D117, take D7 through the **Gorges de Galamus** and turn right onto D14, where the best views of Peyrepertuse are to be had from Rouffiac-des-Corbières.

Peyrepertuse can also be reached from Narbonne, about 60 km (38 miles) away, via D611 through Durban-Corbières or from Perpignan, about 40 km (25 miles) away, via D117 to Maury and D19 to Cucugnan.

QUÉRIBUS

The eleventh-century fortress of Quéribus, eight kilometers (five miles) southeast of Peyrepertuse, was the last Cathar stronghold to fall to the Crusaders, in 1255. Smaller than Peyrepertuse, Quéribus is mostly in ruins, though the *donjon* (keep) is impressive. What merits the rough climb of at least 20 minutes to the top of the sharp 730-m-high (2,400-ft) peak is the magnificent panorama of the plain of Roussillon and the panorama of the Pyrénées. Quéribus lies two kilometers (one and a quarter miles) south of Cucugnan on D123.

Cucugnan is a charming village that is the scene of one of the most popular tales in Daudet's *Letters from My Mill*, *The Curate of Cucugnan*. From Easter to the end of the year, the Théâtre de Poche acting company presents an 18-minute audiovisual rendering of the story at the **Théâtre Achille Mir** (04 68 45 03 69. It is narrated in French, in a flavorful Southern accent, but there is a brochure in English for those whose French is not yet up to par. The program starts automatically every 20 minutes.

The theater is also the place to get information about Cucugnan and assistance with lodging in the area. Cucugnan is four kilometers (two and a half miles) east of Duilhac-sous-Peyrepertuse on D14.

Wine Tasting

Highly respected red *AOC* Corbières wines come from **Domaine du Révérend** (04 68 45 01 13, in Cucugnan, with 20 hectares (48 acres) of vines at the foot of Quéribus, which can be visited daily.

Where to Stay and Eat

The **Auberge de Cucugnan** (04 68 45 40 84 FAX 04 68 45 01 52, at 2 place de la Fontaine, serves fine regional cooking in its dining room in a old stone barn. It is noted for its *coq au vin*, Catalan sausage, guinea hen, rabbit, and wild boar stew. There are fixed-price *menus* at 95, 150, 170 and 240 francs, wine included. The inn rents seven inexpensive rooms. It is closed the first two weeks of September and Wednesdays from January 1 to the end of March.

The **Auberge du Vigneron**** (04 68 45 03 00 FAX 04 68 45 03 08, at 2 rue Achille Mir, also offers five simple, inexpensive rooms and good country cooking in its rustic restaurant, with *menus* at 80 and 185 francs. It is a Logis de France inn.

In Maury, eight kilometers (five miles) south of Cucugnan, **Les Oliviers** (04 68 59 15 24 is a modest 36-place camping ground open from mid-June to mid-September.

AGUILAR

The fourth of the "Five Sons of Carcassonne" is 16 km (10 miles) northeast of Cucugnan in **Tuchan**. It survived a siege by Simon de Montfort in 1210, and the French did not take it until 30 years later. It is the least dramatic of the five fortresses, but has a well-preserved square *donjon* (keep) in the center of a hexagonal array of ramparts with six round towers. They date from the time of Louis IX. There are fine views of the vineyards of Tuchan.

The **Ferme Équestre de Saint-Roch** (04 68 45 47 91, in Tuchan, offers half-day, full-day, or more extended horseback tours of the Cathar sites, an exhilarating way to see them. Rates are 160 francs for a half day, 280 francs for a full day. The farm also rents modest accommodations.

In Tuchan, **Château de Nouvelles** (04 68 45 40 03, a short walk from the ruins of Aguilar, is a leading maker of *AOC* Fitou wines. The wine cooperatives of Cucugnan, Tuchan, and the village of Padern midway between them are also respected producers and welcome wine-tasters daily.

Domaine la Peirière (04 68 45 49 64 is a 20-place campsite in the countryside near Tuchan, about 12 km (seven and a half miles) east of Cucugnan. It is open from May 1 to the end of September.

Tuchan is reached by D14 from Cucugnan.

As you move southward through Languedoc, you'll notice people's features becoming more and more Iberian.

Roussillon

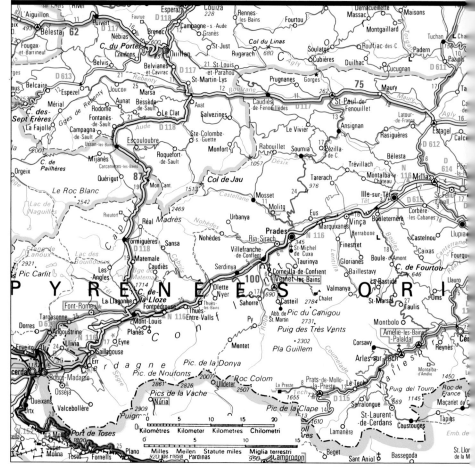

ROUSSILLON IS THE SOUTHERN CORNER of Mediterranean France and the perfect place to wrap up this journey, because in many ways, the two extremities of this region are like bookends. Both have huge ranges of mountains plunging dramatically into the sea, the Alps and the Pyrénées. Both have strong ethnic flavors, Italian and Catalan. It's a toss-up as to which one has the sunnier weather, though Roussillon may have a slight edge, with 325 days of sunshine a year. Nice has its *Train des Pignes* (Pine Cone Train) to the Alpes-de-Haute-Provence, Roussillon its *Petit Train Jaune* (Little Yellow Train) into the Catalan heartland of the Cerdagne in the Pyrénées. We even find the same artists in both places. Besides their better-known stays on the Côte d'Azur, Matisse, Picasso, Chagall, Dufy, and Cocteau all spent important periods in their careers in Roussillon. Travelers who are put off by the ultra-sophistication of the Côte d'Azur should consider taking a run down to Roussillon. Here they will find a place that combines sun, sea, magnificent mountain scenery and first-rate cultural attractions, from tenth-century Romanesque abbeys to the masters of twentieth-century art. It is 467 km (296 miles) by highway from Nice to Perpignan, a perfectly manageable one-day drive.

On the other hand, if gourmet cuisine and luxury living are high on your list of priorities, you will not find much of that in Roussillon. By comparison, the Alpes-Maritimes area (Nice, Cannes, Antibes, Vence, Monaco, etc.) boasts more than two dozen Michelin-starred restaurants, but Roussillon, an area of roughly the same geographical size, has only three. Don't worry, though, you will eat well in Roussillon — this is still France, after all — but on simply prepared dishes such as grilled anchovies, red mullet and other sea fish, trout from Pyrénées streams, fresh vegetables and fruit, of which Roussillon is an important producer. There are far fewer hotels than on the Côte d'Azur too, and barely a handful that attain the level of luxury that is commonplace east of the Rhône.

The good news is that everything is much cheaper in Roussillon, even the handful of Côte d'Azur-quality restaurants and hotels. Another

of Aragon, and in 1172, Counts of Roussillon. This was the golden age of Catalan power, when the Counts of Barcelona rivaled the Counts of Toulouse as supreme lords of the South, and Barcelona ranked with Venice and Genoa as one of the greatest sea-trading powers in the world. The Western Mediterranean became a "Catalan lake."

For a brief, but artistically memorable period from the late thirteenth through the mid-fourteenth century, the Kingdom of Majorca came into existence. It was created in 1276 by King Jaime the Conqueror of Aragon to give his younger son Jaime a kingdom, the elder son Pedro inheriting the throne of Aragon. It was made up of Roussillon, the Balearic Islands and Montpellier, with Perpignan as its capital. Sixty-eight years and two kings later, the ephemeral Kingdom of Majorca was reabsorbed by the Kingdom of Aragon, in 1344, but left an impressive architectural heritage.

In the late fifteenth century, with the marriage of Ferdinand of Aragon and Isabella of Castile, Catalonia fell under Spanish rule. In 1659, after a series of wars, Spain ceded Roussillon to young Louis XIV, and the border was moved south to the Pyrénées. As it had done earlier in the Occitan areas of Provence and Languedoc, Paris imposed the French language and culture on Roussillon and vigorously suppressed everything Catalan.

Today, all people in Roussillon speak French. But a third of them also speak Catalan. While there is none of the violence that marks Basque nationalism at the other end of the Pyrénées, the Catalans are a proud, independent-minded people whose sense of national identity is strong. Street signs are in Catalan as well as French, and the red and yellow flag of Roussillon — blood and gold — is seen as often as the French red, white and blue. After the Spanish Civil War, when Dali, Miró, Casals, and other Catalan artists wanted a taste of Catalonia without going back to a land ruled by Franco, they found it with no difficulty in Perpignan, Collioure, Céret, or Prades. In Roussillon, as in Alsace and parts of the French Basque Country, the traveler often finds himself amazed to realize he is still in France.

advantage for Roussillon is that it has vineyards — interesting ones such as Collioure, Banyuls, Rivesaltes, Côtes du Roussillon — whereas the Alpes-Maritimes has practically none. As in Languedoc, but even more so, here the traveler has the chance to get off the beaten track and explore a splendidly scenic part of France, one that has managed to hold onto its unique Catalan identity.

BACKGROUND

Though most of historic Catalonia now lies on the Spanish side of the Pyrénées, the birthplace of the Catalan nation is in France. It is the high plateau of the Cerdagne deep in the Pyrénées by Andorra, which is predominantly Catalan too. The Catalans made their fortune in iron ore and metal forging here in the early Middle Ages, enabling Count Wilfred the Hairy of Cerdagne to make himself Count of Barcelona in the tenth century. In the twelfth century, his successors made themselves Counts of Provence and Kings

PERPIGNAN

Perpignan is the capital of Roussillon, its only real metropolis, the center of the area's big fruit and wine trade and in recent years, a Mecca for computer businesses and high-technology research. It is a clean, vivacious, attractive city of some 105,000 people that lies eight kilometers (five miles) inland from Mediterranean with the non-navigable Têt River running through it. The Pyrénées loom up to the south, and Mont Canigou, the symbol of Catalan nationhood, exerts its magical presence from 100 km (60 miles) away. It is snowcapped most of the year. Like its Catalan big sister-city of Barcelona, Perpignan is a lively place, delightful to stroll in.

GENERAL INFORMATION

The **Tourist Office** (04 68 66 30 30 WEB SITE www.little-France.com/Perpignan is located at the Palais des Congrès at the far end of the Promenade des Platanes, and there is a small office at the airport. They provide information about the city and some help on the rest of Roussillon. But for complete information on both the city and the outlying areas, contact the **Comité Départemental du Tourisme Pyrénées-Roussillon** (04 68 34 29

94 FAX 04 68 34 71 01 E-MAIL Tourisme.roussillon .france@wanadoo.fr WEB SITE www.pyrenees-orientales.com, at 7 quai de Lattre-de-Tassigny. They are extremely helpful, and their maps and brochures are excellent. If you plan to explore the outlying areas, be sure to pick up their listing of all the hotels, restaurants and camping grounds in Roussillon.

For airport information, call **Perpignan-Rivesaltes Airport** (04 68 52 60 70. The train station, **Gare SNCF** (08 36 35 35 35, is on the west side of the city at the end of Avenue du Général-de-Gaulle. The bus station, **Gare Routière** (04 68 35 29 02, is on Avenue du Général-Leclerc to the west of Place de la Résistance. For buses to towns along the coast, call **Car Inter 66** (04 68 35 29 02. For taxis, call **Accueil Perpignan Taxis** (04 68 35 15 15.

Le Castillet, the medieval fortress that is Perpignan's ground zero.

Car rental agencies are **Avis** (04 68 34 26 71, 13 boulevard du Conflent; **Citer** (04 68 67 31 05, 44 avenue du Maréchal-Juin; and **EuropCar** (04 68 34 65 03, at 28 avenue du Général-de-Gaulle. Bike rental is available at **Cycles Mercier** (04 68 85 02 71, 20 rue Gilbert Brutus.

In case of medical emergency, call the **SAMU** (15.

FESTIVALS AND EVENTS

The **Procession of the Penitents of Sanch** on Good Friday is a colorful, if rather macabre, expression of faith by the Brothers of the Holy Blood (*sanch* in Catalan), who parade through the streets in red robes with sharp-pointed hoods and bare feet carrying an effigy of Christ. **Les Estivales**, a star-studded music, dance and theater festival is held through the month of July at the Palace of the Kings of Majorca, the Campo Santo, and other dramatic locations. A major photojournalism festival, **Visa pour l'Image**, is held in early September, and in mid-September, **Aujourd'hui Musiques** is a two-week festival of new orchestral and operatic compositions and jazz.

WHAT TO SEE AND DO

The **Castillet** is a tall, sturdy fortress that was built as the main gate of the city in the fourteenth century, when it was completely walled, and it is now the dividing mark between the old town and the new. It houses the **Museum of Catalan Popular Arts and Traditions**, also known as the **Casa Pairal**, or "ancestral home" in Catalan, which offers an engaging introduction to Catalan culture. From the roof, there is a vast panorama of the city, the sea, the Corbières, Mont Canigou, and the Pyrénées. It is open in the summer from 9:30 AM to 11:30 AM and 2:30 PM to 6:30 PM, the rest of the year from 9 AM to 11:30 AM and 2 PM to 5:30 PM. It is closed Tuesday and national holidays. Entrance is free.

The **Loge de la Mer** is the most elegant building in the city, a fourteenth-century meeting hall for sea traders that is now occupied by a Quick fast-food franchise, adapted in reasonably good taste. It fronts on the **Place de la Loge**, where the cafés are popular gathering places for the *Perpignanais*. On Tuesday and Thursday nights in the summer, people get up and do the stately Catalan dance, the *sardana*, in the square. Here you can also admire one of Maillol's most famous cast-bronze nudes, *La Méditerranée*. **Place Arago**, a few blocks to the west, is another square with a number of lively cafés.

The **Cathédrale Saint-Jean**, on Place Gambetta a short walk to the east of the Place de la Loge, is an impressive structure with a surface of red brick and pebbles that has a single nave 48 m (158 ft)

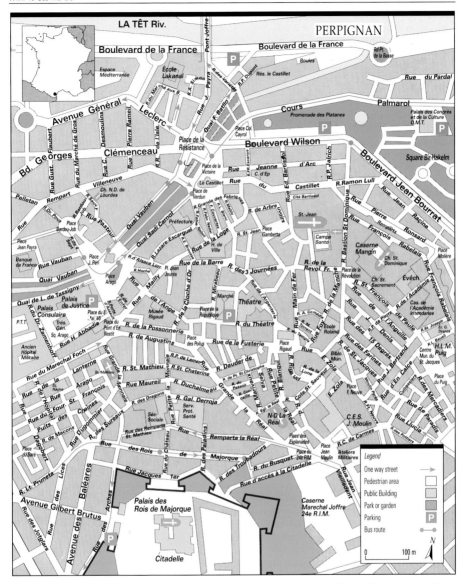

long. It was started in 1324 during the reign of Sanche, the second of the three Kings of Majorca, whose death effigy can be seen in a side chapel, but the church was not consecrated until 1509 and work on it continued into the seventeenth century. Nevertheless, it is the most coherent example of Gothic church architecture in the south of France. Inside, there are many art treasures to admire, including the marble main altar and a number of altarpieces from the sixteenth and seventeenth centuries in side chapels, particularly those in the chapels of Saint Peter and of Saints Eulalie and Julie off the left-hand aisle. As you are leaving the church by the right side, look for the leather-covered door to the corridor that leads to the chapel

containing the *Dévôt Christ*. This is a painfully realistic wooden sculpture of Christ crucified, a German work from the early fourteenth century. According to local legend, the Christ's bowed head is tilting very slowly closer to His chest — it is only a fraction of an inch away now — and when it touches, the world will end. Adjoining the cathedral is the Campo Santo, the only cloister-cemetery in France, made up of four galleries with rows of white marble Gothic porticos.

The **Musée Hyacinthe-Rigaud**, in a seventeenth-century mansion at 16 rue de l'Ange down the street from Place Arago, is named for the leading portrait artist of Louis XIV's court, and it has two excellent portraits by him, one of the elegant

Cardinal de Bouillon and other a self-portrait of the amiable-looking painter. But this is an amazingly eclectic art museum whose collection ranges from the magnificent fifteenth-century Catalan altarpiece *La Retable de la Trinité*, which allegorically depicts the Loge de la Mer, which commissioned it, with the sea at its doorstep, to work by contemporary Catalan painter Antoni Tàpies. It includes three sketches by another noted Catalan, Pablo Picasso. One is of the Countess de Lazerme, his mistress in the mid-1950s, whose home this building was. Among the other works are a delightful pointilist painting by Maillol, *Portrait de Jeune Fille*, nine oils and numerous drawings by Dufy, along with works by Ingres, Brueghel, Marie

Laurencin, Calder, and others. This museum is full of surprises. It is open from 9:30 AM to noon and 2:30 PM to 7 PM from mid-June to mid-September, and it opens at 9 AM and closes at 6 PM the rest of the year. Closed Tuesdays and holidays. Admission is free.

The **Palace of the Kings of Majorca** is inside the medieval **citadel**, which dominates the city from its highest point. It was started in 1276 by King Jaime I to house his court and was completed by the Kings of Aragon when they reabsorbed the Kingdom of Majorca. You can visit the apartments of the king and the queen, the chapel and public rooms, which are handsome spaces with grand walk-in fireplaces, but they are practically empty and give little sense of how people lived and worked here. The most attractive part of the palace is the wide courtyard in which concerts are held in the summer (check at the Tourist Office

for the program). The palace can be visited from 9:30 AM to noon and 2:30 PM to 6 PM in the summer, from 9 AM to noon and 2 PM to 5 PM off-season. Closed Tuesdays and national holidays.

WINE TASTING

If you want to visit a vineyard, but don't have much time for exploring the countryside, visit the **Domaine Sarda-Malet** (04 68 56 72 38, at Mas Saint-Michel, 12 Chemin de Sainte-Barbe, on the south side of Perpignan, actually within the city limits. They make red and white Côtes du Roussillon, the principal *AOC* table wine of Roussillon, and Rivesaltes and Muscat de

Rivesaltes *doux naturel* (sweet apéritif wine), all to perennial critical raves. Their cellar is open weekdays from 8 AM to 1 PM and 2 PM to 7 PM, on weekends by appointment.

WHERE TO STAY

Perpignan is the only place in Roussillon to offer a large choice of hotels, and there are many good choices indeed. A number of hotels participate year-round in a two-nights-for-the-price-of-one program on weekends. The Tourist Office has a list.

Perpignan's deluxe address is **Villa Duflot****** (04 68 56 67 67 FAX 04 68 56 54 05 E-MAIL villa.duflot @little-france.com WEBSITE www.littlefrance.com/ villa.duflot, in a luxuriant private park at 109 avenue Victor-Dalbiez slightly south of the city. It has 24 sunny rooms done in updated 1930s style, some opening directly onto the pool. For a hotel of its quality, the rates are very reasonable, with doubles at 590 to 790 francs. The **Park Hotel*** (04 68 35 14 14 FAX 04 68 35 48 18, at 18 boulevard Jean-Bourrat is a local institution with 67 cushy, traditional-style rooms, moderate in price, and one of the best restaurants in town (see WHERE TO EAT, below). The **Mercure*** (04 68 35 67 66 FAX 04 68 35 58 13 E-MAIL hotel-mercure@altranet.fr, is a tasteful modern hotel with 60 moderately priced up-to-date rooms. It is at 5 Cours Plamarole near the Castillet. The **Poste et Perdrix** (04 68 34 42 53 FAX 04 68 34 58 20, at 6 rue des Fabriques-d'En-Nabot (Place de Verdun), is a hotel with a great deal of character in a town house dating from 1832.

miles) straight east of Perpignan. **Argelès-sur-Mer**, 20 km (12.5 miles) southeast of Perpignan has no less than 56 camping grounds with thousands of places. Other beach towns with a number of camping grounds are **Le Barcarès** with thirteen, **Saint-Cyprien** with five, **Sainte-Marie** and **Torreilles** with six each. For information, contact the Comité Départemental du Tourisme Pyrénées-Roussillon.

WHERE TO EAT

Côté Théâtre (04 68 34 60 00, at 7 rue du Théâtre, is an outstanding gourmet restaurant. Vegetables from Roussillon with fresh coriander

It has 38 neat, clean rooms at a top rate of 260 francs, and is a Logis de France member.

A luxury hotel I include here because I have no other place for it is **L'Île de la Lagune****** (04 68 21 01 02 FAX 04 68 21 06 28, a small modern resort hotel on a little island in an inlet of the Mediterranean, the lagoon of Saint-Cyprien, 19 km (12 miles) to the east of Perpignan. It has a swimming pool and a private beach, 18 tasteful multiple-level rooms and four suites, all with sea views, and one of the finest restaurants in Roussillon (see WHERE TO EAT, below). The average rate for a double room is 850 francs.

Camping

There are a great number of camping grounds along the beaches to the east of Perpignan. The closest are in **Canet-en-Roussillon**, which has nine of them with 2,500 places. It is 11 km (seven

served with warm fresh clams, puff tart of zucchini and Collioure anchovies with basil vinaigrette, and *galinette* (a type of Mediterranean mullet) *bouillabaisse* are a few of the culinary delights that have made Michel Portos the most talked-about chef in Perpignan. The weekday lunch *menu* is 148 francs, more elaborate fixed-price *menus* are 230 and 330 francs. The wine list is superb. The **Chapon Fin**, the gourmet restaurant of the Hôtel Park (see WHERE TO STAY, above), is decorated with Catalan ceramics and has a bright Mediterranean ambiance. It serves *tarte de saumon*, roast scallops in sea urchin sauce, and other inventive dishes, seafood for

The medieval Loge de la Mer, now a fast-food outlet, and one of the many open-air restaurants near the Castillet OPPOSITE LEFT and RIGHT. ABOVE: Catalan sculptor Aristide Maillol's *Méditerranée* at City Hall.

the most part, and has an eminent cellar of Collioure and Côtes du Roussillon wines. Fixed price *menus* start at 125 francs.

For a more popular style of eating, try the **Casa Sansa** (04 68 34 21 84, at 3 rue Fabriques Couvertes near the Castillet, a place I enjoy enormously. It is a big, bustling eatery with a *bodega* atmosphere serving strictly Catalan specialties. Here you may sample *esqueixada de bacalla* (marinated codfish) and *pollastre amb gambas* (chicken and shrimp in Rivesaltes wine sauce), and local wines at moderate prices. For a gastronomic change of pace — the cool, bright taste of Atlantic shellfish and a chilled glass of Muscadet — **L'Huitrière** (04 68 35 56 42 serves fresh oysters trucked down on

lunch *menu* at 130 francs. Closed Sunday nights and Mondays off-season.

HOW TO GET THERE

There are four flights daily from Paris's Orly Airport to Perpignan-Rivesaltes Airport. By train, Perpignan is on the main lines from Paris and Geneva to Barcelona. By bus, Eurolines has service from London and many other cities in Europe, Iberbus has buses from Spain, and Courriers du Midi has daily buses from Montpellier. By car, Perpignan is on the A9 *autoroute* and is the hub of all the other main roads of Roussillon.

ice from Brittany. It is at 12 rue Pierre-Ramiel, west of the Castillet off Boulevard Georges-Clemenceau. The **Brasserie Vauban** (04 68 51 05 10, at 29 quai Vauban, serves honest brasserie fare. The **Grand Café de la Bourse** (04 68 34 25 05, at 2 place de la Loge, is the best place to take in the *sardana* dancing on Tuesday and Thursday nights. For *tapas* and a true Barcelona atmosphere, try **La Bodega Pescador** on Rue Fabriques Couvertes, open till 2 AM.

For gourmet dining by the sea, take a jaunt to **L'Almandin**, the restaurant of L'Île de la Lagune (see WHERE TO STAY, above). Here you may feast on Collioure anchovy blinis with *tapenade, bouillabaisse* of cod, monkfish in crayfish sauce, apricot tart served with fresh wild strawberries, and other compositions of chef Jean-Paul Hartmann which have earned him a Michelin star. Fixed price dinner *menus* start at 195 francs, with is a weekday

EXCURSIONS FROM PERPIGNAN

Perpignan is the jumping-off point for a number of fascinating trips in Roussillon—one to the north, one to the south, and two following the river valleys into the Pyrénées. The distances are short. The northern points of Rivesaltes, Salses-le-Château, and Tautavel are less than half an hour's drive from Perpignan. To the west, Prades, the main town of the Conflent, is only 43 km (27 miles) away. Short distances to the southwest lie the art village of Céret, Amélie-les-Bains, and the Vallespir, the southernmost part of France. To the south of Perpignan are the ancient capital of Elne and the rugged Côte Vermeille (Vermilion Coast), with its charming ports of Collioure and Banyuls-sur-Mer, an easy day-trip by car. If time is short, a trip combining Céret and Collioure could be done in a day.

The only part of Roussillon that is not interesting from a scenic point of view is the Côte Sablonneuse, the 32-km (20-mile) stretch of flat, sandy coast between Port-Barcarès and Argelès-Plage, which has one banal new beach resort after another, along with vast expanses of camping grounds. Otherwise, Roussillon is as intriguing as any other part of Mediterranean France, and the least "spoiled" by mass tourism. The Carinter 66 bus network can take you to all parts of Roussillon, and there is train service to some of these areas. But unless you are a serious hiker or biker, you will have no means of getting out into the countryside once you get there. A car is the best bet, if it is within your means. As in Languedoc, the roads in Roussillon are excellent.

SALSES-LE-CHÂTEAU

As you whip along the A9 *autoroute* between Narbonne and Perpignan, you could easily fly past the Fortress of Salses without even noticing it. Yet this massive, low-lying fort—which is completely intact — was once one of the most important military structures in Europe. It sits in the middle of the narrow plain between the marshes of the Étang de Salses and the rugged slopes of the Corbières that was the only flat, firm land between the Atlantic seaboard and the Mediterranean that an army could easily cross to get to or from the Iberian Peninsula. Its strategic significance became clear in 218 BC when Hannibal convinced the local Gallo-Iberian tribe that controlled it to give his army and 37 elephants free passage on their way north from Spain, and they went on to nearly bring Rome to its knees.

The squat red-ochre stronghold we see today was built in 1497 by King Ferdinand of Spain to defend the then-Spanish border from the French. The walls are 15 m (almost 50 ft) thick at the base, built low to the ground with rounded contours to deflect the fire of the newly perfected cannon. The fortress could billet up to 1,500 troops and there were stables for 300 horses. It proved its worth against Richelieu's invading armies, but lost its usefulness when the Pyrénées became the border in 1659. Vauban is said to have wanted to demolish the fortress, but dropped the project as too difficult and expensive. When you see the bulkiness of the walls, you will understand why.

The Fortress of Salses is 16 km (10 miles) north of Perpignan. It can be reached by car via the *autoroute* if you are traveling in either direction. Park in the Aire de Salses rest area and walk to the fort, a five-minute stroll. However there is no exit ramp for vehicles to Salses. So unless you are continuing north or south on the *autoroute* you should take the N9 to get there. The fortress is open all year from 9 AM to 6:30 PM, to 7:30 PM in the summer, closed on national holidays. For information call (04 68 38 60 13.

TAUTAVEL

In 1971, the skull of the oldest known European was found in a limestone cave in the sheer-cliffed Arago valley 30 km (18 miles) northwest of Perpignan. Tautavel Man lived 450,000 years ago and hunted buffalo, rhinoceros, wild boar, and other game in the plains below. The **Centre Européen de la Préhistoire** (04 68 29 07 76, in Tautavel, opened in 1992, is a modern museum of prehistory with geological exhibits, reconstructions of

the Tautavel Man's habitat, bones of the animals he hunted, and the skull of the Man himself, with an audiocassette in English to lead you through it. Open daily from 10 AM to 12:30 PM and 2 PM to 6:00 PM.

The **Caune d'Arago**, the cave where the Tautavel Man was found, can also be visited in July and August when archaeological digs are in progress. For information, contact the **Tourist Office** (04 68 29 12 08, at the Tautavel town hall, the Mairie.

If you are coming from Salses, take N9 south to D12 west through the hauntingly bleak landscape east of the village of Vingrau and take the local roads to Tautavel, a distance of 27 km

The massive Fortress of Salses OPPOSITE, built in 1497 by King Ferdinand of Spain. ABOVE: The 450,000-year-old Tautavel Man, the oldest human skull discovered in Europe.

(17 miles) in all. Coming from Perpignan, take N9 north to D12. The distance is a few kilometers longer.

Wine Tasting

At the **Château de Jau** (see WHERE TO EAT, below), you can sample their highly esteemed wines, covering a wide range of different types made in Roussillon, from *AOC* Côtes du Roussillon red, *blanc de blanc* (white wine made only from white grapes) and rosés to Vin d'Été, their popular *vin de pays*, as well as Muscat de Rivesaltes, a white *vin doux naturel* (sweet wine), a very dark Rivesaltes, and *AOC* Collioure red table wine, and the Robert Doutres label of *AOC* Banyuls *vin doux*

naturel from the Clos de Paullilles on the Côte Vermeille. The cellar is open weekdays from 8 AM to 5 PM. While visiting the land of the Tautavel Man, you could stop in at the village's excellent wine cooperative, **Les Maîtres Vignerons de Tautavel** (68 29 12 03, at 24 route de Vingrau, which makes the full range of wines of the area. Try one of their aged Côtes du Roussillon to find out how rich, smooth and flavorful the wines of this appellation can be. They are open daily from 9 AM to noon and 2 PM to 6 PM.

Another top winemaker in this area is the century-old **Domaine Cazes** (04 68 64 08 26, at 4 rue Francisco-Ferrer in Rivesaltes, where the Cazes brothers, Bernard and André, make 15 different types of Rivesaltes, Muscat de Rivesaltes, Côtes du Roussillon, and *vin de pays* on their 160 hectare (384 acre) estate, a very large spread for this region. Their wines get consistently high grades in

blind tests by wine experts. Open weekdays from 8 AM to noon and 2 PM to 6 PM.

Where to Eat

The Dauré family's **Château de Jau** (04 68 38 91 38, directly south of Tautavel in Cases-de-Pène, is a winemaking estate that serves a Catalan feast at lunchtime in the summer — *fougasse* (flavored Mediterranean bread), tomatoes and Serrano ham, lamb cutlets and sausage grilled on a fire of dried grape vines, Roquefort cheese, and cinnamon ice cream, served with a different wine at each course — all for 150 francs. The meal is served in a shaded rustic courtyard of the handsome red-ochre eighteenth-century estate house, daily from June 15 to the end of September. Seating is limited, and you would be wise to reserve in advance. You can also visit the contemporary art exhibits put on by the château every summer, which are of a very high level. Independently of the lunch, one can also taste their wine (see above). The Château de Jau is a few kilometers west of Cases-de-Pène on a private road off D117. It is about 10 km (six miles) west of Rivesaltes.

THE ASPRES

Immediately to the west of Perpignan's plain on a straight line with Mont Canigou rises a strange, sparsely populated range of Pyrénées foothills called the Aspres. Its craggy terrain is covered by scrub oaks, wild asparagus, herbs and berry patches, and flocks of goats graze in the shadow of the ancient watch towers, chapels and abbeys that abound in these hills. The main points of interest here are the medieval town of Castelnou and the Prieuré de Serrabone.

To get to Castelnou from Perpignan, take D612 for 14 km (nine miles) to Thuir, where you might want to stop at Pernod-Ricard's **Caves Byrrh** (04 68 53 05 42 to see what is billed as the largest oak vat in the world, with a capacity of more than a million liters, and taste their apéritif wines. Open daily in July and August, weekdays in spring and autumn.

CASTELNOU

This is a beautifully preserved walled village in the heart of the Aspres with the golden stone houses of its 152 people clustered at the foot of an eleventh-century fortress of the Counts of Cerdagne and Besalu. It is noted for its pottery, ironwork and other handicrafts, and its steep, narrow streets, which offer the chance to work up an appetite for another good reason to come here, a meal at l'Hostal.

L'Hostal (04 68 53 45 42 is one of the few restaurants in Roussillon that still prepares *cargolade*, the traditional Catalan dish of snails, pork chops and sausages grilled on an open fire of dried vine clippings, a complicated meal to make that must be ordered in advance. This feast costs 230 francs, wine and dessert included. Normal fare is offered too, with fixed-price *menus* from 110 and 240 francs, wine included. You dine on the big, festive outdoor terrace in fine weather, in the cozy dining room otherwise. It is closed the months of January and February and Mondays and Wednesday evenings, except in midsummer.

To get to Castelnou from Thuir, drive six kilometers (nearly four miles) to the west on D48.

PRIEURÉ DE SERRABONE

Serrabone (04 68 84 09 30 is the oldest Augustinian priory in Europe, started in 1082. At first glance, the extreme austerity of its dark gray schist exterior may give you a chill. But surprises await you inside. First, the entry way, a lovely colonnaded balcony on the edge of a ravine with carvings of monsters on the capitals.

But this is a mere hint of what awaits you inside — an amazing ensemble of sculpted capitals atop the rose marble columns of the tribune representing eagles, lions, griffins, and other fantastic beasts from the *Book of the Apocalypse*, one of the true masterpieces of Romanesque art. The priory also has a 42-hectare (100-acre) botanical garden with more than 1,000 specimens of Mediterranean plants. As from many points around here, there is a marvelous view of Canigou only 16 km (10 miles) to the west. Open daily except public holidays from 10 AM to 6 PM.

To get to Serrabone from Castelnou, drive west on D48, heading toward Canigou. Marvelous vistas are revealed by every twist and turn in the circuitous roads though the Aspres. As you mount, the view becomes more and more open. From the little Romanesque chapel of **Fontecouverte** by the junction with D2 you can see the Mediterranean. Go six kilometers (three and a half miles) south on D2 to Caxias, then right another six kilometers on the road to Col de Fourtou. Turn right there onto D618 and follow it 10 km (six miles) to the north. The access road to Serrabone is on your left.

Serrabone can also be reached more directly from Perpignan via N116 west to Bouleternère and D618 south.

THE CONFLENT

Named for the confluence of streams flowing into the Têt River from the Fenouillèdes, the Canigou Massif and the Cerdagne, the peaceful valley of the Conflent is noted for its peach orchards and market gardens, its access to Mont Canigou, its two Romanesque abbeys, the Pablo Casals Music Festival and the walled city of Villefranche-de-Conflent. It is reached by N116.

PRADES

The commercial hub of the Conflent is Prades, a quiet town of 6,500, known to the outside world as the adopted home of the great Catalan cellist Pablo Casals in the 1940s and 1950s during his self-imposed exile from Franco's Spain and for the renowned **Casals Festival** held from late July to mid-August. For festival information contact (04 68 96 33 07 E-MAIL festival.cassals@wanadoo.fr WEB SITE www.pro.wanadoo.fr/festival.cassals/. For tourist information, contact the **Syndicat d'Initiative** (04 68 96 27 58 FAX 04 68 96 50 95, BP 24, Rue Victor-Hugo, 66502 Prades.

The main concert site is the tenth-century Benedictine **Abbey of Saint-Michel-de-Cuxa** in a pretty little valley just south of town. This outstanding example of Catalan religious art and architecture has a handsome four-story Lombard-style rectangular bell tower, a large pre-Romanesque church consecrated in 974 (the fourth church to be built on this site), a fascinating labyrinthine crypt with a vaulted circular chapel in its center, and an especially lovely cloister — despite the fact that half the capitals of its columns have ended up in New York, at the Metropolitan Museum's Cloisters. A small community of Benedictine monk continues to pursue the monastic life at the abbey.

Streets scenes ABOVE LEFT and RIGHT in the fully walled town of Villefranche-de-Conflent, one of liveliest spots in Roussillon in the summer.

The seventeenth-century **Église de Saint-Pierre** in the center of otherwise uninteresting Prades features a huge 1699 baroque altarpiece by Catalan master wood carver Joseph Sunyer. Forty statues and bas-reliefs of angels, saints, men and animals in leafy and flowery settings, all gilded and painted, surround a majestic Saint Peter on a throne. Put a five-franc coin into the automatic timer to light up this "sculpted opera."

VILLEFRANCHE-DE-CONFLENT

With its stern military ramparts completely surrounding the town and hilltop Fort Libéria adding its touch of menace from the hills above it,

Villefranche-de-Conflent might look unwelcoming at first glance. Wrong. This little town of less than 300 year-round residents is one of the friendliest places in southern France, and one of the most active in the summer, thanks in large part to the initiative of the bright, dedicated young team that runs its tourist and cultural programs. In June, July and August, potters, wood carvers and iron workers open their boutiques, the cafés are in full swing, and a rich program of musical and other cultural events gets under way.

The town lies six kilometers (nearly four miles) south of Prades on N116 in a narrow valley at the confluence of the Têt and Cady rivers, strategically important in the past because it is the only passage between the Cerdagne and the Conflent, via the Têt River Valley. Villefranche-de-Conflent was founded in 1092 by the Count of Cerdagne, who built the original fortress. It was enlarged by

the King of Aragon in the late thirteenth century after the Cathar fortresses to the north fell to the French, but it was destroyed by the French in the war with Spain in the 1650s. After the Pyrénées frontier was established, the indefatigable Vauban came to town (twice, in 1669 and 1679), and laid out the system of ramparts we see today. Seeing that the town was vulnerable to sniping from the hills above it, he ordered **Fort Libéria** to be built up there. In the nineteenth century, Napoléon III had a 1,000-step tunneled stairway built up to it from town (you don't have to climb it; there is an off-road vehicle to take you up there).

Inside those seventeenth-century walls, Villefranche remains a medieval town. The twelfth-century **Église Saint-Jacques** has a dark, haunting mood and a blend of artistic styles from Romanesque austerity to Spanish gilded baroque.

The **Association Culturelle** (04 68 96 25 64, at 38 rue Saint-Jean, is open all year, and directors Guy and Lydie Durbet are more than happy to share their vast fund of knowledge about the region. The **Tourist Office** (04 68 96 22 96, at Place de l'Église, is open in the summer. The staff will find you hotel or guest house accommodations.

Villefranche-de-Conflent is also the place where you connect with the *Petit Train Jaune* to the Cerdagne (see THE CERDAGNE, page 346), and information about that is available at either office.

ABBAYE DE SAINT-MARTIN-DU-CANIGOU

The eleventh-century **Abbaye de Saint-Martin-du-Canigou** (04 68 05 50 03 lies eight kilometers (five miles) south of Villefranche-de-Conflent. To get there, take D116 to the old spa town of **Vernet-les-Bains**, a favorite of Rudyard Kipling, where a clear view of **Mont Canigou** greets you. Continue south on the same road to Casteil and park. The abbey is not accessible by car. Hikers can reach it by a steep, rugged trail, about half an hour each way. Once up there, you will fall under the spell of Romanesque purity of the church and the cloister and even more, the magnificent site on the slope of Canigou. Stairs to the left lead up the hill above the abbey for the best view. It is open all year except in bad winter weather.

Garage Villaceque (04 68 05 51 14, in Vernet-les-Bains provides **jeep rides** to the abbey for 170 francs per person.

The **Tourist Office** (04 68 05 55 35 in Vernet-les-Bains is at Place de la Mairie.

WHERE TO STAY

There are 29 hotels in the Conflent, half of them concentrated in the spa towns of Vernet-les-Bains, which has two three-star and five two-star hotels, and Molitg-les-Bains, which has one of the few four-star hotels in Roussillon (the Château de Riell, see below), one three-star and two two-star hotels. Prades and Villefranche-de-Conflent have perfectly acceptable two-star hotels. For information and help getting rooms, contact the Tourist Offices in the above-mentioned towns. They can also find you *chambres d'hôtes* (bed and breakfasts) and *gîtes*, rural cottages.

The luxurious **Château de Riell****** (04 68 05 04 40 FAX 04 68 05 04 37 E-MAIL riell@relaischateaux .fr WEB SITE www.relaischateaux.fr/riell, is a nineteenth-century mansion in the style of a medieval castle with two swimming pools, two tennis courts, and 24 hectares (60 acres) of private park with a view of Mont Canigou, fireplaces in all 22 antique-furnished rooms, and the only gourmet restaurant in the area (see WHERE TO EAT, below). Double rooms run 1,000 to 1,400 francs. It is a Relais & Châteaux member. Open from April 1 to November 1. It is in Molitg-les-Bains, six kilometers (four miles) from Prades. The hotel will arrange thermal treatments at the local spa.

In Prades, the moderately priced modern 39-room **Pradotel**** (04 68 05 22 66 FAX 04 68 05 23 22 has its own swimming pool. The inexpensive 30-room **Hexagone**** (04 68 05 31 31 FAX 04 68 05 24 89 is next to Prades's large public pool and tennis courts, which visitors are free to use. It is open all year. This is a very friendly little hotel.

In Villefranche-de-Conflent, the **Vauban**** (04 68 96 18 03 FAX 04 68 96 69 66, at 5 place de l'Église in the center of town, has 16 neat, pleasant, inexpensive rooms, open mid-March 1 to the end of October.

Camping

The best camping grounds in the Conflent are to be found in Vernet-les-Bains, which has three, including the **Camping L'Eau Vive** (04 68 05 54 14, by a mountain stream on the Chemin Saint-Saturin. This is a well-equipped 58-place park with a swimming pool, restaurant, bar, washing machines, and rental of tents and campers; open all year. The more modest 100-place **Camping del Bosc** (04 68 05 54 54, at 68 avenue Clemenceau, is open from March 1 to the end of October. In Prades, the simple **Camping Municipal** (04 68 96 29 83, on the Plaine Saint-Martin, has 60 places and is open from April 1 to the end of September.

WHERE TO EAT

In Moltig-les-Bains, the glamorous restaurant of the **Château de Riell** (see WHERE TO STAY, above) features sophisticated Catalan and traditional French cuisine, with items like anchovy puff pastry, lamb roast with thyme and pimentos, filet of sole with poached oysters and caviar, and ice cream with fresh apricots and figs. It is very expensive.

In Prades, **Jardin d'Aymeric** (04 68 96 53 38, at 3 avenue du Général-de-Gaulle, is a plain-

looking little eatery, but don't let that put you off. Good Catalan home cooking awaits you — roast stuffed pigeon, pork cutlets sautéed with eggplant and olive-laced local *tomme* cheese — at very affordable prices. In the little village of Taurinya, on D27 just south of Saint-Michel-de-Cuxa, the **Auberge des Deux Abbayes** (04 68 96 49 53, at 2 place Oratori, is an old country house tastefully converted to a restaurant, serving upscale regional cuisine, with fixed-price *menus* at 110 and 220 francs. There is a lovely garden dining area. Reservations are essential during the Casals Festival.

In Villefranche-de-Conflent the leading restaurant is the **Auberge Saint-Paul** (04 68 96 30 95, at

7 place de l'Église, serving the innovative creations of chef Patricia Gomez, one of Roussillon's finest. There are fixed-price *menus* at 135 and 380 francs. **Au Grill** (04 68 96 17 65, at Rue Saint-Jean, an easygoing eatery in a rustic old Catalan house, serves simple, well-prepared local fare at moderate prices, with fixed-price *menus* from 90 francs, amid ongoing art exhibitions.

HOW TO GET THERE

There are six trains a day from Perpignan to the Conflent, a 45-minute trip to Villefranche. There are also six buses a day, a one-hour and fifteen-minute trip. By car take N116, which follows the valley of the Têt River.

Lively wrought-iron restaurant signs in Villefranche-de-Conflent.

THE CERDAGNE

Villefranche-de-Conflent is the starting point for a 63-km (40-mile) excursion on *Le Petit Train Jaune* to the plateau of the Cerdagne deep in the Pyrénées, the cradle of the Catalan nation. In the summer, open cars are added to enhance the experience. The complete trip southwest from Villefranche to La Tour de Carol at the Spanish border, takes a bit under three hours, but you can get off at any of the 21 stops, if you don't care to go all the way. The section between **Olette**, about 10 km (six miles) from Villefranche, and **Mont-Louis**, 28 km (17.5 miles) away, is the most dramatic. The train

crosses a 16-arch viaduct far above the Têt, as well as another bridge that is 80 m (283 ft) high, and emerges from a long tunnel to reveal the wide, verdant central valley of the Cerdagne and mile-high **Mont-Louis**, the highest fortified city in France, built by Vauban in 1681. The trip from Villefranche to Mont-Louis takes 80 minutes.

The Cerdagne is a ski area, and the next two stops, **Bolquère-Eyne** and especially **Font-Romeu** have major resorts. It also has more sunny days than any other place in France, which is why the government built its solar energy research centers at Font-Romeu and Odeillo, site of the *four solaire*, a gigantic solar oven with 2,000 sq m (21,528 sq ft) of mirrors, the largest in Europe. The next stop is **Estavar** on the border of **Llivia**, a Spanish enclave within the boundary of France. It remained Spanish because of an oversight in the Treaty of the Pyrénées in 1659.

If you want to really get away from it all, get off the train at **Saillagouse**, the next stop, and go to the pretty village of **Llo** three kilometers (two miles) away and check into the **Auberge Atalaya***** (04 68 04 70 04 FAX 04 68 04 01 29, a charming wood and stone inn with 12 delightfully decorated rooms (Madame Toussaint, the owner, is a former decorator), a good restaurant, its own swimming pool, and golf, tennis and horseback riding nearby. The Auberge Atalaya is moderate to moderately expensive in price. It is a Relais du Silence member.

In Saillagouse itself, the Planes Family's rustic **Vieille Maison Cerdane** restaurant and 18-room **Planes Hotel**** (04 68 04 72 08 FAX 04 68 04 75 93, offers a cheerful, well-run, modestly priced alternative. It is at Place des Contes de Cerdagne. They also have a 20-room modern annex, the **Planotel**** which has a pool.

Bourg-Madame and **La Tour de Carol**, the last two towns on the line, are on the Spanish frontier.

Tourist information about the Cerdagne can be obtained from the following **Tourist Offices**: Villefranche-de-Conflent (04 68 96 22 96, Place de l'Église; Mont-Louis (04 68 04 21 97, Rue du Marché; Font-Romeu (04 68 30 68 30, Avenue Emmanuel-Brousse; and Saillagouse (04 68 04 72 89.

If you want to drive to the Cerdagne, take N116 southwest from Villefranche-de-Conflent.

THE VALLESPIR

The **Tech River Valley** winds to the southeast of Mont Canigou to the Pyrénées pass of the Col d'Ares at the Spanish border. The Vallespir, as the area is known, is the southernmost place in France. It is much appreciated by the rest of the nation because it brings the first cherries to the market in the spring. As the early-ripening cherries indicate, the Vallespir is an exceptionally sunny place. Fruit orchards blanket the valleys, and pastures and chestnut forests run up into the hills. Practically any back road you choose to explore in this as-yet-little-discovered area will be a dramatic one, and you will always have Mont Canigou as a reference point to keep you from getting lost.

Céret

This lively hill town 32 km (20 miles) southwest of Perpignan was a favorite retreat of Catalan artists and their friends in the early twentieth century and came to be called "The Mecca of Cubism" because of the work Picasso and Braque did here in 1911 and 1912, when they were collaborating so closely that their paintings were virtually indistinguishable. Gris, Chagall, Kisling, Masson, Soutine and Manolo, Picasso's Catalan sculptor friend who "discovered" Céret, also spent substantial periods here—which accounts for the astounding collection this town of 7,200 has in its **Museum of Modern Art**. There are first-rate works by all these artists and by Matisse (17 sketches he did in Collioure), Maillol, Dufy, Cocteau, Miro, Dali and such present-day names as Arman, Ben, Tàpies, Viallat, and Jean and Jacques Capdeville. The core of the collection is 53 works by Picasso. Twenty-eight are terracotta bowls painted with bullfighting scenes that he made specially for this museum. The building was enlarged and entirely renovated in 1992 and is a model of how modern art works should be displayed. It is open every day from 10 AM to 7 PM from July 1 to the end of August, 10 AM to 6 PM and closed Tuesdays the rest of the year.

Céret has numerous festivals and special events. The main ones are the **Easter procession**, the **cherry market** in April and May, **Feria** (bull-fighting, fireworks, street dances) on the weekend closest to the July 14, and the **Sardana Festival**, a big Catalan traditional dance event held the second to the last weekend in August. For details, contact the Tourist Office.

Where to Stay

The **Terrasse au Soleil****** (04 68 87 01 94 FAX 04 68 87 39 24 E-MAIL terrace-au-soleil.hotel@ wanadoo.fr, on the Route de Fontfrede, is a rambling old farmhouse in the cherry tree-covered hills above town once owned by singer Charles Trenet,

Céret has a wide, animated main street that changes names every block from Boulevard du Maréchal-Joffre, to Jean-Jaurès, to Place Picasso, to Lafayette, but is known here simply as "Le Boulevard." It is shaded by huge plane trees and lined with cafés (including **Le Grand Café**, were Picasso and friends used to gather) and boutiques, and off it, there are old squares with fountains. A **market** is held every Saturday for foods of the region — anchovies, oysters, ham, honey, paella, roast chicken, grilled fish—and local arts and crafts work.

Be sure to pause and look at fourteenth-century **Pont du Diable** (Devil's Bridge) at the entrance to town. Its single arch 45 m (174 ft) wide spans the Tech River at a height of 22 m (72 ft). Cherry orchards cover the hills around town, and Mont Canigou looms benevolently to the west.

The **Tourist Office** (04 68 87 00 53 is at 1 avenue Clemenceau, just off "Le Boulevard."

now a cheerful 27-room hotel with a swimming pool, tennis courts, golf practice hole, and an outstanding restaurant (see WHERE TO EAT, below). The attractive young owners, Pascal and Brigitte Leveille-Nizerolle, have both worked in America. Rooms run 750 to 1,450 francs, suites 200 francs more. It is a Relais du Silence member, open mid-March through mid-October.

Mas Treilles*** (04 68 87 38 37 FAX 04 68 87 42 62 is a handsome cluster of seventeenth-century Catalan stone farm buildings converted with marvelous taste into an eight-room, two-suite hotel. The rooms are very spacious, and almost all have terraces and private gardens, and there is a heated pool. Doubles run 500 to 950 francs, suites

---

OPPOSITE: *Abrivado* at Céret's Feria, the bullfighting festival in July. ABOVE: The *sardana*, the stately Catalan dance, seen in Collioure, is also done in many other towns and villages in Roussillon.

somewhat higher. The restaurant, for hotel guests only, serves refined Mediterranean cuisine. It is on D115 just west of Céret in Pont de Reynès, overlooking the Tech River. Gracious hosts Marie-France and Lazlo Bukk are fluent in English. Open Easter to mid-October.

In the heart of Céret, **Les Arcades**** (04 68 87 12 30 FAX 04 68 87 49 44, at 1 place Pablo-Picasso, has 26 neat, simple rooms, moderately priced to inexpensive. The **Vidal*** (04 68 87 00 85 FAX 04 68 87 62 33 is an old-fashioned, inexpensive 10-room inn at 4 place du 4 Septembre, just off Place Picasso.

CAMPING

Céret has four camping grounds, the best-equipped being the 100-place **Camping Saint-Georges** (04 68 87 03 73, open all year. It has a pool and tennis court. If no space is available in Céret, there are four regular camping grounds and one nudist establishment in neighboring Maureillas-las-Illas.

Where to Eat

The Terrasse au Soleil (see WHERE TO STAY, above) has, as its name indicates, a large sunny terrace, where duck with cherries, sautéed red mullets with a zucchini flan, and other finely-tuned regional dishes are featured at **La Cerisaie**, its Michelin one-star gourmet restaurant (one of the few in Roussillon). There are fixed-price *menus* at 125 and 190 francs. **Le Chat Qui Rit** (04 68 87 02 22, one and a half kilometers (one mile) west of town on Route d'Amélie (D115) in Reynès, is a warm, colorful restaurant with pictures of happy cats all over the place. It is a great local favorite, with bright regional *menus* at 70 francs for a weekday lunch, 170 francs otherwise, a salad bar, and intriguing array of light, summery offerings. There is a cheerful dining deck dotted with big parasols. In the medieval heart of Céret, **Le Pied dans le Plat** (04 68 87 17 65, at Place des 9 Jets, has a dining terrace on the charming, well-shaded little square with an odd fifteenth-century fountain in the middle, where you can savor the Montignac family's modestly priced Catalan and Southwestern home cooking and Breton crêpes. It is open from February to December, daily from June to September, closed Sundays and Mondays at lunch the rest of the time.

How to Get There

Line 35 of the Carinter 66 bus network runs frequent service between Perpignan and Céret and the other towns of the Vallespir. There are about fifteen buses a day. Coming by car from Perpignan, a distance of 32 km (20 miles), the easiest thing is to take the A9 *autoroute* south to Le Boulou and D115 west to Céret. From there the D115 runs southwest along the Tech River and reaches the Spanish frontier at the Col d'Ares.

AMÉLIE-LES-BAINS AND PALALDA

The ancient spa of Amélie-les-Bains, eight kilometers (five miles) to the southwest of Céret on D115, has been drawing people for cures since at least the days of the Romans, and today its waters are prescribed for rheumatism and respiratory problems. The lovely **Gorges du Mondony** begin only a 15-minute walk south of town, and the medieval Catalan village of Palalda, its steep narrow streets all decorated with flowers, is three kilometers (two miles) to the east. It has a little **Museum of Tradition and Popular Arts** with a reconstituted Catalan kitchen and bedroom from the turn of the century. It is open daily from mid-February to mid-December from 2 PM to 6 PM, to 7 PM in the summer.

Like most spa towns, Amélie-les-Bains has a casino.

The **Tourist Office** (04 68 39 01 98 in Amélie-les-Bains is at Quai du 8 Mai 1945.

Where to Stay and Eat

Because of the spa, Amélie-les-Bains has an inordinate number of hotels for a town of 3,300 — one three-star hotel, eight two-star hotels, and 11 one-star establishments. **Castel Émeraude**** (04 68 39 02 83 FAX 04 68 39 03 09 is a big, rambling white hotel with medieval-style twin turrets in a quiet country setting on the bank of the Tech River. It has 59 recently renovated, moderately priced rooms and a well-respected restaurant with *menus* from 95 francs. It is one kilometer west of town on the Route de la Corniche. A Relais du Silence member. The most colorful restaurant in the area is the **Mas Pagris** (04 68 39 38 73, in Montalba d'Amélie, reached by a five-kilometer (three-mile) drive or walk along the Gorges du Mondony. It serves savory dishes made from local products such as wild mushrooms, brook trout, and country sausage. Be sure to try the *boules de picolat*, meatballs cooked in wine and a wild mushroom sauce and served with white beans. A meal costs about 100 francs. In the summer, you dine outside, where the only sound to disturb you will be that of a nearby waterfall.

THE SOUTHERN VALLESPIR

Arles-sur-Tech

Another town of note in the Vallespir, Arles-sur-Tech is known for the lovely **cloister** of its medieval abbey and its Romanesque **Église Sainte-Marie**, which contains a strange tomb, the **Sainte-Tombe**, which keeps filling with a mysterious liquid in a manner that defies scientific explanation. The nearby **Gorges du Fou** is remarkable too. In places it is no more that three meters (10 ft) wide and more than 100 m (330 ft) high.

Corsavy is a tiny, picturesque hill village near Arles-sur-Tech with narrow medieval streets leading up to the ruins of its **castle** and splendid views of Mont Canigou, whose peak is only 12 km (7.5 miles) away.

Arles-sur-Tech's **Tourist Office** (04 68 39 11 99 is on Rue Barjau. There is only one hotel, but it is pleasant and inexpensive, **Les Glycines**** (04 68 39 10 09 FAX 04 68 82 38 08, at 32 rue du Jeu de Paume, a well-maintained old-style establishment from the late nineteenth century with 32 neat, clean rooms and the best restaurant in town.

The largest and best-equipped camping grounds in the southern Vallespir is **Le Vallespir** (04 68 39 05 03, in Arles-sur-Tech. It has 296 places,

There are 10 hotels in Prats-de-Mollo and La Preste (four of them Logis de France) and three modest camping sites, open from April through October. For information about this area, contact the Prats-de-Mollo **Tourist Office** (04 68 39 70 83 at Place Le Fioral.

PERPIGNAN TO THE CÔTE VERMEILLE

The Côte Vermeille (Vermilion Coast) is a string of crystal-clear Mediterranean inlets and sheer cliffs etched into the eastern end of the Pyrénées. The reddish color of the rock gives the coast its name. The cliffs twist along the coast for 20 km

a restaurant, bar, washing machines, a swimming pool, and tennis court and is open from April 1 to the end of October. The pleasantly situated, but modestly equipped 150-place **Camping Riuferrer** (04 68 39 11 06 is open all year.

Prats-de-Mollo

Built on the slopes of an open valley of the Tech 19 km (12 miles) southwest of Arles-sur-Tech, Prats-de-Mollo was a favorite vacation spot of the Kings of Aragon. It has a **Romanesque church**, **medieval ramparts** and the inevitable Vauban fortress, **Fort Lagarde**, on a rocky spur above the town, built to defend the border with Spain, only 14 km (nine miles) to the south. Neighboring **La Preste** is a spa noted for treatment of urinary problems. Napoléon III had a road built to it so he could go for a cure, but the Franco-Prussian War permanently disrupted his plans.

(12.5 mile) from Collioure to Cape Cerbère at the frontier of Spain, and the terraced vineyards of the Banyuls and Collioure *appellations* run up the steep hillsides most of the way. The Côte Vermeille starts 24 km (15 miles) southeast of Perpignan. As you head down there, try to make time for a stop at Elne, which is on the route, halfway between Perpignan and Collioure.

ELNE

Thanks to its steep hill dominating the rich farm plains around it, Elne has been inhabited since time immemorial, and continuously since the sixth century BC. It was the local capital of the Iberians, then the Romans, who made it the capital of Roussillon. Its name derives from Helene, the

Seafood brought in daily by the fishing fleet of Port Vendres.

mother of Emperor Constantine. From 568 to 1602 Elne was an episcopal see, and its large Romanesque **Cathédrale Sainte-Eulalie et Sainte-Julie** dates from the eleventh century. The cathedral's marble **cloister**, built between the twelfth and the fourteenth centuries, is one of the high points of medieval Catalan art, and its imaginative sculptures of fabulous animals, biblical figures, and floral patterns show how the style evolved.

In 1276, Elne lost its status as capital of Roussillon when the King of Majorca moved his court to Perpignan. Today it is a quiet town of 6,000 that makes its living from the fruit and wine trade.

The **Tourist Office** (04 68 22 05 07 is at 2 rue Docteur-Bolte.

Elne is 13 km (eight miles) south of Perpignan and can be reached by frequent trains and Carinter 66 buses. By car, take N114.

COLLIOURE

This town ranks with Cassis and Saint-Tropez as the most beautiful of Mediterranean France's small ports. It has a large thirteenth-century fortress jutting out into the harbor, brightly colored little fishing boats, a church on the water, three beaches, the red-roofed Vieux Quartier, green hills surrounding the ensemble, fortresses atop them, and bright sun and deep blue skies almost every day. "There is no sky more blue in France than in Collioure," said Matisse, who came here in 1905 and fell in love with the light. It was in Collioure that he finally shucked his last formal constraints: "I worked as I felt, only by color," and out of that breakthrough came *Bonheur de Vivre* and *Fenêtre Ouverte*. Derain, who came with Matisse in 1905, painted his dazzling *Phare de Collioure*. When the artists came back in 1906, Dufy, Gris and Marquet

ABOVE: The Côte Vermeille is famed for its anchovies and other seafood. RIGHT: The medieval port of Collioure on the Côte Vermeille, a favorite of Matisse, Derain and many other leading artists of the twentieth century.

joined them, and as a result, Collioure became known as the "Cradle of Fauvism." Twenty full-scale reproductions of works by Matisse and Derain have been mounted at the sites in Collioure where they were painted. Most of the views are little changed from their day.

Collioure's beauty has not been lost on the tourists, be warned. Armies of them arrive in midsummer, swelling the little town to several times its normal population of 2,700.

General Information

The **Tourist Office** (04 68 82 15 47 E-MAIL collioure @little-france.com WEB SITE www.little-france .com/collioure is at Place 18-Juin, one block in from the central beach, the Plage Boramar.

For train information, contact the **Gare SNCF** (04 68 82 05 89. Get **bus information** at the Tourist Office. The buses stop at the main parking lot of the town.

For scuba diving or windsurfing, contact **CIP Collioure** (04 68 82 07 16, 15 rue de la Tour d'Auvergne.

Festivals and Events

On Good Friday evening, the candlelight **Procession of the Brotherhood of the Sanch** is held. On August 16, the **Feast of Saint Vincent** has bullfights, fireworks and a procession up into the hills to Notre-Dame-de-Consolation. A *sardana* **dance festival** is held the first Sunday of September.

What to See and Do

The **Château Royal**, the impressive fortress on the bluff dominating the harbor, occupies a site used by the Phocean Greeks as early as the sixth century BC, and that the Romans later turned into a fortified village. In the Middle Ages, when the Catalan fleet ruled the Western Mediterranean, the Counts of Barcelona built a castle to defend Collioure, Perpignan's outlet to the sea. People in Collioure often refer to the Château Royal as the "Château des Templiers" because of an adjoining fortress the Knights Templar built in the thirteenth century. The royal designation came the following century, when the Kings of Majorca summered here. Spanish kings Charles V and Philip II reinforced the castle in the sixteenth century to protect Collioure from the French, and the fortress took its final shape in the late seventeenth century when Vauban made his inevitable modifications, adding the ramparts that jut out into the harbor. It is open from 10 AM to 5:15 PM June through September, 9 AM to 4:15 PM the rest of the year. In summer, the château hosts art exhibitions and concerts. The Tourist Office can inform you about these.

Across the little fishing harbor from the Château Royal at the end of the pebbly **Plage Boramar** is the seventeenth-century **Église Notre-Dame-des-Anges** with its bullet-shaped bell

tower, converted from an old lighthouse. The interior is murky, especially when you step in from the dazzling sunshine, but let your eyes adjust, and take a look at the nine remarkable gilded wood-carved altarpieces, five of them by the Catalan baroque master Joseph Sunyer, including the huge three level triptych on the main altar.

Narrow streets wind up the hill of the **Vieux Quarter du Mouré**, and at the top sits seventeenth-century **Fort Miradou**.

One place you should not miss is the **Hostellerie des Templiers** on the Quai de l'Amirauté, a hotel, bar and restaurant with an huge collection of art works. The many artists who came to Collioure from the time of Matisse and Derain onward became friends of René Pous, the owner of a local café, and they lavished paintings and drawings on him. Sadly, works by some of the big-name artists, Matisse and Picasso among them, were stolen several years ago. But with 2,000 original works on the walls of the hotel, bar and restaurant, there is no lack of art to peruse. The establishment is now run by René Pous's genial son Jo and his children, and its bar remains the place to plunge into the life of this town.

If you want to see more artworks, the **Musée d'Art Moderne de Collioure** (04 68 82 10 19, at the Villa Pams on the Route de Port-Vendres, has a contemporary art collection and puts on temporary exhibits run by the Musée d'Art Moderne de Céret. For information about their programs, call the museum or check at the Tourist Office.

For an inspiring walk into the hills, climb to the **Ermitage Notre-Dame-de-Consolation**, a hermitage with a number of sailors' ex-votos (offerings made in pursuance of a vow). There are fine views of Collioure, the sea and the mountains throughout the eight-kilometer (five-mile) hike up and back, for which you should allow an hour and a half.

Collioure is famed for its anchovies, and they are grilled outdoors for you along the Plage Boramar. You can also buy delicious fillets of anchovies in jars, marinated in a variety of ways. The leading specialists in this ancient technique are **Roque Salaisons** (04 68 82 04 99, on Route de la Démocratie (N114), or **Desclaux & Cie** (04 68 82 05 25, at the Carrefour du Christ, the intersection of N114 and Rue de la République, the main street down to the port. They have retail outlets at their workshops.

Wine Tasting

The vineyards you will see terraced up the steep, rocky slopes running the whole length of the Côte

LEFT: Collioure's Boramar Beach and its signature campanile, converted from a medieval lighthouse. OPPOSITE: Port Vendres, Roussillon's only deep-water port, has been used by mariners since the time of the ancient Greeks.

Vermeille make two *apellation contrôlée* wines — Collioure and Banyuls. The Collioure wines are deep-colored, exceptionally aromatic dry reds and bright, aromatic rosés, and Banyuls are *vins doux naturels*, sweet wines. It is common for the vineyards of the four communities authorized to make them — Collioure, Port-Vendres, Banyuls-sur-Mer, and Cerbère — to make both. The Collioure *appellation* is small, only 330 hectares (792 acres) of vineyards producing a million liters of wine (as compared to 30 million for Côtes du Roussillon or 45 million for Coteaux du Languedoc).

The **Maison de la Vigne et du Vin** (68 82 49 00, on Place du 18 Juin, across from the Tourist Office, is open from June to September and provides literature on Collioure wine in several languages and arranges wine tasting visits. **Domaine la Tour Vieille** (04 68 82 42 20, one of the most acclaimed producers of both Collioure and Banyuls wines, operates a *cave* in town from Easter to the end of September. It is centrally located on Rue Berthelot. Otherwise, visit the Domaine La Tour Vieille's 10-hectare (24-acre) vineyard at 3 avenue Mirador in the hills above town. Call ahead for an appointment. (For information on *AOC* Banyuls wines, BANYULS-SUR-MER, below.)

Where to Stay and Eat

Collioure is the big resort of the Côte Vermeille, but its hotels are minuscule by Côte d'Azur standards. It has one four-star hotel, six three-star hotels, and six two-star hotels with 323 rooms total in those categories — fewer than the Carlton or the Martinez in Cannes. Prices are relatively low too.

The **Relais des Trois Mas****** (04 68 82 05 07 FAX 04 68 82 38 08, on the Route de Vendres high overlooking Collioure's harbor, has 19 elegant rooms with luxurious baths, four suites, a pool, and health center. It houses a Michelin one-star restaurant, **La Balette**, serving Collioure anchovies marinated in Banyuls wine vinegar, sautéed fillets of red mullet served with *ratatouille* and *tapenade*, and other locally flavored specialties that have earned it one of the rare Michelin stars in Roussillon. It is expensive, with fixed-price *menus* at 195 and 395 francs. The hotel rooms are also expensive, in the 800 to 1,300 franc range. Closed mid-November to mid-December.

Casa Pairal*** (04 68 82 05 81 FAX 04 68 82 52 10, on the Impasse des Palmiers, near the beach, has 28 big, beautifully furnished rooms in a 100-year-old Catalan mansion with a palm-shaded garden and swimming pool, but there is no restaurant. It is a Relais du Silence member, open late March to mid-November. Its rooms run from 380 to 950 francs. **Hostellerie des Templiers**** (04 68 98 31 10 FAX 04 68 98 01 24, at 12 quai de l'Amirauté, has 52 neat rooms in the hotel and its annex. They are renovated regularly, and original art works

are everywhere. Fresh local fish is the restaurant's forte, served in the dining room with a bold mural by Claude Viallat or on the outdoor terrace facing the port and the Château Royal. The restaurant is closed Sunday evenings and Mondays, the hotel and restaurant the month of January. Room and meal prices range from inexpensive to moderate. **Triton**** (04 68 98 39 39 FAX 04 68 82 11 32, a cute old pink hotel on Rue Jean Bart at the Plage de Port d'Avall, Collioure's southernmost beach, has 20 pleasant, well-kept, inexpensive rooms. Reserve one with a balcony and a harbor view (those in the rear are too dark and offer nothing to see).

CAMPING

Collioure has two modest camping sites, **La Girelle** (04 68 81 25 56, and **Les Amandiers** (04 68 81 14 69, both by the Plage de L'Ouille a short walk north of town, open from April to the end of September. If you can't get into one of them, the next town to the north, Argelès-sur-Mer, has 56 camping grounds with thousands of places. **Les Criques de Porteils** (04 68 81 12 73, the closest, is a well-equipped 200-place camp on a cliff overlooking the Plage de L'Ouille, one kilometer (about a half-mile) north of the Collioure train station; open April 1 to the end of September.

How to Get There

There is frequent train service from Perpignan on the Port Bou line (the main line from Paris to the Spanish border) and Carinter 66 bus service from Perpignan's Gare Routière. If you are driving down N114, traffic is especially bad around Collioure in the summer. Stop-and-start conditions are not unusual. A new bypass around Collioure that runs from Argelès to Port-Vendres is a help. But given the volume of traffic in the summer, be prepared for slow going.

PORT-VENDRES

From Collioure, an exciting drive to make is a loop that follows the coast to Banyuls-sur-Mer (see below) and swings up into the hills to return to Collioure on the spectacular Route des Crêtes (see below), the Crest Road along the foothills of the Pyrénées overlooking the Mediterranean.

The town directly south of Collioure is Port-Vendres, the only deepwater port in Roussillon. Ancient Greek mariners used it, and the Romans gave it its name, Portus Veneris, Port Venus. It took its present shape in the seventeenth century, when it became French, and Louis XIV's finance minister Colbert decided to make it a commercial port, and Vauban built his customary forts to protect it. The handsome ensemble of eighteenth-century buildings to the north of the port reflects the prosperity that resulted. Here on the **Place de l'Obélisque** you can see the only monument in

France that celebrates Louis XVI—a 29-m (95-ft) **marble obelisk** that the king gave the town shortly before the French Revolution.

Prosperity continued through the nineteenth and early twentieth century, when Port-Vendres boasted of "the shortest distance in the calmest waters between France and Algeria," and it became a main port for cargo and passenger traffic with North Africa. The loss of Algeria in 1962 dealt a death blow to its large-scale port activities.

Today Port-Vendres, population 5,370, has a faded, B. Traven-like atmosphere, like Tampico in *The Treasure of the Sierra Madre*. It is a cargo port of modest activity, a year-round yacht harbor and a fishing port with the most active fleet on the

worked here in the summers for much of his life and is buried at his farm outside of town. Banyuls is an excellent place for sailing, scuba diving and all water sports and has a good selection of hotels and restaurants. In summer its normal population of 4,662 quadruples.

General Information

The **Tourist Office** (04 68 88 31 58 is on Avenue de la République, on the beach across from the Hotel de Ville, a very helpful and efficient operation. They can give you all the information you need about hotels, restaurants, sailing, scuba diving, and other activities in the area. They also have a long list of furnished rooms and apartments for rent.

Roussillon coast. The **Criée aux Poissons** (fish auction) is held at 4:30 PM at the Quai du Fanal, the fishing fleet's dock at the northern entrance to the harbor. For vacationers Port-Vendres offers numerous little beaches and good access to all water sports. But unfortunately its dramatic landscape is badly marred by too many tasteless modern buildings.

The **Tourist Office** (04 68 82 07 54 is at Quai Pierre Forgas in the center of town.

BANYULS-SUR-MER

This pleasant beach town on a long palm-lined crescent of sandy shore framed by a sweep of the Albères foothills is famous for two reasons: it is the home of Banyuls *vin doux naturel*, a delicious sweet apéritif wine, and it is the birthplace of sculptor Aristide Maillol (1861–1944), who lived and

What to See and Do

Maillol's Tomb is at his farm in a little valley amid hills covered by olive and fig trees a few kilometers from the center of town. The tomb is in the garden, watched over sorrowfully by one of Maillol's hefty nudes, a copy of his War Memorial in Perpignan. Maillol's house and studio have been converted into a museum and can be visited daily from 10 AM to noon. Get precise road directions at the Tourist Office. The tomb is downhill from the road, and you can easily drive right past it without noticing it.

Another Maillol nude, *Harmonie*, is in the little garden in back of Banyuls's Hôtel de Ville.

The **Aquarium of the Laboratoire Arago** (04 68 88 73 73, one of the oldest and most important marine biology laboratories in France, has 39 display

The tomb of Catalan sculptor Aristide Maillol in his native Banyuls-sur-Mer.

tanks containing 250 species of creatures from the Gulf of Lion. It is on Avenue du Fontaulé on the south side of the pleasure-boat port. It is open daily all year from 9 AM to noon and 2 PM to 6:30 PM, and to 10 PM in July and August.

Where to Stay

If you decide to stay overnight in Banyuls, I recommend **Les Elmes**** (04 68 88 03 12 FAX 04 68 88 53 03 WEB SITE www.preso.wanadoo.fr/hotel .les.elmes/, on the Plage des Elmes just north of town — a bright, cheerful 31-room hotel on the beach, very popular with scuba divers. Rooms here are in the moderate range, 280 to 500 francs for a double. A Logis de France member. **Le Catalan**** (04 68 88 02 80 FAX 04 68 88 16 14, on the Route de Cerbère, is a moderately priced modern hotel-restaurant on a hill above town, all 35 rooms have a sea view, and there is a big terrace pool. **Hôtel Llagut**** (04 68 88 00 81 FAX 04 68 88 13 37, at 18 avenue du Fontaulé across from the aquarium, is a Logis de France with 13 inexpensive and moderately priced rooms.

CAMPING

The well-shaded 33-place **Camping du Stade** (68 88 35 66, on the Route du Stade, is open April 1 to the end of October. **Camping Municipal** (04 68 88 32 13 is on Avenue Guy Malé (follow the signs for the Cellier des Templiers). It has 227 places and is open from mid-March to the beginning of November and the first two weeks of December.

Where to Eat

Al Fanal, El Llagut's restaurant, serves respected chef Dominique Trefou's authentic Roussillon cuisine, based on fish and shellfish fresh from Port Vendres. Fixed-price *menus* are 98 and 250 francs. There is an outstanding selection of regional wines. **La Littorine**, the restaurant of Les Elmes, also serves imaginative seafood dishes at reasonable prices.

Wine Tasting

As in Collioure, wine makers in Banyuls-sur-Mer make both *AOC* Collioure and Banyuls *vin doux naturel*. This natural sweet wine is drunk as an apéritif or after dinner. A properly aged Banyuls is considered the only wine to marry with chocolates, and it is good with cigars. You will have no trouble finding it here. It is sold by the glass or the bottle at stands along the beach, or you can visit producers' *caves* and taste it for free. The Grande Cave of the **Cellier des Templiers** (04 68 98 36 92, the largest producer, is right outside town on Route du Mas du Reig (D86). The visit consists of a 20-minute film and a 45-minute guided tour of the vast cellars with their gigantic oak vats and stainless steel tanks and the wooden barrels of wine aging outside in the sun. The wines are aged from

three to fifteen years before being sold. There is free wine tasting at the end of the tour. The cellar is open daily 9 AM to 7 PM April through October, 9 AM to noon and 2 PM to 6 PM and closed Sundays the rest of the year.

The smaller **Cave Cooperative de l'Étoile** (04 66 88 00 10, in the center of town, another fine producer, has a shorter tour of its cellars, also with free wine tasting. It is at 26 avenue du Puig-del-Mas. Open daily except Sunday in summer, weekends in the off-season. Both of these companies also make *AOC* Collioure wine of very high quality.

The young Parcé brothers accomplish wonders with their 30-hectare (72-acre) vineyard, producing extraordinarily delicious and highly acclaimed Banyuls and Collioure wines at their **Domaine de la Rectorie** (04 68 88 18 55. They are at 54 avenue du Puig-del-Mas. Call ahead for a *rendez-vous*.

ROUTE DES CRÊTES

From Banyuls, you have two choices of roads, the coast road that winds along 10 km (six miles) of bleak cliffs to the dreary rail terminus town of **Cerbère** by the Spanish border, or the Route des Crêtes. On the coast road, the cliffs are dramatic at a couple of points, especially **Cap Réderis**, and you might want to drive to the frontier just for the sake of having done it, but frankly, the time it takes doing that would be better spent taking in the scenic pleasures of the Route des Crêtes.

To get to the Route des Crêtes, swing up into the hills in back of Banyuls and take steep, winding D86 northward for spectacular vistas of the Mediterranean from many points. You will pass the ruins of several medieval towers that were part of an elaborate signal network from the time of the Kings of Majorca and Aragon. They allowed watchmen overlooking the Mediterranean to flash signals

deep into Roussillon in a matter of minutes. Park your car below the **Tour Madeloc** about 10 km (six miles) north of Banyuls and walk 15 minutes up to the tower. From its height of 652 m (2,140 ft), it surveys the whole coast from Cap d'Agde in the north well down the Costa Brava in Spain.

Two kilometers (just over a mile) north of the Tour Madeloc is the **Ermitage Notre-Dame-de-Consolation**, the hermitage with sailors' ex-votos on a hill overlooking Collioure.

The road now descends to Collioure, where you can order a glass of Collioure wine and take one more look at the delightful old port with its château and church and brightly painted little fishing boats that so many artists have painted, a fitting way to end our journey through Mediterranean France.

For the resourceful traveler, there are many unspoiled inlets to be found amid the red cliffs of the Côte Vermeille.

Travelers' Tips

GETTING THERE

BY AIR

Nice-Côte d'Azur International Airport, the third busiest in France after Charles de Gaulle and Orly in Paris, serves eight million passengers a year in its two big modern terminals. There are 15 direct flights a day from London on British Airways, British Midland and Easyjet, and Delta has one flight a day from New York. There are more than 45 flights a day from Paris on Air France, Air Liberté, and AOM, and direct flights from 25 other airports in France, from 44 in other European countries, and 14 in Africa and the Middle East. There is bus service every 20 minutes from Nice-Côte d'Azur Airport to Nice's Gare Routière (a 20-minute ride, 21 francs), every hour to Cannes (45 minutes, 70 francs), Monaco (45 minutes, 80 francs), and Menton (75 minutes, 95 francs). There is also frequent helicopter service to Monaco, Sophia-Antipolis, Cannes, and Saint-Tropez.

Marseille-Provence International Airport at Marignane is the second busiest airport in Mediterranean France, with three or four flights a day from London on British Airways depending on the season and about 20 flights a day from Paris on Air France and AOM. It is also Air France's *"Rendez-vous de la Méditerranée,"* its hub for flights between the cities of metropolitan France and airports in Corsica and the main cities of North Africa. **Montpellier Airport** has 10 daily flights from Paris on Air France and a few flights per week from London on Air Littoral and Dan-Air. Other airports with daily flights from Paris are **Toulon–Hyères** (convenient to Saint-Tropez) with 12, **Nîmes–Arles–Camargue** with four, **Avignon–Caumont** with three, **Béziers–Vias** with four, **Carcassonne** with three, and **Perpignan** with four.

As European Union rules encouraging competition have come into play, other French and European airlines have been able to fly to French destinations formerly monopolized by Air France, and prices have fallen. There is a great deal of fluctuation in prices, which are high in the summer and drop off-season, when remarkable promotional deals can often be found. The best bet is to check with travel agents, read the travel sections of newspapers, and hunt for good charters and package deals. The airlines also offer reductions for students, families, and senior citizens.

BY TRAIN

The *TGV*, the *Train à Grande Vitesse* (Very Fast Train), travels on high-speed rails from Paris as far south as Valence, about 80 km (50 miles) south of Lyon, and on normal tracks from there to the south. As of now, the *TGV* gets you from Paris to Avignon in 3 hours and 25 minutes, to Marseille in 4 hours and 25 minutes, Montpellier in 4 hours and 15 minutes, Perpignan in 6 hours, and Nice in 6 hours and 30 minutes. The SNCF (Société Nationale des Chemins de Fer), the French national railroad company, is currently extending the high-speed rails to Marseille, Montpellier, and beyond. This work is scheduled for completion in June 2001.

If you book your train trip well in advance, there are great savings to be had thanks to the SNCF's **Prix Découverte** programs. Prix Découverte J-8 gives you up to 40% (generally between 25% and 30%) off if you book at least eight days — and up to 60 days — in advance. Prix

Découverte J-30 gives you up to 60% off if you book at least 30 days in advance.

For people planning to use the train extensively, the SNCF sells cards authorizing reductions of up to 50%. For passengers 12 to 25 years of age the card costs 270 francs; for people over 60 it is 285 francs; and for those traveling with children under 12 it is 250 francs. For all information, contact SNCF (08 36 35 35 35 WEB SITE www.sncf.fr. Reservations and ticket purchases can be made on the web site.

The **Eurailpass**, which offers unlimited rail travel for a specified number of days throughout Western Europe (except for the United Kingdom), is not a good idea for travelers who want to explore as small an area as Mediterranean France. You have to do a great deal of traveling to make it cost-effective. However, if you do plan to range widely in Europe and want to look into the Eurailpass, call TOLL-FREE (800) 4EURAIL in the United States or (800) 361-RAIL in Canada. To qualify for a low-price Eurailpass, you must purchase it outside Europe. There are substantial reductions for two people traveling together. Any established North American travel agency can sell you these passes. There is also a **France Railpass**

OPPOSITE: The red rocks of the Esterel Corniche west of Cannes. ABOVE: Ferry to the Îles d'Hyères.

that allows three days per month of unlimited travel in France for US$140 each for two adults traveling together, $175 for an adult traveling alone.

To save the effort of long-distance driving, you can ship your car by rail from either Calais or Paris to Avignon, Narbonne or Nice, ride in comfort on a *TGV* or sleep overnight in a compartment, and pick up your car in the sunny South.

In Great Britain, contact Rail Europe ((08705) 848848 WEB SITE www.raileurope.uk, 179 Picadilly, London W1V OBA.

BY INTERNATIONAL BUS LINES

The cheapest way to get to Mediterranean France from London is by **Eurolines (** (990) 143-219 WEB SITE www.eurolines.co.uk, the big European international bus line. A full-fare round-trip ticket between London and Marseille is 1,000 francs. There are reduced fares for travelers under 26 years of age, substantial reductions for children four to 12 years of age, and big reductions off-season. In London the buses leave from Victoria Coach Station You can contact Eurolines in France (08 36 69 52 52 WEB SITE www.eurolines.fr. Travel agents can give you Eurolines's schedules and sell you tickets.

BY CAR

To drive in France, you must be 18 or over. Drivers licenses from other European Union countries, the United States and Canada are accepted in France. People bringing their own cars to France must have proof of ownership and insurance.

The Routes
Most people driving to Mediterranean France from Paris take the **A6** *Autoroute du Soleil* from Paris to Lyon, a distance of 461 km (288 miles), then the **A7** (still called the *Autoroute du Soleil*) down the Rhône Valley. The A7 ends in Marseille, 313 km (196 miles) south of Lyon. For the Côte d'Azur, the **A8** *la Provençale* branches east from A7 just north of Marseille and cuts straight through the center of the Var to Cannes, Antibes, Nice, Monaco, and on to Italy.

For Languedoc-Roussillon, the **A9** *la Languedocienne* branches off from A7 at Orange and runs southwest past Nîmes, Montpellier, Béziers, Narbonne and Perpignan, and down into Spain.

For Carcassonne, the **A61** *Autoroute des Deux Mers* branches westward from the A9 a few miles south of Narbonne.

These toll roads (*autoroutes à péage*) are expensive. To save money, you could take the *Nationale 7* (N7) south from Paris through the Massif Centrale to Lyon, then down the Rhône Valley, paralleling the A6 and A7, and cut east through the Var to the Côte d'Azur. It is free, but very slow.

A colorful alternate route to the Côte d'Azur is the **N85, la** *Route Napoléon,* from Grenoble down through the Alpes-de-Haute-Provence to Cannes.

VISAS

No visas are required by France or the Principality of Monaco for holders of valid United States, Canadian, European Union, Australian or New Zealand passports visiting France as tourists for up to three months. By law, visitors wanting to stay longer than that should obtain long-term visas before coming to France. Tourists in France who decide they want to stay longer than three months and be perfectly legal about it can simply pop

across the Italian or Spanish border, get their passports stamped and come back into France for another three months. But in fact, holders of any of the above-mentioned passports who don't break any laws in France are unlikely to be bothered by any French authorities.

French law requires everyone to carry proof of identification at all times. If you lose your passport, contact your consulate or embassy to get a temporary replacement.

CONSULATES AND EMBASSIES

Consulates and Embassies of major English-speaking countries are the following:
United States Consulate (04 91 54 92 00 FAX 04 91 55 09 47, 12 boulevard Paul-Peytral, 13006 Marseille; or (04 93 88 89 55 FAX 04 93 87 07 38, 31 rue du Maréchal-Joffre, 06000 Nice. United States

Embassy in Paris (01 43 12 22 22 FAX 01 42 66 97 83 WEB SITE www.amb.usa.fr.
British Consulate (04 91 15 72 10 FAX 04 91 37 47 06, 24 avenue du Prado, 13006 Marseille. They have a 24-hour emergency service. British **Embassy** in Paris (01 44 51 31 00 WEB SITE www.amb .grandebretagne.fr.
Irish Consulate (04 93 61 50 63 FAX 04 93 67 96 08, 152 boulevard J-F Kennedy, 06160 Antibes; and ((377) 93 15 70 00 FAX (377) 93 25 25 75, Villa les Bruyères, 1 place Sainte-Devôte, Monte-Carlo, Monaco. Irish **Embassy** in Paris (01 44 17 67 00 FAX 01 44 17 67 60.

The Australian, Canadian, New Zealand, and South African governments have no consulates

in the Mediterranean France region. For inquiries, contact their embassies in Paris:
Australian Embassy (01 40 59 33 00 FAX 01 40 59 33 10 WEB SITE www.austgov.fr.
Canadian Embassy (01 44 43 29 00 FAX 01 44 43 29 97 WEB SITE www.amb-canada.fr.
New Zealand Embassy (01 45 00 24 11 FAX 01 45 01 26 39 E-MAIL nzembassy.paris@wanadoo.fr.
South African Embassy (01 53 59 23 23.

TOURIST INFORMATION

FRENCH NATIONAL TOURIST INFORMATION OFFICES OUTSIDE FRANCE

The French government has travel information offices known as *Maisons de France* in many foreign countries. The main ones in the English-speaking world are as follows:

In the United States
The central phone number is ((900) 990-0040.
Beverly Hills ((310) 271-6665 or 2661 E-MAIL fgto@gte.net, 9454 Wilshire Boulevard, CA 90212.
Chicago ((312) 751-7800 E-MAIL fgto@mcs.net., 676 North Michigan Avenue, Suite 3360, IL 60611 2819.
Miami ((305) 373-8177 E-MAIL acouvez@aol.com, 1 Biscayne Tower, Suite 1750, 2 South Biscayne Boulevard, FL.
New York ((212) 838-7800 E-MAIL info@francetourism.com, 444 Madison Avenue, 16th Floor, NY 10022.

In Canada
Montreal ((514) 288-4264 E-MAIL mfrance@mtl.net, 1981 McGill College Avenue, Suite 490, QUE H3A 2W9.
Toronto ((416) 593-4723 E-MAIL French.Tourist @sympatico.ca., 30 Patrick Street, Suite 700, ONT M5T 3A3.

In Great Britain
London ((0171) 399-3500 E-MAIL piccadilly@mdlf.demon.co.uk, 178 Picadilly, W1V 0AL.

In Ireland
Dublin ((353) 1 679 0813 E-MAIL frenchtouristoffice @tinet.ie, 10 Suffolk Street, Dublin 2.

In Australia
Sydney ((61) 292 31 52 44 E-MAIL french@ozemail.com.au, 25 Bligh Street, NSW 2000.

In Hong Kong
% Air France ((852) 250 19 548 (543) E-MAIL ycmdfhkg@netvigator.com, 21st Floor, Alexandra House, Charter Road, Central.

NATIONAL TOURIST INFORMATION OFFICES IN PARIS

Maison de Tourisme de France (01 42 96 70 00 WEB SITE www.franceguide.com, 20 avenue de l'Opéra, 75001 Paris.
Office du Tourisme de la Principauté de Monaco (01 42 96 12 23 WEB SITE www.monaco-congres .com, 9 rue de la Paix, 75002 Paris.

REGIONAL TOURIST OFFICES

Comité Régional du Tourisme Provence-Alpes-Côte d'Azur (04 91 39 38 00 FAX 04 91 56 66 61, 2 rue Henri-Barbusse, 13241 Marseille.
Comité Régional du Tourisme du Languedoc-Roussillon (04 67 22 81 00 FAX 04 67 58 06 10 E-MAIL contact.crtlr@sunfrance.com WEB SITE www.cr-

---

OPPOSITE: A field of sunflowers in Languedoc. ABOVE: *Pétanque* was invented in Mediterranean France and is played in every village, town, and city.

Travelers' Tips

LanguedocRoussillon.fr/tourisme, 20 rue de la République, 34000 Montpellier.

Office du Tourisme de la Principauté de Monaco ((377) 91 16 61 66 WEB SITE www.monac-congres .com, 2A boulevard des Moulins, MC 98030 Monaco.

DÉPARTEMENTAL TOURIST OFFICES

Mainland France is divided into 95 administrative districts called *départements*, rather like counties in the United States or Great Britain. The tourist authorities of the *départements* are excellent sources of written information about hotels, camping grounds, sports, cultural activities, cuisine, and wines in their areas. Many of their brochures are in English. There are eleven *départements* that are wholly or partially in Mediterranean France, and I strongly recommend contacting them if you're thinking of visiting their areas. Moving from east to west, they are:

Comité Régional du Tourisme Riviera-Côte d'Azur (for the Alpes-Maritimes *département*) (04 93 37 78 78 FAX 04 93 86 01 06 E-MAIL crt06@ nicematin.fr WEB SITE www.crt-riviera.fr, 55 promenade des Anglais, 06011 Nice, for the area from Menton to Cannes, including Nice, the hill towns around Vence, Antibes, and Grasse.

Comité Départemental du Tourisme du Var (04 94 50 55 50 FAX 04 94 50 55 51 E-MAIL cdtvar @toulon, 1 boulevard Foch, BP 99, 83003 Draguignan, for the Esterel coast, the Maures, the Saint-Tropez peninsula, the Îles de Hyères, Toulon, Bandol, and the interior up to the Grand Canyon of the Verdon.

Comité Départemental du Tourisme des Alpes-de-Haute-Provence (04 92 31 57 29 FAX 04 92 32 24 94 E-MAIL CDTL04@wanadoo.fr WEB SITE www .alpes-haute-provence.com, 19 rue du Docteur-Honnorat, BP 170, 04005 Digne-les-Bains, for the Grand Canyon du Verdon, Digne-les-Bains, and the "Lavender Alps" of Haute-Provence.

Comité Départemental du Tourisme des Bouches-du-Rhône (04 91 13 84 13 04 91 33 0182 E-MAIL cdt13@visitprovence.com WEB SITE www .visitprovence.com, 13 rue Roux de Brignoles, 13006 Marseille, for Cassis, Marseille, Aix-en-Provence, Arles, the Alpilles, and the Camargue.

Comité Départemental du Tourisme de Vaucluse (04 90 80 47 00 FAX 04 90 86 86 08 E-MAIL info@ provinceguide.com WEB SITE www.provinceguide .com, 12 rue Collège de la Croix, BP 147, 84008 Avignon Cedex 1, for Avignon, Châteauneuf-du-Pape, Orange, Vaison-la-Romaine, Mont Ventoux, the Dentelles de Montmirail, and the Lubéron.

Comité Départemental du Tourisme de la Drôme (04 75 82 19 26 FAX 04 75 56 01 65 E-MAIL com-externe@cg26.fr WEB SITE www.cg26.fr, 31 avenue Président-Herriot, 26000 Valence, for Nyons, Grignan, and "La Drôme Provençale." Alterna-

tively, La Drôme Provençale has its own WEB SITE www.dromeprovencale.org.

Comité Départemental du Tourisme du Gard (04 66 36 96 30 FAX 04 66 36 13 14 E-MAIL cdtgard @imaginet.fr, 3 place des Arènes, 30000 Nîmes, for Nîmes, the Pont du Gard, Uzès, Beaucaire, and Aigues-Mortes.

Comité Départemental du Tourisme de l'Hérault (04 67 67 71 71 FAX 04 67 67 71 77 E-MAIL tourisme @cge-ol.fr WEB SITE www.cdt.herault.fr/, BP 3067, Avenue des Moulins, 34034 Montpellier, for Montpellier, the foothills of the Cévennes, Sète and the Bassin de Thau, Agde, Béziers, and the Canal du Midi.

Comité Départemental du Tourisme de la Lozère (04 66 65 60 00 FAX 04 66 49 27 96 E-MAIL CDT .Lozere@wanadoo.fr, 14 boulevard Henri-Bourillon, BP 4, 48001 Mende Cedex, for the Cévennes Mountains and the Gorges of the Tarn.

Comité Départemental du Tourisme de l'Aude

(04 68 11 66 00 FAX 04 68 11 66 01 E-MAIL Cdt.aude .Pays.cathare@wanadoo.fr, Conseil Général de l'Aude, Plateau de Grazailles, 11855 Carcassonne Cedex 9, for Narbonne, the Corbières, Carcassonne, and Cathar Country.

Comité Départemental du Tourisme des Pyrénées-Roussillon (04 68 34 29 94 FAX 04 68 34 71 01 E-MAIL Tourisme.Roussillon.france@ wanadoo.fr WEB SITE www.pyrenees-orientales .com, 7 quai Lattre-de-Tassigny, B.P. 540, 66000 Perpignan, for Perpignan, Collioure and the Côte Vermeille, Mont Canigou, and the eastern Pyrénées.

TOURIST INFORMATION AND ASSISTANCE ON THE SCENE

All cities and towns have their own *Office de Tourisme*, and in smaller localities, it is often called the *Syndicat d'Initiative*. Local tourist offices are stocked with free maps and brochures on food, accommodations, sports, outdoors and cultural activities in their area, and the staffs are generally well-informed and very helpful. Some tourist offices will book rooms for you, and many offer guided tours of the principal cultural attractions in their town or city, including tours in English, German and other languages. Tourist offices I have found to be especially helpful in Mediterranean France are those of Menton, Monaco, Nice, Annot, Digne-les-Bains, Cannes, Castellane (for the Grand Canyon du Verdon), Saint-Tropez (town and peninsula), Toulon, Marseille, Aix, Arles, Saint-Rémy, Avignon, Carpentras, Nyons, Grignan, Nîmes, Uzès, Sète, Cap d'Agde, Carcassonne, Limoux, and Villefranche-de-Conflent.

As a general rule, I'd suggest making the *Office de Tourisme* your first stop when you arrive in a

The Cirque de Mourèze, one of many strange natural formations in the Cévennes above Montpellier.

a city or town. If you want to write away for tourist information about any town or city you're interested in, simply address an envelope to "Office de Tourisme," the name of town or city and, if you are writing from another country, obviously, "France." If there is specific information you want, but you don't know French, you can write a note in English. Someone will be able to read it.

GETTING AROUND

BY AIR

Given the short distances between the cities in Mediterranean France and the infrequency of flights, it doesn't make a great deal of sense to fly unless you are in a hurry. However, if you are in a hurry, Air Littoral (08 03 83 48 34, has three flights a day each way between Nice and Marseille (40 to 50 minutes), two between Nice and Montpellier (one hour), and one flight a day connecting Nice and Perpignan (one hour).

BY TRAIN

The train service along the Mediterranean coast is excellent, particularly on the Côte d'Azur, where the local Métrazur service runs trains about every half-hour between Saint-Raphaël and Menton. The only coastal area that is not served by rail is the section between Fréjus and Hyères, including the Saint-Tropez Peninsula. Toulon, Marseille, Arles, Avignon, Montpellier, Béziers, Carcassonne, Narbonne, and Perpignan are also well served by rail. Getting inland by rail is another story.

From Nice, there is the Cuneo line into the Alpes-Maritimes and the *Train des Pignes* (*Pine Cone Train*) into the Alpes-de-Haute-Provence. There is a line from Marseille along the Durance River into the Alpes-de-Haute-Provence, a train from Narbonne to Carcassonne, a train from Perpignan to Villefranche-de-Conflent, and from there the *Petit Train Jaune* (*Little Yellow Train*) into the Cerdagne region of the Pyrénées.

Distances are short. From Nice to Marseille, for example, it is about a two-and-a-half-hour train ride.

BY BUS AND URBAN TRANSPORTATION

There is good bus service between the main towns and cities — Nice, Antibes, Cannes, Fréjus–Saint-Raphaël, Saint-Tropez, Marseille, Aix, Avignon, Arles, Montpellier, Sète, Béziers, Narbonne, Carcassonne, and Perpignan — but service to the interior is infrequent and requires a great deal of patience. The tourist offices have the timetables for the bus services, but you usually have to ask for them. They don't necessarily have them on display.

Public bus systems in the main cities are good, and Marseille has a modern subway system.

BY CAR

Driving in France

One rule of the road you must be extremely careful to obey at all times is *priorité à droite* — the car on the right coming into an intersection has the right of way, unless you are in a traffic circle. But even in an traffic circle, watch out for cars trying to cut in from the right (French drivers are extremely competitive). Drive defensively, in other words.

Seat belts must be buckled in the back seat as well as the front, violators being subject to hefty fines.

Driving under the influence of alcohol carries very heavy fines.

Roads are labeled A for *autoroute*, N for *route nationale*, and D for *route départementale*. The latter generally have good surfaces, but are narrow, especially for American drivers, who are used to wide roads. The speed limit on *autoroutes* (toll highways) is 130 km per hour (81 mph). On the *routes nationales*, non-toll national highways (marked in red on most maps), it is 110 km per hour (68 mph), while it is 90 km per hour (56 mph) on lesser country roads, and 50 km per hour (30 mph) in the city.

Toll roads are marked *péage*.

Car Rental

There are a dozen or more auto rental services operating in the region, large and small, and prices vary widely depending on the time of year, the level of competition and so forth. For Americans, the rates of international companies are considerably cheaper if you make your reservation in advance via an 800 (toll-free) number. The major ones are: **Avis** ((800) 331-1212 WEB SITE www.avis .com; **Budget** ((800) 527-0700 WEB SITE www .drivebudget.com; **Hertz** ((800) 654-3131 WEB SITE www.hertz.com; **National (EuropCar)** ((800) 227-7368 WEB SITE www.nationalcar.com.

Car Leasing

For tourists from outside the European Union who plan to rent a car for 23 days or more, the best price you can get is by a lease-purchase arrangement whereby you pay in advance a fixed rate based on the period of time you plan to use the car and sign a promissory note to purchase the car if you do not return it to the dealer at the end of your trip. For the lowest-priced car, the Renault Twingo, the cost is under US$25 a day for a 23-day period, less for longer periods. Complete insurance coverage is included. The cars can be picked up and returned in many cities in France, including Nice, Marseille

---

Rafting on the Gorges of the Tarn in Languedoc.

and Perpignan. In the United States, contact **Renault Eurodrive** (212) 532-1221 TOLL-FREE (800) 221-1052 or (800) 477-7116 (in the Western states) FAX (212) 725-5379 WEB SITE www.renaultusa.com, 650 First Avenue, New York, New York 10016-3214.

Maps

Kümmerly+Frey/Blay Foldex maps 1:250000 (1 cm=2,5 km), Sheet 14 for Provence-Côte d'Azur, Sheet 10 for Languedoc-Roussillon and Sheet 5 for South-West-Pyrénées are widely available in bookstores, stationery shops and service stations in France.

ACCOMMODATIONS

A full range of accommodations is available in Mediterranean France, and in vast numbers, from some of the most sinfully *de luxe* hotels in the world in Monte-Carlo, Cannes and Saint-Tropez to a sleeping bag in a farmer's field. There are tourist hotels of all levels of quality and price, furnished apartments, houses and cottages, rooms in private homes, nudist colonies and camping and motor home grounds galore. Unlike some parts of the world where you have to scrounge for a decent place to stay, the problem here is one of an embarrassment of choices.

HOTEL CATEGORIES

The French Ministry of Tourism has a rating system for hotels, with (theoretically) five levels ****L (luxury), **** (first-class), *** (very comfortable), ** (comfortable), * (simple, but adequate). I say "theoretically," because lately, the hotels in the four-star-L category have been lumped together with the four-star hotels in the tourist office listings. To find out which is which, just look at the prices. The luxury hotel will be considerably more expensive than the first-class one. Some hotels have no stars. This is not necessarily because they don't merit them. The hotel may be too small to be rated, or the owner may not have felt like filling out the many forms required. The rating system is very complicated, and the differences between hotels of one category and the next may not matter to some clients. For instance, whether the elevator goes to the third or the fourth floor, or the percentage of rooms with private baths can account for the difference between a three-star and a two-star classification. In terms of service, all hotels three-star and above are required to have reception personnel who speak two foreign languages, one of which must be English, and to serve breakfast in the rooms. Unless you demand considerable luxury, a three-star will normally be perfectly satisfactory. For most people, *un bon petit deux étoiles* — a good little two-star hotel — should be quite adequate for a

room with a private bath or shower, which more than 40% of the rooms in two-star hotels are required to have. Lower than two-stars, clean, simple places can be found, but less than 20% of the rooms are required to have private bath or showers. On this level, price rather than comfort is uppermost in the client's mind.

HOTEL PRICES

Generally, the closer to the Mediterranean, the higher the prices, the highest being on the Côte d'Azur, where very expensive hotels are common, and declining as you move westward. Prices also tend to decline as you move inland, though not always (the Alpilles, for instance, is an expensive area). It is possible to find good, reasonably priced hotels on the Côte d'Azur, but you have to look for them. To the west of the Rhône in Languedoc and Roussillon, there are few hotels in the "very expensive" category and prices are considerably lower in general.

The categories of hotel room prices used in this book are calculated on the cost of a standard double room:

VERY EXPENSIVE = more than 1,500 francs
EXPENSIVE = 650 to 1,500 francs
MODERATE = 300 to 649 francs
INEXPENSIVE = less than 300 francs

It should be noted that hotels often have rooms in two different price categories, depending on the location of the rooms in the hotel (with a view or without a view), the furnishings, etc. In our price categories, we are referring to the better quality double rooms in a given hotel.

It is not absolutely accurate but is a good rule of thumb to say that the average price of a room in a given city will drop to half as much as you go down to the next category. For example, in a town where a four-star (****) hotel room goes for 1,200 francs, a three-star (***) will be 600, a two-star (**) 300, a one-star (*) 150.

It should also be noted that the room prices we mention may not correspond exactly to the ones you are quoted when you make your reservation. Prices are subject to change. But they probably will not change by too much.

HOTEL CHAINS AND GROUPS

Relais & Châteaux is an association of prestigious independently owned and operated, small to moderate-sized country inns, superb residences, and sumptuous hotels of great character, generally in magnificent settings. Most are four-star hotels in our expensive (650 to 1,500 francs) price category. The restaurants range in quality from very good to fabulous. For the beautiful Relais & Châteaux catalogue, which is worth getting just to read and look at the pictures, write, call, fax, or e-mail Relais & Châteaux at one of the following locations:

France (01 45 72 90 00 FAX 01 45 72 90 30 E-MAIL resarc@relaischteaux.fr WEB SITE www .relaischateaux.fr., 15 rue Galvani, 75017 Paris.

United States ((212) 856-0015 FAX (212) 856-0193 E-MAIL nyrelais@aol.com, 11 East 44th Street, New York NY 10017.

Great Britain ((0870) 242 00 52 FAX (0171) 828 94 76 E-MAIL relaislondon@easynet.co.ok, Grosvner Gardens House, 35/37 Grosvner Gardens, London SW1W 0BS.

Australia ((02) 9957-4511 FAX (02) 9929-6326, Mary Rossi Travel, Suite 3, The Dennison, 65 Berry Street, North Sydney 2060.

sumptuous all-you-can-eat breakfast buffet for 60 francs. Most have restaurants, which are quite good. Prices vary from city to city, but except for a few short periods throughout the year, in most cities they are in our moderate price category, from about 400 to 650 francs. Their catalogue can be picked up in any of their hotels or ordered from: Mercure Hôtels (01 69 36 80 80 FAX 01 69 36 79 00 WEB SITE www.mercure.com, 2 rue de la Mare Neuve, 91021 Evry. For reservations in France (08 03 88 33 33; United States ((800) 637-2873; United Kingdom ((0181) 283-4580.

Relais du Silence WEB SITE www.relais-du-silence.com is a group of 319 independently owned and operated hotels and inns in Europe

The catalogue is free if you come to the office. There is a charge of 60 francs (US$10) if you want it mailed to you.

The **Mercure** chain has 234 hotels in France, most of them in the three-star category, with 27 in Mediterranean France. Though the chain is part of the Accor mega-group (more than 3,000 hotels worldwide) and most of their guests are business travelers, Mercure hotels are far from cold or impersonal, and they tend to be well-located for tourism. Most are modern, with attractive contemporary decor and soothing color schemes (purples, pastels, coral), but some, such as the Paul Cézanne in Aix and La Vicomté in Carcassonne, are elegant older hotels furnished with antiques. The rooms are quiet and very comfortable (excellent beds, very firm), well-equipped (minibar, cable television, touch-tone phone, modern bathrooms), and the staff is bright and attentive. They have a

and Canada, 25 of them in our Mediterranean French area. Their common characteristic is dedication to peace and quiet. A few are small city hotels such as the elegant Petit Palais in Nice and the sedate Arène in Orange, but most are pleasant country inns, typically with 20 to 30 rooms, many with only 10 or 12, only a few with more than 50. Service is warm and personal. Almost all have restaurants, and the quality varies from very good to excellent (the restaurant of the Terrace au Soleil in Céret has a Michelin one-star rating). The inns have two-, three-, and four-star ratings. Most of them are in our moderate price category (300 to 650 francs), but the four-star establishments such as the Terrace au Soleil and Hostellerie du Vallon de Valrugues in Saint-Rémy-de-Provence are in our expensive category.

One of the many inns in the Camargue oriented to exploring the wildlife-rich region by horseback.

The Relais du Silence catalogue can be ordered from the following addresses:

France (01 44 49 79 00 FAX 01 44 49 79 01 17, Rue d'Ouessant, 75015 Paris. For reservations in France (01 44 49 90 00.

Great Britain ((01736) 79 61 99 FAX (01736) 79 89 55, The Garrick Hotel, Burthallen Lane, Higher Ayer Saint Ives, Cornwall TR26 3AA.

United States ((817) 483-9400 TOLL-FREE (800) 927-4765 FAX (817) 483-7000, HSA Voyages, 5609 Green Oaks Boulevard SW, Arlington, TX 76017.

The **Best Western** group has 160 hotels in France, 26 of them in the Mediterranean area. These are individually owned and operated three- and four-star hotels, all with their own

Central reservation service in the United States TOLL-FREE (800) 528-1234.

Campanile is a chain of almost 400 cheerful, modern two-star hotels and motels in France, England and the Benelux countries, with 41 in our Mediterranean area. The typical Campanile is an American-style double-decker motel with less than 50 rooms run by a hard-working young couple. The standards of comfort and cleanliness are very high. The beds are firm and the bathrooms modern, and there is a television, coffee-maker and touch-tone phone in every room. The decor is rustic, almost to the point of kitsch, and the fare in the restaurants is very simple—grills and buffets are heavily featured (the 35 franc all-you-want

distinct styles, committed to upholding the group's high standards of cleanliness and comfort, and sharing in Best Western's central reservation and marketing systems. In the big cites they range from charming small hotels such as Le Guilhem, a the seventeenth-century gem in Montpellier, to Nice's West End, a big *belle époque* beauty on the Promenade des Anglais. In the coastal areas there are mini-resorts such as the delightful Le Provençal overlooking the sea at the tip of the Giens Peninsula in Hyères, or the graceful four-star Beauséjour in a secluded garden setting in Juan-les-Pins. The hotels are in the moderate and expensive categories. For the free Best Western France hotel guide, write or otherwise contact Best Western France (01 44 87 40 80 FAX 01 44 87 40 84 WEB SITE www.bestwestern.com, 74 avenue Docteur-Arnold-Netter, 75012 Paris. Central reservation service in France (08 00 90 44 90.

breakfast buffet is excellent value). Most Campaniles are in *ZACs* (*Zones d'Activité Commerciale*), modern commercial parks away from the center of town, quiet, but rarely with any local atmosphere. They are especially practical for families and offer a children's *menu* at 39 francs. At the normal room rate of 285 francs, the quality-price ratio is hard to beat (at their 170-room hotel across the Promenade des Anglais from the Nice-Côte d'Azur Airport, the rate is 395 francs, an exception). For the guide to their hotels, call, fax, or write to Campanile Europe (01 64 62 46 46 FAX 01 64 62 46 61 WEB SITE www.campanille.fr, 31 avenue Jean Moulin, 77200 Torcy. The same numbers can be used to make reservations.

Logis de France is an association of 3,710 small and medium-sized family-owned and operated hotels and inns in the three-, two-, and one-star categories, in the inexpensive to moderate price ranges. There are hundreds of them in Mediterranean France, many in off-the-beaten-track places, each different, each reflecting the personality of its owners. Their motto is L'hôtellerie à visage humain (hotel-keeping with a human face). The hotels range from fairly elegant to quite modest, but the standards of cleanliness are good at all levels. The Logis de France guide, which has good maps that show you where all the *logis* are located, is sold by news dealers everywhere in France (100 francs). The *départemental* tourist offices often distribute free pamphlets on the Logis de France in their areas, and there is a Logis de France counter at the Gare Routière (bus terminal) in Nice. The central address is: Fédération Nationale des Logis de France

(01 45 84 70 00 WEB SITE www.logis-de-france.fr FAX 01 45 83 59 66, 83 avenue d'Italie, 75013 Paris. The central reservation number in France is (01 45 84 83 84.

FURNISHED APARTMENTS

Local tourist offices provide lists of furnished apartments, rented by the week, often much cheaper than a hotel if you are vacationing with the family or a group of friends. Ask for the list of *appartements meublés*.

GÎTES

Gîtes ruraux are furnished rural houses you can rent by the week or the weekend at modest rates, from 500 to 3,000 francs a week, depending on size, location and time of year. Booklets for each

département with photos and details can be obtained from Maisons de France overseas, from Offices de Tourisme in the different localities in France, or from the Fédération Nationale des Gîtes de France (01 49 70 75 75 FAX 01 42 81 28 53 E-MAIL info@gites-de-france.fr WEB SITE www.gites-de-france.com, 59 rue Saint-Lazare, 75009 Paris. The booklets are in French with an explanation of the symbols in English, and they run 40 to 80 francs depending on the number of *gîtes* in the *département*. There is also a book of the top-rated *gîtes* and bed and breakfasts in France, *Chambres d'Hôtes Prestige et Gîtes de Charme*, which costs 140 francs.

Reserve as early as possible. The most popular *gîtes* are booked a year in advance.

OTHER TYPES OF ACCOMMODATION

For information on bed and breakfasts, youth hostels and camping in the region, see BACKPACKING, page 39 in YOUR CHOICE.

EATING OUT

For information on Mediterranean French cuisine and wine, see GALLOPING GOURMETS, page 56 in YOUR CHOICE. For information on the top restaurants in the region, see LIVING IT UP, page 42 in YOUR CHOICE.

Throughout the book, we have pointed out restaurants with particularly talented chefs. But watch out: chefs sometimes go elsewhere. So before booking a table at a very expensive restaurant, make sure that the noted chef is still there. If he (or occasionally she) has departed, make inquiries at your hotel or elsewhere about the restaurant's current reputation.

RESTAURANT PRICES

Our price categories are based on the average cost of a meal per person, not including drinks:
VERY EXPENSIVE = more than 600 francs.
EXPENSIVE = 300 to 600 francs.
MEDIUM = 125 to 299 francs.
INEXPENSIVE = Less than 125 francs.

Note that in French the menu is called *la carte*, the word *menu* refers specifically to fixed-price meals of anything up to seven courses, but more commonly three or four, with a limited range of choice for each course. *Menus* can not only represent great value, but often include the most typical local dishes or the specialities of the house.

In many cases, we give prices of fixed-price *menus* or certain dishes. It should be understood that these prices are subject to change at any time.

OPPOSITE: Nice's Hôtel Negresco's Louis XIV Salon with its portrait of the Sun King by Hyacinthe Rigaud. ABOVE: La Grande-Motte on the Languedoc Coast.

TIPPING

IN RESTAURANTS

At the bottom of the menu you will see the phrase *service 15% compris* (15% service charge included). This means that the price of every item listed on the menu has the tip included in it. The prices of the items you order will be added up just as they appear on the menu, and that total is all you are required to pay. In practice, people usually leave a little something if they are happy with the service — an extra five percent, or a 10 franc coin. But they have no obligation to do so if they don't want to.

IN HOTELS

It is customary to give porters 10 francs per piece of luggage and to leave the chambermaids 10 francs a day.

TAXIS

A 10% tip is generally sufficient, but you can give more if the service is particularly good.

THE BASICS

WEIGHTS AND MEASURES

France uses the metric system for all measurements:

Units of Distance
1 km = 0.625 (⅝) mile
1 m = 3.28 ft

Units of Weight
1 g = 0.035 oz
1 kg (kilo) = 2.2 lbs

Units of Volume
1 l = 2.1 US pints = 1.76 UK pints

Temperature
Temperature in France, as in all of Europe, is measured in degrees Celsius (Centigrade): 0°C is the freezing point of water, 100°C its boiling point, room temperature is 20°C (68°F), body temperature is 37°C (98.6°F). For those wanting to convert temperatures to Fahrenheit, a rough approximation is to multiply the Centigrade temperature by two and add 32.

ELECTRICITY

Current in France is 220 volts AC, 50 cycles. While this is compatible with British, Irish, Australian, and New Zealand appliances, you cannot use American standard appliances without a transformer. If you want to use your portable computer in France, it would be wise to get a multi-standard power supply in the United States before leaving on your trip. Sockets take two-prong, round-pin plugs.

DATES AND TIMES

In France, the date is expressed as follows: 1 June 2000, or 1/6/2000 (not 6/1/2000). The time is generally expressed by the 24-hour clock. Thus 8 AM is 8 h or 8 h 00 (*huit heures*) and 8 PM is 20 h or 20 h 00 (*vingt heures*). Noon is *midi* (12 h) and midnight is *minuit* (24 h).

BANKING AND MONEY

Generally banks in the provinces are open Tuesday to Saturday from 9 AM to 4:30 PM and closed Sunday, Monday, and the afternoon before holidays.

EXCHANGE RATES

Most banks can exchange foreign currency and travelers checks. Licensed money-changers display exchange rates. Banks sometimes do not, except in big cities like Marseille and Nice. It is wise to arrange cash exchanges over US$1,000 in advance.
Euro 1 euro = FFr 6.55957
Germany DM1 = FFr 3.35
Switzerland SFr1 = FFr 4
United States $1 = FFr 6.40
United Kingdom £1 = FFr 10.00

CREDIT CARDS

The most widely accepted credit card is Visa, and if you plan to be charging a lot, you would be wise to get one from a bank in your own country before leaving home. MasterCard is accepted almost as frequently. American Express and Diners Club cards are generally accepted in large or deluxe establishments, but modest hotels and restaurants often refuse them because of the high service charges the seller has to pay.

Another virtue of having a Visa card is that it enables you to get cash advances in French francs from banks that honor them. Automated Teller Machines (ATMs) are common in Mediterranean France.

TAXES AND TAX REFUNDS

Americans and other non-Europeans purchasing 2,000 francs or more worth of goods in a single store are eligible for a refund of the value-added tax (the *TVA*, or *taxe sur la valeur ajoutée*). The discounts can range from 10% to 22%, depending on the nature of the goods. You must show your passport to the store staff and ask them to fill out the French customs *TVA* refund form. To get the refund, you have the form processed by French customs (*la douane*) at the airport, on the train or at the frontier post when you are leaving the country. Be prepared to show them the items you purchased, because sometimes they ask. The refund will be either mailed to you or credited to your credit card if you purchased the items on it, which is a lot quicker and easier.

POST OFFICES

Post offices are open from 8 AM to 7 PM Monday through Friday and 8 AM to noon on Saturday. Post

number. (For information about the telephone system in Monaco, see GENERAL INFORMATION, page 117, under MONACO.) For operator-assisted international calls, dial 00+33 plus the country code. For International Information, dial 00+33 +12 plus the country code.

For more details, look in the front part of the Yellow Pages (*Pages Jaunes*), where there are explanations in English and several other languages. Some city codes are listed here (look under *États-Unis* for United States and *Royaume-Uni* for the United Kingdom), but for a more complete list of city codes, get the little booklet called *Le Guide du Téléphone International*, available in France Télécom offices.

offices have bright yellow signs with the words *La Poste* or *PTT*. Stamps can also be purchased in *tabacs* (tobacco shops), large hotels, and some newsstands.

TELEPHONES

France has a good, modern telephone system, and it is quite easy to use.

Making calls out of France

To place calls to foreign countries, dial **00**, the country code, the area code and the phone number. For example, to call Boston, you dial 00+1 (the code for the United States) 617 (Boston's area code), then the phone number. For Great Britain, dial 00+44, followed by the city code (without the "0"), then the seven-digit phone number. To call Monaco, dial 00+377 plus the eight-digit phone

Calling France from a foreign country
Dial France's country code, 33, drop the first 0 of ten-digit phone number, and dial remaining the nine digits.

Pay phones
There are still a few old-fashioned coin-operated instruments on the street or in bars or cafés (normally using a one-franc or two-franc coin), and in some bars or cafés. Sometimes you make your call first and pay the barman after. But most pay phones now operate on *télécartes*, and if you plan to use the phone much, you would be wise to buy one. A *télécarte* is a plastic card with a computer chip in it that entitles you to a certain number of message units. They can be bought in any *tabac* (tobacco shop) or post office and cost from 50 to 120 francs.

Olives at the market in Uzès.

Télécartes can be used for calls to foreign countries as well as domestic. You can also use a Visa card with some pay phones.

EMERGENCY PHONE NUMBERS

Directory inquiries (12.
SAMU (24-hour ambulance service) (15.
Police (17.
Fire (18.

SAFETY

In France, the South has a reputation for crime and corruption. But as far as serious crimes against

he spots something, he snatches it through an open window or opens an unlocked car door and grabs it, and the scooter speeds off between lanes of cars.

If you are traveling overnight on trains, be sure to hide your valuables well. Skillful thieves are known to prey on sleeping passengers in their compartments.

WHAT TO TAKE

You can buy just about any type of product in France that you can in North America, Great Britain or Australia, but, with the happy exception of French wines, it is likely to cost you a good deal more. Clothes are very expensive in France, and

persons or property are concerned, any American city would be delighted to exchange major crime rates with any town or city in Mediterranean France. There is plenty of purse-snatching, pickpocketing, and breaking into cars in tourist areas, and there is occasional nonlethal physical violence to tourists, but the sensible precautions you would take at home should stand you in good stead here as well — namely, stay out of rough neighborhoods, keep your valuables hidden on your body, and don't leave anything of value exposed in your car.

When driving in heavy traffic, you would be wise to lock your car doors and keep your windows rolled up. Lately there has been a rash of thefts from cars by young men on motor scooters. The driver pilots the scooter alongside a row of cars stuck in traffic, while his partner on the back scans them for objects of potential value. When

other than the one or two items they may want to buy to prove that they went there, cost-conscious travelers should bring any clothes they'll need with them. The same goes for over-the-counter pharmaceuticals (aspirin is ridiculously expensive), vitamins, suntan and other lotions, film, mosquito repellent, generally anything you would buy in an American drug store. English-language books cost two to three times as much in France as in Britain or America, and though English language books can be purchased in Nice, Cannes, Aix and Montpellier, the range of titles is not extensive. In the summer, you will not needed a pullover in the evening if you stay near the shore, but in the mountains it can sometimes gets chilly. In the winter, you will be wise to bring some good warm clothes, especially if you find yourself in the path of the *mistral* in Provence or the *tramontane* in Languedoc.

WHEN TO GO

There is rarely any rain in the summer, and temperatures rarely drop below 30°C (87°F) in the daytime. From mid-September to November, there can be rain and occasional storms along the Rhône Valley. Winter is generally dry and sunny. Spring is mild, and there will some rain. In Provence, the *mistral*, the powerful wind that sweeps down the Rhône Valley can arrive at any time of the year, as can the *tramontane* winds in Languedoc.

FRENCH NATIONAL HOLIDAYS

New Years Day, January 1
Easter Sunday and Easter Monday
Labor Day, May 1
Victory in Europe Day (1945), May 8
Ascension Thursday (mid-May)
Pentecost Sunday (late May)
Bastille Day, July 14
Assumption Day, August 15
All Saints Day (*Toussaint*), November 1
Armistice Day (1918), November 11
Christmas Day, December 25

MAJOR FESTIVALS AND EVENTS

Côte d'Azur

LATE JANUARY **Monte-Carlo Rally**, Monaco.
FIRST WEEK OF FEBRUARY **International Circus Festival**, Monaco.
FIRST TWO WEEKS OF FEBRUARY **Fête du Citron** (lemon festival) — music, parades with lavish floats sculpted with lemons, Menton; **Mardi Gras** period; **Carnaval** (Carnival) in Nice — France's biggest, with parades, music, dancing in the streets.
APRIL **Monte-Carlo Open** — international tennis tournament.
MID-MAY **Cannes Film Festival; Bravade de Saint-Torpes**, Saint-Tropez.
SECOND WEEKEND IN MAY **Fête de la Rose**, Grasse.
LATE MAY **Grand Prix de Monaco** — Formula-1 car racing.
MONTH OF JUNE **Festival de la Danse et de l'Image**, Toulon.
JUNE 15 **Bravade des Espagnols**, Saint-Tropez.
JULY **Festival de Musique Classique**, Vence.
EARLY TO MID-JULY **Nice Jazz Festival**.
LATE JULY **Jazz à Juan**, Juan-les-Pins.
JULY/AUGUST **Festival International des Feux d'Artifice** (international fireworks festival), Monaco.
FIRST SUNDAY OF AUGUST **Fête de la Lavande** (lavender festival), Digne-les-Bains; **Fête du Jasmin**, Grasse.
AUGUST **Chamber music festival**, Menton.

END OF SEPTEMBER **Nioulargue** — a huge international sailing event, in Saint-Tropez.
DECEMBER **Fête du Vin**, Bandol.

Provence

FEBRUARY 2 **Chandeleur** (feast of the candles), Basilica of Saint-Victor, Marseille.
GOOD FRIDAY TO EASTER **Corrida**, Arles.
APRIL 25 **Wine Festival**, Châteauneuf-du-Pape; **Fête de Saint-Marc** (patron saint of wine), Villeneuve-lès-Avignon.
EARLY MAY **Fête des Gardians** (cowboys) — rodeo, Arles.
PENTECOST **Fête de la Transhumance** — shepherds' festival, Saint-Rémy-de-Provence.

MAY 24 TO 25 **Gypsy pilgrimage**, Les Saintes-Maries-de-la-Mer.
ALL SUMMER **Pop, rock, and classical music concerts** in the Arena in Nîmes; **bullfights** at the Arena in Arles.
SECOND HALF OF JUNE **Jazz and chamber music**, Aix-en-Provence.
ALL OF JULY **Festival de la Sorgue** — music, theater and dance festival, in Fontaine-de-Vaucluse and Isle-sur-la-Sorgue.
JULY, AUGUST **L'Été de Vaison** — dance, music and theater festival, Vaison-la-Romaine; **Music Festival**, Villeneuve-lès-Avignon; **Medieval Music**, Abbaye de Sénanque, near Gordes.
JULY TO SEPTEMBER **Organa** — organ concerts, Saint-Rémy-de-Provence.

OPPOSITE: The seventeenth-century Old Town of Menton. ABOVE: Façade of the Casino of Monte-Carlo, built by Charles Garnier in 1878.

FIRST HALF OF JULY **Festival International de Folklore de Château Gombert**, Marseille; **Festival Populaire** — folk and popular music, dance and theater, in Port-de-Bouc, near Martigues.

EARLY JULY TO EARLY AUGUST **Festival d'Avignon** — a huge official theater festival, and the **Festival Off**, Avignon; **Festival International d'Art Lyrique et de Musique**, Aix-en-Provence; **Offenbach et Son Temps** — lyric art, dance, and theater festival, in Carpentras.

WEEKEND BEFORE JULY 14 **Les Olivades**, Nyons.

MID-JULY **Soirées Musicales de Saint-Maximin**, Saint-Maximin-la-Sainte-Baume.

SECOND HALF OF JULY **Rencontres Internationales de la Photographie** — major photography exhibitions, Arles.

LAST TWO WEEKS OF JULY **Chorégies d'Orange** — opera and lyric music in the Roman Theater, Orange; **Les Nuits Musicales**, Uzès.

THIRD WEEK OF JULY **Jazz festival**, Salon-de-Provence.

JULY 21 AND 22 **Fête de Sainte-Marie-Madeleine** — with midnight masses celebrated in the grotto, Sainte-Baume.

LATE JULY, EARLY AUGUST **Concours de Boules** — a big *pétanque* tournament organized by *La Marseillaise* newspaper, in Parc Borély Park, Marseille.

LAST SUNDAY OF JULY **Fête de la Tarasque**, Tarascon.

FIRST THREE WEEKS OF AUGUST **Festival International de Piano**, La Roque d'Athéron; **Music and theater festival**, Gordes.

THIRD WEEK OF AUGUST **Provençal Wine Festival** — with parades, *bravades*, theater, in Séguret.

SECOND WEEK OF SEPTEMBER **Fête des Prémices du Riz** (rice harvest festival), Arles.

SUNDAY CLOSEST TO OCTOBER 22 **Fête de Sainte-Marie-Jacobé** — procession and blessing of the sea, Les Saintes-Maries-de-la-Mer.

MONTH OF DECEMBER **Music festival**, Marseille.

DECEMBER 24 Provençal midnight mass throughout the region. Among the most noted are the shepherds' masses at Allauch east of Marseille, Fontvieille, Les Baux, the grotto at La Sainte-Baume, the Arena at Nîmes, and at Séguret.

Languedoc-Roussillon

JANUARY TO MARCH **Traditional carnival processions** every Sunday, Limoux. **Mardi Gras, Feria du Carnaval**, Nîmes.

GOOD FRIDAY **Procession des Pénitents de la Sanch** (Penitents of the Blood), Perpignan, and other processions at Collioure and Arles-sur-Tech.

PENTECOST **Feria de Pentecôte** — 10-day-long bullfighting festival, Nîmes.

EARLY TO MID-JUNE **Printemps des Comédiens**, Montpellier.

JUNE 24 TO 25 **Fête de Saint-Jean** (the Catalan patron saint) — dancing, fireworks, in Perpignan, Céret, Villefranche-de-Conflent.

LATE JUNE, EARLY JULY **Festival International Montpellier Danse** — a huge international dance festival, Montpellier.

LATE JUNE TO LATE AUGUST **Scène d'Été à Pézenas** — crafts, music, theater, traditional dancing, Pézenas.

FIRST WEEKEND OF JULY **Fête de Saint-Pierre** — fishermen's festival, Sète.

EARLY JULY **Festival de la Cité**, Carcassonne; **Festival de Béziers**, Béziers.

MID-JULY TO MID-AUGUST **Festival de Radio France** — international orchestral music, opera, jazz, chamber music, in Montpellier; **Côtes du Roussillon Wine Festival**, Perpignan; **Joutes Nautiques** (nautical jousts), Agde; **Festival**

Médiéval — medieval costume pageant and feasting, Villerouge-Termenès.

JULY 14 **Bastille Day** — fireworks, lighting up of the Cité, Carcassonne.

MID-JULY **International Music Festival** (Casals Festival), Prades.

MID-JULY TO MID-AUGUST **Nuits Musicales du Palais** — classical music, La Grande-Motte; **Festival Mondial du Folklore** (world folklore festival), La Grande-Motte.

LATE JULY, EARLY AUGUST **Fête de la Mer** (sea festival), Agde, Cap d'Agde.

JULY 30 **Festa Major** — religious processions, Arles-sur-Tech.

AUGUST **Tournois de Joutes** — nautical jousting, all month, Sète.

FIRST TWO WEEKS OF AUGUST **Les Médiévales** — medieval costume pageant with jousts, crafts, and music, in Carcassonne.

AUGUST 9 TO 11 **Feria**—bullfighting festival, Collioure.

AUGUST 14 TO 15 **Feria** — running of the bulls, bullfights, parades, and fireworks, in Béziers.

LATE AUGUST **Festival de la Sardane** — traditional Catalan dancing, 400 dancers in costume, Céret.

ABOUT AUGUST 25 **Fête de Saint-Louis** — historical pageants, in Aigues-Mortes; **Fête de Saint-Louis**—nautical jousts, fireworks, and swimming contests, Sète.

EARLY SEPTEMBER **Visa pour l'Image**—international photojournalism festival, Perpignan.

THIRD WEEK OF SEPTEMBER **Feria des Vendanges** — bullfights and related events, Nîmes.

MID-OCTOBER **Fête Votive** — Provençal bullfighting, Aigues-Mortes.

Basic Vocabulary

Yes *oui*;
no *non*
good morning / afternoon *bonjour*
good evening *bonsoir*
good-bye *au revoir*
please *s'il vous plait*
thank you *merci*
you're welcome *je vous en prie*
it's all right *ça va*
what? (as in what did you say?) *comment ?*
what is that? *qu'est-ce que c'est?*
who? *qui?*
where? *où?*
when? *quand?*

THIRD SUNDAY OF OCTOBER **Fête du Vin Nouveau**, Béziers.

FRENCH FOR TRAVELERS

When you're traveling, local people appreciate it if you make an effort to use even a few words in their language. Luckily, everyone already knows the essential phrases to use to greet people in France — "*Bonjour, monsieur*" for men, "*Bonjour, madame*" for women, and "*Bonjour, mademoiselle*" for young women. Always use those phrases, even if they are the only ones you know.

It is considered rude not to preface a request with "Monsieur" or "Madame."

Here are some other words and expressions you may find useful or encounter often in your travels in Mediterranean France.

I don't understand *je ne comprends pas*
speak slowly, please *parlez lentement, s'il vous plait*
do you speak English? *parlez-vous anglais ?*
excuse me *excusez-moi*
how are you? *comment allez-vous?*
what's your name? *comment vous appelez-vous ?*
I'm tired *je suis fatigué*

Days and Months

yesterday *hier*
today *aujourd'hui*
tomorrow *demain*
tomorrow morning *demain matin*
tomorrow afternoon *demain après-midi*
day *jour*

OPPOSITE: Villeneuve-lès-Avignon. ABOVE: The National Conservatory, facing the Palais des Papes in Avignon.

week *semaine*
month *mois*
Sunday *dimanche*
Monday *lundi*
Tuesday *mardi*
Wednesday *mercredi*
Thursday *jeudi*
Friday *vendredi*
Saturday *samedi*
January *janvier*
February *février*
March *mars*
April *avril*
May *mai*
June *juin*

fifty *cinquante*
one hundred *cent*
five hundred *cinq cent*
one thousand *mille*
how much? *combien ?*
what's the price? *quel est le prix ?*

In a Restaurant

I'm hungry *j'ai faim*
I'm thirsty *j'ai soif*
a beer, please *une bière, s'il vous plait*
a draft beer *un pression*
red wine *vin rouge*
white wine *vin blanc*
rosé wine *vin rosé*

July *juillet*
August *août*
September *septembre*
October *octobre*
November *novembre*
December *décembre*

Numbers

one *un*
two *deux*
three *trois*
four *quatre*
five *cinq*
six *six*
seven *sept*
eight *huit*
nine *neuf*
ten *dix*
twenty *vingt*

coffee *café*
tea *thé*
rare (meat) *saignant*
medium *à point*
well done *bien cuit*
hot *chaud*
cold *froid*
waiter *serveur*; waitress *serveuse*
the menu *la carte*
a fixed-price meal *le menu*
the bill (check), please *l'addition, s'il vous plait*
the toilet *les toilettes*
one moment, please *un moment, s'il vous plait*

Shopping

open *ouvert*
closed *fermé*
expensive *cher*
cheap *bon marché*

large *grand*
small *petit*
a little *un peu*
a lot *beaucoup*
all *tout*
nothing *rien*

Directions

right *droit;* to the right *à droite*
left *gauche;* to the left *à gauche*
straight ahead *tout droit*
before *avant*
after *après*
up *en haut*
down *en bas*

Some words you will encounter in the South:

oppidum pre-Roman hill settlement
mas large farm complex
bastide large country estate
beffroi bellfry, bell tower
calanque Provençal fjord
cirque deep, circular depression in the earth made by a previous course of a river
col mountain pass
garrigue rough, treeless lands covered with grasses, wild herbs, and wildflowers
maquis scrub brush
étang pond or swamp
gardian Camargue cowboy
appellation d'origine contrôlée, or *AOC* government standards for the production of top wines
côte coast or, when referring wine, hills (also called *côtes, coteaux* or *costières*

cave cellar
crèche a Nativity scene, or Christmas crib
santons "little saints" in Provençal, small sculpted figures used in *crèches*
mistral strong wind that blows down the Rhône Valley
tramontane strong wind off the Massif Central that blows across Languedoc

For the vocabulary of Mediterranean cuisine, see GALLOPING GOURMETS, page 56 in YOUR CHOICE.

WEB SITES

France is far behind America in computer use in general, but the Internet is starting to catch on, at least as an idea. Many hotels and organizations told us that they hope to have a web site operational "by next year." We'll see. In the meantime, here is a selection of sites that might help prospective travelers plan their trips.

www.blueflag.org

The Foundation for Environmental Education in Europe awards its Blue Flag symbol to the cleanest beaches and marinas in 21 European countries. France has the highest number of Blue Flags in Europe, and Mediterranean France boasts the greatest number of Blue Flag beaches in France. To find out where they are, consult this site. The text is in all major European languages.

www.bouillabaisse.com

At the attractive web site of the famous Miramar fish restaurant in Marseille, you can learn how to make bouillabaisse according to their recipe, read their menu and press articles about the restaurant, and follow links to some of the Miramar's favorite web sites, such as Provence Market and Best of Provence, focusing mainly on the food of Marseille and the Bouches-du-Rhône. Most of the text in French, but some is in English as well.

www.cr-languedocroussillon.fr/ tourisme

The extensive site of the Department of Tourism of Languedoc-Roussillon provides thorough, well-organized coverage of hotels, camping, hiking, golf, tennis, horseback riding, sailing and all others sports, regional cuisine, transportation and other practical travel information for the entire region, from the Gard *Département* on the west bank of the Rhône down to the Pyrénées; in French and English.

www.crt-riviera.fr

The rich multilingual web site of the Comité Régional du Tourisme Riviera-Côte d'Azur covers

OPPOSITE: The village square in Châteauneuf-du-Pape, southern France's most distinguished wine center. ABOVE: A café in Béziers.

just about everything in the Alpes-Maritimes *Département* (Nice, Cannes, Menton, the Corniches of the Riviera and the mountainous back country).

www.franceguide.com

The Maison de Tourisme de France's copious site offers the best Internet introduction for first-time travelers to France, including transportation and travel tips, a geographical breakdown of the country into its main regions with the many appeals of each region, thematic sections on sports, traveling with children, seniors, cultural attractions, special interests such as cooking and wine tasting classes and canal boating, with e-mail links to suppliers and package tour operators. In French and English.

www.lafriche.org

La Friche la Belle de Mai is a former tobacco warehouse in downtown Marseille converted into a cultural clearing house and vast experimental workshop for artists, musicians, actors, theatrical producers, and filmmakers. It aims to "explore new relations of artistic creation with the public, the city and society." La Friche's on-line magazine presents a monthly calendar of avant-garde cultural events in Marseille and elsewhere in Provence.

www.nice-coteazur.org/cityofnice

The solid web site of the City of Nice is particularly good for hotel reservations and information about cultural tourism in Nice.

www.provence-beyond.com

Provence-Beyond is a big Grasse-based private web site devoted to the attractions of the back country of Provence, the Alpes-de-Provence and the Côte d'Azur "beyond" the French Riviera, with lots of good information about the terrain, climate, cultural institutions, festivals, and practical travel information (but no hotels or restaurants), and for US$15 to US$30, Provence-Beyond will lay out personalized itineraries for you (but they will not make any bookings; you have to do that yourself). This is a multilingual site.

www.provenceguide.com

An especially lively and useful source of information and links to e-mail addresses in the Vaucluse, this web site is introduced by the happy Provençal sound of cicadas chirping. There is an overall map of the *département* to click on for detailed maps of the different sections (Avignon, the Lubéron, etc.), and there are click-on boxes and icons for accommodations of all types, gastronomy, local festivals, biking trips through the vineyards of Châteauneuf-du-Pape and the Dentelles de Montmirail, and theme-based outings to cultural and natural sites. In French and English.

www.var-provence.com

Sponsored by a group of 60 hotels of different levels of quality and price in the Var (many of which are mentioned in this book), this web site offers an e-mail reservation service for the member hotels and photos and general promotional text about the Var. This is a multilingual site.

www.pyrenees-orientales.com

The web site of the Comité Départemental du Tourisme des Pyrénées-Roussillon is colorful and well laid-out, with enticing photos of the coastal and mountain areas and excellent maps of the wine areas of the *département*. The text is in French only, but the site is worth visiting for the pictures and maps, and there are links to the Perpignan web site, which is in French and English, and with the very rich Languedoc-Roussillon regional web site, which is in French and English.

GUIDES TO HOTELS AND RESTAURANTS

There are many specialized guides to help you select hotels and restaurants. The *Guide Michelin France* (150 francs) is the bible. Published since 1909, it is the bestselling book in France — more than 600,000 copies a year. (Only the Paris phone directory is distributed in greater numbers, and that is free.) The squat little red tome's 1,500 pages are loaded with valuable information, starting with its widely trusted ratings of hotels and restaurants. To be in the book at all is good. One star designates a restaurant of very high quality, two stars means it is tremendously good, and the famous Michelin three-star rating portends gastronomic nirvana. There are fine little maps of the main towns and cities indicating the location of the hotels and restaurants selected, the tourist offices, and main tourist attractions. It also lists addresses and phone numbers of automobile dealerships and tire shops, phone numbers of airports and golf courses, and gives distances from other towns and cities. Michelin's dozens of funny little symbols (explained in English as well as French) take a while to get used to, but it is well worth the effort to learn how to use this book. No traveler in France should be without it.

Semaine des Spectacles Provence/Côte d'Azur (5 francs) is a pocket-sized weekly guide to entertainment, sports, the arts and outings in the Alpes-Maritimes, Var and Bouches-du-Rhône, and it has a good selection of restaurants. It is in French only.

Le Petit Futé publishes a series of up-to-date guides on the main cities and areas of Mediterranean France, covering just about everything (in French only, 50 to 60 francs).

Veteran Cap d'Agde journalist Georges Renault puts out a little annual guide to restaurants in Cap d'Agde, Marseillan, and vicinity called *le Panse Pas Bête*, with text in French, English, and German. It is available at news stands in Agde, Cap d'Agde, and the area (13 francs).

Le Guide du Routard's *Hôtels et Restos en France* concentrates on food and accommodations in the lower price range. In French only.

Recommended Reading

ARDAGH, JOHN. *The South of France*. London: Mitchell Beazley, 1983; and *France Today*, Penguin, 1987 (updated 1993).

BERRY, LIZ. *The Wines of Languedoc-Roussillon*. London: Ebury, 1992.

BLUME, MARY. *Côte d'Azur, Inventing the French Riviera*. London: Thames and Hudson, 1992.

BRAUDEL, HENRI. *The Mediterranean and the Mediterranean World in the Age of Philip II*, New York: HarperCollins, 1986.

BROMWICH, JAMES. *The Roman Remains of Southern France*. New York and London: Routledge, 1993.

CARO, INA. *The Road from the Past, Traveling through the History of France*. Harvest Books, 1996.

CHARIAL-THUILIER, JEAN-ANDRÉ. *Bouquet de Provence*. London: Pavilion, 1990. Seasonal recipes from owner-chef of the Oustaù de Baumanière in Les Baux-de-Provence.

COOPER, BILL and LAUREL. *A Spell in Wild France*. Mandarin, 1993. About cruising through the Camargue.

DAUDET, ALPHONSE. *Letters from my Windmill*, Penguin.

FISHER, M.F.K. *Two Towns in Provence* and *Map of Another Town*. Boston and Toronto: Little Brown and Company, 1964.

FITZGERALD, F. SCOTT. *Tender is the Night* (many editions).

FORTESCUE, WINIFRED. *Perfume from Provence*. Black Swan, 1993. Reprint of the aristocratic English lady's 1935 account of living in Grasse.

GIONO, JEAN. *The Man who Planted Trees*. London: Harvill Press, 1995.

HARRIS, JOHN P. *An Englishman in the Midi*. BBC Books, 1991. *More from an Englishman in the Midi*. BBC Books, 1993.

JOHNSON, HUGH. *Pocket Wine Book*. London: Mitchell Beazley (annual).

JOHNSON, HUGH. *The Story of Wine*. London: Mandarin, 1991.

JOHNSON, HUGH and HUBRECHT DUIJKER. *Provence, Touring in Wine Country*. London: Mitchell Beazley, 1998.

JOHNSTON, MIREILLE. *The Cuisine of the Sun*. Penguin 1992.

LONG, DIXON and RUTHANNE LONG, DAVID WAKELY, PATRICIA WELLS. *Markets of Provence, A Culinary Tour of Southern France*. San Francisco: Collins, 1996.

MAYLE, PETER. *A Year in Provence* (1990), *Toujours Provence* (1992), and *Encore Provence* (1999). New York: Knopf.

MORE, JULIAN and CARY. *A Taste of Provence*. London: Pavilion Books, 1988.

NAUDIN, JEAN-BERNARD. *Matisse: A Way of Life in Southern France*. Rizzoli, 1998.

OLNEY, RICHARD. *Lulu's Provençal Table*. New York: Harper Collins, 1994.

PAGNOL, MARCEL. *Jean de Florette* and *Manon of the Springs*. Pan, 1987 (or any other book by Pagnol).

PILKINGTON, ROGER. *Small Boat in the Midi*. London: J.M. Pearson, 1989. Cruising on the canals of the South.

ROUQUETTE, YVES. *Cathars*. Toulouse: Editions Loubatières, 1992.

SMOLLETT, TOBIAS. *Travels through France and Italy*. Oxford: Oxford University Press, 1981.

STENDHAL. *Travels in the South of France*. Translated by Elizabeth Abbott. London: Calder and Boyers, 1971.

STEVENSON, ROBERT LOUIS. *Travels with a Donkey in the Cévennes*. Penguin, 1996.

VAN GOGH, VINCENT. *The Letters of Vincent Van Gogh*. Penguin Classics, 1998.

WELLS, PATRICIA. *At Home in Provence*. New York: Scribner's, 1996; London: Kyle Cathie Ltd., 1997.

WYLIE, LAURENCE. *Village in the Vaucluse*. Harvard University Press, 1974.

The Russian Orthodox Cathedral in Nice, the largest Russian church outside the old country.

Quick Reference A–Z Guide
to Places and Topics of Interest with Listed Accommodation, Restaurants and Useful Telephone Numbers

The symbols Ⓕ FAX, Ⓣ TOLL-FREE, Ⓔ E-MAIL, Ⓦ WEB-SITE refer to additional contact information found in the chapter listings.

The symbols Ⓕ FAX, Ⓣ TOLL-FREE, Ⓔ E-MAIL, Ⓦ WEB-SITE refer to additional contact information found in the chapter listings.

389

The symbols Ⓕ FAX, Ⓣ TOLL-FREE, Ⓔ E-MAIL, Ⓦ WEB-SITE refer to additional contact information found in the chapter listings.

The symbols Ⓕ FAX, Ⓣ TOLL-FREE, Ⓔ E-MAIL, Ⓦ WEB-SITE *refer to additional contact information found in the chapter listings.*

397

The symbols Ⓕ *FAX,* Ⓣ *TOLL-FREE,* Ⓔ *E-MAIL,* Ⓦ *WEB-SITE refer to additional contact information found in the chapter listings.*

407

The symbols (F) FAX, (T) TOLL-FREE, (E) E-MAIL, (W) WEB-SITE *refer to additional contact information found in the chapter listings.*

413

Photographs:

All photographs were taken by Nik Wheeler, except for those on pages 19, 197, 198, 199, 213, 245, 261, and 377, by **David Henry**, and 196, by **David Burke**.